Public Speaking

Finding Your Voice

Eleventh Edition

Kathleen J. Turner
Davidson College

Randall Osborn
University of Memphis

Michael Osborn
University of Memphis

Suzanne Osborn
University of Memphis

Portfolio Manager: Karon Bowers
Content Producer: Barbara Cappuccio
Content Developer: Maggie Barbieri
Portfolio Manager Assistant: Dea Barbieri
Product Marketer: Christopher Brown
Field Marketer: Kelly Ross
Content Producer Manager: Melissa Feimer
Content Development Manager: Sharon Geary
Content Developer, Learning Tools: Amy Wetzel
Art/Designer: Blair Brown
Digital Producer: Amanda Smith
Full-Service Project Manager: Integra Software Services, Inc.
Compositor: Integra Software Services, Inc.
Printer /Binder: LSC Willard
Cover Printer: Phoenix Color
Cover Design: Lumina Datamatics, Inc.

Acknowledgments of third party content appear on pages 415–417, which constitutes an extension of this copyright page.

Copyright © 2018, 2015, 2012 by Pearson Education, Inc. or its affiliates. All Rights Reserved. Printed in the United States of America. This publication is protected by copyright, and permission should be obtained from the publisher prior to any prohibited reproduction, storage in a retrieval system, or transmission in any form or by any means, electronic, mechanical, photocopying, recording, or otherwise. For information regarding permissions, request forms and the appropriate contacts within the Pearson Education Global Rights & Permissions department, please visit www.pearsoned.com/permissions/.

PEARSON, ALWAYS LEARNING, and Revel are exclusive trademarks in the U.S. and/or other countries owned by Pearson Education, Inc. or its affiliates.

Unless otherwise indicated herein, any third-party trademarks that may appear in this work are the property of their respective owners and any references to third-party trademarks, logos or other trade dress are for demonstrative or descriptive purposes only. Such references are not intended to imply any sponsorship, endorsement, authorization, or promotion of Pearson's products by the owners of such marks, or any relationship between the owner and Pearson Education, Inc. or its affiliates, authors, licensees or distributors.

Library of Congress Cataloging-in-Publication Data

Osborn, Michael, author. | Osborn, Suzanne, author. | Osborn, Randall, author. | Turner, Kathleen J., author.
Title: Public speaking : finding your voice / Michael Osborn, Suzanne Osborn, Randall Osborn, Kathleen J. Turner.
Description: Eleventh edition. | Hoboken, NJ : Pearson, [2018]
Identifiers: LCCN 2016059882 | ISBN 9780134380926 (pbk.)
Subjects: LCSH: Public speaking.
Classification: LCC PN4129.15 .O83 2018 | DDC 808.5/1—dc23
LC record available at https://lccn.loc.gov/

2016059882

2 18

Student Edition:
ISBN-13: 978-0-13-438092-6
ISBN-10: 0-13-438092-4

á la carte Edition:
ISBN-13: 978-0-13-440129-4
ISBN-10: 0-13-440129-8

This edition is dedicated to Mike and Susie: We cherish both your legacy and the trust you have placed in us.

Brief Contents

Contents

Preface

For more than 2,000 years, educators have recognized that the study and practice of public speaking proves crucial to helping students find their voices. Beyond developing presentation skills and helping them overcome their initial nervousness, what other discipline teaches students to choose and research their topics in a balanced and responsible fashion? To listen critically yet constructively to contrasting views on important issues? To select and combine their words artfully? And to compose messages that are meaningful, coherent, and adapted to the variety of audiences and situations they will encounter in an ever-changing and diverse world? Public speaking courses teach critical abilities that will distinguish your students as competent and well-educated people: more likely to succeed in school, in the workplace, and in the community and more likely to earn a careful hearing when the stakes are high. Thus, it is hardly surprising the course has long enjoyed a special status at the core of higher education, especially in democratic societies that value and rely on the free and open exchange of ideas and information.

Public Speaking: Finding Your Voice, 11th edition represents our best effort to help students and teachers rise to the challenge of finding and developing their own distinct voices. Our approach is eclectic: We draw from both past and present approaches to the process and unique insights from both the social sciences and the humanities to help students understand and develop their public speaking experiences. We believe that a course in public speaking should offer practical advice for achieving success grounded in a broader understanding of how communication works and the ethical considerations inherent in that process. Finally, we appreciate that there is no one right way to teach the course that works for all instructors and all students, and for that reason you will find a variety of applications and materials in each chapter of this book. You will also find that the chapters are thoroughly developed and largely self-contained, allowing instructors the freedom to adapt their sequence to fit their specific courses.

The Roman teacher Quintilian held forth the ideal of "the good person speaking well" as the ultimate goal of an education. Today, we join him in stressing the value of education in public speaking as part of the development of the whole person. That education should not simply help students present better *speeches*, but help them to become better *speakers*. We believe that developing your students' public speaking skills should produce better, more thoughtful consumers as well as producers of messages—all the more important in an age when they are daily bombarded with "fake news" and other forms of deceptive communication. We sincerely hope this textbook will help to nourish ethical as well as effective voices.

What's New in the Eleventh Edition

Revel™

Educational technology designed for the way today's students read, think, and learn

When students are engaged deeply, they learn more effectively and perform better in their courses. This simple fact inspired the creation of Revel: an immersive learning experience designed for the way today's students read, think, and learn. Built in collaboration with educators and students nationwide, Revel is the newest, fully digital way to deliver respected Pearson content.

Revel enlivens course content with media interactives and assessments—integrated directly within the authors' narrative—that provide opportunities for students to read about and practice course material in tandem. This immersive educational technology boosts student engagement, which leads to better understanding of concepts and improved performance throughout the course.

Learn more about Revel
http://www.pearsonhighered.com/revel

Rather than simply offering opportunities to read about and study communication, Revel facilitates deep, engaging interactions with the concepts that matter most. For example, when learning about public speaking, students are presented with a Personal Report of Public Speaking Anxiety (PRPSA). The results of the assessment prompt students to examine their level of apprehension and consider how they could reduce their nervousness in public speaking situations. By providing opportunities to read about and practice communication in tandem, Revel engages students directly and immediately, which leads to a greater mastery of course material. A wealth of student and instructor resources and interactive materials can be found within Revel, such as:

- **Audio Speech Excerpts and Annotations.** In-line audio excerpts of effective and ineffective speaking approaches are enhanced with audio demonstrations, adding dimension and reinforcing learning in a way that a printed text cannot. Full speeches are included at the ends of Chapters 3, 6, 11, 13, 14, 15, and 16, complete with print and audio annotations that explain the choices made by the speaker. Chapter 9 includes a sample formal outline with annotations.

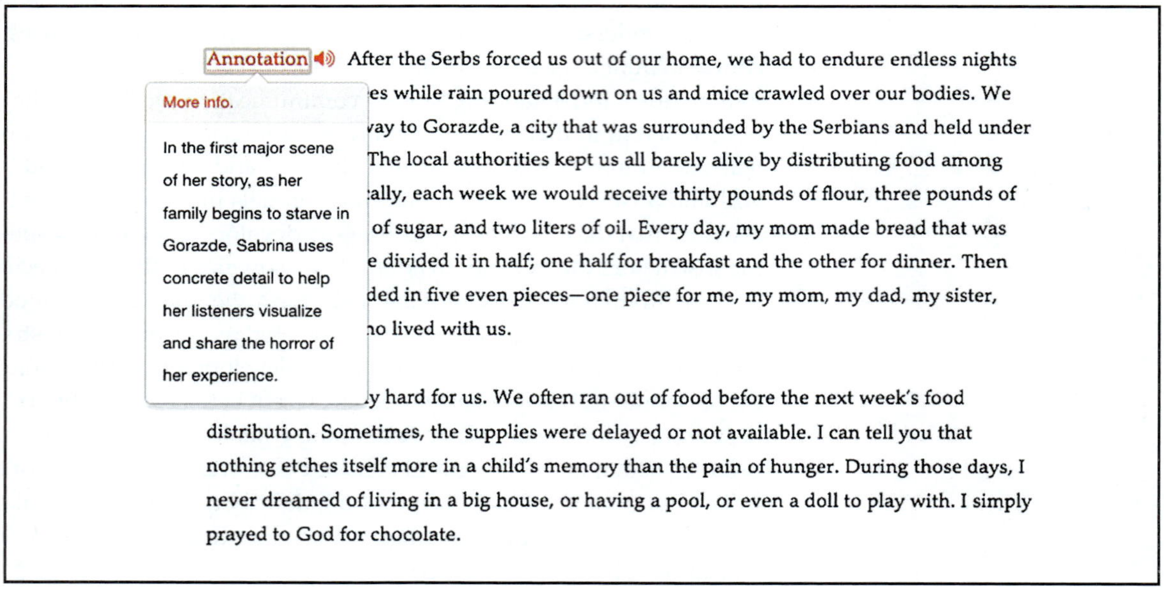

Annotation After the Serbs forced us out of our home, we had to endure endless nights
es while rain poured down on us and mice crawled over our bodies. We
vay to Gorazde, a city that was surrounded by the Serbians and held under
The local authorities kept us all barely alive by distributing food among
ally, each week we would receive thirty pounds of flour, three pounds of
of sugar, and two liters of oil. Every day, my mom made bread that was
e divided it in half; one half for breakfast and the other for dinner. Then
ded in five even pieces—one piece for me, my mom, my dad, my sister,
ho lived with us.

More info.

In the first major scene of her story, as her family begins to starve in Gorazde, Sabrina uses concrete detail to help her listeners visualize and share the horror of her experience.

y hard for us. We often ran out of food before the next week's food distribution. Sometimes, the supplies were delayed or not available. I can tell you that nothing etches itself more in a child's memory than the pain of hunger. During those days, I never dreamed of living in a big house, or having a pool, or even a doll to play with. I simply prayed to God for chocolate.

- **Videos and Video Quizzes.** Video clips of expert advice and speech examples located throughout the narrative boost mastery of the concepts. In Revel, two videos per chapter are accompanied by Video Self-Checks, enabling students to test their knowledge.

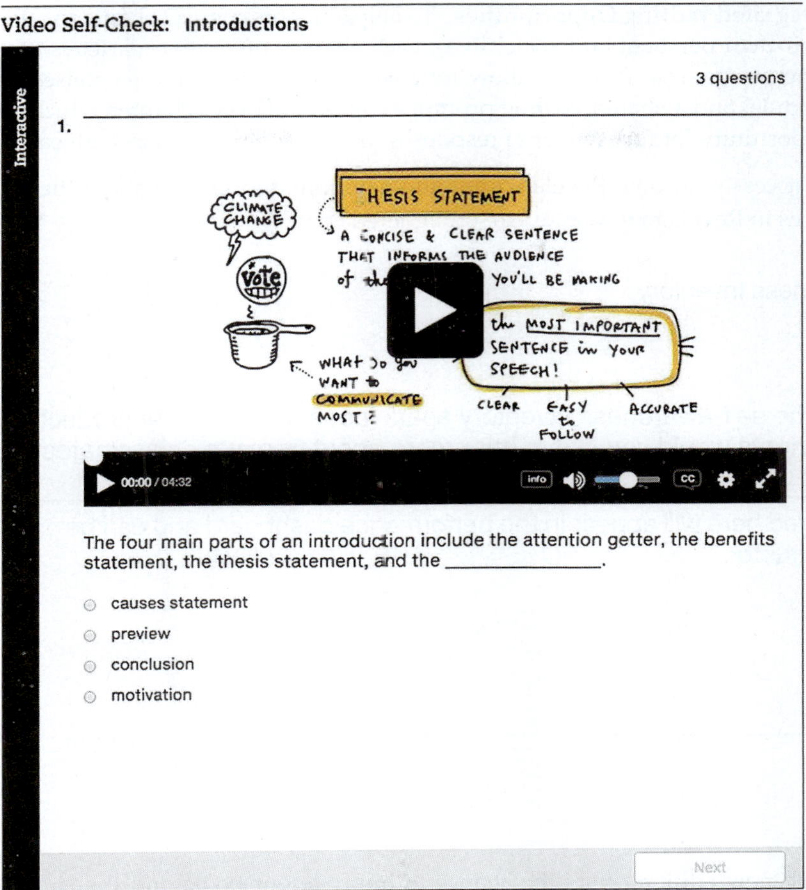

- **New and Interactive Figures.** Interactive figures (such as Figure 1.2: The Transactional Model and Figure 15.1: Toulmin's Model of Argument) give students a hands-on experience, increasing their ability to grasp difficult concepts. By allowing students to examine specific parts of a model and offering accompanying real-life examples, broad and theoretical concepts suddenly become easier to understand.

Figure 1.2 Speech as a Transactional Process

Setting

Message

Channel

Feedback

Interference

Setting

Setting

Setting

Figure 3.1 Major Steps in Speech Preparation and Presentation

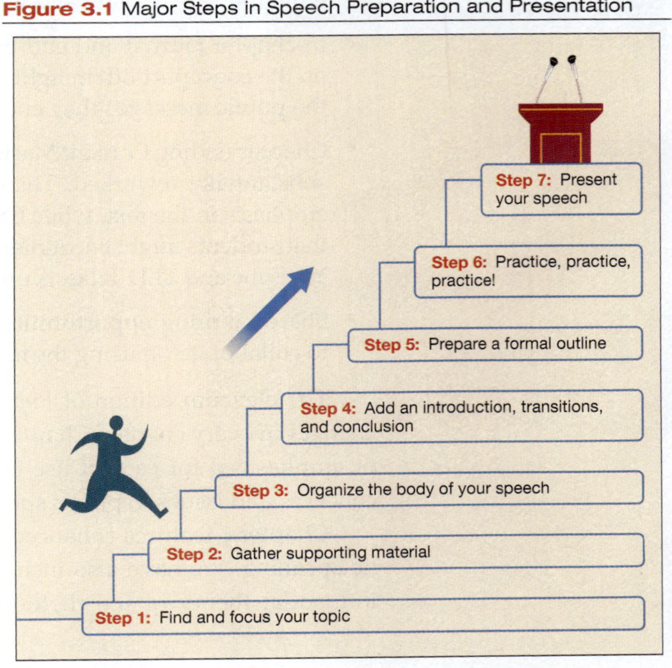

- **Integrated Writing Opportunities.** To help students connect chapter content with their own personal and social lives, each chapter offers two varieties of writing prompts: Journal Prompts allow for free-form, topic-specific responses (one per module) and a Shared Writing prompt at the end of every chapter, which offers an opportunity for focused, brief responses that students can share with each other.

To access your own Revel account and get more information about the tools and resources in Revel, go to www.pearsonhighered.com/Revel.

Journal: The Self-Awareness Inventory

Which elements of the self-awareness inventory spark ideas for your self-introductory speech? Which elements would you like to hear more about from your classmates?

The response entered here will appear in the performance dashboard and can be viewed by your instructor.

Submit

Each new edition offers the chance to improve our book, and the eleventh edition takes full advantage of this opportunity. While preserving the same overall focus and format, every chapter has been thoroughly revised for enhanced accessibility to students. Readers familiar with previous editions will recognize an abundance of new illustrations and examples, pedagogical applications, and online resources.

New features in the eleventh edition of *Public Speaking: Finding Your Voice* include:

- Chapter-opening learning outcomes that have been revised to correspond to each section within the chapter, so that students clearly see the connection between what they are reading and what they are supposed to learn from it.
- In-chapter journal and end-of-chapter writing prompts that have students reflect on the concepts both in light of their own speaking experiences and in response to the public messages they encounter both inside and beyond the classroom.
- Chapter-ending Content Mastery questions and Critical Explorations have also been substantially reworked. The Content Mastery activities reinforce major points of emphasis in the text, while Critical Explorations apply those concepts to examples that students might encounter in their public lives or online through such sources as YouTube and TED Talks. A number of new exercises have been added to each.
- Shared writing opportunities in Revel at the end of each chapter invite students to collaborate on using the concepts to better understand how to find their voices.

The eleventh edition of *Public Speaking: Finding Your Voice* also contains content changes in every chapter. Chapters were reorganized, and some topics were expanded or emphasized for ease of use in the classroom as well as to address contemporary concerns and issues in public speaking.

Chapter 1 features enhanced treatments of the classical origins and ethics of public speaking. We have also included a brief discussion of Lloyd Bitzer's immensely influential theory of the rhetorical situation to illuminate our treatment of public speaking as a dynamic process. The Revel version includes an interactive figure to illustrate public speaking as a transactional process.

Chapter 2 includes an enhanced discussion of the nature and causes of communication apprehension. We have added the classic survey compiled by James McCroskey for assessing communication apprehension, discussions of adopting a communication orientation, means of coping with feelings of anxiety, and a primer with advice for coping with nervousness right before and while making presentations. The Revel version includes an interactive version of the McCroskey survey that can be taken by students in the class, with their answers tabulated and measured.

Chapter 3 includes a revised overview of the process of developing and presenting speeches for early use in the class before students have had the time to read the entire text. The Revel version includes interactive figures, ample audio excerpts and videos, and a multimedia gallery that focuses on noted speakers from history—Sojourner Truth, Frederick Douglass, and Mark Twain.

Chapter 4 has been thoroughly revised and reworked. A new section with guidelines can help students become adept at identifying the effective (and ineffective) aspects of speeches as they listen to them. The "listening problems checklist" has been developed into an interactive Revel feature that allows students to record their answers.

Chapter 5 features enhanced discussions of audience demographics and analysis. New discussions of sexual orientation and socioeconomic status have been added, and we have expanded our discussion of generational distinctions to consider when adapting to a particular audience. The chapter also includes a new focus on determining ways to gather information about your audience. Videos highlight key concepts in Revel.

Chapter 6 provides a revised treatment to choosing and focusing topics both within and beyond the classroom. We have also provided a new mind map to illustrate the process of exploring topic areas. The Revel version offers an interactive fill-in-the-blank exercise on improving flawed thesis statements.

Chapter 7 offers a streamlined description of how to acquire responsible knowledge on topics on the Internet, in the library, and through personal interviews. Clearer and more detailed discussions of conducting research online have also been included.

Chapter 8 offers an enhanced discussion of using supporting materials effectively in speeches. The Revel version provides video and audio excerpts for teaching chapter materials as well as an interactive exercise that allows students to test their knowledge of selecting and combining supporting materials in their presentations.

Chapter 9 offers an enriched discussion for developing clearly structured messages and outlines. Revel includes ample opportunities to hear excerpts and examples of student speeches. An interactive, annotated outline reinforces techniques for strong outlining through video and examples.

Chapter 10 offers an enhanced discussion of the potential advantages and drawbacks of using presentation aids. Revel content includes interactives that highlight how presentation aids can benefit your speech, how presentation aids can damage your speech, deciding which presentation media to use, and finding your voice through PowerPoint.

Chapter 11 features expanded discussions of the functions of using language in speeches as well as the differences between oral and written language use. We have also streamlined our treatment of figurative language for enhanced accessibility. The Revel version offers an interactive feature for teaching the abstract-to-concrete continuum, ample audio excerpts, and two presidential speeches: Franklin D. Roosevelt's first Inaugural Address and Barack Obama's response to the Boston Massacre.

Chapter 12 provides an expanded treatment of extemporaneous speaking as well as a sample keyword outline for use in a presentation. The Revel version features an interactive table drag-and-drop activity to test students' knowledge of the various presentation methods as well as a number of videos to reinforce our discussion of voice, eye contact, and gesturing.

Chapter 13 offers expanded discussions of speeches of explanation and motives that can be used to entice listeners to attend to and remember informative messages. The Revel version provides interactives for teaching pertinent audience considerations and using appropriate speech designs.

Chapter 14 has been revised for accessibility to focus exclusively on the general nature and challenges of persuasive speaking. Our discussions of ethics, the persuasive process, and the types of persuasive speaking have been enhanced, as have our discussions of the problem-solution and refutative speech designs. Numerous examples of speech excerpts, videos, and a host of interactives to test student knowledge of the chapter contents are included in Revel.

Chapter 15 on building persuasive arguments has been reworked thoroughly for enhanced student accessibility. We added treatments of the Toulmin model of persuasive argumentation and enriched our discussions of gathering and using evidence, the primary forms of persuasive reasoning, and engaging disputed propositions pending the predisposition of a particular audience. The Revel version offers new video and audio excerpts, examples, and an interactive to test student knowledge of persuasive fallacies.

Chapter 16 has been streamlined for accessibility and sparked with fresh examples. The Revel version offers numerous video illustrations of ceremonial speaking and a multimedia gallery that highlights such noted historic speakers as Elizabeth Cady Stanton, Martin Luther King, Jr., and Mother Teresa. Interactive features focus on techniques for establishing audience identification and functioning as a master of ceremonies.

Appendix A, "Communicating in Small Groups," provides an overview of speaking and interacting in the context of small work-related groups. Discussions of task and relational communication as related to problem-solving discussions have been added, and our treatments of the roles of group leaders and participants have been developed. An interactive in Revel tests students' knowledge of parliamentary procedure.

Appendix B provides a number of student and professional speeches for additional analysis and includes a new informative speech on the Transpacific Partnership. In Revel, video of Elie Wiesel's Nobel Peace Prize acceptance speech and a student speech are also included.

What Makes This Text Unique?

Over 10 successive revisions, this textbook has inevitably evolved and changed considerably with the times. However, throughout the evolution of the textbook, we have maintained at least five enduring commitments:

- **Emphasizing the ethical significance of public speaking.** From choosing topics to making the actual presentation, every step in the process of developing and delivering public speeches poses important ethical concerns. Throughout this textbook, we emphasize the importance of using information responsibly and honestly. Multiple "Finding Your Ethical Voice" features highlight these and other concerns to amplify our commitment to ethical public speaking.
- **Illuminating the role of public speaking in an increasingly diverse society.** Public speaking classes should provide students with the desire and ability to express the richness of a diverse society and to bridge those symbolic barriers that too often divide us and induce incivility. An appreciation for cultural diversity is a commitment that remains throughout our book.
- **Enhanced emphasis on managing communication apprehension.** We provide an entire chapter on building confidence as a speaker so that students and instructors can face the battle of the nerves early on in their classes. We emphasize the importance of understanding communication apprehension and the value of various

management techniques that can help most students focus and harness their nervous energy into a more dynamic and authentic presentation style.

- **Special preparation for the first speech.** It is difficult if not impossible for students to learn all important concepts before their first speaking assignment because it usually comes early in the semester. For this reason, we include an overview of practical advice and a step-by-step approach to preparing and presenting their first speeches in Chapter 3. We also include a discussion of self-introductory speaking, which is often the theme of the first speaking assignment.
- **A commitment to keeping up with changes in communication technologies.** We have made an increasing effort to account for the constant changes in the way we research and access information, develop and use presentation aids, make presentations using various new media, and speak in the context of mediated small group discussions.

To help students master the material, we offer a number of special learning tools.

- We open each chapter with learning objectives and a chapter outline that prepare students for the chapter content.
- We include epigrams and vignettes at the beginning of each chapter to point out the topic's significance and to motivate readers to learn more.
- We incorporate examples that illustrate the content in a clear, lively, and often entertaining way.
- We include special features in each chapter that help students read productively: "Speaker's Notes" offer guidelines to help students focus on the essentials; "Finding Your Voice" offers exercises and applications that stimulate the learning process; and "Finding Your Ethical Voice" heightens ethical sensitivity.

SPEAKER'S NOTES

Personal Benefits of the Public Speaking Course

This course can help you

- ☐ help reveal yourself as a competent, well-educated person.
- ☐ prepare for important communication situations.
- ☐ become a better communication consumer.
- ☐ develop basic communication skills.
- ☐ control communication apprehension.
- ☐ succeed in college and career.

Finding Your Voice

What If?

Make a list of "what ifs" or concerns that make you nervous about public speaking. You might worry about forgetting what you want to say, confusing your listeners, or talking too long. As you read this chapter, go over your list and develop a plan to counter each one, based on the techniques described here. Which of these techniques do you find proves most useful in controlling your concerns? Which of these techniques do you find the least helpful?

YOUR ETHICAL VOICE

Avoiding Plagiarism

Avoiding plagiarism is a matter of faith among you, your instructor, and your classmates. Be especially alert to the following:

1. Don't present or summarize someone else's speech, article, or essay as though it were your own.
2. Draw information and ideas from a variety of sources, and then interpret them to create your own point of view.
3. Don't parrot other people's language and ideas without giving them credit.
4. Do not recycle work from other classes without checking with your instructor and then sufficiently reworking it.
5. Always provide oral citations for direct quotations, paraphrased material, or especially striking language, letting listeners know who said the words, where, and when.
6. Credit those who originate ideas as you introduce their statements in your speech: "Writer Studs Terkel has said that a book about work 'is, by its very nature, about violence—to the spirit as well as the body.'"
7. Allow yourself enough time to research and prepare your presentation responsibly.
8. Take careful notes as you do your research so that you don't later confuse your own thoughts and words with those of others.

- Marginal definitions are included and designed to help students focus on key terms as they are introduced; in addition, a glossary is included at the end of the book. In Revel, pop-up definitions in the text narrative can be accessed for key term definitions; key terms are also included in a flashcard deck at the end of the chapter.

deliberative speeches
Used to propose, discuss, debate, and decide future policies and laws.

forensic speeches
Used to determine the rightness and wrongness of past actions, often in courts of law.

ceremonial speeches
Used to celebrate or commemorate important events, people, and occasions.

logos
Appeals based on reasoning and evidence.

pathos
Appeals based on emotions.

- We conclude each chapter with a "Final Reflections" summary as well as Content Mastery and Critical Explorations sections, which are also in the Revel version as interactive features.

Final Reflections: A Quest That Deserves Commitment

Paleontologists tell us that a dramatic moment in the story of human evolution occurred several hundred thousand years ago when our early ancestors developed the capacity for speech. It is interesting to consider that each of us—as we discover our voices through preparation, practice, and ultimate success in presentation—replicates in miniature that experience of our species as humans discovered their voices and the incredible power of communication.

For some of us, this experience can be quite dramatic. In his biography of President Lyndon Johnson, Robert Caro tells the story of Johnson's mother, who taught communication to isolated Texas Hill Country children, and of Johnson's cousin, Ava, who studied public speaking with her. When Mrs. Johnson began assigning speech topics, Ava recalls,

> I said "I just can't do it, Aunt Rebekah." And she said, "Oh, yes, you can. There's nothing impossible if you put the mind to it. I know you have the ability to deliver a speech." And I cried, and I said, "I just can't do it!" Aunt Rebekah said, "Oh, yes, you can." And she never let up, never let up. Never. Boosting me along, telling me I could do it. She taught me speaking and elocution, and I went to the state championships with it, and I won a medal, a gold medal, in competitions involving the whole state. I owe her a debt that I can never repay. She made me know that I could do what I never thought I could do.[29]

- Sample classroom speeches found at the end of Chapters 3, 5, 11, 13, 14, 15, and 16 illustrate important concepts. The annotated speeches show how the concepts apply in actual speaking situations. In Revel, audio annotations appear in a pull-down menu next to the content they illustrate or explain and can also be accessed by an audio button, allowing students to hear the annotation. Appendix B contains additional speeches that offer an interesting array of topics, contexts, and speakers.

A Little Chocolate

Sabrina Karic

Reprinted with permission from Sabrina Karic, University of Nevada–Las Vegas.

Annotation I want you to think back to when you were six years old. Then, imagine living in a time, a place, a country, where you constantly heard the noises [gunfire] I just played. I am from the small and tragic country of Bosnia and Herzegovina. While many of you were playing with toys and learning to ride a bike, I was living through a nightmare. I was six years old, certainly not ready to experience war. But one day, I heard my first gunshots and my innocent childhood ended. Almost overnight, my family was plunged into homelessness and poverty.

Instructor and Student Resources

Key instructor resources include an Instructor's Manual (ISBN 0-13-440130-1), Test Bank (ISBN 0-13-440127-1), and PowerPoint Presentation Package (ISBN 0-13-440131-X). In addition to a wealth of exercises and applications for teaching every subject in the text, the instructor's manual offers a comprehensive primer with advice and suggestions for formatting and teaching the course—which can be very helpful for less experienced instructors, especially graduate students who are teaching the course for the first time. These supplements are available at www.pearsonhighered.com/irc (instructor login required). MyTest online test-generating software (ISBN 0-13-440138-7) is available at www.pearsonmytest.com (instructor login required).

For a complete list of the instructor and student resources available with the text, please visit the Pearson Communication catalog at www.pearsonhighered.com/communication.

MediaShare A one-stop media-sharing tool that facilitates interactive learning

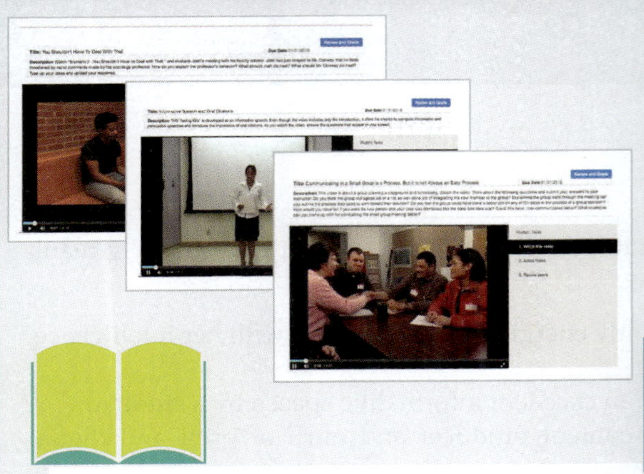

MediaShare is a learning application for sharing, discussing, and assessing multimedia. Instructors easily can assign instructional videos to students, create quiz questions, and ask students to comment and reflect on the videos to facilitate collaborative discussion. MediaShare also allows students to record or upload their own videos and other multimedia projects, which they can submit to an instructor and peers for both evaluation via rubrics and review via comments at time-stamped intervals. Additionally, MediaShare allows students working in a group to submit a single artifact for evaluation on behalf of the group.

MediaShare offers a robust library of pre-created assignments, all of which can be customized, to give instructors flexibility.

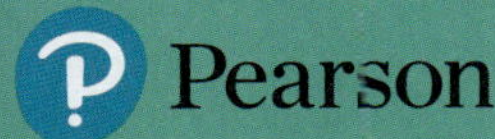

Record video directly from a tablet, phone, or other webcam (including a batch upload option for instructors) and tag submissions to a specific student or assignment.

- Assess students using customizable, Pearson-provided rubrics or create your own around classroom goals, learning outcomes, or department initiatives.
- Grade in real time during in-class presentations or review recordings and assess later.
- Set up learning objectives tied to specific assignments, rubrics, or quiz questions to track student progress.
- Sync slides to media submissions for more robust presentation options.

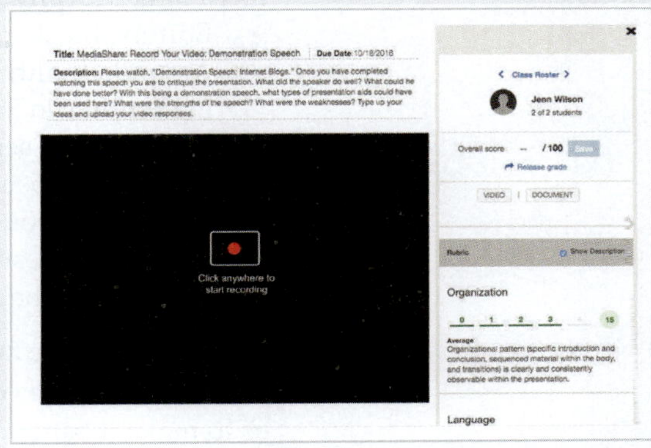

- Set up assignments for students with options for full-class viewing and commenting, private comments between you and the student, peer groups for reviewing, or as collaborative group assignments.
- Use MediaShare to assign or view speeches, outlines, presentation aids, video-based assignments, role plays, group projects, and more in a variety of formats including video, Word, PowerPoint, and Excel.

Time-stamped comments provide contextualized feedback that is easy to consume and learn from.

Create quiz questions for video assignments to ensure students master concepts and interact and engage with the media.

- Embed video from YouTube via assignments to incorporate current events into the classroom experience.
- Ensure a secure learning environment for instructors and students through robust privacy settings.
- Upload videos, comment on submissions, and grade directly from our MediaShare app, available free from the iTunes store and GooglePlay. To download, search for "Pearson MediaShare."

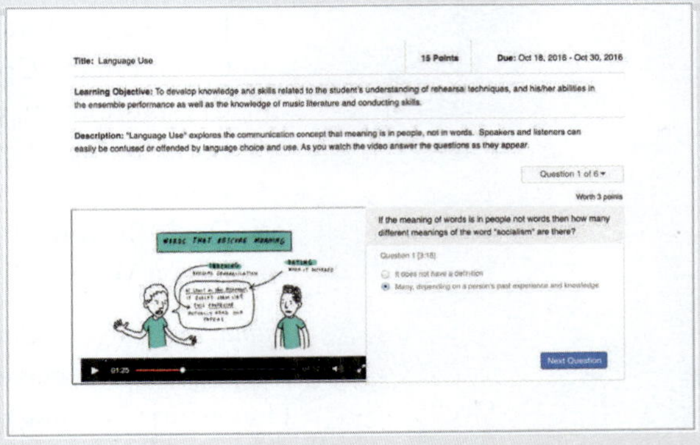

Acknowledgments

For special assistance in the preparation of the eleventh edition, we especially thank the following:

- Amanda Martinez, who constantly energizes her colleagues with her intelligence, innovation, and passion;.
- Kevin Marinelli, who provided an excellent informative speech by a student;
- Barbara Cappuccio, Pearson's content producer and guru of print and digital platforms;
- Karon Bowers, Pearson's publisher in charge of communication;
- Diana Murphy and Amy Smith, excellent instructional assessment developers at Editors, Inc.;
- Amanda Smith, who identified the amazing "Bones" Jones of Doghouse Recording Studios in Salida, Colorado;
- Alverne Ball, senior project manager for Integra;
- And most especially Maggie Barbieri, our wonderful development editor, who has guided us through the rapids of revision with new technology, channelled answers to endless questions with grace and good cheer, stalked the elusive missing pages, and steered the renegade endnotes back to right path. We are very grateful!

Many people have helped our book evolve and succeed over its almost 30 years of existence. We thank our colleagues over all the years who have reviewed our book and helped us to make it better. Hilary Jackson, development editor; Margaret Seawell and George Hoffman, communication editors at Houghton Mifflin; and Nader Dareshori, president of the company, were warm and helpful friends who enjoyed early good fortune with us.

We are grateful to those listed below whose critical readings have inspired improvements throughout several editions:

- Brenda Armentrout, Catawba College
- Richard Armstrong, Wichita State University
- Monette Callaway, Hinds Community College
- Matthew Cecil, Wichita State University
- Haley Draper, Odessa College
- Charles Drinnon, Central Georgia Technical College
- Sheryl Hurner, CSU Stanislaus
- Larry Lambert, Indiana University-South Bend
- Nick Linardopoulos, Rutgers University
- Mark May, Clayton State University
- Peg McCree, Middle Tennessee State University
- Christina L. Moss, University of Memphis
- John Nash, Moraine Valley Community College
- Owen Pillion, College of Southern Nevada
- Crystal Rolison, Cisco College
- Lori Stallings, University of Memphis
- James M. Stewart, Tennessee Technical College
- David Testone, University of Bridgeport
- Reyna Velarde, California State University at Long Beach

Public Speaking: Finding Your Voice welcomes the following new student contributors to the pages of the eleventh edition: Graham Honeycutt, Davidson College (now Graham Honeycutt Coaching); and Stefan Moskovitz, Davidson College.

CHAPTER

Finding Your Voice

LEARNING OBJECTIVES	OUTLINE
This chapter will help you:	
1.1 Understand the personal, social, and cultural benefits of the course.	The Benefits of Public Speaking
1.2 Appreciate the historical roots of and contemporary perspectives on public speaking.	Introduction to Public Speaking
1.3 Appreciate the importance of ethics in public speaking.	Finding Your Ethical Voice

Palomita didn't see why she needed to take a public speaking course. She was majoring in engineering and didn't plan on being active in politics. She wondered what this course would offer her. At the first class meeting, Palomita saw twenty-five other students who looked like they weren't sure they wanted to be there either.

As the course progressed, Palomita discovered a side of herself she never knew. She learned she could get over the initial jitters and make quality presentations—both in traditional formats and through electronic distance presentations. As she explored her topics, she learned more about herself, including her passion for engineering and her desire to prove she could succeed in a nontraditional field for women. She learned about the topics and issues she cares most about, in part by engaging the interests, convictions, and views of her peers. By the time the semester was over, she was well on the way to finding her voice as a public speaker.

"I wanna be somebody that somebody listens to. I wanna be a voice."

—GERON JOHNSON

What does finding your voice mean? Clearly, it goes beyond opening your mouth and making sounds. There are at least three different aspects of finding your voice: becoming a competent speaker, discovering your self-identity, and finding your place in society.

The first aspect involves *learning to be a competent speaker*. To find your voice, you have to know how to make a speech. Despite popular belief, speakers are made, not born. They have to learn—through study, practice, and experience—the art and principles that go into speechmaking. Every chapter in this book elaborates an important dimension of this knowledge.

The second level of meaning involves *self-discovery*. As you "find your voice," you become more confident in yourself. You develop self-esteem and your own style as a speaker. You also develop an increased understanding of why you are speaking. As she spoke successfully, Palomita not only found her voice but also developed a renewed appreciation for her interests and her career goals, which enhanced her sense of identity.

At a third level, finding your voice means *finding your place in society, learning the value of the views and contributions of others*, and *discovering your ethical obligation to listeners*. As you listen to others and as they respond to your words, you develop a sense of your mutual dependency. You learn, as rhetorical scholar Richard Weaver once noted, that "ideas [and the words that convey them] have consequences" and that what you say (or don't say) can be important.[1] We do live in a social world, and our speech or our silence can improve or degrade our surroundings.

"Finding your voice" is a quest that deserves your commitment. This chapter will explain further what this course has to offer and what it asks of you in return.

The Benefits of Public Speaking

1.1 Understand the personal, social, and cultural benefits of the course.

The ability to communicate well in public settings will help establish your credentials as a competent, well-educated person. Learning to present yourself and your ideas effectively can help prepare you for some of the most important moments in your life: times when you need to protect your interests, when your values are threatened, or when you seek approval to undertake a project. The principles you will learn in this class should also make you a more astute consumer of public messages. They will help you sort through the information and misinformation that bombard us on a daily basis. Beyond these important considerations, the public speaking course also offers other *personal, social,* and *cultural benefits*.

Personal Benefits

As you put together speeches on topics you care about, you will explore your own interests and values, expand your base of knowledge, and develop your skills of creative expression. In short, you will be finding your own voice as a unique individual—a voice distinct from all others. As rhetorical analyst Roderick Hart puts it: "Communication is the ultimate people-making discipline. . . . To become eloquent is to activate one's humanity, to apply the imagination, and to solve the practical problems of human living."[2]

Your public speaking course should help you develop an array of basic communication abilities, from managing your communication anxiety to expressing your ideas with power and conviction. These capacities should help you succeed both in school and in your professional life. Not only will you make a better first impression on your faculty, but research suggests that better communicators are better students: they score higher on college entrance exams, maintain better GPAs, and are more likely to stay in school and finish their degrees.[3]

Of course, the professional workplace is even more competitive than college. Every year, the National Association of Colleges and Employers (NACE) surveys hundreds of corporate recruiting specialists who rank communication skills at the top of the list of desirable qualities in potential employees. Because employers "seek key skills that enable workers to use their knowledge effectively in the workplace," NACE advises: "Learn to speak clearly, confidently, and concisely."[4]

Paul Baruda, an employment expert for Monster.com, agrees that "articulating thoughts clearly and concisely will make a difference in both a job interview and subsequent job performance":

> The point is, you can be the best physicist in the world, but if you can't tell people what you do or communicate it to your coworkers, what good is all of that knowledge? I can't think of an occupation, short of living in a cave, where being able to say what you think cogently at some point in your life isn't going to be important.[5]

So unless you plan to live in a cave, what you learn in this course can be vital to your success.

Social Benefits

The benefits of developing your public speaking skills also extend to your life as a responsible citizen. All of us feel compelled to speak out from time to time to defend our interests and values. As you speak out on topics of concern, you enact the citizenship role envisioned for you by those who framed the Constitution of the United States. The First Amendment protects the freedom of speech as well as the right to assemble peaceably and to petition the government to rectify grievances. All of these rights depend on the ability to clearly articulate your views in ways that will connect with your audience.

The political system of the United States is built on faith in open and robust public communication. Indeed, Thomas Jefferson emphasized allowing freedom of speech

SPEAKER'S NOTES

Personal Benefits of the Public Speaking Course

This course can help you

- ☐ help reveal yourself as a competent, well-educated person.
- ☐ prepare for important communication situations.
- ☐ become a better communication consumer.
- ☐ develop basic communication skills.
- ☐ control communication apprehension.
- ☐ succeed in college and career.

as basic to the health and survival of a democratic society. He reasoned that if citizens are the repositories of political power, then their understanding must be nourished by a full and free flow of information and exchange of opinions so that they can make good decisions on such matters as who should lead and which public policies should be adopted.

In your classes, you might speak for or against stronger immigration laws, the government's domestic surveillance policies, the rights of gay people to marry, or the staging of public rallies by such hate groups as the Ku Klux Klan. On campus, you might find yourself speaking out about attempts to alter your college's affirmative action policy, to fire or retain a popular but controversial professor, or to allow religious groups to stage protests and distribute literature on campus. In the community, you might find yourself wanting to speak at a school board meeting about a proposal to remove such "controversial" books as the Harry Potter series or *The Adventures of Huckleberry Finn* from reading lists or the school library. Or you may wish to speak at a city council meeting concerning attempts to rezone your neighborhood for commercial development.

Public speaking classes therefore become laboratories for the democratic process.[6] Developing, presenting, and listening to speeches should help you develop your citizenship skills. Preparation for your role as a citizen is a benefit that serves not just you but also the society in which you live.

Cultural Benefits

As you learn to adapt to diverse audiences, you will also develop a heightened sensitivity to the interests and needs of others—an "other orientation." The public speaking class teaches us to listen to one another, to savor what makes each of us unique, and to develop an appreciation for the different ways people live. Your experiences should bring you closer to meeting one of the major goals of higher education: "to expand the mind and heart beyond fear of the unknown, opening them to the whole range of human experience."[7]

Actress and playwright Anna Deavere Smith values the cultural benefits of public speaking.

This is not only an ethical concern; it is also quite practical. In the world beyond the classroom, in your career, you are likely to encounter a great deal of diversity. How well you can relate to others of different cultural backgrounds may well influence the speed and the extent of your success. Increasingly, organizations recognize that such measures as productivity, creativity, problem

Finding Your Voice

The Story of Your Quest

Keep a journal in which you record your experiences as you navigate this class. As one of your first entries, consider what you think "finding your voice" might mean in your life and career. Formulate at least three personal-growth goals you hope to reach during the course. Then for each of your speeches, keep a record of how you select your topic, develop your ideas, and prepare your presentation. What are your thoughts as you plan and present your speech? In what ways are you making progress toward your goals?

solving, and job satisfaction correlate positively with the effective incorporation and appreciation of a wide variety of viewpoints and experiences.[8] In the words of noted scholar Dr. Brenda J. Allen, *"difference matters."*[9]

Public speaking classes are distinctive in that they make you an active participant in your own education. You don't just sit in class, absorbing lectures. You speak. And as you speak, you help your class become a learning community. It is no accident that the words *communication* and *community* are closely connected. In your class and within this text, you will hear many voices: Native Americans and new Americans, women and men, conservatives and liberals, Americans of all different colors and orientations and lifestyles. As you expand your cultural horizons, you will gain a richer and more sophisticated appreciation of the world around you. You will be encouraged to seek out and consider multiple perspectives on information and on

Sensitivity toward and appreciation of cultural diversity will help you speak effectively to a wide range of audiences.

Finding Your Voice

America: Melting Pot—or Something Else?

A commonly used metaphor for the United States has been that of a "melting pot" that fuses the cultures of immigrants into a superior alloy called "the American character." More recently, however, that metaphor has come under attack as not preparing us for the diversity of audiences we encounter both in classes and in later life. Elizabeth Lozano criticizes the melting pot image and proposes an alternative view of American culture:

> The "melting pot" is not an adequate metaphor for a country which is comprised of a multiplicity of cultural backgrounds. . . . [W]e might better think of the United States in terms of a "cultural bouillabaisse" in which all ingredients conserve their unique flavor, while also transforming and being transformed by the adjacent textures and scents [10]

What metaphor for the American character would you suggest? What advantages and disadvantages does that metaphor have for appreciating the variety that constitutes the United States?

A Speech on Diversity

Find a speech on the subject of diversity. How does the speaker discuss the role of difference in American life? What themes and metaphors can you identify?

controversial issues before committing yourself. You will understand actress and MacArthur Genius Prize winner Anna Deavere Smith when she cherishes "what language is and does and can do . . . not just in the stories of other people, but in their words and the manners in which they speak. What I'm trying to do is reach for that which is not me."[11] As you hear others speak, you discover the many different voices of the American experience. Despite their many differences, all of them are a part of the vital chorus of our nation. Public speaking gives you the opportunity to hear these voices and add yours to them. We will explore these topics in greater detail in Chapter 5.

Introduction to Public Speaking

1.2 Appreciate the historical roots of and contemporary perspectives on public speaking.

The study of public speaking goes back thousands of years, perhaps to those moments when, sitting around ancient campfires, people learned that they could influence and convince others through the spoken word. Here, we offer an overview of the historical roots of public speaking as background for examining key contemporary perspectives.

Historical Roots of Public Speaking

Although the historical roots of public speaking are many, especially noteworthy were those who built—more than 2,000 years ago—a civilization in Athens we still admire as the Golden Age of Greece. These are the people credited with introducing democracy to Western civilization. They also left us a deep appreciation for the importance of public speaking, which served as the major means of disseminating ideas and information. There were no professional lawyers in that era, and citizens were expected to speak for themselves in legal proceedings and to join in the deliberations that shaped public policy. One of their leaders, Pericles, concluded that the ability to speak and reason together was the key to their great civilization:

> For we alone think that a man that does not take part in public affairs is good for nothing, while others only say that he is "minding his own business." We are the ones who develop policy, or at least decide what is to be done, for we believe that what spoils action is not speeches, but going into action without first being instructed through speeches. In this too we excel over others: ours is the bravery of people who think through what they will take in hand, and discuss it thoroughly; with other men, ignorance makes them brave and thinking makes them cowards.[12]

We are heirs to this tradition of "participative democracy" enabled by "participative communication."[13] When citizens gather today to discuss and debate the policies that may govern their lives, they are enacting Pericles' dream of an empowered citizenship. As we explore ideas together, we often enrich our options, learn what causes are important to us, and shape our positions on vital issues. In essence, we are finding our voices.

Perhaps the most important contribution of the Greeks to the study of communication came from Aristotle's *On Rhetoric*, which taught the art of public speaking to the citizens of Athens. Aristotle brought system and order to the already thriving study of public speaking. He codified three major forms of speeches: **deliberative**, used in lawmaking; **forensic**, used in the courts; and **ceremonial**, used during public ceremonies that celebrated great deeds and honored heroes. He also identified three major types of appeals: **logos**, appeals based on logic; **pathos**, appeals based on

deliberative speeches
Used to propose, discuss, debate, and decide future policies and laws.

forensic speeches
Used to determine the rightness and wrongness of past actions, often in courts of law.

ceremonial speeches
Used to celebrate or commemorate important events, people, and occasions.

logos
Appeals based on reasoning and evidence.

pathos
Appeals based on emotions.

emotion; and **ethos**, appeals based on the character of the speaker. Aristotle stressed the importance of using evidence, examples, and stories to support conclusions. He made it clear that finding your voice means not only finding yourself but also learning more about those with whom we communicate.

ethos
Appeals based on the perceived competence, integrity, good will, and dynamism of the speaker.

Aristotle's *Rhetoric* laid the groundwork for the ancient Romans, who would further develop the education of speakers.[14] Cicero, one of the most celebrated orators of antiquity, described rhetoric as "an art made up of five great arts." In his *De Oratore*, he detailed those five arts as how to think through and defend positions (invention), how to arrange and organize arguments (disposition), how to use language effectively (style), how to retain ideas in the mind to recall while speaking (memory), and how to present a speech effectively (delivery).[15] He stressed that ideal speakers should be broadly educated and should understand the culture and values of their audiences. The result became a set of rhetorical canons, or general principles, that would dominate western education into the modern age.

Much of this ancient knowledge focused on *how to communicate*, teaching the art and techniques of public speaking. The second major theme that developed in classical writings concerned *how we ought to communicate*, which considers the power of communication and how it can be used ethically. The Greek philosopher Plato wrote two dialogues that deal specifically with the power of the public oration. The first, *Gorgias*, offers Plato's dark vision of the subject. (You can read *Gorgias* online.) He charged that the public speakers of his time pandered to the ignorance and prejudices of the masses instead of advancing the truth. Too often, these orators told their listeners what they *wanted* to hear rather than what they *needed* to hear. Sound familiar?

In the second dialogue, *Phaedrus*, Plato paints his ideal of the virtuous speaker whose words will help listeners become better citizens and people. (You can read this classic online as well.) Such speakers can be both ethical and effective, even though, Plato observed wryly, this balance may be hard for many speakers to achieve. Plato's vision of the ideal speaker would remain a challenge for communicators of the ages who would follow.

Throughout this text, we draw on the classic tradition to help us understand both *how to communicate* and *how we ought to communicate*. The ancients can help us develop both the techniques and the ethics of speaking in public, whether face-to-face or in the marketplace or in cyberspace. See a sampling of their wisdom in Figure 1.1.

Greek philosopher Aristotle shaped the study and practice of public speaking with his influential work *On Rhetoric*.

Contemporary Approaches to Public Speaking

The classical approach continued to play a prominent role in western education until the modern age, when scholars began to approach public speaking as a subject of serious inquiry as well as a practical art. Contemporary scientists and philosophers continue to enrich our understanding of how communication works as a transactional process and a dynamic force in shaping our lives.

Public Speaking as a Transactional Process. Our natural tendency is to think of a speech as words foisted by one person upon others. Actually, a speech is a complex transaction among seven elements. Of central concern are the speaker, audience, and message; in addition, these elements are affected by the channel, interference, setting, and feedback.

Figure 1.1 Ten Timeless Lessons from the Ancient World

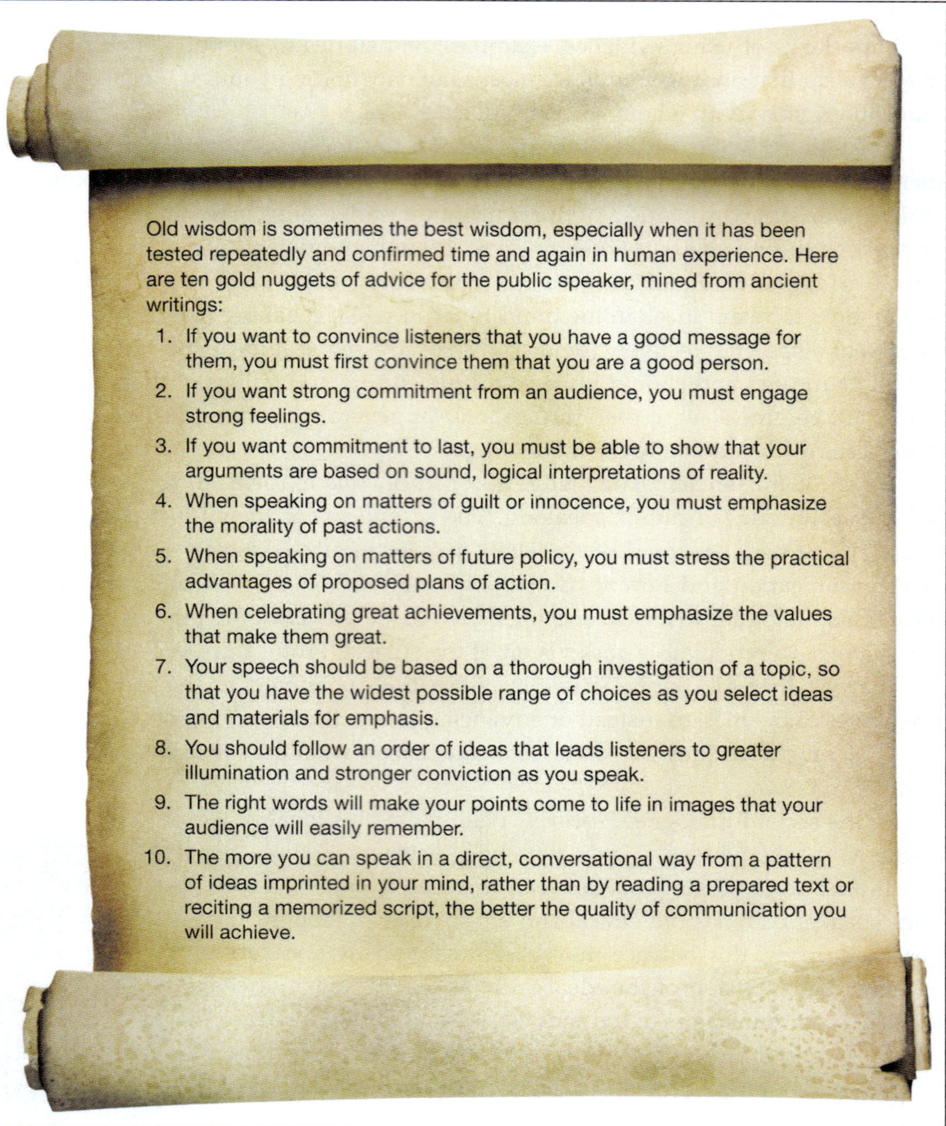
Old wisdom is sometimes the best wisdom, especially when it has been tested repeatedly and confirmed time and again in human experience. Here are ten gold nuggets of advice for the public speaker, mined from ancient writings:

1. If you want to convince listeners that you have a good message for them, you must first convince them that you are a good person.
2. If you want strong commitment from an audience, you must engage strong feelings.
3. If you want commitment to last, you must be able to show that your arguments are based on sound, logical interpretations of reality.
4. When speaking on matters of guilt or innocence, you must emphasize the morality of past actions.
5. When speaking on matters of future policy, you must stress the practical advantages of proposed plans of action.
6. When celebrating great achievements, you must emphasize the values that make them great.
7. Your speech should be based on a thorough investigation of a topic, so that you have the widest possible range of choices as you select ideas and materials for emphasis.
8. You should follow an order of ideas that leads listeners to greater illumination and stronger conviction as you speak.
9. The right words will make your points come to life in images that your audience will easily remember.
10. The more you can speak in a direct, conversational way from a pattern of ideas imprinted in your mind, rather than by reading a prepared text or reciting a memorized script, the better the quality of communication you will achieve.

speaker
Initiates the communication process by framing an oral message for the consideration of others.

Speaker. The **speaker** initiates the communication process by framing an oral message for the consideration of others. Speakers should have a message of value that has been carefully prepared and that deserves serious attention from listeners. Because the fate of speeches depends on how listeners respond, effective speakers need to be audience-centered and alert to the needs, interests, and capacities of their listeners. Ethical speakers believe their messages will improve the lives of listeners by helping their audiences think critically, creatively, and constructively about their topics.

Whether listeners accept a speaker as credible is crucial to the process: If listeners think a speaker is competent, likable, and trustworthy and shares their interests and goals, they will be more likely to accept the message. We discuss ways to establish your ethos or credibility as a speaker in Chapter 3.

audience
The listeners for whom the speaker's message is intended.

Audience. The **audience** for a message consists primarily of the listeners for whom the message is intended; it is "the heart of the public speaking process."[16] As the ancients noted, addressing the audience's concerns is central to the ethical, effective development and delivery of public speeches; otherwise, speakers are just talking to hear themselves speak. The listeners' interests, attitudes, and beliefs all serve as perceptual filters for what the speaker says, so effective speakers adopt an *audience-centered approach*. A conservative member of the Tea Party might bring a much different mindset to listen to your speech than a Move On liberal would. Chapter 5 delves into the process of audience analysis in greater detail.

The notion of "audience" in contemporary society has been complicated by technology. In traditional face-to-face public speaking settings, your audience consists of the listeners who are physically present to see and hear your presentation. Today, readily available computer applications such as Skype and YouTube allow audience members to congregate from different areas and even at different times to consider a message. Indeed, such virtual presentations and meetings have now become so commonplace in the professional workplace that many colleges and universities are developing online courses in public speaking to accommodate the unique opportunities and challenges they present.

The proliferation of technologies has also heightened the difference between what we call primary and secondary audiences. Primary audiences are the people you most want to reach and influence with your message, whereas secondary audiences consist of anyone who might encounter your presentation. For instance, most political campaign speeches are calculated for undecided voters. Strong supporters and strong opponents may or may not benefit from their presentations, but the primary audience for campaigns are people who are willing to hear them but have not yet made up their minds. In today's world, the actual audience members who are present for such presentations are often paid staffers and volunteers who help to create the impression of a live event for television. Messages are written around catchy phrases or sound bites intended to make the evening news, and the primary listeners are typically viewers who are watching from home.

The increasingly important role of social media proved itself during the 2016 presidential election. Republican Jeb Bush announced his candidacy via Snapchat; Democrat Hillary Clinton maintained active Instagram, Pinterest, and Spotify postings; Republican Donald Trump tweeted and retweeted his way into the news on a regular basis and boasted over a million followers on Instagram; and Democrat Bernie Sanders used Facebook Canvas and other means to reach millennials in particular.[17]

Finding your voice as a speaker also asks that you discover your ears as an audience member. If you want others to give you encouragement and a fair hearing, you need to be a good listener in return. What are others saying that you can use? How can you help them grow as a speaker by being a good listener? We say more about what constitutes a good audience later in this chapter and in Chapter 4.

message
The main ideas and information a speaker wants to convey.

Message. Your **message** consists of the words, nonverbal cues, and presentation aids that convey your main ideas, knowledge, and feelings toward your topic. It should be designed around a thesis statement that conveys a clear sense of purpose. You should be able to state your specific purpose in one clear, simple sentence—the simpler, the better. To promote your thesis, your message should follow a design appropriate to the subject and to the needs of listeners. To make the message clear and attractive, you want to use words artfully, and you may use such presentation aids as graphs, charts, or photographs to underscore your point. To make the message credible, you want to offer convincing evidence drawn from reputable sources and sound reasoning. To make your message forceful and impressive, your speech will require presentational skills—your voice, body language, and public presence.

In addition to their main theses, speeches also communicate secondary messages about the speaker, especially the speaker's attitudes and opinions about the particular topic. These primary and secondary messages should be harmonious and mutually supportive, such as "She cares passionately about this subject" or "He has really prepared this speech" or "She's really excited about speaking today." On the other hand, if the audience concludes, "He couldn't really care less about this," or "She hasn't researched these ideas very carefully," the secondary message will often subvert the intended message. Creating a positive relationship among the messages of a speech is vital to the art of public speaking.

channel
Medium that conveys the message to listeners.

Channel. The **channel** consists of the medium used to convey your message to listeners. It may be face-to-face, or it may be transmitted via radio, television, Facebook, Skype, or YouTube. The channel for most public speaking classrooms, engaging small audiences in relatively confined spaces, allows the audience to perceive a great deal about the speaker, and the speaker to pay close attention to the immediate feedback of listeners. Other media change the message in various ways: such audio-only channels as radio concentrate attention on the voice as isolated from the appearance, facial expressions, and gestures of the speaker. Video presentations emphasize facial expressiveness as well as vocal characteristics, often featuring a kind of faux-familiarity suggesting that speakers are talking to us one-on-one, even though there is no direct feedback. Be aware of the effects of distance presentations, in which you speak to an audience removed from your immediate presence, and of asynchronous presentations, in which you speak to an audience whose members view your presentation at different times.

Some social media have profoundly rearranged the channels of public communication. Twitter, for example, forces the creation of messages or tweets in very small bundles of 140 characters. But communicators are apparently not discouraged by this limitation: In 2016, they exchanged about 500 million tweets daily![18] Does such limitation force us to essentialize our thinking, or does it glorify the trivial—or both? The jury remains out.

interference
Distractions that can disrupt the communication process.

Interference. Occasionally, the flow of a message can be interrupted by distractions. These distractions function as **interference** that can disrupt the communication process. Competing sounds drift in through open doors and windows to distract listeners. Laughter from the hallway drowns out your presentation. Acoustical "dead spots" in auditoriums garble the pattern of sound waves, making listening difficult, if not impossible. Someone walks into class late and plops down in the front row. The techno-gremlins play havoc with your computer connection, blocking your transmission.

Being aware of the potential for interference better prepares us to overcome the distraction. Whatever happens, don't let interference disturb your composure. Usually, if you pause and smile, the distractions will fade. Often, a little impromptu humor will disarm the situation and show that you are still in control. We discuss barriers to listening and adapting to the situation in greater detail in Chapters 4 and 5.

setting
Physical and psychological context in which a speech is presented.

Setting. A speech is always presented in a **setting** that can affect profoundly how it is designed, delivered, and received. The setting of a speech refers both to the *physical* arrangements of the space in which the speech is presented; and to the *psychological* mindset of listeners, their knowledge and feelings about your subject and recent events relevant to it, and their expectations concerning you and the occasion.

The *physical setting* includes the actual place where the speech is presented, the time of day, and the size and arrangement of the audience. As discussed above, public speeches in today's world are increasingly presented in virtual settings using various forms of technology that present their own opportunities and challenges. In either case, speakers often have to make on-the-spot adjustments to accommodate the physical setting for making their presentations. Most classroom settings are relatively casual and user-friendly, whereas when speaking in larger venues or outside, you will probably need to animate your voice and gestures or even use a microphone to be heard by everyone present.

For more important presentations, the physical setting is often purposefully chosen or choreographed for maximum effect. It is no accident that political rallies in rural areas are often staged as outdoor events complete with picnics, games, and musical entertainment. Perhaps the most striking example of this in modern history was Martin Luther King, Jr.'s "I Have a Dream" speech, presented in 1963 under the watchful gaze of the Lincoln Memorial in Washington, D.C. The very setting of the speech affected how these listeners—hundreds of thousands of them physically present and millions more listening on radio or watching on television—would respond.

This dynamic speaker seems charismatic and likable.

The *psychological setting* for a speech can obviously be more complicated, especially because it varies from one listener to another. Listeners have expectations because of the *occasion* of the speech; those gathered for a Memorial Day celebration expect a speaker to honor the dead, and may react quite negatively if a speaker decides instead to present her views on tax reform. Audience members may be aware of *recent events*; if you plan a speech either for or against gun control, the psychological setting would change dramatically should there be a mass shooting at a public school on the eve of your presentation. And listeners are influenced by *recent speeches*; if you have planned a humorous presentation and the previous speaker gives a heart-wrenching speech, you will want to determine how to adjust. We consider the physical and psychological setting of speeches in detail in Chapter 5.

Feedback. As you speak, you can pick up cues from your audience that will help you adjust to the ongoing situation. These cues constitute **feedback** that helps you monitor the immediate effectiveness of your message. The need for feedback is one reason to maintain eye contact with listeners and not be glued to your notes or gazing out the window or staring up at the ceiling

feedback
Speaker's perception of audience reactions to the message.

What if listeners are straining forward in their seats? This suggests they may not be able to hear you. You may have to increase the loudness of your voice and raise the energy level of your presentation. What if they look puzzled? You may need to provide an example to clarify your point. What if they are frowning or shaking their heads? Offer additional evidence to convince them.

On the other hand, suppose they are smiling and nodding in agreement. You are on the right track! Sometimes you will sense that listeners are so caught up in what you are saying that you know you are getting through to them. That's the moment when you know you are finding your voice! We discuss feedback further in Chapter 12.

These seven elements—the three central components of speaker, audience, and message, plus the four components of channel, interference, setting, and feedback—all interact to create the greater transactional dynamic that is public speaking. Figure 1.2 offers a visual model of the relationship among these elements.

Finding Your Voice

Communication as Transaction

Attend a scheduled speaking event on campus, and observe the transaction of the seven elements discussed above and illustrated in the model. Was the speaker sensitive to the interplay of these elements? Was the message adapted to the audience and the occasion? Did the speaker respond to feedback? Did interference occur and, if so, how did the speaker and the audience respond? How would a different channel affect the process? Could the communication process have been improved? If so, how?

Figure 1.2 Speech as a Transactional Process

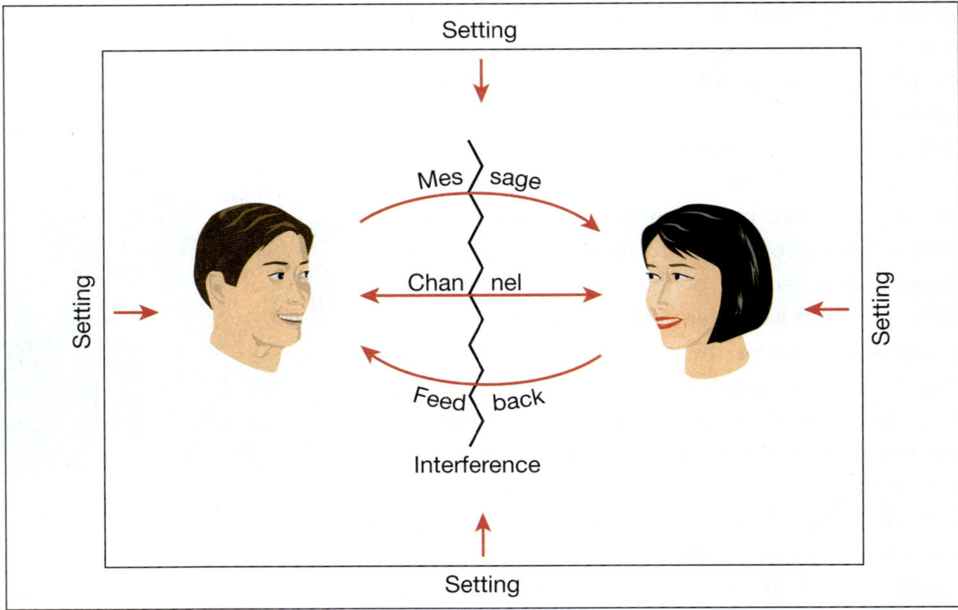

Communication as a Dynamic Process. The transactional model provides a valuable template for understanding public speaking as a constant give and take among the various components of the process: the speaker, the audience, the message, the channel, interference, the setting, and feedback. To understand how public speaking functions to advance and shape our impressions of ourselves and the world around us, we need to consider communication as a *dynamic* as well as a *transactional* process. Whether your purpose is to inform, to persuade, to celebrate, or to listen as a constructive yet critical consumer of ideas, the process of public speaking can *change* and *transform* the lives of the people who participate in it—speakers, listeners, and the communities they form.

Scholars have developed a variety of theories over the past century to better understand the nature of public speaking as a dynamic process. Two of the most influential such approaches are Lloyd Bitzer's theory of the rhetorical situation and Kenneth Burke's theory of identification. According to Bitzer's concept of the **rhetorical situation**, speeches will tend to be effective to the extent they are perceived by primary listeners as a "fitting response" to the needs or exigencies of the public speaking situation.[19] We have already discussed the importance of the psychological setting, including audience expectations regarding the occasion and the context provided by recent events. Every aspect of speechmaking—your purpose for speaking, your choice of topic, your use of language, your style of delivery, your total message—will be more effective when your audience perceives it as an appropriate response to the needs of the immediate and broader situation.

rhetorical situation
The perception that an effective speech provides an appropriate response to the public speaking situation.

According to Kenneth Burke's theory of rhetoric as **identification**, a speech will be effective to the extent that the speaker creates a sense of shared oneness, purpose, and identity with listeners. The idea suggests that speakers create a vision of their audience members as belonging together in one community.[20] The speaker then urges them to *become* that community, to recognize their common interests and goals and to realize what they can accomplish together. Deceptively simple, the theories of rhetorical situation and identification can complement each other to help explain the nature of public speaking as a dynamic process. Just as a good speech should address and define the situation for listeners, it should also prescribe a role for them as a "fitting response" within that situation. Even if only implicitly, all serious speaking conveys a vision of moral community.

identification
A shared sense of purpose and community created between speakers and listeners.

To illustrate how these two theories can work together to enhance the dynamic nature of public speaking, consider Anna Aley's speech protesting slum housing in the student neighborhoods bordering her campus at Kansas State University. Anna spent the first half of her speech defining the situation for her listeners in vivid detail: her own experience living in a moldy, dilapidated apartment with faulty wiring, the thousands of fellow students who live under similar circumstances, and the lack of adequate code enforcement. "You'd better believe there are slumlords in Manhattan," Anna insisted, "and they pose a direct threat to you if you ever plan to rent an off-campus apartment."

The second half of Anna's speech developed a vision of identification for her audience as a community standing up to address this troubling situation. Anna informed her listeners of campus services available to students who had signed their own leases on substandard apartments, circulated a petition to increase campus funding for those services, and exhorted her classmates:

> What can one student do to change the practices of numerous Manhattan landlords? Nothing, if that student is alone. But just think of what we could accomplish if we got all 13,600 off-campus students involved in this issue! Think what we could accomplish if we got even a *fraction* of those students involved!

Anna Aley's speech defined both the rhetorical situation and a vision of identification for her listeners to embody. "It's time we finally got together to do something about this problem," she closed. "Let's send a message to these slumlords that we're not going to put up with this anymore. We don't have to live in slums." Anna's speech is reprinted in full in Appendix B of this text.

Finally, understanding public speaking as a dynamic process can help you to appreciate the power of communication on the wider stage of public affairs. When Martin Luther King, Jr., strove to change racial practices in America, he offered a redress for the legacy of humiliation and segregation that divided Americans along racial lines. In his celebrated speech, "I Have a Dream," King provided a vision of brotherhood and sisterhood to bring the nation together.[21] As his leadership emerged, King's own image seemed to expand. His followers also became heroic figures as they marched through one ordeal after another. These transformations indicate how people can grow when they interact in ethical communication that inspires and encourages them, appealing to what Lincoln called "the better angels of our nature."

Insights about Public Speaking

Compare the insights about public speaking offered by the ancients with those offered by contemporary scholars. What similarities can you identify? What are the differences? What concepts do you think will be the most important as you go through this course? Why?

Finding Your Ethical Voice

1.3 Appreciate the importance of ethics in public speaking.

A course that offers so much requires a great deal in return. It asks that you make a serious commitment of time and dedication to finding your voice as a speaker. It asks also that you respect **public speaking ethics**, standards that determine the rightness or wrongness of public communication behaviors, in both your speaking and your listening. In its "Credo for Ethical Communication," the National Communication Association offers a list of principles to guide you (see Figure 1.3).

public speaking ethics
Standards for judging the rightness or wrongness of public speaking behaviors.

Moral issues can arise in every phase of speechmaking, from selecting the topic to making the actual presentation. For this reason, we offer situation-grounded discussions and "Your Ethical Voice" features throughout this text. In this final section, we discuss three major considerations that underlie ethical public speaking: respect for the integrity of ideas and information, a genuine concern for consequences, and the shared responsibilities of listeners.

Figure 1.3 Credo for Ethical Communication[22]

Source: Used with permission from the National Communication Association, www.natcom.org

Questions of right and wrong arise whenever people communicate. Ethical communication is fundamental to responsible thinking, decision making, and the development of relationships and communities within and across contexts, cultures, channels, and media. Moreover, ethical communication enhances human worth and dignity by fostering truthfulness, fairness, responsibility, personal integrity, and respect for self and others. We believe that unethical communication threatens the quality of all communication and consequently the well-being of individuals and the society in which we live. Therefore we, the members of the National Communication Association, endorse and are committed to practicing the following principles of ethical communication.

- We advocate truthfulness, accuracy, honesty, and reason as essential to the integrity of communication.
- We endorse freedom of expression, diversity of perspective, and tolerance of dissent to achieve the informed and responsible decision making fundamental to a civil society.
- We strive to understand and respect other communicators before evaluating and responding to their messages.
- We promote access to communication resources and opportunities as necessary to fulfill human potential and contribute to the well-being of families, communities, and society.
- We promote communication climates of caring and mutual understanding that respect the unique needs and characteristics of individual communicators.
- We condemn communication that degrades individuals and humanity through distortion, intimidation, coercion, and violence and through the expression of intolerance and hatred.
- We are committed to the courageous expression of personal convictions in pursuit of fairness and justice.
- We advocate sharing information, opinions, and feelings when facing significant choices while also respecting privacy and confidentiality.
- We accept responsibility for the short- and long-term consequences for our own communication and expect the same of others.

Respect for the Integrity of Ideas and Information

In an age when loud assertions of passion and prejudice too often take the place of sound reasoning, when misinformation and outright lies often circulate unchallenged on the Internet, and when some people post messages before thinking about the consequences, it is important to remember and reaffirm that respect for the integrity of ideas and information is a basic principle of ethical communication. This respect requires that you speak from responsible knowledge, use communication techniques carefully, and avoid academic dishonesty.

responsible knowledge
An advanced state of awareness concerning a topic, understanding its major features, issues, latest developments, and local applications.

Speak from Responsible Knowledge. No one expects you to become an expert on the topics you speak about in class. You will, however, be expected to speak from **responsible knowledge**. As we discuss in detail in Chapter 7, responsible knowledge of topics includes

- knowing the main points of concern about your topic;
- understanding what experts say about it;
- appreciating differing points of view on controversial topics;

- being aware of recent events or discoveries concerning your topic; and
- realizing how what you say might affect the lives of listeners.

In short, responsible knowledge is an advanced state of awareness concerning a topic. It is the goal of sound preparation for speaking.

Consider how student Stephen Huff acquired responsible knowledge for an informative speech. Stephen knew little about earthquakes before his speech, but he knew that Memphis was located on the New Madrid fault and that this could mean trouble. He also knew there was an earthquake research center on campus.

Stephen started by going online and then to the library to get basic information. Where is the New Madrid fault? What is the history of its activity? What is the probability of a major quake in the near future? Based on these valuable sources of information, Stephen then arranged for an interview with the director of the earthquake research center. During the interview, he asked additional well-planned questions, including: How prepared is Memphis for a major quake? What kind of damage could result? How could listeners prepare for it? What additional readings would the expert recommend?

All these questions were designed to gain knowledge that would interest and benefit his listeners. Armed with what he had learned, Stephen was well on his way to speaking from responsible knowledge.

Use Communication Techniques Carefully. Unethical speakers can misuse valuable techniques for communicating ideas and information in order to confuse listeners or to hide a private agenda. Consider, for instance, **quoting out of context**. In Chapter 8, we encourage you to cite experts and respected authorities to support important and controversial assertions. This technique is corrupted, however, when speakers twist the meanings of such statements to support their own views and to endorse positions these respected people would never have accepted.

quoting out of context
An unethical use of a quotation that changes or distorts its original meaning.

Politicians are not immune to quoting experts and even each other out of context. President George W. Bush sparked a controversy when his own top scientists accused his staffers of revising and skewing their reports on the likely causes of global warming.[23] Ronald Reagan cited John F. Kennedy as a forerunner to his philosophy of tax cuts to stimulate economic growth, yet Kennedy's economic theories were radically different from Reagan's, and the top tax bracket was more than 90 percent when he took office.[24] Running for reelection in 2012, President Obama cited Reagan as a "wild-eyed, socialist, tax-hiking class warrior" in opposition to Republican challenger Mitt Romney's proposed tax cuts, when in fact Reagan was discussing the need to close tax loopholes that shield the super-rich from paying their share.[25]

Throughout this text, we warn you about how evidence, reasoning, language, humor, presentation aids, and other powerful communication techniques can be abused in specific situations to deceive audiences and undermine constructive communication.

Avoid Academic Dishonesty. In the public speaking classroom, the most discouraging form of academic dishonesty is **plagiarism**, presenting the ideas or words of others as though they were your own.[26] Derived from the Greek term for crooked or treacherous and the Latin term for kidnapping, plagiarism occurs when you parrot an article, book, or presentation without crediting the source in your speech. In effect, you offer the work as if it were your own creation.

plagiarism
Presenting the ideas and words of others as though they were your own.

In public speaking classes, plagiarism can take many forms beyond simply presenting another person's speech as your own. One common variety, called "patchwork plagiarism," consists of cutting passages from multiple sources and splicing them together as though they were one speech, *your* speech. Another common form includes padding your bibliography with sources you did not actually use or consult to meet the research requirements of a speech. Finally, beware of "recycling plagiarism," or presenting papers or speeches completed for other classes—without sufficiently reworking them—as new work for a public speaking class. Of course, many instructors will be delighted and impressed to hear you speak about something related to your broader course of study that you may have worked on for other classes, but be sure to check with them and to make clear how you are significantly altering the materials before reworking past classwork.

There are many good reasons for you to avoid such behaviors. Most colleges and universities regard plagiarism as *a threat to the integrity of higher education* and stipulate penalties ranging from a major grade reduction to suspension or even expulsion from the university. You can probably find your institution's policy on its website or in your student handbook. Your communication department or instructor may have additional rules regarding academic dishonesty.

Another reason to avoid plagiarism in its various forms is the good possibility that *you will get caught*. Instructors are better at spotting academic dishonesty than students may think. Many departments keep files of speeches and speech outlines, instructors do talk to each other, and online resources enable instructors to look up stock speeches that have been lifted from the Internet. Professional associations are constantly updating speech instructors on how to detect plagiarism.[27]

An even better reason for avoiding plagiarism is that it is an *intellectual crime*, the theft and/or abuse of other people's ideas. Just as you would not steal the physical property of others, you should not steal the creative products of their minds. If you credit the thinking of others in your speech by citing your sources honestly, you honor them and at the same time build your credibility. If you plagiarize, you abuse them and convict yourself of a deep character flaw. Give the authors credit for coming up with the ideas and the language; give yourself credit for having done the research!

The most compelling reason for avoiding plagiarism is that *you are cheating yourself*. The plagiarized voice is a fraud. When you plagiarize, you give up your search for your authentic voice and prevent yourself from growing into the communicator you might have become. When you do not prepare your own work, you likely will not speak very well, anyway. You end up compromising all the benefits we have described.

YOUR ETHICAL VOICE

Avoiding Plagiarism

Avoiding plagiarism is a matter of faith among you, your instructor, and your classmates. Be especially alert to the following:

1. Don't present or summarize someone else's speech, article, or essay as though it were your own.
2. Draw information and ideas from a variety of sources, and then interpret them to create your own point of view.
3. Don't parrot other people's language and ideas without giving them credit.
4. Do not recycle work from other classes without checking with your instructor and then sufficiently reworking it.
5. Always provide oral citations for direct quotations, paraphrased material, or especially striking language, letting listeners know who said the words, where, and when.
6. Credit those who originate ideas as you introduce their statements in your speech: "Writer Studs Terkel has said that a book about work 'is, by its very nature, about violence—to the spirit as well as the body.'"
7. Allow yourself enough time to research and prepare your presentation responsibly.
8. Take careful notes as you do your research so that you don't later confuse your own thoughts and words with those of others.

Demonstrate a Genuine Concern for Consequences

Finding your voice also means developing concern for those who listen to you. You become more aware of how your words can influence the lives of your audience as well as your community. Moreover, beyond achieving your specific purpose for an individual presentation, ethical speaking facilitates rational dialogue and decision making as a central process in our society.

We have at present a crisis of civility in public communication. The robust and spirited debate of ideas is an ideal of democracy, but such negative practices as the verbal abuse of opponents and heckling that drowns out other voices undercut that ideal. In such an age, we personally need to set a high standard of honorable communication practices. In a world of increasing incivility, it is up to each of us to preserve and protect the goal of informed and rational decision making made possible only by open, tolerant, and respectful discussion of ideas.[28]

The Shared Responsibilities of Listeners

Finally, no discussion of the ethics of public speaking would be complete without considering the shared responsibilities of listeners. Despite the prominent view of listening as a passive role, listeners play a crucial role in the communication process. Listeners provide the attentive feedback that makes the give and take of authentic communication possible, and they serve as the ultimate arbiters of communication transactions. As such, they bear particular responsibility to listen critically and constructively, as we discuss further in Chapter 4.

It is particularly disheartening to talk with people who have grown so disenchanted with the quality of public discourse that they have chosen to ignore public issues altogether. Unfortunately, nothing does more to reinforce dishonesty and demagoguery in public discussions than ignorance born of cynical indifference among

Finding Your Ethical Voice

As someone who will be giving public speeches in this class, what are ways for you to find your ethical voice?

Finding Your Voice

Becoming a Critic of Public Speaking

"Finding Your Voice: The Story of Your Quest" suggests that you keep a journal in which you describe your experiences as you find your voice. Add speech evaluations to your journal by commenting on effective and ineffective, ethical and unethical speeches as you hear them both in and out of class, whether on campus, through local and national media, on YouTube or TED Talks, or from other sources. As you listen to speeches, ask yourself these questions:

1. Was the speaker credible?
2. Was the speech well adapted to listeners' needs and interests?
3. Did the speech take into account the cultural makeup of its audience?
4. Was the message clear and well structured?
5. Were the language and presentation effective?
6. How did listeners respond, both during and after the speech?
7. Did the setting have any impact on the message?
8. Did the speech have to overcome any interference problems?
9. Did the speech acknowledge the rhetorical situation?
10. Did the speech promote identification between speaker and listeners?
11. Did the speaker demonstrate responsible knowledge and an ethical use of communication techniques?
12. Did the audience members meet their responsibilities as listeners?

otherwise good, intelligent citizens. If public speaking is to be ethical, then listeners must understand and embrace their essential role in the transactional process.

When you reflect on it, playing an honorable role as speaker and listener is a small price to pay for the cornucopia of benefits described in this chapter. At the outset, therefore, a toast: Here's to a successful adventure as you find your voice!

Final Reflections: A Quest That Deserves Commitment

Paleontologists tell us that a dramatic moment in the story of human evolution occurred several hundred thousand years ago when our early ancestors developed the capacity for speech. It is interesting to consider that each of us—as we discover our voices through preparation, practice, and ultimate success in presentation—replicates in miniature that experience of our species as humans discovered their voices and the incredible power of communication.

For some of us, this experience can be quite dramatic. In his biography of President Lyndon Johnson, Robert Caro tells the story of Johnson's mother, who taught communication to isolated Texas Hill Country children, and of Johnson's cousin, Ava, who studied public speaking with her. When Mrs. Johnson began assigning speech topics, Ava recalls,

> I said "I just can't do it, Aunt Rebekah." And she said, "Oh, yes, you can. There's nothing impossible if you put the mind to it. I know you have the ability to deliver a speech." And I cried, and I said, "I just can't do it!" Aunt Rebekah said, "Oh, yes, you can." And she never let up, never let up. Never. Boosting me along, telling me I could do it. She taught me speaking and elocution, and I went to the state championships with it, and I won a medal, a gold medal, in competitions involving the whole state. I owe her a debt that I can never repay. She made me know that I could do what I never thought I could do.[29]

Understanding the multiple benefits of public speaking, appreciating the evolution of perspectives on the process, and valuing the ethical implications involved are the first steps toward winning your own gold medal, whatever form it may take. May you find your voice as a public speaker.

Study Questions

CONTENT MASTERY

1 What are the three types of benefits of finding your voice?

2 What role did public speaking play in ancient Greek and Roman society?

3 What are the three major forms of public speaking and the three main kinds of appeals codified by Aristotle?

4 What seven elements are central to the nature of public speaking as a transactional process? How do they affect each other?

5 How are the rhetorical situation, identification, and community related?

6 How can a speaker meet the challenge of responsible knowledge?

7 What is plagiarism, and why should it be avoided?

8 What are the shared responsibilities of listeners?

CRITICAL EXPLORATIONS

1. What personal and social benefits may be lost to societies that do not encourage the free and open exchange of ideas? Investigate what has occurred in other countries when they deny freedom of expression.
2. Communication has been likened to, among other concepts, a game, a dance, a battle, and a difficult climb over barriers. Which analogy do you prefer, and why? Is there another analogy that you think is better? What do the analogies people prefer reveal about their values and beliefs?
3. Identify an organization that has championed the value of diversity. How has the organization accomplished this? What have been the benefits? What can you apply from this organization to your process of speaking publicly?
4. How does the concept of public speaking as a transactional and dynamic process change your understanding of public speaking?
5. Identify advertisements that illustrate ethical problems in communication. Do the ads make outlandish claims that they fail to prove? Do they make use of demeaning stereotypes? Do they display other shortcomings?
6. As you read NCA's "Credo for Ethical Communication," think of situations in which one or more of these principles may have been threatened or violated. What keeps these principles from being observed and respected more widely?
7. Choose a recent "freedom of speech" controversy from the following options: (1) controlling fake news on social media, (2) restructuring the Internet in order to protect children from pornography, (3) allowing such hate groups as neo-Nazis or the KKK to stage public rallies, (4) permitting religious expression in public schools, (5) publishing university "speech codes" that regulate on-campus expression, (6) amending the Constitution to ban flag burning, or (7) restricting freedom of speech in times of war. Research your chosen issue, and identify the major arguments involved in this controversy, both pro and con. Which of these arguments do you find most persuasive, and why?

8. Social media have provided numerous new forms of communication, both private and public. How are these forms similar to and different from traditional public speaking as it is defined here? In your answer, be sure to consider the following qualities:
   - The spoken aspects of the message
   - The extent to which the message has been carefully designed and prepared
   - Whether the message has been tuned for face-to-face presentation to a particular audience
   - The size of the audience
   - Whether speaker and listeners have distinct, separate roles in the communication process
   - The role of nonverbal communication in the delivery of a message
   - Whether feedback is instantaneous or delayed

CHAPTER 2

Building Your Confidence as a Speaker

LEARNING OBJECTIVES

This chapter will help you:

2.1 Understand factors contributing to communication apprehension.

2.2 Become more confident by managing communication apprehension through a variety of means.

OUTLINE

Betsy Lyles enjoyed success in her public speaking class at Davidson College. But after her first presentation, she wasn't sure that would be the case. Consider her story:

> I felt like I was experienced with public speaking—I had given speeches in high school and had lots of experience reading the lectionary at church. I normally heard positive responses from people about my public speaking; however, standing up to give my first COM 101 speech made me realize that my prior experience didn't mean I was immune to anxiety. When I stood up to give my first speech, I wanted to look confident, but my face was red, my body felt hot, and I began to fidget. I was less than graceful to say the least! It was a problem for me because I didn't want to think of myself as a poor public speaker. I wanted to begin with a high standard for myself and get better from there.

"My mama taught me that anything worth doing in life should be a little scary."

—TERRY McMILLAN

Betsy did indeed "get better from there." After excelling in the class, she even became a tutor at her college's speaking center, helping her fellow students cope with this intimidating barrier to finding your voice.

If, like Betsy, you are feeling a little nervous about public speaking, take comfort in knowing that you are not alone. According to extensive research on the subject, approximately three out of four of us feel some degree of discomfort at the prospect of making public presentations—some of us considerably more than others.[1] As comedian Jerry Seinfeld once quipped, some of us would rather be in the coffin than present the eulogy at a funeral.[2]

Billionaire Warren Buffett credits much of his success to learning to manage communication apprehension.

Nor is this anxiety the sole province of average folks: Well-known public figures such as Prince Harry, Adele, and Warren Buffett are not immune to this fear.[3] Before his debut on *The Late Show*, Stephen Colbert added, "Of course I get nervous! If I don't get nervous I'm not trying!"[4]

In any case, experience has taught us that most students of public speaking feel some degree of anxiety at the prospect of speaking before their classmates—especially with their first few presentations. Such feelings may be particularly challenging for disadvantaged students and students who speak English as a second language. The good news is that, with a little training, a bit of experience, and some of the techniques discussed in this chapter, the vast majority of us can learn not only to cope with and survive these feelings, but to actually cultivate and harness them into developing a more dynamic and engaging speaking style. The late Edward R. Murrow, a pioneer of broadcasting, once said, "The best speakers know enough to be scared. . . . The only difference between the pros and the novices is that the pros have trained the butterflies to fly in formation."[5]

Learning to marshal those butterflies will make a tremendous contribution to finding your voice as a public speaker. The first step is to gain a better understanding of the nature and primary causes of what communication scholars call communication apprehension, which is the focus of the first section of this chapter. The second step, which is the focus of the remainder of this chapter, is to learn some time-tested ways to manage and focus that nervous energy both before and during the course of presenting your speeches.

Understanding Communication Apprehension

2.1 Understand factors contributing to communication apprehension.

Communication apprehension is the range of unpleasant sensations and fears you may experience before or during a presentation. Consider the following scenario:

communication apprehension
Those unpleasant feelings and fears you may experience before or during a presentation.

> The night before your first speech, you go to bed, but toss and turn. The more you think about your speech, the more tense and irritable you feel. The next morning, as you sit waiting for your turn to speak, you are not really listening to the speeches before yours because you feel worried. You hear your name called. Your stomach drops. Your hands start to sweat. Your heart races. Your ears feel hot. Your mouth feels dry. You plod to the front of the room and look up at the audience. Your knees start to shake. Your head starts to spin. You grab the lectern for support.

Do any of these symptoms sound familiar? When your primary symptoms occur before you get up to speak, you are experiencing **anticipatory anxiety**: the fear of public speaking that occurs before your actual presentation.[6] Because you usually know well in advance that you will be giving a speech, you have a lot of time to worry—but you also have plenty of time to manage your concerns. Such apprehensions are at least partially rooted in our exaggerated estimations of the genuine risks involved. When you stand and speak to an audience, you share aspects of yourself for the scrutiny of others. This experience can result in personal growth and self-enhancement, but the risks can be genuinely nerve-racking to less experienced speakers.

anticipatory anxiety
The fear of public speaking that occurs before the actual presentation of a speech.

Presentation anxiety refers to the discomfort you may feel while actually giving your speech—and again, there are ways to manage your apprehensions. The feelings of nervousness you feel just prior to and while speaking are an adrenalin rush, that burst of energy we feel when we encounter what we perceive to be a new and potentially threatening situation It's the same physiological reaction you might feel when you go bungee jumping or run a big race: Your perception sharpens, your heart rate and blood pressure increase, your metabolism changes, and you perspire more.

presentation anxiety
The discomfort you feel while actually giving a speech.

You can gauge your personal level of communication apprehension by completing the questionnaire in Figure 2.1. You may be surprised to find that you didn't score as high on this scale as you thought you might. Beyond that, the most important aspect of communication apprehension to understand is that it is perfectly *natural,* so natural that it is widely shared. Such feelings are not correlated in any way to your level of intelligence, and they do not mean you are "weak or cowardly or neurotic"—it means you're a human being.[7] What's more, *a little nervousness is actually a good thing because you can learn to channel it into positive energy that enlivens your presentation*. Before an athletic or musical performance, are you calm, laid back, and relaxed? No: You're energized and amped up and ready to go! As Beyoncé observed,

Figure 2.1 A Gauge of Communication Apprehension

Personal Report of Public Speaking Anxiety (PRPSA)

Below are 34 statements that people sometimes make about themselves. Please indicate whether or not you believe each statement applies to you by marking whether you: Strong Disagree = 1; Disagree = 2; Neutral = 3; Agree = 4; Strongly Agree = 5.

1.	*While preparing for giving a speech, I feel tense and nervous.*	SA_5 A_4 N_3 D_2 SD_1
2.	*I feel tense when I see the words "speech" and "public speech" on a course outline when studying.*	SA_5 A_4 N_3 D_2 SD_1
3.	*My thoughts become confused and jumbled when I am giving a speech.*	SA_5 A_4 N_3 D_2 SD_1
4.	*Right after giving a speech, I feel that I have had a pleasant experience.*	SA_1 A_2 N_3 D_4 SD_5
5.	*I get anxious when I think about a speech coming up.*	SA_5 A_4 N_3 D_2 SD_1
6.	*I have no fear of giving a speech.*	SA_1 A_2 N_3 D_4 SD_5
7.	*Although I am nervous just before starting a speech, I soon settle down after starting and feel calm and comfortable.*	SA_1 A_2 N_3 D_4 SD_5
8.	*I look forward to giving a speech.*	SA_1 A_2 N_3 D_4 SD_5
9.	*When the instructor announces a speaking assignment in class, I can feel myself getting tense.*	SA_5 A_4 N_3 D_2 SD_1
10.	*My hands tremble when I am giving a speech.*	SA_5 A_4 N_3 D_2 SD_1
11.	*I feel relaxed while giving a speech.*	SA_1 A_2 N_3 D_4 SD_5
12.	*I enjoy preparing for a speech.*	SA_1 A_2 N_3 D_4 SD_5
13.	*I am in constant fear of forgetting what I prepared to say.*	SA_5 A_4 N_3 D_2 SD_1
14.	*I get anxious if someone asks me something about my topic that I don't know.*	SA_5 A_4 N_3 D_2 SD_1
15.	*I face the prospect of giving a speech with confidence.*	SA_1 A_2 N_3 D_4 SD_5
16.	*I feel that I am in complete possession of myself while giving a speech.*	SA_1 A_2 N_3 D_4 SD_5
17.	*My mind is clear when giving a speech.*	SA_1 A_2 N_3 D_4 SD_5
18.	*I do not dread giving a speech.*	SA_1 A_2 N_3 D_4 SD_5
19.	*I perspire just before starting a speech.*	SA_5 A_4 N_3 D_2 SD_1
20.	*My heart beats very fast just as I start a speech.*	SA_5 A_4 N_3 D_2 SD_1
21.	*I experience considerable anxiety while sitting in the room just before my speech starts.*	SA_5 A_4 N_3 D_2 SD_1
22.	*Certain parts of my body feel very tense and rigid while giving a speech.*	SA_5 A_4 N_3 D_2 SD_1
23.	*Realizing that only a little time remained in a speech makes me very tense and anxious.*	SA_5 A_4 N_3 D_2 SD_1
24.	*While giving a speech, I know I can control my feelings of tension and stress.*	SA_1 A_2 N_3 D_4 SD_5
25.	*I breathe faster just before starting a speech.*	SA_5 A_4 N_3 D_2 SD_1
26.	*I feel comfortable and relaxed in the hour or so just before giving a speech.*	SA_1 A_2 N_3 D_4 SD_5
27.	*I do poorer on speeches because I am anxious.*	SA_5 A_4 N_3 D_2 SD_1
28.	*I feel anxious when the teacher announces the date of a speaking assignment.*	SA_5 A_4 N_3 D_2 SD_1
29.	*When I make a mistake while giving a speech, I find it hard to concentrate on the parts that follow.*	SA_5 A_4 N_3 D_2 SD_1
30.	*During an important speech I experience a feeling of helplessness building up inside me.*	SA_5 A_4 N_3 D_2 SD_1
31.	*I have trouble falling asleep the night before a speech.*	SA_5 A_4 N_3 D_2 SD_1
32.	*My heart beats very fast while I present a speech.*	SA_5 A_4 N_3 D_2 SD_1
33.	*I feel anxious while waiting to give my speech.*	SA_5 A_4 N_3 D_2 SD_1
34.	*While giving a speech, I get so nervous I forget facts I really know.*	SA_5 A_4 N_3 D_2 SD_1

Scoring: To determine your score on the PRPSA, complete the following steps:

Step 1. Add scores for items, 1, 2, 3, 5, 9, 10, 13, 14, 19, 20, 21, 22, 23, 25, 27, 28, 29, 30, 31, 32, 33, and 34

Step 2. Add the scores for items 4, 6, 7, 8, 11, 12, 15, 16, 17, 18, 24, and 26

Step 3. Complete the following formula: PRPSA = 72 − Total from Step 2 + Total from Step 1

Your score should be between 34 and 170. If your score is below 34 or above 170, you have made a mistake in computing the score.

High = > 131

Low = < 98

Moderate = 98–131

Mean = 114.6; SD = 17.2

Source: James C. McCroskey, Measures of Communication Bound Anxiety, *Speech Monographs*, 37 (1970), p. 276. The Speech Communication Association.

"I think it's healthy for a person to be nervous. It means you care—that you work hard and want to give a great performance. You just have to channel that nervous energy into the show."[8]

About now you may be thinking, "Okay, so I'm normal and not alone, but I'm still stressed out. Why is this happening to me?" Both external and internal factors contribute to feelings of communication apprehension—a subject to which we now turn.

External Factors

Two external factors often contribute to nervousness about public speaking: an unfamiliar situation and the importance of the occasion.

An Unfamiliar Situation. Almost everybody is somewhat ill at ease in unfamiliar situations, and addressing a large number of people is not an everyday event for most of us.[9] As you become more familiar with the situation, your apprehension should diminish. The best way to become more at ease with the situation is to *practice*. Practice your speech before a group of friends or at your campus communication center. There's even an app for that: VirtualSpeech offers several scenarios with avatar audience members who show engagement in your presentation.[10] If you can arrange it, practice in the room where you will give your speech. If you have access to a computer or smartphone with a video camera, record yourself practicing your speech. Let it rest, view it, look for strengths as well as areas of improvement, and then record yourself again. Can you see the improvement? Be patient with yourself. You will become more confident as the class progresses.

The Importance of the Occasion. People also tend to feel uncomfortable when the stakes are high. In classes, most presentations are graded. Outside the classroom, public speaking may have personal or professional consequences. When a situation matters to us, we often worry in anticipation—which may be worse than the anxiety during the presentation itself. For some, the idea of being recorded while speaking increases the concern because the ephemeral act of speaking will now be saved for (relative) posterity. To help reduce such discomfort, give yourself plenty of time to prepare and practice your speech. Don't wait until the night before to get started. The better prepared you are, the more confident you will be.

Internal Factors

Three kinds of internal factors affect apprehension about public speaking: perfectionism, misconceptions about the audience, and self-sabotage.

Perfectionism. **Perfectionism**—the false belief that your presentation must be flawless to be effective—sets up unrealistic expectations that often contribute to communication apprehension. As a beginning speaker, you may believe that your presentation has to be mesmerizing to not be a disaster. Keep in mind that even professional speakers make little mistakes without destroying or even hurting the quality of their speeches. Indeed, the way they respond to and recover from minor glitches often contributes to the authenticity of their presentations. In the words of Harriet Braiker, an expert on stress management, "striving for excellence motivates you; striving for perfection is demoralizing."[11]

perfectionism
Believing that your presentations must be perfect to be effective.

To paraphrase a colleague's observation, the perfect speech is like the perfect game of golf. It's impossible to complete in 18 strokes, but you keep trying and learning in the process.[12] During a presentation for a job interview, one of your authors realized that she'd forgotten to mention her involvement in high school debate—and then referred back to it later in her speech. Afterward, a colleague noted that he thought he'd just missed the initial reference. She didn't make a big deal of her mind blip, so neither did her audience.

If you look at the speech evaluation forms used in your class, you probably won't see *perfection* anywhere in the criteria. It's all right if you make a few mistakes—if you flub a word or leave out something you meant to include. Your listeners probably won't even notice these flaws unless you call attention to them, and most instructors expect a few glitches, especially with earlier class presentations. It's fine to want to do your best, but cut yourself some slack. As legendary basketball coach John Wooden posits, "If you're not making mistakes, then you're not doing anything. I'm positive that a doer makes mistakes."[13]

Misconceptions about the Audience. You may picture your listeners as predators lying in wait, ready to laugh at your imperfections or pounce on any little mistake. In reality, most audiences, especially those in public speaking classes, want to see you succeed. Remember that most of your classmates are experiencing similar anxieties themselves, and watching others overcome such feelings and speak well helps them to feel better about their own prospects. Indeed, as satirist Pam Ferderbar quips,

> When you stand on the dais and stare blankly into the audience like a cow at dusk, people are thinking, "Holy c**p, I could never do that." Boom. You are a hero. No one needs to know that you begged your boss to send someone else [or wanted to] fake your own death.[14]

Also remember that your listeners will sometimes bring their own issues with them to class. What comes across as indifference or negative feedback from one or two classmates may have more to do with their own preoccupations than their response to your presentation.

illusion of transparency
The mistaken belief that people know what you are thinking and feeling.

Sometimes, beginning speakers actually make themselves more nervous by worrying that others will notice how nervous they are. They suffer an **illusion of transparency**, which assumes that others can see right through them and read their internal states.[15] However, most listeners will not focus on your anxiety as unique unless you call attention to it yourself. As you reflect on your feelings of nervousness while speaking, consider the words of professional speech consultant Dennis Beaver:

> Did a single audience member come up to you and comment on how loud your heart was beating? Or how sweaty your hands appeared? Or how dry your voice sounded? Or what an interesting sound your knocking knees made?[16]

On most occasions, the honest answer to these questions is no. We cannot tell you how many times we've watched student speakers make excellent presentations only to confess after finishing that they were "so nervous" during their speeches. In almost every case, the audience's response was one of genuine surprise and encouragement. On one occasion, we taped a student speech in which the speaker quit toward the end because, in her own words, she was "too nervous to finish." Securing her permission, we showed the recording to future classes, stopping it right before she quit. When we asked the class how nervous she was, they would respond with statements like, "She's doing great" or "She doesn't look *that* nervous." They were usually surprised when we played the rest of her speech.

Finally, even if your listeners do notice that your hands are trembling or your leg is twitching, is this all that bad? They're likely to think that you—like them—are somewhat uncomfortable in front of a group. If you are afraid of sweating profusely, wear a light jacket.[17] If you think you are prone to trembling, use stiff notecards rather than more pliable paper for your key-word outline, and try to incorporate purposeful movements, gestures, and references to presentation aids to focus your energy in positive ways. Hard work and a little experience will help you to cope more effectively with such feelings.

self-sabotage
Focusing on anxieties to the extent that your communicative behaviors confirm and reinforce them.

Self-Sabotage. How often have you heard the expression "the power of positive thinking"? Well, negative thinking can be every bit as powerful—in the opposite

Finding Your Voice

What If?

Make a list of "what ifs" or concerns that make you nervous about public speaking. You might worry about forgetting what you want to say, confusing your listeners, or talking too long. As you read this chapter, go over your list and develop a plan to counter each one, based on the techniques described here. Which of these techniques do you find proves most useful in controlling your concerns? Which of these techniques do you find the least helpful?

direction! Communication scholars and teachers have long noted that negative expectations toward communication have a way of becoming self-fulfilling prophecies when we act on them in a manner that confirms and reinforces them.[18] For example, if you assume that other people are not prone to like you, then you are more likely to interact with others in a manner that is not very likable. The same goes for anticipatory anxieties toward public speaking. The more you assume that you will get nervous, the more likely it will happen when the time comes. Left unchecked, such fears become a form of self-sabotage by which we literally talk ourselves into nervous wrecks before we even stand up to speak.

To use a comparison to popular movies, one of the major causes of communication apprehension is that you have the wrong script running through your head. We cannot say what films of heroic affirmation work for you, but we certainly don't recommend the horror movies that so many beginning speakers seem to associate with public speaking. Instead of succumbing to zombies of your own making, confront them ahead of time and see how you can manage them with a little reality checking. If you are nervous that your presentation will be boring, focus on why you chose your topic and why your listeners should care about it while practicing and making your presentation. Positive thinking is the best antidote to negative thinking and is one of the many strategies for coping with communication apprehension discussed in the remainder of this chapter.

Assessing Your Public Speaking Apprehension

Think of a time that you have felt nervous about speaking or communicating with a group of people. Which of the external and internal factors discussed here best account for your concerns? How can you use this information to manage your apprehension about public speaking?

Managing Your Communication Apprehension

2.2 Become more confident by managing communication apprehension through a variety of means.

In discussing the nature of communication apprehension, we've already offered some suggestions for coping with it. We haven't touched on some of the popular "folksy" advice out there. You may have been told by some well-intended "expert" to picture your listeners in their underwear, to pinch yourself when no one is looking, or to take deep breaths until you hyperventilate. Perhaps the *worst* advice we've heard is to cut back on your preparation and practice because it only makes your more anxious. Of course, this makes speakers *more* apprehensive (and rightfully so) because they aren't prepared to speak.[19] Such advice rarely translates into quick-fix techniques that work for most of us.

You also may have been told that taking a public speaking class will cure you of your communication apprehension. Unfortunately, that is not true. There is no cure for communication apprehension, *but there are ways to help you control it*. The techniques we discuss in this chapter work for most speakers, and they work best when used in combination. Start with one technique and move on to another until you find what helps you most. The techniques we consider are developing a communication orientation; cognitive restructuring; visualization; selective relaxation; and developing your speaking skills through education, preparation, and practice.

Developing a Communication Orientation

If you look over the scenes from your horror movie about giving a speech, you'll find that most of them begin with "I." You think things like "I'm going to really mess this up" or "I'll never remember what I want to say." The difficulty with this perspective: You are focusing on yourself rather than on your audience and your message.

communication orientation

Approaching public speaking as an interactive process rather than a performance.

Shifting to a **communication orientation** helps you move from an "I" emphasis to a "we" emphasis by focusing on public speaking as an interactive communication experience rather than a performance. As we discussed in Chapter 1, authentic communication is a dynamic, transactional process of give and take between speakers and listeners, not a linear process of imposing messages on passive receivers. As you prepare and practice your speech, keep your audience in mind. *What can this speech give to my listeners? How can the speech help them understand this issue?* To help you focus on your message, choose a meaningful topic that you can get excited about. Learn all you can about the topic and how your audience can benefit from it so that you offer something of value. Your goal is to make a connection with the audience on an important topic—not to put on a great performance.

We once had a student who started the semester terrified of public speaking. Beverly conquered her fear by focusing on a topic that was really important yet largely unknown to her audience. Based on her work as a dispatcher for a major trucking firm, she urged her classmates to lobby their congressional representatives to vote for a pending truck safety bill. Her speech was filled with compelling examples of near catastrophes that this legislation would make less likely. She knew her topic, and she genuinely wanted to share her concerns with her listeners. Consequently, she got so caught up with what she was talking about that she forgot to be anxious. The audience was spellbound. When she finished, there was a moment of silence while it all sank in; then the audience broke into spontaneous applause—applause for a well-presented speech and applause for a speaker who had conquered her personal demons. By adopting a communication orientation and finding her voice on a topic of importance to her, she had overcome her anxieties. Her focus on sharing her passion with her audience subdued her nerves.

We advocate what James Winans called public speaking as an *enlarged conversation*.[20] From this perspective, you focus on your conversation with an (admittedly larger) audience, but retain the relaxed and informal tone of the exchange. When you're talking with a friend, you don't tend to be preoccupied with her reaction as much as the enjoyment of the discussion. Apply this perspective to public speaking, and it becomes a natural extension of that communication.

Cognitive Restructuring

cognitive restructuring

Replacing negative thoughts with positive, constructive ones.

Cognitive restructuring expands on our advice for harnessing the power of positive over negative thinking. For every negative thought or fear you experience while preparing a speech, consciously push yourself to offer a constructive rejoinder to replace it. For instance, if you are afraid of sounding stupid, remind yourself that you have done your research and have something important to say to your listeners. If you are worried that everyone will notice how nervous you are, remember that your listeners are less likely to notice or care about it than you are—and most of them are a little nervous themselves. We've already discussed the importance of reframing negative misconceptions about your audience and the need to be perfect. Other examples of cognitive restructuring include:

- *I'll embarrass myself.* What could I possibly do in a short presentation that would be all that embarrassing? Most of my classmates will also make minor mistakes on their first presentations. Even if I trip and fall flat on my face, my classmates will be supportive and impressed by my graceful recovery. So long as I don't actually hurt myself, such slip-ups are commonplace. They won't be a big deal unless I make them one. I should save the embarrassment for occurrences in life that are truly embarrassing—and not minor glitches during a classroom presentation.
- *My mind will go blank.* Even the best speakers experience mental freezes from time to time. If I pause, reorient myself to my notes, and phrase my previous point just a little differently, my train of thought will return to me. Audiences expect summaries within speeches, so they probably won't even notice. If they do, my classmates (and the instructor) will be impressed by my ability to gather my thoughts and continue my presentation
- *I'll make a bad grade if it is obvious that I'm nervous.* I'm taking an introductory level speech course that assumes no prior experience on my part. Most of my classmates are also a little nervous, and my instructor is very aware of this. As long as I prepare good speeches and engage with my listeners while speaking, especially with my first class presentations, a little shakiness alone is not going to hurt my grade.

Write out your own list of fears and concerns you experience while preparing for your next speech, and practice the art of cognitive restructuring by writing positive rejoinders to replace them in your thinking. Figure 2.2 provides suggestions for how to cope with your concerns about communication apprehension.

Visualization

Early on the morning of October 9, 2009, President Barack Obama was awakened with the news that he had won the Nobel Peace Prize. He was scheduled to make a presentation from the Rose Garden at about 11 that morning, so he didn't have much time to prepare his remarks acknowledging the award. CNN television cameras, set up before the scheduled presentation, zoomed in on the window where he was putting the finishing touches on his remarks and getting ready to deliver them. His head would bend down, presumably as he was looking at his manuscript; then it would rise up, and his eyes would close in contemplation of what he was going to say. He was visualizing his presentation. Clearly, **visualization** is not simply a tool for those coping with communication apprehension, but also a vital part of speech preparation.

visualization
Systematically picturing yourself as a speaker and practicing your speech with that image in mind.

Figure 2.2 Examples of Cognitive Restructuring

Negative thoughts . . .	Constructive alternatives . . .
I really don't want to give this speech.	This is my chance to offer my ideas to others.
I'm the only one who is nervous.	Other students are just as nervous as I am.
My speech is going to be boring.	I have good examples and stories to liven up my speech.
I'm not an expert on my topic.	I've done enough research to be knowledgeable about my topic.
I know I'm going to blow it.	I'm ready and I'm going to do a good job.

Athletes often use visualization as a means of preparing for success.

Actors, musicians, and athletes commonly use visualization to calm their nerves and focus them for success.[21] MVP basketball player Stephen Curry practices shooting over and over again, in part so that he can envision achievement. He says it helps him "just to see the ball going in the net."[22] Internationally known cellist Yo-Yo Ma observes that

> Practicing is not only playing your instrument, either by yourself or rehearsing with others — it also includes imagining yourself practicing. Your brain forms the same neural connections and muscle memory whether you are imagining the task or actually doing it.[23]

Follow the example of these accomplished individuals, and visualize yourself as a successful speaker.[24] As you practice your presentation, consciously eliminate all competing distractions from your mind. That way, you can focus exclusively on successfully making your presentation and interacting with your listeners. Take yourself step by step through the course of your speech, envisioning the positive reception of your compelling topic, thoughtful research, and eagerness to communicate. Keep in mind that you want to focus on reaching your listeners with a message that you communicate effectively and enthusiastically. A sample visualization script might read as follows:

> I am walking to the podium in a self-assured manner. I pause and smile at my audience, identifying friendly, receptive listeners. I begin with my well-prepared and practiced introduction to my speech. This good start increases my self-confidence. During my speech, I concentrate on sharing my message with my listeners. I make and maintain eye contact with my audience. I look for feedback from them to tell me that they remain interested and that they seem to understand what I am saying. I grow in confidence as I speak. I deliver my well-prepared and well-practiced conclusion, knowing I have done well on my speech. My audience applauds, and I feel really good about my speech and myself.

Now write your own visualization script. As you write it, picture it as it will happen on the day of your speech. Take this vision of success with you as you enter the classroom on the day of your speech.

Selective Relaxation

selective relaxation
Practicing muscle control techniques to help you reduce physical and psychological tension by relaxing on cue.

Another technique for handling your anxiety is the art of **selective relaxation,** a sequence of muscle control techniques that can help to reduce physical and psychological tension. Begin practicing this technique as you prepare for your first speech. In time, it should help you learn to relax on cue. Follow the sequence outlined here:

1. Find a quiet place where you can be by yourself. Sit in a comfortable chair or lie down, close your eyes, and breathe deeply, in through your nose and out through your mouth. You should feel yourself beginning to relax.
2. Once you feel yourself relaxing, begin slowly repeating a positive cue word, such as *yes*, each time you exhale. Let your mind drift freely. You should soon feel quite relaxed.
3. While you are relaxed and breathing deeply, tense and relax different muscle groups. Begin by tensing your feet and legs: Curl your toes, tighten your calves, lock your knees, and contract your thigh muscles. Hold this tension for several seconds, and think about how it feels. Not very comfortable, is it?
4. Concentrate on breathing deeply again, saying your cue word as you feel yourself relax.

5. Now, repeat steps 1 through 4, moving the focus of tensing and relaxing through your body: First focus on your abdominal muscles, then your hand and arm muscles, and finally your neck and facial muscles. After you have done this a number of times, simply repeating your selected word should trigger a relaxation response.

One benefit of this exercise is that it helps you regulate your breathing, which brings oxygen to your muscles and brain. Another benefit is that once you have mastered the technique, you can practice it unnoticed in many situations. While you are sitting in class waiting to speak, tense your feet and leg muscles; then relax them. If you find yourself getting nervous while you are speaking, say your cue word to yourself. The word alone may be enough to help you relax and return your concentration to your message. One of our students wrote her cue word on her key-word cards, along with reminders to smile and have fun. If this technique doesn't work as well as you would like, try tensing and relaxing a hand as you speak. Just be sure it's down at your side or behind the lectern where it can't be seen.

Education, Preparation, and Practice

Think back to a time in your childhood when you acquired a new ability. It might have been learning to swim or to use a computer. The more you learned and the more you practiced, the more confident you became. The more confident you became, the more eager you were to improve your ability. Before long, you jumped into the deep end of the pool without hesitation or found materials online in creative ways.

The same type of learning relationship exists among education, preparation, practice, and developing your confidence as a public speaker. Simply put, the more you develop your ability to prepare and present speeches, and the more prepared you are to make your specific presentations, the more likely you are to speak with confidence and reassurance. Over the course of this class, you will develop your facility to choose quality topics you can commit to, become responsibly informed so that you can speak with conviction and authority, organize your materials in a manner that will be easier to present, adapt your ideas and reasoning to your particular audience, and present them extemporaneously with your listeners. All of these abilities will be a major benefit to developing your capacity to manage communication apprehension.

No less important will be the considerable work you put into preparing for each specific speech. Keep in mind that practicing is an important part of your preparation. Anxious students sometimes spend a lot of time working and reworking their speeches without leaving enough time to adequately practice their delivery.[25] As discussed in Chapter 12, try to leave yourself ample time for practice, and take an active approach to running through your entire presentation. Stand up, project your voice, and work in movements and gestures as you envision yourself interacting with an imagined audience.[26] If possible, practice where you will make your actual presentation, and practice some more before a live audience.[27] As communication and business professor Matt Abrahams writes:

> To practice effectively, you also need to stand and deliver, even if you are presenting virtually. Hearing your own voice and using relevant, appropriate gestures may improve later recall. You remember more because your mental imagery and physical practice use overlapping neural networks in your brain, improving what's known as memory consolidation, or the process by which a thought becomes cemented in your long-term memory.[28]

Putting It All Together

Do these techniques really work? Will this advice help me? Research related to communication apprehension has established that (1) *such techniques do work for most speakers*, and (2) *they work best in combination*.[29] You should find it much easier to cope with your feelings of anxiety toward public speaking by developing a communication orientation; using the techniques of cognitive restructuring, visualization, and selective relaxation; and gaining some knowledge and practical experience preparing and presenting quality speeches. Consider the advice of Davidson college student Betsy Lyles, whose experiences with communication apprehension opened this chapter:

> To incoming students, I would suggest a couple of things—the first being it doesn't matter how much experience you've had with speaking in the past. Taking a public speaking course and learning about the theories at work behind what you do can be illuminating. And, there's no way not to improve. If possible, have your speeches filmed so you can watch them after your presentation. Make note of what you like and also what you can improve upon. Unfortunately, communication anxiety is a universal problem faced by public speakers *without* a universal solution. Commit yourself to finding solutions that work for you. They might be different from what your classmates do.

When the time comes for putting it all together and making your actual presentation, the following suggestions may help you navigate the last-minute jitters and adrenaline rush associated with presentation anxiety:

- **Compose yourself before and after speaking.** Focus your full concentration on your message, and visualize yourself making your presentation and successfully interacting with your audience. Use selective relaxation to calm yourself, and answer any last-minute negative thoughts with positive reconstructions. When the time comes, avoid a rushed start. Approach the front of the room at a steady pace, establish eye contact, allow that rush of energy to rise and subside, glance at your notes, and begin. Similarly, at the end of your presentation, don't scamper back to your seat as quickly as possible. Maintain eye contact with your audience for a brief pause, and then proceed back to your seat with a steady, confident demeanor.
- **Plan your introductory and concluding remarks carefully.** A smooth and engaging introduction and conclusion will make your speeches much easier and more comfortable to present. For this reason, it may be advisable to memorize your opening and closing remarks as well as your transitions for moving from one main idea or part of your speech to the next. In either case, do not open (or close) your presentations by denigrating yourself for being nervous. The infamous "I'm really nervous but here goes" makes an ineffective opener; such concluding lines as "Whew!" or "Thank goodness that's over!" make unproductive closers. Such comments tend to make members of the audience uncomfortable for speakers, and they usually just serve to make speakers more anxious and less confident in their abilities.
- **Speak clearly and loud enough to be heard by everyone.** Sometimes, nervous speakers tend to race really quickly through their presentations, or they speak ever so slowly and softly. Either version makes it hard for listeners to follow and interact with your presentation. When speaking to more than three to five people at a time, it is really important to animate your voice and gestures more than you usually do. Try to work some variety and cadence into your speaking voice, and make sure you pause and breathe at transitions or when it feels natural.
- **Establish and maintain eye contact from the start.** Eye contact is crucial to authentic audience interaction, and it is really hard to regain once you start reading from your notes or trying to speak from memory while staring at the back wall. This will probably feel awkward at first, but learning to actually interact with your audience while speaking is crucial to developing your skills and contributes to making you feel more confident and comfortable over time. If you are feeling really nervous, try finding a friendly face at the right side, center back, and left side of the room, and then pan back and forth among them until you feel comfortable looking at everyone. By all means, glance at your notes at regular intervals to keep you on track during your presentation, but make it a point not to read from them while speaking.
- **Move in a controlled way.** Purposeful movements and gestures can help speakers channel nervous energy into a more dynamic and engaging delivery style. As discussed in Chapter 12, fluid movements and gestures can complement and

Concerned About . . .	Try This . . .
Unfamiliarity with the situation?	Practice before an audience
Importance of the occasion?	Prepare well in advance
Afraid you'll be scared?	Remember you'll be psyched up
Embarrassing yourself?	Don't sweat the little things
Drawing a blank?	Paraphrase what you just said
Won't be able to finish?	Keep talking; look for a friendly face
I'll shake uncontrollably?	Use gestures and purposeful movement
Predatory listeners?	Classmates want you to succeed
I'll fail if my speech isn't perfect?	No speech is perfect; cut yourself some slack

Figure 2.3 Coping with Your Concerns

contribute to both the tone and the substance of your message. In contrast, fidgety or nervous mannerisms like stroking your forearm or "driving the lectern" distract listeners and compete with your intended message. As discussed in Chapter 10, presentation aids can help speakers cope with communication apprehension because they facilitate purposeful movement.

- **If you should stumble or freeze, make every effort to finish your presentation.** Professional speakers mispronounce words and misstate phrases all the time, and in most cases their listeners hardly notice. If you need to back up and clarify a point, then fine; in either case, your listeners will be impressed by a graceful recovery. If you feel yourself panicking or freezing, then by all means pause, take a breath, sip your water, reorient yourself to your notes, and continue. Work to finish your first few presentations, and remember that managing your nerves will get progressively easier as you gain experience and develop your communication skills.
- **A final thought: *Act confident* even if you may not *feel confident*.** As the old saying goes, "Fake it 'til you make it." As with nervousness and fear, feelings of confidence toward public speaking have a way of becoming self-fulfilling prophecies when we act on them. So walk with confidence to the front of the room, smile for your listeners, establish eye contact, and show them a posed speaker presenting an important message for their consideration. Smiling releases endorphins that trigger a sense of well-being, while also reducing anxiety, lowering blood pressure, and decreasing heart rate.[30] Becoming more self-assured takes time. As you become more experienced at giving speeches and at using the suggestions in this chapter, you will find your confidence growing, and you will be able to convert your fear of speaking into positive, constructive energy.

Figure 2.3 summarizes ways to cope with your concerns about public speaking.

SPEAKER'S NOTES

Twelve Techniques for Handling Communication Apprehension

1. Focus on communicating with your audience.
2. Select a topic that excites you.
3. Carefully research and organize your message.
4. Become responsibly informed about your topic so you can speak with authority.
5. Practice your presentation until it flows smoothly.
6. Get enough sleep the night before your speech.
7. Take a bottle of water to the lectern with you to ease a dry mouth.
8. Learn how to relax on cue.
9. Think positively.
10. Visualize success.
11. Act confident even if you aren't.
12. Take advantage of opportunities to speak in public.

How You Can Help Your Classmates

As you may have noticed, many of the issues of communication anxiety you might experience revolve around how listeners respond to you. Keep in mind that your classmates have similar concerns. You can help relax speakers by the way you respond to them.[31] Come to class prepared to listen. Give speakers your wholehearted attention, and provide them with the positive feedback that is so important to authentic communication. Make it easy for them. If you know students who are extremely anxious, volunteer to serve as a listener when they practice their speeches. Encourage them and compliment them on what they do well. Be the kind of supportive listener you would like to face as you make your own presentations.

Assessing Techniques for Managing Communication Apprehension

Consider the five techniques for managing communication apprehension. Which of these might work for you? How would a combination of techniques operate? If you are reluctant to try a particular technique, why do you hesitate?

YOUR ETHICAL VOICE

Overcoming Communication Anxiety

Consider the ethical implications of communication anxiety. When you are the speaker, what responsibility do you have to your audience to put them before yourself? When you are an audience member, what responsibility do you have to support the speaker? What happens to the process of communication when speakers maintain an "I" orientation? What happens to the process of communication when audiences don't listen?

Final Reflections: Marshaling Your Butterflies

For many students, learning to cope with communication apprehension represents one of the most prominent challenges to finding your voice as a public speaker. Research suggests that a small minority of us are natural performers who never feel anxious when speaking before a crowd. However, for the vast majority of us—your authors included—that last-minute tension before making a presentation never completely goes away, and coping with it is always a work in progress. What you should remember is that this is not necessarily bad. Indeed, the most talented speakers are the ones who learn how to control and then channel that energy into bringing their messages to life for their listeners. By gaining a better understanding of the nature and causes of communication apprehension, and by using some or all of the techniques discussed here to manage it before and during the course of your presentations, you should be prepared to begin the process of making your butterflies fly in formation. And as you marshal your butterflies, you may discover something remarkable. There is indeed "adventure in giving the speech you were afraid to give."[32] As you finish your speech, finding your voice can be exhilarating!

Study Questions

CONTENT MASTERY

1 What are the principle external and internal factors of communication apprehension?

2 How does a communication orientation shift your thinking about public speaking?

3 How does cognitive restructuring work?

4 How can visualization help you control communication anxiety?

5 How can you learn the art of selective relaxation?

6 What are the advantages of education, preparation, and practice?

CRITICAL EXPLORATIONS

1. Revisit the Gauge of Communication Apprehension that you filled out earlier (Figure 2.1). In light of the concepts you have learned in this chapter, map out (a) which factors concern you the most and (b) what you can do to address each one.
2. Invite other students to join you in a support team to improve the quality of assigned speeches. Your support team should
   - work to reduce communication apprehension and increase self-confidence;
   - brainstorm possible topics and discuss strategies for effective speech designs and techniques for audience adaptation;
   - serve as practice audiences; and
   - offer constructive criticism.
3. Consider your recent interactions with social media such as Twitter, Facebook, blog entries, or YouTube. Do you experience communication apprehension when communicating in this way? Why or why not? In what ways is communicating via social media a form of public communication? In what ways is it different from public speaking?
4. Find a speech by one of the people we named as facing communication anxiety: Prince Harry, Adele, Warren Buffett, Stephen Colbert, or Beyoncé. Can you tell that this person is nervous? What does this suggest about the illusion of transparency and the ability to manage communication apprehension?
5. Work on the technique of selective relaxation. Then practice it in the next situation that causes you concern, whether that is a quiz, a test, or meeting a new group of people. How well did this technique work for you? In what ways could you enhance its effectiveness?

Your First Speech:

An Overview of Speech Preparation

CHAPTER

LEARNING OBJECTIVES	OUTLINE
This chapter will help you:	
3.1 Design and develop your first speech for a successful presentation.	Preparing and Presenting Your First Speech
3.2 Create favorable impressions of yourself with your audience.	Influencing the Impressions You Make
3.3 Construct a strong speech introducing yourself or others.	Speeches of Introduction

James was having a hard time getting started on his first speech. He had been asked to introduce himself by explaining one aspect that meant a lot to him and that helped define who he was. James was pretty sure he wanted to talk about his dream of becoming a chef and opening his own restaurant. That much was no problem. But how was he supposed to talk about himself without coming across as self-indulgent? And how was he supposed to already know how to put together and deliver a whole speech when the class had just begun? How could he start?

Then he began to reflect on the reasons he wanted to become a chef: his memories of helping his grandmother prepare holiday meals, his gratitude to the local chef who gave him his first job prepping vegetables in a professional kitchen, and his personal desire to develop healthier variations of the regional dishes he loved. James may not have realized it yet, but as he reflected on the details of his personal story, he was already well on the way to preparing an excellent first presentation. He was beginning to find his voice.

"Without speech there would be no community."

—ERNST CASSIRER

If, like James, you are having a hard time getting started on your first speech, you are certainly not alone. Over the years, we've found that it helps to provide a step-by-step overview for preparing and presenting first speeches—a summary of principles and skills that will be covered in more depth as this book develops. This overview becomes the first section of this chapter. We then discuss the art of managing the impressions we make on others, which is important to all public speaking but especially when addressing an audience for the first time. We close by discussing the speech of self-introduction, often the theme of the first speaking assignment, which helps to develop communication skills that may benefit you in a variety of social and professional contexts.

Preparing and Presenting Your First Speech

3.1 Design and develop your first speech for a successful presentation.

Whatever your first speaking assignment, it helps to work systematically through a series of steps that take you from choosing and focusing your topic through making the actual presentation. Rather than fretting over what you're going to say or how you're going to look, you can follow these steps to develop a coherent and compelling presentation. Figure 3.1, Major Steps in Speech Preparation and Presentation, illustrates this process. As these steps suggest, you need to allow sufficient time for each one. *This makes it vitally important to get started as soon as possible and not to procrastinate until the night before you are scheduled to speak.* A good speech needs time to jell, and you need time to reflect on what you want to say. The more important the speech, the more time you need to devote to it in advance.

As you proceed, keep in mind that speech preparation is rarely a perfectly linear process. You are likely to find yourself working back and forth from step to step. For instance, you might need to return to step 1 and refocus your topic after conducting your research. Even veteran speakers often work through several rough outlines of a speech before getting everything into focus for the actual presentation.

Figure 3.1 Major Steps in Speech Preparation and Presentation

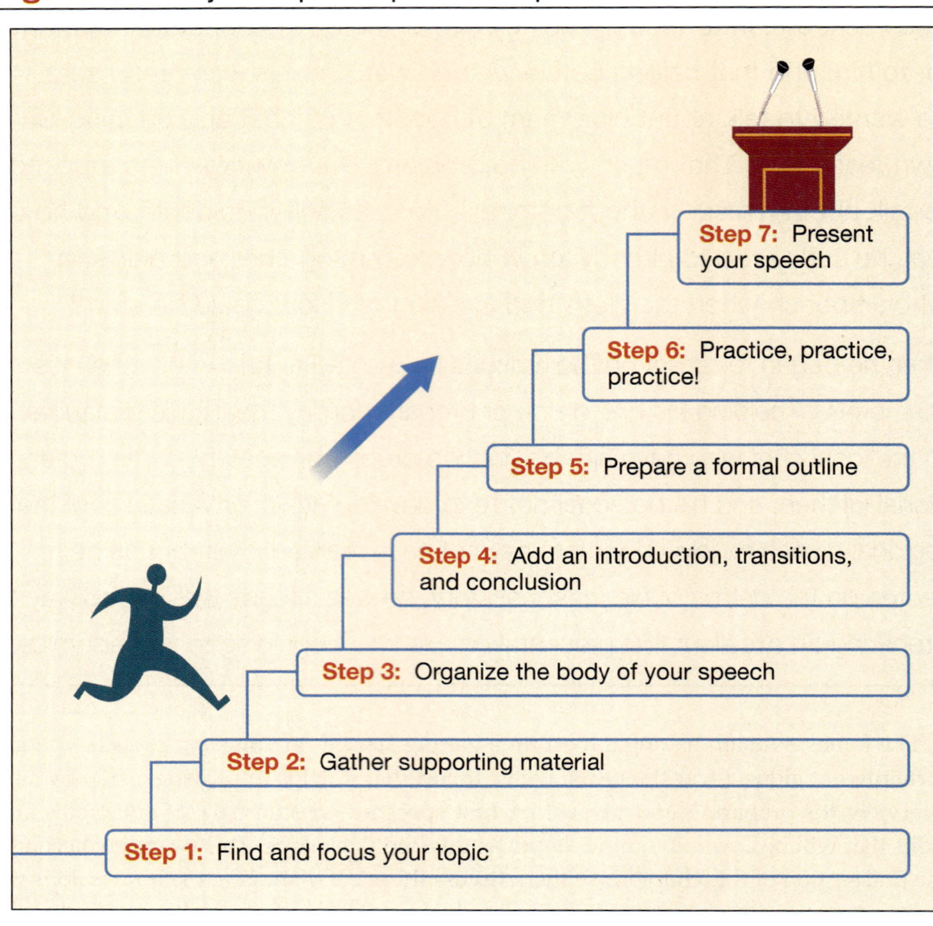

Step 1: Find and Focus Your Topic

Your first step—discussed in more detail in Chapter 6—is to search for a topic that will be appropriate to the assignment, the occasion, audience needs and interests, and your own preferences. When speaking outside the classroom, both the occasion and audience expectations will often determine your choice of topic and purpose. For instance, if asked to present a briefing to fellow employees on how to use a new software package, you pretty much know what you'll be talking about and why you'll be talking.

With classroom assignments, you may have more freedom to choose your own topics and explore your own voice. But your choices will still be limited to some extent by the nature of your speaking assignments. For example, with introductory speeches, you will often tell stories that will help listeners gain a better idea of who you are. With informative speeches, you seek topics on which you can find new and important ideas and information to convey. With persuasive speeches, you identify topics that are controversial or that ask listeners for commitment. With ceremonial speeches, you will celebrate the meaning of a special moment.

Regardless of the occasion or the assignment, good speech topics are important to the speaker and potentially important or interesting to listeners. Simply put, if you have some personal stake in a topic, then you are more likely to invest the interest and work required to make an effective presentation. Likewise, identifying what your audience will find of interest means they will be more likely to listen attentively.

Finally, a good speech topic is one that you will be able to research, prepare, and present in the limited time available to you. The more focused your topic, the more likely you are to provide your listeners with fresh ideas and quality information. For a speech introducing yourself or another, for example, you should not try to tell your entire life story. Instead, focus on one particular experience, goal, or influential person, and use it as a template to suggest who you are or what you hope to become. Similarly, a speech on alcohol abuse in general would not likely tell an audience of college students anything new. However, if you were to focus on a specific initiative to combat binge drinking on your campus or within your fraternity system, then you might have the makings of an excellent informative or persuasive presentation.

Your personal experiences can provide examples and narratives for your speech.

Step 2: Gather Supporting Material

Once you have chosen and focused your topic, you should begin gathering ideas and information to support and expand the major points of your message. When preparing introductory speeches, this typically involves reconstructing the details of your "story" in terms of people and experiences that have shaped you or goals and values that guide you. With later informative and persuasive presentations, you will supplement what you already know by researching the latest facts, events, and expert opinions regarding your topic.

In Chapter 7, we discuss the process of acquiring and critiquing materials to support your points, and in Chapter 8, we talk about the four most common forms of supporting information. Gathering and incorporating supporting materials demonstrates responsible knowledge. Using a blend of these forms—facts and statistics, testimony, examples, and narratives—will help you engage your audience in various aspects of your topic.

facts
Descriptive statements that can be verified as true by observation or by experts.

statistics
Facts that can be measured mathematically.

testimony
Citing the words and ideas of others to support a point.

Facts and Statistics. Because their truthfulness can be verified by independent observers and experts, **facts** are one of the most important and powerful forms of supporting information. For an introductory speech, facts about where you grew up or a cause you care about can enliven your presentation. When speakers address unfamiliar topics, they should provide their listeners with the basic facts they will need to understand them. Persuasive speakers try to show listeners that "the facts are on their side."

Statistics are facts that can be measured mathematically. In an introductory speech, you might use statistics to call attention to the magnitude of a problem you're working to address. Often presented in the form of percentages or contrasting fractions, statistics can be especially effective for tracing the growth or decline of trends such as unemployment or crime rates, or for expressing public opinion on issues such as global warming. As discussed in Chapter 10, graphs and other presentation aids can be particularly effective for emphasizing key facts and presenting large amounts of statistical information.

As you weave facts and statistics into your speeches, keep in mind that they never speak for themselves. You must interpret their meaning artfully to support your assertions, and they are almost always more effective when you provide specific details and cite highly credible sources.

Shooting survivor and former Congresswoman Gabby Giffords used personal experience to speak about gun control.

Testimony. Speakers use **testimony** when they cite the words or ideas of others. When you cite or quote experts or widely respected people in support of your points, you strengthen your credibility. Testimony can also be effective for explaining the meaning of complicated subjects. Eyewitness accounts of events and statements by those whose lives have been affected by your subject can make your speech more authentic and engaging. Finally, quotations from revered documents and respected figures can add eloquence to your

A former slave, Sojourner Truth narrated her experiences in her eloquent speeches on abolition and women's rights.

speech and can invoke shared values and aspirations. Perhaps your introductory speech might note that a guiding principle for you has been an iconic passage from President John F. Kennedy's inaugural address: "Ask not what your country can do for you—ask what you can do for your country."[1] Those eloquent words can lend dignity and importance to your own message.

Examples. **Examples** provide concrete illustrations that help clarify your ideas and ground your speech in reality. Examples say, in effect, "This really happened." They can arouse emotion and move audiences to action.

You can use an extended example that is developed in detail or a series of brief examples. Consider how Jeff Shannon used an extended example to introduce his persuasive speech supporting comprehensive sex education:

> Carla is an attractive and intelligent 15-year-old. Like most young teenagers, she has dreams and aspirations for her future—an education, a career, and maybe someday a husband and family. But, for Carla, realizing those dreams has just become a lot more complicated. She has just joined the growing ranks of single pregnant teenagers.

Whenever you doubt that your listeners may grasp your point or see its relevance to their lives, that is the moment for an example.

examples
Incidents that illustrate a speaker's point.

narratives
Stories that illustrate the ideas or theme of a speech.

Narratives. **Narratives** are stories that illustrate the ideas or theme of a speech. Like examples, stories within your speech can help to engage listeners. Simply put, we humans love a good story, and when artfully presented it is hard not to be drawn into them. Effective narratives call for a lively presentation style and language that is colorful, concrete, and active. They are more fully developed than examples in terms of character, scene, and plot, and they move toward some sort of climax that conveys a clear point or moral. Sabrina Karic's self-introductory speech, reprinted at the end of this chapter, effectively uses narrative to take her audience through her childhood experiences in war-torn Bosnia/Herzegovina.

Taken together, facts, statistics, testimony, examples, and narratives provide the substance of your speeches. Each one serves a unique function; weaving them together demonstrates the complexity of the topic, your understanding of that complexity, and your desire to reach your audience in a variety of ways.

Step 3: Organize the Body of Your Speech

body
The section of a speech that contains your main ideas and the materials that support them.

thesis statement
The central idea of a speech stated as a simple declarative sentence.

Once you've chosen, focused, and researched your topic, you can start to design your actual speech. Try to resist the temptation to start with the introduction. Write the **body** of your speech first, so that you know what you're going to introduce. The body contains the major ideas you wish to develop and their supporting materials.

The first step, as discussed in Chapter 6, is to formulate your **thesis statement** or central idea. This statement, expressed in a simple declarative sentence, should reflect a clear sense of what you intend to say. For instance, in her self-introductory speech, "My Three Cultures," Sandra Balz's thesis statement is "I have become much more aware of how my life is different because of having a mother who is of Palestinian origin but was born and raised in the Central American country of El Salvador" (see Appendix B).

main points
The most important ideas developed in support of the thesis statement.

The next step, as addressed in Chapter 9, is to generate the **main points** that will elaborate, explain, and defend your thesis statement. To find these points, look for the ideas that emerge repeatedly in your research and ask questions suggested by your topic. BJ Youngerman's speech on the art of baseball umpiring discusses three main points: the importance of maintaining order, professionalism, and making the right call the first time (see Appendix B).

design
Standard way to arrange the main points of a speech.

At this point, you should choose a **design** for arranging your main points in a manner appropriate to your topic and purpose. We discuss design options in Chapter 9

Figure 3.2
Outline Format for a Narrative Design

I. Prologue
   A. Describe the setting and background of the story
   B. Introduce the characters
   C. Foreshadow the meaning

II. Plot
   A. Scene 1
   B. Scene 2
   C. Scene 3

III. Epilogue
   A. Show how the story ends
   B. Present the meaning of the story

and in our chapters on informative, persuasive, and ceremonial speaking. For a speech of self-introduction, you might consider one of three kinds of organization:

- a *categorical design* like BJ used, which organizes main points by topics;
- a *chronological design*, which describes events or historical developments in the order they occurred; or
- a *narrative design*, which organizes materials in the form of a story. The narrative pattern uses a prologue, plot, and epilogue (see Figure 3.2 and Chapter 16 on ceremonial speaking).

Speeches of introduction often use a **narrative design** because it is ideal for dramatizing your experiences and reflecting on the lessons you learned from them. Sabrina Karic developed a narrative for her introductory speech, with a **prologue** that illustrates the power of narrative to involve listeners as vicarious participants in her story:

narrative design
A speech structure that develops from beginning to end through a prologue, a plot, and an epilogue.

prologue
The opening of a narrative that establishes the context and setting, introduces the main characters, and foreshadows the meaning.

> I want you to think back to when you were six years old. Then, imagine living in a time, a place, a country, where you constantly heard the noises [gunfire] I just played. I am from the small and tragic country of Bosnia and Herzegovina. While many of you were playing with toys and learning to ride a bike, I was living through a nightmare. I was six years old, certainly not ready to experience war. But one day, I heard my first gunshots and my innocent childhood ended. Almost overnight, my family was plunged into homelessness and poverty.

When you read Sabrina's speech, you will find that the **plot** unfolds through three major scenes: (1) her wealthy family reduced to homeless refugees under siege in Gorazde, (2) Sabrina worrying about her parents who braved enemy lines to seek food for her family, and (3) a joyous reunion tempered by the ongoing horror of the situation.

plot
The body of a narrative that unfolds in a sequence of scenes designed to build suspense.

The opening of her **epilogue** exemplifies the value of narrative for reflecting on who you are or have become in light of a life-changing experience:

epilogue
The final part of a narrative reflecting on its meaning.

> I can't remember how this nightmare ended, but somehow it did. To this day, I vividly remember these moments, and the experience has marked me for life. Now, I appreciate small things. I find satisfaction just taking a walk in the park, thanking God I survived. The experience also made me a fighter, and gave me strength and a will to live that has carried me to this point, and brought me here to share my story with you.

SPEAKER'S NOTES

Checklist for Developing a Narrative Design

- ☐ My prologue describes the setting and context for my story.
- ☐ My prologue introduces the characters in my story.
- ☐ My main points build suspense in my story.
- ☐ My colorful language and dialogue bring the story to life.
- ☐ My epilogue reflects on the meaning of the story.

working outline
A tentative plan that allows you to see the structure of your message as you develop it.

The final step in developing the body of your speech is to prepare a **working outline** that will allow you to see the structure of your message as you develop it. You should support each of your main points with subpoints and with information that substantiates what you have to say. As you proceed, keep in mind that outlining is a tentative process. You may work through several rough drafts before you settle on the final product, which will help you refine your presentation and become familiar with it.

Step 4: Add an Introduction, Transitions, and a Conclusion

introduction
The opening to your speech that gains attention, previews your message, and establishes a favorable connection with your listeners.

Once you've developed the body of your speech, it's time to add an introduction, transitions, and a conclusion. A good **introduction** should arouse the interest of your listeners and prepare them for the message to follow. Often, it will establish your credibility by explaining your personal connection to the topic. It should also point out what listeners may have at stake.

One student speaker offered an effective introduction when she looked up at her listeners after arranging her notes and said: "My message today is very simple: Get off your butts." While her startled listeners watched, she reached under the lectern and produced a large jar of cigarette butts. "This," she said, "is what they call 'butt-ugly.' I gathered these beauties after lunch last Friday in front of the Student Union. That was right after I smoked my last cigarette. Today, I want you to join me. Let's get off our butts together." Her introduction aroused interest and established her credibility to speak on how to quit smoking.

transitions
Connecting elements that cue listeners that you are finished making one point and are moving on to the next.

You should also give careful consideration to **transitions**, how you will move from one point to another and connect them. Good transitions let your listeners know when you've finished one idea and are moving to the next. They often remind listeners of the ideas you have covered up to that point in the speech. You might use short bridging phrases such as "For my next point...," "Having said that...," or "In conclusion...," although sometimes a simple pause or change in vocal inflection can signal listeners that you are ready to move to the next idea. Without carefully planned transitions, you may find yourself resorting to "uhs" and "ers" as you struggle from one point to another.

conclusion
The ending for your speech that reinforces your main ideas and provides your audience with something to remember.

Finally, the **conclusion** should reinforce your message by summarizing main points and leaving your audience something to think about. Often, the conclusion will tie back in to the introduction.

In Chapter 9, we discuss a number of strategies for opening and closing your speeches. Whatever technique you use, keep your introductions and conclusions brief, especially for short speeches. Because they are vital in shaping audience impressions and the flow of your speech, commit them to memory.

Step 5: Prepare a Formal Outline

As discussed in step 3, it is a good idea to create a working outline as you develop your speech. This will help you identify the structure of your presentation and see how the components work together. With informative and persuasive presentations, your instructor may ask you to go one step further to submit a **formal outline** and bibliography. The formal outline represents the final, complete, polished plan of your speech. If you are not given specific instructions, ask if you may follow the discussion and models offered in Chapter 9. Most formal outlines include a title as well as a separately developed introduction, body, and conclusion. All your main and supporting points should be written as complete sentences, and you should include abbreviated source citations that support your points. You should write out the transitions that tie together the main points of your speech.

formal outline
Represents the final, complete, polished plan of your speech.

As for the bibliography, find out whether your instructor has a preferred citation style for listing your sources. We provide samples in Chapter 7 that illustrate the Modern Language Association (MLA) and the American Psychological Association (APA) citation styles. Your instructor may look closely at your bibliography when assessing the quality of your research, so be sure to provide all the information that might be needed to check your sources.

A closing note: Preparing the formal outline and bibliography imposes a discipline on the preparation process that results in a better presentation. Also, with most classroom presentations, it represents the one tangible item your instructor has to evaluate your work after viewing your presentation. Make sure your formal outline and bibliography are computer-generated; neat; and carefully proofed for typos, spelling, and grammar.

Step 6: Practice, Practice, Practice!

Once you have polished and outlined your speech, you should be ready to practice the actual presentation. **Extemporaneous speaking**—which is generally preferred for brief presentations—emphasizes audience interaction and eye contact more than exact wording. You should be thoroughly prepared, and you should know your ideas and materials in the order to be presented. But instead of speaking from memory or reading from a manuscript, you should speak from the general pattern of ideas imprinted in your memory during practice.

extemporaneous speaking
A form of presentation in which a speech is carefully prepared and practiced but not written out, memorized, or read.

Rather than speaking from a formal outline or manuscript, use a **key-word outline**, a brief listing of words and phrases that will cue you to the flow of ideas and major points of emphasis in your speech. Should your mind go blank, you need only glimpse your key-word outline to get yourself back on track. Because they are easier to handle and allow for greater movement, we recommend using three-by-five-inch or four-by-six-inch note cards rather than writing out key words on sheets of paper. Some speakers increasingly make effective use of computer tablets and other electronic prompts. Use large lettering you can read at a glance, keep your notes brief, and look up frequently to maintain eye contact while speaking. Your goal is not to be perfect, and a few bobbles will just add to the naturalness of the communication.

key-word outline
Abbreviated version of a formal outline used in presenting a speech; focuses on cues and points of emphasis.

Again, do not try to speak from memory or read your speech from a formal outline or manuscript! Except for the introduction, the conclusion, and vital transitions, which are often memorized to give speeches a smooth sense of structure and fluidity, the exact wording of your main ideas should occur as you interact directly with listeners. This will give your speech a freshness and naturalness required for effective communication. The goal is to develop a conversational style so that everyone feels you are genuinely speaking to them.

It helps to rehearse your speech in the room where you will present it.

SPEAKER'S NOTES

Practicing Your Presentation

Keep these suggestions in mind as you practice your speech.

1. Visualize yourself making an effective presentation.
2. Focus on your ideas.
3. Speak naturally.
4. Present extemporaneously.
5. Maintain eye contact with your imagined listeners.
6. Practice from your key-word outline.
7. Rehearse until your speech flows smoothly.

Leave yourself an uninterrupted afternoon or evening to practice your presentation. Read over your outline several times until you feel familiar with it. Then develop your key-word outline and practice some more. Practice standing and speaking out loud. Imagine your listeners sitting before you, and pan the room as you maintain eye contact and interact with your imaginary audience. Speak up and animate your voice to bring your ideas to life, working in pauses and nonverbal gestures that feel natural and prompted by your ideas. Glance at your notes while pausing or as you need to. If you can, rehearse in the same room where you will be speaking. If you plan to use presentation aids, practice how you will integrate them into your presentation. Time your presentation to make sure it fits within the assignment's requirements.

When you begin to feel as though you could present the entire speech without notes, try it. If you succeed, you're ready. Put the notes away, get some sleep, and practice a few more times the morning before your presentation.

The Process of Preparing Your First Speech

Before you read through the steps in preparing your first speech, what did you think the process would involve? How did the section's discussion of the steps amplify your understanding?

Step 7: Present Your Speech

Should you find yourself experiencing a last-minute case of the jitters, know that you are in good company. Indeed, communication apprehension is so widespread that we include an entire chapter, Chapter 2, to help you deal with it. For now, keep reminding yourself that this is the first assignment of an introductory course. Again, focus not on yourself but on sharing your message with your audience. Speak loudly and clearly, and discipline yourself to maintain eye contact with your audience. Take comfort in knowing that you will improve substantially during the course of your class. You have so much to gain by finding your voice!

It's your time to speak. You've earned it. Now enjoy the moment with your listeners.

Finding Your Voice

The Speech I Liked Most

What speech from the first round (besides your own) made the greatest impression on you and why? Was it a shared interest in the topic area? Was it an effective presentation style? Was it a compelling or artfully presented narrative? How did the speaker enhance your impression of his or her competence, integrity, good will, and dynamism? What can you learn from this presentation to enhance your own speaking?

Influencing the Impressions You Make

3.2 Create favorable impressions of yourself with your audience.

As you stand to speak, listeners will begin to form impressions of you that will influence how they respond to your messages. Your first speech, whatever its topic, is key to setting the audience's impressions of you for your later presentations. Aristotle called these impressions **ethos**. You can enhance your ethos by cultivating favorable impressions of your competence, integrity, good will, and dynamism. Figure 3.3 illustrates the components of ethos.

ethos
Audience's impressions of a speaker's competence, integrity, good will, and dynamism.

Competence

Competent speakers come across as well informed, intelligent, and well prepared. You can build **competence** by selecting topics in which you have personal experience and by putting together well-organized, effectively worded, well-practiced speeches. You can further build competence by strengthening your knowledge through research and then citing experts and authorities who support your position. For example, if you are speaking on the relationship between nutrition and heart disease, you might quote a medical specialist or a publication of the American Heart Association. Melissa Anderton introduced testimony into her speech in this way: "Dr. Milas Peterson heads the Heart Institute at Harvard University. During his visit to our campus last week, I spoke with him about this idea. He told me...."

competence
The perception of a speaker as being well informed, intelligent, and well prepared.

- She points out the qualifications of her expert.
- The testimony she uses is recent.
- She made a personal contact with her expert.
- She prepared carefully for her speech.

When you cite authorities in this way, you are "borrowing" their credibility to enhance your own.

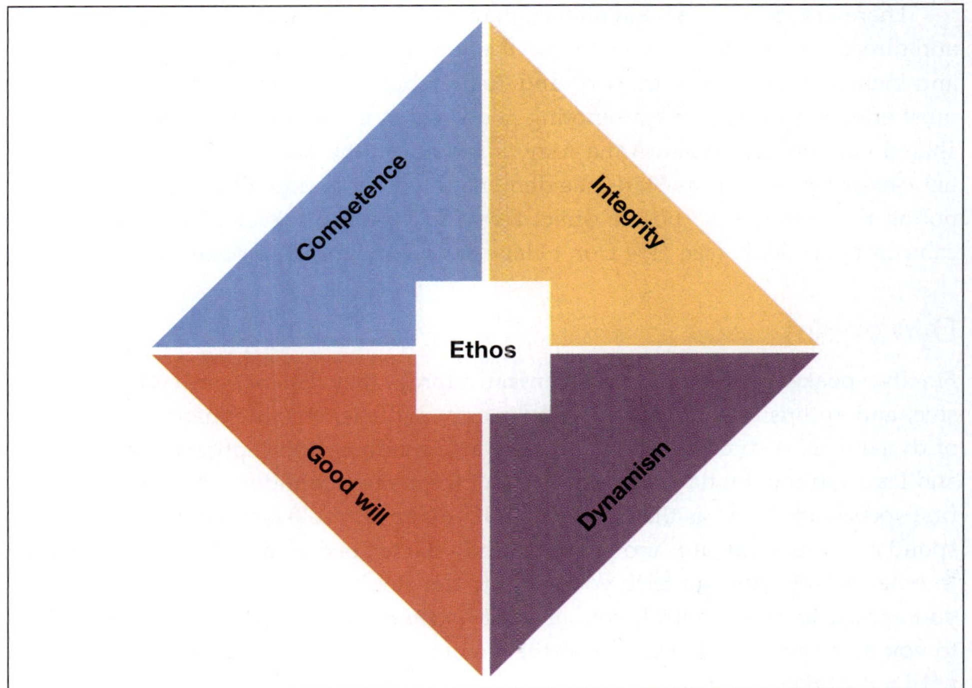

Figure 3.3
The Components of Ethos

Smiling and engaging the audience help speakers demonstrate good will.

Integrity

Speakers cultivate positive impressions of **integrity** by being honest, ethical, and dependable. Listeners will be more receptive to your messages if you are straightforward, personally committed to your message, and genuinely concerned with the consequences of your speaking. The more you ask of your listeners, the more important your integrity becomes. When asking audiences to commit to a course of action, you should make clear your own involvement and willingness to follow your own advice. When addressing skeptical audiences on controversial issues such as reforming health care or increasing restrictions on gun purchases, acknowledge opposing positions before explaining and defending your own.

integrity
The impression of a speaker as being honest, ethical, and dependable.

One of our students, a former gang member named Antonio Lopez, enhanced perceptions of his integrity by citing his own involvement with the gang lifestyle. "I know how this hurt my parents," he recalled. "They didn't want to see video of me shot or arrested on the evening news. I knew I had to change." His openness showed his willingness to trust the members of his audience with sensitive information, and they responded in kind by trusting him.

On the other hand, when another of our students chose to wing his self-introductory speech by talking about how he and his buddies harassed the campus groundhog, his unorganized and unreflective presentation harmed the audience's perceptions of his integrity, and he spent much of the semester trying to overcome that bad impression.

Good Will

good will
The impression that speakers have their listeners' best interests at heart.

Good will means that speakers have the best interests of listeners at heart.[2] Such speakers appear to value the community over their own personal agendas. Good will is crucial to establishing identification, those feelings of shared values, background, and interest that can unite speakers and audiences.[3] As with integrity, good will is hard to repair once it has been violated.

There are many ways to enhance perceptions of good will. An engaging smile and direct eye contact can help. So can the appropriate use of humor, self-disclosure, and inclusive terms such as "we" and "us" to build symbolic bridges. Perhaps the most effective strategy for promoting good will is to emphasize shared values and shared experiences. When Anna Aley talked about the poor quality of housing for her classmates at Kansas State, she demonstrated her good will for her audience by noting that slumlords "pose a direct threat to you if you ever plan to rent an off-campus apartment" (see "We Don't Have to Live in Slums," Appendix B).

dynamism
The perception of a speaker as confident, decisive, and enthusiastic.

> **Ethos**
>
> Identify someone whom you respect. What contributes to that person's ethos? What guidance do your observations provide for your own speaking?

Dynamism

Finally, speakers who convey **dynamism** impress their listeners as confident, decisive, and enthusiastic. Demonstrating energy and excitement enhances perceptions of dynamism. A dynamic speaking style also reinforces perceptions of competence and leadership potential. Even if you don't feel overly confident about making your first speech, try to act as though you are. If you appear self-assured, listeners will respond as though you are, and you may find yourself becoming what you seem to be. In other words, you can trick yourself into developing a very desirable trait! When you appear to be in control, you also put listeners at ease. This feeling comes back to you as positive feedback and further reinforces your confidence. In short, fake it until you make it.

You can enhance dynamism by choosing a topic that you care about. Your enthusiasm endorses your message. We discuss other ways of projecting confidence, decisiveness, and enthusiasm in Chapter 12.

YOUR ETHICAL VOICE

The Ethics of Ethos

To build your ethos in ethical ways, follow these guidelines.

- Do enough research so that you can speak with true competence.
- Cite respected authorities in support of your ideas.
- Interpret information fairly.
- Give sufficient thought to what you will say and how you will say it so that you can concentrate on making connections with your audience.
- Develop a clear organizational structure so that both you and your audience know where you are heading.
- Be honest about where you stand on your topic.
- Have your listeners' best interests at heart.
- Share your enthusiasm for your topic with your audience.

Speeches of Introduction

3.3 Construct a strong speech introducing yourself or others.

Many public speaking classes open with speeches that ask you to introduce yourself or a classmate. Such introductory speeches help you get to know your classmates as you discover the interests, experiences, and quirks that make for interesting individuals. As a consequence, the speeches can create a receptive atmosphere in which you can grow as communicators and discover your voice. These first efforts can also create favorable ethos for later speeches.

In the advice that follows, we shall assume that the assignment asks you to introduce yourself. With only minor adjustments, you can adapt this advice for the purpose of introducing a classmate. In addition, these steps will help you introduce yourself clearly and confidently in a wide range of circumstances. In your life beyond the classroom, you may be called on to say a few words about yourself in the course of formal job interviews, when first joining new groups, in the introduction to longer formal presentations, or even while running for public office. Regardless of the occasion, your ability to tell your story and pursue a meaningful point about who you are and what you believe is an invaluable people skill. It certainly didn't hurt Barack Obama when he introduced himself at the

Finding Your Voice

Self-Introductions and Political Campaigns

Is there a local or national campaign taking place as you take this course? Choose a viable candidate and read or view statements that introduce the candidate to prospective voters. Campaign websites usually include brief campaign biographies as well as "stump speeches" and introductory comments at major political debates. What stories of the candidate's childhood and upbringing do they tell? Do they manifest the attributes of a good narrative as discussed in this chapter? How do they enhance or detract from your perceptions of the candidate's ethos and fitness for political office?

Democratic National Convention in 2004 as "a skinny kid with a funny name who believes that America has a place for him, too."[4]

As you prepare your speech of introduction, ask yourself how listeners might gain a better sense of who you are as a unique individual. Don't try to tell your entire life story in the few brief minutes that are usually allotted for such speeches. Instead, focus on an element that really defines you. If you have any doubts about the appropriateness of prospective topic ideas, check with your instructor.

self-awareness inventory
A series of questions that allow speakers to explore specific ideas for developing their speech of self-introduction.

To help you explore possibilities for your speech, complete a **self-awareness inventory**. Ask yourself the following questions:

1. *How has your **cultural background** influenced you?* How has it shaped the person you are now? How can you explain this influence to others? In her self-introductory speech, Sandra Baltz described herself as a unique product of three cultures. She felt that this rich cultural background had widened her horizons. Note how she focused on food to represent the convergence of these different ways of life:

> In all, I must say that being exposed to three very different cultures—Latin, Arabic, American—has been rewarding for me and has made a difference even in the music I enjoy and the food I eat. It is not unusual in my house to sit down to a meal made up of stuffed grape leaves and refried beans and all topped off with apple pie for dessert.

The text of Sandra's speech may be found in Appendix B.

2. *How has your **hometown** or the environment in which you grew up influenced you?* How were you shaped by it? What stories or examples illustrate this influence? What images of your childhood come to mind? Jimmy Green provided a vivid word-picture to help his audience envision his life growing up in rural Tennessee:

> To share my world, come up with me to the Tennessee River. We'll take a boat ride to New Johnsonville, where Civil War gunboats still lie on the bottom of the river. You'll see how the sun makes the water sparkle. You'll see the green hills sloping down to the river and the rocky cliffs. If we're lucky, we might see a doe and her fawn along the shoreline, or perhaps some great blue herons or a bald eagle overhead.

SPEAKER'S NOTES

Self-Awareness Inventory

1. How has your *cultural background* influenced you?
2. How has your *hometown or childhood environment* influenced you?
3. What *special person* has had a major impact on your life?
4. Were you shaped by an unusual accomplishment or *experience?*
5. Does a favorite *activity* or hobby add meaning to your life?
6. How does your *work* help define you as an individual?
7. What special *goal* or *purpose* in life is meaningful to you?
8. How do your *values* help define who you are?

3. *What **particular person**—a friend, relative, or childhood hero—had a major impact on your life?* Why do you think this person had such influence? Was it an outstanding deed or accomplishment, meaningful mentoring or advice, or an act of kindness that inspired you? Was it a particular experience you shared together? In her self-introductory speech, Marty Gaines explained how she had benefitted from the contrasting influences of her two grandmothers:

> Margaret Hasty was my "Memma," the kind of grandmother that always embraced me with a big hug, and always seemed to have a stash of my favorite cookies nearby. Martha Clark Akers was "Grandmother"—very strict, very formal, and always concerned with my progress in school and whether I was making the "right decisions."

> I guess I preferred Memma's company as a child, but in time I came to realize that I was loved and blessed by both of my grandmothers in equal if different ways. Now, there are days when I just grab my children up and tell them I love them. And I think to myself, "Thank you, Memma." And then there are days when I know that I have to be strong and strict. And I say to myself, "Give me strength, Grandmother."

4. *Have you been marked by some **unusual accomplishment** or experience?* What was it, and how did it affect you? What were the most dramatic moments associated with your experience? In her self-introductory speech reprinted at the end of this chapter, Sabrina Karic tells her story of surviving war and ethnic cleansing as a child and reflects on how she learned to appreciate the small things that so many of us take for granted—such as chocolate!

Your early environment, childhood activities, and favorite hobbies can be rich sources of ideas for speeches.

5. *What **activity** brings meaning to your life?* Remember, what is important is not the activity itself but how it defines you. When he conducted his self-awareness inventory, David Smart decided that playing golf had taught him useful lessons:

> I don't let the little frustrations bother me and I keep going, no matter what happens. In golf, even though you hit a bad shot, you still have to go on and hit the next one. You can't walk off the course just because things aren't going your way. College life is the same way. If you have a bad day or do poorly on a test, you can't just give up and go home. You have to move up to the next tee and keep swinging.

6. *How does the **work** you do make you who you are?* If you select this approach, go beyond describing what you do to focus on how your job has shaped you. Richard Bushart was quite a spectacle as he stood to present his self-introductory speech wearing makeup and a clown suit. But those who were expecting a trivial speech were in for a surprise:

> An adult will think I'm foolish, weird, or just insane. But to a child I'm funny, caring, and a friend. Children have taught me so much.... They have inspired me to dream again and be creative. A child playing in the backyard can take a broom and turn it one way and it's a horse waiting to ride. Turn it another, and it's a hockey stick. Turn it still another, and it becomes a telescope through which she can see the universe.

7. *What are your **goals** or **purpose** in life?* Listeners are usually fascinated by those whose lives are dedicated to some purpose. If you choose to describe some personal goal, be sure to emphasize why you have the goal and how it affects you. Tom McDonald had returned to school after dropping out for eleven years. In his self-introductory speech, he described his goal:

> Finishing college means a lot to me now, even if that means working by day and attending school by night. The first time I enrolled, right out of high school, I "blew it." All I cared about was sports, girls, and partying. Even though I have a respectable job that pays well, I feel bad about not finishing a degree. My wife's diploma hangs on our den wall. All I have there is a stuffed duck!

8. *What **values** or larger cause do you hold dear?* How did they come to have such importance for you? What experiences have helped teach those values to you? What have you done personally or what groups have you worked with to

The Self-Awareness Inventory

Which elements of the self-awareness inventory spark ideas for your self-introductory speech? Which elements would you like to hear more about from your classmates?

advance your cause? Remember that values are abstract, so concrete illustrations will help them come alive for others. As she described her commitment to family values, Velma Black discussed her experiences growing up in a large family in rural Missouri:

> When you are one of thirteen, you learn to get along with others. You have no choice. You learn to work together without whining and complaining. And you learn to love—not noisy shows of affection—just quiet caring that fills the house with warmth and strength.

You may find it awkward to answer some of these questions about yourself. Consider asking friends how they would describe you and what aspects of you strike them as most distinctive. You might even incorporate some of their comments in your speech.

Finding Your Voice

Reflecting on Your First Speech

Describe your personal adventure of preparing your first speech. Which steps identified in this chapter were most difficult for you? Why? What mistakes did you make? What could you have done to avoid such problems? Did you allow enough time before the presentation to develop, polish, and practice it? What have you learned about preparations that might be useful for your next speech? Keep your analysis so you can review it as you prepare later speeches.

Final Reflections: Taking the First Steps

The ancient Chinese philosopher Lao-tzu once said that "a journey of a thousand miles begins with a single step." That may be true, but in the journey to find your voice, your first steps may be the hardest. The purpose of this chapter has been to help you take these initial steps as easily and as successfully as possible.

In the process, we have described not one step but seven. The first is to find a topic that really engages you—that makes you want to learn more and share your knowledge with others. The second is to make yourself at home in the world of research. You learn how to make contact with treasures of learning that await you and how to avoid traps of deception that may have been set by unscrupulous others. The third, fourth, and fifth steps lead you to develop artfully arranged messages that share the power of your new knowledge with others. The sixth step prepares you to present yourself and your ideas in the most favorable light so that people will want to hear you and learn from you. The final step concerns that exhilarating moment when you actually stand before an audience to bring them your message.

All these steps help accelerate the process of finding your voice before a group of fellow travelers as you all take the first steps toward the ultimate destination of effective communication. The next chapters will develop these concepts in greater detail.

Study Questions

CONTENT MASTERY

1 How can you go about finding a topic that will bring out the best in you?

2 How can you develop interesting and responsible content for your message?

3 What different design options can help you structure your message?

4 What are the components of ethos?

5 How can you develop favorable ethos? How can you influence listeners' impressions of you?

6 What is a self-awareness inventory?

7 How can a self-awareness inventory help you develop a speech introducing yourself or others?

CRITICAL EXPLORATIONS

1. Create a list of topics for speeches you might develop during the course of the class term. Can you connect them in some way so that you might learn more about the related, larger topic area as you proceed? How might you build ethos on this larger topic area during your first speech? What cues did you observe from watching the first round of speeches to suggest your classmates might be interested in hearing more about some of these topics? Discuss your ideas with your classmates to gauge audience interest and to benefit from their suggestions.

2. Submit a timeline for the preparation of your first speech, ending with the day you will make your presentation. How much time do you plan to spend on each step in the preparation process?

3. Write a character sketch of someone you believe exemplifies strong ethos. Support and develop this sketch with examples and evidence.

4. Watch a contemporary political speech on YouTube. Evaluate the ethos of the speaker. Did she seem to know what she was talking about? Did he present credible evidence to validate his points (demonstrating competence)? Did the speaker seem honest and open (demonstrating integrity)? Did she seem to have your best interests at heart? Was he pleasant and likable (demonstrating good will)? Was the speaker enthusiastic about the topic of the speech? Did she seem energetic and forceful (demonstrating dynamism)? Explain how the speaker demonstrates each of the dimensions of ethos and how you think this demonstration affects the effectiveness of the speech.

5. Find examples in contemporary advertising emphasizing the testimony of experts or widely respected celebrities. Discuss the differences between these types of testimony. Which ones are effective? In what contexts might they be more effective?

6. You have been chosen to present a speech nominating your favorite professor for a prestigious teaching award—somebody besides your public speaking instructor! How would you go about building a favorable picture of your candidate on each of the dimensions of ethos?

7. How would you evaluate the effectiveness of a recent political campaign in building the ethos of its candidate and/or damaging the ethos of its opponent? Consider the role of political advertising or self-introductory narratives in advancing or hindering these efforts. What part did these efforts play in the results of the campaign?

SELF-INTRODUCTORY SPEECH

Sabrina Karic gave this self-introductory speech to her class at the University of Nevada–Las Vegas. Her speech is built around a narrative that features a personal experience as the shaping force in her life. She tells about surviving the ethnic cleansing that took place in Bosnia and Herzegovina during the early 1990s when she was a child. As she described this situation, her listeners were intrigued by her power and passion.

A LITTLE CHOCOLATE

SABRINA KARIC

Reprinted with permission from Sabrina Karic, University of Nevada–Las Vegas.

In her prologue, Sabrina ducks beneath the table as she plays the sounds of an explosion and gunfire, which startles the audience; then she establishes her credibility to speak from personal experience.

I want you to think back to when you were six years old. Then, imagine living in a time, a place, a country, where you constantly heard the noises [gunfire] I just played. I am from the small and tragic country of Bosnia and Herzegovina. While many of you were playing with toys and learning to ride a bike, I was living through a nightmare. I was six years old, certainly not ready to experience war. But one day, I heard my first gunshots and my innocent childhood ended. Almost overnight, my family was plunged into homelessness and poverty.

In the first major scene of her story, as her family begins to starve in Gorazde, Sabrina uses concrete detail to help her listeners visualize and share the horror of her experience.

After the Serbs forced us out of our home, we had to endure endless nights sleeping under trees while rain poured down on us and mice crawled over our bodies. We finally made our way to Gorazde, a city that was surrounded by the Serbians and held under siege for months. The local authorities kept us all barely alive by distributing food among the families. Typically, each week we would receive thirty pounds of flour, three pounds of beans, one pound of sugar, and two liters of oil. Every day, my mom made bread that was one inch thick. She divided it in half; one half for breakfast and the other for dinner. Then each half was divided in five even pieces—one piece for me, my mom, my dad, my sister, and my cousin, who lived with us.

This was incredibly hard for us. We often ran out of food before the next week's food distribution. Sometimes, the supplies were delayed or not available. I can tell you that nothing etches itself more in a child's memory than the pain of hunger. During those days, I never dreamed of living in a big house, or having a pool, or even a doll to play with. I simply prayed to God for chocolate.

In the second major scene, waiting for the return of her parents, Sabrina describes her growing despair. This dark feeling sets up the happiness she feels over their safe return. She uses an analogy to Christmas to help her listeners appreciate her joy. In this scene, chocolate begins to develop its larger symbolic meaning.

On January 31st of 1993, my parents decided to leave for Grebak, where the Bosnian army was situated. They would have to sneak through enemy lines to get there. If they made it, the Bosnian army would give them food to bring back to us. If they didn't make it—well, we didn't talk about that. If they didn't try, we were all going to starve anyway.

When my parents departed, they had to leave my sister and me on our own. Luckily, we had cousins who lived in Gorazde long before the war began. They took us in, and I can tell you that if it hadn't been for them, we would have starved to death. Days passed, and each day we waited for our parents. And our fears began to grow. We heard rumors that they had run into minefields and been killed. We felt very much alone and scared.

Then on February 7th, a miracle happened. The door opened, and there were our parents! I remember the crying and hugging and kissing. And I remember hope flooding back into our hearts. Our parents explained that although many people had died, God had spared them.

That day, I learned the meaning of gratitude as well as sorrow for those whose parents would not return. But then our thoughts turned to food. My parents had brought so much of it to us! For those of you who celebrate Christmas, I'm sure I can compare my happiness on that one day to all of your holidays, added together. My parents had brought us one unforgettable treasure: Can you guess what it was?

Yes, it was chocolate, a small chocolate bar, broken into pieces during the trip. But my sister and I treasured each tiny piece and ate it very slowly.

In the third scene of her plot, Sabrina jerks listeners back into the daily horror of her situation. The image of a hand grenade interrupting the play of children is especially graphic and memorable.

After the joy of that reunion, we returned to the reality of life around us. It seemed that every day, the explosions were getting closer, louder, and more frequent. I remember one particular day when I was playing with my friends outside our building. Suddenly, we heard a nearby explosion, and all of us dashed for the building. We knew that we had only a few seconds at best. I just got inside the door and closed it, when a grenade exploded right where we had been playing. I fell to the floor and put my hands over my ears, waiting for the ringing to go away. After a few minutes, I peeked outside to see if any of my friends had been hurt. Thank God, all of us had been spared.

In her epilogue, Sabrina reflects on the meaning of her ordeal and invites listeners to look for ways to counter such inhumanity. Note how she applies her experience in global, contemporary ways. At this final point in the speech, chocolate has become a universal symbol for hope.

I can't remember how this nightmare ended, but somehow it did. To this day, I vividly remember these moments, and the experience has marked me for life. Now, I appreciate small things. I find satisfaction just taking a walk in the park, thanking God I survived. The experience also made me a fighter and gave me strength and a will to live that has carried me to this point and brought me here to share my story with you.

And even today, my experience makes me weep for all the children everywhere—Muslim, Jewish, and Christian—in Africa, the Middle East, and elsewhere—all the six-year-olds who experience prejudice and hatred and violence they can't understand. I weep for the loss of their innocence, for the loss of their happiness, for the loss of their lives. Can't we reach out to them and make their world a little more liveable? Can't we bring them a little chocolate?

Becoming a Better Listener

CHAPTER

LEARNING OBJECTIVES	OUTLINE
This chapter will help you:	
4.1 Appreciate your power as a listener.	Your Power as a Listener
4.2 Overcome some basic, common barriers to listening.	Overcoming Barriers to Effective Listening
4.3 Become a more effective and critical listener.	Becoming a Better Listener
4.4 Identify effective aspects of speeches as you listen.	Guidelines for Listening to Speeches
4.5 Become a more ethical listener.	Your Ethical Responsibilities as a Listener

You're making a presentation in your psychology lab. As you stand before the class, you observe the following:

A young woman in the front row is texting on her cell phone.

A student in the back seems to be sleeping off the effects of an all-night party.

Two students in the corner are laughing over something they're holding under their desks.

Another student seems to be working on a lab report, typing furiously on her laptop.

Oh, wait a minute—here is a student who seems ready to listen. His desk is clear of everything except a pen and notebook. He has a supportive look on his face; he's actually waiting for you to make your presentation.

"Know how to listen, and you will profit even from those who talk badly."

—PLUTARCH

As you may have surmised from this opening example, a good listener is sometimes hard to find! According to the American Listening Association, studies suggest that we spend an average of 44 percent of our time listening[1]—and as a student, you spend even more. Yet most of us remember only about half of what we actually hear after listening to presentations and will forget a lot of that over the next 24 hours.[2] Perhaps this is due to the lack of emphasis placed on teaching listening skills in our education system, or perhaps it is due to our tendency to associate speaking with leadership and listening with passivity. As S.I. Hayakawa observed, "Living in a competitive culture, most of us are . . . chiefly concerned with getting our own views across, and we . . . find other people's speeches a tedious interruption of our own ideas."[3] Perhaps closer to home, *listening effectively and ethically is hard work.* Like any other communication skill, it can be developed and nurtured through education and practice—but it takes considerable concentration and effort.

In either case, your ability to listen can make important contributions to your success in school, in the workplace, and in life in general. Obviously, students who do not listen effectively for ideas and information will not perform as well in their classes and will not benefit as much from their educational experiences. In the workplace, poor listening is a commonly cited cause of communication breakdown and organizational dysfunction, which is probably why 73 percent of employers consider listening skills an important criterion when interviewing job applicants.[4] Finally, the ability to listen is crucial to resolving personal conflicts and maintaining healthy relationships with family, friends, and loved ones. When someone doesn't attend to directions, when a partner doesn't pay attention to our frustrations, when a friend doesn't heed our call for help—the relationship suffers.

More important to this class, developing your listening skills will make an important contribution to finding your voice as a public speaker. As you participate in this course, you will spend considerably more time listening to your classmates than making your own presentations. By listening attentively and thoughtfully, you will develop your ability to process ideas and information in a critical yet constructive fashion, and you will develop your appreciation for public speaking as you acquire and hone your own skills. You will also contribute to creating the supportive classroom environment that is so important to both you and your classmates as you discover your own voices. As a listener, you play a crucial role with your participation in the transactional process of communication. You have a shared responsibility for the success and impact of public speaking transactions.

We open this chapter by discussing your power as a listener in the public speaker process. We then address some common listening barriers that present challenges to effective listening. In the third section, we cover the important types of listening and offer advice for developing your listening skills. We then suggest guidelines for assessing public speeches. We close by discussing your ethical responsibilities as you listen to public presentations.

Your Power as a Listener

4.1 Appreciate your power as a listener.

Henry David Thoreau once remarked that "the greatest compliment that was ever paid me was when one asked me what I thought, and attended to my answer."[5] When we think of public speaking and power, we might envision commanding and eloquent speakers moving their audiences as if they were pawns without thought or choice. Yet, as we discussed in Chapter 1, the transactional process of communication makes listeners an essential part of the process; they bring considerable power to public speaking transactions. The most obvious source of power is that listeners are the ultimate arbiters of public speaking messages. As a speaker presents a message, listeners have the power and responsibility to determine the meaning, whether the arguments are well supported with evidence and reasoning, whether the ideas are expressed with passion, and whether they find the advice compelling and worth passing on to others.

As a listener in your public speaking class, you have the power and responsibility to contribute to a supportive and interactive environment that will help your classmates find their voices. Consider the following three experiments:

- In one experiment, students gave speeches on how to select a college. Under the condition of *negative* feedback, their audiences slouched, played with their face or hair or hands, shifted position frequently, doodled, fiddled with objects, looked around, and made no eye contact. As a result, the speakers talked for a shorter length of time, were less fluent and more hesitant, spoke more slowly, and felt less self-confident. Under the condition of *positive* feedback, their audiences sat upright, smiled, nodded, took notes, sat still, and made constant eye contact. As a result, the speakers proved to be more self-confident, fluent, and engaging.
- In a second experiment, students in a college psychology class faced a dull, boring professor who read his notes, spoke in a monotone, seldom gestured, and rarely looked at the students. By instruction of the experimenter, the students started with negative feedback of the sort described in the first experiment and then provided positive feedback, including leaning forward, smiling, and nodding. In response, the professor grew more animated, with an increased rate of speech, greater vocal variety, more gestures, and greater interaction with the students. When the students relapsed into negative feedback at a prearranged signal, the lecturer once again droned on.
- In a third experiment, students in a class agreed ahead of time that the left side of the room would be more visibly and positively responsive for the first half of the period and that the right side would do so for the second half of class. What happened? The professor spoke to the left side of the class for the first half and to the right side of the class for the second half.[6]

So there is a reason your instructor will probably not tolerate using speech rounds for study hall, playing with electronic devices, or whispered conversations in the back of the room. In each of the above cases, actively engaged and constructive listeners actually helped to facilitate a higher quality of public speaking.

Finally, developing your listening skills will help you to become a more effective speaker in at least four ways:

1. You will be better able to adapt to your audience. As you listen to their speeches, you will get a feel for what types of topics and examples might interest them, what authorities they will respect, and how they feel about important issues. Effective listening alerts you to such factors.
2. You will become sensitive to methods that work (or not) in different situations. Not all speaking methods work well all the time. Some you hear will seem brilliant, while others will fall flat. You will develop a sense of which approaches work best with your audience in various situations.
3. You will learn how to evaluate what you hear, what constitutes a credible source of information, and how appropriate types of supporting materials can be used.
4. You can use what you learn from listening to others to help you find your voice. You may hear speeches on topics you never thought you would find interesting, thus expanding your horizons. And you can learn to evaluate your personal positions on issues to see if they will stand up to critical scrutiny.

All of these skills can help you develop and present more effective speeches.

The Power of Listeners in Action

Identify a time when you saw the power of listeners in action—for example, in a class, at a rally, or during a presentation. What did the listeners do to influence the speaker? What resulted?

SPEAKER'S NOTES

Guidelines to Improve Listening through Note-Taking

Following these guidelines will help you listen more effectively both to instructors and to classroom speeches:

1. Familiarize yourself with assigned readings ahead of time, especially for complex subjects.
2. Draw a vertical line on your note paper, leaving a three-inch-wide margin on the right side.
3. Take your notes in outline form on the left side, leaving space between main points.
4. Don't try to write down everything you hear.
5. Be alert for signal words:
   a. *For example* suggests that supporting materia will follow.
   b. *The three steps* suggests a list you should number.
   c. *Therefore* suggests a causal relationship.
   d. *Keep in mind* suggests this is an important idea.
6. Summarize what you hear, and jot down questions in the right margin as they come to mind.
7. Review your notes the same day you take them.

Note that we recommend taking notes by hand rather than using a laptop. Research demonstrates that students who take notes with pen and paper better process and retain information than those who use a laptop—even those who successfully resist temptations to multi-task, text, or surf the web.[7]

Overcoming Barriers to Effective Listening

4.2 Overcome some basic, common barriers to listening.

Even those of us who think we listen well often succumb to one or more common barriers to effective listening. A noisy environment can disrupt effective listening. We may tune out a message as our minds wander, or get sidetracked thinking about personal matters, or come to premature conclusions before we have heard all the speaker has to say. Our own emotions and biases may interfere with the reception of a message.

Figure 4.1 can help you identify some of the problems that act as barriers to effective listening for you. The more items you check on this list, the more you need to work on improving your listening skills. This list will also help you pinpoint which specific areas you should concentrate on.

Figure 4.1 Listening Problems Checklist

Check all items that apply to you.

_____ I find it hard to listen to uninteresting material.

_____ I find it difficult to listen to speeches on issues that I feel strongly about.

_____ I have strong emotional reactions to certain words.

_____ I am easily distracted by noises around me.

_____ I am easily dazzled by a glib presentation.

_____ I find myself thinking up counter arguments when I disagree with a speaker.

_____ I have trouble listening when I have a lot on my mind.

_____ I stop listening when a topic is difficult.

_____ I listen mainly for facts and ignore the rest of a message.

_____ I often jump to conclusions before I have heard a speaker out.

_____ I sometimes text friends or surf the web when I should be listening.

Noise

Physical noise can block effective listening. When physicians in emergency departments change shifts, they frequently brief incoming physicians in the middle of noisy hallways, which can result in tragic misunderstandings that harm the health and well-being of patients.[8] Even in classroom settings that are relatively easy to control, poor acoustics and sources of competing noise can prove a major distraction. In the midst of giving an important job presentation, one of your authors got drowned out by the sound of someone playing the tuba in the room next door. She tried valiantly to speak over the aspiring musician but eventually had to ask a faculty member to deliver a cease and desist request!

Speakers and listeners should work together to resolve or cope with noise problems. Speakers can help by animating their voice and gestures enough to be heard by everyone in the audience. Listeners can provide feedback to let the speaker know there is a problem. Cupping your hand by your ear and leaning forward should help to cue speakers that they need to speak up. If the speaker doesn't respond and you still can't hear, move to a seat closer to the front of the room. If the noise comes from outside, get up and close the window or door, or politely ask those congregating outside the classroom to hold it down.

SPEAKER'S NOTES

Improving Your Listening Skills

Use these suggestions to help improve your listening skills:

1. Identify your listening problems so that you can correct them.
2. Look for something of value in every speech.
3. Be open-minded. Put your biases and problems aside when listening.
4. Control your emotional reactions to what you hear.
5. Ignore general distractions in your environment.
6. Turn off your electronic devices.
7. Reserve judgment until you have heard a speech all the way through.
8. Listen for main ideas. Don't try to write down everything a speaker says.

Inattention

To become effective listeners, we may have to work to overcome boredom, fatigue, and other distractions.

One of the most common barriers affecting listening is simply not paying attention. One cause of this problem is that our minds can process information faster than people speak. Most people talk at about 125 words per minute in public, but listeners can process information at about 500 words per minute. This gap between speaking and listening provides an opportunity for listeners to drift away to other concerns or personal problems.[9]

Chance associations with words may also cause your mind to wander. For example, a speaker mentions the word *arena,* which reminds you that there is a basketball game tomorrow night, which starts you thinking about whether you should get a date, which leads you to wondering if you should ask the person sitting next to you. By the time your attention drifts back to the speaker, it's too late to catch up with the presentation.

Personal concerns are a third cause of inattention. When you are tired, hungry, angry, worried, or pressed for time, you may find it difficult to concentrate. Your personal problems may take precedence over listening to a speaker. Or you simply may have "listening burnout" from too much concentrated exposure to people speaking. If you've ever attended three lecture classes in a row, you will know what this means.

Overcoming inattention requires conscious effort. Get some sleep. Put away all personal devices. Bridge the speaking/listening gap by paraphrasing to yourself what the speaker has just said. Continually check on how you might be able to use or adapt the speaker's comments. When your mind starts to drift, consciously jolt yourself to attention. Try to make listening to presentations a worry-free zone. Maintain eye contact with the speaker, and consciously commit to listening. Figure 4.2 highlights the differences between effective and ineffective listening.

Bad Listening Habits

It is all too easy to acquire bad listening habits. Most of us are sometimes guilty of feigning attention while tuning out a speaker. You may listen just for facts and ignore the major point of a speech.[10] You may try to multitask by texting or checking social media

Figure 4.2 Differences between Effective and Ineffective Listening

Effective Listeners	Ineffective Listeners
1. Focus on the message	1. Let their minds wander
2. Control emotional reactions	2. Respond emotionally
3. Set aside personal problems	3. Get sidetracked by personal problems
4. Listen despite distractions	4. Succumb to distractions
5. Overlook speaker's mannerisms	5. Get distracted by speaker's mannerisms
6. Listen for ideas they can use	6. Tune out dry material
7. Reserve judgment	7. Jump to conclusions
8. Consider ideas and feelings	8. Listen only for facts
9. Hold biases in check	9. Allow biases to interfere
10. Realize listening is hard work	10. Confuse listening with hearing

on your phone and lose your concentration.[11] Too much screen time may lead you into the "entertainment syndrome," in which you want speakers to be lively, funny, and engaging at all times. Unfortunately, not all subjects lend themselves to entertainment.

Overcoming bad habits requires effort. Turn off your cell phone before entering your class—completely off, not just to vibrate. Force yourself to actually pay attention by consciously focusing on the speaker's main ideas and supporting materials. Pay attention to nonverbal cues. Does the speaker's tone of voice change the meaning of the message? Are the speaker's gestures and facial expressions consistent with his or her words? If not, what does this tell you? Focus on what you can get out of a speech beyond its entertainment value.

Biases and Trigger Words

We all have personal preferences and biases that may contribute to poor listening. Perhaps you have strong views on the topic or do not find the speaker to have strong ethos. Unfortunately, such preferences and prejudices can be difficult to control, and failing to recognize them may lead us to too readily accept or reject a speaker's message without really listening.

trigger words
Words that arouse powerful feelings and may interfere with our ability to listen effectively.

In the context of these biases, certain **trigger words** may set off strong positive or negative emotions that become a barrier to effective listening. Positive trigger words like "freedom" and "progress" can blind us to flawed or dangerous messages. Likewise, negative trigger words like "conspiracy" and "fascism" may lead us to filter out messages that might be worth considering. Of course, trigger words invoking slurs and ugly stereotypes will almost always reflect poorly on the speakers' ethos and cause listeners to reject their messages without further hearing what they have to say.

How can you lessen the effect of biases and trigger words? The first step is to recognize that you have them. The past president of the International Listening Association, Professor Richard Halley of Weber State University, suggests that you observe your own behaviors over a period of time and make a list of words that cause you to react emotionally.[12] Then ask yourself the following questions:

- Do I let these words affect the way I respond to messages?
- Could the speaker be using these words to test or manipulate me?
- What can I do to control my reactions?

Coach yourself to identify your reaction to trigger words and topics evoking emotional reactions. Next, decide to listen to the entire message with as open a mind as possible, reserving judgment until you have heard the entire speech. By listening to the entire message, you can avoid jumping to conclusions that may not be grounded in what is being said. Look for something of value in every speech you hear, regardless of the topic or approach. We discuss language and emotions in greater depth in Chapter 11. Figure 4.3 describes some techniques you can use to overcome barriers to effective listening.

Common Barriers to Listening

What do you think are your own most common barriers to effective and ethical listening? How can you address these?

Figure 4.3 Overcoming Barriers to Effective Listening

Challenge	Try this
Noise	Alert speaker; move closer; shut door or window; ask source of noise to quiet down
Inattention	Concentrate by paraphrasing what you hear
Bad habits	Don't fake attention; don't expect to be entertained; don't try to multitask
Biases	Delay judgment; temper emotional responses
Trigger words	Identify them; don't jump to conclusions

Finding Your Voice

Identify Your Trigger Words

List three positive and three negative trigger words that provoke a strong emotional reaction when you hear them. These may include ideals, political terms, and sexist or ethnic slurs. Consider why these words have such a strong impact and how you might control your reactions to them.

Becoming a Better Listener

4.3 Become a more effective and critical listener.

To be articulate, posits Tom Shachtman, requires both "command of the language" and "the ability to take the perspective of the other person"[13]—and the ability to take the perspective of the other person requires listening. To develop your listening skills, you need to understand an important if commonly confused distinction between hearing and listening. **Hearing** is an automatic physical process by which soundwaves affect our eardrums and create noise. For most of us, it simply happens when audible stimuli reverberate in our ears. **Listening** goes beyond hearing to consciously attending, interpreting, analyzing, and remembering the most important parts of a message. As we discussed in the introduction to this chapter, listening is both an active process and an acquired skill that takes conscious effort and practice to cultivate. The first step in developing your listening ability is to gain a better appreciation for the types and functions of listening as they relate to public speaking. The second is to begin developing your applied skills as a critical yet constructive receiver of public speaking messages.

hearing
A physical process in which sound-waves affect our eardrums, creating sound.

listening
An active process and skill that includes attending, interpreting, evaluating, and remembering messages.

Functions of Listening

As with communication in general, different types of listening serve different functions depending in part on the situation. Four types particularly important to public speaking are appreciative listening, empathic listening, comprehensive listening, and critical listening.

Appreciative Listening. When we prioritize **appreciative listening**, we listen for the artistry of a message, whether music, theatre, poetry, or a speech. You may enjoy listening to the presentations of a given speaker for his eloquent language use, her commanding voice and dynamic delivery style, his skillful use of narratives and humor, or the sheer spectacle by which she engages and involves her listeners. If appreciative listening seems frivolous or even elitist at first glance, keep in mind that we learn to give better speeches through a combination of practice and *critique*; and critique entails observing the efforts of others as well as reflecting on our own strengths and areas for improvement. Developing your appreciation for the artistry of public speaking in and of itself will make valuable contributions to finding your voice as you polish your own speaking skills.

appreciative listening
Listening for the artistry of a message.

Empathic Listening. We use **empathic listening** to find the humanity in a message. Empathic listening asks you to enter the world of the speaker, to put yourself in the speaker's shoes, to understand the speaker's perspective.[14] It does not always

empathic listening
Listening to experience the speaker's perspective.

require agreement or even sympathy, but it does encourage you to set judgment aside and to listen with your heart and soul in order to achieve a deeper sense of mutual understanding and identification. Empathic listening is especially important to resolving conflicts and maintaining healthy relationships. In public speaking classes, it helps to create a supportive environment as speakers sense the connection with audience members. It also helps to develop an "other orientation" that is crucial to *all* authentic communication with people who do not already identify or agree with you. Listening is never truly complete unless you learn to empathize. It helps you to grow as a person and to find your own voice by engaging it with the voices of others.

comprehensive listening
Listening that focuses on understanding a speaker's overall message.

Comprehensive Listening. **Comprehensive listening** focuses on understanding the speaker's overall message. Obviously, this includes paying close attention to the speaker's main ideas, supporting materials, and word choice. It also entails careful consideration of the speaker's body language, the use of such nonverbal cues as vocal inflection, gestures, and movement. As we discuss in Chapter 12, a presentation is more effective when a speaker's nonverbal messages complement and reinforce her verbal messages; and when the two modes of communication conflict, most listeners will ascribe more credibility to what they see than what they hear. In either case, we want to recognize both *what* is being said and *how* in order to fully grasp the meaning and significance of the presentation. Effective comprehensive listening depends on concentration, blocking out distractions, and preparing ourselves for what is to come.[15]

critical listening
Listening that carefully evaluates a speaker's message.

Critical Listening. **Critical listening** goes beyond comprehension to carefully evaluating the speaker's message. Critical listeners are open-minded and willing to give a fair hearing even to speakers and ideas they may not agree with, but they accept nothing at face value and are demanding with respect to reasoning, the use of evidence, and choices of wording. They incorporate critical thinking with a healthy skepticism that can help to shield them from the impact of faulty messages and charismatic speakers with questionable motives. As discussed in the next section, critical listeners pay special attention to the use of supporting materials for main assertions, citing credible sources of information, the appropriate use of emotional appeals, language use that clarifies rather than obscures audience understanding, and constructive applications they might derive from the speaker's message.

Questions for Critical Listening

Conscious effort and practice can develop your critical listening skills as you listen to speeches. To guide the process of critical listening, consider the answers to the following five important questions.

1. Does the Speaker Provide Adequate Support for Claims? The reasoning used in a speech should make good sense. Do the conclusions follow from the points and the evidence that precede them? As we further discuss in Chapters 7 and 8, the adequacy of supporting information can be measured using the four R's of *relevance, representativeness, recency,* and *reliability.*

- Evidence is *relevant* when it applies directly to the issue at hand. The speaker who supports the claim that "professional football is destroying family values" with statistics demonstrating a spike in divorce rates would likely raise questions of relevance. Even if we equate rising divorce rates with declining family values, what does this have to do with professional football?
- Supporting materials should also be *representative* of a situation rather than an exception to the rule. A lone act of juvenile violence may or may not be representative of a larger reality, and you would probably want it to be corroborated with more examples and expert opinions rather than jumping to conclusions.

- Information should be the most *recent* available. Recency is especially important when knowledge about a topic is changing rapidly. Citing a study from ten years ago on the threat of domestic terrorism today would fail the test of recency by ignoring current developments and available information on the subject.
- Information should also be *reliable*—we must be able to depend on it. Reliability means that important claims should be confirmed by more than one source, that the sources of information are independent of each other, and that the sources possess appropriate credentials. The more significant and controversial the claim, the more reliable the evidence needs to be.

When evaluating supporting materials, be alert to possible confusion among facts, inferences, and opinions. **Facts** are verifiable units of information that can be confirmed by experts or independent observation. **Inferences** are assumptions or projections we derive from facts and information. **Opinions** add judgments to facts and inferences. For example, "Lee was late for class today" would be a fact. "Lee probably got caught in traffic" would be an inference derived from that fact. And "Lee is an irresponsible student" constitutes an opinion based (at least in part) on that fact. Be alert because unscrupulous or irresponsible speakers and advertisers often blur these distinctions. Facts may or may not justify a particular extrapolation; the inferences and opinions we derive from them require thoughtful consideration from speakers and listeners alike.

facts
Information that can be verified by experts and/or independent observation.

inferences
Assumptions or projections derived from facts and information.

opinions
Personal evaluations or judgments based on facts and inferences.

Finally, you can assume that skillful speakers will use information to paint their positions in the best possible light. There is nothing inherently wrong with that, but you should take it into account when you assess the merits of a message. Watch out for exaggeration. If a proposition sounds unbelievable or too good to be true, it often is. Also consider whether a speaker acknowledges alternative perspectives on issues. How might people from a different cultural background see the problem? How might gender or class differences affect these perspectives? Would solutions or suggestions differ as well? New and better ideas often emerge when we look at the world through a new lens.

2. Does the Speaker Cite Credible Sources? Supporting material should come from sources that are trustworthy and competent in the topic area. Speakers should document their sources carefully and demonstrate as necessary that the sources are experts on their particular topic. If a speaker does not mention a source's credentials or describes them only vaguely, a red flag should go up in your mind. Be especially wary of references like "Studies suggest" and "Experts agree." Ask yourself: what studies or experts are we talking about?

As discussed in Chapter 8, you should also be cautious of speakers and advertisers who distort the intended meaning of expert advice by taking it out of context. It may well be that a majority of dentists would prefer we chew a certain brand of gum over others, but it doesn't follow that those same dentists would recommend we chew gum at all! Always ask yourself, *Where does this information come from? Are these sources really qualified to speak on the topic?* and *Are their opinions and information being accurately represented by this speaker?*

3. Does the Speaker Use Words to Clarify Rather Than Obscure? When speakers want to hide something, they often use incomprehensible or ambiguous language. Such an approach functions to obscure ideas or to intimidate listeners. Introducing people who are not physicians as "doctors" to enhance their testimony on health subjects is one form of vagueness. In Chapter 11, we discuss the use of euphemisms and doublespeak to intentionally mislead listeners or mask a hidden agenda. Such phrases as "corporate restructuring" may be used to mask the unpleasantness of pending job cuts. Another ruse is using pseudo-scientific jargon such as "This supplement contains a gonadotropic hormone similar to pituitary extract in terms of its complex B vitamin methionine ratio." Huh? If it sounds impressive but you don't know what it means, be on the alert. Finally, and as discussed earlier in this chapter,

Critical listeners take into account the emotional aspects of a message—as well as the evidence and reasoning—to understand how a situation has influenced the speaker's view of the world.

watch out for the use of trigger words or inflammatory language that may elicit emotional reactions that undermine critical listening.

4. Does the Speaker Use Emotional Appeals Appropriately? As we discuss in Chapter 14, there is nothing inherently wrong or unethical about invoking emotional appeals such as compassion, fear, or even anger when presenting a speech. Vivid examples and compelling stories demonstrate the speaker's passion for a subject and help to involve listeners at a deep level—which is especially important to persuasive speaking. Indeed, you should be cautious of speakers who deliberately ignore the emotional aspects of a situation. You simply cannot fully understand an issue until you know how it affects others, how it makes them feel, and how it colors their view of the world. Suppose you were listening to a speech on climate change that contained the following statement: "The United States has 5 percent of the world's population but produces 25 percent of the world's carbon dioxide emissions." Although these numbers are impressive, what do they tell you about the human impact of climate change? Consider how much more meaningful this material might be if accompanied by stories of how people's lives have been affected by rising seas and severe weather events.

You should be even *more* skeptical of speakers who rely exclusively on emotional appeals to substitute for rather than to complement the use of evidence and reasoning. Often, such speakers are simply not adequately informed, so they are speaking from what "they've heard" with a few emotionally charged observations. At worst, speakers who rely exclusively on stoking emotional reactions without regard to the accuracy or adequacy of their claims are called **demagogues**. Former Senator Joseph McCarthy was one of the most notorious demagogues in modern American history. He rose from relative obscurity to immense popularity during the early 1950s by fueling fears of a vast communist conspiracy within the United States government. Eventually, he was disgraced when his exasperated fellow senators voted to censure him in 1954. To this day, the word "McCarthyism" is still synonymous with anticommunist hysteria and demagoguery during the Cold War.[16]

demagogues
Leaders who pander to popular prejudices and emotional appeals without regard to truth or reason.

5. What Constructive Applications Can I Derive from the Speaker's Message? Beyond critiquing the use of evidence, language, and emotional appeals, critical listening is never complete until we give thoughtful consideration to the potential constructive applications of a speaker's message. We have already discussed the value of appreciative listening to developing your presentation skills. Most speakers genuinely believe in what they have to say, and there is usually some potential value in listening even to messages we might not be predisposed to accept. We might learn valuable new information or gain a richer perspective and understanding of how others perceive or experience topics and issues we care about. We find and nurture our own voices when we seek to reconcile them with carefully considered opposing voices.

For example, you might be opposed to standardized testing and other educational reforms referred to as Common Core. By listening to a quality presentation in favor of Common Core, you might come away with an enhanced appreciation for the challenges facing public school teachers and the need for stronger minimal standards to better prepare young people for college and the professional workplace. The questions you ask yourself and the speaker might contribute to a higher quality of discussion on the topic. Taken together, critical and constructive listening can help both speakers and listeners to find and sharpen their voices.

The Four Types of Listening

Of the four types of listening discussed in this section, which one would you most like to develop more? Why?

SPEAKER'S NOTES

A Dirty Dozen Red Flags for Critical Listening

These red flags should alert you to potential problems in a message:

1. No strong evidence provided
2. Evidence and conclusions that aren't connected
3. Information inconsistent with what you know
4. Opinions or inferences presented as facts
5. Claims of exclusive knowledge
6. Outlandish promises or guarantees
7. Sources of information not identified
8. Questionable sources of information
9. Overdone emotional appeals
10. Missing emotional appeals
11. Vague or incomprehensible language
12. Trigger words and inflammatory language

Finding Your Voice

Listening in Challenging Situations

Find speeches outside your class—on YouTube, on TED, or elsewhere—that challenge you as a comprehensive and critical listener. What external or internal barriers in the speaker, the situation, and yourself make it hard for you to listen effectively? What might you miss as the result of impaired listening? How might you overcome this problem?

Guidelines for Listening to Speeches

4.4 Identify effective aspects of speeches as you listen.

Now you have the opportunity to put the power of listening into effect. When you hear a speech, use a combination of appreciative, empathic, comprehensive, and critical listening to offer a fair hearing while keeping an open and assessing mind. The following guidelines will help you identify the qualities of a good speech.

Strong delivery skills encourage listeners to be attentive.

Substance:

- Are the main ideas supported with sufficient information that is recent, relevant, reliable, and representative?
- Are facts and statistics, testimony, examples, and narratives used appropriately?
- Are sources cited properly in the speech?
- Does the speech promote identification among topic, audience, and speaker?
- Is the language clear and appropriate?
- Do presentation aids follow the criteria for effective design and delivery?
- Are questions handled well, with wrap-up provided?

Applying Concepts from the Guidelines for Listening to Speeches

Apply the concepts from the guidelines for listening to speeches to a speech outside of class. How does the structure of the guidelines help you identify particular aspects of the speech? Do your answers to each question provide insights into your overall reactions to the presentation?

Structure:

- Does the introduction engage and orient the audience?
- Can you identify the main points of the speech?
- Are transitions used to tie the speech together?
- Does the conclusion help you remember the speech?

Presentation:

- Is the speech presented extemporaneously?
- Are notes used unobtrusively?
- Does the speaker maintain good eye contact?
- Is the speech presented enthusiastically?
- Is the speaker's voice expressive, with good rate, loudness, and pauses?
- Is the speech free of such vocal fillers as *um, like,* and *you know*?
- Do gestures and body language complement ideas?
- Does the speech fit the time limits of the assignment or situation?

Overall:

- Does the speaker come across as genuinely committed and sincere?
- Did you find the central message compelling? Why or why not?
- What did you learn that was new or of value from listening?
- What were the strongest and weakest points of the presentation?

SPEAKER'S NOTES

Recommendations for Oral Critiques

You may be asked to respond, formally or informally, to a speaker in the classroom or in the community. When you do so, the following guidelines can be helpful:

1. Be supportive of the speaker's efforts.
2. Begin with a positive statement.
3. Phrase suggestions tactfully, such as, "Did you consider...?" and "Help me understand why...."
4. Avoid vague comments such as, "I didn't like it." Be as specific as possible so the speaker can benefit from your feedback.
5. When you point out a problem, offer a suggestion for improvement.
6. End with a positive statement.

Your Ethical Responsibilities as a Listener

4.5 Become a more ethical listener.

The ideal of effective listening is incomplete without the ethics of listening. Given that listeners play a central role in participating in the dynamic transactional process of public speaking, they have important obligations both to the speaker and to the consequences of a presentation. You should honor what philosopher Eugene Garver calls the ethical bond between speaker and audience.[17]

First, you have an ethical obligation to the person speaking. You should exert a conscious effort to filter out distractions, follow the speaker's message attentively, and provide the engaged feedback that is so important to authentic communication. Avoid prejudging a speech simply because you may not respect a speaker or because you anticipate disagreeing with what will be said. Put aside prejudices based on lifestyle or cultural differences. Given our diverse and complex society, "listening across differences becomes a necessary feature of social life."[18] We broaden our perspectives and develop our own voices by listening carefully to the voices of others. Finally, emphasize strengths as well as weaknesses when asked to critique a speaker's presentation, and offer constructive advice on how the speaker might improve. The guidelines for oral critiques are summarized in the Speaker's Notes box above.

No less important, you have a shared obligation for the impact and consequences of the speeches you hear. As we discussed earlier in this chapter, listeners have the power and responsibility to interpret and evaluate the speaker's message. With that power comes responsibility, not only for how you react or respond to a speaker's message, but for its potential impact on the lives of other people. You also have a shared responsibility for the quality of public discussion that emerges from public speaking transactions. Nothing fuels dishonest and manipulative speaking so much as the indifference of poor listeners. We all benefit when speakers and listeners take their ethical obligations seriously.

Considering the Ethics of Ineffective Listening

Think of a time when you did not listen effectively. In retrospect, what are the possible ethical implications of that breakdown?

YOUR ETHICAL VOICE

Evaluating the Ethical Dimensions of a Speech

Public speeches can give rise to a host of ethical problems. To test the ethical dimensions of speech, ask yourself these questions:

1. Does the speaker demonstrate responsible knowledge of the topic?
2. Does the speaker show respect for the audience?
3. Does the speaker seem concerned about the impact of the speech?
4. Does the speaker orally document sources of information?
5. Does the speaker avoid inflammatory language?
6. Does the speaker avoid exaggerating claims?
7. Does the speaker use emotional appeals appropriately?

Final Reflections: The Golden Rule of Listening

The ancient Greek philosopher Epictetus posited that "We have two ears and one mouth so that we can listen twice as much as we speak."[19] When we practice the art of effective listening, we enact a form of the Golden Rule: *Listen to others as we would have them listen to us*. Effective listening strengthens relationships and organizations; improved listening enriches friendships and leads to positions that may turn a job into a career. As one observer noted, "The best leaders are very often the best listeners. They have an open mind. They are not interested in having their own way but in finding the best way."[20]

As you learn to become a better listener, you will also learn to become a better speaker. Listening to your classmates make presentations, you will learn what interests them, how they feel about various issues, and what techniques might work best when you are speaking. The free flow of ideas in the classroom can also give rise to novel topics you may want to explore in the process of finding your voice.

In the end, there is a circularity in the relationship between speaker and listener. When we listen effectively to others, we help them become better communicators. As they become better communicators, they make it easier for us to listen. Finding your voice can be contagious: In a positive classroom setting, students may find their voices together. Listen louder,[21] and you will find your voice.

Study Questions

CONTENT MASTERY

1 What power do you have as a listener?

2 What are the common barriers to effective listening?

3 What are the major functions of listening used for speeches?

4 What questions can help you become a more critical listener?

5 How can you provide a helpful and supportive critique of a speech?

6 What should you do to become an ethical listener?

7 How can becoming a more effective listener benefit you?

CRITICAL EXPLORATIONS

1. Review the discussion of the power you have as a listener. Is this a perspective you have encountered before? Do you have difficulty accepting it? If so, why? What are the implications for you as a listener?

2. Complete the checklist of listening problems in Figure 4.1. Working in small groups, discuss your listening problems with your classmates. Develop a listening improvement plan for the three most common listening problems in your group.

3. Think of a time when not listening effectively put you in a difficult situation. What problems did this cause? What could you have done differently? Share your insights with a classmate, and discuss the similarities and differences in your experiences.

4. One way to improve your concentration is to keep a listening log in one of your other classes. As you take class notes, put an X in the margin each time you notice your attention wandering. By each X, jot down a few words pinpointing the cause: for example, "used *men* as generic term." After class, count the number of times your mind drifted, and note the causes. Can you identify a pattern of reactions? This exercise will help you identify the conditions that bring on inattention and will make you more aware of your tendency to daydream. Once you realize how often and why you are drifting away, you can more easily guard against this.

5. Think of a person you like to listen to (such as a speaker or teacher). List all the adjectives you can that describe this person. Think of another person you do not like to listen to. List the adjectives that describe this person. Compare the two lists. What does this exercise suggest about effective critical listening?

6. Review your class notes from one of your lecture courses. What do they suggest about your comprehensive listening abilities? Were your notes coherent? Were you able to identify the main points, or did you try to write down everything that was said? Was the material easy to follow and understand? How might you change your comprehensive listening to result in better notes and deeper understanding?

7. Evaluate a contemporary political speaker on ethical grounds using the questions in the Your Ethical Voice feature in section 4.5. Be sure to differentiate between the ethical uses of speech techniques and the moral consequences of the message. What insights does this generate on the ethical implications of listening?

CHAPTER

Adapting to Your Audience and Situation

LEARNING OBJECTIVES

This chapter will help you:

5.1 Adjust your message to the demographic characteristics of listeners.

5.2 Understand how psychographics might influence listeners.

5.3 Determine ways to gather information about your audience.

5.4 Understand the rewards and challenges of audience diversity.

5.5 Adjust your message to the speaking situation.

OUTLINE

After another round of proposed tuition hikes, you've decided to run for the student senate. You feel the hikes will be especially hard on students who, like yourself, are working their way through college. You also think the raises will result in less minority representation on campus. You are convinced that the administration has not done enough to trim spending and that the existing student government has not been outspoken enough on this issue.

"Orators have to learn the differences of human souls."

—PLATO

During the course of your campaign, you are invited to speak at an outdoor rally sponsored by the Black Student Association (BSA), and—with your instructor's permission—you plan to present your message to your public speaking class as your persuasive speech. Of course, your general message and purpose for speaking will remain the same, but the different audiences and situations will suggest different strategies and points of emphasis. The BSA is committed to promoting and retaining minority enrollment, so it makes sense to focus on that aspect of the issue when speaking at their rally. And, because you'll be speaking outside to a large audience, you should find out whether some sort of amplification will be available. As you prepare your presentation for your public speaking class, you should make sure that your speech will meet the criteria of the assignment as stipulated by your instructor. Because public speaking assignments are usually brief, you should streamline your presentation by focusing exclusively on your most important ideas and information as relevant to your classmates.

It may seem ironic, but a crucial part of finding *your* voice is determining how to adapt to different audiences on different occasions. Just as you adjust your communication when you speak to your best friends, your parents, or your professors, the enlarged conversation of public speaking is *audience- and situation-centered*. Every aspect of preparing and presenting your speeches—from choosing your topic to making the actual presentation—should be developed with your audience and situation in mind. Of course, this raises important ethical questions.

We've all heard waffling politicians who reverse their positions from audience to audience—and we certainly aren't advocating that unethical approach. But given the multiple facets of your own identity and interests, the complexity of various topics, and the variety of people and occasions for public presentations, adaptation plays a key role in connecting you with your listeners in meaningful ways. It demonstrates that you have carefully considered not only what you want to say but what your audience wants and/or needs to hear. You simply cannot find your voice until you learn to adapt and share it with others, and understanding your audience is a key part of that process.

You've probably already begun to develop a sense of your classmates and the setting in which you'll be speaking, but be cautious about putting too much emphasis on such superficial cues as dress or personal mannerisms. As a next step, you want to develop a systematic analysis to discover:

- How much your listeners know about your topic;
- How interested they are in the subject;
- How they feel about your topic;
- What appeals might be best to reach them; and
- What challenges the speaking situation might pose.

In this chapter, we first consider getting to know your audience by analyzing their demographics and psychographics. We then offer ways to gather information about your listeners and how to use that information in addressing today's diverse audiences. We close by considering the physical and psychological dimensions of the public speaking situation to which you want to adapt.

Understanding Audience Demographics

5.1 Adjust your message to the demographic characteristics of listeners.

The first step in getting to know the members of your audience is to consider their demographic characteristics. **Demographics** of an audience—literally translated as "measurement of the people"[1]—include their age, gender, sexual orientation, education, race and ethnicity, socioeconomic background, and group affiliations. Politicians and advertisers spend a lot of money studying the interests and concerns of targeted groups, and for good reason. Such information can provide valuable clues for tailoring and adapting your messages to the needs and predispositions of your audience.

demographics
General characteristics of listeners, including age, gender, sexual orientation, education, race and ethnicity, socioeconomic background, and group affiliations.

Demographic affiliations provide an important set of indications for audience analysis, but they should be used with care—especially when considering the relatively small audiences for most public speaking situations. Such information may provide valuable insights on large groups of people *in general*, but it tells us very little about your specific listeners *as unique individuals*. Each of us is a composite of overlapping and sometimes competing demographic affiliations, and there are always exceptions to every rule. You cannot afford to ignore the potential importance of demographic factors, but you should never use them as a basis for making sweeping presumptions.

As you begin your audience analysis, consider how the following demographic variables might influence the way your audience receives your message.

Age

Since the days of Aristotle, speech educators have taught that younger audiences tend to be more pleasure loving, more idealistic, and more willing to consider new ideas for changing the world. Older listeners tend to be more set in their ways, more concerned with maintaining the social order, and more concerned with having a comfortable existence. Those in the full bloom of adulthood, Aristotle argued, present a balance between youth and age, being confident yet cautious, judging cases by the facts, and being willing to consider new ideas in a critical yet constructive frame of mind.[2] Contemporary research supports the relationship between age and openness to persuasion that Aristotle identified.[3] The presidential elections of John F. Kennedy in 1960 and Barack Obama in 2008, both orchestrated around messages of change and faith in a better future, were anchored by the overwhelming support of young, first-time voters.[4]

Finding Your Voice

Where Do Your Listeners Fit In?

Look up polling information on today's college students online at any of the major polling sites. Some helpful resources include the Pew Research Center and the Education Research Institute. From what you have observed in this course, consider how your classmates compare with the demographic and attitudinal information you find in national polls. Which demographic factors in your audience are similar to those in the polls? Which factors differ? What do the similarities and differences suggest about how you can approach this audience in your speeches?

More recently, scholars and advertisers have focused on age in terms of generational identification. The idea is that people who come of age during the same period of time tend to share experiences, world views, lifestyles, and dispositions that distinguish them from other generations. For instance, much has been written about the "Baby Boomers," who came of age during the 1960s and are generally characterized as more idealistic and progressive than their parents' generation, which had been hardened by the Great Depression and World War II.[5] Some studies suggest that the current generation of "millennials" represents a resurgent idealism or optimism tempered by an emphasis on individual responsibility. They are more comfortable with new technologies, more tolerant of diversity, and more willing to adapt to a constantly changing world.[6] See Figure 5.1 for general traits that have been identified for various generations as well as major events affecting their world view.

Older generations often describe younger generations in less flattering terms: self-absorbed, less hard-working, and less interested in social and political issues. In part, this appears to be a cyclical phenomenon; Generation X-ers may mutter about Millennials much as their Baby Boomer parents once muttered about them! You can learn more about the latest generation of young college students by reading the annual report of UCLA's Higher Education Research Institute on first-year college students.[7]

Figure 5.1 Generational Identification[8]

Generation	General Traits	Select Major Events	Major Media
Post-Millennial/Generation Z (born 1997–2012)	Technologically savvy; time will tell!	Recession	To be discovered
Millennial/Generation Y (born 1981–96)	Idealistic, entrepreneurial, less religious, technologically sophisticated, appreciative of diversity	September 11, 2001; Columbine High School shootings, digital revolution	Smartphones
Generation X (born 1965–80)	Well educated, independent, skeptical, low levels of political involvement, ethnically diverse, value work-life balance	Iranian hostage crisis, Reagan Revolution, Challenger disaster	Computers
Baby Boomer (born 1946–64)	Tolerant, optimistic, individualistic, politically involved, environmentally conscious, consensus-seeking	Vietnam War, Watergate, Civil Rights Movement, Women's Movement	Television

Gender

Knowledge of your audience, such as the younger generation's comfort with and interest in new technologies and social media, will help you adapt your message to meet their needs and expectations.

Gender roles have changed significantly over the past half century. In 1968, just 37 percent of American women held full-time jobs outside the home, and the jobs they held typically offered little pay and little power. Today, women make up 47 percent of graduates from American law schools, and they are the primary breadwinners in 40 percent of American households.[9]

While their findings are widely disputed, some scholars argue that men and women have different styles of communication. Men, we are told, are more verbally aggressive and competitive in their communicative behaviors, more concerned with "winning arguments," and more interested in exerting control over the situation. Women, we are told, are more focused on maintaining social connections, nurturing mutual growth and self-discovery, and accommodating contrasting positions.[10] In general, women do tend to be more liberal than men. They are more likely to support spending increases on education, more concerned about environmental protections and gay rights, and more accepting of government providing for children in need and the elderly.[11] Women also vote more than men and have consistently outvoted their male counterparts in recent presidential elections by margins ranging from 4 million to nearly 8 million votes.[12]

Again, there are exceptions to every demographic tendency, and you should be especially cautious of invoking or relying on gender stereotypes that make sweeping generalizations about men or women before any audience. It may well be that women in general are more liberal than men, but some of the most prominent conservatives in America today are women. You should also be wary of various forms of **sexist language**, which tends to be especially offensive when used in formal presentations. In addition to obviously disparaging labels, this includes irrelevant references to gender such as "*male* nurse" or "*female* game warden." Singular references can prove problematic with the generic "he," as in "a surgeon needs to wash his hands thoroughly before every procedure." You can use "she or he," or even better, use the plural "they" as a more accurate and elegant solution: "surgeons need to wash their hands thoroughly before every procedure." Finally, watch out for colloquial terms that carry gendered connotations such as "darling" for women or "guys" for referring to gender-mixed audiences.

sexist language
Using disparaging labels and references to gender, making irrelevant references to gender, or using masculine nouns or pronouns when the intended reference is to both sexes.

Sexual Orientation

We live in an age of revolutionary change with respect to gender norms. The once-standard categories of male and female have evolved: Facebook offers almost sixty gender identities, and gay, lesbian, and transgender characters star in movies, prime-time and daytime television programs, and such on-demand services as Netflix.[13] Terms have morphed, such as Latino to Latino/Latina to Latinx to be more inclusive. Although public acceptance has grown, the variety of sexual orientations is not new: As early as 1948, researcher Alfred Kinsey found that "37% of males and 20% of females had homosexual experiences during their lifetime."[14] As communication scholars suggest, rather than being fixed, increasingly sexual identities are seen as "multiple, unstable, and fluid social constructions intersecting with race, class, and gender, among others."[15]

Attentiveness to how individuals prefer to be referred to will go a long way. You should refrain from referring to sexual orientation as a preference or choice of lifestyle. Terms like "homosexual" have been used so derogatively for so long that many prefer "gay" or "lesbian" or increasingly the acronym LGBTQ (lesbian, gay, bisexual, transgender, or questioning). Many ugly stereotypes of gays and lesbians overlap with ugly gender stereotypes. For instance, gay men may be characterized as "less of a man" because they are seen as overly effeminate, and lesbians may likewise be disparaged as overly masculine. In some circles, transgendered individuals are still perceived to be simply gender confused. Of course, these stereotypes are not only hurtful but most often simply wrong, and you should again be cautious about jumping to presumptions based on sexual orientation. Gay and lesbian couples, for instance, are generally better educated and more affluent than their heterosexual counterparts.[16] There are a lot of devoutly religious people in the LGBTQ community, and in such prominent conservative groups as the Log Cabin Republicans.

Education

The educational focus and level of your listeners can be valuable indicators of their knowledge and interest in a topic area. They can help you determine the level at which you should address your topic and whether you need to explain basic ideas or define language specific to your topic area. For instance, if you are addressing a group of advanced accounting majors, you can probably assume they already know what a Roth IRA is; with more general audiences, you should probably offer a brief definition and explanation before proceeding with the rest of your speech.

Education is generally a poor indicator of political preference, and you should be cautious of the common stereotype of universities as bastions of liberal indoctrination. However, you can expect educated listeners to be generally more informed on and more interested in current affairs, more tolerant of differing cultures and lifestyles, and more willing to listen to new ideas and fresh perspectives with an open mind. You can also expect them to be more critical and demanding consumers of messages. Educated listeners are more likely to expect you to engage opposing views when arguing disputed positions and to use knowledge as responsible evidence. If you are not well prepared, educated listeners are more likely to question your credibility for future presentations.[17]

Race and Cultural Background

This demographic includes race and ethnicity as well as geographical identity, defined as "the relationship between identity and place"[18] (e.g., nation, region, and the urban-rural continuum). The United States is host to one of the most racially and culturally diverse populations on Earth. The U.S. Census recognizes the categories of Caucasian, African-American, Native American, Hispanic, Latino/a, Asian, and Pacific Islander, but these categories don't even begin to account for the wealth of immigration to this nation from every corner of the globe.[19] What's more, most Americans are composites of multiple overlapping racial and cultural backgrounds and influences. Needless to say, discussions of race and culture in America have become increasingly more pressing and complicated than the overly simplified categories of "white," "black," and "other."

All of this diversity is rightfully celebrated as a source of great pride and national strength, but it can pose significant challenges to meaningful communication. People from different backgrounds often have different experiences, interests, and viewpoints that can become a source of misunderstanding and potential conflict. Consider, for example, the different perspectives that urban and rural audiences may have on the issue of gun control. Urban listeners may be more prone to associate guns with crime and violence in the streets, whereas rural audiences may associate guns with hunting, recreation, or symbols of freedom. On other subjects, American citizens may have a hard time understanding the challenges faced by undocumented workers living in this country. Northerners and southerners often have misconceptions about each other.

All humans are members of the same genetic family and, over the past few decades, experts have increasingly emphasized the extent to which racial and cultural differences are conditioned or constructed through a lifetime of interacting with significant others and members of our immediate communities.[20] This does not mean these differences are not real or meaningful, but it does suggest that they can be constructively engaged through thoughtful and considerate communication. Later in this chapter, we devote an entire section to discussing the challenges of addressing diverse audiences: the importance of learning more about the cultures you are engaging, using the right supporting materials, engaging shared values, and—of course—choosing your words carefully. Again, we encourage you to learn and employ the terms your listeners use to identify themselves and to be especially cautious of stereotypes, off-color humor, offensive labels and terms, and irrelevant markers such as "*Hispanic* police officer" or "*black* doctor." You should also be cautious of references that might be perceived as coded or **symbolic racism**, as when people speak of "protecting the integrity of our neighborhoods" to convey an obvious discomfort with the prospect of having members of other ethnic groups for neighbors.

symbolic racism
Indirect racism that uses code words or subtle contrasts to suggest that one race is superior to another.

A major barrier to effective and ethical cross-cultural communication is **ethnocentrism**, which refers to the popular tendency to presume that our own culture is "correct" and that other perspectives are wrong. As with all biases, the first step to overcoming ethnocentrism is to recognize it at play in our own thinking and communicative behaviors. We once heard the story of a woman standing in line at a store, speaking on her phone. When she hung up, the man behind her chastised her, saying "If you want to be in this country, you need to speak English!" She responded, "Sir, I was speaking Navajo; if you want to speak English, go to England." To avoid the impression of ethnocentrism in your speeches, *show respect for the humanity of all people, and recognize that this common humanity transcends our differences*.

ethnocentrism
The tendency of any nation, race, religion, or group to believe that its way of looking at the world is right and that other perspectives are wrong.

Socioeconomic Status

Socioeconomic status refers to the economic well-being or class of your listeners. According to the U.S. Census, nearly 50 million people in this country live at or below the poverty line,[21] and a majority of middle- or working-class Americans are considerably less well off in terms of real income and assets than they were just a few decades ago.[22] Obviously, class differences can exert tremendous influence on the way your listeners will perceive and experience a given topic. Those of us who are better off may have a hard time appreciating the stress of having to choose between feeding our children and providing them with health care. As interpersonal communication scholars Marsha Houston and Julia T. Wood argue, class includes not just current income but the assumptions that people make about economic (in)security and the attendant social and material benefits.[23] Those with less financial stability are more likely to live near their families, to pursue inexpensive leisure activities, and to follow more traditional gender roles. One of our students suggested that he felt greater affinity with other lower-class students than with his fellow white students because the former would never simply assume that he could go out for dinner or get a new book without carefully considering the costs.

As with all demographic variables, you should use caution when considering the socioeconomic status of your listeners, because sweeping presumptions often do not hold true. Yes, wealthier people are more likely to vote Republican and working-class people are more likely to vote Democrat, but there are a lot of exceptions to both rules, and those tendencies may be changing. What's more, the very subject of socioeconomic status has become a volatile issue in American public discourse. Politicians who speak out against economic inequities and injustices can expect to be assailed by their critics for being divisive and promoting class warfare, which may explain why so few of them choose to do so. Finally, be cautious about the terms you use in reference to your listeners. Americans have a great historic reverence for the middle class, and nine out of ten like to be associated with it regardless of their actual status.[24] Most people living paycheck to paycheck do not like to be called "poor" or "lower class," and even well-to-do people tend to cringe when you call them "rich"—especially when it is time to pay taxes!

Finding Your Voice

The Importance of Groups

Of the groups you belong to, consider the one that means the most to you. What is it about being a part of this group that brings you the greatest satisfaction? Is it the social interaction? The opportunity to do something of value for society? The respect you receive from it? What does your membership say about you as a person? What do your classmates' memberships say about them? Are there more similarities than differences? How might this information be useful to you as you choose topics and prepare your speeches?

Group Affiliations

The groups to which people belong often reflect their interests, attitudes, and values. Knowing the occupational, political, religious, and social group memberships of your audience members can help you design a speech that better fits their interests and needs.

Occupational Groups. Your listeners' occupational affiliations or career aspirations can provide insight into how much they know about a topic, the vocabulary you can use, and which aspects of a topic should be most interesting to them. An audience of health care providers, for example, can be expected to already know about the latest strains of flu viruses. Knowledge of occupational interests also suggests the kinds of authorities that listeners will find most credible. If many of your classmates are business majors, for instance, they likely will find information from the *Wall Street Journal* more convincing than information from *USA Today*. You can gather information on various occupational groups by consulting specialized publications and websites. For instance, the American Bar Association, the American Marketing Association, the Society of Hispanic Engineers, and the National Communication Association all have websites and publications that offer ideas and insights about various audiences.

Political Groups. Knowledge of your listeners' political affiliations can provide valuable insights into strongly held moral and ideological convictions. Such knowledge is especially important for developing speeches on such controversial issues as gun control, immigration, and health care reform. Many people are willing to divulge their political affiliations, but they can be tricky to ascertain. Sometimes, the nature of the speaking occasion and sponsoring group can provide helpful clues. For example, a banquet hosted by your local chamber of commerce will likely attract a mostly conservative or pro-business audience. General surveys (see Figure 5.3) can be useful for analyzing the dynamics of smaller classroom audiences, and students with strong political ties will often make them known in the course of class discussions and their own speeches.

Keep in mind that we live in an age of declining party loyalty and adherence to party doctrines. Some Democratic and Republican politicians take positions on issues that are at odds with those of their own party, as the 2016 presidential election campaigns made abundantly clear. Growing numbers of younger Americans now define themselves as "Independents" who evaluate issues and candidates on an individual basis.[25] We encourage you to be cautious about attributing too much to political affiliation and to supplement what you learn with more specific information regarding your audience and intended message.

Religious Groups. Knowing the religious affiliations of listeners can suggest underlying social and cultural attitudes and values, and many denominations advocate specific positions on timely political issues. According to a recent Gallup survey, Mormons tend to be slightly more conservative than Protestants, who in turn tend to be slightly more conservative than Catholics, who tend to be slightly more conservative than Jews.[26] While some 70 percent of Americans identify as Christians, increases in immigration and cultural diversity have swelled the ranks of Muslims, Hindus, and Buddhists in this country. Finally, roughly 33 percent of Americans aged 18 to 29 now identify themselves as having "no religious affiliation" whatsoever. And while many of them claim to be "spiritual" in their own way, they tend to be decidedly more liberal than their more religious counterparts.[27]

A word of caution: You can't always assume that because people are members of a particular religious group, they will embrace all of the teachings of that group. Catholics differ, for example, on whether women should be ordained as priests and whether birth control is a sin; not all Jews keep a kosher kitchen. One thing you can count on, however, is that audiences are usually sensitive about topics related to their religious convictions. As a speaker, you should be aware of this sensitivity and be attuned to the religious makeup of your audience. Appealing exclusively to Christian values before an audience that includes members of other religious groups will likely diminish the effectiveness of your message with everyone in your audience.

Social Groups. Often, we are born into a religious group, raised in a certain political environment, and end up in an occupation as much by chance as by design. But we choose our social groups on the basis of our interests. Membership in social groups can be as important to people as any other kind of affiliation—and in some cases, even more important. Photographers may join the campus film club, businesspeople may become involved with the local chamber of commerce, and environmentalists may be attracted to the Sierra Club.

Knowing the group affiliations of your listeners can help you design a speech that fits their interests, concerns, and needs.

Knowing which social groups are represented in your audience and what they stand for is important for

Finding Your Voice

Using Public Polls to Adapt to Your Audience

Choose a topic of interest to you or one assigned by your instructor and explore three public opinion polls from the respected research organizations listed in this section. How does each source frame the topic? What questions does each one ask? How do their results compare? What insights might this exercise offer for a speech on this topic?

effective audience adaptation. A speech favoring measures to control pollution might take a different focus, depending on whether it is presented to the Rotary Club or to the Audubon Society. With the Rotary Club, you might stress the importance of a clean environment in persuading businesses to relocate to your community; with the Audubon Society, you might emphasize the effects of pollution on wildlife. As with political affiliations, people tend to make their important group memberships known to others around them. Be alert to such information from your classmates, and consider it while planning and preparing your speeches.

Some Words of Caution

As we discussed in the introduction to this section, becoming aware of demographic factors is an important first step in getting to know your audience. Such knowledge can be useful for identifying likely points of shared interest, for framing appeals, and for avoiding sources of misunderstanding. You should be cautious about relying too heavily on any one demographic factor when analyzing your audience. Most audiences are more diverse than you might realize. Today's college classrooms are generally much more varied in terms of minorities, economic levels, and nontraditional students than those of just a generation ago. And, even if your classmates all *look* the same, you can safely assume that most class audiences represent a healthy mix of political, religious, and other demographic categories. The multiple demographic affiliations of individuals often work together but sometimes may compete with each other to shape how they might receive your message. For instance, a listener might be a liberal Democrat on most issues while staunchly opposed to abortion because of personal religious convictions.

Perhaps more important, there is a very fine line between demographic sensitivity and stereotyping. Most public speaking audiences are relatively small, and what tends to be true for larger sections of society is often wrong when applied to specific individuals. Some of the most ardent critics of affirmative action are prominent African Americans. Some of the harshest critics of the Catholic Church's opposition to birth control are themselves devout Catholics. Even when your demographic presumptions are accurate and seemingly positive, most people become uncomfortable when they feel they are being spoken to as members of groups rather than as individuals. This is especially true when speakers do not share these affiliations. The lesson should be clear: Remember that your listeners may not conform to stereotypes. Respect their individuality. You can find general information on demographic influences from a variety of sources, including public opinion polls posted by reputable sources such as the Gallup Organization, the National Opinion Research Center, the Pew Research Center, the Zogby Poll, and the Roper Center for Public Opinion Research. Then adapt what you find to the particular beliefs, attitudes, values, and relevant motives of your audience.

Using Demographics to Guide Your Speech Selection

What have you observed about the demographics of your classmates up to this point? What do you still not know? How will this information help guide your preparation of your next speech?

SPEAKER'S NOTES

Avoiding Racist and Sexist Language

To avoid racist and sexist innuendos in your speeches, keep these guidelines in mind:

1. Do not use slang terms to refer to racial, ethnic, religious, or gender groups.
2. Avoid using the generic *he* and gender-specific titles such as *meter maid*.
3. Avoid stereotypic references, especially those that imply inferiority or superiority.
4. Stay away from sexist, racist, ethnic, or religious humor.

Understanding Audience Psychographics

5.2 Understand how psychographics might influence listeners.

The **psychographics** of the audience refers to the beliefs, attitudes, values, and motives that shape listeners' behavior. A better feel for the psychographics of your particular audience, along with your analysis of their demographics, can help you focus your specific purpose and message, choose the most effective appeals, decide which authorities to cite, and determine which examples and stories might work best in your speeches.

psychographics
The beliefs, attitudes, values, and motives that influence the behavior of listeners.

Beliefs

Beliefs express what we know or think we know about subjects. They are typically acquired directly through experience and education and indirectly from friends, family members, and trusted authority figures. They may be based on verifiable facts, such as "The price of higher education has increased dramatically over the past five years." Or they may reflect subjective opinions, such as "Higher education is the way to a good job," or even popular lore, such as "Southerners make the best chefs." At their worst, beliefs may express demeaning stereotypes about races, religions, or cultures.

beliefs
What we know or think we know about subjects.

Information about your listeners' beliefs can suggest what additional information you need to provide or what misinformation you may need to correct. For instance, if you are presenting a speech arguing for limits on government access to individuals' social media, you will probably want to find out if your audience members *believe* that the government is monitoring our social media transactions and whether it is legal for them to do so. The first claim should be easy to establish with news reports and expert testimony, but it is complicated by the fact that the government has not been forthcoming about divulging such information in the past. The second claim is trickier because it raises an ongoing and sometimes heated debate between beliefs about personal privacy versus national security. Your listeners may have already developed strong feelings or attitudes on the issue.

Attitudes

Attitudes are more strongly held thoughts and feelings that predispose us to respond positively or negatively toward a given subject—whether we like or dislike, or approve or disapprove of people, places, events, or ideas. Because they are more specific than beliefs, attitudes are typically a better indicator of your listeners' willingness to consider and act on your message. They may also be harder to influence,

attitudes
Strong thoughts and feelings that predispose us to respond positively or negatively toward specific subjects.

so they require your best use of evidence and reasoning. As we will discuss further in Chapter 14, with skeptical audiences it is usually a good idea to establish common ground before addressing differences. You should also emphasize facts and expert opinions more than emotional appeals. On some occasions, you might even consider adjusting your specific purpose to give your speech a better chance for a favorable reception.

Consider our sample speech above opposing government monitoring of social media. If you anticipate that your listeners will have already developed strong feelings that prioritize national security over personal privacy, then you should gather convincing information and be ready to address your audience on their own terms. In addition to emphasizing the importance of protecting us from terrorist attacks, supporters of government surveillance programs will likely feel that reports of government spying on individuals are exaggerated and that most of us have nothing to worry about unless we're up to something wrong. With really skeptical audiences, you might consider limiting your objective to enlightening your audience about the issue or to calling for more transparency and disclosure as to the nature and extent of government monitoring.

Values

values
The moral principles that suggest how we should behave or what we should believe.

Our most important beliefs and attitudes are anchored by our personal, social, religious, and political **values**—the moral *principles* we live by that suggest how we should behave. Values provide us with standards for evaluating the rightness or wrongness of ideas and behaviors and may include such ideals as honesty, fairness, accountability, faith, and patriotism.

Values are at the core of our identity. As principles that govern our behavior and our way of seeing the world, they are even more resistant to change than strongly held attitudes and beliefs. For that reason, effective speakers rarely try to challenge or change the core values of their listeners. As we will discuss in Chapter 14, it is much easier to reason from values the audience shares with the speaker. Again, if you were arguing for measures to limit government access to social media before a skeptical audience, you might do well to open by stressing the widely shared value of freedom in America and by citing the Fourth Amendment to the U.S. Constitution, which guarantees us the right to be free from unreasonable search and seizure. What good is national security if we sacrifice the freedoms we would fight to defend? Such references to shared values can increase identification with your audience, even when you are not completely or immediately successful in persuading them to accept your conclusions.

Motives

motives
Widely shared psychological needs, desires, and impulses.

Motives are widely shared psychological needs, desires, and impulses. Motivational appeals work by identifying a connection between your message and a sense of need in the minds of your listeners. Because they are so widely shared, such appeals may help to create common bonds among today's diverse audiences.

Sometimes speakers make their appeal to motives explicit, as when a financial adviser opens her presentation by saying "Everyone dreams of a secure retirement, but that begins with making sure your credit is good." On other occasions, motivational appeals are implied in a good speech. For instance, a presentation that raises consciousness of a spike in violent crime near your college will engage your classmates' need to feel safe on campus. Psychologists and marketing researchers have been studying motivational appeals since the early twentieth century.[28] Perhaps the most influential contribution to this discussion is Abraham Maslow's five-tiered hierarchy of needs, which posits that lower-level physical and security needs must be satisfied before our higher-level needs for belonging, esteem, and self-actualization come into play.[29] Consider the ways in which your speeches might invoke the following widely shared motivations.

Physical Well-Being. As Maslow argued, all of us have physical needs for such basics as food, water, clean air, and sleep. We also have a basic need to feel reasonably healthy and comfortable. Commercials for fitness and weight-loss products often play to this set of needs. One student speaker caught the attention of his classmates as he appealed to this need in the introduction of his speech on the benefits of yoga:

> No pain, no gain! Right? No, wrong. If workout routines leave you heading for the medicine cabinet, look for another way to get your body and heart in shape. An exercise program that combines yoga and power walking improves both your body tone and your cardiovascular system.

Safety and Security. We all need to feel free from such threats as crime and natural disasters. Commercials for home security systems typically appeal to this need, as do politicians supporting policies to combat terrorism. Appeals to safety and security needs usually arouse a sense of fear, and are almost always more effective when the aroused fear is coupled with a constructive rejoinder. Revisiting our earlier example, a speech documenting a spike in violent crime near your campus would probably be more effective if you provide your listeners with advice on how to keep themselves safe or even how to get involved and become part of a proposed solution. Yet be careful: When fear appeals come across as too obvious or exaggerated, your listeners may feel manipulated and react negatively to you and your message. Fear appeals that stereotype groups of people as a threat are especially problematic.

Knowledge. People are naturally curious and have a deep-seated need to understand the world. We want to know what things are, why they are happening, how they work, and what we can do to make them work better. In today's rapidly changing world, speeches that explain and describe the use of new technologies in the workplace might fulfill this need. Joseph Van Matre's student speech on the use of videogame simulations in medical fields, education, the business world, and the military was well received by his classmates, who were not familiar with these applications (see this speech in Appendix B).

Relationships. Human beings are social creatures, and we all have a need for the affection, companionship, acceptance, and support of others. Our friends and families help define who we are and make the world a less lonely place. The need for social bonds is often used in advertising, suggesting that you risk losing friends if you don't use the right deodorant or wear a particular brand of shoes. Speeches that encourage listeners to join clubs or groups typically address our relational needs.

Achievement and Recognition. Most people like to feel they are successful, and like to be recognized for their accomplishments. Appeals to our need for achievement are commonly used by motivational speakers, as they encourage us to take charge of our lives. Recognition appeals are often used in commercials for expensive new cars as a way to tell others that we've arrived. Speakers may arouse the need for recognition when they compliment their audiences in their introductory remarks. Compliments can put listeners in a positive frame of mind, making them more receptive to your message.

Personal Growth and Satisfaction. Beyond material success and achievement, most people like to feel that they are developing their inner potential—that they are growing in a meaningful way. Definitions of personal growth may vary from person to person and culture to culture. People may derive their sense of satisfaction from having a job they love, becoming independent, developing artistic talents, or even pursuing a passion such as jogging. Appeals to this need are sometimes subtle but are common in advertising, as in commercials for online universities. As with achievement and recognition appeals, they are also commonly used by motivational speakers.

Pleasure and Recreation. All of us need to have fun from time to time—especially college students, who often find themselves overwhelmed with assignments, tests, and speeches to give, not to mention full- or part-time work. Appeals to this need are a staple of advertising, as in commercials for luxury vacations, expensive "grown up" toys, and alcoholic beverages. Your speeches can engage this need by introducing your listeners to new recreational activities or affordable nearby places for weekend getaways.

Tradition. Most people identify with traditions such as holidays and patriotic celebrations that give them a sense of roots. Many of our core values are steeped in traditions. Appeals to tradition are so common in public speaking that we treat them as a primary source of persuasion in Chapter 14 and of ceremonial identification in Chapter 16. People feel a particularly strong desire to reaffirm traditions in times of crisis, such as natural disasters.

Appeals to tradition may help establish identification that bridges cultural barriers. Consider the following passage, in which student speaker Stephanie Herrera describes the celebration of Christmas in Mexico:

> People walk through the neighborhood in a *posada*. This means "where they stop." The stops along the way are beautifully decorated homes where the walkers sing carols and are given gifts of food—like cookies and candies. The *posada* is a parade to honor Niño Dios, which means "baby God" in English.

Stephanie's reminder that Christmas is celebrated across cultures helped bring her listeners together and made them receptive to the rest of her message.

Altruism. The decision to volunteer at a soup kitchen or contribute to a charity reflects our basic need for altruism.[30] People derive satisfaction from feeling they are helping others and making the world a better place. Commercials urging us to feed children in underdeveloped countries draw on this need, as do speakers encouraging us to volunteer in our communities. Beth Tidmore used this appeal when she described the benefits of the Special Olympics for children with disabilities:

Beth Tidmore invoked her listeners' need for altruism when she encouraged them to volunteer for the Special Olympics.

> They experience courage and victory—and, yes, they also experience defeat. They get to interact with others with disabilities and with people without disabilities. And their mental disability is not a problem. It's not weird. Their biggest achievements aren't recognized with a medal. Their biggest achievements take place over time in the growth they make through being a part of the Special Olympics.

We all experience the psychological motives discussed here in varying degrees, and we all respond

Motives in Speeches	
Physical Well-Being	Having enough to eat and drink, enjoying a comfortable temperature, being free from pain
Safety and Security	Feeling safe and secure, being free from fear
Knowledge	Satisfying curiosity, answering questions about how things work in the world
Relationships	Satisfying desires for affection, companionship, acceptance, and support
Achievement and Recognition	Accomplishing goals, overcoming obstacles, winning awards and honors
Personal Growth and Satisfaction	Developing your potential, improving your performance, doing your job well
Pleasure and Recreation	Having a good time, going on vacation, having fun for its own sake
Tradition	Having a sense of roots, doing things as they have always been done, honoring ancestors, appreciating your history
Altruism	Taking care of others, providing comfort and aid, giving to charities, volunteering service, promoting the general well-being

Figure 5.2 Motives in Speeches

to them differently. For example, while most older people place a higher value on personal safety than on recreation, former President George H. W. Bush celebrated his ninetieth birthday by going skydiving! If you've ever moved alone to a new town, then you've probably experienced a heightened need to make friends. Finally, members of different cultures may define and prioritize these needs in differing ways. Some cultures favor traditional ways over innovation and individual achievement. Americans may be praised for valuing achievement through hard work, but criticized for their excessive need for comfort.

The use of psychographic appeals is sometimes controversial. For example, advertisers are often criticized for advocating reckless consumer spending and for inundating us with unrealistic and unhealthy images of idealized beauty. Likewise, politicians are often criticized for exploiting our fears. As we discuss in Chapter 15, motivational appeals can be used ethically to gain attention and move people to action, but their exaggerated use may cause listeners to react negatively to both you and your message. Appeals to motives must stand on a foundation of strong evidence and be used thoughtfully in relation to both the audience and the topic.

Identifying Motives in Advertisements

Find five advertisements, and identify the motives each one uses to appeal to its audience. How successful do you find each appeal, and why? If you substitute another motive, which one would it be and how would it alter the appeal?

YOUR ETHICAL VOICE

Putting Motives in Action

You are working on a speech urging your classmates to vote in an upcoming election. Which of the motives we have discussed might you appeal to? How would you use these appeals? What ethical issues should you consider as you make such appeals?

Gathering Information about Your Audience

5.3 Determine ways to gather information about your audience.

Knowing that the demographics and psychographics of your audience can help guide everything from the topic you select to how you deliver your presentation, the next question is: How do you gather that information? With classroom audiences, some information can usually be obtained through observation. Simply look around and appreciate the variety of your classmates. Listen carefully during conversations before and after class as well as the first round of speeches for statements that might reveal occupational interests or cultural and group affiliations. When preparing for unfamiliar audiences outside the classroom, you may have to obtain such information on your own. Sometimes, the person or group inviting you to speak can provide useful information. So can exploring the websites and literature available about the group and its members.

When you have the opportunity, you can gather more precise information on your audience through the use of surveys. Free online resources such as Facebook, Twitter, and Survey Monkey can be useful for sampling the opinions of connected friends and followers. The General Audience Survey (see Figure 5.3) can help you gather information on demographic affiliations and general interests, and the Topic-Oriented Audience Survey (see Figure 5.4) can be customized for gathering more specific information that explores what your listeners know about your topic, how they feel about it, and how they might respond to different sources of information about it.

closed-ended questions
Questions that stipulate a limited number of answers for respondents to select such as true-false, multiple-choice, and scaled questions.

Should you decide to develop your own survey, give careful consideration to the types of questions you ask and the way you word them. **Closed-ended questions**

Figure 5.3 General Audience Survey

General Audience Survey

Age: ___

Year: ___Freshman ___Sophomore ___Junior ___Senior ___Other:

Major:

Race/Ethnic Background (check all that apply):

___African American ___Asian American ___Caucasian ___Latinx/Hispanic American

___Native American ___Other: ______________

Political Preference:

___Democrat ___Republican ___Independent ___Other: ______________

Religious Preference: ____

Career Ambitions: ____

Hobbies and Recreational Activities: ________________________________

What I believe is the most important public issue facing us today: ________________

Figure 5.4 Topic-Oriented Audience Survey

Topic-Oriented Audience Survey

Please circle the answer that best represents your position for each question.

Have you heard of ____________________ before? [add your topic]

Yes No Not sure

How interested are you in this issue?

Very Somewhat Not Very

Rate your thoughts and feelings toward this topic on the following scales:

strong ___:___:___:___:___ weak

decisive ___:___:___:___:___ indecisive

active ___:___:___:___:___ passive

good ___:___:___:___:___ bad

dangerous ___:___:___:___:___ safe

Please place a check beside each of the sources of information on this topic you would find credible.

_____ Fox News
_____ CNN
_____ *Wall Street Journal*
_____ MSNBC
_____ *Washington Post*
_____ Bill O'Reilly
_____ Rachel Maddow
_____ Stephen Colbert
_____ Hillary Clinton
_____ Donald Trump

In general, how do you feel about this topic? ________________________
____
____

stipulate a limited number of choices for respondents to select. You have probably taken a number of surveys asking you to respond to questions as "true" or "false." Other closed-ended questions may offer a variety of possible responses. For instance, a demographic question may ask your classmates, "What year are you in school? _______ freshman _______ sophomore _______ junior _______ senior." Finally, scaled questions may ask respondents to place their reactions along a continuum of five responses ranging from "strongly agree" to "agree" to "undecided" to "disagree" to "strongly disagree." Such Likert scales, as they are commonly called, can help to measure the intensity of your listeners' attitudes toward your subject or message.

Closed-ended questions of the true-false, multiple-choice, and scaled format are commonly used for conducting audience surveys because they can provide useful feedback. They are relatively easy to administer and to respond to, and they encourage respondents to provide concrete answers to difficult questions. The results can be easily tabulated to provide a valuable template for assessing your audience as a whole with respect to a given topic or message. How many of your prospective listeners agree or disagree with the government monitoring our use of social media? How strongly do they feel about this issue?

The drawback of using closed-ended questions is that they are limited in terms of providing quality feedback as to how audience members actually think and feel about your issue. For instance, two or more respondents might support the use of government monitoring of social media but for vastly different reasons. For this reason, many surveys close with one or a few **open-ended questions** that invite respondents to provide and elaborate answers on their own terms. For instance, if you asked the same respondents above, "Generally speaking, how do you feel about the government monitoring our social media?" you might get a variety of answers. Some may respond that they generally believe you should support the government but admit to not having given the subject much thought. Some may be prone to support any initiatives that promote national security regardless of consequences, whereas others might be prone to support such surveillance but only under certain circumstances that protect the privacy rights of most Americans. These are important distinctions that can prove really valuable to you as you hone and focus your presentation.

open-ended questions
Questions that allow respondents to answer in as much detail as they choose.

Open-ended questions have their drawbacks as well. They are more time-consuming both to take and to evaluate and pose difficulties for surveying large groups of people. They also tend to provide inconsistent feedback that makes it hard for you to draw more general conclusions about your audience as a whole.

Regardless of what type of questions you choose to include in your survey, you should be careful with the way you structure and word them to ensure an accurate and unbiased assessment. Keep your questionnaires short, use simple questions that address a single idea, and use language that is clear and concrete. Avoid the use of technical jargon and colloquial references that may confuse respondents who speak English as a second language. Try to avoid the use of terms like "always" and "never," and make a conscious effort to avoid rigging your questions by inserting your own biases or implied answers. Even subtle changes in your choice of words can skew listeners' responses. Consider the different answers you might get from the same person if you asked "Do you support government monitoring of social media to protect us from terrorism?" versus "Do you oppose government monitoring of social media because it infringes on your privacy rights?"

Finally, while administering your survey, make it a point not to sway responses by revealing your position on your topic. Encourage your respondents to provide additional feedback. Tell your respondents not to add their names to the survey, and ensure them that their responses will be kept anonymous. As you tabulate your feedback, keep in mind that any survey provides only a general snapshot of where your audience stands. Compare what you learn from a questionnaire with what you hear as you listen to others talking about the issue in question as well as what you discover during your research. Then, use your findings in your presentation to demonstrate that you have sought to understand your audience: "According to the recent survey that you filled out for me, 25 percent of you did not know that the government is keeping tabs on our use of social media, and more than half of you expressed discomfort with the idea. Today, I'm going to explain why you are right!"

Developing a Survey to Gather Information

Jot down what you have already observed about your classmates. What does this information tell you? What else would you like to discover? How would you develop a survey to gather that additional information?

The Rewards and Challenges of Audience Diversity

5.4 Understand the rewards and challenges of audience diversity.

Chances are the audiences that you will address in class, at work, or in your community will be considerably more diverse than those of your parents' generation. And that diversity will only increase in the future. According to the U.S. Census Bureau, by mid-century more than half of all Americans will be members of minority groups, more than one in five will be elderly, and nearly one in five will be foreign born.[31] Learning to appreciate and interact with that diversity can be incredibly rewarding. It can enrich your thinking and expand your horizons, and it can help you become a more effective and ethical speaker. But it can also pose several challenges. How can you adapt to the variety you are likely to find in an audience for a public presentation? You can rise to these challenges by learning more about the *cultural backgrounds* of your listeners, speaking from *shared values*, using *supporting materials* thoughtfully, and *choosing your words* carefully.

Become Familiar with the Audiences' Cultural Affiliations

The best way to learn about different cultures is to reach out to those who belong to them. Locate websites that provide perspectives on different cultures. Consider attending social events or open houses hosted by organizations representing different minority, international, or religious groups on your campus. Reach out to others around you with respectful curiosity to learn more about them. Such contacts will often acquaint you with people who can offer advice for adapting your ideas, selecting supporting materials, and avoiding language that might be offensive. Such contacts may also help you grow and find your voice as you address diverse audiences.

Speak from Shared Values

While values and the way we prioritize them may vary across cultures, most Americans share such values as hard work and individual freedom. Focus on shared values rather than differences to emphasize commonalities. In his keynote address before the Democratic National Convention in 2004—a speech largely credited with catapulting him to national prominence—then Senator Barack Obama transcended the potential barriers of politics, race, and culture by emphasizing a shared patriotism. "There is not a liberal America and conservative America," he

Finding Your Voice

Sampling Audience Diversity

With your instructor's permission, form small groups of class members who differ in age, gender, ethnicity, or other demographic features. Have the members write down their five most important needs, wants, and wishes. Then compare the lists and make note of the similarities and differences. Use this information to learn about each other. Consider how both the commonalities and the dissimilarities might be helpful in planning speeches.

insisted, "there is only the United States of America. There is not a Black America and a White America and a Latino America and an Asian America—there's the United States of America."[32]

Finally, try to invoke values that appeal across cultures. Such values as honesty, fairness, justice, charity, self-determination, and respect for tradition can make connections beyond ostensible boundaries. When Malala Yousafzai spoke at the United Nations on the day declared in her honor, she stressed:

> Malala Day is not my day. Today is the day of every woman, every boy and every girl who have raised their voice for their rights. There are hundreds of human rights activists and social workers who are not only speaking for human rights, but who are struggling to achieve their goals of education, peace and equality.[33]

Her appeal to the shared values of human rights, education, peace, and equality created bonds among youth ambassadors and world leaders from almost 200 countries.

Use Supporting Materials Thoughtfully

As we will discuss in Chapter 8, facts and statistics, testimony, examples, and narratives provide support for your presentations. Different cultural groups may find different types of support important. Some groups may be persuaded by facts and expert testimony. Others might value the voices of elders or religious leaders. Still others might be engaged more by stories and dramatic examples. Try to determine what kinds of supporting materials your specific audience will find most convincing. If you are especially uncertain about audience preferences, use a variety of supporting materials: provide facts and expert opinions to validate your main ideas, look for quotations by authorities your listeners will respect, and engage your listeners with stories and examples.

When cultural differences exist in your audience, *emphasize the use of narratives*. All people tell stories, and nothing can bring diverse groups together more effectively than narratives that help them discover their shared humanity. Former Vice President Al Gore reflected on this power of narrative in his attempts to promote peace talks between the Israelis and their Palestinian neighbors. The situation looked hopeless, he remembered, when a "miracle" occurred. In Gore's words, "The breakthroughs came when they told stories about their families. I have seen time and time again how storytelling brings people together."[34]

Choose Your Words Carefully

Speakers who bridge cultural diversity use the language of inclusion. The use of pronouns such as *we* and *our* instead of *them* and *their* can enhance your chances for establishing common ground. Conversely, avoid language that calls attention to differences between yourself and your listeners.

Be careful that your words do not confuse listeners. When audience members are unfamiliar with your topic, it helps to use lay language and define terms that might be misunderstood. Presentation aids can clarify and amplify your most important ideas and information. If your audience includes listeners for whom English is a second language, avoid slang terms and colloquialisms such as "he left it all out on the floor" or "she hit the wall." These and similar expressions can bring utter confusion to those who are new to our language and its idiosyncrasies.

Invoking shared values and choosing your words carefully can bring listeners together, even when issues threaten to drive them apart.

By all means, avoid the use of words that invoke ethnic, religious, and gender stereotypes. Do not try to copy the communication style of other cultures, which almost always comes across as inappropriate, if not offensive. If you try to speak a language that is not your native tongue, be sure you get the pronunciation right. In one political race, a candidate offered a speech that he hoped would win the support of the Cuban expatriate community in Florida. As he concluded, he shouted: "*Patria o muerte, venceremos!*" ("Fatherland or death, we shall overcome"). He did not understand the icy reaction he got until someone explained that those words were the trademark sign-off of Fidel Castro.[35]

Appreciating the Diversity of Your Audience

Write down the cultural affiliations you can identify for your classmates. How can you use shared values, supporting materials, and language to adapt to your audience?

Adjusting to the Speaking Situation

5.5 Adjust your message to the speaking situation.

In addition to understanding and adjusting to your audience's demographics and psychographics, you need to consider the **speaking situation** in which you will make your presentation. The situation includes not only the *occasion* for speaking but also the *physical* and *psychological settings*.

speaking situation The occasion for speaking as well as the physical and psychological settings.

The Occasion

As you prepare your speeches, consider why people will gather to hear you. Listeners have expectations about what type of presentation they will hear. When attendance is mandatory, as in work-related or classroom presentations, you want to give extra thought to attracting and sustaining attention. Your task is to transform a captive audience into an enthusiastic one. Similarly, if your presentation accompanies a meal, you will compete with food, service, and conversation.

As we note in Chapter 6, expectations surrounding the occasion will often dictate your choice of topic and purpose for speaking. For instance, if you are making an award presentation at a banquet, then you should focus primarily on the nature of the award and the worthiness of the recipient. The expectations of the occasion will also influence how we dress and our style of presentation. Obviously, formal occasions require formal attire; in addition, they guide your manner of presentation and your language choices.

Audience members may become annoyed when speakers violate their expectations about what is appropriate regarding the occasion. Obviously, if listeners expect an award presentation for a fellow employee and you focus most of your presentation on your own contributions, your listeners will likely be irritated and may question your ethos and status within the organization. We once attended an opening session for a convention of choral conductors, featuring a presentation by the chair of the National Endowment for the Arts. Although the opening of the presentation addressed the audience directly, she quickly transitioned to what was obviously a boilerplate speech on the arts generally—and in the process, she lost the attention and respect of her audience.

The Physical Setting

The physical setting includes the place where you will be speaking, the time of your presentation, and the size of your audience. Like the occasion, these factors will affect how you speak.

Place. The place where you will speak can pose several challenges. For example, will a lectern be provided? Is there a stage? Do windows offer a competing view or an opportunity to connect with your topic? The answers to those questions might influence your planning and practice for the presentation. If you plan to use an electronic presentation aid, make sure you have an electrical outlet as well as the proper technology and that your aid displays clearly. When speaking outdoors or in a really large room, you might need to use a microphone to project your voice. Classroom settings are usually small and speaker-friendly, but you can never be sure. We taught a course at a major university that was undergoing renovations. We never knew when we were going to have to suddenly project our voices loudly enough to compete with a rumbling jackhammer!

If you are speaking online, it will help to know where your audience is located. They might be in a central location or widely dispersed; they might view your presentation simultaneously or on a delayed feed. Choose a location without a distracting background. Although you may be tempted to wear your pajamas, dress according to the audience and the occasion. Keep an erect posture, and limit your gestures. Most important, enunciate clearly and use dynamic vocal inflections. Although the visual elements remain important, researchers have found that your voice carries more weight with online presentations.[36] Regardless of where you will speak, familiarize yourself with the place. Think about whether you want to move a desk or table or rearrange the seating to facilitate your audience's appreciation of your speech. If possible, practice your presentation there. Such preparation will make you more comfortable, which is especially helpful for coping with communication apprehension.

Time. When are you more focused? At the beginning of the semester? First thing in the morning? Right after lunch? The amount of time you are allotted to speak, the time of day, the day of the week, and even the time of the year can affect the way listeners receive your message. When speaking early in the morning, at the end of a long workday, or on Mondays—when listeners are still adjusting to the weekend being over—you may need to be especially dynamic and to use vivid supporting materials and presentation aids. Even snowy winter days or sunny spring days can sometimes put listeners in a distracted state of mind.

With shorter presentations, the limited amount of time you have increases the importance of streamlining your message. You must focus quickly on your most important ideas and choose your most relevant and impressive supporting materials. You should also plan focused introductions and conclusions that give your message punch and power. Avoid Winston Churchill's admitted shortcoming: "I'm going to make a long speech because I've not had the time to prepare a short one."[37]

Audience Size. Finally, the size of your audience affects your speaking. Smaller audiences allow for more interaction, which invites a more casual presentation. On the other hand, larger audiences may call for a more formal manner of speaking, while still inviting a sense of enlarged conversation. Your voice should be animated and your gestures more emphatic so that you can easily be seen and heard by everyone. Since you cannot make or sustain eye contact with everyone, you should choose representative listeners in various sections of the audience and pan back and forth so that everyone feels included. Presentation aids and lettering should be large and bold enough to be intelligible to your most distant listeners. If you are speaking via a webcast or recording, look directly into the camera and, by proxy, into your audience's eyes.

The size of your audience should affect your manner of presentation.

SPEAKER'S NOTES

Checklist for Analyzing the Speaking Situation

Use this checklist to be sure you don't overlook anything important when analyzing the speaking situation:

1. What are the audience's expectations, and how can I take them into account?
2. How can I adjust to the place where I will speak?
3. How will the time or timing of my speech affect the audience?
4. How large will my audience be?
5. Is there any late-breaking news relevant to my topic?
6. Have others addressed relevant topics with this audience?

The Psychological Setting

The psychological setting for your speeches may be influenced by the context of recent events or by speeches that are presented before yours.

Recent Events. When listeners enter the room the day of your speech, they bring with them information about recent events. This information affects the way they receive and evaluate your message. Citing recent developments early in your speech can help you establish the importance and timeliness of your topic. On the other hand, failing to acknowledge or account for recent events can damage both the effectiveness of your message and your ethos. For instance, we once had a student present a speech that was highly critical of the "war on terror" right after a major and well-publicized attack on American soil. The speech was otherwise very thoughtful, well supported, and well developed. The fact that the speaker failed to even acknowledge the attack and was obviously not prepared for subsequent questions about it left a negative impression on his listeners.

Jody Cross learned that her speech on leadership to middle managers would come at a challenging time: The company's directors had instituted a major change without consulting them, resulting in a disgruntled and distrustful group. Rather than regretting that she'd ever said yes to the engagement, she embraced the opportunity because "audiences like this are in deeper need of assistance." Instead of starting with her qualifications, she began by addressing her listeners' need for appreciation, recognition, understanding, and motivation. As a result, she observed, "You could actually see their physical presence change," from stiff and resistant to open and relaxed.[38]

Recent Speeches. Many speaking occasions—such as award dinners, political rallies, and class presentations—feature a number of speeches presented in succession. The speeches presented before your presentation can have a **preliminary tuning effect** on the thinking, mood, and receptivity of your audience. This effect sometimes requires last-minute adjustments—usually in the introduction to your speech. For instance, if the speaker before you makes a truly outstanding presentation, you might do well to acknowledge that before launching into your own speech. If your speech follows an effective presentation on a depressing subject such as human slavery, you might want to rethink the humor you had planned to open your speech. It is easier to consider alternatives as part of your preparatory practice rather than at the spur of the moment, so anticipate how you might be able to adjust.

preliminary tuning effect
The effect of previous speeches or other situational factors in predisposing an audience to respond positively or negatively to a speech.

The preliminary tuning effect can be quite challenging when a previous speaker makes a compelling argument against the position you intend to take in your speech. This sometimes happens in public speaking classes. For example, suppose you are going to present a speech supporting legislation to protect the habitat of an endangered species. The speaker before you has made a powerful and well-supported argument that passing the proposed law would do substantial damage to the local economy. Rather than criticizing the speaker, it is usually better to gracefully thank the speaker

Figure 5.5 Audience Analysis Worksheet

Audience Analysis Worksheet

	Factor Description	Adaptations Needed
Audience Demographics	Age: ______	______
	Gender: ______	______
	Education: ______	______
	Sociocultural Background: ______	______
	Group Affiliations: ______	______
	Interest in Topic: ______	______
	Knowledge of Topic: ______	______
Audience Psychographics	Audience Beliefs: ______	______
	Audience Attitudes: ______	______
	Relevant Values: ______	______
	Motivational Appeals: ______	______
Speaking Situation	Time: ______	______
	Place: ______	______
	Occasion: ______	______
	Audience Size: ______	______
	Context: ______	______

Adapting to Your Audience

Identify ways that adapting to your audience would be unethical and ways that you could adapt ethically. What criteria do you use to draw the line?

for raising an issue that you both believe is important. You might then transition into your presentation with something like, "Now let me tell you the other side of the story."

Bringing It All Together. The audience analysis worksheet in Figure 5.5 will help you consider all the factors we have discussed in the chapter as you plan for the audience and situation of your speech. When you have sized up the situation, adding this knowledge to your analysis of audience demographics, psychographics, and diversity, you will be ready for the next challenge of focusing and constructing your message.

YOUR ETHICAL VOICE

Guidelines for Ethical Audience Adaptation

Keep the following guidelines in mind as you consider adapting your message to your audience:

1. Change your strategies, not your convictions.
2. Use the exploration of your audience's characteristics to examine your own position in greater depth.
3. Appeal to shared needs and values to bridge cultural differences.
4. Resist stereotypes and biases that may lead you to misjudge others.
5. Address and correct impulses toward ethnocentrism.
6. Avoid sexist, racist, ethnic, or religious humor.
7. Show respect for the common humanity of your listeners.

Final Reflections: Looking Beyond Yourself

What am I going to talk about? What will I say? How will I do? What will the audience think of me? Will my grade be okay? It is a natural thing for beginning speakers to be preoccupied with the first-person pronouns *I*, *me*, and *my*, especially when they know their performances will be graded. These are all common, understandable concerns. Often, as we discussed in Chapter 2, this focus on yourself is a major cause of communication apprehension.

Central to addressing these concerns is turning that focus from yourself to your connection with your audience. Who are they, and what kind of background experiences, interests, and attitudes do they bring with them? What can you say that might be useful to them? How might you expand the horizons of their lives?

We have offered ways to better understand your listeners. What beliefs, attitudes, values, and motives do they have? What appeals will move them to adopt a new course of action? As audiences become more culturally diverse, how can you speak across these differences to draw listeners together? And how might the setting of the speech—both physical and psychological—affect your efforts?

These are all questions prompted by this chapter, and they all point you outward beyond yourself. To answer them successfully is to increase your control of the power of the spoken word, and that raises a final ethical question: How will you use this new power? Will you exploit or manipulate others to serve your own purposes? We are not advocating that you pander, ingratiate, or knuckle under to your audience. We *are* advocating the value of adapting your messages to the humanity of your listeners and to the demands of a given moment.

Scholar Donald C. Bryant characterized the function of rhetoric as "adjusting ideas to people and people to ideas."[39] Understanding your audience and exploring ways to connect them to your ideas—and to connect yourself to the audience—will strengthen your ability as a public speaker and as a person. The Guidelines for Ethical Audience Adaptation developed here can help you maintain your moral bearings as you seek, discover, develop, adapt, and ultimately find your voice.

Study Questions

CONTENT MASTERY

1 What are the demographic characteristics of audiences? How can you adjust your message to these characteristics?

2 In what ways can psychographics influence listeners?

3 What is the difference between beliefs and attitudes, and how might these affect the reception of a message?

4 How can you put values and motives to work for you in messages?

5 How can you gather information about your audience's demographics and psychographics?

6 How can you meet the challenges of audience diversity in order to reap the rewards?

7 What constraints can the physical speaking situation impose, and how can you cope with them?

8 What challenges does the psychological setting for a speech suggest, and how can you adjust to make your message more effective?

9 What ethical guidelines should you keep in mind as you adapt to your audience and situation?

CRITICAL EXPLORATIONS

1. Before your next speech, develop a topic-oriented audience survey based on Figure 5.4. Ask permission from your instructor to distribute it to the class to complete in either paper or electronic form. How could you adapt your speech according to what you discover?
2. Choose a controversial issue, and explore at least two public opinion polls that offer findings relevant to this issue. How do the questions in each compare? Are there any differences among the findings? If you used one of these polls in a speech, should you feel an ethical obligation to acknowledge the other polls as well, especially if they differ?
3. Watch a persuasive speech on YouTube, and identify the motivational appeals used in it. How skillfully does the speaker use these appeals? What other motives might the speaker have used? What does this suggest about ways you could use motivational appeals in your presentations?
4. Have you ever heard speeches that were not adapted to the situation? What happened? Did the speakers address a subject that was inappropriate for the occasion? Did they ignore the perspectives of the audience? Did they go on too long? Was the delivery not adjusted to the size of the room and audience? How would you have advised them to better adapt?
5. Investigate a cultural group different from your own. Identify the pattern of values you think are particular to the group, as revealed in their writings, websites, and speeches. If you were to prepare a speech for an audience of members from that group, what kinds of appeals might you use? What might you have to be careful about in your speech?

6. You have been invited to present a speech on genetically modified organisms (GMOs) to

   a. a biology class at a local high school.
   b. a meeting of the Rotary Club.
   c. a gathering at the Senior Citizens Center.
   d. your class.

   How might you adapt the speech to these various audiences? Explain and defend your approach.

CHAPTER

Finding Your Topic

LEARNING OBJECTIVES

This chapter will help you:

6.1 Learn the qualities of a good speech topic.

6.2 Discover topic possibilities through brainstorming, interest charts, and mediated prompts.

6.3 Explore a promising topic area through mind mapping and topic analysis.

6.4 Refine your topic for speaking.

OUTLINE

What Is a Good Topic?

Discovering Your Topic Area

Exploring Your Topic Area

Refining Your Topic

Lindsey Yoder won the first Michael Osborn Public Speaking Contest at the University of Memphis with the powerful speech that appears at the end of Chapter 14. Lindsey was then invited to present her speech on human trafficking to a community rally that involved hundreds of activists, church members, police officials, and city leaders. We asked Lindsey how she had selected the topic for her speech.

"I did not choose my topic," she said. 'It chose me."

"We miss the possibility of being surprised by what is hidden in plain sight right in front of us."

—ALEXANDRA HOROWITZ

If this were the way classroom speeches were usually generated, there would be no need for this chapter. Unfortunately, Lindsey's experience is the exception rather than the rule. Most of us need help finding, refining, and adapting the topics of our speeches so that they fit assignments and the needs of our listeners. We have to follow a search process to generate the best of these topics. This chapter will describe this process, showing how you can conduct it successfully.

In the communication world that awaits you beyond the class, topics impose themselves on you: Work concerns, community affairs, and political issues of the moment may all provide the impetus for your speaking. But the public speaking classroom typically offers one great advantage: It allows you to explore the universe of possible topics to find those best suited to help you find your voice. This freedom to select your topic helps you exercise your creativity and realize your potential.

What Is a Good Topic?

6.1 Learn the qualities of a good speech topic.

Many people panic when asked to give a speech. Students often get that deer-in-the-headlights look: "What am I going to talk about? What the heck am I going to do?" Students aren't alone in this panic. The dean asked one of the authors to speak to a campus convocation, and her first thought was, "Me?! What do I possibly have to say that anyone would want to listen to?"[1] Be comforted by the fact that there are indeed ways of identifying and developing good topics.

The first requirement of any speech topic is that it meet the expectations of your audience with respect to the occasion and the immediate situation. For instance, if you give a briefing at work on the progress of a given project, present an award at a sports banquet to an outstanding member of your team, or speak out against a proposed ordinance before your local city council, then your choice of topic and purpose for speaking will be largely guided by the nature of the occasion and audience expectations.

With classroom speeches, of course, a good topic must fit your assignment. Your instructor may ask you to present an introductory, informative, persuasive, or ceremonial speech and may stipulate more specific requirements such as timing, use of supporting materials, presentation aids, and formal outlines and bibliographies. But class presentations typically give you considerably more freedom to choose and explore topic ideas that are important to you and that you feel should be important to your listeners. This provides you with a unique opportunity to find and explore your voice and, in the process, enrich the lives of your listeners by sharing new information or a new perspective.

Regardless of the occasion, a good topic is one that *involves you, engages your listeners,* and *can be managed responsibly* given the time allotted for preparing and presenting your speech.

A Good Topic Involves You

Imagine yourself speaking successfully:

> You're enthusiastic about what you're saying. Your face shows your involvement in your topic. Your voice expresses your feelings. Your gestures reinforce your meaning. Everything about you says, "This is important!" or "This is interesting!" or "This will make a difference in your lives!"

Once you can identify a subject that makes you feel this way, you may well have found your topic, or—like Lindsey Yoder—your topic may have found you.

Your topic does not have to be an earthshaking issue, but it should be something your listeners ought to know more about. Trivial topics, such as "how to twirl a baton" and "how to kick a football," waste the time of both the speaker and the listeners. Such overworked topics as "don't drink and drive" also waste time unless they offer listeners a new and fresh slant.

Above all, your topic should be important to you personally and should help you develop as a speaker. What are *you* interested in? What do you like to do? What piques your curiosity? What do you talk about with friends? What have you learned in a class that really intrigues you? What annoys you? It's much easier to engage an audience if you yourself know what's interesting about a topic. Moreover, it takes time to think through your ideas, research them, organize what you discover, and practice your presentation. If your topic is important to you, it's much easier to invest the time and effort required to speak responsibly.

A Good Topic Engages Your Listeners

Picture an audience of ideal listeners:

> Their faces are alive with interest. They lean forward in their seats, intent on what you are saying. They nod or smile appropriately. At the end of your speech, they want to ask you questions about your ideas or voice their reactions. Long after your speech, they are still thinking about what you said.

What topic will help you create this kind of audience response? By now, you probably have heard the first speeches in your class, and you know something about your listeners. Ask yourself, "What are my audience's interests? What do they care about? What do they need to know more about?" Graham Honeycutt, while a student at Davidson College, noted that the best speakers "really search deep down and find how a topic relates to them, and then feed on that to see how they can create a similar reaction in their audience."

A passion for sports can prompt ideas for speech topics.

A Good Topic Is One You Can Manage

The final test of a good topic is whether you can acquire the knowledge you will need to speak responsibly on it. The time you have for the preparation and presentation of your speech is limited, and some topics are incredibly complicated. Consequently, you should select a *manageable part* of your topic area to develop for your presentation. For example, instead of trying to cover the entire subject of terrorism—its causes, sources, kinds, purposes, leaders, and so on—it would be much better to focus on one aspect, such as your community's plan in case of a terrorist attack. This more limited topic would focus more closely on your audience's particular interests and should help you prepare a responsible presentation.

Think of your search for the right topic as a process that goes through phases of discovery, exploration, and refinement.

- In the **discovery phase**, you uncover promising topic areas.
- In the **exploration phase**, you focus on specific speech topics within these areas.
- In the **refinement phase**, you identify the general and specific purposes of speeches you might give on these topics and write out your thesis statements.

It is important to realize that *this process takes time*. Give yourself *at least* a week to select your topic, do your research, outline your speech, and practice your presentation. You will find that this time is well invested. Nothing comforts you more on the eve of a presentation than knowing you are well prepared.

discovery phase
Identifying broad topic areas that might generate successful speeches.

exploration phase
Examining broad topic areas to pinpoint more precise topics for speeches.

refinement phase
Framing the general and specific purposes of a speech's topic and a thesis statement.

Developing a Realistic Timeline

Develop a realistic timeline for the discovery, exploration, and refinement of the topic for your upcoming speech.

Discovering Your Topic Area

6.2 Discover topic possibilities through brainstorming, interest charts, and mediated prompts.

Students often have great ideas for topics—but they don't recognize them as such. Three techniques—brainstorming, interest charts, and mediated prompts—can help you discover promising topics for speeches.

Brainstorming

Brainstorming is a technique that encourages free associations in the search for a topic area. Ask yourself, *What kinds of topic areas could I explore for my next speech?* At the top of a sheet of paper, write down the first idea that occurs to you. Below this idea, write down as many relevant ideas as come to mind. Do not try to think critically about these ideas until you have a sizable list. Let your mind wander. Once you've developed the list, go back and critique them one at a time to see what emerges. We encourage you to use paper rather than an electronic device because that way you can draw connections among what you've written down—but perhaps a computer will work well for you.

brainstorming
Technique that encourages the free play of the mind to generate a list of ideas that can then be carefully considered and critiqued for possible topics.

You may discover, as one student of ours did, that such free-wheeling generation of ideas can be productive and creative. Zachary came to our office one day early in the term with a serious case of topic anxiety. After we convinced him that his symptoms were not terminal, he accepted our invitation to participate in brainstorming. Zachary wrote down "Wyoming" at the top of his legal pad. He then wrote down the following associations: trout, Yellowstone, fire, drought, George Anderson (a well-known fly fisherman), catch and release, and wolves. He studied this list closely. "You know," he said, "I could speak on 'Fire and Water in Yellowstone: Too Much of One, Too Little of the Other.'" And eventually he did.

Interest Charts

An **interest chart** is a systematic projection of your own interests and those of your audience. They can be useful for discovering and exploring prospective topic areas. The classical writers on rhetoric were the first to discover that the mind follows certain habitual paths that are productive in creative thinking. You have already followed such paths if you developed the self-awareness inventory suggested in Chapter 3.

interest chart
Visual display of speaker or audience interests, as prompted by probe questions.

Figure 6.1 Your Interest Chart

The productive possibilities you explored in that chapter can be easily adapted and enlarged here. They appear in the form of questions that guide the mind:

1. What *places* do you find interesting?
2. What *people* do you find fascinating?
3. What *activities* do you enjoy?
4. What *objects* intrigue you?
5. What *events* stand out in your mind?
6. Which *ideas* do you find exciting?
7. What *values* are important to you?
8. What *problems* concern you most?
9. What *campus concerns* do you have?

You can use your responses to these queries, supplemented by what you learn about yourself and others from social media, to develop a chart that projects a comprehensive visual display of your interests. To create such a chart, write out brief responses to the probe questions. Try to come up with at least five responses for each question. Your interest chart might then look like that in Figure 6.1.

Once you have completed your personal interest chart, make a similar chart of audience interests. What places, people, events, activities, objects, ideas, values, problems, and campus concerns seem to spark discussions in class or on social media? Study the two charts together, looking for shared interests. To do this systematically, make a three-column **topic area inventory chart**. In the first column (your interests), list the subjects you find most appealing. In the second column (audience interests), list the subjects that seem most interesting to your listeners. In the third column, match columns 1 and 2 to find the most promising areas of speech topics. Figure 6.2 shows a sample topic area inventory chart.

topic area inventory chart
A means of determining possible speech topics by listing topics you and your listeners find interesting and then matching them.

In this example, your interests in cycling and hiking coincide with the audience's interest in unusual places, and that connection suggests a possible topic area: "weekend adventures close to campus." Similarly, your concern for physical fitness pairs with the audience's interest in deceptive advertising to generate another possibility: "exercise rip-offs." Your concern over tuition costs intersects with audience interests in economic problems, leading to "keeping college affordable." Finally, your interest

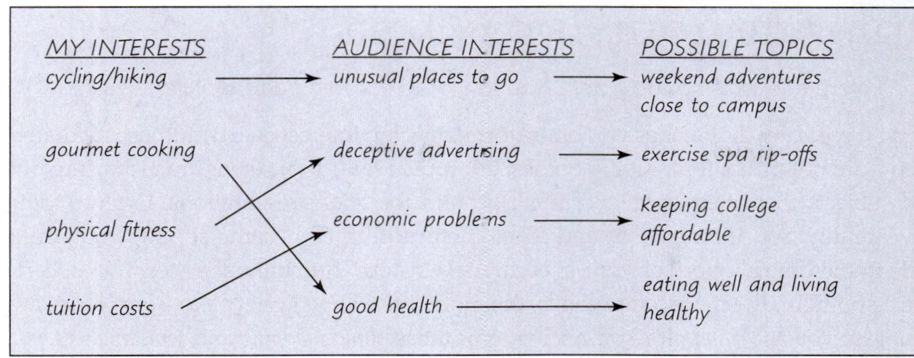

Figure 6.2 Topic Area Inventory Chart

in gourmet cooking resonates with audience concerns over good health to suggest the topic area of "eating well and living healthy."

Our students have used interest charts to identify such topics as the superiority of wooden roller coasters, how to escape riptides, the benefits of sleep, the Korean educational system, tsunamis, the domestic adoption system, organ donation, child soldiers in Africa, energy drinks, and respecting Muslim head coverings. Who knows what you could find through this process?

Mediated Prompts

If brainstorming and interest charts don't produce enough promising topic discoveries, **mediated prompts** provide another excellent source. When using such prompts, you jump-start the creative process by scanning newspapers, magazines, and electronic media for ideas. Go through the Sunday paper, scan *Time* and *Newsweek* or quality periodicals such as *The Atlantic* or *Smithsonian*, or read the daily headlines of the *New York Times* or *Wall Street Journal* online. Explore a dictionary using the initial of your first or last name, and see what ideas the words there might spark. The Osborns, for example, might find oak, oatmeal, observatory, obsession, oceanography, ocelot, omnivorous, onyx, opportunity, ostrich, overcome, oyster, and ozone—a wealth of ideas for presentations!

mediated prompts
Sources such as newspapers, magazines, and electronic media that can suggest ideas for speech topics.

The Internet offers some special resources if you are selective. If you search the words "speech topics," you may find a few gems among the garbage. Explore the websites of organizations of interest, whether the National Women's History Museum, the Baseball Hall of Fame, the International Museum of Muslim Cultures, or the National Museum of African American History and Culture. Investigate such Internet search indexes as Lycos Topics. You may find promising ideas on such outlets as Twitter, Tumblr, Facebook, and Pinterest to see what is trending. In addition, some sites are especially helpful. See, for example, the "Topic Selection Helper" developed by Ron St. John of the University of Hawaii's Maui Community College Speech Department (go to the Public Speaking Web Guide website).

As you scan media resources, consider the headlines, advertisements, and pictures. What catches your attention? The headline "Travel Money Tips Offered" might inspire you to speak on "champagne travel on a beer budget." Or the personals section in the classified ads might prompt a speech on "the dangers of Internet dating services." You might be intrigued by the different fonts that are used or by the subjects or framing of photographs and illustrations.

The media-prompts technique has one great advantage: The topics it generates are timely. But be cautious. Mediated prompts can suggest ideas for speeches, but you can't simply summarize a single article and use it as a speech. The article provides a starting point for your thinking; then you want to do further research and integrate these sources into your own voice. *Your* speech must be *your* message, designed to appeal to *your* specific audience. You should always bring something new to your topic—a fresh insight or a special application for your listeners—based on ideas gleaned from processing a number of resources.

Techniques for Discovering Topics for Future Speeches

How do the techniques of brainstorming, interest charts, and mediated prompts help you to identify ideas for speeches that you might not have thought of otherwise? Were some of the topics "hidden in plain sight," as Horowitz's opening quotation suggests? How can these techniques make discovering topics for future speeches easier?

Exploring Your Topic Area

6.3 Explore a promising topic area through mind mapping and topic analysis.

topic areas
Promising but broad subjects that need to be honed into topics for briefer presentations.

What you typically discover as you brainstorm, develop interest charts, and use mediated prompts are not actual topics for speeches, but **topic areas**. Topic areas are promising but broad subjects that often cover too much ground for brief presentations. Explore topic areas carefully, and then narrow and focus them until they become specific enough to handle in the time allotted for your speech. As Winston Churchill once noted, "A speech is like a spotlight; the more focused it is, the more intense the light."[2] Two techniques are available to you as you explore promising topic areas: *mind mapping* and *topic analysis*.

Mind Mapping

mind mapping
Changes customary linear patterns of thinking into visual representations of relationships to encourage creative exploration.

Mind mapping disrupts the customary linear patterns of thinking in order to free our minds for creative exploration.[3] These habitual patterns can prevent us from thinking fully and freely about subjects. For example, most of us, when we write down our thoughts, start at the top of the page and work down. Mind mappers turn the sheet of paper so that its length is horizontal rather than vertical (what on the computer is known as the landscape orientation). Then, instead of starting at the top of the page, they begin at the center, where they place the topic area they wish to explore. Instead of flowing down the page, thinking radiates out from this center so that it forms a more natural circular pattern of ideas rather than a linear one. These satellite thoughts can be ringed by even more particular associations that can help us visualize new ideas as we develop them.[4] Using contrasting colors can further stimulate creativity. For those dedicated to online work, such apps as MindMeister and Popplet may prove helpful for mind mapping.

To see how mind mapping works, let's assume you have carefully completed the interest charts. You have discovered your strongest interest is in American politics. You think this interest will be shared by many of your listeners. This convergence of interests has produced a promising topic area, political reform. You have already begun to read about this subject and have started to accumulate information. To explore this topic area using mind mapping, place it at the center of your page, as indicated in Figure 6.3.

As your mind roams freely around this central idea, you come up with five major satellite ideas: "Finances," "Electoral College," "Media," "Voting," and "Reform Groups." As you reflect on each of these satellite ideas, you develop even more specific associations that radiate from each. Looking at these ideas as they form a spatial pattern, you can see any number of possible topics for your speech. One of these might connect three of the major satellite ideas by focusing on how the U.S. Public Interest Group combats the influence of wealthy PACs to increase voter turnout. Or you might decide you want to focus on efforts to suppress voting in your home state.

Mind mapping is a free-form exploratory technique that can be highly creative. The next technique we discuss offers a more systematic, disciplined way to explore topic areas.

Finding Your Voice

Discovering Your Topic Area

Use brainstorming, an interest chart, and mediated prompts to discover at least three promising topic areas on which you could speak. Rank these topic areas in order of preference, and explain how you discovered these areas and why you ranked them this way.

Figure 6.3 Mind Map of Political Reform

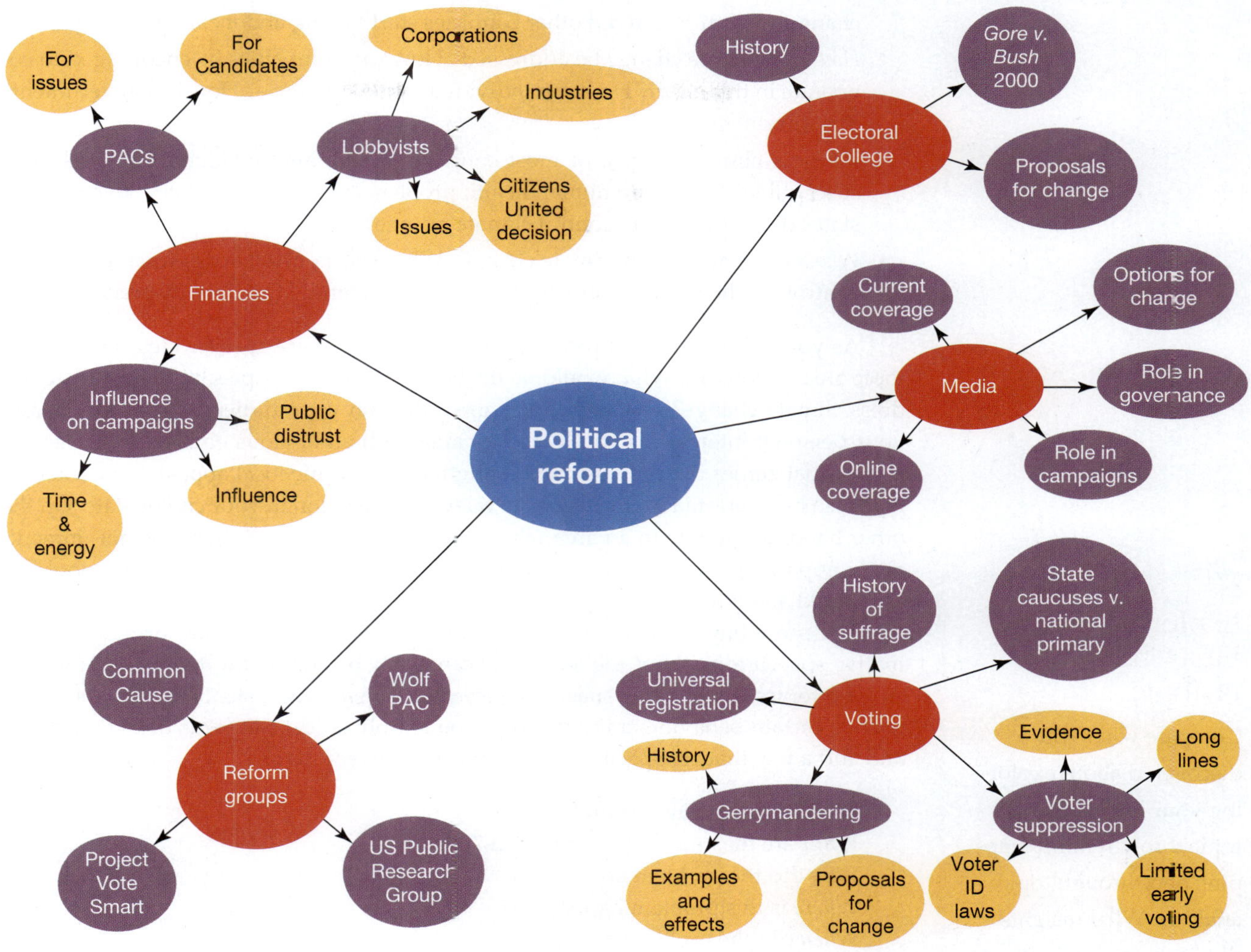

Topic Analysis

The beginning course in journalism introduces fledgling reporters to the basic questions they need to ask as they investigate a story: *Who? What? When? Where? Why? How?* As one journalist-blogger notes, "Journalism purists will argue your story isn't complete until you answer all six questions. It's hard to argue this point, since missing any of these questions leaves a hole in your story," while "getting answers to these six questions can really help you get all the information needed."[5]

The noted scholar Wayne Booth has endorsed these questions as a more general method of exploring the value of topics: "Decide which questions stop you for a moment, challenge you, spark some special interest."[6] For the public speaker who is exploring the possibilities of a topic area, these six questions constitute the technique we call **topic analysis**. Let's consider climate change as a topic area and see how these questions might prompt inquiry:

topic analysis
Using questions often employed by journalists (*who, what, when, where, why,* and *how*) to explore topic possibilities for speeches.

- *What* is climate change? What are the major causes of it? What are the contributing causes in our community? What part can individuals play in reducing it? What can government do to control it? What is the role of international organizations?
- *Why* do we have climate change? Why do some countries and some companies resist reducing greenhouse gas emissions?

- *When* did climate change first become an issue? When was the first important book about climate change published? When were the first U.S. laws relating to climate change passed? When did other countries start talking about climate change?
- *How* can climate change be addressed? How can companies be encouraged to cooperate in this effort? How can individuals help the cause? How can governments play productive roles?
- *Where* is climate change of most concern? Where are endangered species most susceptible? Where are human health problems most acute? Where have cities or states done the most to control climate change?
- *Who* suffers most from climate change? Who is responsible for enforcing emission controls? Who brought climate change most forcefully to public awareness?

As you consider the six prompts, write down as many specific ideas about your topic area as you can. What would be the best topic for your speech if you were to address climate change? That depends a great deal on your audience, your locale, and your personal interests. If you live in an area with an obvious emissions problem, a speech that zeroes in on that situation might have specific local appeal. Your listeners may also be interested in the history of relevant legislation in your city or state. On the other hand, if you live in an area where the impact of climate change is not immediate or apparent, you may have to work hard to convince listeners that they should be concerned about it.

The preceding topic analysis was geared to exploring what are primarily informative speech topics, but the technique can easily be adapted to the analysis of persuasive topics. Because persuasion concerns problems and asks us to change or not change certain behaviors and attitudes, you simply adjust the focus of the questions and add a few that are specific to the persuasive perspective:

Who is affected by this problem?
What are the most important issues?
Why did the problem arise?
Where is this problem happening?
When did the problem begin?
How is this problem like or unlike previous problems?
How extensive is the problem?
What options are available for dealing with the problem?

After you have discovered and explored topic areas, several topics should emerge as promising possibilities for your speech. As you ponder these options, keep in mind how well they fit the assignment, whether you could speak on them in the time available, whether you will be able to research them responsibly, and how useful they might be for listeners.

Exploring Your First Choice of Topic

Compare what you discovered about exploring your first choice of topic through mind mapping and through topic analysis. What insights did each approach offer? What did you learn from one that you didn't from the other? How can you use these techniques for presentations outside this class?

Finding Your Voice

Exploring Your Topic Area

Use mind mapping and topic analysis to explore the preferred topic area you identified in "Finding Your Voice: Discovering Your Topic Area." List, in order of preference, three promising topics for speeches that emerge from this exploration. How and why did these topics emerge? Why did you rank them as you did?

Refining Your Topic

6.4 Refine your topic for speaking.

Having discovered and explored a promising topic area, you should be ready for the final phase of topic selection: refining and focusing the topic in preparation for speaking. To complete this phase, consider the *general purpose* of your speech, determine your *specific purpose*, and prepare a *thesis statement*.

General Purpose

Invitations to speak outside class will usually specify the **general purpose** of your speech: "Could you help us understand changes in the tax code?" or "Would you tell us why you are opposed to changes in the tax code?" or "Will you help us thank the senator for her leadership in changing the tax code?" Speeches that would address such questions seek understanding, offer a position on a controversial issue, and express appreciation, respectively. They correspond to the three general purposes: to *inform, to persuade,* and *to commemorate:*

general purpose
The speaker's intention to inform or persuade listeners or to commemorate some person or occasion.

- *The general purpose of a speech to inform is to share knowledge with listeners.*
- *The general purpose of a speech to persuade is to advise listeners what to believe or how to act and to offer them reasons to follow such advice.*
- *The general purpose of a ceremonial speech is to commemorate the meaning and/or importance of an occasion, event, or person.* Ceremonial speeches include eulogies, toasts, after-dinner speeches, and tributes.

Your instructor may specify the general purpose of your speech as part of your assignment. Being clear about your general purpose will guide the rest of the process of refining your topic.

Specific Purpose

Determining your **specific purpose** helps you narrow your topic until it comes into sharp focus. It states precisely what you want your listeners to understand, believe, feel, or do. Having your specific purpose clearly in mind helps direct your research so that you don't waste valuable time wandering around the library and surfing the Internet for materials that will prove irrelevant. You should be able to state your specific purpose clearly in a single phrase.

specific purpose
The speaker's particular goal or the response that the speaker wants to evoke.

Let's look at how a specific purpose statement can give focus to a speech:

Topic area:	The Artistry of Dr. Seuss
General purpose:	To inform

Jess Bradshaw loved the books of Dr. Seuss when she was a child. Now an undergraduate student, she remained fascinated with his books, suspecting that their simplicity might result from a quite sophisticated creative process. However, her topic area, as stated here, would be much too vast and general to cover in a five- to six-minute speech. She would never be able to consider the entire range of ideas that might be associated with it, much less provide examples and supporting content. After all, Dr. Seuss wrote many books, any number of which might well be mentioned in developing such a topic. And "artistry"? That's certainly a vague and probably extensive subject. Clearly, Jess's topic area needed to be

Effective speeches develop a central idea, allow speakers to speak with conviction and passion, and promise listeners important information and insights.

refined, narrowed, and focused in a specific purpose statement, or she would confound both herself and her audience.

As Jess read more about Dr. Seuss, she found a really interesting interview with him that spelled out how he had created *The Cat in the Hat*. This book, she decided, would provide her point of focus. And the incredible story of how he labored to create such a simple-seeming text would be a further point of refinement. Jess came up with the following:

Specific purpose: To inform my audience of Dr. Seuss's creative persistence as he composed *The Cat in the Hat*.

Jess had just made a major move in refining her topic. Now she was ready to test and possibly improve her specific purpose statement.

Testing Your Specific Purpose Statement. Developing a successful specific purpose statement is one of the most important steps in topic refinement. The following tests should help you:

1. *Does the specific purpose promise new information or fresh advice?* You may be greeted with yawns if you propose "to inform listeners that drunk driving is dangerous." You will have tied yourself to a tired topic. When you tell listeners something they have already heard many times, you waste their time and yours. On the other hand, tracing the history of Mothers Against Drunk Driving (MADD) or comparing the effects of driving while drunk with driving while texting would add a novel perspective.
2. *Can you accomplish your specific purpose in the allotted time?* If you propose "to persuade listeners that health care in the United States is too costly and inefficient," you have bitten off far more than you can chew. Many students worry that they will struggle to fill the allotted time, but usually, once they explore the topic area, they discover there is more than enough information. Remember, in a five-minute speech, you have only about 700 words to get your message across—roughly a page and a half of single-spaced, 12-point type. You may need to limit your remarks to, for example, the health care crisis in your community in order to meet time restrictions. That strategy might also be more interesting to your listeners.
3. *Have you avoided the double-focus trap?* It is sometimes difficult to make that final decision to narrow your topic to a single point of emphasis. It may be tempting to fall into the trap of double focus: "to inform my listeners of hiking *and* camping opportunities in Shenandoah National Park." If you attempt to address both these subjects in any meaningful way, you may go beyond your time limit. The "and" in such statements is often a red flag that signals a double-focus problem.
4. *Have you avoided the triviality trap?* When you speak to twenty-four people for five minutes, you will be taking up two hours of their collective time. What are you offering them in return? If you promise to inform them about "how to mix a martini" or "how to change a tire," you are likely to leave your listeners feeling short-changed. They may react with a blunt, "So what?" You want to convince listeners that you have a specific purpose that promises them important information, insights, or advice so that, by the end of the speech, they feel they have invested their time wisely.
5. *Have you met the test of relevancy?* In selecting her topic, Jess Bradshaw asked several of her classmates about whether they shared her background as early fans of the Dr. Seuss books. She looked for ways to connect her topic to their interests. However, what might be a good topic for one audience might not be so relevant to another. If your specific purpose is to propose raising the eligibility age for Social Security benefits to a youthful audience, you might struggle to close the relevancy gap between the two. Making a connection to a younger audience would be easier if you instead discussed ways students can reduce the debt burden many of them acquire during their college years.
6. *Have you avoided the technicality trap?* Sometimes, speakers forget that listeners may not share their technical vocabulary. They are puzzled when listeners respond with

dazed, bewildered looks and the question, "Huh?" A speaker who promises "to inform listeners of the principles of thermonuclear energy" or "to inform my audience about the intellectual evolution of Kant's meta-ethics" is stepping directly into this trap—unless the audience is an advanced class in physics or philosophy. If, in contrast, the audience is a beginning public speaking class, then the speaker has not factored the audience's background into the topic selection. This failure often becomes evident when speakers write out their specific purpose statements.

7. *Have you avoided signs of bias?* If you offer as your specific purpose "To persuade my audience that we should fire our *dumb* football coach," or "to inform my audience of the *stupidity* of the Paleo diet," judicious listeners could well conclude that your mind is so closed on this subject that you have not been able to judge evidence fairly and dispassionately. Your obvious bias would prevent you from being a trustworthy speaker on this topic.

Improving Your Specific Purpose Statement. Refining your specific purpose can help enhance your speech. Let's look at three examples of flawed specific purpose statements and see how they might be improved:

1) Flawed: To persuade my audience that driving while distracted is dangerous
Improved: To persuade my audience not to text while driving

The first version of the specific purpose is vague, and it tells the audience nothing new. Who would argue that driving while distracted is not dangerous? The improved version focuses more precisely on a contemporary problem and seeks a specific result.

2) Flawed: To inform listeners of major attractions at Yellowstone and Glacier National Parks
Improved: To inform listeners of exciting destinations in Yellowstone National Park

The first version of the specific purpose here presents a classic double-focus problem. Choose one or the other, as in the improved version, so that you can develop its appeal in greater detail.

3) Flawed: To persuade listeners to take their medications on a regular basis
Improved: To persuade listeners of the immediate and long-term health benefits of a sustained exercise program

In addition to being vague, the flawed specific purpose could present a major relevancy problem, as most traditional college-age students are not confronted (yet!) with long lists of daily required medicines. Ongoing exercise programs, on the other hand, are desirable throughout a lifetime.

SPEAKER'S NOTES

Testing Your Specific Purpose Statement

Your specific purpose statement must pass all the following tests:

1. Does it project a speech that will offer new information and/or fresh advice?
2. Can you accomplish your purpose in the time allotted for the speech?
3. Do you focus on a single topic, avoiding double focus?
4. Do you focus on an important topic, avoiding triviality?
5. Would your speech be relevant to your particular audience's interests and needs?
6. Is your speech appropriately geared to your audience, avoiding overly technical language and subject matter?
7. Is your specific purpose free from bias?

Thesis Statement

thesis statement
Summarizes in a single sentence the central idea of your speech.

Writing your **thesis statement** or central idea is the final refinement in preparing a topic for a speech. The thesis statement summarizes in a single sentence the message of your speech. You should be able to easily articulate it in a single breath. If you have to pause in the middle of the statement, your thesis statement is probably too long. For example, Jess Bradshaw's speech concentrated on this thesis statement: "*The Cat in the Hat* is the incredibly simple product of an incredibly complicated creative process." B. J. Youngerman focused his persuasive speech in defense of Walmart on the following thesis statement: "Walmart is a positive force in American public life." Such sentences, notes scholar Wayne Booth, "state a potential claim" that the speeches themselves must demonstrate or prove.[7]

Most speakers like to integrate the thesis statement into the introduction of their speech so that listeners will know their intentions from the outset. Should you choose to do this, we recommend that you do not blatantly proclaim, "My thesis statement is. . . ." Instead, integrate it smoothly into the introduction. The thesis statement should arouse interest and provide sharp focus for the speech. Effective speeches are structured to develop a central idea. When that idea is obscure, there is no central focus to hold the structure of thoughts together. The speech then rambles about in a disorganized way and leaves no lasting impression on the audience. When listeners ask, "What exactly are you trying to say?" or "What would you like us to do?" chances are the thesis statement has not been clearly realized or well stated.

At times, however, speakers may omit the thesis statement from their introductions. When presenting persuasive messages before highly skeptical audiences, for example, it is sometimes advisable to introduce your subject area and make your case for your position before actually stating it toward the end of your speech. This may give your presentation a better chance of receiving a fair hearing. On other occasions, speakers may omit the thesis statement altogether from their presentations, leaving it to be constructed by listeners from cues within the speech. But this technique also entails considerable risk because listeners may miss the point.

Most of the time, your specific purpose will be revealed in your thesis statement, but the two are not identical. *The specific purpose expresses what you want to accomplish; the thesis statement summarizes what you intend to say.* One student developed a relationship between the specific purpose and thesis statements of a speech as follows:

Specific purpose:	To persuade listeners that binge drinking is a serious problem on our campus
Thesis statement:	Today, I want to discuss a major problem on campus—binge drinking—and what we can do about it.

Note that the speaker did *not* say, "My thesis statement is that. . . ." Instead the thesis statement is smoothly woven into the presentation.

hidden agendas
Actual motivations and goals that speakers keep secret, making it difficult to evaluate their intentions.

In ethical speaking, the thesis statement will usually reveal the speaker's specific purpose; at the very least, it will not disguise it. *But let the listener beware!* Speakers sometimes hide their actual intentions. If you consider the **hidden agendas** of cult leaders, or sometimes even business leaders and leaders of nations, you can see how serious this problem can become. When people offer you "just the facts" but really want to sell you a product or service, or when they purport to be protecting the voters as they line their own pockets, or when they give vivid images to solicit your donation without telling you how the organization will use your funds, the speakers' hidden agendas come at your potential risk. In short: *The greater the distance between the hidden specific purpose and the thesis statement disclosed in the speech, the larger the ethical issue.*

Refining Your Purpose Statement

Write out your specific purpose statement and use the seven tests to refine it.

The refinement phase of topic selection is like looking at a topic successively through the lenses of a microscope. When you identify the general purpose, specific purpose, and thesis statement of a speech topic, you bring the topic into sharper and sharper focus. At the end of the process, what was at first broad and vague should now have become precise. You should be ready to conduct the research and planning that will develop your topic into a successful speech.

YOUR ETHICAL VOICE

The Ethics of Topic Selection

Ethical problems can infiltrate the process of topic selection for speeches. To avoid many of these problems, follow these guidelines:

1. Do not select a topic that could be hurtful, such as how ethnic slurs have evolved.
2. Do not select a topic that potentially invites illegal activity, such as how to make a pipe bomb.
3. Do not select a topic on which you cannot obtain responsible knowledge.
4. Do not purposely obscure your thesis statement in order to hide your specific purpose.

Finding Your Voice

Refining Your Topic

Refine the preferred topic identified in "Finding Your Voice: Exploring Your Topic Area" until you have determined its general purpose, specific purpose, and thesis statement. What are the strengths and limitations of the speech you might give on this topic? As you answer this question, be sure to consider the assignment, the time limits, and audience needs and interests as well as the intrinsic value of the topic.

Final Reflections: The Great Chain of Communication

Cicero, the renowned Roman orator and communication theorist, once wrote that public speaking is an art made up of five great arts: creating the content of a speech, organizing its ideas, expressing them in effective language, committing the speech to memory, and presenting the speech powerfully. These arts are obviously all connected and form the great chain of the communication process.

This chapter helps you forge the first link in Cicero's chain, developing something worthwhile to say. Until you have a clear, compelling idea of what you want to talk about, it is useless to discuss any of the other arts.

There are moments when we have little choice in selecting speech topics: Problems arise in the workplace, and we must address them. Or we may be invited to speak at public meetings as experts or concerned citizens on issues of immediate concern. On such occasions, we are constrained by the urgencies of the moment and by our own background of competence.

But the public speaking classroom typically offers freedom to explore a wide range of issues and interests before you speak. Sometimes, the topic you finally select will come to you in a flash of intuition. Even if it does not, there are systematic ways to ensure that you are on the right track before you commit to a speech. As we have seen, these systems involve discovering potential topic areas, exploring them for possible topics, and refining these topics until they focus precisely on our audience and our goals.

Finding your topic—one that fascinates and excites you, that you can commit to and become passionate about, that justifies your investment of time and energy—is also an essential step in finding your voice

Study Questions

CONTENT MASTERY

1 What is a good speech topic?

2 How can you find promising topic areas?

3 How can you develop effective interest charts?

4 How can you explore fertile topic areas to focus on the best topics?

5 Why can mind mapping be an effective tool for exploration?

6 How can you refine your chosen topic in preparation for speaking?

7 How are the specific purpose and thesis statements related, and how can they differ?

CRITICAL EXPLORATIONS

1. Complete a chart of your interests, including at least three entries in each of the suggested categories. With the help of classmates, complete a topic area inventory chart that lists audience interests as well. Based on the interaction of your interests and theirs, rank the most promising topic areas.
2. In connection with the interest chart exercise just discussed, develop a mind map around the most promising topic area. In what ways does this exercise produce specific ideas for speech topics?
3. Follow up the mind map from question 2 by using the topic analysis method to explore the most promising topic areas. How does the application of the questions of *who, what, where, when, why,* and *how* help clarify and develop the topic options?
4. Choose the best topic ideas that emerge from your topic analysis, and frame possible specific purpose and thesis statements for them. Keep in mind the virtues of simplicity, clarity, specificity, ethicality, and appeal to your anticipated audience. Are the specific purpose and thesis statements closely aligned? Would you have enough time in your speech to cover the content suggested by these statements?
5. Develop a topic briefing in which you propose a topic or series of topics you would like to explore in classroom speeches. At the discretion of your instructor, present your topic briefing either as a written proposal or as an oral presentation to a small group or to the class as a whole. Explain why you want to give these speeches and how listeners might benefit from them. Identify any problems you might have in presenting the topic and how you plan to deal with them. List the major sources of information you plan to draw on in preparing your speeches.

   If presented orally, your presentation should invite questions and suggestions.
6. Discuss the defects in the following specific purpose statements:
   - **a.** To inform the audience about how to swing a golf club
   - **b.** To inform the audience about nuclear physics
   - **c.** To inform the audience about indoor and outdoor gardening
   - **d.** To persuade the audience to boycott our stupid commencement ceremonies
   - **e.** To persuade listeners to support our foreign policy in the Middle East

f. To inform listeners how to reduce their tax burdens
g. To inform listeners about the theory of electricity

7. Identify three topics you believe would be unethical to develop for classroom speeches. Explain and defend your position.

INFORMATIVE SPEECH

At various moments in this chapter, we have referenced the experience of Jess Bradshaw in developing her topic concerning the artistry of Dr. Seuss. What follows is the final product of her careful preparation, as the speech was presented to her Davidson College class. Concerning how she came up with her topic, Jess reports that she had loved the Seuss books since childhood and suspected that many in her audience would share her fond memories of them. Her biggest problem in topic development, she says, was narrowing the topic, making the hard decision to get rid of interesting but less relevant information.

PULLING A CAT OUT OF A HAT

JESS BRADSHAW

Reprinted with permission from Jessica Bradshaw.

Have you read *The Cat in the Hat*?
Of course you have. I'm sure of that!
And how about *Green Eggs and Ham*? Did you dig that Sam-I-Am?
Or *Yertle, the Turtle* you got from Aunt Myrtle?
And did you enjoy the grouchy Grinch?
Of course you did—that was a cinch!

What Dr. Seuss gave you, as he proclaims in his opening of *The Cat in the Hat*, was good fun that is funny. His books may not seem all that complex, realistic, or even deep, but it was not without much work that Theodore Seuss Geisel, otherwise known as Dr. Seuss, was able to make you laugh and smile. Indeed, *The Cat in the Hat* is the incredibly simple product of an incredibly complex creative process. Geisel was amazingly persistent in developing, writing, and editing what would become a classic in children's literature.

The speech follows a narrative pattern, telling the story of how a classic work was composed. In developing the story, Jess makes effective use of expert testimony. This paints a favorable impression of her ethos as a competent, responsible person whose information can be relied on. This impression would create a positive presumption in favor of speeches she would later give on other topics.

The idea behind *The Cat in the Hat* did not come in one great moment of inspiration; instead, it was the result of over four months of brainstorming, drafting, rejecting, and brainstorming again. As told by Philip Nel, in *Dr. Seuss: American Icon*, William Spaulding, the educational director of Houghton Mifflin Publishing Company, challenged Geisel to write a story using only 225 words from a list of 348 words that first graders were able to recognize by sight or phonics. Geisel accepted the challenge, expecting to spend a few weeks on the project, according to Ruth MacDonald, author of the book *Dr. Seuss*.

Geisel, writing in the *New York Times Book Review*, reported searching for weeks for a topic before finally receiving his answer in a dream. Rushing off to his typewriter, he wrote thirty-two pages of *The Queen Zebra* before realizing that the words "queen" and "zebra" were not on the list. Four months later, Geisel was still working on the assignment, this time attempting to write a story about a bird without using the word "bird"—because it too wasn't on the list! But without the word, he was unable to get the project off the ground. Sorry. Bad pun!

By then, according to *The New Yorker* article "Cat People: What Dr. Seuss Really Taught Us," Geisel had reached a moment of crisis:

> I thought it was impossible and ridiculous and I was about to get out of the whole thing; then I decided to look at the list one more time and to use the first two words that rhymed as the title of the book—cat and hat were the ones my eyes lighted on.

The use of direct quotations from Geisel is much more striking and colorful than if Jess had used paraphrasing to summarize his thoughts. The exact, colloquial words give the speech an air of freshness and authenticity it otherwise would have lacked.

But writing *The Cat in the Hat* took as much persistence as the brainstorming for it required. "You got an idea and then found out you had no way to express yourself," Geisel states in *American Icon*. But Geisel worked through the difficulties in a complex process that he described in the *New York Times Book Review:*

> The method I used is the same method you see when you sit down to make apple strudel without the strudel.... You take your limited, uninteresting ingredients and day and night, month after month, you mix them up into thousands of combinations. You make a batch. You taste it. Then you hurl it out the window. Until finally one night, when it is darkest just before dawn, a plausible strudel-less strudel begins to take shape before your eyes!

And for nine months, Geisel worked at editing the strudel-less strudel that is the beloved *The Cat in the Hat*. Later, in *American Icon*, he described the process: "To produce a 60-page book, I may easily write more than 1,000 pages before I'm satisfied. The most important thing about me, I feel, is that I work like hell—write, rewrite, reject, re-reject, and polish incessantly." According to Seussentennial, the official website for the Dr. Seuss Enterprises, Geisel purchased an old observation tower in La Jolla, California, where he worked eight hours a day for nine months manipulating the 225 words he used in *The Cat in the Hat*. That amounts to 67 hours per word!

To reports of his genius, Geisel retorted, "If I'm a genius, why do I have to work so hard? I know my stuff looks like it was all rattled off in 28 seconds, but every word is a struggle and every sentence is like the pangs of birth."

But eventually his persistence paid off. According to *Publisher's Weekly*, *The Cat in the Hat* is the sixth best-selling children's book of all time. So the next time you're sitting in your tower, on the third floor of the library, working on that paper idea, remember the persistence of Theodore Seuss Geisel in developing, writing, and editing *The Cat in the Hat*. And even in your gloom, maybe you will smile, remembering what Dr. Seuss himself went through.

Having completed the remarkable narrative of how Dr. Seuss pulled a cat out of a hat, Jess ties her speech directly to the experience of her listeners. A little Seuss-like persistence might help them develop their assigned papers, she suggests. This lighthearted turn in the speech brings it to a graceful close.

Building Responsible Knowledge

CHAPTER

LEARNING OBJECTIVES

This chapter will help you:

7.1 Learn basic strategies for conducting, evaluating, and recording research.

7.2 Find and evaluate information on the Internet.

7.3 Locate and evaluate information in the library.

7.4 Conduct personal interviews to add to your knowledge of your topic.

OUTLINE

Getting Started

Researching on the Internet

Researching in the Library

Conducting Personal Interviews

As a student, Marisol lived on a tight budget. However, she had always felt that it was best to buy "green" products whenever she could afford it, even if they cost a bit more. She believed these products came from companies that respected the earth as much as she did. Marisol especially thought it was important to buy sustainably harvested seafood because she loved the ocean and wanted to do all she could to protect marine ecosystems.

"Learn, compare, collect the facts! Always have the courage to say to yourself, 'I am ignorant.'"

—IVAN PETROVICH PAVLOV

Marisol felt that this would make a good topic for her persuasive speech. She could educate her classmates on the virtues of spending the extra money for sustainably harvested fish and raise awareness among her peers about vital issues of marine ecology. She was excited about her topic and ready to begin her research.

Marisol began her research by noting the price differences between regular and sustainably caught seafood at her local specialty grocery store. Her next step was to search the Internet. The amount of information she found was overwhelming and sometimes contradictory. While she found plenty of websites espousing the merits of sustainable fisheries, others suggested that in many cases the process of certifying sustainable seafood amounts to little more than a marketing ploy. These sites contended that the commercial fishing industry dupes consumers to pay more with advertising that claims "certified sustainable" products, when in fact such "greenwashing" simply masks the same old environmentally harmful business practices.[1]

Which sources were telling the truth? Marisol soon realized that it would take more reading and considerable reflection before she would be ready to speak on this subject. She would need to learn more about the major issues and latest developments surrounding her topic, what the scientific experts and opposing interest groups have to say about it, and how it might affect the lives of her listeners beyond paying higher grocery bills. Marisol was well on the way to developing a base of responsible knowledge that would allow her to present an outstanding speech.

Becoming responsibly informed like Marisol earns you the right to speak. It allows you to present quality information or advice, and it demonstrates your mind and character for your audience. No less important, *learning how to become responsibly informed* on the subjects you care about will make a tremendous contribution to finding your voice as a public speaker. In this chapter, we discuss some basic research strategies and tools to help you do just that. We open with some general principles for getting started that can help to streamline the process, and then proceed to discuss the three most common resources for researching topics that are available to most college students: the Internet, libraries, and interviews with experts or people with unique insights.

Getting Started

7.1 Learn basic strategies for conducting, evaluating, and recording research.

Personal experience, such as surviving breast cancer, can be a rich source of stories and examples, adding credibility and interest to a speech.

How do you acquire responsible knowledge? You already have many of the skills you need to get started. When you want to find out about the latest movies to be released, the best places to get pizza in your town, or the way to get to the next level in your favorite computer game, what do you do? You go online, you read some relevant publications, and you talk to knowledgeable people whose opinions you trust and respect. That is research, and you already know how to do that—or at least how to get started. Indeed, you have been doing research for years!

Of course, you cannot become an expert in the short amount of time you have to research topics for class speaking assignments, but with a disciplined and methodical approach you can certainly learn enough to speak responsibly. As discussed in Chapter 4, **responsible knowledge** includes a general grasp and understanding of:

responsible knowledge
Comprehensive knowledge of a topic area that includes major features and issues, expert opinions, latest developments and local applications, relevance to listeners, and opposing views.

- the main issues or features of your topic;
- the most respected authorities on your topic and what they say about it;
- the latest developments and local applications;
- how your topic might affect the lives of listeners; and
- on controversial topics, the prominent opposing views.

In this section, we discuss some preliminary strategies and principles for getting started on your quest for responsible knowledge: assessing your prior knowledge and experiences, setting your research objectives, evaluating what you discover, and recording the information for future use in your speeches.

Assess Your Prior Knowledge and Experiences

The first step in researching any topic is to take stock of what you already know. Citing your personal expertise or interest in a topic can add credibility and authenticity to your speeches, greatly enhancing perceptions of your ethos as a speaker. Your personal experiences can offer a rich source of illustrative examples and stories that can help to make it easier for your listeners to identify with you and your message.

Sometimes, you can arrange to acquire direct experience as part of your research, especially with local topics. Suppose you are planning a speech on how local television stations prepare newscasts. You might find some quality information online and through publications, but think of how much more engaging your presentation might be if you also conducted an interview with a local broadcaster, or if you arranged to visit a local newsroom and take in the atmosphere and excitement of an actual live broadcast.

As valuable as it is, personal experience is rarely sufficient to provide all the information you will need for your speech. Your personal knowledge may be limited, the sources from which you learned may have been biased, or your experiences may not have been typical. Even people who are acknowledged authorities on a subject look to other experts to give added weight to their messages. Use your personal knowledge as a starting point, and expand it through other sources.

Set Your Research Objectives

Once you have assessed your prior knowledge and experiences, you should determine what additional information you will need in order to speak responsibly about your topic. Consider your focused thesis and specific purpose statements, as discussed in Chapter 6, and use them as touchstones to guide your investigation. Ask yourself: What facts and figures, testimony, examples, and narratives can I use to support my ideas and illuminate their importance for my listeners? What experts, activists, or respected figures could I invoke to lend authority and credibility to my assertions? What recent events or developments should I acknowledge and work into my presentation? Finally, what resources are likely to provide me with the highest quality of useful information on this topic?

As you proceed with your research, *try to work from the general to the specific.* That is, you should start by acquiring a general knowledge of your topic area and then focus on discovering the specific, more in-depth knowledge that will qualify you to speak responsibly. As you conduct your initial readings, you may find yourself refocusing your central ideas and purpose for speaking. Marisol, for instance, began her research by reading about the merits of sustainably caught seafood in general. As she became more informed, she focused more specifically on the controversies surrounding the process and conditions for certifying wild-caught seafood as sustainably harvested.

Finally, do not forget the importance of using your time effectively and efficiently. It takes time and effort to become responsibly informed, and you should leave yourself enough time to prepare your speech and practice your presentation. Even if it is obvious enough, the maxim bears repeating: *Do not wait until the day before your presentation to start researching your topic!* Give yourself time to read and reflect on the materials you discover, and be prepared for the inevitable false starts, beguiling tangents, and unexpected frustrations as well as the joys of coming across the perfect materials that are part of all research projects.

Evaluate What You Discover

It is hard to overemphasize the importance of evaluating the quality of the information you find before using it in your speeches. A single flawed or exaggerated piece of information pulled from an untrustworthy source can ruin an otherwise excellent presentation and do lasting damage to your ethos. Think of yourself as a detective: You examine clues, interrogate sources, and develop theories to answer the riddles of your topic.[2] Your speeches should impress listeners that you are a credible source of ideas and information, open-minded and willing to consider the facts as you find them, cognizant of contrasting views and opinions, and genuinely concerned with how your topic might intersect with their lives.

Whether you find your information on the Internet, in the library, or through conducting personal interviews, you should evaluate it in terms of the four Rs of relevance, representativeness, recency, and reliability, as discussed in Chapter 4:

- *Relevance* concerns the extent to which supporting materials apply directly to your topic and purpose for speaking. Try to avoid getting sidetracked by reading materials you encounter that are interesting but extraneous to your immediate topic and message.
- *Representativeness* means the extent to which supporting materials depict a situation as it typically exists. Consider the extent to which your information will be received as characteristic of the point you are making rather than an exception to the rule.
- *Recency* refers to the timeliness or currency of supporting materials. Especially with late-breaking or fast-evolving topics, such as the latest flu virus, make sure

you have the most up-to-date information that accounts for recent events and developments.

- *Reliability* concerns the overall credibility of supporting materials. As a general rule, the more important or controversial your topic, the more important it is to provide sources of information that will be perceived as credible and trustworthy. Consider the credibility of both your sources and the sources that your sources cite, and make it a point to consult multiple perspectives whenever possible to correlate your most important assertions and information—especially if that information comes from obscure publications, activist websites, or social media posts.

Record Your Findings

Having her subject in mind, Marisol plunged into her research. Soon, she was reading articles and books, expanding her knowledge of the wild fish controversy. It was so interesting that she moved hastily from one reading to another, confident that she would remember the particulars of each source later.

Finally, she sat down to design and plan her speech. For her opening, she would use that fascinating quotation on greenwashing. Now, *who* said it? And *where* did she find it? Marisol was stumped. Several precious lost hours later, as she backtracked through these readings, Marisol finally found the quotation—and discovered that it was not quite what she had remembered!

Marisol's experience makes our case. You need a system for recording *what* you discover *at the time* you discover it. Don't wait to start taking notes until after you've read multiple sources of information, so that you're scrambling to find that perfect material that you know you read somewhere. Whether you are writing in a notebook or working with a computer, we suggest you use a systematic approach to accurately record the information you find, your sources and the information you will need to cite them in your bibliography, and the impressions and ideas you develop about your topic while conducting research.

We suggest that you develop a folder devoted to research on your topic. Within this folder, create a **research log**, a file in which you can jot down ideas as they occur during your exploration. Rather than trusting an often overloaded memory, this becomes "control central" for your investigation. Your log is also a place to develop a list of key terms as you uncover them and to pinpoint the readings you want to pursue. Your research log can trace the evolution of your thinking. You might even end up modifying your specific purpose and thesis statement in light of your discoveries. The research log becomes the story of your research investigation, from the initial questions to the construction of your case.

research log
File in which you jot down ideas, list key terms, and prioritize readings.

Then, develop a **source file** to record the complete information you will need to document the sources you consult in your bibliography. Each entry should contain the authors' names as published on the source (when provided), the title of the article or web page, the publication or website that published the source, the date published or posted, the complete URL address (if your instructor prefers), the date you accessed your materials, and a brief description or explanation of the kinds of information the source provides. With printed materials, you may also need to provide the names of editors, specific page numbers, and the physical location where a book was published. Check with your instructor to see if she has a preferred style for citing sources in your bibliography. Figure 7.6 at the end of this chapter provides sample entries using the American Psychological Association (APA) and the Modern Language Association (MLA) formats. For a more comprehensive overview of both styles, consult the Purdue University Online Writing Lab (OWL).

source file
Contains complete information for citing your consulted sources on your bibliography.

Figure 7.1 Sample Source File Entry

[*Source data*]
Oosterveer, Peter, and Simon Bush. *Governing Sustainable Seafood*. New York: Routledge, 2016.

[*Explanation*]
explores nutrition, economics, and regulation of sustainable seafood from a social scientific perspective

You also may want to add to your source file a short explanation of the material, information about the author's credentials, and your own reactions. These notes will make it easier for you to find the sources you found useful for particular purposes as well as remind you of sources you've already seen that proved less useful. See the sample source file entry in Figure 7.1.

subject files
Contains the precise information you discover and gather while conducting your research.

documents file
Contains articles downloaded from search engines or pages you scanned into your computer.

Next, develop a set of **subject files** for recording information that might be useful in your speeches. Your subject file entries should contain the precise facts and statistics, paraphrased testimony and verbatim quotations, and examples and narratives you discover while conducting your research. Each entry should also provide abbreviated references in parentheses to the sources of that information as documented in your source file. Researchers sometimes organize their subject file entries in terms of divisions that emerge during their research. For example, Marisol soon discovered that much of the information she gathered clustered into three major areas: the virtues of sustainably harvested seafood, controversies over the process of certification, and the environmental impact of commercial fishing. See Figure 7.2 for a sample subject file entry.

You may find it helpful to build a **documents file** in which you place articles you have downloaded from search engines or pages you have scanned into your computer so that they are readily accessible. Be sure to identify the source of such selections on the document itself. See Figure 7.3 for an example of Marisol's initial documents file. Online resources for collecting electronic documents, often with the ability to offer your own comments, include Livebinders, Padlet, Pinterest, and Social Bookmarks. Several of these allow others to post links on your topics as well.

Developing a Research Plan

Develop a research plan for your next speech using the concepts from this section. What resources do you feel will be most useful for researching your particular topic?

Of course, this system of recording your research can be adapted for your own personal uses. Many researchers, for example, like to combine their source and subject file entries. Just make sure you document your information and sources adequately and accurately. Not only will it spare you the last-minute

Figure 7.2 Sample Subject File
Barton Seaver

[*Subject heading*]
Environmental Impact

[*Subject entry*]
According to Barton Seaver, chef and seafood expert, "Sustainable seafood represents a healthy relationship with our oceans that can endure forever. When humans consume seafood, we leave an indelible mark on the ecosystem. It is critically important for our own well-being—and that of the oceans—that we understand the impacts of our choices." (Nat Geo)

Is Sustainable-Labeled Seafood Really Sustainable? : NPR
Sustainable seafood guides | WWF
The Piscivore's Dilemma | Outside Online
TEDTalks Barton Seaver - Sustainable Seafood? Let's Get Smart
Making seafood sustainable American experiences in global perspective—Mansel G. Blackford
Sustainability and the UK's Major Food Retailers, Jones, Comfort, and Hillier

Figure 7.3 Sample Initial Index to Documents File

agony of having to go back and reread your sources at the last minute, it may help you to avoid the **accidental plagiarism** that occurs when we unwittingly misrepresent our sources or present their ideas or words without remembering who said it.

accidental plagiarism
Various forms of unintentional academic dishonesty due to sloppy research techniques.

SPEAKER'S NOTES

Avoiding Accidental Plagiarism

The following advice can help you avoid unintentional dishonesty that occurs through sloppy research:

1. Keep careful records throughout your research process.
2. Consult with your instructor or reference librarian when you are in doubt about how to cite a source.
3. Take thorough notes that document your sources of researched information, and make it a point to distinguish your own ideas and information from those you derive from your sources.
4. Record quotations accurately, and always cite your sources when quoting or paraphrasing the words of others.
5. Do not quote or paraphrase others out of context: make sure your use of supporting materials represents the source's intended meaning.
6. When in doubt, cite your sources. Your listeners will be impressed and it will enhance your ethos as a speaker.
7. Run your completed work through an online plagiarism checker such as *Turnitin.com*. You can probably do this free of charge through your school's online resources.

Researching on the Internet

7.2 Find and evaluate information on the Internet.

Over the past few decades, the Internet has become an incredibly popular and useful resource for research. By going online, you can access a wealth of free information that can help to jump-start your quest for responsible knowledge. Over the next few pages, we discuss some of the most commonly used tools for conducting online research and then offer some advice for evaluating the information you find.

Search Engines A **general search engine** allows you to search the Internet for sites containing a given keyword or phrase. The results are typically organized in terms of relevance, popularity, or date of placement on the Web. The most popular general search engines include Google, Yahoo, and Bing. Use a combination of these to yield a broader variety of responses, as each provides somewhat different responses. As an option, you might use a **metasearch engine**, such as Info.com, Dogpile.com, or Metacrawler.com, which provides links to sources from a variety of other search engines. In either case, search engines can help to provide a broad

general search engine
An Internet search engine that allows you to enter keywords and find related websites.

metasearch engine
A search tool that compiles results from multiple search engines.

overview of general speech topics, but because they are often limited in the quality and depth of information they provide, they should be used only as a starting point for conducting your research.

When using general or metasearch engines, make sure your antivirus and spyware programs are up to date and running before you explore new websites and services. Also, be aware that many search engines make money by selling advertisements. As a result, the first few sites listed in your results may be there only because they paid for that privilege and not because the information contained is especially useful. For example, British Petroleum created quite a stir at the height of the Gulf oil crisis when it purchased the right to preferentially place its materials in search results for "oil spill" and similar terms. To see this premium placement as anything other than a commercial enterprise can lead your carefully planned research astray.

Perhaps the greatest challenges to conducting responsible research on the Internet are the sheer amount of posted materials and the lack of editorial oversight and quality control. Indeed, searching topics by keyword alone on the Web is a bit like shopping thrift stores. There are plenty of gems out there, but you usually end up sifting through a lot of trash to find them—and you don't always find what you're looking for. You can either expand or focus your searches by using the site's advanced search options and by consulting the advice we outline in "Speaker's Notes: Tips for Refining Internet Searches."

Most search engines offer the option to choose the kind of source that best suits your purpose. Once you have your search results, you can narrow your findings by type of source. For example, when Marisol Googled "sustainable seafood," she got nearly a million results! She clicked the "News" link to narrow her results to news articles pertaining to her topic. Then she went back to her initial results page; clicked the "Images" option on the results pages; and then, under usage rights, clicked "labeled for non-commercial reuse." As a result, Marisol got photos, logos for organizations, and a Seafood Watch ratings illustration that proved to be very useful as presentation aids for her speech.

subject directory
An organized list of links to websites on specific topics.

Subject Directories You can also focus your searches by using free online subject directories. A **subject directory** organizes links on topic-specific materials such as humanities, natural sciences, politics, technology, entertainment, and sports. Because they are focused on specific subjects and compiled and screened by humans, they tend to yield more selective and often higher-quality results than general search engines. The Open Directory Project, for example, is useful for searching popular topics and for

SPEAKER'S NOTES

Tips for Refining Internet Searches

The following tips can help you expand or focus your searches:

1. Use AND to limit your search to sites that include both terms or phrases: mammogram AND ultrasound.
2. Use OR to broaden your search to sites that include either term: Memphis OR barbecue.
3. Use a minus sign (a hyphen flanked by spaces) to restrict your search by excluding sites containing the term or phrase following the sign: Lions - Detroit.
4. Use NEAR when words should be close to each other in the document: pollution NEAR climate change.
5. Use quotation marks to restrict your searches to a given phrase: Baltimore Preparatory School results in 2.5 million hits, whereas "Baltimore Preparatory School" results in 279 hits.
6. Use "site:" following a term or phrase to restrict your search to a given site or domain. For example, typing "oil spill site:whitehouse.gov" will limit your search results to presidential statements on the topic; "Afghanistan site:edu" will limit your search results to articles posted on educational websites.
7. When all else fails, read the instructions under "Advanced Search Tips" on your search engine home page.

searching by category. The Library of Congress, Academic Index, and Google Scholar can help you locate a wealth of high-quality materials and publications that general search engines will usually not uncover. By searching subject directories on greenwashing, Marisol was able to find articles published in the *Journal of Business Ethics, Environmental Health Perspectives*, and the *Tulane Law Review*. These were useful, more specific resources for her speech.

Useful Websites

Several free access websites can be valuable resources for finding quality information. LibrarySpot.com, for instance, is an award-winning site that offers links to encyclopedias, dictionaries, and a wealth of other research tools you might find in the reference section of a library. Google News has an archive that allows you to search news stories by topic, date, source, and location; and sites posted by Gallup and the Pew Research Center offer highly credible polling information on a wide variety of topics and issues. Wikipedia remains controversial with many professors because it relies on public input to edit its articles. Yet it offers more than 39 million entries, many of which provide links to valuable resources, and studies suggest that changes to the editing process have vastly improved the quality of its articles.[3] Nonetheless, we encourage you to be cautious and to consult your instructor before using information gathered from Wikipedia in your speeches.

Many sites posted by the government can provide valuable information on a wide range of topics, including voting patterns in American politics, procedures for immigrating to the United States, the latest housing scams, and even how to start your own non-profit organization. USA.gov offers a portal for accessing documents published by federal, state, and local governments, where Marisol found resources that included revised "Green Guides" from the Federal Trade Commission, advice on green marketing from the U.S. Small Business Administration, and legal cases in states from Florida to Washington. American FactFinder provides a wealth of information gathered by the U.S. Census Bureau regarding the demographic, social, and economic makeup of communities. WhiteHouse.gov posts all the major speeches, press releases, and position statements by the president, and House.gov and Senate.gov provide access to congressional materials.

The Internet is an increasingly valuable resource for speech ideas and responsible knowledge, but materials should always be evaluated carefully.

For topics in the arts, check out websites for such organizations as the Metropolitan Museum of Art, Artcyclopedia, Artchive, Soundpiper, Music and History, Artists House Music, Music Online, Theatre History, and the American Alliance for Theatre and Education. For information about people, go to the various Who's Who sites (e.g., American, International, Women, Asian Americans, Online), the Dictionary of Hispanic Biography, Contemporary Black Biography, and the biography section of LibrarySpot. For information on cultures, look up the Latino American Experience, Princeton University Asian-American Studies, My Jewish Learning, Muslim Culture, African-American Web Connection, or Black Thought and Culture. For information on corporate and nonprofit organizations, consult U.S. Business and Industry Council, Global Market Information Database, Business Insights, and Associations Unlimited. For topics on the sciences, try Science Daily, Science News, and National Geographic. For comprehensive online collections of current and historic American speeches, see American Rhetoric and Voices of Democracy.

Of course, there are a lot more free websites available to you than we could possibly discuss here, such as eHow, about.com, YouTube, and Hulu, as well as websites for major news organizations and daily newspapers. One problem with conducting research online is that many of the most authoritative journals and publications are no longer available free of charge. However, you should be able to access most of them (and a whole lot more) through your school library's paid electronic databases, which we discuss in the next section. For more information on researching your topics online, we recommend you visit "Finding Information on the Internet: A Tutorial," posted by the library at the University of California, Berkeley.

Social Media

Social media sites like Facebook, Twitter, and Pinterest allow individual users to create and share content and to sound off with comments or "likes" on everything from sports teams to celebrity controversies to the latest political developments. Several organizations may be involved with your topic—business associations, advocacy groups, or individuals—who have social media accounts and post commentaries or news stories on a regular basis. While these posts are often not edited for accuracy, quality, or bias, they can provide valuable information and can point you in rewarding directions during the preliminary phase of your research. For instance, by searching the words "sustainable seafood" on Facebook, Marisol found numerous posts by activists and scientists as well as links to more reputable sources that she would not likely have found on her own.

You should be especially cautious, however, when surfing social media sites for information on topics for your speeches. While most of the sites strive to monitor and close the accounts of malicious organizations, you should be ever cognizant of disinformation, outright bigotry, and general silliness floating around on all of these sites. Always double check or corroborate any information you find posted on social media sites—especially startling facts, quotations, and examples without sources—and never cite social media sites as a source of researched information in your speeches or your bibliography without the permission of your instructor.

> You can't believe everything you read on the Internet.
>
> —Abraham Lincoln

Evaluating Online Resources

While evaluating the information you find online, keep in mind that virtually anyone can put anything on the Internet. While websites are sometimes taken down due to offensive content or copyright infringements, most are subject to little, if any, editorial constraints. This makes it especially important to use your critical thinking skills and evaluate the information you find as carefully as possible. Start by determining what kind of website you are viewing.

Determining What Kind of Website You Are Viewing As you search online, consciously distinguish among advocacy, information, commercial, and personal

Finding Your Voice

Discovering Advocacy Websites

Use the World Advocacy website to locate a specific website that advocates for a cause or controversial issue that interests you, such as immigration laws, health care reform, gun control, or clean energy alternatives. Locate an information website on the same topic, and describe the differences between the two sites. Do you detect an agenda beyond being informative in either or both sites? What tips you off? How can you find additional resources to place this information in context?

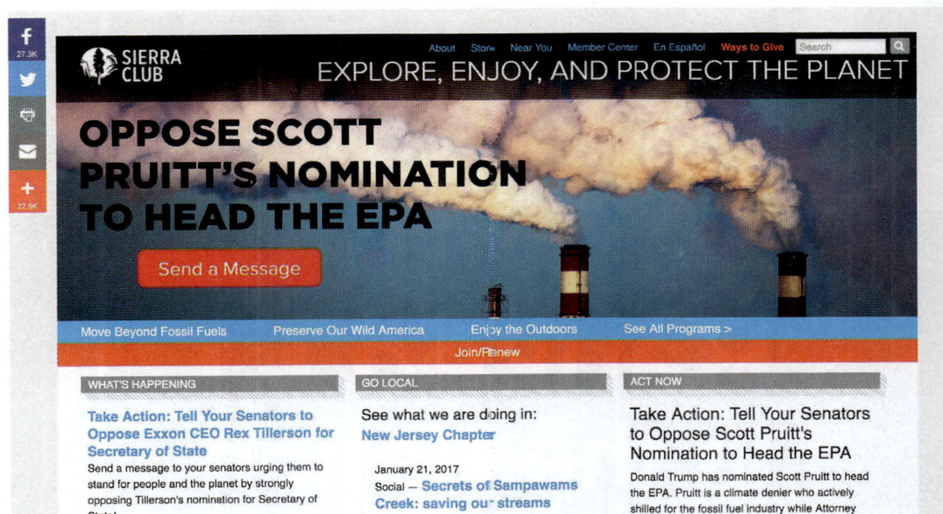

Figure 7.4 Advocacy Website Home Page

Source: Sierra Club, www.sierraclub.org. Used with permission.

websites. As with social media, the websites of commercial ventures and individuals can sometimes lead you in valuable directions, but they are generally not as useful for conducting research as advocacy and information sites. The purpose of an **advocacy website** is to raise consciousness or to persuade people to think or act with respect to a given issue or proposition. An advocacy site might ask for contributions, try to influence voting, or simply strive to promote a cause. Some examples of advocacy sites include the Sierra Club, Citizens Against Government Waste, and the Southern Poverty Law Center.

advocacy website
A website with the major purpose of raising awareness or persuading people to act.

The Sierra Club home page, shown in Figure 7.4, illustrates the features of an advocacy website. The top ribbon bears a truncated mission statement: "Explore, Enjoy, and Protect the Planet." Windows across the top menu document the organization's past and ongoing work promoting environmental causes. The "What's Happening" column provides links to news stories and other sources of information; the "Go Local" column highlights state and regional activities; and the "Act Now" column promotes the group's agenda and beats the drums for donations.

Like the Sierra Club home page, many advocacy websites provide quality information and links to other credible sources of information, but such sources typically present only one perspective on an issue. Therefore, you should carefully evaluate what you read, strive for balance by discovering what opposing groups and advocates have to say, and corroborate any information that is especially compelling or important by cross-referencing it with other, less partisan sources.

The purpose of an **information website** is to provide factual information on a specific topic. Information websites may include research reports; current world, national, or local news; government statistics; or simply general information such as you might find in an encyclopedia or almanac. For example, both Mayo Clinic and MedlinePlus are excellent sources of information about health issues. The material on the Mayo Clinic website has been prepared by physicians and editors associated with the medical institution; the material on the MedlinePlus website comes from the government-sponsored National Library of Medicine.

information website
A website designed to provide factual information on a subject.

Figure 7.5 shows the Mayo Clinic home page. Even though this website is registered in the commercial domain (.com), the focus is primarily on providing health-related information. Note some of the differences between this information home page and the advocacy home page shown in Figure 7.4. While you are subjected to the occasional advertisement, you are not asked for a donation, and the website is not specifically designed to sell you any products.

It is not always easy to differentiate between advocacy and information websites. Some nonprofit sites walk a fine line between informing and advocating without damaging their credibility. For instance, the home page of the American Red Cross

Figure 7.5 Information Website Home Page

Source: By permission of Mayo Foundation for Medical Education and Research. All rights reserved.

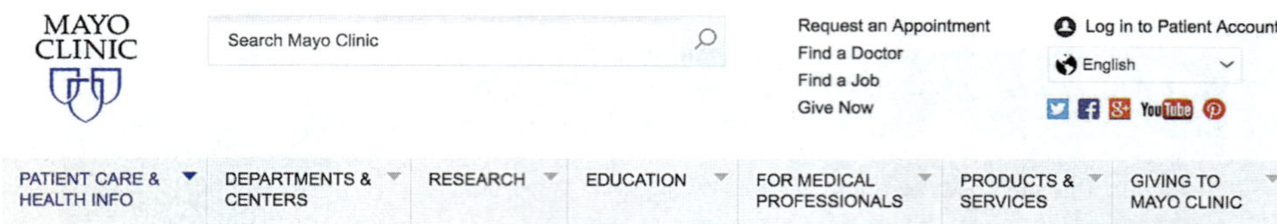

offers links to a wealth of highly credible information on disaster relief efforts, but it is presented in a manner that is obviously calculated to arouse your sympathies and evoke your financial generosity. Some advocacy sites seek to mask their persuasive agendas behind the appearance of informative expertise and objectivity. Be especially wary of anonymous studies, "fact sheets," and news stories posted by partisan activist groups, and watch out for blatant disinformation that fabricates or distorts information beyond reason to advance a hidden agenda.

Evaluating Online Information

As we noted earlier, *recency* is crucial when addressing current events, disputed issues, and topics relating to science and technology. With such topics, most of your online information will likely come from news sources and popular periodicals, information and advocacy websites, and government documents. Most reputable sites will date archived information. When they don't, you have to rely on the date the site was last updated, depend on the credibility of the host site or sponsoring agency, or seek information elsewhere.

Reliability is especially important when evaluating information retrieved from Internet sources. The reliability of a source usually boils down to its *authority, accuracy*, and *objectivity*. **Authority** refers to the credibility and expertise of a given source of information with respect to a particular issue or subject area. As a general rule, websites posted by credible organizations cite their sources, offer links to other reputable sources, and make it easy for you to identify their sponsoring agencies. You can search most organizations by their names or URL addresses. If it is hard to determine who is sponsoring a website, you should probably not use it.

authority
Criterion for evaluating the credentials of a source.

Accuracy refers to the precision or truthfulness of information. Again, the best way to ensure the accuracy of researched information is to use sites hosted or sponsored by credible sources—but even this can be tricky to ascertain. For instance, there are a lot of "spoof" news sites online—some of them quite entertaining—and it can be easy to fall victim to sources that look like "the news" when we like what we're reading. One such site, NationalReport.net, posted the "news" that, shortly before her death, Nancy Reagan endorsed Hillary Clinton for president—and the liberal-leaning but presumably more reputable Bloomberg Politics fell for it.[4] Again, credible sites usually document sources and provide links to other credible information. Watch out for statistical information and studies generated by advocacy organizations and

accuracy
Criterion for evaluating the correctness of information by checking it against other information.

SPEAKER'S NOTES

Checklist for Evaluating Internet Materials

When using the Internet to do research, use the following checklist to evaluate the information you find.

1. What type of website have I accessed? Advocacy? Information? Other?
2. Is the author or sponsoring agency identified?
3. Does the author or sponsoring agency have appropriate credentials to address the issue?
4. Does the material contain links to other information on the subject or citations of available print resources?
5. Is the material impartial, or does it seem biased?
6. Do other authorities confirm the information found on the website?
7. Is the material up to date on time-sensitive topics?
8. Is the material covered with enough breadth and depth?

commercially funded "think tanks" with an obvious interest in the outcome. Be wary of information that seems purposefully obscure and inaccessible to the average reader. As always, check any information you find on obscure websites that seems "too good to be true" by consulting other, less partisan sources of information.

Objectivity concerns the extent to which information on websites is free from personal feelings, bias, and hidden agendas. Most recognized experts and mainstream news organizations have a vested interest in maintaining their ethos as balanced sources of ideas and information. Most reputable advocacy and commercial websites are honest about their preferences and strive to present information reliably and accurately. However, knowing that a source has an agenda should cue you to look for additional information from differing perspectives. As mentioned earlier, the advocacy sites that try to hide their objectives are the ones you really must watch out for. The lack of an "About Us" or "Mission Statement" link on the site serves as a clear indication that it may be peddling disinformation. For example, racist and anti-Semitic groups have been known to disguise their messages of hatred by developing what at first glance look like benign informative websites.

objectivity
Criterion for evaluating whether or not a source provides an unbiased or balanced perspective.

We close with a caveat that bears repeating: *because anyone can put anything on the Internet, it is very important for you to be a thoughtful and critical consumer of online ideas and information.* For an excellent tutorial on assessing the quality of websites, we recommend "Evaluate Web Pages," which is posted by the Widener University Library. The Annenberg Center for Public Policy offers a site entitled FactCheck.org, which lists and assesses informative and advocacy websites dealing with public issues.

Evaluating Internet Resources

Find two Internet resources relevant to the topic for your next speech, and evaluate the information they provide.

Researching in the Library

7.3 Locate and evaluate information in the library.

In this age of the Internet, we sometimes forget the tremendous resources libraries can provide for in-depth research. Most college and large municipal libraries offer the following advantages:

- **Reference or Research Librarians:** These people are among the most valuable resources in the library. Librarians know how to access a wide variety of informative resources and are paid to help people conduct quality research in an efficient manner. Some libraries even offer research consultations with the reference librarian that you can schedule from your computer. As Wayne C. Booth and his colleagues note in *The Craft of Research*, "You can't learn the ropes of research if you don't know where they are, and you won't find where they are unless you ask."[5] Don't hesitate to call on the expertise of these well-informed people who really want to help.

- **Carefully Evaluated Materials:** Whereas virtually anyone can post materials on the Internet, the resources available to you in research libraries have more often been compiled, edited, appraised, and categorized by scholars and journalists using high standards of truthfulness and intellectual integrity. For many topics, your college or local library offers a quality of information you simply will not find online or through interviews with available experts.
- **Online Catalog:** The online catalog lists the books and periodicals available in the library, tells you where the items are located, and indicates whether the items are available, have been checked out, or have been placed on reserve. You can search for books by author, title, subject, or keyword. When you find a book that looks interesting to you, look for the call number on the catalog entry. With that in hand, you can go directly to the stacks and find your book.
- **e-Books:** Most libraries subscribe to hundreds of thousands of electronic books and e-texts on a variety of topics. You can usually find these through your library's online catalog or through a listing on the library's website.
- **Reference Area:** This area contains encyclopedias, yearbooks, dictionaries, almanacs, and atlases. Specialized encyclopedias, such as the *International Encyclopedia of the Social and Behavioral Sciences*, cover specific topics in greater detail, while specialized dictionaries are available on all sorts of topics from American slang to zoology. Almanacs and yearbooks such as *Facts on File* can provide credible and timely compilations of facts and figures, and biographical resources such as *Who's Who* can help to identify qualified experts on your topics. Books of quotations, such as *Bartlett's Familiar Quotations* and *Ancient Echoes: Native American Words of Wisdom*, can provide valuable material for the introductions and conclusions of speeches.
- **Electronic Databases:** Most colleges and universities provide free access to a variety of subscription databases that allow you to search and download full-text versions of popular, scholarly, and government publications. Often, you can access these materials from your personal computer at home. You should check to see which of the following your library offers.
  - *Periodical and newspaper databases:* These databases allow you to locate timely articles relevant to your topic in leading newspapers such as the *New York Times* and in popular periodicals such as *Time* and *The Atlantic*. One such database is LexisNexis Academic, which provides full-text access to more than 45,000 information sources, including articles from more than 500 leading newspapers around the world. Others are ProQuest and Ethnic Newswatch. Some popular periodicals, such as *Scientific American*, are perceived as highly credible and objective, whereas others may be less acceptable to a critical audience.
  - *Scholarly databases:* While popular journals, reference materials, and news publications can provide a general overview of your topics and specific information on the latest developments, scholarly books and journals will generally provide the most in-depth knowledge of the topics they cover. Articles published in scholarly journals go through a process of **peer review**, which means they are checked by experts in the field for quality and accuracy before they are approved for publication. The Book Review Index provides reviews and summaries that can help to focus your search, and the bibliographies of scholarly works can help you determine the most respected or most often cited researchers on a given subject. The following databases cross various disciplines and fields of knowledge to provide a comprehensive picture of scholarship up to the present:

    JSTOR catalogues more than 1,000 academic journals in various disciplines.

    EBSCOhost provides links to special databases covering scholarly journals and publications. Among these databases are Academic Search Premier,

peer review
Process by which articles in scholarly journals are checked by experts in the field for quality and accuracy before being approved for publication.

Humanities Abstracts, and Communication and Mass Media Complete.

InfoTrac OneFile accesses more than 100 million articles in areas from economics and sociology to science and medicine.

Libraries are an excellent resource for in-depth research on a speech topic.

- **Government Documents Area:** Many libraries still maintain collections of federal, state, and local government publications in hard copy, although most current documents are now available and more readily accessible in electronic form.
- **Nonprint Media Archives:** Collections of DVDs, CDs, films, videos, recordings, and microfilms can be found in the media archives.
- **Special Collections Area:** Many libraries have areas that provide access to local publications, resources, and unique archives that can help you adapt your speeches to the needs and interests of your surrounding community. For example, in its Mississippi Valley collection, the University of Memphis houses a world-famous archive of materials relating to the Memphis Sanitation Strike of 1968 during which Dr. Martin Luther King, Jr., was assassinated.

Before you go to the bricks-and-mortar version, take some time to explore your school library's website. Follow the links on the home page to familiarize yourself with the wealth of information and services provided. Look for an online virtual tour and for a floor plan showing where the various materials are kept. Additionally, many libraries have subject-specific research guides available on their website with tabs for suggested reference materials, books, journal articles, and databases. You will likely be amazed to find that your library is much more than just a warehouse for books and magazines.

Finding Your Voice

Expanding Your Sources of Information

Go to Procon.org, and choose a controversial topic on which you already have a strong opinion. Read the arguments, both pro and con, for this topic. Do those posting the arguments seem credible? How can you tell? Do you find that you are open to both sides of the argument, or do you evaluate the postings based on your original opinion? After reading both sides of the issue, reevaluate your feelings about this topic. Has your opinion changed, or do you feel stronger in your convictions? What resources in your library might clarify your thinking?

Evaluating Information from the Library

Because printed and online resources available through research libraries are generally subject to more exacting standards of academic rigor, we may be more inclined to let our guard down and accept them as valid without question—which can sometimes lead us astray. Quality advocacy is still advocacy, perhaps all the more dangerous and seductive because of its quality. The mere fact of being in print or available through your library does not by itself confer truth. You should consider the credibility of all the sources and information you research for use in your speeches, an important part of that *reliability* test we mentioned previously.

As you assess the credibility of an author, ask yourself: *Is this person an expert on my topic? What are the author's qualifications?* Remember that scientists and college professors are not necessarily experts on every subject. You should be able to assess the credentials of most experts (such as their professional associations) and determine what other experts have to say about them by searching their names, enclosed in quotation marks, in a general search engine. When assessing authors who are journalists, evaluate the credibility of those who are cited in their articles.

> **Discussing Your Topic with Your Librarian**
>
> Talk with a librarian at your library about your topic for your next speech. What do you learn from this discussion that you would not have found on the Internet?

You should also consider the publication in which the material appears. Professional journals are generally seen as more credible than popular magazines and newspapers. In turn, popular periodicals vary in terms of their credibility. For most audiences, mainline newspapers are considered more credible than tabloids, and upscale magazines such as *The Smithsonian* are more credible than *Reader's Digest*. Popular periodicals may also reflect political or social biases. For example, *The Nation* offers a liberal perspective on contemporary issues, and the *National Review* presents a conservative outlook. Consequently, as you select authors and publications to cite in your speeches, consider how their reputations might affect the way your listeners respond to your message.

Finally, remember that the timeliness or *recency* of information is critical for topics addressing current events, controversial issues, and the latest developments in science and technology. Printed materials—especially book publications—can grow stale and outdated before you get a chance to read them, so make it a point to seek out the most up-to-date information available.

Conducting Personal Interviews

7.4 Conduct personal interviews to add to your knowledge of your topic.

Personal interviews can provide special information, stories, and opinions not available through Internet or library research. An interview with a local expert or a community member directly affected by your topic can clearly demonstrate to your listeners how your topic may have an effect on their lives or the lives of those in their communities. For example, if you were researching a speech on crime at your university, an interview with the head of campus security on what forms of crime are most often reported, whether crime rates on campus have risen or fallen over the past few semesters, and what students can do to better protect themselves and their property could add a great deal of credibility to your speech. Your classmates would likely appreciate the special effort you made to enhance their listening experience by making the subject directly *relevant* to their lives.

As valuable as they can be, interviews also pose some challenges. Finding the right person to interview can be difficult. You need to make sure your expert has the appropriate qualifications to offer information and perspectives you can use confidently. Also, personal interviews should be the last stage of your research strategy. Before asking a person for his or her valuable time, you must make sure your questions cannot be easily answered online or through library research. You need sufficient knowledge of your subject before you can ask intelligent questions and be able to listen critically to the answers. To maximize the effectiveness of an interview, use these strategies:

- Conduct interviews during the final phase of your research process.
- Check local news sources to help you identify qualified prospects for interviews.
- Although it is generally preferable to conduct an interview face to face, you can identify widely recognized experts for possible Skype, Facetime, telephone or e-mail interviews through your initial online and library research.
- Survey the research interests of your school's faculty members to identify additional interview possibilities close at hand.

Once you have identified a good prospect for an interview, you move on to *schedule the interview*, *prepare your questions*, and *conduct the interview*.

Personal interviews can provide special information, stories, and opinions and can add credibility to your speech.

Schedule the Interview

The best way to ask for an interview is to contact the prospect directly. Express your sincere interest in the subject, and explain that you are preparing a public speech on a topic that is important to you both. Most people will be flattered that you recognize their expertise and value their opinion and will likely grant you the interview if they can. Discuss the kind of questions you wish to ask and how much time you will need. Schedule a specific date and time for the interview, and follow up with a confirmation e-mail. It may be helpful to record the interview, but *never do so without permission*.

Prepare Your Questions

Complete most of your library and Internet research before you conduct the interview so that you know what questions to ask and can converse intelligently on the subject. You should also have a clear idea of the purpose of your interview. What do you hope to learn from this person? Write out interview questions that are relevant to your specific purpose.

Plan open-ended questions that invite discussion. If you ask questions that call for a yes or no answer, that is likely all you will get. Phrase your questions carefully so you don't suggest the answers you want to receive, and save any controversial questions for late in the interview, after you have established rapport. Then ask touchy questions tactfully: "According to a recent article published in the campus newspaper, university officials have a history of discouraging students from bringing charges of sexual assault on this campus. Can you comment on that?" If asked with sincerity rather than hostility, this type of question can produce the most interesting and useful part of your interview.

Order your questions in a logical sequence so that one question flows into the next. Consider your time limitations and plan your questions accordingly.

Conduct the Interview

Dress appropriately in accordance with the context to show that you take the interview seriously. Arrive a few minutes early. Bring along a notepad for taking notes, extra pens, your list of questions, and your recording device if you have permission to record the interview. Make sure your device works properly and that you know how to use it. Given the potential failures of technology, take notes during the interview—even if you are recording. Just note the highlights of your subject's answers. Trying to write everything will slow down the interview and may have a negative impact on your exchange.

Introduce yourself and remind your subject of the purpose of the interview. You might break the ice by discussing something you admire about the person's work and telling her why you wished to interview her. Then proceed with your list of prepared questions, but use these only as a guide. Be open to asking questions you had not planned but that come up in the course of the interview—you'll often find interesting material that way. Let the expert do most of the talking; you're there primarily to listen. Allow the person you are interviewing to complete the answer to one question before you ask another. Adapt to the flow of conversation.

Be alert for opportunities to follow up on answers by using probes, mirror questions, and reinforcers. A **probe** is a question that asks a person to elaborate on a response: "Could you tell me more about . . . ?" A **mirror question** repeats part of a response to

probe
A question that asks a person to elaborate on an answer.

mirror question
A question that repeats part of a previous response to encourage further discussion.

reinforcer
A comment or action that encourages further communication from someone being interviewed.

encourage additional discussion: "So you're saying that . . . ?" A **reinforcer** provides encouragement for the person to communicate further. Smiles, nods, and such comments as "I see" are reinforcers that can keep the interview moving. If you feel the interview beginning to drift off course, you can often steer it back with a tactful transition. As the interview draws to a close, summarize the main points you heard and how you think they may be useful in your speech. A summary allows you to verify what you have heard and reassures the expert that you intend to use the information fairly and accurately. Thank your expert for her time.

After you have completed the interview, go over your notes as soon as possible and write out your expert's responses to important questions while the exact wording is still fresh in your mind. It is much easier to fill in the blanks immediately afterward than to wrack your brain after an interval of time. Finally, follow up with a thank-you note in which you report the successful results of your speech.

SPEAKER'S NOTES

Guidelines for Interviewing for Information

To conduct an effective interview for information, follow these guidelines:

1. During your preliminary research, identify possible interview prospects.
2. Make contact with the person you wish to interview.
3. Research your topic thoroughly before the interview.
4. Plan a series of questions that relate to your specific topic.
5. Act professional: Be on time, dress appropriately, and be courteous.
6. Ask positive, open-ended questions that encourage discussion.
7. Let the expert do most of the talking, but don't hesitate to ask for clarification or additional information.
8. Summarize the main points of the interview, and thank the expert for her time.

The Personal Interview

Identify two people who would be good prospects for a personal interview for your next speech. What perspectives could they offer that you cannot find otherwise? What are three questions you would ask and why?

Evaluating Information from Personal Interviews

Generally speaking, you should be less vulnerable to bad information gained from personal interviews. By the time of the interview, you will be armed with a good deal of library and Internet research, know the general features and issues surrounding your subject, and have acquired some in-depth knowledge about them. Therefore, if the interviewee should make really partisan or outlandish statements, you should be able to detect such claims for what they are.

On the other hand, you should approach the interview with some gratitude to the interviewee for consenting to talk with you. If the person is charming, affable, and flattering, you may find yourself *wanting* to agree with what he says, no questions asked. Be aware of this personal tendency, and be cautious: You can be grateful to a person without endorsing what he has to say, especially if other respected sources of knowledge you have consulted hold different views.

YOUR ETHICAL VOICE

Guidelines for Ethical Research

To be sure your research meets the ethical standard of respect for the integrity of ideas and information, apply the following guidelines:

1. Allow sufficient time for research.
2. Investigate differing perspectives on your topic.
3. Access credible sources of information.
4. Never fabricate or distort information.
5. Take careful notes on what you read.
6. Avoid plagiarism by indicating in your notes which ideas are yours and which come from other sources.
7. Cite your sources in your presentation.

SPEAKER'S NOTES

Checklist for Acquiring Responsible Knowledge

Use this checklist to ensure that you have covered all the bases in your research.

1. ___ I have engaged in the basic strategies for starting research, including assessing my own knowledge and experiences, establishing research objectives, evaluating resources, and recording findings.
2. ___ I have sought knowledge from reputable sources on the Internet.
3. ___ I have explored resources in the library and consulted with librarians to enhance my search.
4. ___ I have conducted personal interviews with experts.
5. ___ I have sought the judgments and opinions of experts on my topic.
6. ___ I have sought information that would be the most useful to my listeners.
7. ___ I have sought examples and stories that will bring my subject to life and illustrate its relevance.
8. ___ I have tested all of my research findings in terms of relevance, representativeness, recency, and reliability.

Final Reflections: Empowering Your Voice

In this chapter, we compared researchers to detectives, trying to figure out how clues, testimony, and evidence fit together and what their juxtaposition tells us. We asked some of our colleagues and advanced students to describe the meaning of research to them, using whatever comparisons came to mind. One described research as a treasure hunt, in which one seeks those gems of knowledge that will enrich a message. Another described it as an archaeological dig, in which one sifts through the writings of others in search of valued discoveries. Still others invoked comparisons to voyages of discovery, opening a succession of doors, or acquiring the raw materials for giving their speeches a solid foundation.

We opened this chapter with the narrative of Marisol researching her speech on sustainable seafood. For Marisol, research was a time for self-correction and redirection. As she read up on her topic, she came to suspect that she had indeed been "greenwashed" by unscrupulous marketers who promised to protect wild fish populations but actually endangered them by hoodwinking the buying public. She then refocused her concerns on the controversies surrounding the certification of wild-caught fish as sustainably harvested

Who can say what your research adventure might mean to you? Beyond any particular discoveries, you will be acquiring the ability to find, evaluate, and verify information—in short, to think critically—in ways you can use throughout your life to help you understand and verify what is going on in your world. And that, indeed, helps you find and empower your voice.

Study Questions

CONTENT MASTERY

1 What are the four dimensions of responsible knowledge that need to be developed in the course of your research?

2 What basic strategies should you use to develop responsible knowledge?

3 What are the strengths and limitations of personal experience as a source of responsible knowledge?

4 What kinds of resources does the Internet offer?

5 What special problems does the Internet present in terms of determining the credibility of sources? How can you evaluate a website for credibility?

6 What special advantages can the library offer as a source of responsible knowledge?

7 What criteria should you use to evaluate resources from the library?

8 How can personal interviews be used to strengthen your speech?

CRITICAL EXPLORATIONS

1. As you view news, be alert for stories that contain opinions disguised as information. What tips you off to the deception?
2. For your speech topic, find three websites with URLs that end in .com, three that end in .org, and three that end in .edu. Evaluate each in terms of the four Rs: relevance, representativeness, recency, and reliability.
3. Explore the Internet, seeking answers to the following questions. Keep a record of how long it takes you, what resources you use, and the results of your search.
   a. What was the population of the city in which you were born in the year of your birth?
   b. Who won the Pulitzer Prize for literature in the year you were born? For what work was this awarded? For what other works is the author noted?
   c. What actress won the Academy Award for best supporting actress in the year you were born? What movie was she in?
   d. What noteworthy event took place during the month and year you were born? When and where did this happen?
   e. What television show had the highest Nielsen ratings when you were 6 years old?
   f. Select the contemporary figure you most admire. When was he or she born? What awards has he or she received?
4. In question 3 above, substitute a parent or guardian for yourself. Then use the library instead of the Internet to locate the answers to these questions. Keep track of how long it takes you to find the information, where you find it, and the results. Compare the two sources in terms of efficiency and quality of information.
5. You are preparing an informative speech on the latest research technology available through your school's library, and the research librarian has graciously agreed to an interview. Prepare a list of five questions you will ask in the interview.

6. Prepare a formal bibliography of the readings you consult as you develop your next speech. Follow either the APA or the MLA style format illustrated in Figure 7.6, depending on your instructor's preference.

Figure 7.6
Citation Guide

Book, Print

MLA: Oosterveer, Peter, and Simon Bush. *Governing Sustainable Seafood*. Routledge, 2016.

APA: Oosterveer, P., & Bush, S. (2016). *Governing Sustainable Seafood*. New York, NY: Routledge.

Scholarly Journal Article with One Author, Print

MLA: Levenshus, Abbey Blake. "Building Context-Based Knowledge of Government Social Media Communication through an Ethnographic Study of the US Coast Guard." *Journal of Applied Communication Research*, vol. 44, no. 2, 2016, pp. 174–193.

APA: Levenshus, A. B. (2016). Building context-based knowledge of government social media communication through an ethnographic study of the US Coast Guard. *Journal of Applied Communication Research*, *44*(2), 174–193.

Scholarly Journal Article with Two Authors, Print

MLA: Enck, Suzanne, and Megan E. Morrissey. "If Orange Is the New Black, I Must Be Color Blind: Comic Framings of Post-Racism in the Prison-Industrial Complex." *Critical Studies in Media Communication*, vol. 32, no. 5, 2015, pp. 303–317.

APA: Enck, S., & Morrissey, M. E. (2015) If orange is the new black, I must be color blind: Comic framings of post-racism in the prison-industrial complex. *Critical Studies in Media Communication*, *32*(5), 303–317.

Magazine Article, Print

MLA: Switek, Brian. "Dawn of the Dinosaur" *Smithsonian*, Apr. 2016, pp. 82–86.

APA: Switek, B. (2016, April). "Dawn of the dinosaur." *Smithsonian, 46*(11), 82–86.

Newspaper Article, Print

MLA: Safer, Jeanne. "A Politically Mixed Marriage." *Wall Street Journal*, 26 Mar. 2016, p. C3.

APA: Safer, J. (2016, 26–27 March). A politically mixed marriage. *The Wall Street Journal*, p. C3.

Article in an Edited Collection or Chapter of a Book in an Anthology, Print

MLA: Turner, Christopher R. "Product Placement of Medical Products: Issues and Concerns." *Handbook of Product Placement in the Mass Media,* edited by Mary-Lou Galician, Haworth Press, 2004, pp. 159–170.

APA: Turner, C. R. (2004). Product placement of medical products: Issues and concerns. In M. Galician (Ed.), *Handbook of product placement in the mass media* (pp. 159–170). New York, NY: Haworth Press.

eBook

MLA: Davidson, Jeanette R. *African American Studies*. Edinburgh UP, 2010. *Introducing Ethnic Studies E-book*, public.eblib.com/choice/publicfullrecord.aspx?p=624263

APA: Davidson, J. R. (2010). *African American studies* (Introducing ethnic studies). Edinburgh: Edinburgh University Press. Retrieved from http://public.eblib.com/choice/publicfullrecord.aspx?p=624263

Online Newspaper Article

MLA: Fritz, Angela. "Scientists Say Antarctic Melting Could Double Sea Level Rise." *Washington Post*, 30 March 2016. www.washingtonpost.com/news/capital-weather-gang/wp/2016/03/30/what-6-feet-of-sea-level-rise-looks-like-for-our-vulnerable-coastal-cities/. Accessed 15 April 2016.

APA: Fritz, A. (2016, March 30). Scientists say Antarctic melting could double sea level rise. *Washington Post*. Retrieved from https://www.washingtonpost.com/news/capital-weather-gang/wp/2016/03/30/what-6-feet-of-sea-level-rise-looks-like-for-our-vulnerable-coastal-cities/

Online Magazine Article

MLA: Ross, Ashley. "No Kidding: We Have No Idea How April Fools' Day Started." *Time.com*, 31 March 2016. time.com/4276140/april-fools-day-history/. Accessed 1 April 2016.

APA: Ross, A. (2016, April 1). No kidding: We have no idea how April Fools' Day started. *Time.com*, March 31, 2016. Retrieved from http://time.com/4276140/april-fools-day-history/

Website with an Organizational Author

MLA: Arthritis Society, The "Arthritis Facts and Figures." *The Arthitis Society,* 2016. arthritis.ca/understand-arthritis/arthritis-facts-figures. Accessed 16 December 2016.

APA: The Arthritis Society (2016). Arthritis facts and figures. Retrieved from https://arthritis.ca/understand-arthritis/arthritis-facts-figures

Speech, Recorded

MLA: Hadid, Zaha. "Acceptance Speech for the Pritzker Architecture Prize." Pritzker Architecture Prize Ceremony. 31 May 2004. The State Hermitage Museum, St. Petersburg, Russia. https://www.youtube.com/watch?v=hMC6EXASP2Q. Accessed 20 January 2017.

APA: Hadid, Z. (2004, May 31). *Acceptance speech for the Pritzker Architecture Prize*. Speech presented at the Pritzker Architecture Prize ceremony, The State Hermitage Museum, St. Petersburg, Russia. Retrieved from https://www.youtube.com/watch?v=hMC6EXASP2Q

Speech, Live

MLA: Coates, Ta-Nehisi. "Reynolds Lecture on Race Relations." 16 November 2016. Davidson College. Address.

APA: Coates, T. (2016, November 16). *Reynolds lecture on race relations.* Davidson College.

Personal Interview

MLA: Alexander, Anne A. Personal interview. 22 August 2016.

APA: Because personal interviews do not provide recoverable data, they are not included in the reference list according to APA style guidelines. They should, of course, be cited in your speech and listed in your bibliography as follows: Alexander, A. (2016, August 22). Personal communication.

Sources:

MLA Handbook for Writers of Research Papers, Eighth Edition, 2016

Publication Manual of the American Psychological Association, Sixth Edition, 2010

https://owl.english.purdue.edu/owl/section/2/11/

https://owl.english.purdue.edu/owl/section/2/10/

Supporting Your Ideas

CHAPTER

LEARNING OBJECTIVES

This chapter will help you:

8.1 Use facts and statistics to ground your speech in reality.

8.2 Present expert, lay, and prestige testimony to add credibility.

8.3 Provide examples to show how your subject affects individual lives.

8.4 Develop narratives to add action and interest to your speech.

8.5 Select the most appropriate combination of supporting material to use in your speech.

OUTLINE

Facts and Statistics

Testimony

Examples

Narratives

Selecting and Combining Supporting Materials

The Golden Gate Bridge has occupied a prominent place in the American imagination since it opened in 1937. Its architects, engineers, and construction workers had to triumph over fierce winds, dense fogs, swirling tides, a channel nearly 400 feet deep, and a span of water over two miles wide. Thus, it stands as a monument to the human power to overcome vast forces of nature. Today, at a time of deep political and religious divisions between populations, the bridge (like so many such bridges around the world) may promise that we can build connections between separated people, even when the task of doing so seems formidable.

"It is wrong always, everywhere, and for everyone, to believe anything upon insufficient evidence."

—WILLIAM JAMES

Think of speeches as bridges that carry messages that can connect speakers and audiences. And think of yourself as a builder of these symbolic bridges. To be successful, you must learn how to construct structures of thought that rest on solid pillars of supporting materials. To be a good builder, you must know your materials and what they can support. You need to know how to select and use them wisely. Just as a bridge must carry heavy weights and withstand storms and high winds, your speech must withstand doubt and controversy. When you rise to speak, you must be confident of its structural integrity.

When you hear an assertion, such as "animal cloning is dangerous to human beings," think of your likely reaction: Who says so? What is the basis for that claim? Why should I accept this? **Supporting materials**—facts and statistics, testimony, examples, and narratives—are the pillars, braces, and cross-braces of serious speechmaking. The effective and ethical use of supporting materials encourages others to take your ideas seriously. Such materials give strength and human appeal to the voice you are discovering and developing.

supporting materials
The facts and statistics, testimony, examples, and narratives that are the building blocks of substantive speechmaking.

At this point, you should have gathered a wealth of information and begun to generate your main ideas, as discussed in the previous two chapters. In this chapter, we discuss the four forms of supporting materials that constitute this information, point out how to put them to work in your speeches, and discuss how to combine them to maximum advantage.

Facts and Statistics

8.1 Use facts and statistics to ground your speech in reality.

As discussed in the previous chapter, your first objective when researching any topic is to get the facts straight. Facts and statistics are indispensable to responsible speaking—especially when addressing informative or persuasive topics. When audience members get the impression that the facts are in your favor, they are likely to give you attention and respect.

Facts are statements that can be verified as true or false by experts or independent observation. Sojourner Truth was born into slavery. The National Communication Association boasts almost 8,000 members. Former U.S. Treasurer Rosario Marin and

facts
Descriptive statements that can be verified as true or false by independent observation or by experts.

media entrepreneur Cathy Areu established the National Association of Latina Leaders (NALL) in 2003. Jack Dorsey sent the first tweet on March 21, 2006. On January 1, 2017, thirty-nine people died in a nightclub in Istanbul, Turkey, as a result of a terrorist attack.

Very few people would question that these statements are factual. What they *mean*, however, and what we should do about them may be vigorously debated. Examine a term like *terrorist*: how it should be defined and whether it is rightfully applied in a particular case can be especially controversial.

Statistics are facts measured mathematically. In our "show me the numbers" culture, statistics are useful for describing size precisely, making predictions, illustrating trends, and demonstrating important comparisons. The following illustrates how statistics can provide support.

statistics
Facts that can be measured mathematically.

> According to the Centers for Disease Control and Prevention, the percentage of children aged six to eleven years in the United States who were obese increased from 7 percent in 1980 to nearly 18 percent in 2014. Similarly, the percentage of adolescents aged twelve to nineteen years who were obese increased from 5 percent to nearly 21 percent over the same period.[1] These are ominous trends for the health of this country.

We typically listen carefully and respectfully to such statistical claims. In democratic societies, public opinion polls that demonstrate "the will of the people" can strongly influence policy decisions.

Using Facts and Statistics

Because they can be verified, facts and statistics provide a powerful resource for validating important and controversial assertions. However, it is essential to remember that—despite the commonplace assumption—*facts do not speak for themselves.* They aren't like bricks that are unchanging, no matter what the context. *You* must explain what they mean. You select them to make some point and then interpret them. Developing the ability to frame facts effectively is vital to finding your voice.

Consider this statement: "According to a U.S. Department of Labor report issued on March 4, 2016, the unemployment rate in this country was 4.9 percent."[2] This is certainly a factual statement, but what does it mean? One person might argue, "That's an alarming number of people who remain out of work. The president's policies are a failure." Another might answer, "That represents a huge drop from 9.7 percent in 2010. The president's policies are working."

These dramatically different claims interpret the meaning of the fact. Which one is correct? Ironically, both could be, based on these statements alone. You might strengthen your case for either claim by providing additional evidence, but keep in mind that facts and figures cannot just stand alone. *You must explain to listeners how they relate to your message and what it is that they demonstrate.* According to Richard Alldritt of the United Kingdom Statistics Authority, their effective use "requires both knowledge of the subject and a real empathy with the user. . . . You have to believe in the good that statistics can do, and [you have to] care about the user."[3] Look for ways to place facts and statistics in a context that will be meaningful for your audience. You can tell your audience that in a single year almost 45,000 people died in car accidents; how do they understand the magnitude of that number? See what happens when you provide a perspective: That number is "the equivalent of a fully loaded passenger jet crashing with no survivors every day for a year. If everyone wore seat belts, more than half of these deaths could have been avoided."[4] Using the "human scale principle" contextualizes points by casting them in everyday terms.[5]

The preceding example illustrates another important decision to make when presenting facts and statistics: whether to state them in general or precise terms. Is it more effective to say that worldwide, 2.078 billion people have social media accounts, or to say that more than 2 billion people have social media accounts?[6]

Figure 8.1 Pie Graph

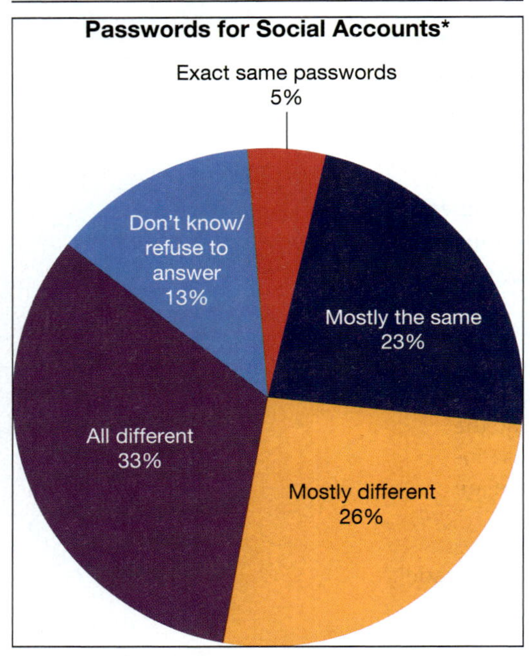

Source: Based on data from Bankrate Money Pulse survey, Sept. 15-18, 2016,http://www.bankrate.com/finance/consumer-index/money-pulse-1016.aspx#ixzz4OJjrRDh1 (accessed October 27, 2016)

Presenting statistics in the rounded-off manner of the first statement can have more impact and be more easily remembered. On the other hand, there are some audiences and situations for which the exact numbers could be significant. Your college audience of critical listeners might be such an audience; global social media use might be such a subject. Decide whether the general or the precise way of expressing facts will work best for you, your audience, and your topic. If you are uncertain on this point, our advice is to err on the side of precision.

Presentation aids can effectively communicate large amounts of factual and statistical information. If you want to explain how few people properly protect their media accounts, you could rattle off a series of statistics—or you could show a pie graph (Figure 8.1) that quickly demonstrates only a third of those surveyed use distinctive passwords for each account.[7]

Facts and figures are vital to responsible knowledge and ethical speaking, but be careful not to overemphasize them. A flood of vaguely relevant dates, events, and percentages will likely make your audience's eyes glaze over. Be selective in determining which facts and figures will be most effective, and use a variety of supporting materials to complement them. When considering the use of facts and figures in your speeches, evaluate them using the *four Rs*, and make it a point to distinguish "the facts" from the *inferences* and *opinions* that we and others derive from them.

Applying the Four Rs. For most speech topics, your research should yield an array of facts and statistics. You want to make sure that these meet the requirements of the four Rs as discussed in Chapter 7: relevance, representativeness, recency, and reliability.

First, you should make sure that facts and figures are *relevant* to your topic and central ideas. This can be challenging when you come across fascinating facts and figures about a subject. You might be tempted to mention them just because they seem so interesting—"hey, did you realize that *temulent* means 'drunken' or 'intoxicating'?"[8]—but if they deflect listeners from your central thesis, you will likely confuse and distract them.

Second, make sure that specific facts are *representative* of the larger reality you are addressing rather than an exception to the rule. Penguins are birds but cannot fly; that does not prove that birds cannot fly. Be wary of whether general conclusions actually apply to the situation you are describing. You might declare that 84 percent of adults use the Internet—but if you don't specify that you're referring to the United States, someone might point out that worldwide access is only 46.4 percent.[9]

Third, your facts should pass the test of *recency*. The ancient Greek philosopher Heraclitus posited that "the only thing that is constant is change"[10]—so the timeliness of your information is important. Especially for late-breaking or evolving topics, yesterday's fact may be today's illusion. For example, a report on the incidence and treatment of HIV/AIDS from 1995 will be vastly different from the findings of a current report. On such topics, you should be careful to cite the most up-to-date data available.

Last, you should consider facts and statistics for *reliability*. They should come from recognized experts, respected research institutions, and news outlets that have a reputation for balance and objectivity. Be careful about the increasing number of sources that appeal to particular audiences. More liberal listeners may likely be suspicious of outstanding facts and numbers culled from Fox News, whereas conservative listeners may have similar issues with MSNBC. Depending on your audience, relying exclusively on such sources may lead listeners to discredit your speech, however reasonable and well-constructed.

This criterion poses particular challenges in the age of the Internet, when sources may be knowledgeable experts or inexperienced amateurs. Some websites initially might look like reputable news sources but may turn out to be a front for a corporation, an advocacy group, or a bemused individual with a penchant for inventing material. Don't use them until you have checked out their credentials and are convinced of their reliability. Watch out for blatant **disinformation** or sensational facts that have been willfully fabricated or distorted beyond reason in order to advance a hidden agenda.[11] As a general rule, always find more reputable additional sources for incredible facts and statistics you find on social media posts and obscure Internet "news" sites. When in doubt, corroborate!

disinformation
Information that has been fabricated or distorted in order to advance a hidden agenda.

Finally, be mindful that statistical predictions represent probability, not certainty, and that even credible statistics can be distorted by partisan interest groups. Speakers for both major political parties often spin the same or similar statistics to reach opposing conclusions. In the 2016 presidential campaign, for example, candidates used the same figures about immigration to argue for a bewildering variety of "reforms" ranging from a "path to citizenship" to mass deportation.[12] The same point goes for popular polling data. The vast majority of Americans support some concept of immigration reform, but their ideas as to what constitutes reform vary wildly. Be wary *who* "the people" are and *what* "the people" want when citing them to support your claims.

Finding Your Voice

Detecting Disinformation

Find a news story you believe is biased or constitutes disinformation. Using the four Rs, evaluate the story's use of facts and statistics. How does it present facts and statistics as opposed to inferences and opinions? What would a more balanced story include?

For example, consider how quickly disinformation about the April 2013 Boston bombings got circulated and even picked up by reputable TV and cable news outlets. Reporters and commentators, as well as those on Twitter and other social media, tried to reconstruct events and analyze leads in the chaotic days following the tragic bombings, resulting in some wild speculation and conjecture on threads of information as well as the garbling of true stories. How can you judge the accuracy of such news stories, even in the heat of "breaking news," especially when some of the information (such as the "captured" tweet or the lockdown situation in Boston) *is* accurate and provides vital communication?

Distinguish Facts from Inferences and Opinions. In addition to evaluating facts and statistics, you should make a conscious effort to distinguish them from inferences and opinions. **Inferences** refer to the conclusions we derive from factual information, whereas **opinions** add an element of personal evaluation and conviction. For instance, it is a fact that 44 percent of the victims of sexual assault in this country are younger than 18 years old.[13] From that fact, we might reasonably *infer* that children as a group are especially vulnerable to sexual assault. We might also *opine* that our efforts to prevent sexual crimes against young people are insufficient. Sometimes it is difficult to recognize where the facts end and the inferences and opinions begin. Indeed, if we used the simple word "distressing" to introduce this statistic, it would add an element of opinion to our very presentation of the facts.

inferences
Conclusions derived from events and factual information.

opinions
Expressions of personal evaluation and conviction.

This is not to suggest that inferences and opinions are less substantive than facts and figures. Indeed, they are vitally important for interpreting the *meaning* of factual information, the *how* or *why* a problematic reality came into being and *what* we should do about it. But they are more personal and subject to dispute than settled facts, and you should expect important inferences and opinions to be supported with factual information and credible sources. Consider, for example, the claim that "the Mazda MX-5 is the best affordable sports car on the market." Now contrast that with "According to the 2016 *U.S. News* analysis of six published reviews and test drives, 'the Mazda MX-5 Miata ranks number one in quality among affordable sports cars.... [It] is exceptionally athletic and more engaging to drive than most of its similarly-priced rivals.'"[14] Obviously, both statements are ripe with inferences and opinions, but the second is arguably much more convincing.

Of course, there is nothing inherently wrong with expressing honest convictions and feelings in a speech. Freedom of speech assures us of the right to do just that. But our voice has more power when our expressions include thoughtful, considered reasons.

For more on the uses and misuses of statistics, see the brief but excellent online primer compiled and maintained by Robert Niles, "Statistics Every Writer Should Know." See also our discussion of fallacies in Chapter 15.

Finding Relevant Statistics

Find a set of statistics relevant to the topic for your next speech, and identify different ways in which the data might be used. How can you ensure that you are using these statistics accurately and ethically?

SPEAKER'S NOTES

Interpreting Facts and Statistics

Follow these guidelines for using facts and figures in your speeches.

1. Demonstrate how a fact fits the points you are making.
2. Decide whether to present your statistics in general or precise terms.
3. Select the most appropriate facts and statistics so you won't overwhelm your listeners.
4. Support controversial claims with facts from more than one source.
5. Test facts for relevance, representativeness, recency, and reliability.
6. Avoid using sources that are obviously biased.
7. Carefully distinguish between facts and fact-based interpretations and opinions.

Testimony

8.2 Present expert, lay, and prestige testimony to add credibility.

You use **testimony** when you quote the words or summarize the ideas of others to support and illustrate your points. Using testimony is like calling witnesses to speak on your behalf. You add their ethos to yours when you show that their opinions and observations confirm the views you present. We'll consider the three forms of testimony and then turn to ways to use them appropriately.

Types of Testimony

The three forms of testimony are expert, lay, and prestige. Each one contributes a different kind of authentication to your speech.

testimony
Citing the words and ideas of others to support a point.

expert testimony
Citing the words of people or institutions qualified by training or experience to speak as authorities on a subject.

Expert Testimony. **Expert testimony** comes from people who are qualified by training or experience to speak as authorities on a subject. An interpersonal communication scholar can speak to forming friendships; a nutritionist can address the strengths and weaknesses of the food pyramid; a gerontologist can articulate the values of befriending an older citizen; an accountant can talk about the implications of tax codes. Such support can be especially useful when you are not a recognized expert and when your topic is complicated, unfamiliar, or controversial.

When you use expert testimony, remember that competence is area-specific: Your experts can speak as authorities only within their area of expertise. An interpersonal communication scholar, for example, wouldn't necessarily be reliable on the subject of the food pyramid. Note how Gabrielle Wallace, whose speech appears in Appendix B, wove the testimony of *three* expert sources together to support her speech comparing French and American eating customs:

Citing expert testimony adds substance to your speech.

> According to Paul Rozin, a nutritionist at the University of Pennsylvania, French portion sizes on average are about 25% smaller than American portions—which might explain why Americans are roughly three times more likely to become obese than French people.
>
> A factor that might account for this is the French upbringing. Mireille Guiliano, author of *French Women Don't Get Fat*, says that the French are not conditioned to overeat. Instead, they are taught to eat only until they are full, and then stop! A recent University of Pennsylvania study confirmed this tendency. The study compared the eating habits of students from Paris and Chicago. It found that French students stopped eating in response to internal cues, like when they first started feeling full or when they wanted to leave room for dessert. The American students, on the other hand, relied more on external cues. They would, for example, eat until the TV show they were watching ended, or until they ran out of a beverage. There's no question that eating habits are a vital point of difference between the French and American cultures.

This was powerful testimony, enhancing the credibility of both the speaker and the speech. Just think of how much weaker the speech would have been had Gabrielle *not* cited these authorities, relying simply on her own assertions. Much of its power lay in how Gabrielle established the credentials of her experts.

It's important that you guard against bias as you select expert testimony. Also be aware, however, that on some occasions the perception of bias can actually enhance the usefulness of a source. One of the most powerful forms of testimony, **reluctant testimony**, occurs when people testify *against* and *despite* their apparent self-interest.[15] Consider Amanda Miller's speech criticizing the U.S.-sponsored "School of the Americas" as a source of right-wing terrorism in Latin America. From her audience analysis, Amanda knew that many of her listeners were conservative Republicans, and she feared that some of them might dismiss her message as a left-wing "apology for America." So she decided to open her speech by citing a prominent conservative, well known for his patriotism and his willingness to use American military power and influence abroad:

reluctant testimony
Invoking the words of sources who appear to speak against their own interests.

> "If any government sponsors the outlaws and killers of innocents, they have become outlaws and murderers themselves, and they will take that lonely path at their own peril." President Bush spoke these words to the world shortly after the attacks on the World Trade Towers.

By citing a person held in such high regard by her listeners, Amanda invited them to look at her issue through an ironic lens Once they knew what many graduates of the School of the Americas had actually done, they would conclude that the United States had acted in a manner that was contradictory to our own national values and interests. The rest of her speech was well received because of the way she had adapted her message to the political leanings of her audience.

lay testimony
Citing the words or views of ordinary people on a subject.

Lay Testimony. **Lay testimony** represents the wisdom of ordinary people. It may come from people who have first-hand experience with a topic or issue, or from those who simply have strong feelings about it. While not appropriate for validating complex or disputed ideas, lay testimony helps illustrate real-life consequences and adds authenticity to your speech. It is highly regarded in democratic societies, in which the experiences and opinions of everyday folk are greatly valued.

As he addressed the annual meeting of the Public Broadcasting System, Bill Moyers used lay testimony to emphasize the value of public radio and television:

> There was a cabbie [in New York City] named Youssef Jada. He came here from Morocco six years ago.... Youssef kept his car radio tuned to National Public Radio all day and his television set at home on Channel Thirteen. He said—and this is a direct quote—"I am blessed by these stations." He pointed me to a picture on the dashboard of his 13-month-old son, and he said: "My son was born in this country. I will let him watch Channel Thirteen so he can learn how to be an American."
>
> Think about that.... Why shouldn't public television be the core curriculum of the American experience?[16]

You can find effective lay testimony in your own backyard. The audience analysis you conduct, supplemented with informal interviews with your listeners, can provide lay testimony that you can then use in your presentation. You can create special bonds of identification with your listeners when you quote them in your speech.

Lay testimony is a common staple of news stories, letters to editors, and responses to online blogs and postings. Often these are colorful, if sometimes dubious, sources of popular opinion. Opinion polls, such as Gallup International's year-end feature "The Voice of the People," also can serve as a powerful form of collective lay testimony. Representing the voice of the people, such testimony is especially potent in societies in which "the people" is a positive symbol that represents the final repository of political power.[17]

prestige testimony
Citing the words of an admired public figure or text.

Prestige Testimony. **Prestige testimony** associates your message with the words of an admired figure or text such as Thomas Jefferson or the Declaration of Independence. While such sources do not typically provide expertise with respect to your particular topic, their words can lend a heightened elegance and wisdom to your speeches. Because of this quality, prestige testimony is often used as a source of inspiration in ceremonial speaking.

Bill Moyers used lay testimony to illustrate the importance of public radio.

In his "Speech on Race," delivered during his first campaign for the presidency, Barack Obama relied heavily on prestige testimony. He cited the Constitution of the United States ("We the people, in order to form a more perfect union"), William Faulkner ("The past isn't dead and buried. In fact, it isn't even past"), and the Bible ("We are commanded to do unto others as we would have them do unto us. Let us be our brother's keeper, Scripture tells us. Let us be our sister's keeper.").[18] This combined prestige testimony from an iconic political document, a noted author, and a sacred text lent considerable eloquence to Obama's argument.

Using Testimony Effectively

As you use testimony, be sure your reference reflects the overall meaning and intent of its author. Never twist the meaning of testimony to make it fit your purposes, an unethical practice called **quoting out of context**. Political campaign advertising is often rife with this abuse. For example, during a political campaign in Illinois, one state representative sent out a fund-raising letter that claimed he'd been singled out for "special recognition" by *Chicago* magazine—and indeed he had. He had been cited as "one of the state's ten worst legislators."[19]

quoting out of context
An unethical use of a quotation that changes or distorts its original meaning.

Consider the best ways to use each kind of testimony. For *expert* testimony, for example, you want to stress the credentials of the specialist as appropriate to the topic. If the testimony is recent, and if it appears in a prestigious publication, let listeners know that as well.

Again, *lay* testimony can be really effective for adding a note of popular authenticity to your messages. If you decide to use testimony from survey data, be sure it meets the criteria of reliability and recency. Also, be aware that polls measure the popularity of a subject but not necessarily its rightness or wrongness. Don't assume a majority opinion at a given moment equates with ethical or even factual correctness. In his classic treatise *On Liberty*, John Stuart Mill warned of what he called "the tyranny" of majority opinion.[20]

If you are using *prestige* testimony, think about how your listeners might feel about the person or text you are citing. You should also consider whether associating with this person or text will increase your credibility as a speaker and the believability of your message. As with lay testimony, prestige testimony should not usually be used to verify facts. Figure 8.2 provides some guidelines for evaluating testimony.

Finding Examples of Testimony

On a single topic, find examples of expert, lay, and prestige testimony. What role can each type play in supporting your points? What are the limitations of each?

Figure 8.2
Checklist for Evaluating Testimony

General

- ___ Is this testimony relevant to my purpose?
- ___ Am I quoting or paraphrasing accurately?
- ___ Am I using the appropriate type of testimony for my purpose?

Expert Testimony

- ___ Have I verified the credentials of my source?
- ___ Are my expert's credentials appropriate for my topic?
- ___ Will this expert be acceptable to my listeners?
- ___ Is my expert free from vested interest?
- ___ Is this testimony consistent with that of other authorities?
- ___ Does this testimony reflect the latest knowledge on my topic?

Lay Testimony

- ___ Does this testimony demonstrate the human applications of my topic?
- ___ Does this testimony enhance identification with my topic?
- ___ Are the people cited likable?
- ___ Is polling data from a reputable organization?
- ___ Is polling data recent?

Prestige Testimony

- ___ Do my listeners believe this person or text is prestigious?
- ___ Does this testimony add grace and dignity to my speech?
- ___ Does associating with this person or text enhance my credibility as a speaker?
- ___ Does associating with this person or text enhance the credibility of my speech?

As you frame testimony for use in your speech, decide whether to quote or to summarize what others say. When you repeat the exact words of others, you are using a **direct quotation**. When quotations are too long or complex to present word for word, you can **paraphrase** or restate what others have said in your own words. Generally speaking, direct quotations are the more powerful form of support. They are useful when statements are brief and eloquent or when the exact wording is important for the point you are making. They are also effective for supporting complex or controversial assertions before skeptical audiences.

direct quotation
Repeating the exact words of others to support a point.

paraphrase
Rephrasing or summarizing the words of others to support a point.

Write out quotations on separate note cards to preserve the exact wording. Give some thought to how you will blend them into your speech: for example, "According to..." or "In the words of...." Pause as you read the words to increase their impressiveness, and maintain eye contact with listeners during the pauses.

SPEAKER'S NOTES

Using Testimony

Keep these guidelines in mind as you plan the use of testimony in your speeches.

1. Use *expert testimony* to validate information.
2. Use *lay testimony* to build identification and add authenticity.
3. Use *prestige testimony* to enhance the stature of your message.
4. Select sources your audience will respect.
5. Quote or paraphrase materials accurately.
6. Point out the qualifications of experts as you cite them.

Examples

8.3 Provide examples to show how your subject affects individual lives.

Just as pictures serve as graphic illustrations for a printed text, **examples** serve as verbal illustrations in a speech. They bring a speech to life by offering specific instances that exemplify or encapsulate your point. In her speech on "The Price of Bottled Water," Katie Lovett offers a series of examples to bring home her point: "There are vitamin waters, nicotine waters, caffeine waters, electrolyte-enhanced Smart Water, the 'orbtastic' Aquapods that target kids, Bling H_2O which sells for $35 a bottle, 'Hello Kitty' water for cats, and yes, even a 'diet' water called 'Skinny.'" Examples involving real people help listeners relate to your message by showing the human side of situations. Say, for example, you want to show that stuttering can be overcome. You could assert that fact and cite an expert in speech pathology. But think of how much more effective your speech would be if you also cited examples of famous people who have succeeded despite speaking impediments, such as Marc Anthony, Emily Blunt, Shaquille O'Neal, Tiger Woods, Marilyn Monroe, and Winston Churchill. In doing so, you offer specific representatives who embody your point.

examples
Incidents that illustrate a speaker's points.

When examples are drawn from your personal experience, they help establish your credibility to speak on the topic. Joseph Van Matre, for example, discussed his favorite video game before addressing their uses by fitness trainers, educators, the military, and the business world (see Appendix B). This helped to establish his ethos. By citing shared interests and experiences with your listeners, you create a bond with them. You share understanding, which can lead in turn to identification.

Because of the power of examples in oral communication, speakers often use them to open speeches. Austin Wright began his persuasive speech on government abuse of individual rights with the following example:

> On September 26, 2002, Canadian citizen Maher Arar boarded a flight home from a family vacation in Tunisia. During a layover in New York City, American authorities detained Arar, interrogating him for the next twelve days. After repeatedly denying any connection to Al Qaeda, Arar was shackled and loaded onto a private, unmarked jet headed for Syria, where he was tortured for the next ten months.

Because they are more concrete and colorful than abstract words, examples can more easily arouse emotions. They can touch people with the humanity of situations, even though listeners may come from different cultural backgrounds. When Dolapo Olushola wanted to reach out to her American listeners concerning the plight of AIDS orphans in her native sub-Saharan Africa, she talked about one representative child with whom she had worked as a volunteer. To magnify the poignancy of the example, she showed photos, which touched the heartstrings of listeners. Several responded by volunteering to help her raise money.

Finally, examples provide emphasis. When you make a statement and follow it with an example, you are pointing out that what you have just said is *important*. Examples amplify your ideas. They say to the audience, "This deserves your attention." Examples are especially helpful when you introduce new, complex, or abstract material. Not only can they make such information clearer; they also allow time for the audience to process what you have said before you move on to your next point.

Using Examples Effectively

The most common strategy for using examples in speeches is simply to reference them as specific illustrations of a more general statement or point. Such uses are typically concise and to the point. Sometimes a series of brief examples can help to drive home an idea. In a speech to the National Prayer Breakfast, for example, rock star and social activist Bono used this technique while exhorting American leaders to set aside 1 percent of the federal budget for African relief programs:

> One percent is not merely a number on a balance sheet. One percent is the girl in Africa who gets to go to school, thanks to you. One percent is the AIDS patient who gets her medicine, thanks to you. One percent is the African entrepreneur who can start a small family business, thanks to you. One percent is not redecorating presidential palaces or money flowing down a rat hole. This one percent is digging waterholes to provide clean water.[21]

Using an example of someone who has overcome a speech impediment, such as Emily Blunt, embodies your point.

On some occasions, speakers may choose to develop their examples in further detail for greater emotional impact. Chris Christie, governor of New Jersey, used this technique when he described how one child responded to Hurricane Sandy in his 2013 State of the State Address:

> I met nine-year-old Ginjer. Having a nine-year-old girl myself, her height and manner of speaking was immediately familiar and evocative. Having confronted so many crying adults at that point I felt ready to deal with anything. Then Ginjer looked at me, began to cry, and told

> me she was scared. She told me she had lost everything; she had lost her home and her belongings. She asked me to help her.[22]

factual example
An example based on something that actually happened or really exists.

Generally speaking, the most effective examples for use in speeches are based on actual events or the experiences of real people. Such **factual examples** provide strong support for your ideas because they actually did happen: They authenticate the point you are trying to make. Joseph Jimenez, CEO of Novartis, used the following factual example to support a more positive view of his pharmaceutical company:

> We believe . . . it is our obligation to offer low-cost generics to lower health care costs around the world.
>
> Here's just one example. We introduced generic enoxaparin in this country last year. This is a medicine that helps prevent blood clots. It matters because clots can break free, and cause a deadly blockage in the lung. When we introduced a generic version, it saved the U.S. government $700 million. That's a big deal.[23]

hypothetical example
An example offered not as real but as representative of actual people, situations, or events.

In comparison to a factual example, a **hypothetical example** is not offered as real so much as *representative* of actual people, situations, or events. This kind of example can be useful when factual examples are not available or when their use would not be appropriate. While generally not as authoritative as their factual counterparts, hypothetical examples can still be very effective. Of course, you should make sure they are representative of the issue or situation you are addressing. Consider the following hypothetical example, which illustrates the growing problem of childhood obesity:

> Let me introduce you to Madison Cartwright. Madison is twelve years old. She's four feet eleven inches tall. She weighs 155 pounds. Her body mass index is over 29. This means that Madison is one of the more than nine million children and teenagers in this country who can be classified as obese.
>
> How does this affect her? Not only is she a prime candidate for health problems such as childhood diabetes, but she also has other problems. She loves softball, but has difficulty playing because she gets short of breath. So she sits in the bleachers and watches her classmates. Madison is very smart, but she hates school. She is often the butt of "fat" jokes and teasing by her classmates. Instead of playing outside or socializing with friends after school, Madison goes home and watches TV by herself. Her self-esteem is very low.
>
> Is Madison a real person? Well, yes and no. You may not find someone with her name at the middle school you attended, but you will find many Madisons in the seventh grade there. Childhood obesity in the United States has reached epidemic proportions.

Always alert your listeners to the hypothetical nature of your example. You can do this by beginning your example with an introductory phrase such as "Imagine yourself . . ." or "Picture the following. . . ." Or, as in the preceding example, you can let listeners know near the end.

Regardless of what kinds of examples to use, you should give careful consideration to how you want them to function in your speeches. Do you want to personalize a point? To buttress an argument? To clarify what you mean? Then look for, or create, examples that serve your purpose. You want to make sure your examples fit your point, are representative, and will be believable (see Figure 8.3). Otherwise, you risk distracting and confusing listeners. If your examples seem far-fetched, listeners will grow suspicious of both you and your speech. Keep in mind that what works well with one audience may not click with another. Ask yourself if the example will fit well with the experiences, motivations, and interests of your listeners. You should risk offending listeners only when they need to be shocked into attention before they can be informed or persuaded.

____	Is this example relevant to my topic and purpose?
____	Does this example fairly represent the reality of a situation?
____	Will this example make my ideas more understandable?
____	Will this example make my point more memorable?
____	Will my listeners find this example believable?
____	Is this example appropriate for this audience?
____	Is this example in good taste?
____	Is this example interesting?

Figure 8.3 Checklist for Testing Examples

To work well, examples should be interesting, colorful, and dynamic, so select specific features that will make them come to life. Emphasize concrete details. Name the people, times, places, and groups in your examples. You could mention a postal carrier, but your listeners will relate more if you name Luis Francesco with the United States Postal Service. When Joseph Jimenez wished to emphasize that "caring and curing" is the theme of his pharmaceutical company, he chose the following example:

> ...We're joining the WHO [World Health Organization], the Gates Foundation and others to work to end leprosy, a disease that goes all the way back to the Bible.
>
> It's a terrible disease with an intense social stigma. In ancient times, people with it were forced to wear cowbells, so everyone else could hear them coming and get away.
>
> ...But we make a therapy to treat leprosy and cure it. And with it, people can live a normal life. That's why we're committed over the next 10 years to providing the therapy free to everyone who needs it.[24]

When you keep examples concise but striking in this way, you stimulate listeners to provide details on their own, and their imaginations fill out the example.

Use examples selectively. Examples can work well to open and close speeches, to clarify your main ideas, and to ground your speech in reality. But don't make your speech a running series of examples when what you really need is a combination of facts, statistics, and testimony to affirm that your examples are valid and representative of the situation you are addressing. These additional kinds of supporting materials help demonstrate the legitimacy of your examples.

Finally, use transitions to move smoothly from statement to example and from example to statement. Such phrases as "For instance..." and "As you can see..." work nicely.

Finding Factual and Hypothetical Examples

On the topic for your next speech, find a factual example or create a hypothetical example. Then use the checklist in Figure 8.3 to assess its value for your speech. What steps should you take to improve the example as supporting material? Note that this may include finding a new example and going through the process again.

SPEAKER'S NOTES

Using Examples

Let the following suggestions guide your use of examples in speeches.

1. Use examples to emphasize major points.
2. Use examples to attract and hold attention.
3. Use examples to clarify abstract ideas.
4. Use examples to personalize your points.
5. Name the people and places in your examples.
6. Use factual examples whenever possible.
7. Keep examples concise and to the point.

Narratives

8.4 Develop narratives to add action and interest to your speech.

narratives
Stories that illustrate the ideas or theme of a speech.

A **narrative** is a story that conveys an idea or establishes a mood. And we humans are storytellers![25] Since the dawn of time—probably before we started putting together abstract arguments and chains of thought—we've used stories to entertain each other, celebrate heroic deeds, teach and reaffirm values, and interpret the often chaotic ebb and flow of human experience. As filmmaker Jean-Luc Godard observes, "Sometimes reality is too complex. Stories give it form."[26]

Like examples, narratives provide concrete illustrations of abstract ideas and issues, engage listeners in the speech, and help to cross the barriers that often separate people. But more than examples, they describe a sequence of actions—beginning, middle, and end—that unfolds over time. The compelling drama of a well-constructed narrative engages the listeners in asking, *What happens next? How will this turn out?* We use narratives to remember the past, to illustrate our ideals, and to transmit our cultural traditions from one generation to another. Americans, for instance, have long been fond of "rags to riches" stories celebrating our commitment to hard work and individual responsibility—not to mention riches! These sorts of stories help to define who we are and what we value.

You can draw narratives from many sources—history, fairy tales, parables from the Bible or the Koran, literature, ancient Greek and Roman myths, or popular media. You might create a story specifically for the purpose of your speech. Or you might tell stories that re-create real-life experiences: The incredible story of how Dr. Seuss wrote *The Cat in the Hat* is central to Jess Bradshaw's "Pulling a Cat Out of a Hat," the speech that concludes Chapter 6. As discussed in Chapter 3, narratives documenting personal experiences are common in self-introductions, but they also can be useful in all forms of public speaking to establish identification and credibility. In that wonderful compendium of narratives called *Arabian Nights*, Tahir Shah posited that "Stories are a communal currency of humanity."[27]

Types of Narratives

embedded narratives
Stories inserted within speeches that illustrate the speaker's points.

The forms of narrative often found in speeches are *embedded, vicarious experience*, and *master narratives*. **Embedded narratives**, which occur at specific points within the overall structure of a speech, are the most commonly used form. Such narratives are often included as part of the introduction or conclusion of a speech. Your narrative might be solemn and serious or humorous and lighthearted, but it should make a point that supports your speech. Using pauses and transitions will signal listeners that you are beginning or ending the story.

Maya Angelou often used narrative to illustrate ideas in her speeches.

Student speaker Brandon Marshall concluded his inspirational speech by telling a story:

> You would be amazed at how many people I hear complain about the "obstacles" in their lives. So often, whenever we face obstacles, we just put our heads down and quit. The Native Americans used to say that when you prayed for strength, the gods would often send you some sort of tribulation, so that you could overcome it.
>
> I was driving with my friend the other day down Poplar Avenue when I saw a homeless man, fighting his way up the sidewalk in his second-hand wheelchair. I had seen him before, digging through trash at Overton Park,

> pulling out half-eaten bananas and old sandwiches. This particular day, he was stuck at a small section of concrete that had been worn away to rocky gravel. The whole way down the street until I couldn't see him anymore, I watched him push and push, only to move maybe a foot. Now that's an obstacle.
>
> So the next time you're in the midst of a struggle, don't focus on yourself. Look at the situation as an opportunity to become a stronger individual, and ask yourself what you can do for someone else.

Using this embedded narrative in his conclusion ensured that those in the audience had a thoughtful perspective to take with them.

Speakers who want to involve the audience often use a **vicarious experience narrative**. Such a narrative invites listeners into the action so that they imagine themselves participating in the story. A vicarious narrative will often begin with a statement such as "Come along with me..." or "Picture yourself...."

vicarious experience narrative
Speech strategy in which the speaker invites listeners to imagine themselves enacting a story.

Finally, sometimes a speech will develop a single **master narrative**. In this case, the use of narrative does not support your speech—it *is* your speech. Your entire speech is told in the form of a story. Master narratives are common with testimonials and with introductory speaking, as we saw illustrated in Sabrina Karic's "A Little Chocolate." This speech, which narrates Sabrina's experiences as a child in war-torn Bosnia, may be found at the end of Chapter 3. Review that chapter for its discussion of how to design your presentation around a master narrative.

master narrative
A speech structured around a story that reveals some important truth.

Using Narratives

Even though storytelling may come naturally to us as humans, there is an art to presenting stories orally. The first step is determining when you should use a narrative. Don't just toss in a story; select one that will illuminate your speech in a way that is directly relevant to your topic and purpose for speaking. Save narratives for special moments, and avoid the temptation of stringing together tales that lack a clear focus.

The most effective narratives are fresh and dramatic, offering a vividly described scene, clear character development and interaction, and a plot that moves toward some sort of climax or—in the case of humorous narratives—a punch line. They present characters and actions that seem believable, so that they can help listeners make sense of problems and situations.[28]

The same concepts for developing the prologue, plot, and epilogue in longer narratives that we described in Chapter 3 can be applied to embedded narratives. Note how vividly—even though briefly—Sandra Baltz described the setting in her prologue for the story opening her speech on scarce medical resources:

> On a cold and stormy night in 1841, the ship *William Brown* struck an iceberg in the North Atlantic.

She continued in the plot to provide a vivid account of what happened:

> Passengers and crew members frantically scrambled into the lifeboats. To make a bad disaster even worse, one of the lifeboats began to sink because it was overcrowded. Fourteen men were thrown overboard that horrible night. After the survivors were rescued, a crew member was tried for the murders of those thrown overboard.

In her epilogue, Sandra reflected on the meaning of this action, relating it to her speech:

> Fortunately, situations like this have been rare in history, but today we face a similar problem in the medical establishment: deciding who will live as we allocate scarce medical resources for transplants. Someday, your fate—or the fate of someone you love—could depend on how we resolve this dilemma.

Figure 8.4
Evaluating Narratives

___ Is the narrative relevant to my topic and purpose?
___ Does the narrative fairly represent the situation?
___ Will the story help listeners make sense of my points?
___ Will the narrative draw listeners into the action?
___ Is the narrative appropriate for this audience?
___ Will the story provide appropriate role models?
___ Will the story enhance identification among listeners, topic, and speaker?
___ Will the narrative make my speech more memorable?
___ Does the story set an appropriate mood for my message?
___ Is the narrative fresh and interesting?
___ Does the story flow well?
___ Is the narrative believable?
___ Is the narrative in good taste?

Assessing the Use of a Story in a Speech

Identify a story that you have heard in another class, or in a favorite movie or video. What was the story? Using the concepts of this section, assess its use. What point did it illustrate? Was it told effectively? Could it have been improved?

Bringing a story to life calls for dramatic language and skillful presentation. You can bring the characters and action alive through your words. Let listeners see what you're describing by using colorful language that evokes visual images. Use voice and dialect changes to signal that a character is speaking, and use dialogue. Paraphrasing can save time, but it robs a story of power. Let your characters speak for themselves!

Practice telling your story so that you get the wording and timing just right. Polish and memorize the punch lines of humorous tales: The story exists for them. Carefully planning and rehearsing your narrative will allow you to get caught up in telling the story, which in turn will help your audience experience your narrative with you. You can take advantage of the more intimate nature of storytelling by moving out from behind the lectern and closer to your listeners. You can pause to increase the impact of important moments in your story, especially when something you say evokes astonishment or laughter. A well-prepared, focused story provides dramatic, compelling support for your point. As a Hopi American Indian proverb holds, "Those who tell the stories rule the world."[29]

For more on the art of storytelling, see the online tutorial "Effective Storytelling," developed by Barry McWilliams. Figure 8.4 provides some guidelines to help you evaluate using narratives in speeches.

Finding Your Voice

Your Favorite Story

Think back to your childhood and recall your favorite story. Prepare a brief presentation (less than three minutes) of this story. Practice presenting it as if you were telling it to a group of first graders. Working in small groups, share your story with other group members. Listen to their stories. What storytelling techniques seemed most effective? What made some of the stories less effective?

SPEAKER'S NOTES

Using Narratives

Keep the following suggestions in mind as you plan narratives to use in a speech.

1. Use stories to involve the audience with your topic.
2. Make the characters in your stories come to life.
3. Use changes in voice and dialect for different characters.
4. Use dialogue rather than paraphrase.
5. Use colorful, vivid language.
6. Practice telling your stories so that they flow smoothly.

Selecting and Combining Supporting Materials

8.5 Select the most appropriate combination of supporting material to use in your speech.

Good journalists seek multiple sources of information before publishing a story. Effective, ethical speakers seek similarly broad and representative supporting materials—both to gain and demonstrate responsible knowledge and to appeal to a variety of audience preferences. In responsible speaking, the four forms of supporting materials—facts and statistics, testimony, examples, and narratives—rarely stand alone and apart from each other. In combination, they lend great strength to your speech. Facts and figures ground your message in reality, while expert testimony provides credibility to your claims. Lay testimony brings your message home to ordinary folks and popular opinion, while prestige testimony aligns you with respected authority figures. Examples reinforce facts and figures by focusing on the experiences of representative individuals and situations. Narratives tell stories that add drama and sometimes humor to your message. Examples and narratives can also engage the audience's feelings in support of your position.

How you combine these forms of supporting materials leaves room for individual artistry. Sandra Baltz began her speech on scarce medical resources by telling the dramatic story of the shipwrecked *William Brown* we quoted earlier in this chapter. Having aroused audience interest, she went on to introduce facts and figures that established the real dimensions of the problem she was discussing. She followed this by telling the moving story of an individual whose fate was very much affected by the medical resources problem. She concluded by offering a solution proposed by experts in the medical resources field. This particular combination of supporting materials strengthened her message and gave resonance to her voice.

Citing several credible sources helps establish the validity of your points. As Austin Wright built his case against the government's use of faulty databases in the War on Terror, he carefully supported each of his vital points with at least two credible sources of information. See his speech at the end of Chapter 15.

Different situations will call for different emphases as you combine supporting materials. Your choice of materials should reflect careful consideration of the challenges posed by your particular speech.

- If your topic is *controversial,* rely primarily on facts, statistics, factual examples, and expert testimony.
- If your ideas seem *abstract,* bring them to life with examples and narratives.
- If a point is highly *technical,* define key terms and supplement facts and statistics with expert testimony.
- If you need to *arouse emotions,* use lay testimony and vivid examples or narratives.

- If you need to *defuse emotions,* emphasize facts, statistics, and expert testimony.
- If your ideas are *novel or unfamiliar,* provide key facts and illustrative examples, define and explain basic terms and concepts, or provide analogies based on the experience of your listeners.

Above all, keep your audience at the center of your thinking, and ask yourself these critical questions: Which of these materials will make the biggest impression on my listeners? Which of these materials will listeners be most likely to remember? Which of these materials will listeners find most credible? Which materials will most likely make listeners want to act?

Whatever combination of supporting materials you select, make sure to cite your sources in ways that help your audience understand the value of your research. Be sure to give the original authors credit for their insights, and give yourself credit for being smart enough to see their value. Unlike this book, where we can provide citations in notes at the end, speakers need to incorporate the key information orally. Your listeners can't see your bibliography or your formal outline, so you want to make it easy for them to gauge the value of your sources. Plan ahead of time how you will provide your oral citations:

- "As the *Wall Street Journal* pointed out in an article from November 2017, . . ."
- "According to a Gallup poll conducted one month ago, . . ."
- "In an article published in the March 2017 issue of the *Journal of the American Medical Association,* Dr. Christopher R. Turner of the University of Wisconsin Medical Center stated . . ."
- "In the words of Yo-Yo Ma, famed cellist and winner of the J. Paul Getty Award, . . ."

Determining how to smoothly incorporate such information will boost your ethos by demonstrating the ethos of your sources.

Finally, the use of supporting materials can sometimes raise ethical questions, as we see in "Your Ethical Voice: The Ethical Use of Supporting Materials." Keep the guidelines discussed here in the forefront of your thinking.

Identifying Examples of Supporting Material

For your next speech, identify one example of each kind of supporting material. What function can each kind serve? Where do you need to gain additional information?

YOUR ETHICAL VOICE

The Ethical Use of Supporting Materials

To be certain you are using supporting materials in ethical ways, follow these guidelines.

1. Provide the date, source, and context of information cited in your speech.
2. Don't present an inference or opinion as though it were a fact.
3. Remember that statistics are open to differing interpretations.
4. Protect your listeners from biased information.
5. Don't quote out of context to misrepresent a person's position.
6. Be sure examples are representative of the reality you are addressing.
7. Don't present hypothetical examples as though they were factual.
8. Use narratives to illustrate key points, not to substitute for them.

Final Reflections: Developing a Well-Supported Voice

At the beginning of this chapter, we likened the structure of a well-supported speech to that of the Golden Gate Bridge. That beloved bridge joins Marin County with San Francisco. It is as impressive now as it was when it opened eighty years ago. But the great speeches of our time may attempt even more spectacular feats as they strive to connect distant cultures and audiences that may be deeply suspicious of each other. At the rare moments when they are successful, these speeches stand at the pinnacle of human achievement.

Your challenge in constructing a message to deliver to your listeners may seem far less daunting, but nevertheless it is considerable. Like those who build the great bridges that bear many times their own weight, you want to make, choose, and use supporting materials in the right way. Combine facts and statistics, testimony, examples, and narratives to build a message that is considerably stronger than the sum of its parts. And if you've ever watched somebody present an obviously suspect piece of information to support an important or disputed claim, you also know that, like a bridge, a speech is only as strong as its weakest support.

This quality of strength is certainly one you want associated with the voice you are discovering. Think of other desirable qualities you might like to add to that emerging voice. Would "credible," "colorful," "appealing," "moving," and "interesting" be among them? You can create all of these impressions by selecting and using effective supporting materials. Develop these materials, and you can add these qualities to your voice.

Study Questions

CONTENT MASTERY

1 How do facts and statistics strengthen your speech?

2 How do expert, lay, and prestige testimony differ?

3 What special advantages can examples bring to your speech?

4 How can narratives make a speech more effective?

5 How can you determine which kinds of supporting material to use in your speech?

6 Why should you use a combination of supporting materials?

7 Why is it important to cite your sources orally in your presentation?

8 What ethical standards should guide your selection and use of supporting materials?

CRITICAL EXPLORATIONS

1. Access *Vital Speeches of the Day* online, and open the free sample issue. Look for a speech that contains statistical information. Were the statistics convincing? Were sources clearly identified? Did the speaker make the information come alive? What advice would you give the speaker on how to make more effective use of statistics?
2. Evaluate the use of testimony in two of the student speeches in Appendix B. Do the speakers use enough testimony? What types are used? Are they appropriate to the purpose? Do the speakers introduce the qualifications of their sources?
3. Share your reactions to a current commercial based on prestige or celebrity testimony. How relevant is the celebrity to the product being sold? How effective is the ad? What drawbacks might there be to this type of advertising?
4. Develop an example or a narrative to illustrate one of the following abstract concepts:

   love
   compassion
   dedication
   courage
   justice

   How could this narrative or example help you in a speech?
5. Find a commercial that tells a story in order to sell a product. What narrative qualities make these ads effective or ineffective?
6. Which types of supporting materials in what combinations might help you build a case for or against the following claims?
   a. We should increase spending on preschool education.
   b. We should cut taxes paid by small business owners.
   c. Security measures on campus are inadequate.
   d. We should emphasize restoring the environment over creating jobs and providing health care.
   e. The use of drones in modern warfare is permissible.

   Explain and defend your choices.

CHAPTER 9

Structuring and Outlining Your Speech

LEARNING OBJECTIVES

This chapter will help you:

9.1 Develop speeches that are simple, well ordered, and balanced.

9.2 Understand the design options as you arrange the main points of your speech.

9.3 Prepare introductions and conclusions.

9.4 Complete a formal outline.

OUTLINE

"Every discourse ought to be a living creature; having a body of its own and head and feet; there should be a middle, beginning, and end, adapted to one another and to the whole."

—PLATO

Overheard at the Student Union:

"I've got to take Intro Biology this semester. I can take Forsyth or Bennett. Have you had either of them?"

"Yes, both. Forsyth is a really funny guy. Keeps you laughing."

"Sounds like my kind of guy."

"Well, there is one small problem: Dude is totally disorganized. Jumps all around in his lectures. Hard to take notes."

"Hmmm. How about Bennett?"

"Not so funny. But she knows her stuff. She's easy to follow and makes it easy to learn."

"Okay. I think I know my choice."

Any real doubt who this student selected? Everyone likes to be entertained, but most people prefer well-organized speakers, especially when the message is important. Indeed, studies suggest that students learn more from teachers who are well focused and that they are annoyed by instructors who ramble and jump from one idea to another.[1]

Well-organized speeches are easier to follow, understand, and remember.[2] Being well organized will enhance audience perceptions of your competence; what's more, it will help you be more confident.[3] When you invest time to find a good topic, refine and research it, and gather vital information about it, you want to focus all these discoveries in a well-structured speech that listeners will find valuable and easy to grasp, and that you will find easy to remember. Clearly, developing a well-organized speech is an important phase in the process of finding your voice.

Research confirms that students learn how to structure messages more effectively in public speaking classes, and that these skills also transfer to improved writing.[4] Developing organizational skills is also important to finding your voice as an ethical speaker because ethical speaking encourages critical thinking and responsible listening. In this chapter, we discuss some basic principles of a well-structured speech. We then take you step by step through the process of constructing speeches from generating and arranging speech materials to polishing your formal outline.

Principles of a Well-Structured Speech

9.1 Develop speeches that are simple, well ordered, and balanced.

Reading a book is like reading a map: If you lose your place, you can back up and figure out how to find the route again. Listening to a speech is like embarking on a journey when you aren't quite sure where you're going: If you lose your place, you can't rewind the speaker to figure out where you are; you just have to hang on for the ride and hope for the best—and that is *not* a comfortable feeling.

So as you design your speech, think of it as taking your audience on an *oral journey*, one for which they cannot look at the map. You want a simple structure, explicit organization, clear connections, and sufficient repetition so your listeners will benefit from the ride. A well-planned oral journey will create better reception, better comprehension, and better retention of your message. Moreover, it will be easier for *you* to keep in mind and to deliver clearly and confidently. The principles of a well-structured speech reflect the importance of *simplicity*, *order*, and *balance*. Keep these fundamental concepts in mind as you build your presentation.

Simplicity

A simple speech is easier for speakers to present effectively, and for listeners to grasp and remember. You achieve **simplicity** in your speeches when you *limit the number of main ideas*, use *wording that is concise and direct*, and *repeat your key points* for emphasis.

simplicity
Suggests that a speech has a limited number of main points and that they are short and direct.

Limit the Number of Main Points. As a general rule, the fewer the main points in a speech, the better. You want your listeners to be able to follow your presentation, and they can only process so much in a short period. In addition, the supporting ideas and materials you need to develop each point take time. As a consequence, short speeches—whether in the classroom, the workplace, or a community group—should usually develop no more than three main points. Don't spread yourself too thin.

All this means that you want to go through a disciplined process of critical thinking: What are your most important points? What are your key supporting ideas and materials for those points? In an oral presentation, you want to emphasize focus and depth over breadth of coverage. For instance, if you were researching and developing a speech in favor of welfare reform, you might initially come up with several ideas and impressions:

- We have too many welfare programs.
- Most of our programs are underfunded.
- Some programs spend money wastefully.
- Some programs duplicate coverage.
- People who genuinely need assistance are sometimes denied.
- Recipients have little input as to what is needed.
- Traditional welfare programs can foster a culture of dependence.

Each of these points may be important. However, when presented in such random fashion they will likely confuse and overwhelm your listeners—and perhaps you as well. As you prioritize your points and supporting materials, you might begin to hammer out the following simpler and more coherent train of thought:

Specific purpose: To persuade the audience that our current approach to welfare needs to be revised.

Thesis statement: Our approach to welfare doesn't work.

First main point: I. It doesn't work because it's inadequate.
Subpoints:
A. Existing programs are not sufficiently funded.
B. People who genuinely need help are left out.

Second main point: II. It doesn't work because it's inefficient.
Subpoints:
A. There are too many duplicate programs.
B. There is too much wasted money.

Third main point: III. It doesn't work because it's insensitive.
Subpoints:
A. It creates dependence that stifles initiative.
B. It robs recipients of self-respect.
C. Recipients have little input.

This simpler structure makes the message easier to follow—both for you and for your audience. The thesis statement offers an overview of the message. Each main point elaborates and develops the thesis statement. The subpoints organize and focus the secondary ideas so that they support the main points. Important but overlapping ideas can be combined, while interesting but irrelevant ideas and materials can be discarded. In the process of simplifying your ideas and information, you have already begun developing a structurally coherent answer to the question of why approaches to welfare are not working.

A well-organized speech, including well-planned and designed presentation aids, is easy to follow.

Phrase Main Points Clearly. Express your main points as simple, direct statements. You might initially phrase your main point as "Our approach to welfare does not work because it is inadequate both in terms of funding and not getting the right aid to the right people." As you rework the point, you come up with a clearer version:

Our approach to welfare does not work because it is inadequate.

A. Existing programs are not sufficiently funded.
B. People who genuinely need help are left out.

By separating and streamlining the concepts, you make them easier to follow. Straightforward statements also facilitate the third guideline for simplicity: repetition.

Repeat Key Points for Emphasis. Clearly stated ideas can more easily be repeated, which reinforces your central thesis. In the revised example above, the central message of "Our approach to welfare doesn't work" is reinforced by repeating the point "It doesn't work because..." while introducing each of the system's three main shortcomings. This method of **parallel construction**, repeating much of the wording of main points while emphasizing their different points of focus, emphasizes that these are the main points. To the eye, this repetition may look clumsy and boring, but to the ear, it makes them easy to follow and remember—especially as you develop the subpoints within each main point.

parallel construction
Using the same or similar word patterns to articulate and contrast your main ideas.

Repetition is built into the standard format of well-organized speeches. Speakers preview their messages in the introduction, repeat these messages as they develop them in the body, and repeat these messages again as they review them in the conclusions of their speeches.

Order

order
A consistent pattern used to develop a speech.

Order in a speech requires a clear, consistent pattern of development from beginning to end. A well-ordered speech follows a clear structure on two levels. First, it opens by introducing the message and orienting the audience, continues by developing the main ideas in the body of the speech, and ends by summarizing and reflecting on the meaning of what has been said. As the old saw goes, "Tell them what you're going to tell them, then tell them, then tell them what you've told them." Second, the main points within the body of the speech adhere to a clear design scheme that develops the thesis statement clearly. That design might be, for example, categorical, problem-solution, or narrative, as discussed later in this chapter.

It may be tempting to begin with the introduction—after all, that's where your speech will start, right?—but resist that temptation. To build an orderly speech, you should design and construct the *body* of your speech first because that is where you will present, illustrate, and substantiate your message. Once you have structured the body, you can prepare an introduction and a conclusion custom-tailored for your message.

Balance

balance
Suggests that the introduction, body, and conclusion receive appropriate development.

Balance means the major parts of your speech—introduction, body, and conclusion—should receive appropriate development. For most speaking occasions, and certainly for classroom speeches, you will be given specific time requirements, which you

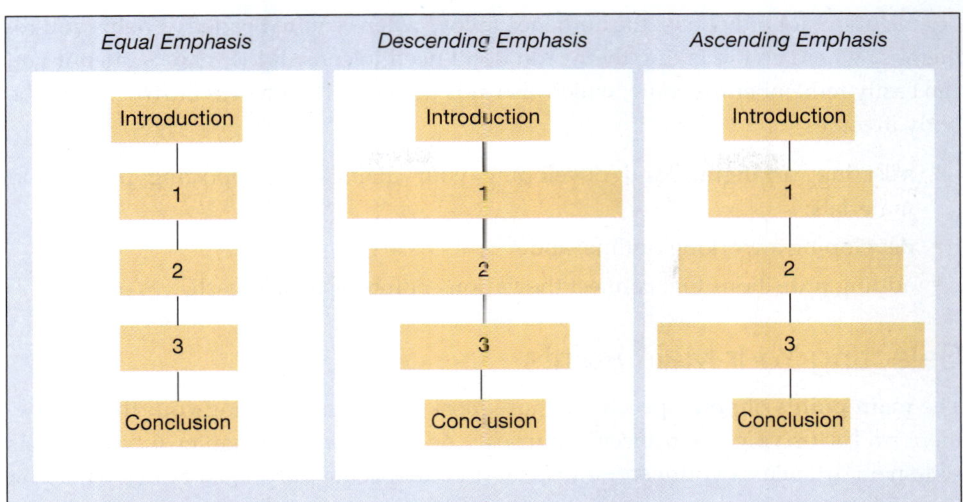

Figure 9.1
Balanced Speech Designs

should keep in mind as you plan your message. You really don't want to finish your first main point only to find out you have sixty seconds left to finish two other main points and the conclusion. The following suggestions can help you plan a balanced presentation:

1. *The body should be the longest part of your speech.* This is where you develop your main ideas in full. The introduction and conclusion serve as a frame for the body of your speech, so you don't want this frame to overpower what it should showcase. Again, because this is the most important part of your speech, we suggest you construct the body before developing your introduction and conclusion.
2. *Balance the development of each main point in your speech.* If your main points seem equally important, strive to give each point *equal emphasis.* This strategy would seem appropriate for the message outlined earlier on the three *Is* of welfare—inadequate, insufficient, insensitive—in which each point seems to merit equal attention. If your points differ in importance, you might start with the most important point, spending the most time on it, and then present the other points with a *descending emphasis,* according to their importance. For example, if you are presenting a problem-solution speech in favor of health care reform before an audience of listeners who do not believe we need health care reform, you should probably spend most of your time establishing the existence of the problem and then just touch on prospective solutions. However, to the extent your audience already agrees that we need health care reform, you might use an *ascending emphasis* that touches briefly on the problem and focuses primarily on prospective solutions and how audience members might become actively involved in promoting them.
3. *Especially with short presentations, your introduction and conclusion should be brief and approximately equal in length.* Introductions often run slightly longer, but the combined length of both should be less than the body of your speech.

Applying Simplicity, Order, and Balance

Find an advertisement, and examine the extent to which it uses simplicity, order, and balance. Could the application of these principles improve the message's reception?

Structuring the Body of Your Speech

9.2 Understand the design options as you arrange the main points of your speech.

The **body** of your speech contains your main points and the materials to support them. As you take your listeners on your oral journey, you don't want them to feel like you're a drunken cab driver, dashing down streets and careening around corners, or a lackadaisical navigator who's taking them on some random scenic excursion. A clear

body
The section of a speech that contains your main ideas and the materials that support them.

organization not only helps the audience follow where you're headed, it helps you remember where you're taking them: You don't need to consult the map as often if you can easily remember the route, which also aids delivery. The process of structuring the body involves

- selecting, arranging, and developing your main and supporting points and materials;
- developing a working outline; and
- adding transitions that connect the various points of your speech.

Selecting Your Main Points

main points
The most important ideas developed in support of the thesis statement.

The **main points** of your speech are those most vital to establishing your thesis statement and satisfying your specific purpose. As we noted in Chapter 6, your thesis statement articulates your central idea, and your specific purpose specifies what you want your listeners to understand, agree with, do, or appreciate as a result of your speech. Your main points develop your thesis statement in a way that meets your specific purpose.

Sometimes, the main points will emerge clearly from your topic and purpose for speaking. If your thesis statement is "Throwing pottery is an enjoyable and rewarding pursuit," and your specific purpose is to inform your audience how to throw pottery, then the main points that seem logical would be

1. preparing the clay;
2. fashioning the pot; and
3. completing the piece.

At other times, your main ideas will emerge and evolve as you conduct your research. For instance, if you are researching a speech on the mistreatment of women in Afghanistan under the Taliban, you will quickly discover a broad range of possible considerations, more than you could ever hope to cover in a single speech. But from this mass of information you might identify three areas of focus:

1. Women are denied access to education, health care, and the right to work.
2. Women are routinely subject to physical and psychological violence.
3. Women who speak out or assert themselves face frightening recriminations.

You may decide to build your main points from these areas of emphasis: Perhaps you want to focus on the three restraints articulated in the first area or to combine the second and third into your speech. Each main point should articulate a single idea, following the principle of simplicity. Using the visual technique of mind mapping that we discussed in Chapter 6 may help you see priorities and connections more easily.

Arranging Your Main Points

Once you have chosen your main points, your next decision is determining how to arrange them. Making that decision depends on your material, your purpose, and your audience. Keep in mind that your audience will more easily follow you on your oral journey if you offer a clear map they can follow.

Note that, while some topics practically beg for a certain organizational pattern—for example, the speech above on throwing pottery lends itself to a sequential pattern—other topics are amenable to several different patterns. No single design is *inherently* good, bad, boring, or exciting; it depends on how you use it. If you find yourself struggling to make your main points fit one particular pattern, try experimenting with another couple of options. In the process of exploring the alternatives, you may discover a clearer way to focus your material, a better route for taking your audience to the desired destination.

There are many patterns available to you: *categorical, comparative, spatial, sequential, chronological, problem-solution, refutative,* and *narrative*. All of these patterns reflect the different ways we think about subjects as well as what we discover about them during research. We introduce them here and develop them in later chapters in connection with the types of speeches that typically use them. We provide a more detailed discussion of categorical, comparative, spatial, sequential, chronological, and causation designs in our chapter on informative speaking. We develop problem-solution and refutative designs in further detail in our chapter on persuasive speaking. In our chapters on speeches for special occasions, we further consider the narrative design.

Categorical. The **categorical design**, sometimes called the topical design, arranges the main ideas of a speech so that they reflect major points of emphasis uncovered during research. You might explore the topic of synesthesia, a neurological condition in which senses overlap. Upon investigation, you discover that the three types that most intrigue you are when letters and numbers evoke particular colors, when sounds evoke tactile sensations, and when sounds evoke certain colors. Your three main points then express these three kinds of synesthesia.

categorical design
Arranges the main ideas of a speech so that they reflect major topics or points of emphasis.

Specific Purpose: To inform listeners about three key forms of synesthesia

Thesis Statement: Synesthesia entails the involuntary linkage of different senses.

Main Points:

I. With grapheme-color synesthesia, people see letters and numbers in various colors.
II. With auditory-tactile synesthesia, people feel tactile sensations when they hear particular sounds.
III. With chromesthesia, people hear sounds that evoke specific colors.

Each component constitutes a main point about a form of synesthesia, and each one holds equal importance.

Comparative. A **comparative design** explores the similarities and differences among elements. For example, a speaker might develop a speech comparing three major features between the cities of New York and London, such as emphasizing them as centers of arts and entertainment, business, and politics. This kind of comparison would be *literal,* based on comparing the same kinds of elements.

comparative design
Explores the similarities and differences among elements.

Another kind of comparative design is *figurative,* which works by relating a subject to a different realm of experience or reality. In her informative speech on nutrition, Thressia Taylor made a potentially boring subject come to life by comparing it to taking care of a car.

Specific Purpose: To inform listeners of the importance of good nutrition

Thesis statement: Feed your body the same way you would care for a classic car.

Main Points:

I. Proteins provide the octane in your gasoline.
II. Carbohydrates give you energy and fast acceleration.
III. Good fats keep you well lubricated and running smoothly.

Good comparative designs spark interest and often appreciation for the speaker's creativity. By relating the unknown to the known, they can make subjects easier to understand.

spatial design
Arranges the main points of a speech as they occur in actual space, creating an oral map.

Spatial. A **spatial design** arranges the main points of a subject as they occur in actual space, often taking listeners on an imaginary tour. For example, if you are asked to address a group of incoming students on the resources available to them in the library, you might use a floor plan as a presentation aid as you point out where different departments are located. An effective spatial design provides your listeners with a verbal map. You want to select points of emphasis carefully to help your listeners retain this map so that you don't overburden them with excessive detail.

In contrast, if you were to use a categorical design in such a speech, you might ask this question: "Where in the library might you find major resources for your speeches?" You might then focus on current periodicals, book holdings, and government documents as the main points for developing your speech. Either design offers advantages and disadvantages; your choice between them would again be determined by your purpose and the needs of your audience.

sequential design
Explains the steps of a process in the order in which they should be taken.

Sequential. A **sequential design** explains the steps of a process in the order in which they should be taken. Most demonstration or "how to" speeches use a sequential design scheme. For instance, if you were to present our sample speech above on how to throw a pot, you would use a sequential design. Speeches following the sequential design often make use of presentation aids, such as models or flow charts, to demonstrate the steps of a process.

chronological design
Explains the events or historical developments in the order in which they occurred.

Chronological. A **chronological design** explains events or historical developments in the order in which they occurred. Chronological designs often survey the pattern of events that led up to a present-day situation. D'Angelo Crawford described such a pattern as he explored the history of the T-shirt.

Specific purpose: To inform listeners how the T-shirt has become an important item of clothing

Thesis statement: The evolution of the T-shirt demonstrates changing uses of clothing.

Main Points:
I. T-shirts were first designed for sailors to spare sensitive people the sight of hairy armpits.
II. T-shirts were used as outerwear in the tropics during World War II.
III. T-shirts now often display pictures or personal or political messages.

Chronological presentations are effective when speakers keep their presentation of events simple, in the order in which they occurred, and related to the specific purpose of the speech.

causation design
Considers the origins or consequences of a situation or event.

Causation. A **causation design** traces the origins or consequences of a situation or event, proceeding from cause to effect or from effect to cause. Causation designs are often used to explain current developments and forecast future events. Alexandra McArthur used a causation design to show how tourism can have a negative impact on developing nations.

Specific Purpose: To persuade listeners that tourism can harm developing nations.

Thesis Statement: Tourism can cause economic, sociological, and political problems for developing nations.

Main Points:
I. Tourism can encourage the unequal distribution of wealth and the loss of capital to foreign investors.
II. Native workers resent exploitation and abuse.
III. Tourism reinforces class inequities and dislike of foreign nations.

The causation design can provide the framework for both informative and persuasive speeches.

Problem-Solution. The **problem-solution design** focuses attention on a problem and then provides an answer to it. Because life constantly confronts us with difficulties, the problem-solution pattern is one of the most frequently used speech designs, especially in persuasive speeches. In an effective problem-solution speech, you first convince listeners that they have a problem that they must deal with. Then you show the audience that you have a solution that makes sense, that is practical and affordable, and that will improve their lives.

problem-solution design
Focuses attention on a problem and offers a solution for it.

The **motivated sequence** offers an elaborated version of the problem-solution pattern. This popular design, first developed years ago by Professor Alan Monroe, follows five steps: (1) drawing *attention* to a situation, (2) demonstrating a *need* to change it, (3) explaining how a plan might *satisfy* this problem, (4) *visualizing* the results of following or not following the speaker's advice, and (5) issuing a call for *action*.[5] Several generations of student speakers—not to mention infomercials—have used the motivated sequence variation to great advantage.

motivated sequence
Expanded version of the problem-solution design that emphasizes the steps of attention, need, satisfaction, visualization, and action.

Refutative. The **refutative design** proceeds by defending a disputed thesis and confronting opposing views with reasoning and evidence. Found in debates over public policy, this pattern of thought proceeds by identifying and engaging key opposing arguments and concerns. Nick McDonald demonstrated this pattern as he defended birth control education programs in public education.

refutative design
A persuasive design in which the speaker engages opposing views.

Specific purpose: To persuade my audience that birth control education programs belong in public schools.

Thesis Statement: We should support comprehensive sex education in our public schools.

Main Points:

I. Opponents of teaching sex education in our schools argue that they promote sexual promiscuity.
II. However, credible research documents a striking reduction in teen pregnancies in schools that offer such education.
III. Therefore, birth control education programs offer hope for one of our largest social problems: children having children.

In Chapter 14, we elaborate a five-part refutative process for speeches that focus exclusively on engaging and defending disputed propositions. Those who follow this design should be careful not to let their refutations degenerate into personal attacks. Respect your opponents by refuting them with solid evidence and reasoning.

Narrative. The speech that follows a **narrative design** tells a story. In contrast to designs that follow a linear pattern of development, a narrative design follows a dramatic pattern that proceeds from *prologue* to *plot* to *epilogue*, as we discuss in Chapters 3 and 16. The prologue introduces the story by setting the scene for action. It foreshadows the meaning of the speech and introduces the main characters. The plot is the body of the narrative, in which the story unfolds through a scene or series of scenes that build to a climax. The epilogue reflects on the meaning of the story by drawing a lesson from it that audience members can apply. Narratives help illustrate concepts and add human interest to a speech.

narrative design
Speech structure that develops a story from beginning to end through a prologue, plot, and epilogue.

The preceding designs are often used in combination. For example, our earlier discussion of three forms of synesthesia suggests a categorical design. But such a speech might also incorporate a cause-effect pattern to explain how the condition originates or combine with a comparative design to reveal how synesthetes and nonsynesthetes experience the world. Again, we discuss these designs in more detail as they become particularly relevant to informative, persuasive, and ceremonial speaking, as indicated in Figure 9.2.

Figure 9.2
Design Options

Categorical	Arranges points by their natural or customary divisions.
Comparative	Compares different ideas to reveal their similarities and differences.
Spatial	Arranges points as they occur in physical space, taking listeners on an imaginary tour.
Sequential	Arranges points in order of their occurrence, as in the steps of a process.
Chronological	Arranges points in terms of their historical development over time.
Causation	Presents the causes and/or effects of a problem.
Problem-Solution	Discusses a problem, then offers a solution.
Refutative	Strives to persuade listeners by answering opposing arguments.
Narrative	Follows the form of a story with a prologue, plot, and epilogue.

Developing Your Main Points

subpoints
The major divisions of a speech's main points.

sub-subpoints
The major divisions of a speech's subpoints.

In the process of identifying your main points, you will find materials to constitute the subpoints and sub-subpoints that will support them. Main points are general statements, while **subpoints** supply more specific materials that flesh them out, make them credible, and bring them to life. In complex units of thought, **sub-subpoints** perform the same kind of service for subpoints. In effect, subpoints and sub-subpoints answer basic questions any critical listener might ask, such as: How do I know this is true? What does it mean? Why should I care?

To illustrate these thoughts, imagine you are developing one of the earlier main points concerning feeding your body the way you would care for a classic car. To support the general claim that proteins provide the octane in your gasoline, you could define what proteins are, cite a medical center's report on the value of protein, and explain the kinds of foods that provide protein. Even more specific facts, examples, and testimony from physicians and nutritionists could serve as sub-subpoints.

In short, strengthening both main points and subpoints means using supporting materials. As we discussed in Chapter 8, *facts*, *figures*, and *expert testimony* help to support ideas that are disputed, complicated, or new to your audience. *Examples* and *narratives* engage listeners by showing how your ideas apply to specific situations.

The different forms of supporting information are almost always more effective when used in combination. An ideal model of support includes the most relevant facts and statistics, the most authoritative testimony, and at least one story or example that clarifies your ideas and brings them to life. Again, if you were supporting the point about the importance of protein, you might look for credible statistics and expert testimony to document why it is significant, and for real-life examples and narratives to put a human face on the scientific data. Figure 9.3 provides an ideal format for supporting a point.

Developing a Working Outline

We can imagine that the word "outline" elicits at least a few eye-rolls. Aren't outlines those tedious, boring tasks that you do just to satisfy instructors? Well—not if you understand how outlines can help you develop a clear, coherent speech in a way that will build your confidence. Outlining is a process that allows you to see the structure and interrelation of your ideas and materials as you develop them. With outlining, you can untangle your thoughts and information, getting them down in black and white where you can shape them into a coherent pattern.

Figure 9.3
Format for Supporting a Point

Statement: ______________________________
____

(Transition)

1. Factual information or statistics that support statement:

____

____

(Transition)

2. Testimony that affirms statement:

____

____

(Transition)

3. Example or narrative that illustrates statement:

____

(Transition)

Restatement: ______________________________
____

The first step is to develop a rough or **working outline**—a *tentative* plan illustrating the pattern of your main and supporting points and how they fit together. A working outline serves as a sketch or a rough draft so you can see relationships, identify common threads, and recognize and rectify gaps. Rather than a hoop to jump through, an outline provides assurance that you have clear main points that are well supported and coherently arranged.

working outline
A tentative plan showing the pattern of a speech's major parts, their relative importance, and the way they fit together.

The two most basic and interrelated principles of outlining are *coordination* and *subordination*. The principle of **coordination** suggests that all statements at a given level of your outline should be of similar importance; thus, the three main points concerning the mistreatment of women under the Taliban appear to share the same approximate significance. The principle of **subordination** requires that supporting ideas and materials descend in importance from the general to the specific as the outline moves from main points to subpoints to sub-subpoints. Use *indentation* to show in your outline that subpoints are subordinate to main points, and indent again to show the subordinate status of sub-subpoints. Note how this process of indentation is indicated in Figure 9.4, Format for a Working Outline.

coordination
Placing statements equal in importance on the same level in an outline.

subordination
Arranging materials in an outline in an order of descending importance from the general to the specific—from main points to subpoints to sub-subpoints, and so on.

A working outline of our main points describing the various forms of violence against women under the Taliban might take the following form:

Main point: Women are subject to various forms of violence under the Taliban.

Subpoint A: Women subject to high rates of domestic abuse

Sub-subpoint 1: Wives and daughters regarded as property of husbands and fathers

Sub-subpoint 2: Taliban ignores reports of domestic abuse

Subpoint B: High rates of sexual assault

Sub-subpoint 1: Young girls forced into arranged marriages—older men

Sub-subpoint 2: Gang and honor rapes by rival factions

Sub-subpoint 3: Victims reporting assaults branded social outcasts

Subpoint C:	Resisting women face frightening recriminations
Sub-subpoint 1:	Arbitrary humiliation and flogging by Taliban officials
Sub-subpoint 2:	Macabre forms of public punishment

As you develop a working outline of the body of your presentation, consider these key questions:

- Have you adequately supported your thesis statement?
- Have you satisfied your purpose for speaking?
- Are your main ideas arranged using a sensible design scheme?
- Is the overall structure of your body balanced and appropriately developed?

Be honest with yourself. It's better to be frustrated during the process of developing your speech when you have the opportunity to revise than to be regretful later. Outlining is a corrective as well as creative process, and you may go through several drafts as you polish and develop your speeches. Each time, you will have a clearer idea of what you want to say and how you want to say it, and you will be that much closer to finding your voice.

Adding Transitions

transitions
Connecting elements that cue listeners that you are finished making one point and are moving on to the next.

Once you have identified, developed, and outlined your main ideas, you can plan transitions. **Transitions** are verbal and nonverbal cues that let your audience know you are finished making one point and are moving on to the next. Transitions serve as *oral*

Figure 9.4
Format for a Working Outline

Topic: ______
Specific purpose: ______

INTRODUCTION

Attention material: ______
Thesis statement: ______
Preview: ______

(**Transition** to body of speech)

BODY

First main point: ______
  Subpoint: ______
    Sub-subpoint: ______
    Sub-subpoint: ______
  Subpoint: ______

(**Transition** to second main point)

Second main point: ______
  Subpoint: ______
  Subpoint: ______
    Sub-subpoint: ______
    Sub-subpoint: ______

(**Transition** to third main point)

Third main point: ______
  Subpoint: ______
  Subpoint: ______

(**Transition** to conclusion)

CONCLUSION

Summary statement: ______
Concluding remarks: ______

signposts that assure the audience you know where you are leading them on this oral journey; they function as reminders (e.g., the helpful sign that assures you are still going south on I-77!); turn signals (we're taking a left turn here because that keeps us headed toward our destination); and explanations (we've reached an intersection; what is its significance?). Effectively planned transitions connect the main points of the body of your speech and tie the body to the introduction and conclusion. They help your audience follow the overall structure and direction of your message.

For example, after you voice your thesis statement, you might say something of this sort: "How do we know this is true? Let's consider the evidence." This transition would move you effectively into the body of your speech.

After developing your first main point, you might say: "So now we see that the latest facts support what I'm saying. What about the experts? How do they feel about this situation?" This transition would help listeners interpret the significance of what you have just established. The two questions would then move you on to your next point.

When you complete that demonstration, you might say: "So both the facts and the experts support what I'm saying. But how does that affect people's lives? How could it affect you?" This transition would help listeners remember what you have demonstrated. Again, the questions would lead you toward your next point, involving stories and examples.

News accounts of mistreatment of Afghan women prompted a well-constructed speech.

You might then move into your conclusion: "So the facts favor my position. The experts agree. And the impact on your life and the lives of those you care about could be vital. So what should you do about it?" Now you would be ready in this imagined persuasive speech to point listeners toward the action you want them to take.

Some transitions are quite subtle. A brief pause coupled with a change in vocal inflection can effectively cue your audience that you are moving on to the next point or part of your speech. Simple terms and short phrases such as "for my next point" can also be effective. Finally, preview and summary statements can serve as effective transitions between the parts of a speech; previews lead into the body and summaries lead into the concluding remarks. With longer or more complicated presentations, an **internal summary** within the body of a speech can help to remind your listeners of points you have already covered before moving on. Internal summaries are especially useful in problem-solution speeches when transitioning from your discussion of a problem to offering prospective solutions or a course of action. Keep these brief and to the point so that they highlight only major ideas, as in this example from a speech supporting caps on greenhouse gas emissions:

internal summary
A transition that reminds listeners of major points already presented in a speech before proceeding to new ideas.

> So now we know that global warming is real and getting worse. We know it exacts a frightening economic and environmental toll. And we know that human pollution and greenhouse gas emissions are a major contributing cause of climate change. The only question is, What are we going to do about it? Experts agree that the following measures could help make a real difference.

Whatever techniques you use, plan your transitions carefully. Good transitions will make your speeches easier to present as well as follow and can be helpful for coping with communication apprehension. Otherwise, you may ramble from point to point through awkward pauses and vocal fillers such as "uh" and "you know." In Figure 9.5, we offer a comprehensive list of common short transitions for use in your speeches.

Developing a Working Outline

Develop a working outline for your next speech. How does it help you identify an appropriate design? What gaps do you find in your supporting materials and your reasoning? How does this help you strengthen your presentation?

Figure 9.5
Common Transitions

To Indicate	Use
Time Changes	until, now, since, previously, later, earlier, in the past, in the future, meanwhile, five years ago, just last month, tomorrow, following, before, at present, eventually
Additions	moreover, in addition, furthermore, besides
Comparison	compared with, both are, likewise, in comparison, similarly, of equal importance, another type of, like, alike, just as
Contrast	but, yet, however, on the other hand, conversely, still, otherwise, in contrast, unfortunately, despite, rather than, on the contrary
Cause-Effect	therefore, consequently, thus, accordingly, so, as a result, hence, since, because of, due to, for this reason
Numerical Order	first, second, third, in the first place, to begin with, initially, next, eventually, finally
Spatial Relations	to the north, alongside, to the left, above, moving eastward, in front of, in back of, behind, next to, below, nearby, in the distance
Explanation	to illustrate, for example, for instance, case in point, in other words, to simplify, to clarify
Importance	most important, above all, keep this in mind, remember, listen carefully, take note of, indeed
The End of the Speech	in short, finally, in conclusion, to summarize

Finding Your Voice

Structuring Your Speech

Ask your instructor to help you set up a self-help group of three to five classmates to work on the next speech assignment. Share working outlines with each other, explaining what the strategy is behind your proposed structure and how your outline satisfies the principles of coordination and subordination. Demonstrate that you have adequate supporting material for each main point. Revise your working outline in light of the suggestions you receive.

Introducing and Concluding Your Speech

9.3 Prepare introductions and conclusions.

Once you have structured the body of your speech, the next step is to prepare an introduction and a conclusion. Listeners tend to be most affected by what they hear at the beginning and end of a speech. Introductions and conclusions set the tone of the entire message and often contain its richest language and clearest statement of your main ideas and purpose. In this section, we identify some basic functions and offer advice for effectively introducing and concluding your speeches.

Pope Francis builds an ongoing relationship with listeners by appealing to shared interests and values.

Introducing Your Speech

Your **introduction** should get the audience interested in taking that oral journey with you by capturing their attention, establishing your ethos as a credible speaker, and previewing your message so it is easier for your listeners to follow.

introduction
That part of your speech that should capture listeners' attention establish your ethos, and preview your message.

Capturing Attention. All too often, speakers open their presentations with something like "Good morning, my speech is on . . . ," which actually has the effect of turning listeners off. You want the opening lines of a speech to arouse attention and curiosity, convincing listeners that they have something to gain from following you on this oral journey. Among the most commonly used strategies for capturing attention are *acknowledging the audience, location, or occasion; invoking shared interests* and *values; urging audience participation; using appropriate humor; opening with a narrative; opening with a quotation;* and *startling the audience.*

Acknowledging the audience, location, or occasion. In speeches given outside the classroom, speakers often begin with a few remarks acknowledging the audience, the location, or the purpose or meaning of the occasion. Such references are usually brief and should convey a touch of eloquence. Consider the following words from the introduction of a speech by President John F. Kennedy at a White House dinner honoring Nobel Prize winners:

> I think this is the most extraordinary collection of talent, of human knowledge, that has ever been gathered together at the White House, with the possible exception of when Thomas Jefferson dined alone.[6]

Invoking shared interests and values. Speakers who seem to differ from listeners in obvious ways will often begin their speeches by appealing to shared interests and values. They create a platform of identification on which they can build the remainder of their speech. An example of this kind of opening occurred when Pope Francis addressed the Congress of the United States in 2015, stressing their common bonds of sharing the American continent:

> I am most grateful for your invitation to address this Joint Session of Congress in "the land of the free and the home of the brave." I would like to think that the reason for this is that I too am a son of this great continent, from which we have all received so much and toward which we share a common responsibility.[7]

He also previewed the theme of his presentation with an allusion to Luke 12:48: "For unto whomsoever much is given, much shall be required." These references helped him to create a shared sense of identification and purpose as he proceeded with his presentation.

Urging audience participation. Another common technique is to solicit the participation of audience members. Posing a well-worded series of questions, requesting a show of hands, or getting your audience to repeat a catchphrase aloud can be very effective. However, not all such strategies require a direct response. The simple use of inclusive pronouns such as *we* and *our* can help to promote identification and involvement. Another technique is the use of **rhetorical questions** that are not intended to provoke a response so much as to engage curiosity. For instance, knowing that most of his classmates were familiar with popular video games, University of Arkansas student Joseph Van Matre opened his speech on

rhetorical questions
Questions that have a self-evident answer or that provoke curiosity, which the speech then proceeds to satisfy.

The use of humor in an introduction gains audience attention and draws listeners and speakers together.

their constructive applications with the following rhetorical questions:

> If I say the word *gamer,* what words come to mind? Antisocial? Geek? Dropout? Well, how about fighter pilot? Fitness guru? Or intelligence analyst? I'm not a hard-core gamer, but I do enjoy the company of my Wii from time to time, as well as an occasional round of Madden football with my friends. So when I heard in a radio interview that video games actually have many constructive educational and professional applications, I was intrigued and decided to do some reading. What I learned was highly surprising.

Using appropriate humor. Appropriate humor offers some real advantages. Effective humor at the beginning of a speech can put both listeners and speakers at ease with the speaking situation and can sometimes make it easier for speakers to tackle sensitive topics. In his remarks to the Radio and Television Correspondents' Association dinner in 2007, President George W. Bush used humor to address his historically low approval ratings: "A year ago, my approval rating was in the 30s, my nominee for the Supreme Court had just withdrawn, and my vice president had shot someone. Ah, those were the good ol' days."[8]

Because laughter is shared, it can also function to promote identification, drawing speakers and listeners together. As the French philosopher Henri Bergson noted, "Laughter appears to stand in need of an echo. . . . Our laughter is always the laughter of a group."[9]

Unfortunately, humor can also be one of the most abused techniques for opening a speech. Some speakers have the mistaken notion that if they just tell a joke at the beginning of their speeches—any joke—listeners will like them and listen to their message. There's no way of knowing how many listeners have suffered, and how many speakers have bombed, over this misconception!

The truth is that humor may not work well for everyone. Moreover, it can be grossly inappropriate for some topics on some occasions, and any kind of humor based on ethnicity, gender, religion, or sexual orientation is always unacceptable.

Should you decide to open your speech with humor, keep it fresh, relevant, and brief so that it does not upstage your message. Canned jokes pulled from primers and online collections are rarely effective, and you should be cautious about relying on humor to cope with communication apprehension. While effective humor can put both speaker and audience at ease, humor that falls flat can have just the opposite effect. Remember that there are other ways to come across as likable and to capture audience attention. Explore your strengths as a speaker and play to them: this is a vital part of finding your voice and gaining confidence as a speaker.

SPEAKER'S NOTES

Using Humor

Keep the following in mind when considering the use of humor in your speeches.

1. Don't use humor just to be funny. Keep it relevant to your topic.
2. Use humor to put audience members at ease and increase their receptivity to your ideas.
3. Avoid religious, ethnic, racist, or sexist humor, all of which speak poorly of you.
4. If you must poke fun at someone, let it be yourself.
5. Don't use humor that might trivialize a serious topic.
6. Avoid planned humor if you are really anxious about speaking.

Opening with a narrative. Storytelling can be a powerful means of creating identification with your audience. Narratives educate us by helping us remember the past and celebrate shared moral commitments. Effective narratives use vivid, graphic language to help us envision abstract topics and issues in concrete human terms. Stories may be either imaginary or based on real-life experiences and historical events. Depending on your purpose for speaking, they can be lighthearted and humorous or somber and serious.

In either case, introductory narratives should be brief. Consider the opening narrative to Ashlie McMillan's introductory speech on scuba diving:

> Imagine you're sitting aboard a dive boat. It's rocking back and forth. You can feel the sun beating down on you. You can feel the wind blowing on you. You smell the ocean, the salt water. You can hear the waves crashing up against the boat. You put on your dive pack with your heavy oxygen tank and you walk unsteadily across the deck of the rocking boat. And all of a sudden you plunge into a completely different environment. All around you is vast blueness and infinite space, a world completely different from the one you left above. But all you have to do is turn on your back and look above and you see the sunlight streaming in through the top of the water. And you can see the world that you left behind.

Ashlie's skillful use of action words—such as *rocking, blowing,* and *crashing*—and her vivid appeals to the senses made this scene come alive for her listeners and placed them in the middle of it. See Chapters 8 and 16 for more advice on developing narratives in your speeches.

Opening with a quotation. Starting with a striking quotation or paraphrase from a highly respected text or figure can both arouse interest and dignify your speech. For instance, references to revered political documents such as the Declaration of Independence or to well-known authors such as George Orwell and Maya Angelou can be very effective.

However, opening quotations need not come from such elevated sources. University of Arkansas student Guy Britton introduced his speech concerning illegal immigration with the following ironic quotation: "An anonymous author once said: 'The early North American Indian made a great mistake by not having an immigration bureau.'"

Quotations should be short, to the point, and relevant to your purpose. Several excellent collections of quotations are available online, including Quoteland, RefDesk's Quotations, Brainy Quotes, Creative Quotations, and Bartlett's Quotations.

Startling the audience. Sometimes speakers open with a shocking piece of information intended to startle listeners into close attention. Landon West used this technique to introduce his informative speech:

> I want to introduce you to a person whom I have known for a very long time. He is like many of you. He knew that he could be anything that he wanted to be, given the chance. But there was something about him that his peers would never let him forget: he was fat! (Shows enlarged photo.) The more he began to accept that he was going to live life obese, the more his willingness to contribute diminished. Who is this person? Well, he doesn't really exist anymore. This is me, just a year and a half and 100 pounds ago. I was a statistic for the epidemic of obesity that plagues this country.

With this opening, Landon did more than create intense interest. He also justified himself as an authentic speaker on the obesity problem and enhanced his own ethos. By confiding in his audience, he came across as a trusting person whom they could trust in return.

As effective as this technique can be, you should use it carefully. If your opening is too sensational, you run the risk of its upstaging the rest of your speech. Keep your use of startling information within the boundaries of good taste. Remember, the point is to startle those in your audience into listening, not to traumatize or offend them.

SPEAKER'S NOTES

Capturing Attention

The following strategies can help you gain attention in the introduction of your speech.

1. Acknowledge the audience, location, or occasion.
2. Invoke shared interests and values.
3. Solicit the audience's involvement and participation.
4. Engage your listeners with relevant humor.
5. Open with a narrative that relates to your topic.
6. Begin with a striking quotation.
7. Startle your audience with powerful information or a novel approach.

Establishing Your Credibility. The second major function of an effective introduction is to establish your credibility as a speaker. In Chapter 3, we discussed the importance of listeners forming favorable initial impressions of your ethos: *Why should your audience believe that, for this oral journey, you know where you're taking them (competence)? Can they trust you to lead them in the right direction (integrity)? How do they know you have their best interest at heart (good will)? Will you make the trip an engaging one (dynamism)?* Outside the classroom, you may enter a speaking situation with some initial ethos based on what listeners know or have heard of your reputation and experience. A good introduction before you stand and speak can further prime listeners to give you a favorable hearing.

In classroom situations, however, it's up to you to use your introduction to establish special reasons that qualify you to speak. Do you have a wealth of knowledge to share on this topic? Have you had special personal experiences that brought the importance of this topic home to you? Do you bring special work experience to bear? In your introduction, tell your story about such experiences, or cite credible sources your listeners will accept. They will conclude that you bring authentic interest and credentials to your topic, and they will listen more closely to what you have to say.

When you establish favorable ethos in the introduction of your speech, you signal that you have found your voice. When you show that you are likable, sincere, competent, and dynamic, your listeners want to identify with you. Your effectiveness as a speaker and your value as a spokesperson for your cause are magnified.

preview
The part of the introduction that identifies the main points to be developed in the body of the speech and presents an overview of the speech to follow.

Previewing Your Message. The final function of an introduction is to preview the body of your speech. The **preview** indicates the main points you will cover and offers your listeners an overview of the speech to come. A good preview should help them follow your message and serve as an effective transition into the body of your speech. Invoking our metaphor of the oral journey: Just as your thesis statement should tell your listeners the destination and reason for your journey, your preview statement should outline the primary routes you will take to get them there. That way, your audience will know what to look for along the ride.

Explicit preview statements are common to informative and persuasive presentations and can be especially useful for speeches addressing unfamiliar, complicated, or technical topics. They need not be of the mundane "In this speech, I'm going to talk about these three points" variety. For her speech informing her Davidson classmates of how French people can eat indulgent foods while still remaining healthy, Gabrielle Wallace offered this more elegant preview:

> To understand the French paradox, we must take a close look at how they combine food choices, their consumption of beverages, and the cultural attitude they have developed toward food.

As the mother of a Newtown, Connecticut, shooting victim, Scarlett Lewis called on her personal experience to enhance her credibility as she spoke at a fundraiser for the organization set up in her son's memory: The Jesse Lewis Choose Love Foundation.

In speeches developing a narrative design as discussed in Chapters 3 and 16, the preview may take the form of a prologue, using a foreshadowing technique: "I never expected that my life would be forever changed by what would happen that day." When speakers foreshadow their stories, they don't tell their listeners exactly what will happen, but they do alert them that something important will take place. This prepares them to listen intently to the story.

Concluding Your Speech

A good **conclusion** should give your speech a sense of closure and leave your listeners with something to remember. Just as opening your presentation with, "Hello, my speech is about..." would not likely be effective, neither would ending it with, "Well, that's it." If you are lost for ideas, think of your speech as wrapping up the oral journey you promised your listeners in the introduction. Your conclusion should assure them that their destination has been reached. Giving them something to remember that journey is like offering them a postcard to take with them. For most short presentations, an effective conclusion should summarize your message (as necessary) and provide some concluding remarks.

conclusion
The ending for your speech that reinforces your main ideas and provides your audience with something to remember.

Summarizing Your Message. Sometimes with really short or casual presentations, an explicit summary statement of your message is not necessary or even desirable. However, for longer or more complicated presentations, they can be really useful for reminding your listeners of what they have heard and for transitioning from the body of your speech into your concluding remarks. It signals the audience that you are about to finish.

Go beyond simply repeating your main points; instead, use this as a chance to reflect on and reinforce the central message of your speech. Consider the conclusion to Gabrielle Wallace's speech:

> For the French, eating is an important part of their lives. It is engrained in their culture and permeates their daily existence. The three factors of eating correctly, drinking wisely, and making a meal an enjoyable experience are what keep the French paradox alive.

Providing Concluding Remarks. Although a summary statement can offer listeners a sense of closure, concluding remarks that stay with your listeners will help seal that effect. Many of the techniques that create effective introductions can also be used to develop memorable conclusions.

Echoing your introduction. Sometimes called a "bookend," a conclusion that applies the same technique used in the introduction can provide a nice sense of closure. For example, you might finish a story that you started in the introduction or refer back to your startling information, rhetorical question, or opening quotation. Referring back to the introduction can be an effective means of letting listeners know that you are bringing your message full circle. For instance, one student speaker who opened with the example of Earl Washington's wrongful conviction for murder concluded her plea for judicial reforms by stating: "There are more Earl Washingtons out there, and they're counting on us!"

Restating the relevance of your message to your audience. At the beginning of a speech, you should involve your listeners by showing them how your message relates directly to their lives. In the conclusion, you should remind them of what they personally have at stake. Consider Doneal McGee's closing plea in a speech opposing "abstinence only" sex education in American high schools:

> These kids are our future, and their problems will become ours in many ways. Babies having unplanned babies out of wedlock are more likely to end up quitting school and on welfare, producing expensive wards of the state and swelling the ranks from which a vast majority of troubled children arise. We have no choice but to support the responsible teaching of sex education in our high schools. They're our kids, and our future may well hang in the balance!

Issuing a call to action. In persuasive speeches, concluding remarks often urge listeners to take the first step to confirm their commitment to action and change. Beth Tidmore used this technique to conclude her speech urging her classmates to volunteer for the Special Olympics:

> Becoming a volunteer is the best way that you can help. If you can't give a weekend, give a couple of hours. If you can't become a leader, just become a cheerleader. Show up. Be a happy smiling face. It's the best way to give to charity, because you can see the results right in front of you. You can see the shiny medals, the triumphant finishes, the happy faces, the screaming fans. And you know that you're helping someone else and giving of yourself to them.... Can drives need cans. Blood drives need blood. And, the Special Olympics need volunteers. They need warm hearts and open minds. In Special Olympics, everyone is a winner—especially the volunteers!

Persuasive speeches designed to recruit volunteers often end with a call to action.

Asking rhetorical questions. When used in an introduction, rhetorical questions can help arouse attention and curiosity. When used in a conclusion, they give your listeners something to think about after you have finished. Elinor Fraser opened a speech opposing the use of cell phones while driving in the following way: "How many of you were chatting on your cell phones while driving to class this morning?" After a speech that established the danger of such behavior in graphic terms, her final words were "So now that you know the risk you are running, are you going to use your cell phones again while you're on the way home? If so, let me know so I can drive in a different direction."

Closing with a story. Just as stories can effectively introduce a speech, concluding narratives can help your audience experience the meaning of your message. To end her speech on dangerous off-campus housing conditions, Anna Aley told the following story about her neighbor:

> I got out of my apartment with little more than bad memories. My upstairs neighbor was not so lucky. The main problem with his apartment was that the electrical wiring was done improperly; there were too many outlets for too few circuits, so the fuses were always blowing. One day last November, Jack was at home when a fuse blew—as

> usual. And, as usual, he went to the fuse box to flip the switch back on. When he touched the switch, it delivered such a shock that it literally threw this guy the size of a football player backwards and down a flight of stairs. He lay there at the bottom, unable to move, for a full hour before his roommate came home and called an ambulance. Jack was lucky. His back was not broken. But he did rip many of the muscles in his back. Now he has to go to physical therapy, and he is not expected to fully recover.

Closing with a quotation. Brief quotations that capture the essence of your message can make for effective conclusions. For example, if you open a speech with a historical quotation, another on the same theme or from the same person might provide an elegant sense of closure. Arkansas student Guy Britton, who opened his speech on illegal immigration with a humorous quotation, achieved a nice bookend effect by closing with another example of the same technique: "Jay Leno once said: 'This problem with illegal immigration is nothing new. In fact, the Indians had a special name for it. They called it white people.'" Guy's sly humor took some of the ethnocentric steam out of a hot-button issue.

Closing with a metaphor. A memorable metaphor can end your speech effectively. As we discuss in Chapter 11, metaphors combine objects or perspectives that are apparently unalike so that we see unexpected relationships. In the conclusion of a speech, an effective metaphor may reveal hidden truths about the speaker's subject in a memorable way. Another University of Arkansas student, Simone Mullinax, closed her classroom tribute to her grandmother by concluding with a metaphor that had run throughout her speech:

> Years from now I will be teaching my granddaughter to build the perfect key lime pie. And I will be thinking about my grandmother, whose love seeps into all the crust that holds me together. We will work the fillings together and we will know just what to top it off with to make it perfect. And we will bake pies like friends hold conversations, the intricacies hidden beneath the taste and the impressions lasting beyond the words

Using strategic repetition. Repetition helps implant ideas in the minds of your listeners. The form of repetition discussed earlier called parallel construction—in which certain phrases are repeated in close succession for added emphasis—can make for conclusions that are both elegant and dramatic.

> So now we see why our welfare program just doesn't work. It doesn't work because it's inadequate. It doesn't work because it's inefficient. And it doesn't work because it's insensitive. It's time for a better idea.

Selecting and Using Introductory and Concluding Techniques

Because introductions and conclusions are so crucial in shaping audience impressions and setting the tone for your speech, you should give them considerable thought. Because they are so vital, we suggest that you write them out and commit them to memory.

As you review your research notes, look for materials that might be effective openers and closers. The following guidelines may help:

- Consider relevance to your message and the mood you wish to establish. Some messages and occasions call for a light touch, while others are more serious.
- Consider the members of your audience and what techniques might best tune your message to their needs and interests. We discuss audience analysis and adaptation in Chapter 5.

Using Effective Introductions and Conclusions

Find a short speech, and concentrate on the introduction and the conclusion. To what extent does the speaker follow the guidelines of this section? To what extent does the speaker differ from these guidelines? How effective do you think the introduction and conclusion are, and why?

- Keep it brief! The combined length of your introduction and conclusion should be considerably less than the body of your speech.
- Do what you do best. Some people are natural storytellers; others are funny; still others are better with striking statistics or quotations. Play to your strengths.

Finding Your Voice

Critiquing Through Outlining

Select one of the speeches from Appendix B, or a speech from a source such as C-SPAN, YouTube, or TED Talks, and prepare a working outline of it. Does the outline clarify the structure of the speech? Does it reveal any structural flaws? Can you see any different ways the speaker might have developed the speech? Write an alternative introduction and conclusion using a different technique. Compare the new with the original. Which works better, and why?

SPEAKER'S NOTES

Checklist for a Working Outline

You can trust your working outline if the following statements accurately describe it:

1. My topic, specific purpose, and thesis statement are clearly stated.
2. My introduction contains attention-getting material, establishes my credibility, and focuses and previews my message.
3. My main points represent the most important ideas on my topic.
4. I have an appropriate number of main points for the time allotted.
5. Each subpoint supports its main point with more specific detail.
6. Every subdivision contains at least two entries.
7. My conclusion contains a summary statement and concluding remarks that reinforce and reflect on the meaning of my speech.
8. I have planned transitions to use between the introduction and body, between each of my main points, and between the body and conclusion of my speech.

Preparing Your Formal Outline

9.4 Complete a formal outline

formal outline
The final polished and fully developed plan for your speech.

Once you have developed your working outline and have a good idea of how you will introduce and conclude your speech, you can turn it into your **formal outline**. The formal outline represents the final polished plan or roadmap for your oral journey. It should provide a fully developed structural overview of your main ideas and supporting materials in the order to be presented, and a list of your researched materials. We provide you with a sample of a formal outline at the end of this chapter.

Most formal outlines include

- a heading with a title, topic, and specific purpose statement;
- an introduction, including attention material, thesis statement, and preview;
- the fully developed body of your speech, following the principles of coordination and subordination;
- a conclusion offering a summary statement and concluding remarks; and
- a list of works consulted or cited, as your instructor indicates.

Heading

The heading of a formal outline should offer a title, your topic, and a specific purpose statement. While your topic and specific purpose statements are vital to planning effective speeches, they are usually not stated in the speech itself. To avoid creating false expectations or confusing your audience (and yourself!), finish your formal outline before determining your title. Sometimes speakers opt to state their titles as they open their speeches, which can help to focus and engage your listeners. Consider the way Betsy Lyles wove references to her title, "The Abused Women of Afghanistan," into the introduction of her speech:

> Of course, such brutalities are hardly unknown to *the abused women of Afghanistan*. But this was the spring of 2009—nearly eight years after the so-called liberation of the Afghan people by a U.S.-led coalition of forces. *The abused women of Afghanistan* need your support now for efforts to defend their basic human rights.

A Clearly Structured Body

The body of your outline should consist of your main and supporting ideas and materials in the order to be presented. Using a precise and abbreviated system for coordinating and subordinating these materials in your formal outline will help you see how they support and connect with each other.

- Label your main points with Roman numerals (I, II, III), in order of their appearance in your presentation.
- Label your subpoints with capital letters (A, B, C), and indent them further to show their subordination to the main points.
- Label your sub-subpoints with Arabic numbers (1, 2, 3), and indent them even further to show their subordination to the subpoints.
- If you need sub-sub-subpoints, label them with lowercase letters (a, b, c), and indent them to show their subordination to the sub-subpoints.

While the entries in a working outline are often sentence fragments, indicating their tentative, evolving status, *each main and supporting point of a formal outline should be worded as a complete, simple sentence containing only one idea.* For instance, where you might have entered "Bad eating harmful" as a main point in your working outline, you would rewrite it as "Bad eating habits are harmful" for a formal outline. As you develop main points with supporting subpoints, the qualifying and dependent clauses within your main points, as well as supporting ideas and information, can become subordinate points.

Also, remember the importance of developing at least *two* subdivisions when adding subordinate points to your outline: If you have subpoint A to support main point I, then you need to have subpoint B. The same holds for developing sub-subpoints and sub-sub-subpoints. If you only have one supporting point for an assertion, then it is not really subordinate and can probably be combined with the point it supports. For instance, the assertion that "Bad eating habits are harmful because they are unhealthy" is really a single point and could be simplified to "Bad eating habits are unhealthy." On the other hand, the statement "Bad eating habits are harmful because they are unhealthy and can damage your self-image" provides a tangle of supporting clauses that could be clarified through outlining as follows:

I. Bad eating habits are harmful.
   A. They are unhealthy.
   B. They can damage your self-image.

Breaking down complex sentences into an outline format helps focus what you are going to say, suggesting what you should emphasize and further support while clarifying the structure and logic of your speech.

The Introduction, Conclusion, Transitions, and Presentation Aids

As discussed earlier in this chapter, your introduction, conclusion, and vital transitions should help you frame a well-structured presentation. Because all three of these components are so important to setting impressions, orienting your listeners, and encouraging the overall fluidity of your presentation, many instructors prefer to have you write them out verbatim, as illustrated in our sample formal outline at the end of this chapter. That doesn't mean you have to present them word-for-word as written, but they provide a firm sense of how you plan to open and close your speech and move from one main point to the next, making for a smoother, more comfortable presentation. Should your instructor request that you outline the introduction and conclusion, do *not* include them as the first and last main points along with the body of your presentation. Mark them off as distinct sections complete with separate numerals and letters for indentation. That way the main points of your body will be numbered as I, II, and III, so they will be easier to remember.

Your formal outline should also include references to when you plan to display and use presentation aids. While you could simply write "show chart" or "display photograph" at the end of the sentence where you plan to use them on your formal outline, that would pass up the opportunity to determine how you will blend your aids into your speech. Think of how you can present them for maximum effect: "According to the National Science Foundation, as this chart shows..." or "Women in Afghanistan who are not covered head to toe in burqas (show photograph) are subject to harsh punishment."

Oral Citations and Source Citations

oral citations
Providing your listeners with essential information about the sources you use in your speech.

source citations
Brief references to your sources within a formal outline.

Your formal outline should include direct references to the sources you will cite orally during your presentation. Because your audience cannot look at the list of works you have consulted, these **oral citations** assure them that you have conducted sufficient research to speak from responsible knowledge. Oral citations of respected sources are especially important for substantiating claims that are complicated, time-sensitive, or controversial. "Speaker's Notes: Guidelines for Oral Documentation" will help you construct effective oral citations.

In addition to oral citations, you should include abbreviated **source citations** within your formal outline for each piece of supporting information you use. Source citations help to demonstrate the thoroughness of your research as integrated into your presentation and should be included in parentheses at the end of the points or subpoints to which they apply. In most cases, the author's last name or an abbreviated title in *italics* or quotation marks plus a page number will suffice—for example, (Branch, p. 14) or (*Parting the Waters*, p. 52). List the author's last name with an abbreviated title if you are citing more than one work by the same author. If the author is a group or organization, list its name in abbreviated form.

SPEAKER'S NOTES

Guidelines for Oral Documentation

To develop effective oral citations, follow these guidelines:

1. Identify the publication in which the material appears.
2. Identify the time frame of the publication (usually the year is sufficient unless the material is time-sensitive).
3. Offer highlighted credentials for the experts you cite.
4. Select direct quotations that are brief and that will have an impact.
5. Avoid presenting every detail of the written citation.
6. Provide more extensive oral citations for controversial and time-sensitive material.

Works Cited or Consulted

Finally, most instructors will ask you to submit a bibliography or list of **works cited** along with your formal outline. A works cited list should include only those sources of information that you actually refer to in your presentation. Some instructors may also ask for a list of **works consulted**, which includes all of the works you read and found informative, even those you did not actually cite or use in your presentation. Still other instructors may ask you to annotate your list of works cited or consulted by including a one- to three-sentence description addressing the nature or value of the ideas and information each entry offers.

works cited
A list of the sources mentioned in your presentation.

works consulted
A list of all the works you read in preparation for your presentation.

In any case, your list of referenced sources is crucial to documenting your research and demonstrating your acquisition of responsible knowledge in support of your claims. Do not pad your list with sources you found online or in the library but did not actually consult, which is a form of academic dishonesty that instructors take very seriously. Provide full and proper citations so that you can refer curious listeners or your instructor to the exact sources of information. In order to list your references in proper form, refer to the sample formats provided in Chapter 7 that illustrate the Modern Language Association (MLA) and American Psychological Association (APA) styles. Your instructor may indicate a preference between these two styles. Longer, more developed primers on both styles are easy to find online. We highly recommend the tutorial posted by the Purdue University's Online Writing Lab (OWL).

Formal Outlines: A Few Precautions

Formal outlines have one great advantage. They impose a discipline on the preparation process that can help you develop a substantive speech that rises to the high standards of responsible knowledge. They also have one great disadvantage: If used during your presentation, they can suck the life right out of a speech. You can end up reading from them rather than speaking in a fresh, direct, and extemporaneous way to the listeners in front of you. The *only* time you should read during your speech is when you are quoting the words of someone else because the exact wording is dramatic, impressive, and vital. Refer to Chapters 3 and 12 on developing a key-word outline for use while practicing and presenting your actual presentation.

We close on a practical if obvious point: If your instructor requires you to submit a formal outline and list of references as part of a formal speaking assignment, remember that it will be one of the few tangible items he or she will have for evaluating the work you did prior to making your presentation. If you turn in a sloppy rough draft with incorrect formatting and handwriting scribbled in the margins, then you will obviously not make a good impression. Formal outlines should be computer-generated; clean; and free of misspellings, grammatical errors, and typos. Ask your instructor if you can model your formal outline on the sample we provide at the end of this chapter.

Developing a Formal Outline

What do you find to be the most difficult part about developing a formal outline? What does that suggest about the challenges you may face in the presentation itself?

Final Reflections: Deep Roots of Structuring and Outlining

The various design options we have discussed are templates we use to understand the world and to grasp its meaning for our lives. We want to know how things come to be, so we seek causes and effects. We often divide subjects into categories that reflect our interests; for example, when we are considering a proposal, we may consider it in terms of its *cost, benefits,* and *likelihood of success*. This becomes one of the most popular forms of categorical order. Chronological order reflects our orientation in time, and sequential design speaks to our need to know step-by-step processes. Spatial order reflects how we situate ourselves within the world. For example, an environmentalist may look at mountains in terms of plant and animal life at different altitudes, while mine owners might see the same mountains in terms of the seams of coal they contain. The persistence of the problem-solution pattern speaks to the continual appearance of difficulties that must be dealt with if we are to live successfully.

We are also creatures who need to see a pattern completed once it has begun. A discussion of causes does not satisfy us when we can't see the effects. If you discuss a problem, we want to see a solution; likewise, any discussion of solutions seems senseless if we aren't given a clear understanding of the problem. In short, we want closure to satisfy the patterns of expectation we bring to our experience.

Being a successful speaker calls for an ability to arrange what you have learned into intelligent patterns of knowledge that listeners will find easy to access and hard to forget. You want to be able to build a structure of reasons so compelling that the conclusion will seem irresistible to fair-minded listeners. As you find your voice, you will come to place great value on the disciplines of structuring and outlining.

Study Questions

CONTENT MASTERY

1 What are the three principles of a well-structured speech?
2 What design options can help you arrange the main points of your speech?
3 How can you develop and support your main points?
4 What functions do transitions serve?
5 How can you develop a working outline of your speech?
6 What are the different ways you can introduce and conclude your speech?
7 What are the major distinguishing features of a formal outline?

CRITICAL EXPLORATIONS

1. Read and evaluate a speech from Appendix B. How well does it satisfy the principles of effective structure? What design option does the speech exemplify? How well does it develop its main points? How effective is its introduction and conclusion? Does it make good use of transitions? How might it have been improved in these respects?
2. For your next speech, develop a formal outline, following the model provided at the end of the chapter. Exchange these with several classmates before you speak, and ask for their reactions and suggestions.
3. Find two commercials: one you believe is effective, the other ineffective. Can you identify structural reasons for the difference?
4. Working in small groups, share summaries of the research you have done for your next speech. What are the main points suggested by these summaries? What would be an appropriate design for these points? Explore different options, and explain why you chose the design you did.
5. Suggest an appropriate structural design for the following specific purposes:
    a. To inform listeners where they might see a grizzly bear in the wild
    b. To inform the audience about sexist advertising practices
    c. To inform listeners about the ideal way to prepare for an examination
    d. To persuade listeners to help control global warming
    e. To persuade listeners to vote for a particular candidate in the next election
    f. To inform listeners of major events in the woman's suffrage movement
    g. To persuade listeners that tax cuts can stimulate the economy
    h. To inform listeners of the story behind Amelia Earhart's last flight
    i. To persuade listeners that drones are not an appropriate means of ensuring national security
6. The following list of items provides the raw materials for an informative speech on auctions. Design a working outline for them, from the specific purpose statement to the conclusion. Compare these outlines in class, and seek consensus on what

might be the best outline and why. What changes would you need to make to turn this into a formal outline?

a. The right type of auction for you is not hard to find.
b. The first principle of auctions is that merchandise always goes to the highest bidder.
c. Set a maximum amount you are willing to pay, and do not bid beyond it.
d. Quote National Association of Auctioneers' definition of auctions.
e. Have you been to an antique or art store lately, only to be blown away by the astronomical prices?
f. Today, we've considered how auctions work, how to find them, and how to make good buys at them.
g. Choose an auction according to what you want and what's available to you.
h. To inform my audience how to make auctions work for them
i. Auctions are available on the Internet and in the classified section of most Sunday newspapers.
j. Once you find your auction, consider the following four tips for making the buy.
k. Auctions are a fun and economical way to make purchases.
l. Be alert for when your item goes up for sale.
m. Estate auctions liquidate the belongings of an entire family, or estate, usually after an illness or death.
n. There are many types of auctions.
o. Having worked around auctions for several years, I've come to know and appreciate this fascinating form of free trade.
p. Today, I'm going to tell you how auctions work, where to find them, and some basic tips for making smart buys.
q. There is a better way to purchase the rare, valuable, or just out-of-the-ordinary items you fancy.
r. Art and antique auctions offer such collectibles as paintings, furniture, jewelry, coins, and stamps.
s. Auctions are a fascinating alternative for making purchases.
t. So maybe I'll see you at an auction someday, and you, too, can learn to duck the ridiculous prices of "fine" shopping.
u. Determine if the merchandise is in good shape.
v. Municipal auctions feature both government property that is no longer needed and property that has been acquired through bankruptcy or legal proceedings.
w. Determine if the merchandise is what you really want.
x. Arrive early to inspect the merchandise to see if it's worth buying.

SAMPLE FORMAL OUTLINE

Reprinted with permission from Betsy Lyles, Davidson College

HEADING

Title: The Abused Women of Afghanistan
Topic: Plight of the Women of Afghanistan
Specific Purpose: To win support for efforts to protect women in Afghanistan.

INTRODUCTION

Attention Materials: Orbal could hardly believe the news from her native homeland. A nineteen-year-old girl had just been executed in public for adultery. That same month, a public gathering of women had been attacked by an angry mob and pelted with stones, an outspoken advocate for women's issues had been gunned down in broad daylight, and the president had just signed a law making it illegal for women to refuse sex on demand to their husbands (Taylor). Of course, such brutalities are hardly unknown to the abused women of Afghanistan. But this was the spring of 2009—nearly eight years after the so-called liberation of the Afghan people by a U.S.-led coalition of forces.

Thesis Statement: The abused women of Afghanistan need your support now for efforts to defend their basic human rights.

Preview: We will consider how the U.S. invasion brought hope to Afghanistan's women; how these hopes are now being dashed; and, finally, how you might help in this struggle for human dignity.

(**Transition:** "First, let's revisit the hour of their promised liberation.")

BODY

I. The U.S.-led invasion in 2001 brought great promises and hopes for the women of Afghanistan.
 A. President George Bush and other Western leaders emphasized liberation in making their case for war to the Afghan people.
  1. The BBC News reports that American bombers dropped leaflets depicting the mistreatment of Afghan women ("Silent Scream").
  2. UN Secretary General Kofi Annan (*show photo*) insisted that "there cannot be true peace and recovery in Afghanistan without a restoration of the rights of women" (United Nations).
  3. First Lady Laura Bush (*show photo*) explicitly associated the invasion with advancing their cause.
 B. The new Afghan constitution guarantees equal rights for women ("Women in").
  1. Women are once again voting and serving in public office.
  2. In some areas women now have access to rudimentary education, health care, and a level of freedom they have not experienced in decades.

(**Transition:** "However, the reality does not always live up to the promise.")

II. Afghan women fear that their newly gained freedoms are already being rolled back.
 A. The central government under Hamid Karzai is incapable of or unwilling to protect women.
  1. According to CBC News, the Taliban has banned women from working and stoned women who protest ("The Women").
  2. "Warlords" dominate the Loya Jirga, which is the or Afghan legislative body ("Overview").
   a. According to the warlord chair of that assembly, "God has not given you [women] equal rights because under his decision, two women are counted as equal to one man" ("Women of").
   b. The warlords' philosophy is that a woman should be "treated like an animal" and "kept like a slave" (RAWA).

Betsy's introduction gains attention by combining two techniques: *opening with a narrative* and *startling the audience*. Essentially, she tells a story that shocks her listeners with its graphic detail.

The body of the speech combines two prominent design options. First, its main points develop (1) the promise of the invasion for women's rights, (2) the disappointment over the results, and (3) the renewed hope now embodied in the RAWA organization. While it develops within this categorical design, the speech also follows the problem-solution pattern of identifying a problem (disappointed hope) followed by a solution (renewed hope as represented in the work of RAWA).

To develop the first main point, Betsy relies on subpoints and sub-subpoints based on testimony from world leaders.

To develop the second main point, Betsy creates a structure of subpoints and sub-subpoints built on alleged factual evidence and testimony. Any one of the sources she uses might be suspect on grounds of bias. Knowing this, she depends on an impressive array of concurring evidence to support her claims.

To establish her third main point, Betsy builds through her subpoints and sub-subpoints a detailed picture of the work of RAWA to support the conclusion that the group deserves audience support. This impression would be further strengthened had she presented factual evidence confirming the success of RAWA's work.

3. President Hamid Karza (*show photo*) has signaled his willingness to sacrifice women's rights for reconciliation.
    a. He is engaged in talks with "moderate" elements of the Taliban ("UN Head").
    b. News has recently surfaced of a secret "reconciliation law" granting amnesty for all crimes committed before 2002 ("UN Head").
    c. In 2009, he signed the infamous "rape law" that makes it illegal for women of the Shia minority to deny their husband's sexual advances on demand (Abawi).

B. Reports of violence and oppression against women are again on the rise ("Women of").
1. Corrupt local officials typically ignore reports of domestic abuse and sexual assault.
2. Many schools have been shut down by a reign of terror and violence.
    a. Girls have been harassed, mutilated, and even killed for attending classes.
    b. Less than 10% of Afghan girls in rural areas have access to education.
3. In many areas women still live in obvious fear of harsh recrimination for behaviors deemed un-Islamic.

(**Transition:** "There is a little light in all this darkness. I want to tell you now about a remarkable group of women who have been fighting for these rights for over thirty years.")

III. The Revolutionary Association of the Women of Afghanistan (RAWA) is the most prominent organization for women's rights and social justice in Afghanistan.

A. RAWA sponsors a number of humanitarian projects.
1. They create educational opportunities (*show photo of schools*) for women and their children.
    a. They operate fifteen primary and secondary schools in Afghan refugee camps.
    b. They provide home-based schooling for women and girls where it is still unsafe to attend school.
2. They provide health care (*show photo of health care*) to abused women and children.
    a. They operate small hospitals that provide free care.
    b. They operate mobile health teams that travel throughout the troubled regions of Afghanistan and Pakistan.
3. They provide vocational training and financial support (*show photo of training*) to help Afghan women support their families and become self-sufficient.
    a. They encourage chicken farms, weaving shops, and bee-fostering projects.
    b. They offer small loans to start small businesses.

B. In addition to such humanitarian projects, RAWA sponsors a website (*show website*) to educate the world about the treatment of women in Afghanistan.
1. The website offers an overview of the situation of Afghan women in five different languages.
2. The website lists the restrictions that the Taliban has placed on Afghan women.
3. The website posts "horrible photos" of Afghan women driven to set fire to themselves to escape their fates.

IV. So how can you light a small candle in the Afghan darkness?
  A. Go to the RAWA website (*show RAWA.com*) and find out how you can get involved.
  B. Demand that our president and our legislators not abandon the women of Afghanistan.

(Transition: "So we see that the view of Afghanistan through the eyes of women is not a happy one.")

CONCLUSION

Summary statement: It's a story that started with high hopes as the United States invaded Afghanistan. Then those hopes and promises began to shrivel as fundamentalist values once again spread and stained the fabric of Afghan culture. But RAWA holds high the beacon of hope for the abused and forgotten women of Afghanistan. These heroic fighters for women's rights deserve your commitment, because, as Martin Luther King Jr. said right before he died, "We are all tied together in a single garment of destiny." Go to RAWA.com and find out how you can help.

Concluding remarks: My friend Orbal, herself a RAWA activist, choked back tears as she relayed the story of an eleven-year-old neighbor that had been abducted, beaten, raped, and then traded for a dog by a local warlord. Orbal and women like her have choked back enough tears. Get involved! We must not forget the women of Afghanistan.

Betsy's summary statement offers a skillful review of the main points of the speech. It invokes a powerful appeal to listeners based on stirring images that contrast fundamentalist values with the hope represented by RAWA. The concluding remarks return to the opening narrative to provide a sense of closure and to make a final appeal to the feelings of listeners.

WORKS CONSULTED

Abawi, Atia. "Afghanistan 'Rape' Law Puts Women's Rights Front and Center." *CNN.com/asia*. Cable News Network, 7 April 2009. Web. 27 March 2010.

"Letter to the United Nations." *Revolutionary Association of the Women of Afghanistan (RAWA)*. Revolutionary Association of the Women of Afghanistan (RAWA), 28 April 2007. Web. 2 April 2010.

"Overview on the Situation of Afghan Women." *Revolutionary Association of the Women of Afghanistan (RAWA)*. Revolutionary Association of the Women of Afghanistan (RAWA), n.d. Web. 2 April 2010.

"RAWA's Social Activities." *Revolutionary Association of the Women of Afghanistan (RAWA)*. Revolutionary Association of the Women of Afghanistan (RAWA), n.d. Web. 5 April 2010.

"Silent Scream." *BBC News World Edition*. BBC, 8 April 2002. Web. 27 March 2010.

Siun. "McChrystal Digs In, Afghan Women Say Get Out." *Rethink Afghanistan*. Brave New Foundation, 13 July 2009. Web. 14 Apr. 2010.

Taylor, Rupert. "Women's Rights Abused in Afghanistan: Ancient Prejudice Against Females Is Hard to Defeat." *Middle Eastern Affairs*. Suite101.com, 20 April 2009. Web. 27 March 2010.

"UN Head in Afghanistan Meets with Militant Group." *Yahoo! News*. Yahoo Inc., 25 March 2010. Web. 26 March 2010.

United Nations. "The Situation of Women in Afghanistan." *Afghan Women Today: Realities and Opportunities*. The United Nations, 2002. Web. 26 March 2010.

"Women in Afghanistan." *Independent Lens: Afghanistan Unveiled*. Independent Television Service, 17 November 2004. Web. 26 March 2010.

"Women of Afghanistan." *CBC News Online*. CBC, 1 March 2005. Web. 26 March 2010.

CHAPTER

Presentation Aids

LEARNING OBJECTIVES

This chapter will help you:

10.1 Appreciate how presentation aids can help—or hinder—your speech.

10.2 Understand the functions served by different types of presentation aids.

10.3 Select the most appropriate means of presenting your aids.

10.4 Plan, design, and prepare presentation aids.

10.5 Use presentation aids well.

10.6 Use presentation aids ethically.

OUTLINE

Jon was struggling for ideas to introduce his speech on the educational challenges facing children with dyslexia. He knew he needed to provide his listeners with a basic understanding of his topic before discussing the latest tools and methods for instruction, but all of the definitions he found seemed so abstract and dry. He could simply explain that dyslexia is a learning disorder that makes it hard to read and write by scrambling your ability to process and connect letters, words, and sounds—but what would that really tell his listeners about the experiences of people coping with the condition?

He then came up with a novel idea. He would open his presentation by projecting the following passage on a slide and asking his classmates to recite it out loud with him:

> "bifficulty on reading ir l϶arniny two reed,...
> alwags aggompanieb ɓy bifficulty on riding,
> end particulately on pseling."[1]

As his classmates struggled through the end of his passage, Jon continued, "Easy, huh? This is what I go through every day. Every time I crack open a book. Every time I try to do homework. Every time I sit down to gather and write out my thoughts. Like millions of Americans—and some people you know—all of my life I have struggled to overcome the challenges of a learning disability called dyslexia." Jon's creative ingenuity paid off. His classmates listened enthusiastically to the rest of his presentation and then peppered him with questions and observations.

"My task is to make you hear, feel and see. That and no more, and that is everything."

—JOSEPH CONRAD

Jon's introduction illustrates the potential for presentation aids to help you more effectively find and share your voice as a public speaker. **Presentation aids** are visual, auditory, and tactile supplements that can enhance the clarity and effectiveness of your presentations. When used appropriately, the right aids can provide your audience with concrete illustrations and direct sensory experiences that can be much more effective for communicating some messages than words alone.

presentation aids
Visual, auditory, and tactile supplements intended to enhance the clarity and effectiveness of a presentation.

For instance, if you were discussing the finer points of an Australian didgeridoo, you might describe it as an instrument with a pliable mouthpiece attached to a hollow tube without holes. But think of how much more vivid your presentation would be if you supplemented that description with photographs, or played an audio recording, or brought an actual instrument to class for a brief demonstration. Your verbal descriptions of the didgeridoo's distinctive sounds would then truly come to life for your audience.

With the development of computer technologies, the types and uses of presentation aids are multiplying rapidly. In this chapter, we open by discussing some of the potential advantages and disadvantages of using presentation aids. We then describe some of the more prominent types of presentation aids, indicate some popular traditional and contemporary media for presenting them, offer advice for preparing and presenting them, and close with some ethical considerations for using presentation aids in your speeches.

The Advantages and Disadvantages of Presentation Aids

10.1 Appreciate how presentation aids can help—or hinder—your speech.

As Jon's demonstration of the effects of dyslexia for his audience shows, the effective use of presentation aids that are thoughtfully considered and well-constructed can benefit your presentations in a number of ways. However, aids that are sloppy, poorly conceived, or ineffectively presented serve as a liability for the speaker. Figure 10.1 summarizes the major advantages and disadvantages of presentation aids.

Figure 10.1 Major Advantages and Disadvantages of Presentation Aids

Presentation Aids Help Your Speeches When They:	Presentation Aids Hurt Your Speeches When They:
• Add authenticity and emphasis to your words	• Distract your listeners
• Promote the audience's understanding	• Confuse your listeners
• Add variety and interest to your speeches	• Damage your credibility
• Enhance your credibility as a speaker	• Damage your delivery
• Improve your delivery skills	• Put you at the mercy of technology
• Make your speeches more memorable	

Advantages of Presentation Aids

Presentation aids can benefit your speeches by:

- **Adding authenticity and emphasis to your words.** When you show listeners what you are talking about, you demonstrate that it actually exists and highlight its importance to your presentation. If your audience can actually see the differences between digital cameras and film cameras, they are more likely to be convinced that one is better than the other.
- **Promoting the audience's understanding.** Words are abstractions that can evoke a variety of meanings for different people. As a speaker, you help listeners experience and interpret your messages more accurately when you supplement your words with presentation aids to enhance their understanding. It is easier to give directions to someone when there is a map that both of you can see. Similarly, it is easier to explain the steps in a process when listeners are shown each part of the sequence.
- **Adding variety and interest to your speeches.** Just as pictures and boxed materials may be used to break up long stretches of text in a book, presentation aids can be used to break up long stretches of words in a speech. Visual and auditory aids provide variety and sensory stimulation that can enhance your audience's interest and attention to your presentations—particularly in today's visually oriented society.

- **Enhancing your credibility as a speaker.** They tell listeners you put extra effort into preparing your speech with their interest and understanding in mind. Speakers who use presentation aids are judged to be more professional, better prepared, more credible, more interesting, more concrete, and more persuasive than speakers who do not use such aids.[2] In some organizational settings, audiences expect speakers to use presentation aids, such as PowerPoint slides. If you don't have them, the audience may be disappointed, and your credibility may suffer.
- **Improving your delivery skills.** Using a presentation aid encourages movement as you display your aid. Movement energizes a speech, getting you away from the "stand behind the lectern/talking head" mode of delivery that many audiences find boring. If you have communication apprehension, purposeful movement—such as pointing to something on an aid as you display it—provides a constructive outlet for nervous energy. It directs your attention away from yourself and toward your message and your audience.
- **Making your speeches more memorable.** Research suggests that audiences have better recall of an informative presentation when visual images are used and that recall is even better when those images are in high-quality color.[3] Advertisers, for example, know that the combination of verbal and visual elements can "produce more mental images and lead to a more favorable attitude," which in turn aids recall of the message.[4] Presentation aids are easier to remember than words because they are concrete. A photograph of a hungry child may linger in your memory, thus increasing the influence of a speech urging you to contribute to a charity.

Disadvantages of Presentation Aids

Presentation aids can damage your speeches by:

- **Distracting your listeners.** They can draw attention away from your message if they are not used properly. For example, if your audience has difficulty reading an aid, they will strain to see it rather than listen to you. If they are passing around your handouts, objects, or photographs, they will be distracted from what you are saying. If you display an aid and then forget to refer to it, they may find themselves staring at it and wondering why it's there. If projected pictures are gruesome, some may be too upset to listen.
- **Confusing your listeners.** Closely related, the wrong aids can actually confuse your listeners about your intended message. Aids that are interesting but not directly relevant can be annoying as well as confusing. Blurry images, unclear graphs, and overloaded slides likely result in an audience that is more mystified than enlightened. Responding to a PowerPoint slide concerning the conflict in Afghanistan that included eight different colors, 12 bubbled entities, almost 100 names, and a confusing mess of connecting arrows, General Stanley McChrystal famously observed, "When we understand that slide, we'll have won the war."[5]
- **Damaging your credibility.** Aids that are poorly planned, sloppy, ineffectively used, or inaccurate may cause serious damage to your ethos for speaking. Listeners may think you did not care enough about your speech to invest the time and effort needed to prepare an effective presentation aid. Even worse, they may think you are incapable of preparing one.
- **Damaging your delivery.** If you look at your presentation aids more than your audience, you risk losing the strong eye contact and interaction with your audience that is so important to an effective presentation. That in turn may further damage your ethos: Don't you know your material well enough to talk to the audience rather than to the aid? Practice using your presentation aids as you practice your speech, and think of how you will integrate them smoothly without losing contact with your listeners.

Using Presentation Aids

Find a speech online that includes presentation aids. Using the checklist in this chapter, how well did the speaker use them? What could the speaker have done to improve their use?

- **Putting you at the mercy of technology.** Make sure the physical location of your speech will accommodate your planned use of computers or other electronic media for presenting your aids. Even then, be prepared to improvise and "soldier on" when the techno-gremlins play havoc with your plans. It happens!

In short, presentation aids can either help or hinder your speech. An aid may be beautifully rendered, or wonderfully funny, or impressive to behold—but if it does not help you find your voice on this topic with this audience, you should not use it.

You have a multitude of presentation aids from which to choose, as the following sections suggest. Investigate the specific options you have as well as the benefits and challenges of each. In determining which types of aids and media would be the best, ask yourself these questions: *How will a presentation aid help my audience understand my thesis, main points, and supporting materials? How will a presentation aid empower my voice?*

Types of Presentation Aids

10.2 Understand the functions served by different types of presentation aids.

Sometimes beginning speakers make the mistake of choosing a *medium* such as a handout or PowerPoint before giving careful consideration to what *types* of visual aids would be best suited to their most important ideas and information. The most frequently used types of presentation aids include people and other animals, objects and models, graphic representations, and pictures.

People and Other Living Creatures

Intentionally or not, you are always a presentation aid for your speeches. As further discussed in Chapter 12, your body movements, hand gestures, facial expressions, vocal characteristics, and even your choice of clothing can and will make important contributions to how your messages will be received. As a general rule, we suggest that you dress for the occasion or just a little nicer, but sometimes your choice of attire can be used to communicate more specific messages. For instance, if you were discussing your military service abroad as part of your introductory speech, then wearing your military uniform might really enhance your credibility. Similarly, a registered nurse might enhance his credibility to discuss a breaking medical issue by wearing his scrubs or work clothes while speaking.

Speakers often use physical movements to demonstrate how to perform a process such as a yoga exercise or artistic technique. One of our students, Lazetta Crawford, incorporated a number of key dance steps to illustrate her speech on stepping, an African American dance form that combines footsteps, the spoken word, and hand claps to produce complex rhythms and sounds. Not only did her demonstration help to clarify her subject, it added a degree of liveliness and interactive immediacy that was enthusiastically received by her listeners.

You can also use other people as presentation aids. One of our students, Neomal Abyskera, used two of his classmates to illustrate the lineup positions in the game of rugger, as played in his native Sri Lanka. At the appropriate moment, Neomal said, "Pete and Jeff will show you how the opposing players line up." While his classmates demonstrated the shoulder grip position, Neomal explained its role and function. The demonstration was more understandable than if he had simply tried to describe the position verbally or had used stick-figure drawings.

While more seasoned speakers can sometimes pull it off effectively, we do not recommend that beginning speakers put their listeners on the spot by asking for unscripted volunteers. It can be really uncomfortable when nobody agrees to volunteer and sometimes even more so when somebody does and then proceeds to ham it up. Your volunteers should be willing participants, and they should meet with you ahead of time to practice your presentation. Be tactful, but make sure they understand that their role is to help you communicate your message as opposed to distracting from it. If possible, have them sit in the front row or off to the side during your presentation so that they can quickly and easily come forward and then sit down again without distracting your listeners.

Demonstrating key dance steps involved in stepping provides interest and clarity.

Finally, on some occasions and for some topics, speakers may use well-trained pets or other animals as presentation aids. For instance, a student with disabilities might bring a dog trained to help her perform everyday tasks that most of us take for granted. However, we caution you to remember that *less well-trained* pets—not unlike humans—often get excited or nervous when placed in an unfamiliar context before an unfamiliar crowd. If your dog breaks free and accosts everyone in the front row with kisses, it may be endearing to some but will probably not contribute much to your presentation. Check with your instructor before bringing live animals to class for use as presentation aids, and make sure that doing so will not constitute a violation of university or college rules.

Objects and Models

Displaying the actual objects you are discussing can gain attention, increase understanding, and add authenticity to your speech. If using actual objects creates a problem, you might consider a model.

objects
Specific items that illuminate an article or parts of a process.

Objects. Specific **objects** can provide valuable illustrations and engage audience attention. For instance, you might use a fly-fishing rod while discussing casting techniques or a set of decorations used to celebrate Día de los Muertos, the Mexican holiday honoring the deceased. To explain how a real-life stroke contributed to her "stroke of insight" as a neuroscientist, Dr. Jill Bolte-Taylor used an actual human brain to describe how the two hemispheres of the brain function.[6] The success of her presentation depended on her credibility as a scientist, her comfort in handling the brain, and her assessment that her audience would be far more fascinated than turned off by its use.

As illustrated by our fishing rod example, "how to" speeches are usually more effective when speakers demonstrate how to use the necessary tools or objects for completing a process. We once had a student bring a pumpkin and carving kit to demonstrate the process of preparing a jack-o'-lantern. As she displayed her skills, she told stories that recounted legends surrounding the use and meaning of jack-o'-lanterns. Her presentation aid and her words helped each other: The demonstration enlivened her speech, and the stories gave the demonstration depth and meaning. When she came to her closing remarks, she reached under the lectern and produced a finished jack-o'-lantern complete with illumination. The effect was memorable.

Using a simple object can be all the more effective in this age of electronic wizardry. On some occasions, objects may be presented as symbolic representations of a broader point or mood that speakers wish to convey. A law enforcement officer, for

Demonstrating a process becomes clearer with an object as a presentation aid.

instance, might display a badge to emphasize her commitment to law and order. One U.S. senator recently held forth and then tossed a snowball before his colleagues to counter what he called "the hysteria on global warming."[7]

When Andrew Evans brought a glass of water to the front of the room for his persuasive speech on faith and reason, we thought he just wanted it in case his throat got dry. Instead, in the middle of his speech he picked it up to suggest that the water represented human reason and the glass, faith. Noting that the water can be transferred from one container to another but cannot stand on its own without any support, he suggested that reason has to have some kind of faith—in God, in science, in something—to support it. For the wide variety of perspectives in his audience, this simple presentation aid proved thought-provoking.

When using objects as presentation aids, make sure they are large enough for everyone in your audience to see, and do not pass small objects around for your audience to look at during brief presentations because they tend to distract listeners. Of course, *objects that are dangerous, illegal, or potentially offensive, such as drugs or pornography, should not be used in classroom speeches*. One speaker unwisely chose to demonstrate fire safety by setting fire to paper in a trash can, resulting in the evacuation of the building and the arrival of the fire department. Even replicas of dangerous materials can cause problems. One of our students brandished a very realistic-looking toy semiautomatic weapon that he pulled from beneath the lectern during the introduction of a speech on gun control. Several audience members became so unnerved that they could not concentrate on his message.

model
A replica used to represent an object.

Models. When objects are too large, too small, not available, or too fragile or precious for use in a public setting, a **model** can sometimes make an effective substitute for use as a presentation aid. Toy dolls, for instance, have long been used to teach parenting skills to adolescents and expectant first-time parents.[8] One of our students, George Stacey, brought a slightly smaller-than-life-sized model of a person to demonstrate cardiopulmonary resuscitation (CPR). Computer graphics are beginning to replace the use of scaled-down models to represent buildings and physical locations, but a little creative improvisation can be effective in the classroom. We once had a student make an excellent presentation on home security systems using his daughter's dollhouse for a model. When using models as presentation aids, you should hide or cover them when not in use so that they do not distract from your presentation.

Graphics

graphics
Visual representations of information, such as sketches, maps, graphs, charts, and textual materials.

Graphics, such as sketches, maps, graphs, charts, and textual materials, provide visual representations of ideas and information. Because they will be displayed for only a short time and from a distance during your speech, they should be instantly clear and easy to read. Each graphic should focus on developing one idea or related set of information. Your choice of colors should contrast sharply from the background in a manner that projects your intended message. We cover such considerations in greater depth under "Preparing Presentation Aids" later in this chapter.

Sketches. Sketches are simplified representations of your subject. Of course, preparing sketches entails a measure of artistic skill, but they can be very effective for communicating some messages in some contexts. One student speaker used a sketch transferred to a transparency to illustrate the measurements one should take before buying a bicycle. While talking about how to make bar-to-pedal and seat-to-handlebar measurements, he pointed to the appropriate areas of the bike on the sketch.

Maps. As a representation of physical space, a map can be really useful for speeches describing spatial relationships and providing directions. For instance, if you were introducing incoming students to the resources available in your college library, a simplified map of your library would help you explain how to find those resources. In a speech on the major attractions in Yellowstone Park, Tiffany Brock used an outline map of the park to show the route from the South Visitor's Center to Old Faithful, Mammoth Hot Springs, and the Grand Canyon of the Yellowstone River. Seeing the map helped listeners put the locations and distances into perspective.

Maps can also be useful for highlighting the locations of important occurrences and putting problems into perspective. One of our students used a simplified map to help his listeners see the projected results of a series of earthquakes along the New Madrid fault in the central United States (see Figure 10.2). Because commercially prepared maps typically contain too much detail, the best maps are those that you create or find specifically for your speech, making them simple, relevant to your purpose, and uncluttered.

Figure 10.2 Map as Presentation Aid

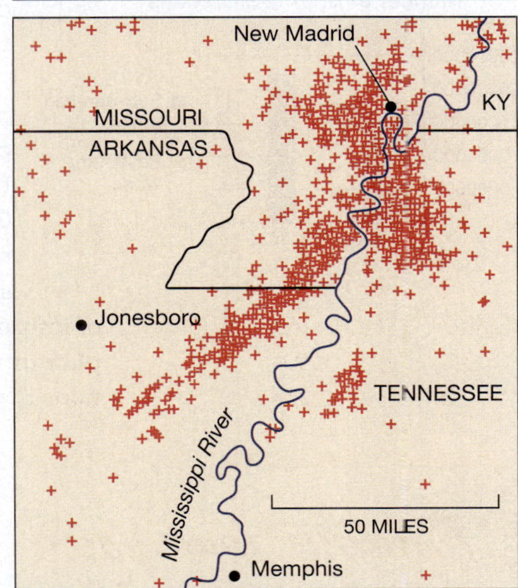

Source: U.S. Geological Survey, Department of the Interior/USG

Graphs. Mrs. Robert A. Taft, wife of a prominent former senator and leader of Washington society, once commented, "I always find that statistics are hard to swallow and impossible to digest."[9] Nowadays, it is certainly hard to swallow the sheer quantity of numbers we hear on a regular basis, and it is even harder to digest and make sense of them when a lot of figures are presented to us orally during a single presentation. But a well-designed graph can make statistical information much easier for listeners to understand and appreciate.

A **pie graph** shows the size of a subject's parts in relation to one another and to the whole. The pie represents the whole, and the slices represent the parts. The segments, or slices, are percentages of the whole and must add up to 100 percent. The most effective pie graphs for use as presentation aids have no more than six segments because too many slices make a graph difficult to read. The pie graph in Figure 10.3 shows the extracurricular activities of college students.

pie graph
A circle graph that shows the size of a subject's parts in relation to each other and to the whole.

A **bar graph** shows comparisons and contrasts between two or more items or groups. Bar graphs are easy to understand because each item can be readily compared with every other item on the graph. Bar graphs can also have a dramatic visual impact. Figure 10.4 is a *horizontal* bar graph that illustrates the relative

bar graph
A graph that shows comparisons and contrasts between two or more items or groups.

Figure 10.3 Pie Graph

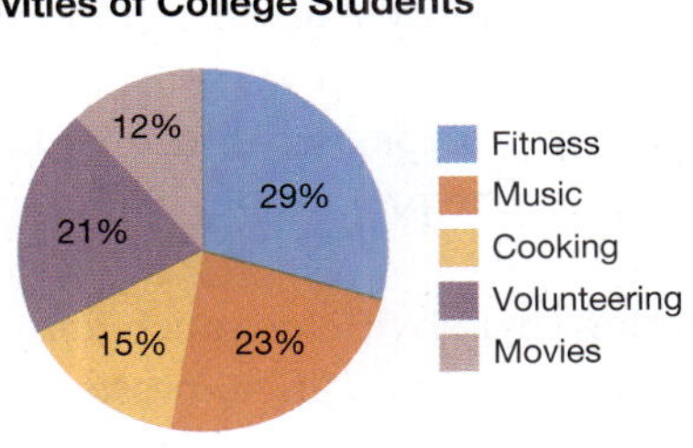

Figure 10.4 Horizontal Bar Graph

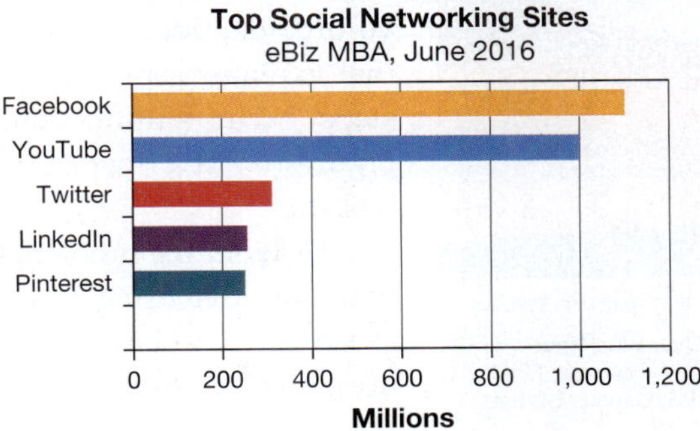

Figure 10.5 Vertical Bar Graph

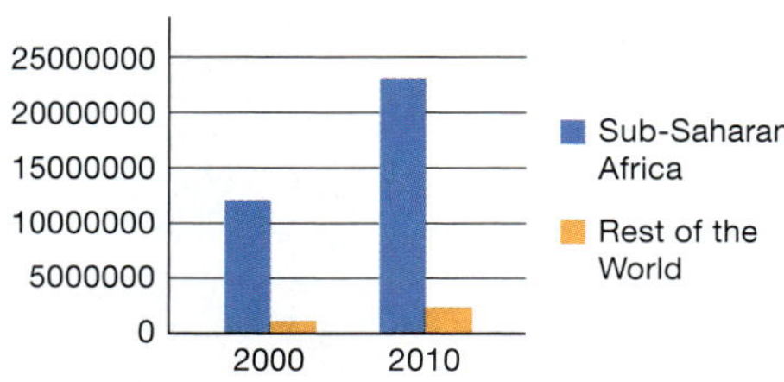

popularity of the top five social networking sites. Figure 10.5 offers a *vertical* graph prepared by Dolapo Olushola for her speech illuminating a tragic crisis created by the HIV/AIDS epidemic in Africa. When the variables on the vertical axis need longer titles, horizontal charts often provide greater legibility.[10]

Some bar graphs make use of pictographs, or stylized drawings, in place of linear bars. For example, images of cannons—each representing a certain amount of expenditure—might be used for a bar graph comparing the size of our military budget with that of other industrialized nations. One of our students used images of beer bottles to contrast the maximum number of recommended alcoholic beverages per week with estimated consumption levels on her campus. The effect was to dramatize the importance of information that might have otherwise come across as obvious or preachy. If you plan to use pictographs in your presentation aids, be sure they are simple depictions that do not distract from the impact of your material.[11]

Finding Your Voice

Exploring Graphs

Using the same set of statistical information, prepare rough drafts of a pie graph, a bar graph, and a line graph. What aspects of the data does each version highlight? What aspects are less evident in each version? Which version makes the information clearest and most striking for an audience? Which version would seem to work best for you as a speaker? How would you present the graph during a speech? What point would you use it to make or strengthen?

line graph
A visual representation of changes across time; especially useful for indicating trends of growth or decline.

flow chart
A visual method of representing power and responsibility relationships or describing steps in a process.

A **line graph** demonstrates changes across time, and it is useful for showing trends in growth or decline. Figure 10.6 shows the level of education achieved by Americans from 1940 to 2015. The upward-sloping lines confirm the steady increases over time in the numbers of people earning high school and college degrees and the diminishing numbers of people with less than a high school education. When you plot more than one line on a graph, use distinct colors. Limit the number of lines to three at most so that you don't confuse your audience.

Figure 10.6 Line Graph

Population Age 25 and over by Educational Attainment: 1940–2015

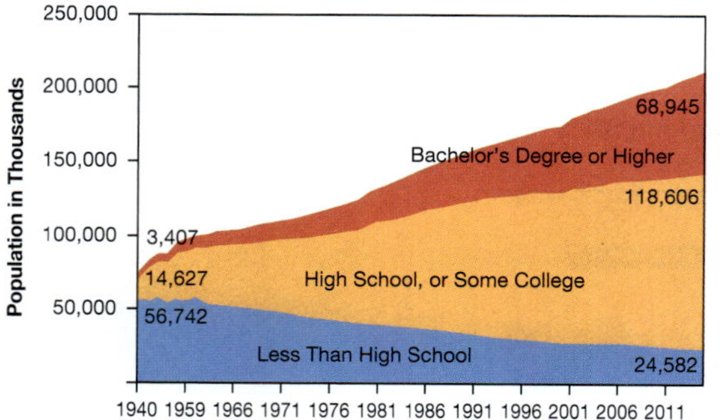

Source: Percent of People 25 Years and Over Who Have Completed High School or College, by Race, Hispanic Origin and Sex: Selected Years 1940 to 2015, U.S. Census Bureau. U.S. Department of Commerce.

Charts. Charts provide visual summaries of relationships that are not visible. Charts can be quite complex, so the speaker's challenge is to simplify them without distorting their meaning. The listeners must be able to understand a chart instantly and to read it from a distance.

One frequently used type of chart is a flow chart. A **flow chart** can show the steps in a process, the hierarchy and accountability in an organization, or the genealogy of a family tree. In a flow chart that explains a process, the levels, lines, and arrows indicate what steps occur simultaneously and what steps occur sequentially. Figure 10.7 is a flow chart that indicates the process of developing a website.

To avoid the problem of cluttering charts with too much information, consider using a series of charts, presented in succession. It is much better to have several clean, clear charts than one that tries to do too much, overloading both the audience and the speaker in the process.

Textual Graphics. **Textual graphics** are visuals that contain words, phrases, or numbers. Displaying the key words of a message can help to emphasize the importance and memorability of your most important ideas and information, and they can help your audience follow longer or complicated messages more easily. For example, for a speech describing the steps for completing a process such as preparing a flower arrangement, a series of slides numbering the steps in that process might be really effective.

Perhaps the most commonly used form of textual graphic is a simple **bulleted list** of key points. When preparing bulleted lists for use in your speeches, begin with a centered title, and then list your materials in the order to be discussed. Use a color for text entries that contrasts strongly with the background for clearer projection, and limit any list of textual information on a single aid to no more than six lines and no more than six words per line. A single word or short phrase is almost always more effective than a complete sentence. While addressing a marketing task force charged with developing and publicizing a campus communication center, one of your authors used the bulleted list featured in Figure 10.8.

Another frequently used type of textual graphic presents an **acronym** composed of the initial letters of words to help your audience remember your message. One speaker chose the topic of how military language has seeped into everyday use. As one example, she offered the term "snafu," commonly used to refer to a mistake, problem, or confusion that is par for the course, and then showed the image in Figure 10.9 to depict the word's origin as an acronym. When preparing such a graphic, use the acronym as a title, then list the words under it. Use size and/or color to make the first letters of the words stand out.

Figure 10.7 Flow Chart: Creating a Website

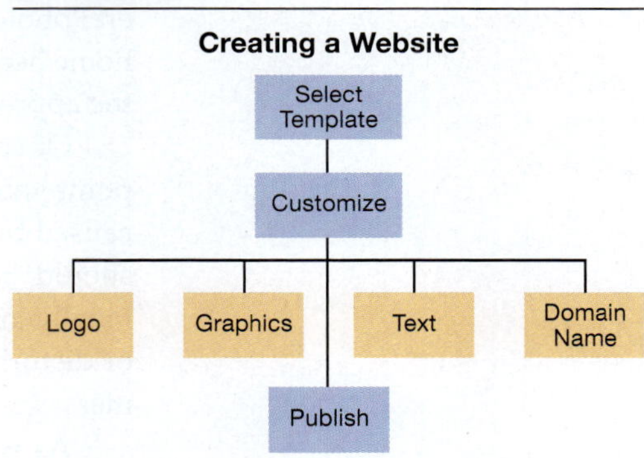

Figure 10.8 Bulleted List

Marketing Task Force

- Mission Statement
- Current Image
- Target Market
- Desired Image

Figure 10.9 Acronym Graphic

SNAFU

SITUATION
NORMAL:
ALL
FOULED
UP!

Pictures

Pictures and photographs can be powerful presentation aids. A good photograph can authenticate a point in a way that words cannot. Like vividly described examples, they can transport your listeners and engage them on an emotional level. For instance, if you were presenting a speech on the devastation caused by a recent hurricane, you would likely find and share information on the strength of the storm, the extent and cost of property damage, and the number of people displaced or worse. Think of how much more effective your presentation might be if you also displayed a photo like the one in Figure 10.10 of a house that has been split in half by a hurricane.

Figure 10.10 Projected Photograph

textual graphics
Visuals that contain words, phrases, or numbers.

bulleted list
A presentation aid that highlights ideas by presenting them as a list of brief statements.

acronym
A word composed of the initial letters of a series of words.

Pictures can also help make connections with your audience. When Jody Cross spoke to the Kansas City Association of Realtors, she included the group's logo and several photographs of homes from their own website. By doing so, Jody not only brought home her point about using visual images to connect with her audience, she also earned the appreciation of her listeners for demonstrating that she understood them.

Of course, the pictures you choose should accurately represent your topic or the point you are making. You shouldn't use a stock photograph to illustrate the damage caused by a specific storm, for example, and—as discussed later in this chapter—you should be cautious of using images that may have been altered or manipulated. Finally, on most occasions, you should avoid the use of pictures that are so graphic or disturbing that they might upset your listeners and distract them from your actual message.

As with all presentation aids, the pictures you project or display should be relevant to the point you are making while you display them, and they should be large enough for everyone in the audience to see. As a general rule, photographs should be at least 11 by 17 inches for speeches in small boardrooms or classrooms and considerably larger when addressing larger audiences in larger venues such as an auditorium. As with small objects, you should not distribute small photographs for your listeners to look at during your presentation because they will tend to distract attention from your actual presentation.

On most occasions, you should limit the number of pictures for brief presentations because too many may overwhelm your audience and undermine their capacity to emphasize your most important points. However, on some occasions, a series of artfully narrated pictures in succession can be really effective—for example, to encourage your classmates to visit a nearby travel destination or to trace the career and evolution of a noted artist or photographer. As we discuss in the next section, today's technology makes it increasingly easy to weave pictures and other presentation aids seamlessly into your presentations.

> **Using Effective Presentation Aids**
>
> Identify three of the four types of presentation aids in speeches you have seen. What made them effective? What made them ineffective?

Presentation Media

10.3 Select the most appropriate means of presenting your aids.

The many *types* of presentation aids can be shared with your audience through a variety of presentation *media*. Traditional media include *flip charts, posters, handouts, chalk or marker boards, transparencies, videotapes,* and *audiotapes*. Newer presentation media use computer programs such as *PowerPoint* and *Prezi* that can incorporate slides, films, DVDs, and sound. These newer media have become the standard for presentations in organizational and educational settings. Although you may be best acquainted with the computer versions, familiarity with other media allows you greater creativity as well as options when technology is not available.

Traditional Media

Many speakers head immediately for newer presentation media. Yet traditional media still offer a variety of useful opportunities for showing presentation aids.

flip chart
A large, unlined tablet (usually a newsprint pad) placed on an easel so that as each page is filled up it can be flipped over the top.

Flip Charts. A **flip chart** is a large, unlined tablet placed on an easel so that each page can be flipped over the top when you are done with it. Most flip charts are newsprint pads that measure about 2 feet wide by 3 feet high. They are convenient, inexpensive, and adaptable to many settings. One speaker used flip charts to show how he developed caricatures for his editorial cartoons. Because flip charts are meant to be used spontaneously, they are especially useful at meetings when subjects come up that should be written out so that they can be analyzed and understood.

Although flip charts can be effective in some group communication settings, they don't work as well in classroom speeches. Their use suggests that the speaker did not care enough to prepare a polished presentation aid that would be easy for the audience to see. Writing on a flip chart also forces speakers either to stop speaking while they write or to speak while facing away from the audience, which may offset any gain from using the charts.

Finding Your Voice

Alternative Media

Consider this scenario: Due to a complicated legal battle, all computer-generated programs have been temporarily withdrawn from the market—but you still need to give a presentation, and you need to illustrate several of your points. How could you use traditional media to give voice to your ideas in ways that would engage your audience?

Chalk and Marker Boards. A chalk or marker board is available in almost every classroom and many corporate conference rooms. Like flip charts, chalk and marker boards should not be used for more formal presentations, but they can be really effective for spontaneous improvisation. For instance, if you notice that some of your listeners look confused as you make a short presentation, you might write a few words or draw a simple diagram to clarify your most important points. Because you inevitably lose eye contact with listeners while writing on a board, do not use this medium for anything that will take more than a few seconds to write or draw. Never use chalk or marker boards simply because you did not want to take the time to prepare a more polished presentation aid.

Posters. Posters can be used to display pictures, sketches, maps, charts, graphs, or textual graphics. In an average-size room with a small audience, posters about 14 by 17 inches may work best; they are easier to handle than larger sizes. You can place the posters face down on the lectern or table and display them as you refer to them. You can also use the back of a poster to remind you of names of people or to cue you to the next point in your presentation. One student had trouble remembering the name of the president of Iran, a brief but important reference in his speech. He wrote it on the back of the large photograph of the man, so when he raised it to show the audience, he could read "Hassan Rouh-ha-ni."

Handouts. Handouts are useful when your subject is complex or your message contains a lot of statistical information, and they can extend the impact of your speech and validate the information you have presented. Pass them out *after* your speech so listeners have something to remind them of what you said. If you distribute a handout before you speak, the audience will read it rather than listening to you. If it is absolutely necessary for listeners to refer to a handout during your presentation, it is better to guide them through an enlarged version where you can control what portions they see at a time. Never distribute handouts during your speech. This is a sure-fire way to disrupt your presentation and confuse or lose listeners. Multipage handouts are multi-distracting.

Transparencies, Projections, and Slides. Transparencies, projections by document cameras, and slides allow listeners to see graphics or photographs more easily, especially when audiences are large or spread out in a big room. Business speakers often prefer them to posters or flip charts because they look more professional.

Transparencies are easier to use than slides because you don't have to darken the room when you show them. They are simple and inexpensive to make. You can write on a transparency while it is being shown, adding spontaneity to your presentation. You can also use a pen or pencil as a pointer to direct your listeners' attention to features you want to emphasize.

Document cameras can project either transparencies or hard copy onto a large screen. To explain how to read music, for example, you might show the score of Handel's *Messiah* while playing a recorded section, pointing to the various parts in the score as the instruments and choral parts enter the piece.

When you show slides with a carousel projector, the room usually has to be darkened. Unfortunately, this means that the illuminated screen becomes the center of attention rather than you. One major disadvantage of using transparencies, document cameras, or slides is that often you must speak from where your equipment is located. If you have to stand behind listeners or in the middle of the audience to run the projector, you will be talking to someone's back. If remote-controlled equipment is not available, your best solution may be to practice having a classmate change the projections or slides on cue.

Generally speakers now prepare transparencies and slides on personal computers. You can purchase transparency sheets for use with most printers. You can also draw or print your material onto plain paper and convert it to a transparency on a copier. If you have access to only a black-and-white copier or printer, you can use opaque markers to add color. Framing your transparencies will avoid glare from light showing around the outside edges of the projection.

When you arrange slides in a carousel, be sure they are in the proper order and that none of them are upside down and/or backward. Today, most personal computers are packaged with software that allows you to prepare and present slides without a carousel projector. We discuss this in greater detail in our section on new media.

Video and Audio Resources. Video and audio resources such as DVDs, videotapes, computer recordings, and CDs can add variety to your presentation. Make sure in advance that the place where you will be making your presentation has the proper equipment to work with your materials.

Video resources are useful for transporting the audience to distant, dangerous, or otherwise unavailable locations. Although you could verbally describe the beauty of the Montana Rockies, your word-pictures can become more powerful if reinforced with actual scenes projected electronically.

Using video poses special problems for speakers. Moving images attract more attention than the spoken word, so they can easily upstage you. In a short speech, keep the focus on the speaker by limiting video and audio clips to thirty seconds or less. A videotape segment must be edited so that splices blend cleanly, and such editing takes special skill and equipment. A simpler means is to transfer this material onto a CD, which can be done on most personal computers with a DVD/CD burner. For certain topics, carefully prepared videos can be more effective than any other type of presentation aid. A student at Northwest Mississippi Community College who was a firefighter used videotape in an informative speech on fire hazards in the home. By customizing the video to fit the precise needs of his speech, he was able to show long shots of a room and then zoom in on various hazards. He prepared the video without sound so that his speech provided the commentary needed to interpret and explain the pictures. Using this technique, he made his subject much more meaningful for listeners.[12]

Audio resources may also be useful as presentation aids. Sabrina Karic started her self-introductory speech on growing up in war-torn Bosnia and Herzegovina with a recording of a loud explosion and gunfire, during which she ducked beneath the table as the audience jumped (see "A Little Chocolate" at the end of Chapter 3). When in doubt about the wisdom or practicality of using such aids, consult your instructor.

SPEAKER'S NOTES

Deciding What Presentation Media to Use

Let the following suggestions guide your selection of presentation media.

When you need to . . .	try using . . .
☐ adapt to audience feedback	☐ flip charts or chalk or marker boards
☐ display maps, charts, graphs, or textual graphics	☐ posters or computerized programs
☐ present complex information or statistical data	☐ handouts or slides
☐ display graphics or photos to a large audience	☐ slides or transparencies
☐ authenticate a point	☐ audio and video resources
☐ make your presentation appear more professional	☐ computerized programs

PowerPoint, Prezi, iPad Apps, and More

Computer-generated presentations have become ubiquitous. When properly designed and used well, they can bring together text, numbers, pictures, music, video clips, and artwork to create polished and compelling slides, videos, animations, and audio materials. Used poorly, they will bore, confuse, and annoy your audience—and perhaps you as well. In *Presentations* magazine, Rebecca Ganzel pictured the following scenario:

computer-generated presentation
The use of commercial presentation software to join audio, visual, textual, graphic, and animated components.

> It's that nightmare again—the one in which you're trapped in the Electronic Presentation from Hell. The familiar darkness presses in, periodically sliced in half by a fiendish light. Bullet points, about 18 to a slide, careen in all directions. You cringe, but the slides keep coming, too fast to read, each with a new template you half-remember seeing a hundred times before: Dad's Tie! Sixties Swirls! Infinite Double-Helixes! A typewriter clatters; brakes squeal. Somewhere in the shadows, a voice drones on. Strange stick people shake hands and dance around a flow chart. Typefaces morph into Word Art.
>
> But the worst is yet to come. As though you're watching a train wreck in slow motion, you look down at your hand—and *you're holding the remote.*[13]

If swirling backgrounds and flashy transitions attract more attention than your ideas, they will overpower your voice. Yet electronic presentation aids can provide vivid, engaging enhancements that bring your ideas alive for your audience. Moreover, in certain settings, such presentation formats are simply expected. Using them well will set you apart from the countless speeches that commit "Death by PowerPoint."

PowerPoint Presentations and Their Cousins. Undoubtedly, the most ubiquitous form of presentation software is PowerPoint. Why is PowerPoint so popular? For starters, it is the most widely available software of its type, coming prepackaged on many computers sold to businesses and educational institutions. PowerPoint is also fairly easy to use. The software contains templates and comes with a step-by-step online tutorial. Apple's version of presentation software is Keynote. Some users—especially Mac devotees—find it more straightforward with better graphic design and multimedia interfaces than PowerPoint. However, some run into problems of incompatibility in a PowerPoint-dominated world.[14] Android users have a similar alternative in SoftMaker Presentations Mobile, an inexpensive app that can create PowerPoint-like slides on the go. As presentation software, it is a less agile cousin to PowerPoint, but it can also import PowerPoint shows from a variety of sources, including Dropbox and Google Drive. Although other programs are proliferating—for

Figure 10.11
A Satiric PowerPoint for the Gettysburg Address

Source: Reprinted with permission from Peter Norvig, "The Gettysburg Powerpoint Presentation," http://norvig.com/Gettysburg/.

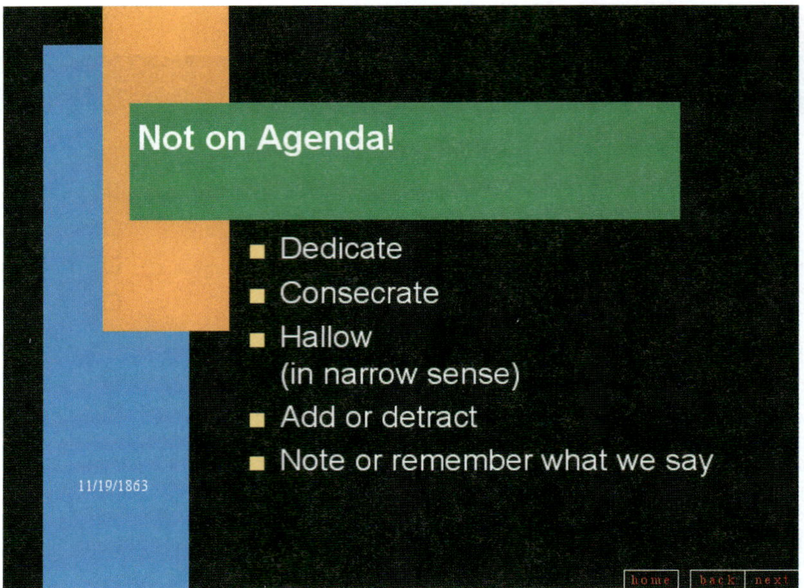

example, Apache OpenOffice, Impress, Kingsoft Presentation Free, Slide Bureau, Google Presentation, and Zoho, and such animation programs as Reallusion and Powtoon, to name a few—PowerPoint still dominates the market.

PowerPoint is not only the most used but also the most frequently *misused* type of presentation aid, in part *because* it is so easy to use. Who has not been subjected to poor PowerPoint presentations that annoy the audience, mask the message, and harm the speaker's credibility? Peter Norvig, the director of research for Google, endured one too many of these suffocating speeches. He responded by creating a tongue-in-cheek PowerPoint version of the Gettysburg Address (see Figure 10.11) that "captured the main phrases of the original, while losing all the flow, eloquence, and impact."[15]

Yet used well, PowerPoint can be a powerful tool that amplifies your voice instead of masking it. Attorney Mark Lanier showed the potential of PowerPoint in a significant trial charging Merck, the company producing Vioxx, with causing the death of Bob Ernst. After addressing the jury and introducing them to Bob's widow, Carol (Lanier's client), the lawyer displayed a family photograph of the couple as he told anecdotes and family history. His next slide retained the image of the couple, but this time without the background, as he talked about what started to go wrong. The next slide showed Carol and the blank background, but now Bob's figure was replaced with a big empty outline such as you see at murder scenes. Against this slide, Lanier told the jury that Bob Ernst was dead. By pairing verbal and visual storytelling, Lanier eventually won the trial for his client, even in a conservative part of the country not prone to awarding damages against a large company.[16]

Using PowerPoint well requires an understanding that it is fundamentally a *visual* medium. Moreover, it is a *design* medium rather than a brainstorming medium. If your first instinct is to create your speech in PowerPoint, step away from the computer, and reconsider. If your second instinct is to cut and paste what you've written, step away from the computer, and reconsider. Presentation designer Garr Reynolds observes that, if you attempt to merge a document for a written presentation into slides for an oral presentation, all you end up with is a "slideument" that doesn't serve either purpose well.[17] And, if you do end up with a "slideument," your audience will read faster than you can speak, and in the process everyone—including you—will be bored. As graphic designer Robin Williams notes, "The problem is not really that you are reading the slide—*the problem is that you have put everything you're going to say on that slide.*"[18]

When Amazon CEO Jeff Bezos introduced the Kindle Fire HD, he wanted to emphasize that the new version of the e-reader had an eight-week battery life. He might have put it as one entry in a long line of bulleted points. Snooze! To pack a greater punch, Bezos showed a calendar with the months September and October. September 6, which was the day of his presentation, was highlighted in red. Bezos explained that if turned on during his presentation, the Kindle Fire's eight-week battery would last until the end of October. That's a powerful image that most likely will not be forgotten.[19]

Gabrielle Wallace used a similar approach in her informative speech on the apparent contradiction of the French eating and drinking well but rarely gaining weight. Rather than using PowerPoint to list her thesis, detail her main points, and repeat her quotations, she paired her discussion of how the French dine with photographs of red wine, fruits, vegetables, and bread. Instead of putting her prelunch audience to sleep, she had us drooling over her vibrant visual images and hanging on her every word.

Conceptualizing your PowerPoint as a fundamentally visual presentation aid is an important first step. In addition, other basic principles can help you find your voice:

- Follow the *basics of preparation* detailed in the next section, with particular attention to using a simple template, contrasting colors, clear images, and minimal language.
- *Pare your language* to the absolute minimum. The rule of thumb is no more than six lines per slide, with no more than six words per line—but that does not mean that you should cram thirty-six words onto a slide. Focus on your key words, and determine whether, like Jeff Bezos, you would get a bigger bang from "eight weeks' worth of battery life" or a highlighted calendar.
- As you design the slides, *step back from the computer* to get a better idea of how it will look to your audience. Nancy Duarte of Duarte Designs suggests measuring your computer screen diagonally and then translating inches into feet: For a 17-inch computer screen, for example, stand 17 feet away. That will give you a better way to gauge the visibility of your slides when they are projected than you have by sitting right next to the monitor.[20]
- If one slide contains material you will discuss sequentially, such as before-and-after pictures or the bulleted list of Figure 10.8, *use the "entrance" code* to make subsequent portions appear at the click of the mouse. Structure each slide similar to a billboard, for which you only have three seconds to process the information as you zoom by.[21]
- At the points in your presentation when you do not need an aid, *insert blank slides or hit the "b" key* for a black screen so that your audience will not be distracted.
- Make sure your slides don't overwhelm your presentation. You don't want your speech to become just a voice-over for a slide show.
- Be sure to *proofread* your slides carefully—and have others proofread for you. It's really embarrassing, distracting, and harmful to your ethos to have major typos projected for all to see.
- *Check your presentation in the room* where you will present. What's clear when right in front of you on the computer may appear murky when it's projected.
- After you've finalized your presentation, *save it as "PowerPoint Show"* so that you can immediately open to the first slide rather than having to click your way into it.

Slate's technology columnist Farhad Manjoo observes, "When people write annoying e-mails or make inscrutable spreadsheets, we don't blame Outlook and Excel; we blame the people. But for many of us, PowerPoint software is synonymous with the terrible output it often generates."[22] Follow the guidelines above, and you will give a good name to PowerPoint and a better name to yourself. Avoid committing "suislide" by displaying a PowerPoint slide like that in Figure 10.12.[23] The tutorials accompanying PowerPoint often encourage the use of busy templates, bullet points, animation schemes, and other distractions; choose wisely, with your audience in mind.

Figure 10.12 How *Not* to Use PowerPoint

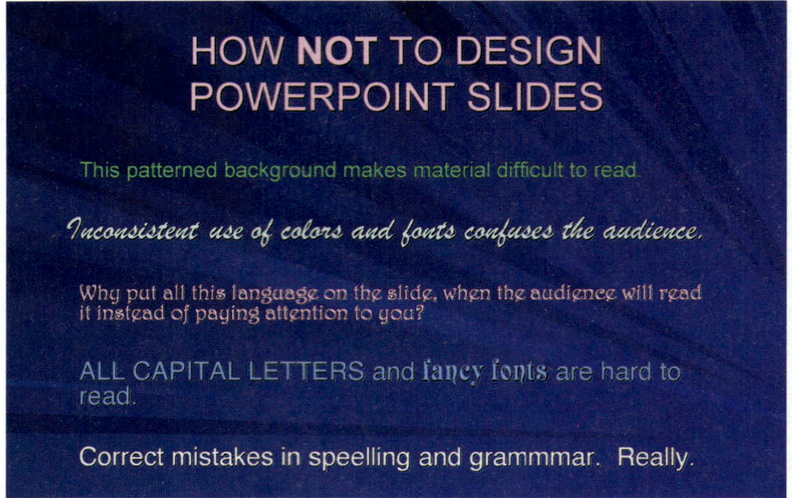

Prezi Presentations. Whereas PowerPoint uses a linear approach with one slide appearing after another, Prezi allows a three-dimensional approach to explore the interconnections. Rather than one slide following another, Prezi emphasizes interconnections and relationships by using a "canvas" on which you place your concepts. You can group ideas, layer concepts, zoom in to focus in more detail on one aspect, and then zoom out to return to the big picture. As with PowerPoint, you can incorporate images, videos, sound, and language. Dr. Scott Titsworth of Ohio University explains,

> Prezi allows you to visually travel inside ideas. As a child did you ever go into your backyard and use a magnifying glass to look at things? You get a broad view and then zoom down to see very fine details to learn more about the big picture. Prezi does that for you in presentations. You create everything for your presentation on a big canvas, and can embed smaller pictures or clusters of ideas within that larger picture (this can create some very cool surprises for those in the audience). . . . Prezi allows you to think about ways in which holistic visual designs can enhance and augment a spoken narrative.[24]

Prezi offers a visually stimulating, layered, almost cinematic approach to presentation aids. Katie Lovett used Prezi to develop a powerful persuasive speech against bottled water. She took her audience inside the marketing strategies, consumer misconceptions, and environmental effects, showing relationships and consequences in a dynamic way that had us mesmerized. Although she found it relatively easy to learn,

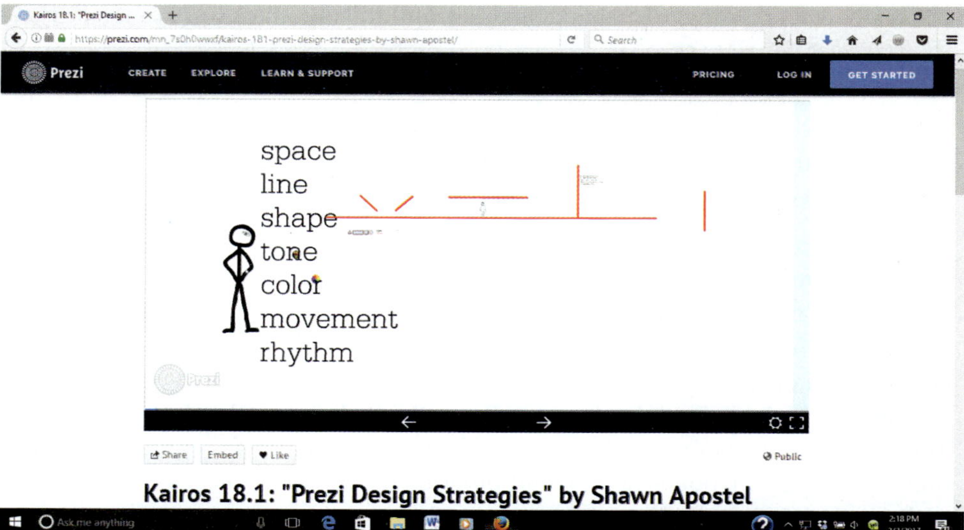

This online guide to the design of Prezi presentations demonstrates the effective use of key components.

Prezi Designed by Dr Shawn Apostel.

she did caution that she so enjoyed playing with the software that she had to rein herself in. Other students have found it more difficult to figure out, particularly if they are unaccustomed to visualizing their information.

Graphic design professor Shawn Apostel suggests that good Prezis start with visual metaphors.[25] Those metaphors often form the overall shape of the presentation, either used at the beginning and ending or revealed only as a zoom-out at the conclusion. Examples include the influence of jazz bass players in the shape of a guitar, an explanation of the process of designing a new public school library displayed as a tree, and budgeting for a college student conceived as income versus debts on a set of scales. In each case, the Prezi moves from the macroscopic view to more microscopic perspectives and back again. In the Prezi on jazz bass players, for example, the overview of the guitar then moves along the guitar's neck as a timeline, with various players placed along the frets in chronological order. Short video examples are embedded along the way.

Effective Prezis do not need to be this complicated, however. Apostel advises using shapes as simple as a circle or a square to frame your presentation or a background image such as a cloud.[26] Apostel's Prezi on designing such presentations, illustrated above, begins with a canvas that shows his major concepts, delves into each one in turn, and then pulls back to remind viewers of the outline.[27]

Give your audience the overview at the outset, to serve as a visual preview, and then move through each point in turn. If you prepare your audience for movements among areas and use big jumps in perspective sparingly, they will mean more, and your audience won't suffer motion sickness.

Using Prezi does pose certain challenges. With its constant changes, Prezi does not serve longer presentations well, as it's likely to cause "Prezilepsy."[28] Like Keynote in a PowerPoint world, not all technology is equally receptive. Some Prezi users report that the presentations work better on Macs than on PCs; others have not been able to get the program to work with a remote control mouse. Prezi.com contains a description, tutorials, and sample presentations on a wide variety of topics. The basic format is available to the public free of charge; students and educators can receive a more advanced free version by registering. Apostel offers a useful tutorial on Prezi.com that can guide your development of a presentation aid. One caution about examples of Prezis you will find online: Many are designed as self-contained messages as opposed to a presentation aid, so they include far too much text to be used for a speech.

iPad Apps. Two applications may be especially useful for iPad aficionados: Haiku Deck and Pixxa Perspective. Haiku Deck draws its name from a form of Japanese poetry that is beautiful and evocative in its simplicity. That form evokes the goal of this software's developers: The three young men from Seattle wanted a format for iPads that would be clean, concise, and fun. Key to the success of Haiku Deck: the numerous ways to incorporate images—from your own iPad, from websites (including social media), or from their vast store of illustrations available through Creative Commons without copyright entanglements and with automatic attribution. Searching that store of illustrations proves as simple as typing in a key word or two—for example, "mountains" or "winter scenes"—and looking through the options.

This easy access to visual images combines with sharp constraints on the number of words that can be included on each slide. Haiku Deck allows only two lines of language and only five items per bulleted list. Such "radical simplicity," as one user calls it, can be both an advantage and a disadvantage: Although the software emphasizes clean, clear visual storytelling, it may create challenges for those who are not comfortable working within its restrictions.[29] In addition, its current version does not allow for sound, transitions, or animations, although these capacities may be added soon.

Haiku Deck is free, with additional resources available for a small fee. Online tutorials and blogs can assist in the construction of slide decks. Currently, it can be used on iPads, iPhones, and the web, and you can use the iPhone as a remote for the presentation. You can export your presentation to PowerPoint or Keynote after uploading it on the Haiku Deck site, or you can share it via Facebook, Twitter, or e-mail—a handy way to get additional guidance from your instructor before the presentation.

A second application for iPads is Pixxa Perspective. Unlike the predominantly free Haiku Deck, Pixxa Perspective charges for a variety of apps. Yet for that charge, Perspective provides the capacity for not only text, images, and diagrams for each "scene" or slide, but also interactive motion charts. If you wanted to show, for instance, the relationship between tuition costs and initial salaries after graduation, you could post a graph and then put it in motion to show the changes in the correlations or to pass through the data from various years. A spreadsheet can be turned into charts quickly. Perspective has also added the capacities to incorporate both sound and video.

Like Haiku Deck, Perspective presentations are available only for iPads and can be tweeted and e-mailed. Unlike Haiku Deck, wireless connections may allow projection to a large screen, and Perspective can be used to record your presentation for playback and analysis.

As you might imagine, some users—especially those who are not familiar with the technology—may find that Perspective poses more challenges to learn than Haiku Deck, even with online assistance. In either case, adapt the guidelines for developing effective PowerPoint presentations, and prepare for the prospect that the techno-gremlins that lurk in *any* technology may wreak havoc, especially for people who are not as comfortable with the software and are nervous about their presentations to boot.

What Will They Think of Next? Although PowerPoint, its younger relative Prezi, and new iPad arrivals overshadow other presentation media, other technologies that can be incorporated into speeches spring up regularly. Clickers or their free online version in Socrative, for example, can be used during an informative speech to let the listeners test themselves on their knowledge of the topic or during a persuasive speech to identify how audience members react to particular ideas and proposals. PowerPoint now comes in a version for tablets, and smartphones have an app for that.

One commencement speaker made an ingenious use of modern technology. Addressing graduates at Queens University of Charlotte, Eric Newton of the nonprofit Knight Foundation showed them brief videos about three nonprofit organizations and then asked them to use their cell phones to text their choice of the three. The winning organization received a $50,000 check on the spot. Newton then challenged the graduates:

> Doesn't it feel good to give?... Tonight, my hope is that students walk away with a clearer understanding of the incredible power of digital media. We have the ability, at our fingertips, to make an instant difference in the lives of those in need, and it is our responsibility as noble citizens to do just that.[30]

By asking the graduates to bring their cell phones (not that they needed much urging), Newton created suspense. By asking them to vote and then acting on the results, he involved the audience in an immediate way. By showing them what a difference their digital involvement made, he capitalized on the opportunity to demonstrate that small actions have big consequences and that each person can indeed make a difference.

Technological innovations proliferate at such a rapid pace that from the beginning of any given semester to its end, more presentation media will probably appear. Tried and true or new and sexy, presentation aids can help you find your voice if you prepare and use them well.

Using Software Programs as Presentation Aids

Find a presentation online that uses one of the presentation software programs listed here. What are the strengths of this program for the kinds of speeches you deliver? What are the challenges such a program poses? How could you address those challenges?

Preparing Presentation Aids

10.4 Plan, design, and prepare presentation aids.

Once you have decided what types of aids you want to use and what available media will be most appropriate for sharing them, you should begin the process of planning and preparing your presentation aids for maximum effect. As our discussion so far suggests, presentation aids can either make or break a speech. Before plopping yourself in front of your computer, take some time to read back through your notes and consider how particular aids could most enliven and enrich your most important ideas and information. Experts recommend that you start by experimenting with rough drafts using good old-fashioned pencil and paper, or the ever-handy sticky notes, for developing your initial ideas.[31] This process will allow you adequate time to let your ideas incubate, grow, and develop.[32]

Once you have selected the appropriate types of aids and media to give voice to your ideas, create them following basic principles of *design* and *color*. "If the content…can't be understood because of poor design," PowerPoint consultant Dave Paradi points out, "there is no way it can be an aid to the presenter."[33]

Principles of Design

A good presentation aid is simple, easily seen, appropriately focused, and well balanced. Consider the basic principles of *simplicity, visibility, emphasis,* and *balance* as you plan and prepare your materials. Look at your aids from the perspective of an audience member to see if they meet these criteria. As graphic designer Alex W. White quips, "One definition of good design is the balance between monotony and the designer's self-indulgence."[34]

Simplicity. Each presentation aid should focus on illustrating a single idea or related set of information. Beginning speakers often try to cram too much information into a single aid, which distracts listeners as they try to figure out what everything is and what it means. We had one student divide a standard 2- by 3-foot poster into twelve segments, glue samples of medicinal herbs in each box, and then print its name and use under each sample. Needless to say, only listeners in the front row could actually read any of the print, and the aid created more confusion than illumination. He would have been better served had he used a series of smaller posters, each featuring one herb, displayed as he talked about each one in turn.

Consider how much language is really necessary on your aid. Think back to the opening of this chapter: As a listener, would you be more engaged by the speaker reading a slide with the definition of dyslexia from *Black's Medical Dictionary* or by the visualization of what a dyslexic might see? You might be tempted to use moving objects, flying text, or repeated sound effects. Surveys report that these "special effects" regularly make the Top Ten list of annoying presentation features.[35]

Visibility. The size of any presentation aid must be appropriate to the setting in which it is used. Listeners in the back of the room must be able to see and read your presentation aids without straining. Bringing a full-sized canoe into a small room will prove both cumbersome for you and overwhelming for your listeners. Bringing a six-inch model or photograph of a canoe may be more manageable, but those beyond the first row will be irritated that they can't see it.

Visual images should also make it easy for audience members to understand your intended message. That photograph of your first date might be a riot, but if most of your audience can't tell who's in it or what the setting is, you'll have to figure out a better way to share it. You may love the way a chart of the impact of a tornado ripping through Oklahoma represents its complexity and the scope of the disaster, but if your

Figure 10.13 Choosing the Right Typeface

Empowering your voice:	Shouting over your voice:
Baskerville	Algerian
Bodoni	Brush Script
Franklin Gothic	Curlz
Garamond	Old English
Rockwell	Snap

audience can't make heads or tails of the elaborate connections, it will drown out your own voice.

Make sure the words on your presentation aids are clearly legible, or risk committing another sin from the Top Ten.[36] For slides, for example, use at least a 24-point type font for titles, 14-point for subtitles, and 12-point for other text. Choose an easily read typeface that emphasizes your ideas rather than itself. Figure 10.13 can help you distinguish appropriate typefaces to empower your voice. On rare occasions, you might employ one of the fancier fonts, but as a rule stick to those that are clearly legible from a distance. When preparing poster boards or flip charts, plot letters that are at least an inch and a half in size (preferably a little larger), and use wide markers in strong colors to make sure that those in the back of the room can see clearly.

Finally, just as audience members should be able to easily read and interpret visual materials, they need to be able to easily hear your audio materials. If the sound of a recording or video is so soft that your listeners can't hear, then your point about the differences in hip-hop styles will be lost. If it's too loud, you risk blasting them out of the room and upstaging your actual message.

Emphasis. Your presentation aids should emphasize your most important ideas and supporting materials. Your listeners' eyes should be drawn immediately to what you want to illustrate. On the acronym chart (see Figure 10.9), the first letter of each word stands out. The map of Yellowstone Park mentioned earlier contained only the attractions the speaker planned to talk about and the route between them. Had she added pictures of bears to indicate grizzly habitats, drawings of fish to show trout streams, and photos of mountains to designate the terrain, the presentation aid would have been cluttered and distracting.

Choose only the aspects of the image, the language, or the sounds that are most directly relevant to the point you want to make, and focus on those. Full sentences and complex diagrams also make the dreaded Top Ten list.[37] As designer Robin Williams advises, you want to "get rid of superfluous stuff. You don't need all kinds of gewgaws sitting on your slide cluttering up your information."[38] Illustrating the workings of an airplane cockpit will make more sense to your audience if you highlight each control as you discuss it.[39] When in doubt, leave the details out. Let your spoken words provide the elaboration.

Balance. Presentation aids that are balanced are pleasing to the eye. You achieve balance when you position textual materials so that they form a consistent pattern. Don't overload a slide or try to use every square inch of a posterboard. Plot center points carefully while planning your aids, and use the margins and white space to frame your materials and focus your listeners' attention.

Principles of Color

As many of the illustrations in this chapter show, color adds impact to presentation aids. Colorful presentation aids tend to attract and hold attention better than black-and-white ones. Color also can convey or enhance meaning. A speech about crop damage from a drought, for example, might use an enlarged outline map with natural colors to reinforce the message: the least affected areas in green, moderately damaged areas in yellow, and severely affected areas in brown.

Color can also be used to create moods and impressions. Figure 10.14 shows some of the reactions that various groups might have toward colors. For most Americans, blue suggests power, authority, and stability (blue chip, blue ribbon, royal blue). Using blue in your graphics can evoke positive reactions toward a proposal. Red signals excitement or crisis (in the red, red ink, "I saw red"). Line graphs tracing a rise in campus crimes might be drawn in red to convey the urgency of the problem. On the other hand, you should avoid using red when presenting financial data unless you want to focus on debts or losses. In American culture, green is associated with both money (greenbacks) and environmental concerns (Greenpeace), but medical personnel associate it with infection. Cultural differences also influence how people interpret colors. In the United States, for example, white is associated with weddings, baptisms, confirmations, and other joyous rituals. In Japan and India, however, white is a funeral color, associated with sadness. Go online to Webdesignabout.com to explore more culturally based color associations.

Figure 10.14 Meanings of Colors

	Movie-goers	Financiers	Doctors
Blue	Tender emotions	Reliable	Cold
Green	Playful	Profitable	Infection
Yellow	Happy	Highlighted/ important	Jaundice
Red	Exciting	Unprofitable	Hot/radioactive

Source: Courtesy of La Puerta Books and Media.

The way you use colors in combination can convey subtle nuances of meaning. An **analogous color scheme** uses colors that are adjacent in the color spectrum, such as blue, blue-green, and green. This type of color scheme shows the differences among elements, while suggesting their close connection and compatibility. For example, a pie graph could use analogous colors to represent the students, faculty, and administration of a university. The different colors suggest that, although these parts are separate, they belong together. In this subtle way, the presentation aid implies that these components of a university should work together.

analogous color scheme
Colors adjacent on the color wheel; used in a presentation aid to suggest both differences and close relationships among the components.

complementary color scheme
Colors opposite one another on the color wheel; used in a presentation aid to suggest tension and opposition.

monochromatic color scheme
Use of variations of a single color in a presentation aid to convey the idea of variety within unity.

A **complementary color scheme** uses colors that are opposites on the color wheel, such as red and green. Complementary color schemes suggest tension and opposition among elements in a speech. Because they heighten the sense of drama, they may enliven informative speaking and encourage change in persuasive speaking.

A **monochromatic color scheme** uses variations of a single color. The acronym graphic (Figure 10.9) uses a monochromatic color scheme. These schemes suggest variety within unity. A monochromatic color scheme would be inappropriate for bar graphs or line graphs because they require more contrast to be effective.

Figure 10.15 illustrates these three types of color schemes. Find an online tool to assist with color choices, such as AdobeColor.com, ColorHunter.com, or Palleton.com.

The colors you use for letters and numbers in a presentation aid should contrast sharply with the background. As Figure 10.12 demonstrates, patterned or shaded backgrounds can make words difficult to read. For most occasions, speakers use lighter colors for backgrounds and strong primary colors such as dark blue and green for lettering. We do not recommend using red letters against a light background because it tends to bleed, which makes the words blurry and difficult to read. When speaking in rooms with bright lighting, lighter backgrounds—especially brilliant whites—can create glare. On such occasions, you might want to choose a darker background scheme, and use lighter colors such as white for projecting textual messages.

Analyzing the Use of Presentation Aids

Return to the presentation you selected using one of the presentation software programs. Analyze its presentation aids using the principles of design and color.

Color contrast is especially important for computer-generated slides and transparencies. Because projection creates a lower resolution, colors will appear less distinct when projected than they do when seen on a computer monitor. Such colors as pastel pink, light blue, and pale yellow, and hues with a grayish tinge, may not be strong enough for good

Figure 10.15 Types of Color Schemes

ANALOGOUS	COMPLEMENTARY	MONOCHROMATIC
students	problem	beginning
faculty	solution	middle
administration		end

graphic emphasis in any type of presentation aid. The rich burgundy background that looks so great on your computer might look more like muddy water once it is projected. Run a sample, and project it to see how the final colors will actually look to an audience. If the results are not what you expected, try other colors until you are satisfied. Keep uppermost in your mind the maxim from designer Garr Reynolds: "Think communication—not decoration."[40]

SPEAKER'S NOTES

Checklist for Preparing Presentation Aids

Each presentation aid should meet these criteria:

_____ My aid emphasizes a key point in my presentation.

_____ Each aid focuses on only one major idea.

_____ My aid is easy to see or hear.

_____ Each presentation aid is as simple as I can make it.

_____ My images and print are large enough to be seen from the back of the room.

_____ My aid has good color contrast that helps to project it effectively.

_____ I use colors and lettering consistently.

_____ I have ample margins at the top, bottom, and sides of my aid.

_____ I have checked for spelling errors.

_____ I have checked the room where I will give my speech and know that my presentation aid will work there.

_____ I know how I will show each aid at the appropriate point and how I will hide it before and after.

_____The audio portion of my aid can be clearly heard throughout the room.

Using Presentation Aids

10.5 Use presentation aids well.

Even the best-designed presentation aids require skillful use to enhance a speech. As we discussed each type of presentation aid, we made suggestions on how to use it in a speech. Here, we bring these suggestions together and extract some general guidelines.

First, be sure to *practice* using your presentation aids so that you can integrate them smoothly into your speech. Otherwise, you may find yourself fumbling around and referring to them awkwardly after making a point, or forgetting to reference them altogether until the end of your speech. Plan for transitions such as, "As you can see on this chart . . .," and practice your references to them while maintaining eye contact with an imagined audience. Stand to the side of your aids while speaking so that listeners can easily see them, and point to what you are talking about so they can easily follow with their eyes. By all means, be sure you aren't committing the number one sin on the Top Ten list of annoying presentations: speaking to or from your presentation aids.[41]

Take the opportunity to check out the site where you will be speaking ahead of time to consider *the logistics of displaying and using your presentation aids*. Step back and view them from the back row. Can you read them without straining? Is everything spelled correctly? Is your eye drawn to what is most important? Have you positioned your materials for easy viewing? Do the images look balanced? Do you need an easel for a poster board or flip chart? Should you bring masking tape or push pins? If you plan to use objects, models, posters, flip charts, and other physical aids, consider how you will display them while speaking and how you will conceal your aids both before and after using them.

Check out any electronic equipment you will use (e.g., computer, document camera, or DVD player), and practice using it in the room in which you will speak. Do you need an extension cord or a remote mouse? Can you control the level of light in the room so your presentation aids can be seen? What works on your personal computer, for example, might not work on the classroom computer. Be certain that any equipment in the classroom is working properly and that you can operate it. If you are using computerized materials on a CD, DVD, or jump drive, be sure it is compatible with the equipment in the room.

Again, you should try not to display presentation aids until you are ready to refer to them, and you should cover or conceal them afterward so that they do not distract attention from your speech as it progresses. A blank screen will not compete with your voice; a display of what you've already addressed or are about to discuss will. For the same reasons, you should avoid distributing small objects or photos for your listeners to look at during the course of a short presentation. If you have prepared handouts, the best time to distribute them usually comes after you speak. You want them to focus on you and your message, not what is coming around the room that they have not yet seen.

A simple but important point: Be prepared to improvise when things go wrong. Nothing ruins an otherwise good presentation so much as when speakers panic because the projector will not light up or because the classroom computer will not connect to the Internet. Consider how you will handle the situation if the techno-gremlins are at play, if the vase that is the centerpiece of your presentation breaks, or if the downpour on the way to class smudges your beautiful charts. Foresight will enable you to address these situations more calmly, and your listeners will likely be impressed by your ability to make on-the-spot adjustments and a decent presentation regardless.

Finally, for most brief speeches, avoid the common tendency to overuse presentation aids. Remember, their primary function should be to emphasize and clarify your most important ideas and information. When you flip to yet another aid to illustrate every single point you make, the accumulation tends to undermine that purpose. Of course, there are exceptions to this rule. As discussed earlier, for some presentations, a succession of narrated pictorial images can be really effective, and many speakers use a succession of textual graphics to help their listeners follow longer, more complicated presentations. Presentation aids that are barely relevant or just interesting may distract attention from your central message.

Before each speech, review the list of *what* and *what not* to do while using presentation aids in Figure 10.16.

Improving the Use of Presentation Aids

Find a speech that incorporates presentation aids, and analyze how well the speaker uses them according to the guidelines in this section. What advice does the speaker's use of presentation aids best exemplify? What advice would you offer him or her to improve the use of presentation aids?

Do	Don't
1. Practice using your aids.	*1.* Try to "wing it" using your aids.
2. Display aids only when referring to them.	*2.* Leave aids in view throughout speech.
3. Stand to the side of the aid as you speak.	*3.* Stand in front of aids as you speak.
4. Point to what is important on the aid.	*4.* Make listeners search for what's important.
5. Maintain eye contact with listeners.	*5.* Deliver your speech to your aid.
6. Distribute handouts after your speech.	*6.* Distribute handouts during speech.
7. Limit the number of aids in your speech.	*7.* Become a voice-over for a slide show.

Figure 10.16
The Dos and Don'ts of Using Presentation Aids

Ethical Considerations for Using Presentation Aids

10.6 Use presentation aids ethically.

Presentation aids can be a tremendous resource for public speaking that is both ethical and effective, but they can also be used to distort information and mislead listeners. Comparative line or bar graphs, for instance, can be manipulated through simple framing and context to support opposing conclusions using the same factual information. Figure 10.17 provides two bar graphs illustrating considerably different takes on the relative participation of people of color as board members for Fortune 500 companies. By using only 10 percent of the actual board population for context, the first graph gives the impression that diverse groups—and African Americans in particular—are well represented, whereas the second graph, which contextualizes the same numbers against the backdrop of the entire board population, paints a less impressive picture.[42] Make sure your presentation aids present information in an appropriate context.

You should also credit your sources of information on your presentation aids. Be sure to include this information in smaller (but still visible) letters at the bottom of any material you plan to display, as Figure 10.17 shows. Citing your source on your presentation aid verifies the information presented and reminds you to mention the source in your oral presentation. Finally, be conscious of relevant copyright and fair use laws when reproducing or approximating presentation aids from other published sources—especially if your speech will be reproduced for financial or commercial gain. Such sites as Images.Google.com and ARTStor offer search options to pull up only those representations labeled for noncommercial reuse or for noncommercial reuse with modifications.

Some of the most interesting ethical questions involve the use of film and visual materials. For example, the most famous photographer of the Civil War, Mathew Brady, rearranged bodies on the battlefield to enhance the impact of his pictures. Eighty years later, another American war photographer carefully staged the now celebrated photograph of U.S. Marines planting the flag at Iwo Jima.[43] In 2015, a widely distributed photograph purported to show four National Geographic staff members running from a bear.[44] On one hand, these famous images are fabrications: They pretend to be what they are not. On the other hand, they may bring home reality more forcefully. In other words, the form of the photos may be a lie, but the lie may reveal a deeper truth. Are these photographs unethical, or are they simply artistic?

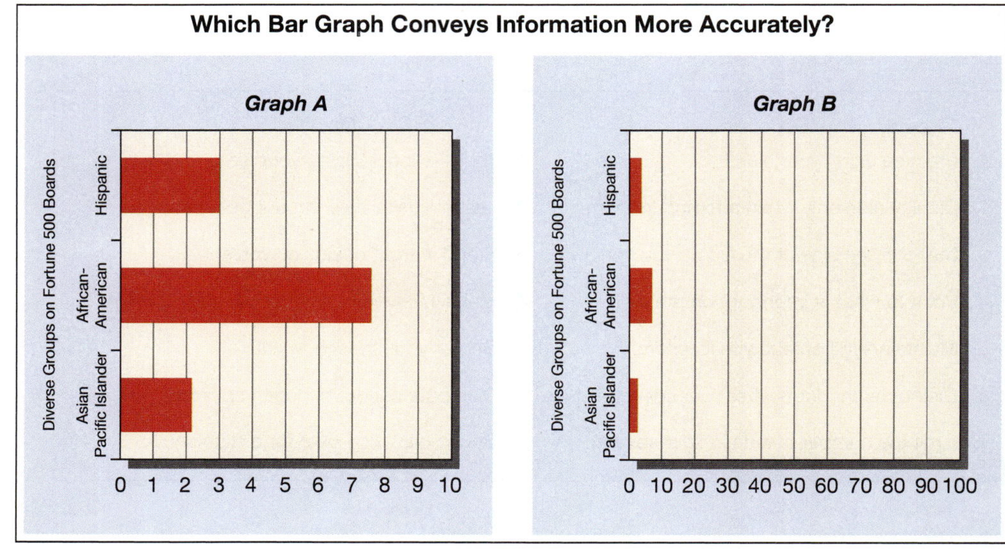

Figure 10.17 Bar Graphs That Are Misleading and Not Misleading in Presenting the Same Material

Source: Based on Alliance for Board Diversity, "Missing Pieces: Women and Minorities on Fortune 500 Boards—2010 Alliance for Board Diversity Census, (2011). © Michael Osborn.

With today's technology, the potential for manipulating and distorting visual images looms ever larger. Consider how often negative ads during political campaigns work by plucking unflattering still images of opposing candidates from video, often with their eyes half closed or their mouths gaping open. During his first presidential run in 2008, Barack Obama's supporters noted that many of the images used to depict him in opposing ads grew progressively darker over the course of the campaign.[45] Of course, these allegations created quite a stir, and his opponents scoffed at any suggestion of conscious intent. In either case, such distortions can certainly tap into and reinforce what Lincoln might have called our lesser angels, and can be particularly harmful when it comes to making such important decisions as choosing a president. Blind adherence to the old adage that "seeing is believing" presents pitfalls in this contemporary age.

To be an ethical communicator, you should alert your listeners whenever you manipulate images so that they reveal your messages more forcefully. You should also be able to defend your creation as a better representation of the truth. As a listener, you should develop a skeptical attitude about images and seek additional evidence if there is any question concerning their validity.

Using Presentation Aids Ethically

Sketch out a presentation aid for your next speech. Design one that presents the information in an unethical manner and one that presents the information in an ethical manner. What are the implications of each choice for you, your audience, and your topic?

YOUR ETHICAL VOICE

The Ethical Use of Presentation Aids

Follow these guidelines to avoid unethical use of presentation aids:

1. Be certain charts or graphs do not distort information.
2. Be aware of how the visual representation of material suggests a particular perspective.
3. Never manipulate visual images to deceive your audience.
4. If you alter an image to reveal some deeper truth, let the audience know.
5. Cite the source of your information on a presentation aid.
6. As a listener, be on guard against the power of presentation aids to deceive you.

Final Reflections: Amplifying Your Voice

When poorly conceived, designed, and used, presentation aids can overpower your voice. We once had a student who volunteered with the local rescue squad. He gave a persuasive speech urging his classmates to join the squad. After his introduction, he announced, "Now we are all going outside," where we found an emergency vehicle. While the speaker tried to tell listeners about the equipment, they were climbing in and out of the vehicle. He lost their attention completely and was never able to complete his speech.

When thoughtfully conceived, designed, and used, presentation aids can empower your voice, giving nuance, power, and character to your speech. In her informative speech on the fashions typical of the three major tribes of her native Nigeria, Dolapo Olushola used an imaginative mix of a map, photographs, and fabrics to help her audience understand the cultural significance of clothing. Seeing the quality of the actual materials, as well as how they created distinctive styles of dress, produced visual immediacy and appreciation.

Imagine yourself as a member of the audience: What kind of aid would help you as a listener? What would engage your interest, increase your understanding, and improve your retention? How could the speaker share enthusiasm for a topic in creative ways? And what would be overkill?

And always remember the bottom line: A presentation aid should *aid* the presentation, not *be* the presentation.

Study Questions

CONTENT MASTERY

1. How can presentation aids help your speech? How can they be problematic?
2. How do you decide which type of presentation aid you should use?
3. What kinds of media are at your disposal for creating and using presentation aids? What are the advantages and disadvantages of each kind?
4. How do you plan and design effective presentation aids?
5. What are the guidelines for using presentation aids well?
6. What ethical considerations guide your design and delivery of presentation aids?

CRITICAL EXPLORATIONS

1. Your speech assignment includes the requirement to use a presentation aid. Consider how you will approach the assignment to maximize the effect of your presentation aid. Make some notes on what you would illustrate with which types of aids and why, and then share these with your classmates. If they disagree with your choices, what does that suggest about how you need to adapt to your audience?
2. You want to give a speech about backpacking in Colorado. For what aspects of the speech might you use a person, an object, a model, and a picture?
3. Select a speech from Appendix B, and prepare a rough draft of a presentation aid that might have been used with it. Consider how the aid might have helped the speech and what principles of design and use would influence its effectiveness.
4. Return to the topics presented at the end of Chapter 8 on supporting materials. What types of presentation aids would effectively amplify your voice for each of these topics?
   a. We should increase spending on preschool education.
   b. We should cut taxes paid by small business owners.
   c. Security measures on campus are inadequate.
   d. We should emphasize restoring the environment over creating jobs and providing health care.
   e. The use of drones in modern warfare is permissible.

   Explain the types of aids you would use as well as the presentation media you would choose, and defend your choices.
5. Now that you've decided which types of presentation aids would be the most effective for each of the topics in question 4, explore the implications of your means of presentation. For example, what would be the advantages and disadvantages of using a poster or a transparency as opposed to a PowerPoint or Prezi?
6. Select one of the presentation aids you have developed for questions 4 and 5, and explain how you would prepare it using the principles of design and color.
7. Like an international PowerPoint version of a chess match, Pecha Kucha uses a "20 × 20" rule: 20 PowerPoint slides automatically shown for only 20 seconds each, requiring the presenter to hone a carefully crafted presentation to fit six minutes and forty seconds. Go to the Pecha Kucha website, select an example, and determine how well the speaker uses PowerPoint.
8. Go online to a site like TED, and find a presentation using presentation aids. How appropriate are the aids to the presentation? How well designed are they? How well does the speaker use the aids? Do the presentation aids appear to present the material ethically?

CHAPTER

Putting Words to Work

LEARNING OBJECTIVES

This chapter will help you:

11.1 Learn the power of language to shape perceptions, arouse feelings, unite listeners, and move them to action.

11.2 Understand what makes oral language special.

11.3 Appreciate the six Cs of using language effectively, especially in extemporaneous speeches.

11.4 Learn how to use specific techniques of language to magnify your voice.

OUTLINE

What Speakers Can Do with Words

The Special Characteristics of Oral Language

The Six Cs of Using Oral Language

How Techniques of Language Can Magnify Your Voice

A legislator was asked how he felt about whiskey. He replied, "If, when you say whiskey, you mean the Devil's brew, the poison scourge, the bloody monster that defiles innocence, dethrones reason, creates misery and poverty—yes, literally takes the bread from the mouths of little children; if you mean the drink that topples Christian man and woman from the pinnacle of righteous, gracious living into the bottomless pit of degradation, despair, shame and helplessness, then certainly I am against it with all my power.

"But if, when you say whiskey, you mean the oil of conversation, the philosophic wine, the ale that is consumed when good fellows get together, that puts a song in their hearts and the warm glow of contentment in their eyes; if you mean Christmas cheer; if you mean the stimulating drink that puts the spring in an old gentleman's step on a frosty morning; if you mean that drink, the sale of which pours into our treasury untold millions of dollars which are used to provide tender care for our crippled children, our blind, our deaf, our dumb, pitiful, aged and infirm, to build highways, hospitals, and schools, then certainly I am in favor of it.

"That is my stand, and I will not compromise."[1]

"Give me the right word and the right accent, and I will move the world."

—JOSEPH CONRAD

The "Whiskey Speech," a legend in southern politics, was originally presented some years ago by N. S. Sweat, Jr., during a heated campaign to legalize the sale of liquor by the drink in Mississippi. Because about half of his constituents favored the initiative and the other half were opposed, Representative "Soggy" Sweat decided to handle the issue with humor.

Although some might read Sweat's statement as simply another slick-talking politician evading a highly contentious issue, it also illustrates the power of language to influence the way we perceive, contemplate, and interact with the world around us. Words can reveal the world in many ways. They can be magnets that draw us together or wedges that drive us apart. They can arouse or dull our feelings. They can goad us into action. Clearly, the words we use and how we use them are not just the pretty packaging we use to adorn our more substantive ideas and information. They play an important role in shaping who we are and what we believe. As a consequence, the effective and ethical use of language is crucial to finding your voice as a public speaker. Before you can move the world with your messages, you must first discover the right words and share them with your listeners.

In this chapter, we discuss how to make the power of language work for you. First, we talk about the power of words to shape perceptions, arouse feelings, unite listeners, and move them to action. We then offer some advice for putting words to work in your speeches by better understanding what distinguishes an oral style and some basic principles of effective language use for extemporaneous presentations. We close by exploring some special techniques you can use to magnify the power of your messages and your voice as a public speaker.

What Speakers Can Do with Words

11.1 Learn the power of language to shape perceptions, arouse feelings, unite listeners, and move them to action.

Given that words form, frame, and express understandings among people, we can understand linguist Steven Pinker's characterization of humans as "verbivores" who draw sustenance from language.[2] To better understand the ways in which language nurtures our lives, this section outlines what words can do: *shape perceptions, arouse feelings, bring listeners together,* and *move them to action.*

Shape Perceptions

To listen to speakers is to see the world as they see it. We look at subjects through the speaker's windows. When actress Viola Davis accepted an award at *Variety*'s Power of Women luncheon, for example, she painted a vivid picture of her childhood:

> I was one of the 17 million kids in this country who didn't know where the next meal was coming from. And I did everything to get food. I've stolen for food. I've jumped in huge garbage bins with maggots for food. I have befriended people in the neighborhood who I knew had mothers who cooked three meals a day for food. And I sacrificed a childhood for food and grew up in immense shame.[3]

This vivid personal portrait helped her audience see her world through her perspective and explained her dedication to the cause "Hunger Is" and its goal of eradicating hunger.

Shaping perceptions can be vital when listeners have no prior experience with the subject. When astronauts first walked on the moon, they had to express what they saw in terms that made sense to our earthbound understandings. They had to describe what had never before been seen. The conversations between space and mission control were filled with passages such as the following:

> I'm looking out here at this mountain and it's got—it looks like somebody has been out there plowing across the side of it. It's like one sort of terrace after another, right up the side.[4]

But of course, the perspectives offered through language may be enchanted and misleading. For example, many writers and orators in the South became incredibly popular after the Civil War by offering idealized images of slavery and plantation life before the war. These images were used to justify not only the past but the continuing mistreatment of African Americans for more than a century after the war.[5] This may seem like ancient history, but such images of the past can linger. In response to a lawsuit alleging racist and sexist practices in her business dealings, Paula Deen, cooking show host and Emmy Award–winning television personality, revealed that she accepted such romantic notions as an accurate reflection of that tragic period. Having hired an exclusively African American crew to serve a wedding party, Deen reflected that the "entire staff was middle aged black men, and they had on beautiful white jackets with a black bow tie. I mean, it was really impressive. [They] . . . represented a certain era in America. . . . I would say they were slaves."[6]

Soon after, Paula Deen's hit television show was taken off the air. Obviously, the power of words to shape perceptions poses a serious ethical responsibility. Appreciating how language fashions conceptions and understandings, and how words can close the gap separating speakers and listeners, constitutes an important way to find your voice.

Arouse Feelings

The right words can arouse strong feelings and even change attitudes to reinforce your message and purpose for speaking. For instance, when we use terms like "cowardly" and "barbaric" in reference to acts of terrorism, we involve our listeners by engaging their sense of disgust and moral outrage. Emotional appeals are especially important with topics that are distant in time, such as the passage of the Voting Rights Act in 1965; or distant in space, such as the suffering of refugees in far-off lands. Emotional appeals are also important for topics that might not seem relevant to most college students, such as Alzheimer's disease, which wreaks havoc on mostly older people and their immediate family members. The right words can transport your listeners and take them there.

denotative meaning
The dictionary definition or objective meaning of a word.

connotative meaning
The emotional, subjective, personal meaning that certain words can evoke in listeners.

The way you use and define words can have a tremendous impact on arousing or deflating the emotional effect of your messages. Using the **denotative meaning** of a term, or its dictionary definition, may defuse a potentially unsettling quality of your message. For example, the denotative definition of alcohol is "a colorless, volatile, flammable liquid, which is widely used as a solvent, drug base, explosive, or intoxicating beverage."[7] **Connotative meaning**, on the other hand, invests a term with strong personal associations and motivations. Consider the contrasting definitions of alcohol offered by Soggy Sweat at the beginning of this chapter. The "intoxicating beverage" is no longer just a chemical substance but rather "the poison scourge" or "the oil of conversation."

As we discuss in Chapter 8, vividly described examples and compelling narratives can help to promote emotional involvement with a message. That is why commercials that encourage you to contribute to charities to alleviate the suffering of impoverished children typically focus on the plight of a single child rather than bombarding you with statistical information. Similarly, Sally Duncan opened her student speech on Alzheimer's with the story of her own grandmother. After expounding on the life of a cultured, eloquent woman with a master's degree who taught English classes for years, she read aloud her "last letter from Nanny" that dramatically illustrated the affliction:

> Dear Sally. I am finally around to answer your last. You have to look over me. Ha. I am so sorry to when you called Sunday why didn't you remind me. Steph had us all so upset leaving and not telling no she was going back but we have a good snow ha and Kathy can't drive on ice so I never get a pretty card but they have a thing to see through an envelope. I haven't got any in the bank until I get my homestead check so I'm just sending this. Ha. When you was talking on the phone Cathy had Ben and got my groceries and I had to unlock the door. I forgot to say hold and I don't have Claudette's number so forgive me for being so silly. Ha. Nara said to tell you she isn't doing no good well one is doing pretty good and my eyes. Love, Nanny.

The use of emotional appeals in public speaking has always been a subject of ethical controversy, especially when such appeals are used to *substitute for* rather than to *strengthen* sound reasoning and credible evidence. But there is nothing inherently irrational about feeling compassion for the victims of a natural disaster or outrage when we hear of pedophilia in our schools and religious institutions. Of course, assessing the rationality of emotional appeals can be subjective. Many critics of the War in Iraq accused our leaders of abusing the anger and fear that so many Americans felt in the wake of the terrorist attacks of 9/11. Others apparently disagreed, at least early on. The decision to invade proved very popular at the time, as most politicians in Congress—Democrats and Republicans alike—voted to support it.

Bring Listeners Together

In many situations, speakers seek to convey a shared sense of purpose to unite their audiences. As we discussed in Chapter 1, Kenneth Burke emphasized the concept of identification, which occurs when speakers create a shared sense of purpose and community through communication. Such connections are especially important when individual action is not enough; skillfully used language can bring people together to accomplish important shared goals.

This power of language is particularly evident during times of grief when tragedy reminds people of their need for one another. During the dark days of April 2013, as the nation mourned the victims of the bombings at the Boston Marathon, President Barack Obama spoke at the memorial service held for victims and used the occasion to affirm national purpose and identity:

President Obama's use of inclusive language and appeals to our national identity brought listeners together at the interfaith prayer service for the victims of the Boston Marathon bombings.

> I'm here today on behalf of the American people with a simple message. Every one of us has been touched by this attack on your beloved city. Every one of us stands with you.
>
> Because, after all, it's our beloved city, too. Boston may be your hometown, but we claim it, too. It's one of America's iconic cities. It's one of the world's great cities. . . .
>
> Our faith in each other, our love for each other, our love for country, our common creed that cuts across whatever superficial differences there may be—that is our power. That's our strength.[8]

Consider here the emphasis on "we" and "our"—the great pronouns of inclusion—and such phrases of identification as "one of America's iconic cities."

Not only times of crisis but times of celebration call for language that brings people together. As we discuss in Chapter 16, special occasions like presidential inaugurals, college graduations, and award presentations often call for speeches that are rich with references to shared values that bind us together into communities, and vivid verbal pictures that show us our values in action. Such speakers often tell stories that teach us to treasure our traditions using language that is colorful, concrete, and graphic. Note how President Ronald Reagan used such language in his second inaugural address to call up memories of heroes and to strengthen the image of the American heritage:

> Hear again the echoes of our past. A general falls to his knees in the harsh snow of Valley Forge, a lonely President paces the darkened halls and ponders his struggle to preserve the Union, the men of the Alamo call out encouragement to each other, a settler pushes West and sings a song, and the song echoes out forever and fills the unknowing air.
>
> It is the American Sound. It is hopeful, big-hearted, idealistic—daring, decent and fair. That's our heritage. That's our song.[9]

You, too, can use the power of words to unite your listeners as you find your voice. The right words and phrases, used in the right places, can create a lasting picture.

Move Listeners to Action

As we discuss in Chapter 14, effective language use is crucial in moving audiences from agreement to action. Getting involved entails risk, and your words should convey to listeners that a situation or problem warrants their involvement, that you are a knowledgeable and trustworthy source of information, and that your proposed course of action is sound and will make a difference. As with emotional appeals, vividly described examples and narratives can help to involve listeners as active participants in your message. Finally, it helps to provide specific instructions for action so that your audience can take that first step, which in turn will help to solidify their commitment.

Consider how Anna Aley used language to convince her listeners that action is necessary, that her ideas are sound, and that success is possible. In her speech urging students to act to improve off-campus housing conditions (see Appendix B), Anna painted vivid word pictures of deplorable off-campus housing. She supported these descriptions with both factual examples and her personal experiences. She also reminded listeners that, if they acted together, they could bring about change:

> What can one student do to change the practices of numerous Manhattan landlords? Nothing, if that student is alone. But just think of what we could accomplish if we got all 13,600 off-campus students involved in this issue! Think what we could accomplish if we got even a fraction of those students involved!

Anna then proposed specific actions that did not demand great effort or risk. In short, she made commitment as easy as possible. She ended with an appeal to action:

> Kansas State students have been putting up with substandard living conditions for too long. It's time we finally got together to do something about this problem. Join the Off-Campus Association. Sign my petition. Let's send a message to these slumlords that we're not going to put up with this anymore. We don't have to live in slums.

Anna's words expressed both her indignation and the urgency of the problem. Her references to temporal considerations—"too long" and "it's time"—called for immediate action. Her final appeals to join the association and sign the petition were expressed in short sentences that packed a lot of punch. Her repetition of "slumlords" and "slums" motivated her listeners to transform their indignation into action.

Anna also illustrated another strategy of language that is important when you want to move people to action: the ability to develop dramas showing what is at stake and what actions listeners should take.[10] Such depictions draw clear lines between right and wrong. Be careful, however, not to go overboard. Ethics require that you show respect for all involved in a conflict. As both a speaker and a listener, be wary of melodramas that offer stark contrasts between good and evil, because such depictions often distort reality.

Evoking a Response in a Speech

Identify a time when you were moved by a speaker to change your perception about an idea, to feel differently or more deeply about an issue, to renew your commitment to a group or cause, or to take some kind of action. What did the speaker say to evoke this response in you?

YOUR ETHICAL VOICE

Managing Powerful Language

To use the power of words in ethical ways, follow these guidelines:

1. Let your words illuminate rather than distort your subject.
2. Use words to support reasoning, not substitute for it.
3. Use words not to divide people but to bring them together.
4. Use language to celebrate past traditions and strengthen shared values.
5. Use words to provide positive visions of the future.
6. Avoid using language that misleads or confuses the listener.
7. Avoid language that degrades people.

The Special Characteristics of Oral Language

11.2 Understand what makes oral language special.

In the previous section, we discussed the power of language for shaping audience perceptions, arousing emotional involvement, bringing listeners together, and moving them to action. But how can you use the power of words in your own speeches to help you find and express your voice in meaningful ways?

Think of times when speakers sounded like they swallowed a dictionary, delivering a presentation for generations to come rather than for their immediate audiences. Were you bored to tears? At least part of the difficulty may be that the speakers used language designed for *written* rather than *oral* use. The best speeches are those developed for the ear—not for the eye.[11]

To understand the special power of oral language, consider how it differs from written language.

- **Oral language is less formal.** Because speaking is, as we pointed out in Chapter 1, an "enlarged conversation," oral language is more relaxed than written language, including colloquialisms and contractions. Someone receiving an award is not likely to articulate, "Oh, yes; my goodness; this is such a privilege" as to exclaim, "Oh, yeah!!" Essays often avoid such contractions as "isn't"; speeches frequently use them. A journalist might write, "One thousand, two hundred fifteen students dropped out of Bay County high schools last year." A speaker would want to make it easier for listeners to grasp the magnitude of the problem by rounding off the numbers: "More than twelve hundred students dropped out of Bay County high schools last year!"
- **Oral language is more colorful and intense.** Speakers want their audiences to become involved in the presentation, and one way to do that is to include colorful, intense words. These qualities are vital to the effectiveness of speaking, as many studies have demonstrated.[12] When Gabrielle Wallace discussed the paradox of how the French eat well and yet don't gain weight (found in Appendix B), she helped her audience feel the experience linguistically:

  > The French thoroughly enjoy the delight of food itself. They enjoy using all five senses when eating. My stepfather, when tasting a new wine, swirls it to watch the color, and slowly takes in a small amount to absorb the flavor. The owner of a French bakery where I work back home often puts baguettes up to his ear and squeezes them to hear their crunch and test their quality. Claude Fischler, a French sociologist at the University of Pennsylvania, notes that when asked to respond to the words "chocolate cake," Americans say "guilt" whereas the French say "celebration."

  In addition, sentence fragments and slang expressions can add to color and intensity to speeches. Note how University of Arkansas student Joseph Van Matre drew in his listeners with slang expressions and punchy sentence fragments at the beginning of his speech on video games (see his speech in Appendix B):

  > If I say the word "gamer," what words come to mind? Antisocial? Geek? Dropout? Well, how about fitness guru, educator, or intelligence analyst?

- **Oral language is more personal and interactive.** For speeches to be effective, the words must engage listeners personally. As we saw with President Obama's speech after the Boston Marathon bombing, speakers use such inclusive pronouns as "we" and "us" to promote closeness with listeners. They may evoke a "you are there" feeling that helps listeners experience the action described in the speech. Notice how Stephanie Lamb, a student at the University of Arkansas, used words to create this sense of vicarious participation at the beginning of her speech:

  > We've all seen it. Driving down the road in the heat of traffic in the early morning on your way to school or in the late afternoon during rush hour. You glance at the driver in the car beside you, and you see him talking on his cell phone and gesturing. The traffic picks up, but the driver is so absorbed in his cell phone conversation that he fails to notice that traffic has come to a stop. Wham! Another fender-bender.

Speakers often use such interactive language at the beginning of their speeches. They may ask rhetorical questions that engage listeners directly, as Joseph Van Matre did in his speech on video games.

- **Oral language must be instantly understood**. Audiences face constraints that readers do not. Communication consultant Jerry Tarver reminds us that listeners cannot "reread" words that are spoken, so oral language must be simpler. Complicated words are liable to perplex the audience and make them lose focus as they try to figure out what those terms mean. A compound, complex sentence structure is likely to confuse not only listeners but also speakers. Speakers often use repetition and parallel structures to help audiences follow their presentations, and they include more examples and narratives to make sure listeners get the point.[13] Revisit Viola Davis's comments about searching for food in the subsection on sharing perceptions to see how she used these techniques to connect with her audience.

These examples illustrate the *informal, intense, personal,* and *immediate* qualities of oral language. And, as we shall see in Chapter 12, speakers use pauses and changes in loudness and pitch to clarify and reinforce meaning. Such oral resources are not available in written communication.

Appropriate Language for Oral Delivery

Look up the description for this course in your college's or university's catalog, and consider how you might rewrite it into language appropriate for oral delivery. What changes did you make and why?

SPEAKER'S NOTES

Features of Oral Language

1. Oral language is less formal.
2. Oral language is more colorful.
3. Oral language is more personal.
4. Oral language is more interactive.
5. Oral language uses simpler words and more repetition.
6. Oral language uses more examples and narratives.
7. Oral language must be instantly understood.

The Six Cs of Using Oral Language

11.3 Appreciate the six Cs of using language effectively, especially in extemporaneous speeches.

Given the special characteristics of oral communication, how can you use language effectively in your speeches? To answer that question, we open this section by discussing what we call the six Cs of using oral language ethically and effectively: *clarity, conciseness, color, concreteness, correctness,* and *cultural sensitivity*. We close with some practical advice on using language in extemporaneous speaking.

Clarity

We have already noted the importance of being instantly understood so that your listeners are not confused or perplexed. If your words are not clear, listeners will not follow your message. To be clear, you need to first understand what you want to say and find words that convey your ideas as directly and simply as possible. Your goal is to have the audience understand as closely as possible what you intend to say. A key is to be mindful of how your audience members may interpret the language you use and to remember that they can't read your mind.

One factor that reduces clarity is the unnecessary or undefined use of **jargon**, the technical language specific to a profession. Jargon is useful as a shorthand for those "in the know," but it will confuse an audience who doesn't share that technical

jargon
Technical language related to a specific field that may be incomprehensible to a general audience.

vocabulary. A business manager, for example, might address her equally experienced colleagues using terms like "end-user perspective" to refer to the experiences of their customers, but most listeners would likely be confused if not lost by such language. All of us have various areas of expertise and knowledge of specialized terms, and we may sometimes use them without realizing that they can serve as a barrier to communication. Avoid the unnecessary use of jargon, and always stop and define any important terms with which your listeners may not be familiar.

A similar problem arises when speakers use words that are overblown and pretentious. A vivid example occurred when sign makers wanted to tell tourists how to leave the Barnum museum. Rather than drawing an arrow with the word "Exit" above it, they wrote "To the Egress." Apparently Barnum meant this as a joke and most of his patrons realized it as such, but there is no telling how many visitors left the museum by mistake, thinking they were going to see that rare creature—a living, breathing "Egress."

Sometimes speakers may deliberately avoid clarity, whether to be delicate or to mislead listeners. Terms and phrases used to soften and obscure unpleasant truths are called **euphemisms**. Many euphemisms are relatively harmless, as when we refer to a friend who has gained weight over the holidays as "festively plump," or when sports broadcasters refer to football players who fumble a lot as having "ball security issues." At their worst, the use of euphemisms, jargon, and other forms of linguistic ambiguity degenerates into **doublespeak**, when people—especially powerful leaders—use them to deliberately mislead their listeners to advance their own agendas.[14] In times of war, terms like "surgical strikes" and "collateral damage" may be used to mask the brutality of combat, and business executives may use terms like "corporate restructuring" to disguise the reality of pending layoffs. Figure 11.1 offers examples of doublespeak.

euphemism
Words that soften or evade the truth of a situation.

doublespeak
Words that point in the direction opposite from the reality they supposedly describe.

Public television commentator Bill Moyers once warned of the dangers of this misuse of language:

> If you would . . . serve democracy well, you must save the language. Save it from the jargon of insiders who talk of current budget debate in Washington as "megapolicy choices between freeze-feasible base lines." Save it from the smokescreen artists who speak of "revenue enhancement" and "tax-base erosion control" when they really mean a tax increase.[15]

How can you avoid such violations of clarity and ethics? One way is through **amplification**, which extends the time listeners have for thinking about an idea and helps them bring it into sharper focus. You amplify an idea by defining it, repeating it, rephrasing it, offering examples of it, and contrasting it with more familiar and concrete subjects. In effect, you tell listeners something and then expand what you have just said.

amplification
The art of developing ideas by restating them in a speech.

Conciseness

In discussing clarity, we talked about the importance of amplification in speeches to expand understanding. Although it may seem contradictory, you must also be

Figure 11.1 Doublespeak

When they say:	What they often mean is:
Marital discord	They're fighting
Downsizing	Firing
Making a salary adjustment	Cutting your pay
Initial and pass on	Let's spread the blame
Quick thinking	Offers good excuses for errors
Collateral damage	We killed innocent people

concise, even while you are amplifying your ideas. You must make your points quickly and efficiently. In a presentation at the University of Kansas, Gabby Murnan exhorted her fellow students to challenge themselves through new experiences—in short, to "find your bold."[16] This snappy, succinct phrase clearly summarized her point.

Simplicity and directness help you be concise. Thomas Jefferson once said, "The most valuable of all talents is that of never using two words when one will do."[17] Straightforward, uncomplicated language and constructions enhance your listeners' understanding. You do not want to be subject to the pithy criticism that Abraham Lincoln provided of a verbose speaker: "He can compress the most words into the smallest idea of any man I know."[18]

maxims
Brief and particularly apt sayings.

One way you can achieve conciseness is by using **maxims**, compact sayings that encapsulate general beliefs. Such adages as "You can't tell a book by its cover" or "The grass is always greener on the other side" capture attention and compress ideas into a short phrase, which can summarize your points or provide a counterpoint. Because they quickly summarize widely accepted perspectives, the brevity of maxims provides dramatic impact. To reinforce his point that we need to actively confront the problems of racism, sexism, and homophobia, Haven Cockerham, vice president of human resources for Detroit Edison, came up with this striking maxim: "Sometimes silence isn't golden—just yellow."[19]

Yet as culturally bound sayings, your audience needs to know the maxims, or be able to quickly process them, to be effective. In addition, they should not be substituted for a carefully designed and well-supported argument. But once you have developed a responsible, substantive speech, maxims might provide a way to reinforce your message.

Color

Oral language is, as we noted earlier, more colorful and intense than written language. Colorful language is vivid and animated. It often expresses the speaker's involvement and feelings by using the fragments, rhythms, and colloquialisms of everyday conversation. A popular local professional wrestler once described his role as a bad guy in colorful terms: "I was meaner than a damn rattlesnake and tougher than a two-dollar steak."[20]

Colorful words paint striking pictures for listeners that linger in the mind. Jennifer Lee, the writer and director of *Frozen*, painted a graphic image of the effects of being bullied growing up:

> Eventually, you drink the bully koolaid and self-doubt takes over. People talk about the dangers of rose-colored glasses, but let me tell you, the lenses of self-doubt are far worse. They are nasty. Thick and filthy . . . they're covered in swamp scum and mold—there's like a family of snails living on them. And they're nearly impossible to see past.[21]

neologism
An invented word that combines previous words in a striking new expression.

Sometimes, you can form a distinctive word by creating a **neologism**, an invented word that combines previous words in a striking new expression. You might relate how you did not volunteer but were "voluntold" to serve on a committee, or how learning that an exam won't be given leads to "cancelelation." In her speech urging the purchase of hybrid cars, Davidson student Alexandra McArthur framed a colorful conclusion based on a combination of "hybrid" and "hubris":

> If you do end up buying a hybrid, as you drive around town looking trendy, cruising past the gas stations, you may start feeling pretty good about yourself and talking about your car any chance you get. This new form of pride, commonly called *hybris*, may be annoying to your friends but is nothing incurable. I'm sure they will forgive you when they get their first hybrid.

One form of especially colorful language is **slang**, the informal style and vocabulary used by a particular group. Slang is often expressed through colorful colloquial expressions such as "Show me the money" and "This is a real dumpster fire." You may have been advised not to use slang in your writing courses when it violates the rules of "proper" English, but it can be very effective in public speaking given the right audience and occasion. As poet Carl Sandburg noted, slang is "language that rolls up its sleeves, spits on its hands, and goes to work."[22]

Colorful language and a lively presentation bring speeches to life.

Slang has its uses in speeches: its color can add energy to your message and be a source of identification with your listeners. But use it with caution. Sometimes such expressions are not appropriate, as on formal occasions requiring a high level of decorum. Moreover, you need to be certain that your audience will understand your expressions because slang is culturally specific. As always, you should also avoid using ethnic slang or other words that your audience might find offensive. Finally, slang should be used sparingly—to emphasize a point or add a dash of humor and color.

slang
The informal style and vocabulary used by a particular group.

Concreteness

One way to engage your listeners with colorful language is to use specific, immediate, tangible terms. Concrete terms offer particular, demonstrable examples, whereas abstract terms refer to broad categories and ideas. Look at the difference, for example, between "building materials" and "concrete," or between "hard work" and "doing the reading, going to class, taking good notes, and studying in advance." Concrete language adds interest and clarifies ambiguities.

The more concrete your language, the more pictorial and precise the information you convey. Consider how Olivia Jackson began her speech advocating study abroad as a part of higher education:

> A fresh coat of snow covers the peaks of the Alps. Rain pelts the window, slowly rolling down onto the windowsills. It is only October and I need a scarf, a heavy winter jacket, and boots to walk outside. The radiators on the bus are belching heat, causing the windows to fog up. Using my scarf, I rub an oval through which I gaze at the passing scenery. The bus roars down the autoroute, passing the pharmacy's flashing green cross, a Carrefour super store, and numerous small boutiques that line the narrow street. Little cars are lined up at the stoplight waiting as the tram zips by and bicyclists hurry to cross the street before the stream of cars commences. This was a typical morning for me in France during my fall term this past year. Every morning, I would see new people, notice different buildings, and watch the city of Grenoble awaken.

The striking, exciting images Olivia creates in our minds both gain our attention and help support her later argument that study abroad programs enhance the educational experience. Your language should be as concrete as the subject permits. Figure 11.2 illustrates this continuum of abstract to concrete language.

Correctness

Nothing can damage your credibility more than the misuse of language. As we noted above, the occasional use of slang can be really effective depending on your audience and occasion, but glaring mistakes in grammar and pronunciation can make you

Figure 11.2 Abstract to Concrete Continuum

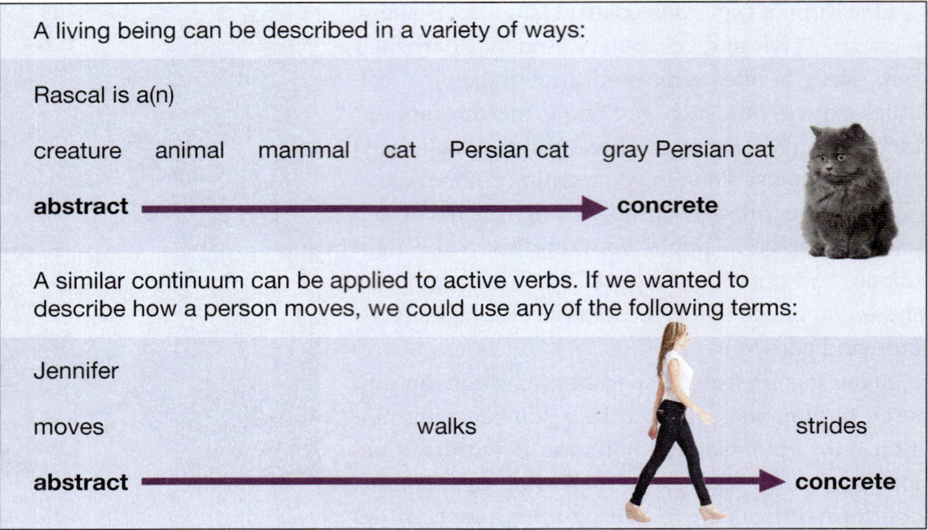

seem uneducated and even ignorant. While touting his education plan, one prominent politician told listeners that the most important consideration should be, "Is your children learning?"[23] Hopefully, they would not miss the lesson on subject–verb agreement! Other common grammatical errors that make listeners cringe are listed in Figure 11.3.

Mistakes in word selection can be as damaging as mistakes in grammar. People often err when using words that sound similar. Such confusions are called **malapropisms**, after Mrs. Malaprop, a character in an eighteenth-century play by Richard Sheridan. She would say, "He is the very *pineapple* of politeness," when she meant *pinnacle*.[24] Perhaps all of us are guilty of using malapropisms from time to time,

malapropisms
Language errors that occur when a word is confused with another word that sounds like it.

Figure 11.3 Correcting Grammatical Errors

1. Using the wrong tense or verb form:
   Wrong: He *done* us a big favor.
   Right: He *did* us a big favor.
2. Lack of agreement between subject and verb:
   Wrong: *Is* your classmates giving speeches?
   Right: *Are* your classmates giving speeches?
3. Using the wrong word:
   Wrong: *Caricature* is the most important factor in choosing a mate.
   Right: *Character* is the most important factor in choosing a mate.
4. Lack of agreement between a pronoun and its antecedent:
   Wrong: A hyperactive *person* will work *themselves* to death.
   Right: Hyperactive *people* will work *themselves* to death.
5. Improper use of pronoun used as subject:
   Wrong: *Him* and *me* decided to go to the library.
   Right: *He* and *I* decided to go to the library.
6. Improper type of pronoun used as object:
   Wrong: The speaker's lack of information dismayed my students and *I*.
   Right: The speaker's lack of information dismayed my students and *me*.
7. Double negative:
   Wrong: I *don't never* get bad grades on my speeches.
   Right: I *never* get bad grades on my speeches.

and politicians are certainly not immune. One former U.S. senator declared that he would oppose to his last ounce of energy any effort to build a "nuclear waste *suppository*" in his state.[25] The Speaker of the Texas legislature once acknowledged an award by saying, "I am filled with *humidity*."[26]

The lesson is clear. Brush up on your grammar, and use a current dictionary to check the meaning and pronunciation of any word you feel uncertain about. For additional help, refer to the website developed by Professor Paul Brians of Washington State University to help students avoid common errors of language use.[27]

Cultural sensitivity requires adaptation and respect, as well as the careful choice of language.

Cultural Sensitivity

Because words can either elevate and inspire or hurt and humiliate your audience, you need to exercise **cultural sensitivity** in your choice of language. Looking back into the history of human communication, you will find little about cultural sensitivity and inclusivity. The ancient Greeks, for example, worried only about speaking to other male Athenians who were "free men" and citizens. Today, with our increasing awareness of different lifestyles, racial diversity, and the pursuit of gender equity, cultural sensitivity has become a crucial standard for both effective and ethical language usage.

cultural sensitivity
The respectful appreciation of diversity within an audience.

Sometimes plural constructions are not only more inclusive but more accurate than singular constructions. For instance, the reference "speakers should respect their audiences" would usually be preferable to "a speaker should respect his audience." Avoid unnecessary modifiers, such as "black doctor" or "male nurse." Using the terms that groups use for themselves generally shows respect for these individuals, whether people with disabilities, gays and lesbians, or Korean Americans. As Rosalie Maggio observes, using respectful, fair, and accurate language really is p.c.—personal courtesy.[28] As mentioned earlier in the chapter, the experience of Paula Deen, author, restaurant owner, and television personality, confirmed the importance of cultural sensitivity, to her dismay. In the wake of a lawsuit charging that racial slurs and jokes about women, Jews, and blacks were common in the kitchen of one of Ms. Deen's restaurants, the Food Network dropped her popular television program, and prominent corporate sponsors discontinued using her as a spokeperson. In response, she said: "I want to apologize to everybody for the wrong that I've done. . . . Inappropriate, hurtful language is totally, totally unacceptable."[29]

A lack of cultural sensitivity almost always has negative consequences. At best, audience members may be mildly offended; at worst, they will be irate enough to reject both you and your message. For more on this subject, see our discussion of audience diversity and cultural sensitivity in Chapter 5.

Language and Extemporaneous Speaking

As we discuss in Chapter 12, most short speeches should be presented extemporaneously, which emphasizes audience interaction over exact wording. The key is to know your ideas and materials so well that you are open for authentic interaction: to back up and repeat or clarify ideas as necessary, to respond to audience feedback, and to accommodate those inevitable distractions and technical glitches. You do want to give especially careful attention to how you will open and close your speeches; to your transitions for moving through the major points and ideas; and to whatever special

> **Analyzing Language**
> Analyze the language of three advertisements. How does each one use the six Cs? Could the advertisers use them more effectively? What does this exercise suggest about how you can use language in your presentations?

techniques you intend to incorporate, such as metaphor and antithesis, as discussed in the final section of this chapter. However, if you try to present your speech verbatim from a manuscript or from memory, you risk being more in your head or in your notes than making a connection with your audience.

The process of planning and preparing the words you will use for extemporaneous speeches should begin when you have finished a first draft or coherent outline and overlaps with the process of practicing for the delivery. Read your speech *out loud* to yourself several times until you begin to feel comfortable with it; saying the words will help you refine and remember your speech. Always look to shorten and simplify your sentences so they flow smoothly and are easy to pronounce, and think of where you will pause for effect or give yourself a chance to breathe and glance at your notes. This process should make for presentations that are not only more eloquent but easier to present—which is helpful if you are coping with communication apprehension. When you feel like you know your speech thoroughly and are beginning to word your main points just a little differently each time, you should be really close and ready to move on to the next step of practicing for your actual presentation.

How Techniques of Language Can Magnify Your Voice

11.4 Learn how to use specific techniques of language to magnify your voice.

There are critical moments in a speech—often at the beginning or the ending or as arguments reach their conclusions—when you want your words to be especially effective. At these and other moments, you can call on certain techniques of language to enhance the power of your voice.

Identifying, understanding, and utilizing these techniques is called *rhetorical style*. Over the centuries, many such techniques have been identified; they seem to be grounded in our nature and to have evolved to meet basic needs for effective communication. Here, we discuss three broad categories of techniques especially useful for public speaking: techniques of *figurative* language; techniques that change the customary *order* of words; and techniques that exploit the *sounds* of words for special effects.

Using Figurative Language

figurative language
Words used in surprising and unusual ways that magnify the power of their meaning.

Figurative language uses words in unusual ways to create fresh understandings. We focus here on six forms that may be especially useful for public speakers: *metaphor, enduring metaphor, culturetype, simile, personification*, and *powerful terms*.

metaphor
An implied comparison that connects subjects not usually related to create a surprising perspective.

Metaphor. "A speech is a bridge of meaning that connects a speaker and a listener." Such expressions often help listeners understand unfamiliar ideas or gain new appreciation for familiar ones. A **metaphor** offers an implied comparison between subjects and ideas that are not usually related. Effective metaphors add color and perspective to your message in ways that can be startling and revealing.

Metaphors are often useful for introducing and concluding a speech because they establish the speaker's unique perspective on a subject and give final expression to it. In his speech following the Boston bombings, Obama both opened and closed with the same metaphor: "Scripture tells us to run with endurance the race that is set before us." The expression was particularly apt, given the setting of the Boston Marathon and the situation.

Metaphors used as a conclusion can offer a final frame of understanding that interprets the speech for listeners. Student speaker Alexandra McArthur finished her speech warning listeners not to accept at face value the pictures of foreign countries painted in travel brochures: "Tourism may be an economic band-aid for the gaping wound of poverty." Such an unusual metaphor is easily remembered.

Because metaphors can be so powerful, you should select them carefully and use them with restraint. First, *the gravity of the metaphor must match the seriousness of your subject.* Just as you would not typically wear cut-offs to a funeral, you should not use certain metaphors to express certain ideas. At a commemoration of a loved one, for example, you would not suggest that "her face was a perfect oval, a circle that had its two sides gently compressed by a Thigh Master." The quality of bagels served in your university cafeteria might not be the best, but you would likely come across as silly if you characterized it as representing "our darkest hour"! The lesson is clear: Be sure the dignity of the metaphor matches the subject to which it is applied.

Second, *mixed metaphors can confuse listeners and lower their estimation of your competence.* In 2013, the United States underwent *sequestration,* the indiscriminate across-the-board reduction of funds for federal programs. One commentator on the effects of sequestration noted:

> The conventional wisdom now seems to be that . . . the Obama administration cried "wolf!" unnecessarily. Sorry, but the wolf is here all right: he's just eating the seed corn stored out of sight in the warehouse, as opposed to the food on the table.[30]

Most of those in the audience were left scratching their heads trying to figure out why wolves, who are carnivorous creatures of the forest, would be eating corn in a warehouse.

Third, *avoid trite metaphors* such as "I was on an emotional roller coaster." Overuse has turned these metaphors into clichés that no longer have any impact. Not only are they ineffective but using them may damage your ethos. Tired comparisons suggest a dull mind.

Finally, *avoid the use of metaphors to dehumanize people.* Researchers have found that metaphors are often used to justify degrading and scornful attitudes toward entire groups of people.[31] Rhetorical scholar Randall L. Bytwerk notes that leading up to World War II, the Nazis described Jewish people using metaphors of vermin. In the logic of that metaphor, the "solution" to the "problem" was extermination—with the inhuman result of concentration camps and gas chambers.[32]

Enduring Metaphor. One special group of metaphors taps into shared experiences that persist across time and sometimes cultural boundaries. These **enduring metaphors**—or "archetypal metaphors" as they are sometimes called—are especially popular in speeches, perhaps because they appeal to deep motives and can bring people together. They connect their subjects with such timeless themes as light and darkness, storms and the sea, the family, mountains and valleys, diseases and cures, and seasonal change. A brief look at three of these metaphors demonstrates their potential power to magnify meaning.[33]

enduring metaphors
Metaphors of unusual power and popularity that are based on experience that lasts over time and crosses many cultural boundaries.

Light and Darkness. From the beginning of civilization, most people have made negative associations with darkness and positive associations with lightness. The dark is cold, unfriendly, and dangerous, whereas light brings warmth, safety, and a restored sense of control. When speakers use the light–darkness metaphor, they usually equate problems or bad times with darkness and solutions or recovery with light. Olivia Jackson spoke of her grandfather's experience with Alzheimer's disease as a "dark abyss of emptiness and forgetfulness" and as a "descent into darkness."

Of course, all rhetorical figures are subject to ethical misuse. Images of light and darkness are often used to oversimplify complicated disputed issues in terms of good versus evil, which makes it difficult if not impossible to find common ground and mutually agreeable solutions. Moreover, throughout much of our history, white

Light and darkness, storms, and the sea are often sources of enduring metaphors that can magnify meaning in a speech.

supremacists have used the association of darkness with evil to justify deplorable attitudes and treatment of African Americans. But speakers have also made persistent use of the image to couch more ennobling messages. In a speech encouraging her classmates to join the fight against sexual slavery in the twenty-first century (reprinted in full at the end of Chapter 14), Lindsey Yoder closed by imploring: "Dare to reach out your hand into the darkness, to pull another hand into the light."

Storms and the Sea. A storm metaphor is often used to describe serious problems. Often, the storm occurs at sea—a dangerous place under the best of conditions. When political problems are the focus of the speech, the "captain" who "steers the ship of state" can reassure us with his or her programs or principles—and make them seem very attractive in the process. In his first inaugural address, for example, President George W. Bush said that "through much of the last century, America's faith in freedom and democracy was a rock in a raging sea."[34]

As with metaphors of light and darkness, the image of the ship of state on stormy seas may be used to advance morally questionable ends. It may be used to justify unquestioning obedience to authority and the loss of individual liberties typically suffered by the crew. Especially during times of perceived crisis, it can lend a romantic, attractive appearance to strong authoritarian government that may suppress outspoken dissent and democratic systems.

The Family. Family metaphors express the dream of a close, loving relationship among people through such images as "the family of humanity."[35] As he asked listeners to rise above race, Barack Obama appealed to such images: "Let us be our brother's keeper, Scripture tells us. Let us be our sister's keeper."[36] Such metaphors can be very useful when listeners feel alienated from each other. Family metaphors can then be a powerful force to bring listeners together and to develop identification. Wade Steck demonstrated the potential of such metaphors as he was describing his experiences at the University of Memphis Frosh Camp Program, his introduction to college life:

> When I got to Frosh Camp, they made me feel at home. First thing they did was to break us into "families" of ten to twelve people who would share the same cabin for those few days. Each "family" had its counselors, carefully selected juniors and seniors who were actually called your "mom" or "dad." . . . The thing I liked most were the Fireside Chats. At night under the stars, watching the logs burn, . . . people would just relax and talk. I discovered that many of those in my family shared my concerns and anxieties.

As with other enduring metaphors, even images of family bonds and affection can be misused. They can give an artificially attractive appearance to abusive and exploitative relationships. In the realm of public debate, they may gloss over important differences that need to be openly and intelligently discussed. In the years leading up to the American Revolution, British politicians commonly referred to Great Britain as the "mother country" and dismissed the grievances of American colonists as the ramblings of "rebellious children." These familial images justified autocracy. One problem with such images is that they can be absorbed by those belittled by them. Until the colonists themselves were freed from the idea that they "belonged" to the mother country, they could never hope to be free.

Finding Your Voice

Enduring Metaphors in Contemporary Communication

Look for examples of enduring metaphors as used in contemporary public communication (e.g., speeches, editorials, blogs, advertising, social media, or movies). Why do you think they were chosen to illustrate or make the point? How do they work? Are they used appropriately under the circumstances? What alternate metaphors might have been used, and how would that change the conception of the situation? How can they connect with motivation as it is explained in Chapter 5? Can you see any ethical problems with their use?

Culturetypes. **Culturetypes** are powerful and widely shared images or metaphors that are more specific to the values, identity, and goals of a particular group or culture. For instance, we Americans like to characterize our leaders as "self-made" people who rose to power or wealth as a result of hard work, intelligence, and self-reliance. And while the image is not unique to western culture, we also like to declare "wars" on everything from poverty to drug abuse to terrorism. Perhaps the most enduring culturetype in the American mind is the symbol of the frontier. While running for president in 1960, John F. Kennedy challenged us as Americans to be the "pioneers of a New Frontier . . . in an age where we will witness not only breakthroughs in weapons of mass destruction, but also a race for mastery of the sky and the rain, the ocean and the tides, the far side of space, and the inside of men's minds."[37]

culturetypes
Terms that express the values and goals of a group's culture.

Similes. A **simile** is a variation of metaphor that indicates to listeners when a comparison is coming. Such words as "like" and "as" are signals that alert listeners and introduce the comparison. A union organizer in India encouraged her listeners to think of the union as being like an umbrella: with the union, they won't get hot in the sun, and they won't get wet in the rain.[38] One of the most memorable similes we have heard was framed by a student who had once been wounded while parachuting in a war zone. He described the tracer bullet as "a force that spun me around like a twisted yo-yo at the end of a string." Very few of us had shared that experience, but most of us were familiar with yo-yos. Aided by the simile, we could easily imagine the moment.

simile
A language tool that clarifies something abstract by comparing it with something concrete; usually introduced by *as* or *like*.

Personification. **Personification** treats inanimate subjects, such as ideas or institutions, as though they had human characteristics and form. Personification makes it easier to arouse feelings about people and values that might otherwise seem abstract and distant. Here is how one student used personification effectively in a classroom speech:

> The university must be more caring. It must see that its investments make a statement to others about its morality. When it supports companies that are destroying the environment, it endorses what they are doing. It becomes a silent partner in that destruction, and might as well be cutting down rain forests itself.

personification
A figure of speech in which nonhuman or abstract subjects are given human qualities.

Powerful Terms. In every culture, specific words are immensely popular and therefore serve as a powerful resource for identification with your audience as you shape their perceptions of your message. Rhetorical theorist Richard Weaver has written extensively of **god and devil terms** with strong positive and negative connotations in western culture. Words like "progress," "modern," and "efficient" tend to serve as god terms because they elicit positive responses, whereas the tendency for words like "drugs" and "terrorism" to elicit negative responses casts them as devil terms.

god and devil terms
Powerful terms that have strongly positive or negative connotations in a culture.

Finding Your Voice

The Culturetypes of Our Time

What words would you nominate as culturetypes in contemporary society? Find examples of the use of these words in public communication. How do they work? Are there ethical problems with their use?

In her speech, "The Price of Bottled Water" (see Appendix B), Katie Lovett argues that the bottled water industry has co-opted emerging god terms from the environmental movement to advertise its products:

> Bottlers seize upon public anxiety over municipal tap water supplies, supposedly offering us the safety that tap water cannot. As a result, the National Resources Defense Council has found that "pure," "pristine," and "natural" are some of the most commonly used god-terms found in marketing and on labels.

Katie offers evidence that such god terms encourage inaccurate assumptions that bottled water provides superior safety.

ideographs
Compact expressions of a group's basic political faith.

Communication scholar Michael Calvin McGee identified an especially potent group of terms he called **ideographs**. These words express in shortened form a country's basic political values.[39] McGee and his students argue that words like *freedom*, *democracy*, and *equality* are important because they are shorthand expressions of political identity.[40] It is inconceivable to many Americans that other nations might not embrace the idea of "equality" or wish to have a "democratic" form of government. Expressions such as "*freedom* fighters" and "*democracy* in action" have unusual power for us because they are ideographs.

Because they are so powerful, you should be especially cautious of the appropriateness of such terms with respect to your audience, your message, and the occasion. Keep in mind that one person's "freedom fighter" can be another person's "terrorist." What one person means by "democracy" isn't necessarily what another does. What's more, such terms and their meanings tend to evolve and change over time and within certain subsets of a culture. For much of the past century, for instance, the word "socialist" has been one of the most reviled devil terms in American culture. Yet in 2016, a self-proclaimed "democratic socialist" waged a serious and very popular campaign for president.[41]

Ideographs and god/devil terms often do ethical work by reminding us of our heritage and suggesting that we must be true to our values. But be sure to look beyond the generalities and consider the motives behind their use as well as their applicability to the topic at hand. As a speaker, you should use them sparingly; as a listener, you should inspect their appropriateness carefully.

To identify aspects of unethical use of god/devil terms and ideographs, consider the following questions:

1. *Is this really what it claims to be?* Does the development of weapons of mass destruction really represent "progress"? Are "freedom fighters" actually thugs?
2. *Are those who use these claims credible sources of information?* For example, are those who advance the "science" of cryonics, the preservation of bodies by freezing them in hopes of discovering how to restore life to them on some future occasion, really "scientists"? Or are they exploiters out to take your money?

3. *Do these claims reflect an ethical sense of values?* For example, lopping off the top of a mountain to strip-mine coal may be a highly "efficient" form of mining, but what effect does it have on the environment?
4. *What kinds of actions are these words urging us to endorse or undertake?* For example, should we be asked to support or even die for "democracy" in a nation whose citizens may prefer some other form of government?

Changing the Order of Words

We expect to find words in certain predictable patterns. *Antithesis, inversion,* and *parallel construction* are three techniques that deliberately change the ways words are normally ordered in messages. Their primary functions are to draw attention to the thoughts they express and to reveal the speaker in a favorable light.

Antithesis.

Antithesis arranges different or opposing ideas in the same or adjoining sentences to create a striking contrast. Used effectively, antithesis can enhance your ethos by conveying a clear and decisive grasp of alternatives. The classic example is John F. Kennedy's oft-cited exhortation in his inaugural address: "Ask not what your country can do for you—ask what you can do for your country."[42] Beth Tidmore used the technique well in her speech on Special Olympics: "With the proper instruction, environment, and encouragement, Special Olympians can learn not only sport skills, but life skills."

antithesis
A language technique that combines opposing elements in the same sentence or adjoining sentences.

Inversion.

Inversion reverses the expected order of words in a phrase or sentence to make ideas more memorable. The "Ask not" in the Kennedy example above illustrates this technique. But inversion goes beyond reversing the expected order of words. In a baccalaureate address presented at Hamilton College, Bill Moyers commented on the many contradictions in contemporary life and concluded: "Life is where you get your answers questioned."[43] Here, the inversion of the conventional order of responses following inquiries makes a witty, striking observation.

inversion
Changing the normal order of words to make statements memorable.

Both antithesis and inversion follow the pattern of saving the stronger idea for last. Given what communication scholar Jerry Tarver calls the "basic differences imposed by time" on oral communication, you are generally more effective when you lead your listeners to your key concept, particularly if you contrast a negative with a positive.[44] An example: in his commencement address at Davidson College, President Bobby Vagt noted that "perfection is not a state of being, but a process of becoming."[45] Note how much more powerful that is than "perfection is a process of becoming, not a state of being."

Parallel Construction.

Parallel construction repeats the same pattern of words in a sequence of phrases or sentences for the sake of impact. We discussed the use of parallel construction for framing the main points in a speech in Chapter 9, but parallel construction can occur at any critical moment in a speech. When used in the conclusion of a speech, the repetition of the pattern of words can make a message memorable. Lindsey Yoder ended her speech on human trafficking with the following eloquent parallel construction:

parallel construction
Wording points in a repeated pattern to emphasize their importance and to show how they are both related and contrasted.

> The quiet screams of our people call for us desperately. Let us be the generation to hear them. Let us be the generation to change the world. Let us be the generation to end modern slavery.

Using the Sounds of Words to Reinforce Their Meaning

As they are pronounced, words have distinctive sounds. At least two techniques, alliteration and onomatopoeia, arrange these sounds in ways that draw special attention to the ideas they contain.

Alliteration.

Alliteration repeats the initial sounds in a closely connected pattern of words. Such popular phrases as "animal aggression" and "dressing down"

alliteration
The repetition of initial consonant sounds in closely connected words.

onomatopoeia
Words that sound like the subjects they signify.

The Power of Language

Select one form of figurative language, one way of manipulating the order of words, and one instance of exploiting the sound of words, and create a tribute to your best friend. How do these techniques help you think differently about the power of language to magnify your voice?

are striking and memorable due to their use of alliteration. In Great Britain's political battle over how closely British economic policy should be tied to the European Union, one Conservative Party leader expressed his position by combining alliteration with animal metaphors and a distinctly British culturetype: "Better to be a British bulldog than a Brussels poodle."[46] His expression made a striking impression and was featured in media accounts.

Onomatopoeia. **Onomatopoeia** (on uh mah tuh pay' uh) is the tendency of certain words to imitate the sounds of what they represent. Onomatopoeia has the quality of conveying listeners into a scene by allowing them to hear its noises, smell its odors, taste its flavors, or touch its surfaces. The technique awakens sensory experience.

Think of Olivia Jackson's speech about studying abroad, which we discussed as an example of concrete language. She also uses onomatopoeia when she says the radiators were "belching heat" and the tram "zips by." Suppose you were trying to describe a scene of refugees fleeing from war and starvation. You might describe an old woman and her grandson as they *trudge* down a road to nowhere. The very sound of the word *trudge* suggests the weary, dusty, discouraged walk of the refugees. Water might *splash, squirt*, or *drizzle*; a bird might *tweet, warble*, or *chirp*. Because it invokes an actual sense of the experience it signifies, onomatopoeia offers a kind of "3-D" experience with language and tends to stick in your mind.

These various ways to magnify the power of language are summarized in Figure 11.4. As you consider how you might use them, remember that your language should not seem forced or artificial. For these techniques to work, they should seem to arise naturally and spontaneously in your speaking, and they should fit both you and your subject. Use them sparingly so that they stand out from the rest of what you say. When artfully employed, they can increase the power of words so that they reinforce your message and help make your voice significant.

Finding Your Voice
Do Words Work for You?

Analyze how you used the power of language in your last speech. Did you have to overcome any barriers to perception or feeling among your listeners? Did you measure up to the standards suggested by the six Cs? How did listeners respond to your message? What special techniques did you use? How could the discussion in this section help you improve future presentations?

Final Reflections: Give Me the Right Word

We end this chapter where we began: reflecting on Joseph Conrad's eloquent observation, "Give me the right word and the right accent, and I will move the world." Most of us have little desire to move the world, but we would like to convince others to give our thoughts serious consideration.

Words, we now see, can enlighten us or blind us, enflame us or benumb us, bring us together or drive us apart, inspire us to act or encourage inaction, and define who we are and are not. Words can heal or injure us. There is no greater lie than the saying

Figure 11.4 Magnifying the Power of Language

Using Figurative Language		
Technique	**Definition**	**Example**
Metaphors	Unexpected figurative comparisons	An *iron curtain* has descended across the continent.
Enduring metaphors	Metaphors that transcend time and cultural boundaries	The development of the Internet marked the *dawn* of a new way of learning.
Culturetypes	Words that express the values, identity, and goals of a group	We will not allow this *war* on the *sanctity of marriage*.
Similes	Figurative comparisons using *like* or *as*	The jellyfish is *like a living lava lamp*.
Personifications	Attributing human characteristics to things or events	Liberty *raises her flame* as a beacon.
God/devil terms	Powerful terms that have strongly positive or negative connotations in a culture	The company is devoted to the ideal of *modern, efficient, progressive science.*
Ideographs	Words that express a country's basic political beliefs	All we ask is *liberty* and *justice*.
Manipulating the Order of Words		
Technique	**Definition**	**Example**
Antithesis	Presenting contrasting ideas in parallel phrases	There is a *time to sow* and a *time to reap*.
Inversion	Changing the expected word order	This insult *we did not deserve*, and this result *we will not accept.*
Parallel construction	Repetition of words/phrases at beginning or end of sentences	*It's a program that . . . . It's a program that . . . . It's a program that . . . .*
Exploiting the Sounds of Words		
Technique	**Definition**	**Example**
Alliteration	Repetition of initial sounds in closely connected words	Beware the *n*attering *n*abobs of *n*egativism.
Onomatopoeia	Words that imitate natural sounds	The creek *gurgled* and *babbled* down to the river.

you may have chanted as a child: "Sticks and stones may break my bones, but words can never harm me." Think about when you used this phrase: When someone called you a dirty so-and-so, and your feelings were hurt!

Words can indeed harm, but developing our ability to use words can make us more effective, both as people and as communicators. When we acknowledge that powerful words can affect how we see and feel about our world, whether we come together in effective action groups, or whether we nurture our shared values and identity, we have taken a major step toward developing our ways with words.

The next step is to set the standards and guidelines of growth. The goals of clarity, conciseness, color, concreteness, correctness, and cultural sensitivity can light our path toward language development. Become curious about words: As you study and read, keep a dictionary and a thesaurus at hand. Look up words that are unfamiliar to you. Try them on for size to see what they can do. As you expand your language capacity, you enhance your perspective on the world and your potential for communication.

Finally, experiment with the techniques we have identified. Framing metaphors and similes, for example, exercises your capacity for analogical, creative thinking. Indeed, each of the basic techniques brings unique, important possibilities to communication—that is why they are basic.

In short, the right words can help you develop awareness, find your voice, and give it power.

Study Questions

CONTENT MASTERY

1 What four accomplishments can speakers achieve when they use words effectively?

2 What makes oral language special?

3 How can the six Cs guide your choice of language for a speech?

4 Define the following techniques and describe their functions:

- **a.** Metaphor
- **b.** Enduring metaphor
- **c.** Culturetype
- **d.** Simile
- **e.** Personification
- **f.** God and devil terms
- **g.** Ideograph

5 What advantages can inversion, antithesis, and parallel construction bring to public speaking?

6 What can speakers accomplish by using alliteration and onomatopoeia?

CRITICAL EXPLORATIONS

1. The example that opens this chapter presents arguments for and against the consumption of whiskey. Rephrase these arguments using denotative language. How does this affect the power of the arguments?
2. Develop a metaphor to express an idea about the following abstract concepts: *love, freedom, justice,* and *poverty*. Do these metaphors help communicate the ideas? How?
3. View a speech on YouTube. Does it demonstrate how language can shape perceptions, arouse feelings, bring people together, or incite action? How well does the speech perform these functions?
4. Look for maxims in political rhetoric (such as speeches, ads, or position statements). Are the maxims effective? Why or why not?
5. Look for advertisements to find examples of the special techniques of using language we have discussed. How do these forms of expression shape your perception of the subject?
6. Did you grow up in a cultural background that differs from mainstream American culture? If so, what culturetypes or ideographs can you identify that were distinctive in that different culture? Can you remember what functions these forms of expression performed?
7. Ohio State University President Gordon Gee had a problem with cultural sensitivity as he explained at a public meeting why Notre Dame had not been invited to join the Big Ten: "You can't trust those damn Catholics. . . . The fathers are holy on Sunday and they're holy hell the rest of the week." After his remarks were widely published, he apologized, explaining, "They were a poor attempt at humor." Shortly thereafter, he resigned. Can you find other examples of the lack of cultural sensitivity in public communication?

SELF-INTRODUCTORY SPEECH

In her self-introduction presented at Vanderbilt University, Ashley Smith used three contrasting photographs—each representing a different lifestyle—to structure her speech. This device also illustrates the cooperation of the visual and the verbal—pictures and words—to complete her message. The photographs offer the surface details, but the words explain how they are representative of ways of life and what she learned from these exposures. In effect, they bring the photographs into focus for her speech.

THREE PHOTOGRAPHS

ASHLEY SMITH

Reprinted with permission from Ashley Smith.

Photographs often tell stories that only a few can hear. I would like to tell you the story told to me by three snapshots that hang in my room in suburban Jacksonville, Florida. If you saw them, you might think them totally unrelated; together, they tell a powerful tale.

Ashley's sharp, clear use of images helps shape listener *perceptions* and arouses *feelings* by overcoming barriers of distance. The touch of dialogue adds action to the picture.

"Ashley, *levantete!*" I heard each morning for the month that I spent in Costa Rica as an exchange student. I would wake up at 5:30 to get ready for school and would stumble off to the one shower that the family of five shared. I had to wash myself in cold water because there was no warm water—that usually woke me up pretty fast! I then got dressed and breakfast would be waiting on the table. Predictably it would be fruit, coffee, and gallo pinto, a black bean and rice dish usually served at every meal.

We would then walk to school and begin the day with an hour and a half of shop class. After shop we would have about 15- to 20-minute classes in what you and I might call "regular" academic subjects: math and Spanish, for example. Those classes had frequent interruptions and were not taken very seriously. The socialization process was quite clear: These children were being prepared for jobs in the labor force instead of for higher education. Each afternoon as we walked home we passed the elite school where students were still busy working and studying. The picture in my room of my Costa Rican classmates painting picnic tables in the schoolyard reminds me of their narrow opportunities.

The Botswana picture personifies the cultural deprivation Ashley criticizes. Again, the combination of picture and words explains and magnifies her feelings and invites identification from her listeners.

The second photograph on my wall is of a little girl in Botswana. She's nearing the end of her education and has finished up to the equivalent of the sixth grade. She will now return to a rural setting because her family cannot afford to continue her schooling. To add to the problem, the family goat was eaten by a lion, so she had to return to help them over this crisis.

But she didn't miss out on much—most likely, she would have gone on into the city and ended up in one of the shantytowns, one more victim of the unemployment, poverty, even starvation endured by the people. Her lack of opportunity is due not so much to class inequalities as in Costa Rica, but more to the cultural tradition of several hundred years of European exploitation. Recently there has been extensive growth there, but the natives have been left far behind.

The third photograph offers a transition into Ashley's personal plan of action. We see that for her it reflects a way of life that hides the reality she had found elsewhere that now calls her into a life commitment.

The third photograph in my room is of four high school students, taken where I went to school in Jacksonville, Florida. We're all sitting on the lawn outside school, overlooking the parking lot full of new cars that will take us home to warm dinners and comfortable beds and large homes and privileged lives. Many of us—including myself for most of my life—took this world for granted. But now, for me, no more. I may have gained a lot in my travels, but I lost my political innocence.

One thing I gained is an intense desire to become an educator. I want to teach people to succeed on their merits despite the social and economic inequalities that they're faced with. And I want to learn from them as well. I want to teach the boy who never mastered welding that he could own the factory. And I want him to teach me how to use a rice cooker. I want to teach the girl who is exhausted each afternoon after walking to the river with a jar on her head to gather water that she could design an irrigation system. But I also want her to teach me how to weave a thatched roof. I want to travel and teach and learn.

Three photographs, hanging on my wall. They are silent, mute, and the photographer was not very skillful. But together they tell a powerful story in my life.

Ashley uses personification to focus sharply on her life goals and to represent them to her listeners.

Delivering Your Speech

LEARNING OBJECTIVES	OUTLINE
This chapter will help you:	
12.1 Understand the importance of delivery for effective speaking.	The Power of Delivery
12.2 Become versatile in various methods of presentation.	Methods of Presentation
12.3 Develop your physical voice for better communication.	Developing Your Physical Voice
12.4 Develop more effective body language.	Developing Your Body Language
12.5 Practice for successful delivery.	Practicing Your Presentation for Delivery
12.6 Become flexible in answering questions and making mediated speeches.	Developing Flexibility: Answering Questions and Making Mediated Speeches

Thomas had worked long and hard on his speech. He had selected a topic that excited him and that he knew his audience could learn from, his research had expanded his knowledge, and he had organized his main ideas and materials carefully. Yet he knew he wasn't ready yet because now he needed to turn his hard work into a presentation that would bring his ideas to life and engage his listeners. Thomas knew that by practicing carefully and repeatedly, he could have a genuine enlarged conversation with his listeners.

When he stood up in front of the class, he stood tall, gestured freely, looked at all of the audience, and spoke in a clear, firm voice. He spoke with such energy and enthusiasm, with such joy and passion, that we *wanted* to listen to him and take his ideas seriously. He communicated in ways that magnified his ethos, exhibiting the qualities of competence, character, good will, and dynamism that we described in Chapter 3.

"The success of your presentation will be judged not by the knowledge you send but by what the listener receives."

—LILLY WALTERS

"Finding your voice" means far more than simply sounding and looking good at the lectern. Rather, finding your voice means finding the causes that call you to speak, discovering what you want to say about them, and framing these messages with all the skill and power they deserve. Nevertheless, all your reflection, investigation, and planning will come to naught unless your speeches come to life in the actual delivery.

That's what this chapter is about—preparing you for presentation. We discuss the power of effective delivery and various methods of delivery. We then help you develop two great resources, your physical voice and your body language, and how to practice your presentations to use these successfully. We close with some advice for handing question-and-answer sessions and making mediated presentations.

The Power of Delivery

12.1 Understand the importance of delivery for effective speaking.

Delivery refers to the actual physical presentation that enacts your speech by engaging with your listeners. While the topic, research, organization, and language of a speech constitute essential aspects of preparation, a presentation can only accomplish its goals when it brings your message to life by stimulating authentic interaction with your listeners. Good delivery not only gives your speeches a better chance of receiving a positive hearing, but an engaging style of presentation will almost always enhance the audience's perceptions of your ethos.

delivery
Presenting a speech to an audience, integrating the skills of nonverbal communication with the speech content.

Regardless of what method of delivery you choose for speaking, *an effective presentation should sound natural and conversational*—so that you are talking *with* listeners, not *at* them. Your goal should be an **expanded conversational style** that is direct, spontaneous, colorful, and tuned to the responses of listeners.[1] The nonverbal messages you communicate through vocal characteristics, face and hand gestures, eye contact, and physical movements should complement the content and intended tone of your verbal message. Your listeners should understand that you are genuinely interacting with them and that you are genuinely committed to your message and its effective communication.

expanded conversational style
A presentational quality that while somewhat more formal than everyday conversation, preserves its directness and spontaneity.

While obviously more formal and planned out, an effective delivery style should retain some of the natural spontaneity of an everyday conversation. Approach your presentation from a communication orientation that focuses on your message and engaging your listeners rather than on yourself as a performer. Set aside your expectations for perfection and lofty eloquence and focus instead on "help[ing] your audience understand your message."[2] Even if you should stumble over a few words, listeners will tend to find you more likable and trustworthy for making the effort to engage them. Finding your voice means discovering and learning how to use your own personal style more effectively.

Underlying the obvious requirements for an effective delivery are the deeper requirements of *attitude*. As both speaker and listener, *you should want to communicate*. This point may seem obvious, but we remember another student in whom this desire to communicate seemed oddly lacking. She had done well in high school speaking contests, she told us in her first speech, and thought of herself as a good speaker. And in a technical sense, she was right. Her voice was pleasant and expressive, her manner direct and competent. But there was a false note, an overtone of artificiality that made it difficult for listeners to engage and identify with her message. We sensed that she believed that *she* was more important than her audience and her ideas.

immediacy
A quality of successful communication achieved when the speaker and audience experience a sense of closeness.

Finally, an engaging presentation style helps to produce a sense of **immediacy** or closeness between speakers and listeners.[3] Immediacy contributes to establishing identification—that shared feeling of oneness and purpose as discussed in Chapter 1. It encourages listeners to open their minds to you and to be influenced by what you say.[4] You can encourage immediacy by reducing the actual distance between yourself and listeners. If possible, move closer to them. Smile at them when appropriate, maintain eye contact, use gestures to clarify and reinforce ideas, and let your voice express your feelings.

Appreciating Effective Delivery
Think of a time when you found a speech to be incredibly boring. Could the speaker have presented the same message using different delivery techniques to pique your interest?

To summarize, *effective delivery makes your ideas come alive while you are speaking*. It blends nonverbal with verbal communication so that reason and emotion, heart and head, and mind and body all work together to advance your message. The remainder of this chapter helps you move closer to a presentation that reaches this goal.

Methods of Presentation

12.2 Become versatile in various methods of presentation.

The four most commonly recognized methods for making presentations are *impromptu speaking, extemporaneous speaking, reading from a manuscript*, and *memorized text presentation* (see Figure 12.1). Although classrooms frequently emphasize impromptu and extemporaneous delivery, you may encounter situations in which you need to use a manuscript or offer a memorized presentation.

Impromptu Speaking

impromptu speaking
Speaking on the spur of the moment in response to an unpredictable situation with limited time for preparation.

Impromptu speaking is speaking on the spur of the moment in response to unpredictable situations with limited time for preparation. Such speaking is sometimes called "off the cuff," a phrase that suggests you could put all your notes on the cuff of your shirt or, if you followed the practice of one contemporary political speaker, in the palm of your hand (we don't recommend either practice!). Even in a carefully prepared speech, there may be moments of impromptu speaking—times when you must make on-the-spot adjustments to the audience's feedback or respond to questions at the end of your speech.

Many situations call for impromptu speaking. During class, you often answer a question or comment on a point just made by your professor. At work, you might be

Figure 12.1 Methods of Presentation

Method	Use	Advantages	Disadvantages
Impromptu	When you have no time for preparation and practice	Allows spontaneity, permits responses to feedback, and enables speaker to rise to the demands of the situation	Does not permit polishing, is often less well organized, and limits research and use of supporting material
Extemporaneous	For most public speaking occasions	Allows structured spontaneity and permits responses to feedback	Requires considerable research, preparation, and practice; experience leads to excellence
Manuscript	When exact wording is important or time constraints are strict	Allows planning of precise wording, can be timed within seconds, and may be important for mediated presentations	Demands an ability to read conversationally and inhibits responses to feedback
Memorized	When you will be making a brief remark, such as a toast or award acceptance	Allows planning of eloquent wording, can sound well polished, and enables speaker to talk without using notes	Must be written out in advance, can emphasize memory over communication with the audience, and can sound phony and inauthentic

asked to make a presentation in five minutes. Or in meetings, you may decide to say a few words about a new product or program. In these cases, you make impromptu speeches.

When you have just a few minutes to prepare, focus on the task at hand. Start by *determining your purpose*. What do you want the audience to know? Why is this important? Next, *decide on your main points*. Since impromptu presentations are usually quite short, you may have time for only one main point, and you should not tackle more than three. If you can, jot down a memory-jogging word for each idea in a skeletal outline that will help keep you focused.

As you speak, *don't dash through your remarks*. A slower delivery gives you time to think ahead, allows your audience time to absorb what you're saying, and minimizes "ums," "likes," and "you knows." Stick to your main point or points. If you have more than one point, incorporate simple transitions as you go: "My first point is.... Second, it is important to.... Finally, it is clear that...." Keep your presentation short, and end with a summary of your remarks.

Many impromptu speakers like to use the **PREP formula** to develop their main ideas: State the *p*oint, give a *r*eason and *e*xample, and then restate the *p*oint.

PREP formula
A technique for making an impromptu speech: State a *p*oint, give a *r*eason and *e*xample, and restate the *p*oint.

*P*oint:	You should buy a hybrid car.
*R*eason(s):	Hybrid cars are good for the environment—and good for your pocketbook!
*E*xample:	If you drive 10,000 miles a year, you could easily save $600 a year on gas alone.
Restatement of *P*oint:	Drive green and keep more green. Buy a hybrid!

Finally, if yours is one of a number of successive impromptu presentations during a meeting, you might need to make on-the-spot adjustments to account for or incorporate ideas and information presented by earlier speakers. Most impromptu speaking situations are relatively casual. No one expects a polished presentation on a moment's notice. However, the ability to organize your ideas quickly and effectively and to present them confidently puts you at a great advantage in any setting. The principles of preparing speeches you are learning in this course will help you become a more effective impromptu speaker in a variety of contexts.

Extemporaneous Speaking

extemporaneous speaking
A form of presentation in which a speech, although carefully prepared and practiced, is not written out or memorized.

The extemporaneous method of delivery is generally preferred for achieving an enlarged conversational style while speaking. As discussed in Chapter 3, **extemporaneous speaking** emphasizes eye contact and audience interaction over exact wording. Your speech needs to be well prepared and thoroughly practiced, and you should have a firm grasp of your main ideas and supporting materials in the order to be presented. But instead of speaking from memory or reading from a manuscript, you speak from key words and prompts that will allow you to focus on the sequence of your ideas as you develop your speech, your underlying message, and the actual process of interacting with your listeners while speaking. With a little practice, the extemporaneous method will help you to cultivate a spontaneous and natural-sounding presentation style that will make it easier to establish immediacy with your listeners. You will not be a prisoner to your text, and each presentation will vary according to your audience, the occasion, and the particular demands of the moment.

Because extemporaneous speaking depends on interaction with the audience to be effective, speakers often employ references or strategies to promote listeners' participation—usually while introducing or concluding their presentations. As discussed in Chapter 9, requesting a show of hands, asking for direct verbal feedback, or using a well-phrased rhetorical question can be very effective for engaging your listeners. One student at Davidson, speaking on the importance of proper nutrition to her 9:30 a.m. class, began by asking the audience how many had eaten breakfast that morning. She then incorporated their answers into her presentation. Such interaction encourages listeners to become involved as co-participants in constructing the meaning of your message, as discussed in Chapter 1. It becomes their creation as well, which—as discussed in Chapter 15— is especially important when persuading listeners to get involved and take action.

Finally, because it requires speakers to master the overall pattern of thought within their speeches, extemporaneous speaking emphasizes the importance of *thorough preparation and practice*. In the next section of this chapter, we discuss the process of cutting your speech down to key words and preparing for your actual presentation. To give your presentations a stronger sense of structure and fluidity, you may want to memorize your opening lines, your concluding lines, and your strategies for transitioning from one point or part of your speech to the next. But while you are developing and supporting your main ideas, you should leave yourself open to engaging and interacting with your listeners.

The key is learning to monitor and respond to feedback from the audience while you are speaking. As most of that feedback will be nonverbal, good eye contact is especially important. On occasion, you may need to make spontaneous adjustments to feedback that signals *confusion, lack of interest*, and *disagreement* before moving on to your next point. Being well prepared will enable you to make these adjustments during your presentation.

Feedback That Signals Confusion. Listeners' puzzled expressions can signal that they don't understand what you are saying. You may need to define an unfamiliar word or rephrase an idea to make it simpler. You could add an example or a quick story to make an abstract concept more concrete. It might help to compare or contrast an unfamiliar idea with something the audience already knows and understands. When you detect signs of misunderstanding, you can say, "Let me put it another way." Then provide a different explanation that might clarify the matter for anyone who is confused.

Feedback That Signals Loss of Interest. Bored listeners wiggle in their seats, drum their fingers, or develop a glazed look. To get them to reengage, you can provide an example or story that makes your message come to life, or you can involve listeners by asking a question that calls for a show of hands. You can startle them with a bold statement and remind them of the importance of your topic. Keep in mind that enthusiasm is contagious: *your* interest can arouse *theirs*. Move from behind the lectern and get closer to them. Whatever happens, do not become disheartened or lose faith in your speech. In all likelihood, some people—probably more than you think—find your message interesting.

Feedback That Signals Disagreement. Listeners who disagree with you may frown or shake their heads to indicate how they feel about what you are saying. A number of techniques can help you soften disagreement. If you anticipate resistance, work hard to establish your ethos in the introduction of your speech. Listeners should see you as a competent, trustworthy, strong, and likable person who has their best interests at heart.

To be perceived as competent, you need to *be* competent. Arm yourself with a surplus of information, examples, and testimony from sources your audience will respect. Practice your presentation until you are comfortable with it. Set an example of tolerance by respecting positions different from your own.

You may find that, although you differ with listeners on issues, you agree with them on goals. Stress the values that you share. Appeal to their sense of fair play and their respect for your right to speak while avoiding angry reactions and inflammatory language. You should be the model of civility in this situation. Think of these listeners as offering an opportunity for your ideas to be heard.

Reading from a Manuscript

When you make a **manuscript presentation,** you read to an audience from either a text or a teleprompter. Manuscript presentations are most useful when exact wording or eloquence is particularly important, or when time constraints are strict. Many mediated presentations, for example, must be timed within seconds. Manuscript presentations may also be the best option for presenting really long or complicated speeches that would be exceedingly difficult to reduce to key words and present extemporaneously.

manuscript presentation
A speech read from a prepared text or teleprompter.

Although certain circumstances may call for manuscript delivery, such presentations can pose real challenges. The first begins with the preparation of the manuscript. Most of us don't write in a natural oral style. The major differences between *oral* and *written* language, covered in Chapter 11, bear repeating. Good oral style uses short, direct, conversational speech patterns. Even sentence fragments can be acceptable. Speakers need to use repetition, rephrasing, and amplification more than writers. Developing a sense of rhythm and using imagery are especially important in oral style. Too often, written manuscripts overshadow the need for adapting to spoken language.

Another common drawback occurs when, having prepared and scripted an excellent presentation word for word, speakers simply do not practice enough to truly interact with their listeners while speaking. Unless speakers are comfortable with the material, they can end up glued to their manuscript rather than communicating with listeners through eye contact and adaptation to feedback. A failure to practice thoroughly also inhibits a lively delivery with vocal variety.

President George W. Bush, for example, struggled with manuscript presentations early in his presidency. Yet when he spoke to rescue workers at the still-smoking

Annie Lennox, British singer-songwriter, gave such a skillful manuscript speech at Berklee College of Music that many thought she was using extemporaneous delivery.

ruins of the World Trade Center in the wake of the terrorist attacks of 9/11, his impromptu remarks responded to the concerns of his audiences, both immediate and removed. As a result, Bush had met the "challenge of a leader," which was to have his speech "capture the needs and mood of his country," for the first time.[5] Later, Bush would give successful manuscript speeches, but it is interesting that he first found his voice in the give-and-take of impromptu speaking.

Successful manuscript speeches retain the conversational, communicative flavor of impromptu and extemporaneous speaking while working from prepared, scripted remarks. When singer Annie Lennox gave the commencement speech at Berklee College of Music in Boston, she presented the address so well that those of us hearing it on the radio did not even realize that she was not using extemporaneous delivery. Viewing the video of the speech revealed that she did indeed have a manuscript. Her oral style, familiarity with the speech, and connection to the audience made her presentation effective.[6]

Again, and for some of the reasons discussed here, most public speaking professors prefer the extemporaneous method of delivery, and you should consult your instructor before considering the use of a manuscript for classroom presentations. That said, most people will make manuscript presentations from time to time. The following suggestions may help you to do so more effectively:

- Use a large font to prepare your manuscript so you can see it without straining.
- Use light pastel rather than white paper to reduce glare from lights.
- Double- or triple-space the manuscript, and leave adequate margins for presentation cues and last-minute revisions
- Use the top two-thirds to three-quarters of the page to facilitate eye contact.
- Mark pauses with slashes, or break phrases into bullet points.
- Highlight material you want to emphasize by capitalizing or italicizing it.
- Practice speaking from your manuscript so that you can deliver it well and maintain as much eye contact as possible with your audience.
- Think about incorporating some "planned ad libs" that will seem spontaneous and help connect with your audience.
- Don't panic if you stray a bit from the manuscript in delivery. Your audience won't know unless you signal it to them, and some spontaneity helps enliven the presentation.

If the opportunity arises, make a video recording of your rehearsal. Review the recording and ask yourself the questions in the checklist in Figure 12.2.

Figure 12.2
Assessing Manuscript Delivery

View a recording of your presentation, and ask yourself:

- Do I sound as though I'm talking with someone or as if I'm reading a text?
- Do I maintain eye contact with my imaginary audience?
- Do I pause effectively to emphasize the most important points?
- Does my body language reinforce my message?

Revise and continue practicing until you are satisfied.

Memorized Text Presentation

memorized text presentation
Speeches committed to memory and delivered word for word.

Memorized text presentations are committed to memory and delivered word for word. Memorized presentations are useful for making short presentations when the exact wording or eloquence is particularly important, such as presenting a toast or receiving an award. Because the introduction and conclusion of a speech are especially important—the introduction for gaining audience attention and the conclusion for leaving a lasting impression—their wording should be planned and rehearsed with special care.

In general, you should avoid trying to memorize anything much longer than a minute or two because this method of presentation poses many problems. Speakers who try to memorize their speeches can get so caught up with *remembering* that they forget about *communicating*. The result often sounds stilted or sing-songy, and nervous speakers may freeze when they get lost in their words or omit important parts of their speech. Speaking from memory also tends to inhibit eye contact and adapting to feedback. It can keep you from clarifying points when audience members signal that they don't understand or from following up on ideas that seem especially effective. Another problem with memorized speeches is that they often must be scripted word for word in advance. As we noted with manuscript speaking, many people struggle to write in an oral style.

If you must memorize a speech, commit it so thoroughly to memory that you can concentrate on communicating with your audience. If you experience a "mental block," keep talking. Restate or rephrase your last point to put your mind back on track. If this doesn't work, you may find yourself forced into an extemporaneous style and discover that you can actually express your ideas better without the constraints of exact wording.

Monitoring and Responding to Feedback

Watch a speaker you admire. You might look for a presentation at an awards ceremony by a noted actor, activist, or sports figure; or you might search for clips of a favorite politician addressing an issue you care about. How does that person monitor and respond to feedback? What effect does that have on the communication between speaker and listeners?

Developing Your Physical Voice

12.3 Develop your physical voice for better communication.

It may seem strange to say that to find your voice, you must develop your voice. But when utilized properly, the human vocal apparatus can be a rich and expressive instrument of communication. As poet and author Maya Angelou observed, "Words mean more than just what is set down on paper. It takes the human voice to infuse them with deeper meaning."[7] Consider the following simple statements:

I don't believe it.
You did that.
Give me a break.

How many different meanings can you create as you speak these words, just by changing the ways you say them?

The quality of your voice affects your ethos and your message. If you sound confident and comfortable with your own identity and if listening to you is a pleasant experience for your audience, listeners are likely to raise their estimation of you. But if you sound tentative, people may think you are not very decisive, perhaps not even convinced by your own message. If you mumble or speak with a monotone, they may think you lack self-confidence or have something to hide. If you are overly loud or strident, they may conclude you are not very likable.

While most speakers do not need to make radical changes to improve their speaking voices, minor improvements can produce big dividends. With a little effort and practice, most of us can make positive changes. Think of your voice as providing the music to the lyrics of your words. Your favorite performers vary their delivery, using a range of notes, tempos, and volume levels juxtaposed with the language of their songs to create meaning. You have an opportunity to convey layers of meaning in your message as your voice brings your speech to life. In her commencement speech at the Berklee College of Music in Boston, singer Annie Lennox not only used rich vocal textures and tones in her presentation but also sang snippets of the songs that had influenced her career. Her mix of pitch, rate, and volume added both zest and interest to a speech well tailored to the audience and the occasion.[8]

The first step in learning to use your voice more effectively is to evaluate how you usually talk. Record yourself while speaking and reading aloud. As you listen to yourself, ask these questions:

- Does my voice convey the meaning I intend?
- Would I want to listen to me if I were in the audience?
- Does my voice present me at my best?

If your answers are negative or uncertain, look at how the concepts in this section can help you discover ways to better find your voice. Save your original recording so that you can hear yourself improve as you practice.

Pitch

pitch
The position of the human voice on a scale ranging from low and deep to high and sharp.

habitual pitch
The vocal level at which people speak most frequently.

optimum pitch
The level at which people can produce their strongest voice with minimal effort and that allows variaticn up and down the musical scale.

Pitch is the placement of your voice on a scale ranging from low and deep to high and sharp. Like singers, speakers can use a wealth of tones to be expressive. For effective speaking, find a pitch level that is comfortable and that allows maximum flexibility and variety. Each of us has a **habitual pitch**, the level at which we speak most frequently. We also have an **optimum pitch**, the level that allows us to produce our strongest voice with minimal effort and that permits variation up and down the scale.

To experiment with how to use pitch effectively, read the following paragraphs from N. Scott Momaday's *The Way to Rainy Mountain*. Use your optimum pitch level, with pitch changes to provide meaning and feeling. To make the most of your practice, record yourself so you can observe both problems and progress.

> A single knoll rises out of the plain in Oklahoma, north and west of the Wichita Range. For my people, the Kiowas, it is an old landmark, and they gave it the name Rainy Mountain. The hardest weather in the world is there.... In the summer the prairie is an anvil's edge. The grass turns brittle and brown, and it cracks beneath your feet. There are green belts along the rivers and creeks, linear groves of hickory and pecan, willow, and witch hazel. At a distance in July or August the steaming foliage seems almost to writhe in fire.... To look upon that landscape in the early morning, with the sun at your back, is to lose the sense of proportion. Your imagination comes to life, and this, you think, is where Creation was begun.[9]

Use this exercise to explore the full range of variation around your optimum pitch and make you more conscious of the relationship between pitch and effective communication. Then record yourself reading the passage again, this time exaggerating the pitch variations as you read it—even to the point of feeling silly. If you have a narrow pitch range, you may discover that exaggeration makes you sound more effective.

In contrast, try reading these phrases:

– Lord, help me become the person my dog thinks I am.
– I'm not running on all syllables today.
– It can rain on my parade—it's still my parade!
– Those students are graduating "magna cum miracle!"

The rhythms, and humor suggest different uses of your optimal pitch.

When you speak before a group, don't be surprised if your pitch seems higher than usual. Pitch is sensitive to emotions and usually goes up when you are under pressure. You can follow the professionals' practice of warming up your voice before you speak, including humming your optimum pitch softly to yourself, so that you start out on the right level. Or you might try this warm-up exercise:

> Whether the weather be cold,
> Or whether the weather be hot,
> We'll be together
> Whatever the weather,
> Whether we like it or not![10]

Finding Your Voice

Developing Your Optimum Pitch

You can use the following exercise to help determine your optimum pitch.

Sing the sound *la* down to the lowest pitch you can produce without feeling strain or having your voice break or become rough. Now count each note as you sing up the scale to the highest tone you can comfortably produce. Most people have a range of approximately sixteen notes. Your optimum pitch will be about one-fourth of the way up your range. For example, if your range extends twelve notes, your optimum pitch would be at the third note up the scale. Again, sing down to your lowest comfortable pitch, and then sing up to your optimum pitch level.[11]

Record this exercise (perhaps on a cell phone, computer, or digital camera), and compare your optimum pitch to the habitual pitch revealed during your first recording. If your optimum pitch is within one or two notes of your habitual pitch, you should not experience vocal problems related to pitch level. If your habitual pitch is much higher or lower than your optimum pitch, you may not have sufficient flexibility to raise or lower the pitch of your voice to communicate changes in meaning and emphasis. You can change your habitual pitch by practicing speaking and reading at your optimum pitch.

Rate

Your **rate**, or the speed at which you speak, helps set the mood of your speech. As with pitch, effective speakers often use deliberate changes in rate, pauses, and sustained sounds to give texture to their presentations. For example, when *Law and Order: Special Victims Unit* star Mariska Hargitay spoke on domestic violence to the National Press Club, she used a fast, light pace as she talked about whipping out her cell phone to take a photograph of the vice president when she met him. Once she moved to delineating the statistics on domestic violence, however, she used a slower, more deliberate rate.[12] These variations involved the duration of syllables, the use of pauses, and the overall speed of presentation.

rate
The speed at which words are uttered.

The rate and stress patterns within a speech produce its **rhythm**, an essential component of all communication.[13] Rhythmic variations enable you to point out what is important and make it easier for listeners to comprehend your message. For example, if you have been speaking rapidly and then suddenly slow your pace, pausing to highlight the contrast, you will call attention to what you are saying. This, your vocal change suggests, is important.

rhythm
Rate and stress patterns of vocal presentation within a speech.

People who feel intimidated by the speaking situation often speed up their presentations and run their words together—a rapid-fire delivery suggesting the speaker's desire to get it over with and sit down! At the other extreme, some speakers become so slow and deliberate that they almost put themselves and their audiences to sleep. As we noted in Chapter 4, the typical rate for extemporaneous speaking is approximately 125 words per minute. You can check your speed by timing your reading of a chosen text. If you allow time to pause between important points in a way that is appropriate for an interactive delivery style, your reading may run slightly longer. If you took less

Mariska Hargitay of TV's *Law and Order: Special Victims Unit* varied her rate of speech to add texture to her speech on domestic violence and the founding of the Joyful Heart Foundation.

than fifty seconds, you are probably speaking too rapidly for most listeners to follow and engage your presentation.

Pausing before or after a word or phrase can highlight its importance. It gives your listeners time to contemplate or respond to what you have said. You might want to pause during your presentation to allow for laughter, to let the audience process a compelling example or startling statistic, or to give your listeners a chance to realize the intended answer of a rhetorical question. In his commencement address at Wake Forest, for example, Stephen Colbert used pauses to deliver punch lines successfully, as in his comment that "Of course, we mustn't forget the parents, who to get you students to this day have sacrificed so many things [pause]—primarily money!"[14]

The effective use of pausing can also build suspense and maintain interest as listeners anticipate what you will say next. Moreover, pauses can clarify the relationships among ideas, phrases, and sentences, and are often used—as discussed in Chapter 9—as effective transitions to cue your listeners that you are through making one point and moving onto the next. In the introduction of her speech reprinted in Appendix B, Ashlie McMillan asked her audience to close their eyes and imagine themselves living day to day as a dwarf. At the end of this hypothetical exercise, she paused before she introduced her cousin and her amazing obstacles and abilities. As Sir Ralph Richardson, the esteemed British actor, noted, "The most precious things in speech are the pauses."[15] While practicing your presentation, consider when and how you might use pauses for maximum effect.

Although pausing can be really effective, the wrong use of silence within a speech can work against you. *A short, deliberate pause conveys meaning; a long hesitation signals confusion, uncertainty, and/or a lack of preparation.* Some speakers habitually use "ers" and "ums," "wells" and "okays," "likes" and "you knows" in the place of pauses without being aware of it. These **vocal distractions** may fill in the silence while the speaker thinks about what to say next, or they may be signs of nervousness. They may also be signals that speakers lack confidence in themselves or their messages.

vocal distractions
Filler words, such as "er," "um," and "you know," used in place of a pause.

Sometimes simply becoming aware of such vocal distractions is enough to help you control them. Work to eliminate such fillers from your daily conversations so that you do not have to worry about cutting them out during presentations. Practicing your presentation also diminishes vocal distractions. When you are comfortable with what you're going to say and how you're going to say it, you are much less likely to need those vocalized pauses or to use "okay," "well," or "you know" as transitions instead of language that will help your listeners follow your points. Remember, the goal is to decrease your vocal distractions—not to get rid of every single one. A few are natural; too many affect your credibility.

Finally, keep in mind that different cultures have different norms and expectations regarding rate and rhythm while speaking. These differences can sometimes create misunderstandings that become barriers to communication and may sometimes surface as ugly stereotypes. In the United States, for example, some northerners still stereotype southerners as less intelligent because they tend to speak a little more slowly, and some southerners still stereotype northerners as rude and verbally aggressive because they tend to speak more quickly. Such superficial thinking mars opportunities to listen and learn. Moreover, you should be thoughtful while speaking and listening to more effectively communicate with others who happen to speak a different rhythm than yourself.

Finding Your Voice

Minimizing, Um, Vocal Distractions

Worried that you might be including too many vocal distractions in your presentations? Try this exercise, adapted from one developed by Professor Pat Baker of Davidson College:

1. Record your presentation as you practice one of the major points for your speech.
2. Then play it back, counting the "uhs" (or "likes" or whatever). Write the total number here: _______
3. Divide by the number of minutes you spoke to determine your baseline per minute: _______
   Divide this number by two to get your baseline per 30 seconds: _______
4. Record your presentation again, focusing on delivering 30 seconds' worth. Play it back, and again count the vocal distractions for that period.
5. Do this several times, trying to decrease the number of vocal distractions each time. Then consider increasing the time to 45 seconds or 1 minute.

Volume

No presentation can be effective if the audience can't hear you. Nor will your presentation be successful if you overpower listeners with a voice that is too loud. When you speak before a group, you usually need to speak with a greater volume than you do in general conversation. The size of the room, the presence or absence of a microphone, and background noise may also call for adjustments. To adjust your loudness, take your cues from audience feedback. If you are not loud enough, you may see listeners leaning forward, straining to hear. If you speak too loudly, they may unconsciously lean back, pulling away from the noise.

As with culturally influenced rates of speaking, different cultures have different norms and expectations concerning appropriate volume. For example, in some Mediterranean cultures, a loud voice signifies strength and sincerity, whereas in some Asian and Native American cultures, a soft voice is associated with good manners and education.[16] When members of your audience come from a variety of cultural and ethnic groups, try to moderate your delivery and be sensitive to your listeners' responses.

As with pitch and rate, you can develop your voice for volume through vocal exercises either using a chosen text or while practicing your actual presentation. The celebrated Greek orator Demosthenes taught himself how to project his voice by speaking over the sound of crashing waves.[17] You may or may not have a beach handy, but you can certainly create competing sounds of noise to speak over. Try practicing over the sounds of your favorite music or YouTube. Adjust the volume just loud enough to force you to project and animate your voice forcefully in order to be heard by all the listeners of your imagined audience.

To speak with proper volume, you must have good breath control. You need enough force to project your voice so that you can be heard at the back of a room. You also need enough breath to finish phrases and provide appropriate pauses. Breathing exercises, such as the one we offer in "Finding Your Voice: Developing Your Voice through Breathing," can help you develop good breath control while speaking. As any singing or acting instructor will tell you, breathing deeply from the diaphragm will give your voice more volume and staying power. On the other hand, shallow breathing produces less air control and a weaker speaking voice—sometimes resulting in awkward unplanned pauses or even dizziness and hyperventilation.

BJ Youngerman effectively used changes in volume in his speech about his experience as a baseball umpire.

Finding Your Voice

Developing Your Voice through Breathing

To check whether you are breathing properly for speaking, stand with your feet approximately 8 inches apart. Place your hands on your lower rib cage, thumbs to the front, fingers to the back. Take a deep breath—in through your nose and out through slightly parted lips. If you are breathing correctly, you should feel your ribs moving up and out as you inhale.

Then take a normal breath and see how long you can count out loud while exhaling. If you cannot reach fifteen without losing volume or feeling the need to breathe, you need to work on extending your breath control. Begin by counting in one breath to a number comfortable for you, and then gradually increase the count over successive tries. Do not try to compensate by breathing too deeply. Deep breathing takes too much time and attracts too much attention while you are speaking. Use the longer pauses in your speech to breathe, and make note of your breathing patterns as you practice your speech.

Finally, you should vary the volume of words and phrases in your speech, just as you change your pitch and rate, to express ideas more effectively. Changes in volume are often used to express emotion. The more excited or angry we are, the louder we tend to become. But don't let yourself get caught in the trap of having only two options: loud and louder. Decreasing your volume, slowing your rate, pausing, or dropping your pitch can also express emotions quite effectively.

Davidson student BJ Youngerman demonstrated the importance of variations in volume as he reenacted a scene from his experience as a baseball umpire. In the confrontation between himself and a coach, BJ contrasted the angry loudness of the coach with his own quieter, more controlled vocal manner as an umpire. Read the scene aloud, and, as you play both roles, explore your own capacity to produce both louder and quieter speech:

Me: "He's out!" (with hand motion)

Coach: "You've got to be kidding me, Blue! He was a good 10 feet beyond the base before the ball got there. That's horrible!"

Me: "Coach, it's a judgment call. I called it like I saw it. Please get back to your dugout."

Coach: "Blue, that was the worst call I've ever seen. You're totally blind."

Me: "Coach, this is your final warning: Get in the dugout."

Coach: "Well just because you got cut in Little League doesn't mean you have to take it out on these kids!"

Me: "That's it! You're done!" (waves arms to signify ejection of coach)

Had BJ delivered this entire exchange using the same volume throughout, the lack of contrast would have robbed the example of much of its power. Instead, the vocal contrasts accompanied his vigorous gestures to stimulate interest in his presentation on being an umpire.

Finding Your Voice

Can You Hear Me Now?

To acquire more variety in volume, practice the following exercise recommended by Ralph Hillman: "First, count to five at a soft volume, as if you were speaking to one person. Then, count to five at medium volume, as if speaking to ten or fifteen people. Finally, count to five, as if speaking to thirty or more people."[18] If you record this exercise, you should be able to hear the clear progression in loudness.

Variety

Have you noticed a continuing refrain in these discussions of pitch, rate, and volume? Variety is the spice of life, including public speaking. You recognize the importance of vocal variety when you hear speeches that lack it. Speakers who drone on in a monotone convey that they have little interest in their topic or their listeners or that they fear the situation they are in. Variety can make speeches come to life by adding color and interest.

Again, short speaking exercises using a favorite text can help you develop an array of vocal qualities to express meaning and feeling while making your presentations. You might choose the text sample we provide above from *The Way to Rainy Mountain*, or use this as an opportunity to become more intimately familiar with the verbal style of a favorite novelist, poet, or songwriter. Choose a passage that will take you about a minute to read, and perform it out loud. Make deliberate changes in pitch, rate, and volume to convey differing meanings and moods from the same words. Children's stories—often written to help young people develop their vocabularies and oral style—can be particularly useful. It is hard to beat such classics as Dr. Seuss' *The Cat in the Hat*, *Myrtle the Turtle*, and *Green Eggs and Ham*, or Judith Viorst's *Alexander and His Terrible, Horrible, No Good, Very Bad Day*. Whatever text you choose, record yourself and compare your readings with your initial self-evaluation recording to see if you are developing variety in your presentations.

Vocal Considerations

People often make judgments about others on the basis of their speech patterns. If you slur your words, mispronounce familiar terms, or speak with a dialect that sounds unfamiliar to your audience, you may be seen as uneducated or have a difficult time establishing identification. Of course, some speaking impediments are grounded in physical impairments that are best treated by a licensed speech therapist. However, most speakers can benefit by correcting minor errors in articulation, enunciation, and pronunciation, and by being cognizant of the challenges and opportunities posed by differences in ethnic and regional dialect.

Articulation. **Articulation** is the way you produce individual speech sounds. Some people have trouble making certain sounds. For example, they may substitute a *d* for a *th*, saying "dem" instead of "them." Other sounds that are often misarticulated include *s*, *l*, and *r*. Severe articulation problems can interfere with effective communication, especially if the audience cannot understand the speaker or if the variations suggest lack of education. Again, with extreme cases, the services of a speech therapist may be necessary, but minor articulation issues can usually be improved through conscious effort and practice.

articulation
The manner in which individual speech sounds are produced.

Enunciation. **Enunciation** is the way you pronounce words in context. In casual conversation, it is not unusual for people to slur their words—for example, saying "gimme" for "give me." However, careless enunciation causes credibility problems for public speakers. If you repeatedly use references such as "Howarya?" for "How are you?" in the course of making a formal presentation, it may well damage your ethos before most public speaking audiences. Check your enunciation patterns on the recordings you have made to determine whether you should articulate words more clearly. If you do, concentrate on precise enunciation as you practice your speech. Be careful, however, to avoid the opposite problem of inflated, pompous, and pretentious enunciation, which sounds phony. Strike the balance between sloppy slurring and overly precise articulation.

enunciation
The manner in which individual words are articulated and pronounced in context.

Pronunciation. **Pronunciation** involves saying words correctly. It includes both using the correct sounds and placing the proper accent on syllables. Because written

pronunciation
The use of correct sounds and of proper stress on syllables when saying words.

Matt Damon made effective use of his native Boston accent when speaking in New England.

English does not always indicate the correct pronunciation, we may not be sure how to pronounce words that we first encounter in print. For instance, does the word *chiropodist* begin with a *sh,* a *ch,* or a *k* sound? What syllables should be emphasized?

If you are not certain how to pronounce a word that is unfamiliar, highly technical, or foreign to you, consult a dictionary. A number of online pronunciation guides from such sources as Merriam-Webster or Macmillan dictionaries can help. Online discussions of your subject with streaming video may help to verify your pronunciation of unfamiliar or technical terms, and online news stories may help you to correctly pronounce the names of important foreign leaders. An especially useful print reference is the *NBC Handbook of Pronunciation*, which contains 21,000 words and proper names that sometimes cause problems.[19]

Sometimes even well-educated people may habitually mispronounce common words if they have become accustomed to doing so in casual conversation. For instance, many people mispronounce the word *government* as "goverment," *athlete* as "athalete," and *ask* as "axe." Former President George W. Bush attracted considerable attention and some ridicule for habitually mispronouncing the word *nuclear* as "*nucular*."[20] Because such mishaps can damage your ethos as a speaker, be sure to verify the pronunciation of troublesome words as you practice your speech and become comfortable with their correct form.

dialect

A speech pattern associated with an area of the country or with a cultural or ethnic background.

Dialect. A **dialect** is a speech pattern typical of a geographic region or ethnic group. Your dialect usually reflects the area of the country where you were raised or lived for any length of time and is often indicative of your cultural and ethnic identity.[21] In the United States, there are three commonly recognized regional dialects: eastern, southern, and midwestern. Additionally, there are local variations within the broader dialects. For example, South Carolina boasts the Gullah dialect from the islands off the coast, the low-country or Charlestonian accent, the Piedmont variation, and the Appalachian twang.[22] And then there's always "Bah-stahn" [Boston], where you "pahk the cah" [park the car] before you go to the "pahty" [party]!

Everyone sees someone as speaking differently from themselves, and there is no such thing as a superior or an inferior dialect. Of course, it doesn't hurt to speak the same dialect as your primary listeners, and unfortunately there are still some people who cling to negative stereotypes associated with regional and ethnic dialects. Not too long ago, many teachers encouraged people with historically stigmatized dialects to master "standard English" and learn the art of code-switching for making formal presentations. However, there is nothing about an Irish accent that makes activist Bono any less eloquent, and Bill Clinton's southern accent doesn't seem to hinder his efforts to reach individuals across the country.

As a general rule, you should model your speaking voice on the standard for educated people from your geographic area or ethnic group, and you should be cautious of culturally specific phrases and words that might not be familiar to listeners from different backgrounds. Beyond that, you should cultivate your own unique speaking voice as an expression of who you are and as a way to connect your ideas, knowledge, and convictions with other people. As consultant Ty Boyd advises, "play the horn you were born with."[23] When inaugurated as president at a southern institution, Dr. Carol Quillen used effective self-deprecating humor by sharing advice she'd received: "We know you are from the northeast—bless your heart!—but let us finish our *own* sentences."[24]

Assessing Your Own Speaking Voice

Given the discussion in this section of developing your voice for better delivery, assess your own speaking voice. How can you improve your use of pitch, rate, volume, and variety for your next speech?

YOUR ETHICAL VOICE

Persistent Questions about Presentation

Audiences often raise ethical and practical questions concerning the presentation aspects of public speaking. The following mini-scenarios offer a sampling of such questions and doubts:

1. "He talks so slowly. Does he *think* slowly, too?"
2. "She talks so fast. Is she trying to put something over on me?"
3. "I don't like his hairstyle or his clothes. Can a person with such bad taste be telling the truth?"
4. "She has a peculiar accent—probably foreign. How can she possibly understand my problems?"
5. "He just mispronounced a word. Could his thinking be flawed as well? Can I trust such an ignoramus?"
6. "She looks uncomfortable—kind of buried in her notes and not looking us in the eye. If she's not confident as a speaker, should I be confident in following her advice?"
7. "He sounds too good, too polished. Can I trust him?"

Assuming you are the person to whom such questions are asked, how would you answer them? What advice would you offer to counter such distrust?

Developing Your Body Language

12.4 Develop more effective body language.

Communication with your audience begins before you ever open your mouth. **Body language** refers to communication achieved through the use of facial expressions, eye contact, movement and gestures, and even physical appearance.[25] In the courtroom, lawyers strive to convey an air of confidence and leadership through body language. Trial consultant Constance Bernstein advises attorneys to "win trials nonverbally" through strong presentations of not only their cases but also themselves. She emphasizes the importance of eye contact as a way to "address each juror individually." She stresses standing tall and firm so that "you will feel more grounded." She advocates using gestures "to anchor your message," both because they are memorable and because "your hands are invisible connections to jurors." And she recommends speaking in a way that conveys assurance and poise:

body language
Communication achieved using facial expressions, eye contact, movements, and gestures.

> When you are in the courtroom fearing the worst, do not let anyone sense your anxiety. Take a deep breath and relax.... Opposing counsel will be dismayed by your confidence; the judge will be impressed by your calmness; and the jurors will view you as self-confident and thoroughly prepared.[26]

Attorneys seek Bernstein's counsel to help craft and deliver successful presentations. Her advice echoes ours for public speaking: You can amplify your voice using facial expressions and eye contact, movement and gestures, and clothing and personal appearance to underscore and magnify your message. Although we discuss these as separate types of body language, in practice audiences interpret them as a totality.[27]

Facial Expression and Eye Contact

The eyes are the most important element of facial expressiveness. In mainstream American culture, frequent and sustained eye contact suggests honesty, openness, and respect. We may think of a person's eyes as windows into the self. If you avoid looking at your audience while you are talking, an American audience may assume you are drawing the shades on these windows. A lack of eye contact suggests you do not care about listeners, you are putting something over on them, or you are afraid of them.

Note that other cultures view eye contact differently. In China, Indonesia, and rural Mexico, traditionally people lower their eyes as a sign of deference. In general, people from Asian and some African countries engage in less eye contact than those from the mainstream American culture.[28] Some Native Americans may even find direct eye contact offensive or aggressive. Therefore, with culturally diverse audiences especially, don't conclude that listeners who resist eye contact are necessarily expressing their distrust or refusal to communicate.

When you reach the lectern, turn, pause, and engage the eyes of your audience. This signals that you want to communicate and prepares people to listen. During your speech, try to make eye contact with all sectors of the audience. First, look at people at the front of the room, then shift your focus to the middle and sides, and finally look at those in the rear. You may find that those sitting in the back of the room are the most difficult to reach. They may have taken a rear seat because they don't want to listen or be involved. Eye contact is one way you can gain and hold their attention. Be sure not to stare at just one or two people. You will make them uncomfortable, and other audience members will feel left out.

Smile as you start your speech unless a smile is inappropriate to your message. A smile signals your good will toward listeners and your ease in the speaking situation—qualities that should help your ethos.[29] From your very first words, let your face reflect and reinforce their meaning. An expressionless face suggests that the speaker is afraid or indifferent. A frozen face may be a mask behind which the speaker hides. The solution lies in selecting a topic that excites you, concentrating on sharing your message, and having the confidence that comes from being well prepared.

You can also try the following exercise. Utter these statements using a dull monotone and keeping your face as expressionless as possible:

> I am absolutely delighted by your gift.
> I don't know when I've ever been this excited.
> We don't need to beg for change—we need to demand change.
> All this puts me in a very bad mood.

Now repeat them with *exaggerated* vocal variety and facial expression. A happy medium between the two offers a lively vocal quality without forcing it. You may find that your hands and body also want to get involved. Encourage such impulses so that you develop an integrated system of body language.

Movement and Gestures

Most actors learn—often the hard way—that if you want to steal a scene from someone, all you have to do is move around, develop a twitch, or swing a leg. Before long, all eyes will be focused on that movement. This cheap theatrical trick shows that physical movement sometimes can attract more attention than words. All the more reason that your words and gestures should work in harmony and not at cross purposes!

Let your gestures grow out of your message naturally. Stand tall with good posture so that you can breathe easily and project confidence. Start with your hands and body in a position that allows free action. For example, you cannot gesture if your hands are locked behind your back or jammed into your pockets or if you are grasping the lectern like a life preserver. Instead, let your hands rest in a relaxed position—at your sides, on the lectern, or in front of you at waist level. As you execute a gesture, let yourself move naturally and fully. Don't raise your hand halfway and then stop with your arm frozen awkwardly in space. When you have completed a gesture, let your hands return to the starting point, ready to emphasize the next important point.

Peter Dinklage used effective gestures that underscored his meaning in his speech at Bennington College.

Research suggests that adopting a superhero stance in private—feet wide apart, hands on your hips, shoulders thrown back, head held high—generates a psychological and physiological sense of confidence. Try assuming this open, expansive position in private before you speak, and you are likely to feel more powerful and self-assured.[30]

As with all body language, your gestures and movement should be consistent with, and complement, what you are saying. When Peter Dinklage of *Game of Thrones* fame spoke to the graduating class of Bennington College, he mostly rested his hands gently on the lectern, which made his use of gestures more effective. When he repeated the "wisdom" that others proffered in preparation, for example, he shared, "know that there is no wrong speech"—at which point he shrugged shoulders, raised his hands in the air, and shook his head.[31]

You may have developed a strategic awareness of body language as you practice—for example: "When I reach this moment in the speech, I've got to stop, pause, look hard at listeners, and use gestures to really drive home my point." But body language should always *appear* natural and spontaneous. Gestures should never *look* contrived or artificial. For example, you should avoid framing a gesture to fit each word or sequence of words you utter. Perhaps every speech instructor has encountered speakers like the one who stood with arms circled above him as he said, "We need to get *around* this problem." That's not good body language!

This also means you should avoid random movements, such as pacing back and forth, twirling your hair, rubbing your eyes, jingling change in your pockets, or "driving" the lectern. Once you are aware of such mannerisms, it is easier to control them. Try a video recording (perhaps with a cell phone or digital camera) as you practice for your next speech. Just as audio recordings can reveal aspects of your voice that are surprising, so can video recordings reveal unsuspected habits of movement to correct. If your campus has a communication center, the consultants there can also coach you.

Don't assume there is a universal language of gesture. Rwandans, for example, learn an elaborate code of gestures that is a direct extension of their spoken language.[32] In contrast, American gestural language is far less complex and sophisticated. Still, it can perform important communication functions, such as reinforcing, amplifying, and clarifying the spoken word.

The Factor of Distance. From **proxemics**, the study of how humans use space during communication, we can derive two additional principles that help explain the effective use of movement during speeches. The first suggests that *the actual* **distance** *between speakers and listeners can affect their sense of closeness or immediacy*. Presidential speeches offer a compelling illustration of this principle. When making formal presentations before Congress or other large organizations, they usually speak from a position that places them *above* and somewhat *distant from* their listeners. This deliberate use of space emphasizes the power and formality of the office and enhances their presidential stature. On less formal occasions such as town hall meetings, they strive to be more interactive and personable with their listeners, to speak to them at their own level, and to come across as "just plain folk." Control of proxemics in all such cases helps them establish the desired persona of a citizen-leader who enjoys unusual power but is still "one of us." You can rest assured that their advisers are very aware of these proxemic effects!

proxemics
The study of how human beings use space during communication.

distance
Principle of proxemics involving the control of the space that separates speaker and audience.

Finding Your Voice

Toward a Livelier Presentation

As you practice your next speech, record yourself or work with a partner and deliberately try to speak in as dull a voice as possible. Stifle all impulses to gesture. Then practice speaking with as colorful a voice as possible, giving full freedom to movement and gesture. Then analyze the two versions. Which aspects create a colorful and expressive presentation that makes your ideas seem more lively and vivid? How can you incorporate these aspects into your presentation to your audience while still being comfortable with the speech?

When making informal presentations such as most classroom speeches, it is usually a good idea to reduce the amount of unnecessary distance between yourself and your listeners. Some speakers manage to accomplish this while using a lectern, but for others that stand can become a formidable barrier to establishing identification. Some speakers may come across as glued to or hiding behind the lectern, whereas shorter speakers—through no fault of their own—may literally disappear from view. One judge counsels attorneys to avoid lecterns altogether, arguing that "they create artificial barriers between lawyer and juror."[33] Try speaking either beside or in front of the lectern so that your body language can work for you.

At the same time, you don't want to move so close to listeners that you make them feel uncomfortable. If they pull back involuntarily in their chairs, you know you have violated their sense of personal space. A healthy balance can be achieved by gauging your audience's responses. In addition, moving purposefully—without pacing—can engage your audience and provide an appropriate outlet for your energy.

elevation
Principle of proxemics dealing with power relationships implied when speakers stand above listeners.

The Factor of Elevation. The second principle of proxemics suggests that **elevation** *also affects the sense of closeness between speakers and listeners*. As illustrated by our example of presidential speaking, addressing your audience from a position of elevation places you in a "power position" over your seated listeners. Because of that presumed association, speakers may find that this arrangement discourages identification with some listeners. For this reason, speakers who want to strike a less formal tone of interaction will sometimes sit on the edge of a desk or stand in front of the lectern in a more relaxed and less elevated stance. On some occasions before really small audiences, they may actually choose to speak from a sitting position or move to the same elevation as their listeners.

Reducing the physical distance between the speaker and audience can enhance identification with the speaker as being "one of us."

Clothing and Personal Appearance

Your clothing and grooming can affect how you and your message are received.[34] As Goffman notes, your personal appearance should be consistent with the overall impression you want to give.[35] How we dress can even influence how we see ourselves and how we behave. A police officer out of uniform may not act as authoritatively as when dressed in blue. A doctor without a white jacket may behave like just another person. You may have a certain type of clothing that makes you feel comfortable and relaxed. You may even have a special "good luck" outfit that raises your confidence.

When you are scheduled to speak, dress in a way that makes you feel confident while also appropriate to the audience and the occasion. Find out if the occasion calls for formal, casual-dress, or informal attire, and dress at the expected level or just a little nicer. Most gatherings for public speaking are relatively formal, and if you show up significantly underdressed you will likely convey a lack of regard for the occasion and your audience, or even an arrogant sense of entitlement—as if you're too important, intelligent, or powerful to concern yourself with the rules of decorum.[36] On the other hand, if you address an informal gathering like an outdoor barbecue or a sports banquet wearing a fancy formal suit or dress, that too can create a barrier to identification. As we noted in Chapter 10, your appearance can serve as a presentation aid that complements your message. Like any other aid and body language in general, it should never be a distraction that competes with your words for attention.

Bringing It All Together

In his classic book *The Presentation of Self in Everyday Life*, Erving Goffman emphasizes the importance of creating consistency among the verbal and nonverbal elements of expression. To achieve a harmony of impressions, *your vocal characteristics, body language, and clothing/personal appearance must reinforce your verbal language.*[37] If your face is expressionless as you urge your listeners to action, you are sending inconsistent messages. If you seem flustered and uncertain as you urge listeners to be confident and calm, your impressions will be badly out of sync. As a general rule, whenever your verbal and nonverbal messages seem contradictory, listeners will tend to attribute more credibility to your nonverbal messages. Be sure your body and words both "say" the same thing, and be sure your body gives voice to the concepts and moods you want to express.

Learning to use your body language effectively will enhance your impact beyond public speaking. From courtrooms to business to personal relationships, understanding the value of coordinating message and delivery will improve communication in your life.[38]

Identifying Verbal and Nonverbal Aspects of a Message

Identify a speaker who makes you uncomfortable. Can you locate disparities between the verbal and nonverbal aspects of the message that would explain your discomfort?

Finding Your Voice

Critiquing Presentation Practices

Attend a guest lecture or speech or view a presentation on TED or YouTube (such as Jennifer Lee's commencement speech at the University of New Hampshire or Betty White's acceptance speech at the Screen Actors Guild awards). Was the speaker's voice effective or ineffective? Why? How would you evaluate the speaker's body language? Did the speaker read from a manuscript, make a memorized presentation, or speak extemporaneously? Was the speaker adept at moving from one mode of presentation to another? How flexible was the speaker in answering questions?

Practicing Your Presentation for Delivery

12.5 Practice for successful delivery

It takes a lot of practice to sound natural. Although this statement may seem contradictory, it should not be surprising. Speaking before a group is not your typical way of communicating. Even though most people seem spontaneous and relaxed when talking with a small group of friends, something happens when they walk to the front of a room and face a larger audience of less familiar faces. They often freeze or become stilted and awkward, which is uncomfortable for everyone. The key to overcoming this problem is to *prepare and practice* until you can respond fully to your ideas as you present them to your audience.

Remember that public speaking is a *process*, not a product: Start by developing your presentation sufficiently in advance of the scheduled date so that you have the opportunity to refine and grow comfortable with your message. Heed the maxim that "It takes one hour of preparation for each minute of presentation time."[39] Then follow the advice on how to get to Carnegie Hall: Practice, practice, practice! Steve Jobs's renowned presentations of Apple products succeeded because he started working on the event well in advance and then devoted the forty-eight hours before each one to polishing the presentation. His engaging, nonchalant informality came "after grueling hours of practice."[40]

Don't fall into the trap of avoiding practice because it reminds you that you are not confident about your upcoming speech: That is a recipe for a self-fulfilling prophecy![41] Instead, rehearse your speech until your voice, face, and body can express your feelings as well as your thoughts. Constance Bernstein, founder of Synchronics Group Trial Consultants, advises lawyers to be so familiar with their arguments that "you will be able to deliver them without faltering—without losing eye contact."[42]

As discussed in Chapter 3, practice begins by reading through your formal outline or manuscript several times *out loud* to yourself until you begin to feel comfortable with the structure and flow of your message. Reading aloud or "speaking the speech" provides several benefits:

- **It will enhance your memory.** Actually vocalizing the words engages your brain in ways that simply reading them will not. It also helps you become more comfortable with the message.
- **It will provide a more accurate estimation of time.** You can think through a presentation in about three-quarters of the time you need to deliver it. Think of how you feel when an instructor keeps you beyond the allotted class time, and use that to help you stay within the specified limits.
- **It will enable you to make adjustments to enhance orality.** That compound-complex sentence that looked so good on paper leaves you breathless and confused when you say it out loud. It's better to discover and correct that difficulty during practice than during delivery.

Once you begin to feel like you know your speech, break it down to a key-word outline on note cards as illustrated in Figure 12.3, and continue practicing until you are ready. Key words provide prompts that can be viewed at a glance while speaking to help keep you on track. They should be concise and large enough to read at a glance so you don't disrupt the flow of your presentation. Especially if you plan to speak without a lectern, we recommend note cards because they are easy to handle for extemporaneous presentations. Use a separate card for your introduction, your conclusion, and each main point. Add cues for referencing presentation aids or planned variations in your delivery style, and write out longer quotations in full on a separate card. Number your cards for a graceful recovery in case you drop them while making your presentation. It happens!

Practice your entire presentation. Stand up while you speak; project your voice loudly enough to be heard from the back of the room; and work in your nonverbal gestures, pauses, and vocal variations as you interact with an imagined audience before you. Practice handling and introducing presentation aids so they can be integrated smoothly into your speech. Practice reading important quotations until you can present them naturally without having to look at every word. If possible, practice your speech in your actual classroom or a similar classroom in order to familiarize yourself

Figure 12.3
A Sample Key-Word Outline

Place the introduction, each of the four main points, and the conclusion on *separate* note cards. Note that the outline follows the guidelines of *not* numbering either the introduction or the conclusion, only the main points. In addition, put your quotations and oral citations on separate note cards.

INTRODUCTION

Symptoms of global warming *(hit these hard)*

The "Greenhouse Effect" *(need good eye contact)*

Must understand the second to control the first

BODY

I. Greenhouse effect = natural process
   A. Makes earth livable
   B. Now we've unbalanced (summary Schneider)
      1. Too much CO_2 and methane
      2. Record temperatures
         a. 2000s warmest decade
         b. 2016 hottest year on record! *(be dramatic)*
      3. Threatens all living things—including us! *(be emphatic)*

II. First cause: Loss of trees (*Time* 2015)
   A. Cutting
   B. Clearing (Univ of Washington study, 2017)
   C. Burning *(pause for effect)*

III. Second cause: Emissions (Union: Card 1)
   A. Farming
      1. Tilling
      2. Rice farms
      3. Cattle
   B. Industrial
      1. Smokestacks
      2. Trucks
      3. Airplanes *(pause for emphasis)*

IV. Third cause: Personal consumption (*U.S. News* 2014)
   A. Population and prosperity
      1. More people = more consumption
      2. Higher standards = more consumption
   B. Single largest cause (*NY Times* Oct. '16) *(emphasize strongly)*
      1. Fossil fuels = 90% of personal energy use
      2. Cars on road increased almost 4x since 1950 (*L.A. Times* Dec. '16) *(repeat for emphasis)*

CONCLUSION

Listen, watch, smell *(slow down and emphasize)*

Questions from the future *(really hit them with these)*

with the physical setting. Finally, picture your listeners responding positively to what you have to say. Address your ideas to them, and visualize your ideas having impact.

Although it may sound contrary to the spirit of conversational spontaneity, force yourself to use your key-word cards both during practice and during your actual presentation. Sometimes students become so familiar with their speeches that they open their presentations from memory as if speaking on auto-pilot. This often works well for about a minute until they stumble over their words and then find themselves fumbling back through their notes. Even when you know your next point, make it a point to glance at your notes at planned intervals during your presentation. When using note cards, hold them in your nondominant hand, and shuffle them with your dominant hand as you move from point to point. If you plan to speak from a lectern, position them so that you can maintain strong eye contact with your listeners while speaking. In either case, do not try to hide the fact that you are using notes.

If they are available and willing, ask a few trusted friends or family members to listen to your speech and offer constructive feedback. If your campus has a communication center, then by all means take advantage of the special advice and support of peer coaches. Ask others: Was it easy for them to follow you? Did your ideas seem clear and soundly supported? Were you speaking loudly and slowly (or quickly) enough? Do you have any mannerisms (such as twisting your hair or saying "you know" after every other sentence) that distracted them? The suggestions of others may be more objective than your self-evaluation, and you will get a feel for speaking to real people rather than to an imagined audience. Moreover, research confirms that speakers who practice before real audiences receive higher evaluation scores later.[43] Recording your practice can also be beneficial—as long as you remember to look for *both* strengths and areas to improve.

Making a Key-Word Outline for Your Speech

Make a key-word outline for your next speech. What are the most challenging aspects of narrowing your formal outline to a few key words? What are the advantages of working from a key-word outline?

Once you begin to feel like you could present your entire speech from just a glance at your key-word cards, try it. If you can, you should be ready. Put your notes away and get some rest—especially if it's getting late and you have to make your presentation in the morning! On the day you are assigned to speak, get to class early enough to look over your outline one last time so that it is fresh in your mind. Take the time to focus on your speech. Although financial consultant Suze Orman regularly goes on the speaking circuit, she insists that "when I'm on my way to a speaking engagement, you cannot talk to me about another project. All I'm doing is thinking about that speech. That way, when I get there, everything is clear."[44]

If you are still feeling a little nervous, revisit the advice we offer for coping with communication apprehension in Chapter 2. Visualize yourself presenting your speech successfully. If you have devoted sufficient time and energy to your preparation and practice, you should be able to manage the butterflies for your first few presentations, and a little experience should make you feel increasingly confident for future presentations. For now, enjoy the experience of sharing your ideas with your audience, and remember the perspective of Jody Cross, owner of the consulting firm Leaders Speak: "Perfection is not the goal—connection is!"[45] With practice, you will be able to achieve that connection. The checklist provided in "Speaker's Notes: Practicing for Presentation" summarizes our suggestions for practicing.

YOUR ETHICAL VOICE

We have emphasized the importance of practicing your delivery of your presentation, primarily so that you feel more comfortable and can adapt more easily to your audience's feedback. Preparation and practice also entail an ethical obligation to your audience. Consider: If you have 25 people in your audience and you speak for 10 minutes, you are responsible for 250 minutes, or more than 4 hours, of their collective time. What commitment does that place on you as a speaker? What obligation would you feel as an audience member?

SPEAKER'S NOTES

Practicing for Presentation

To practice your presentation, follow these suggestions:

1. Practice standing up and speaking aloud, if possible in the room where you will be making your presentation.
2. Practice first from your formal outline, then gradually work your way to your key-word outline as you become proficient with your material.
3. Work on maintaining eye contact with an imaginary audience.
4. Practice integrating your presentation aids into your message.
5. Check the timing of your speech. Add or cut as necessary.
6. Continue practicing until you feel comfortable and confident.
7. Present your speech in a "dress rehearsal" before friends or at your campus communication center. Make final changes based on their suggestions.

Developing Flexibility: Answering Questions and Making Mediated Speeches

12.6 Become flexible in answering questions and making mediated speeches.

Finding your voice as a speaker includes mastering the various methods of presentation, developing your voice and nonverbal skills for maximum effect, and practicing for effective delivery. In addition, it means developing flexibility for a variety of special speaking situations. In Chapter 5, we discuss the importance of adapting to various aspects of public speaking situations, including the occasion, the physical setting, and audience size. Here, we address the challenges and opportunities of *handling question-and-answer (Q&A) sessions* and *making mediated presentations.*

Handling Questions and Answers

On many speaking occasions, members of the audience will be given the opportunity to ask questions after your speech. Some instructors like to incorporate time for Q&A sessions after students give speeches because it tends to stimulate the audience's interest and interaction and can help speakers develop their ability to deliver impromptu remarks. The following suggestions should make handling questions easier for you.[46]

- **Prepare for questions.** Try to anticipate what you might be asked, think about how you will answer those questions, and do the research required to answer them authoritatively. Practice your speech before friends or peer tutors, and urge them to ask you tough questions.
- **Paraphrase the question as the beginning of your answer.** This is especially important if the question was long or complicated and your audience is large. Paraphrasing ensures that everyone in the audience hears the question. It gives you time to plan your answer, and it helps verify that you have understood the question. Paraphrasing also enables you to steer the question to the type of answer you are prepared to give.
- **As you answer, maintain eye contact with the audience.** Note that we say, "with the *audience*," not just "with the questioner." Look first at the questioner, and then make eye contact with other audience members, returning your gaze to the

questioner as you finish your answer. The purpose of a question-and-answer period should be to extend the understanding of the entire audience, not to carry on a conversation with one person.

- **Defuse hostile questions.** Reword emotional questions in more neutral language. For example, if you are asked, "Why do you want to throw our money away on people who are too lazy to work?" you might respond with something like, "I understand your frustration with the current programs; we need to explore why they aren't helping people break out of the cycle of unemployment." Don't be afraid to use such questions to help you make a closely related point.[47]
- **Don't be afraid to concede a point or to say, "I don't know."** Such tactics can earn you points for honesty and can help defuse a difficult question or hostile questioner. You can offer to find the information and get in touch with the questioner later, or you can say that particular aspect was outside the realm of your research.
- **Keep your answers short and direct.** Don't give another speech. Vice President Joe Biden of Delaware, while highly regarded as a foreign policy expert, entered the 2008 presidential campaign with a reputation for being a compulsive talker and for putting his foot in his mouth. At the first nationally televised debate for Democratic Party hopefuls, the moderator skewered him with an unfriendly question:

  Moderator: An editorial in the *Los Angeles Times* said, "In addition to his uncontrolled verbosity, Biden is a gaffe machine." Can you reassure voters in this country that you would have the discipline you would need on the world stage, Senator?
  Senator Biden: Yes.
  (Audience laughter. Long moment of silence)
  Moderator: Thank you, Senator Biden.
  (More laughter)[48]

- **Handle nonquestions politely.** If someone starts to give a speech rather than ask a question, wait until he or she pauses for breath, and then intervene with something like, "Thank you for your comment," or, "I appreciate your remarks." Continue with, "You have asked, then, about . . .," and select one aspect of the statement to which you want to respond. You might also respond, "That's an interesting perspective. Can we have another question?" Maintaining eye contact with the entire audience will facilitate this goal. Stay in command of the situation.
- **Bring the question-and-answer session to a close.** The time allotted for Q&A is often limited. As you approach that time or as your audience begins to fall silent, call for one or two final questions and then bring your presentation to a close. Quickly summarize your message again to refocus listeners on your central points, like a bumper sticker for your oral journey. When Tom Ross, former president of Davidson College, met with a group of parents and alumni, one parent of a current student offered a heartfelt tribute to the quality of her daughter's education. Ross smiled at his audience and said, "I can't think of a better way to end this evening than with that!"[49]

Stepping into the audience to take questions, as celebrity chef Robert Irvine did during a demonstration, gives the speaker a chance to increase the influence of the speech.

Making Mediated Presentations

In today's age of ever-evolving technology, it is increasingly likely that you will make presentations across vast distances and even time using various forms of electronic and computer media. You may find yourself creating an online training program, speaking on closed-circuit television, Skyping an interview, recording instructions at work, using community access cable channels to promote a cause, or appearing on commercial television. Each of these mediated formats requires not only developing your physical voice and your body language but also making particular adaptations to deliver your messages well.[50]

With most mediated presentations—at least for the present—you will not be able to see your audience while speaking. In fact, with today's Internet, you may not even know who your audiences may eventually be. You won't be able to adapt to feedback, so as you develop your presentation, you need to work to keep the message clear. Use colorful, concrete language so that your audience remembers your points. Use previews and internal summaries to keep viewers on track. If you want to incorporate presentation aids, make sure they are appropriate to the medium. It's unwieldy to use large easel posters online, for example, but you can effectively incorporate videos. (See related considerations in Chapter 10.)

Despite the fact that you cannot see the faces of your viewers, you want to keep a conversational tone. Imagine yourself speaking to individuals, but be sure to speak slowly enough that your audience can follow you. Use those extemporaneous skills to good effect; if you need to use a teleprompter to stay within a time limit, practice using the guidelines for manuscript speaking.

Set up the camera so that it frames your head and the top of your shoulders at eye level. You don't want the audience via the camera looking down on you, nor do you want them peering up your nostrils. Look directly at the camera so that your viewers will see you looking at them. Beware of two contradictory tendencies: either to stiffen up or to overact. You don't want to be a talking head: you want your voice and facial expressions to convey your interest in the topic and your audience. At the same time, the camera magnifies all your movements and vocal changes, so use restrained head movements and underplayed facial expressions as well as moderate changes in volume. Rely on pauses and on subtle changes in tempo, pitch, and inflection to drive your points home.

Because the camera brings you close to viewers, it also magnifies every aspect of your appearance. Consider what the backdrop will be. If you can, minimize the distractions; many a YouTube presentation has been marred as viewers try to figure out what's posted on the refrigerator or what clothes are hanging in the closet. The backdrop will influence your choice of dress: If you have light hair or if the backdrop will be light, wear dark clothing for contrast. If you have a dark skin tone, consider a light or neutral background and lighter-colored clothes. Make sure your clothes fit well and look good, as wrinkles, stains, pulls, and gaps will be magnified on screen. Dressing conservatively will keep the focus on you and your message. Avoid glittery or dangling jewelry, shiny fabrics, and flashy prints and stripes that might "swim" on the screen and distract viewers. Avoid white or light pastels, which could reflect lights and create glare. Both men and women need makeup to achieve a natural look on camera. Have powder available to reduce skin shine or to hide a five o'clock shadow. Use makeup conservatively because the camera will intensify it.

Remember that the microphone picks up *all* sounds, including shuffling papers, clicking pens, and tapping on a lectern. If you use a stand or handheld microphone, position it about ten inches below your mouth. The closer the microphone is to your mouth, the more it picks up unwanted noises like whistled *s* sounds or tongue clicks. Before you begin your speech and after you finish, always assume that any microphone or camera near you is live. Don't say or do anything you wouldn't want your audience to hear or see.

Assessing a Question-and-Answer Session

Watch a question-and-answer session (e.g., a news conference, a talk show, or a corporate presentation after a crisis). How well does the individual handle the questions? How could following the guidelines in this section improve the session?

All of the advice about preparation and practice, from rehearsing in the space if possible to being fully comfortable with your message, applies to mediated presentations as well. Keep your voice conversational, your body relaxed, and your face friendly even as you look into the eye of the camera.

Certain media, such as television, require strict time limits; if the producer says you have five minutes, it does not mean you have five minutes and five seconds. In such cases, you may want to use either a teleprompter (which is best used with practice) or carefully prepared manuscript (also requiring practice), and time yourself while preparing your presentation.

If you make a mistake, keep going. Sometimes "mistakes" are actually improvements; other times, the audience won't even notice if you just continue. If appropriate, smile when you finish and continue looking at the camera to allow time for a fade-out.

Final Reflections: Poetic Presentations

It is now clear that no one is going to give you your voice. You have to find it for yourself—and to convince others you have found it as you stand before them. As Thomas discovered in our opening scenario, topic, research, and design constitute necessary but not sufficient preparations for effective delivery. You need to practice the presentation until you are comfortable with what you want to say and how you want to say it, so that you can concentrate on making the connection with your audience. Developing your vocal qualities and your body language will enable you to bring the speech to life. More confident presentational styles lead to more confident presentations, which in turn lead to even more confident presentational styles—whether speaking in front of the class, interviewing for an internship, or addressing a convention. As you step to the front of the room when you are asked to speak, do so confidently. Project the realization that you have something worthwhile and important to say that listeners should consider carefully.

Speechwriter Peggy Noonan observed that "a speech is poetry: cadence, rhythm, imagery, sweep! A speech reminds us that words, like children, have the power to make dance the dullest beanbag of a heart."[51] Extemporaneous or manuscript, presentation or question-and-answer session, face-to-face or mediated—whatever the context, effective delivery turns language into interactive poetry, forming an essential part of finding your voice.

Study Questions

CONTENT MASTERY

1 What role does delivery play in your presentation?

2 What are the four forms of presentation? What are the advantages and disadvantages of each?

3 How can your physical voice enliven your message?

4 What can body language contribute to your presentation? How can it detract?

5 How can you prepare effectively for your presentation?

6 What steps will enhance your question-and-answer sessions?

7 How does giving a presentation in a mediated format differ from a face-to-face speech?

CRITICAL EXPLORATIONS

1. Find a speech that uses a manuscript or memorized delivery (e.g., at C-SPAN or Annie Lennox's 2013 commencement speech at Berklee College of Music). What did the speaker do to enhance the presentation? What did the speaker do that distracted from the presentation? What could the speaker have done to improve? Then find a speech that uses extemporaneous delivery (e.g., at TED.com). What did the speaker do to enhance the presentation? What did the speaker do that distracted from the presentation? What could the speaker have done to improve?
2. Develop a list of statements, such as, "I'm tired," "That's hilarious," and "What a wonderful story you have told." As you read these statements, exaggerate changes in pitch, rate, and volume to create differing moods and meanings. For example, try reciting "That's very interesting" in a voice that conveys boredom, then excitement, then disdain. Experiment with how many meanings you can generate for these statements with different changes of your voice.
3. During a conversation with a friend, try limiting your facial expressions, eye contact, movement, and gestures. How long does it take your friend to become aware that something is different? How do you feel when you are talking conversationally but limiting your body language? How does this exercise suggest ways that you can develop your body language appropriately when giving a speech?
4. Map out a practice schedule for your next speech. How can you use practice to encourage using your voice clearly and powerfully in your presentation?
5. Consider your last speech. If you had a question-and-answer session afterward, how could the guidelines in this chapter have helped? If you did not, consider how the guidelines in this chapter might have prepared you for one.
6. Say one of your presentations is so good that your intructor would like you to give it again, this time to be posted on YouTube. How would you modify your presentation for the mediated form?

CHAPTER

Informative Speaking

LEARNING OBJECTIVES	OUTLINE
This chapter will help you:	
13.1 Realize the importance of informative speaking.	Informative Speaking: An Overview
13.2 Prepare speeches that create a vivid description, demonstrate a process, or explain how something works.	Types of Informative Speaking
13.3 Use different techniques to help listeners learn and remember.	Helping Listeners Learn
13.4 Understand the options for designing informative speeches.	Designs for Informative Speeches
13.5 Appreciate briefings as a particular kind of informative speaking.	Briefings: A Special Case of Informative Speaking

In ancient Greek mythology, Prometheus was punished by the other gods for teaching humans how to make fire. According to the myth, these jealous gods knew that people would no longer be dependent upon them for their survival. They could now keep themselves warm, cook their own food, and use the extended light to create and share more knowledge as they huddled around their campfires. Eventually they would use this power to build their own civilizations and chart their own destinies. His fellow gods had every reason to be concerned. Prometheus had just delivered the first significant informative speech.

This tale reminds us of the extent to which human civilization and progress depends on the sharing of knowledge and information. Breakthroughs in medical research, communication technologies, and early detection systems that alert us to natural disasters help us to better cope with challenges to our existence and contribute to the quality of our lives. The free and open exchange of information is especially crucial to democratic societies in which our collective fate depends on the will of knowledgeable citizens and rational decision making.

"The improvement of understanding is for two ends: first our own increase of knowledge; secondly, to enable us to deliver that knowledge to others."

—JOHN LOCKE

Learning to make effective and ethical informative presentations will contribute substantially to finding your voice as a public speaker. Presenting quality information in a balanced and responsible fashion will benefit you regardless of whether your general purpose is to inform, persuade, or celebrate. Responsible informative speaking reinforces respect for the integrity of ideas and information, which is an important standard of ethical speaking as discussed in Chapter 1. It also reinforces respect for the importance of understanding the listeners' perspectives, which is essential for the audience-centered approach to public speaking that we have stressed throughout this text.

Developing your informative speaking skills can also help you to find your voice in the classroom and in the professional workplace. As a student, most of the presentations you will make in your courses will be primarily informative. Should you become a journalist, you will need to convey information and explain its significance in an accurate and succinct fashion. If you become a teacher, presenting information in a manner that motivates your students may be vital to their success. Working as a manager, you will likely present oral reports or briefings as well as train new employees. Government agencies, from the Department of Agriculture to the National Park Service, send representatives to speak to and inform various constituencies.

In this chapter, we examine the importance of informative speaking, address types of informative speeches, offer advice for motivating your listeners to listen to and remember your messages, and cover the major design formats used to structure informative presentations. We close by addressing the *briefing*, a prominent form of informative speaking you may be asked to present in business or professional settings.

Biz Stone, Twitter co-founder and a great storyteller, speaks to corporate groups to provide new information and ideas to employees.

Informative Speaking: An Overview

13.1 Realize the importance of informative speaking.

informative speaking

Functions to enlighten listeners by sharing ideas and information.

Informative speaking enlightens listeners by sharing ideas and information so that they can make better decisions. As an informative speaker, you want listeners to pay attention to your message and understand it. Your purpose is not to convince them to change their minds or behavior but to offer a balanced presentation of relevant information so that they can more responsibly reach their own conclusions. For instance, Jessica Floyd presented an informative speech on the dangers of the Zika virus. The dangers she described were vivid, and Jessica provided quality information to explain the nature and origins of the virus, measures being taken to treat and contain it, and specific advice to avoid contracting it. But she wasn't looking to convert her listeners or advance a disputed proposition or course of action. What they did in response to this new knowledge was up to them. If you find yourself arguing with other perspectives, your topic may be more appropriate for a persuasive speech.

informative value

A measure of how much new and important information or understanding a speech conveys to an audience.

By sharing knowledge, an informative speech reduces ignorance. It does not simply repeat something the audience already knows. Rather, the **informative value** of a speech is measured by *how much new and important information or understanding it provides the audience*. As you prepare your informative speech, ask yourself the following questions:

- Is my topic *significant enough* to merit an informative speech?
- What do my listeners *already know* about my topic?
- What more do they *need to know* to accomplish my purpose?
- Do I *understand my topic* well enough to help my audience understand it?

It is clear that informative speakers carry a large ethical burden to develop and share responsible knowledge of their topics. In Chapters 7 and 8, we discuss the acquisition and use of responsible knowledge as conveying an understanding of the major issues and features associated with your topic, what the most respected authorities have to say about it, latest and local developments, and the potential effect on the lives of your listeners. A responsible informative speech should cover all major positions on a topic and be supported by strong information that satisfies the four Rs of relevance, representativeness, recency, and reliability.

Although informative speakers may have strong feelings on a subject, it is unethical to deliberately omit or distort important information. Speakers who are unaware of information because they have not done sufficient research act irresponsibly. As you prepare your speech, you should read for balance and seek out materials from sources that offer different perspectives on your subject.

YOUR ETHICAL VOICE

The Ethics of Informative Speaking

As you prepare your informative speech, keep these ethical considerations in mind.

1. Be sure you can defend the morality of your choice of topic.
2. Do sufficient research to speak responsibly.
3. Present all information that is important for the audience's understanding.
4. Mention all major positions on a topic when there are different perspectives.
5. Do not omit relevant information because it is inconsistent with your perspective.
6. Do not distort information.

Finally, informative speaking can pose a special challenge for speakers. Self-introductory speeches often reveal fascinating insights into the personalities of speakers. Persuasive speeches offer the drama of controversy surrounding issues. Ceremonial speeches can entertain and inspire. In contrast, informative speeches can sometimes seem rather dull. On the other hand, many of the informative speeches we have heard in class, including those cited in this chapter, captivated us. What can we learn from these successful speakers so that you can prepare informative presentations that are both engaging and beneficial for listeners?

First, these speakers selected good topics. They chose topics they were genuinely interested in that yielded quality information, and they emphasized their importance and interest for listeners.

Second, these speakers used their time well. They selected topics early enough to leave adequate time to conduct responsible research, to reflect on what they had learned, and to adapt their materials to their particular audience. They used their time to contemplate how to pique their listeners' interests, to introduce them to new ideas, and to enlarge their perspectives.

Third, these speakers organized their speeches well. They introduced their topics in a manner that engaged the audience's attention and established a clear specific purpose for speaking. They developed their main ideas using a coherent and sensible design, and they prepared a memorable conclusion that emphasized their most important ideas and information.

Fourth, these speakers provided colorful, striking content. They provided memorable facts, figures, and testimony to challenge their listeners with unexpected information. They used vivid examples, narratives, and language to awaken feelings and bring their ideas to life. They emphasized the relevance and importance of the materials to the lives of their listeners.

Fifth, they put a lot of energy into their presentations. They set a varied and lively pace using vocal inflection, pauses, and nonverbal gestures and movement for emphasis. Their voices came alive to reflect the importance of their messages.

Approaching Your Informative Speech

Identify a time when you learned information from a speaker. Why do you recall this instance? What did the speaker do to help you acquire that information? How can you use the insight about this speaker's approach in your informative speech?

Types of Informative Speaking

13.2 Prepare speeches that create a vivid description, demonstrate a process, or explain how something works.

It is often said that we live in the Age of Information. Yet, as Caleb Carr observes, mere information "is not knowledge."[1] We turn information into knowledge when we share it and explain its meaning and significance for others. That is the essence of informative speaking, which fulfills three basic human needs:

1. *We want to expand our knowledge and awareness of the world.*
2. *We want to learn skills that are beneficial or enjoyable.*
3. *We want to understand the nature, workings, and implications of important aspects of phenomena.*

These three needs relate directly to the three major types of informative speaking: speeches of *description*, speeches of *demonstration*, and speeches of *explanation*.

Speeches of Description

Many informative speakers seek to create a vivid portrait of an activity, event, object, person, or place. A **speech of description** should give the audience a clear image of your subject. Depict the beauty of your favorite travel destination; the reverberating sound in Renaissance cathedrals; or the sights, sounds, and tastes of New Orleans during Jazz Fest. Take your listeners through an oral observance of Ramadan, Yom

speech of description
An informative speech that uses vivid language to illustrate an activity, object, person, or place.

Kippur, or Christmas as celebrated in Scandinavia. Describe the horrid conditions of the Robben Island prison where Nelson Mandela spent 18 years of his life; the devastation and suffering wrought by Hurricane Katrina; or the process by which tartar turns to plaque on your teeth, similar to barnacles on a ship's hull.

Speeches of description are most effective when they provide concrete and colorful words to create an image of your subject that complements the tone of your message. Consider this depiction of Capitol Reefs National Park in central Utah:

> Tucked beside a sparkling stream on a sheer rock surface you find ancient etchings and paintings. These vivid, angular petroglyphs record the experiences and beliefs of the Fremont culture that lived here more than three thousand years ago. One human-like figure sports large shoulders, tapered hips, and stick arms, fingers, and legs. Adorned with an elaborate curved horn headdress and a sunburst shield, the figure's posture suggests one ready for either a hunt or a dance. Nearby, figures of frolicking deer, hefty bighorn sheep, and scurrying lizards cavort across the rock. A sprinkling of circles, spirals, and stars dance amid hand- and footprints.

Can you see the ancient artwork? If so, the speaker's pictorial language has done its descriptive work. We provide a further discussion of descriptive language use in Chapter 11.

The effective use of such presentation aids as images, objects, and audio recordings can also help your listeners see and hear what you want to convey. Your topic and purpose can also suggest the appropriate choice of design. The speaker above used a spatial design to take her listeners on a visual tour of the Capitol Reefs National Park, whereas a speech describing Christmas in Scandinavia as distinct from the United States might use a comparative design.

speech of demonstration
An informative speech that shows the audience how to do something.

speech of explanation
An informative speech that offers information about the nature, workings, and implications of abstract and complex subjects.

Speeches of Demonstration

The **speech of demonstration** shows an audience how to do something. Dance instructors teach us the Texas two-step. CPR instructors teach us procedures that save lives. Cooking shows offer demonstrations. In our classes, we've had students present demonstrative speeches on topics ranging from how to start your own investment portfolio to how to restore antique furniture. The tip-off to the speech of demonstration is the phrase *"how to."* What these examples have in common is that they demonstrate a process and empower listeners by showing them how to perform it—or at least how to understand what is involved in the process.

Speeches of demonstration show the audience how to do something.

A speech of demonstration is most effective when it provides listeners with clearly demarcated steps for completing a process. This is often aided by the effective use of presentation aids as discussed in Chapter 10. For instance, if you presented a speech on how to play the dulcimer, bringing the actual instrument to class would help both to demonstrate the process and to create interest by allowing your listeners to hear its sweet sounds. PowerPoint and other multimedia packages can also help to clarify the steps in a process. When you are making a speech of demonstration, "show and tell" is usually much more effective than just "tell."

Speeches of Explanation

A **speech of explanation** offers information about the nature, workings, and implications of subjects that are abstract or complicated. You might explain the physics of sneezing, the way a government agency functions (or is supposed to function), or the documented benefits of art therapy. You could trace how the concept of "equality" has evolved over the years, explore some of the special effects of the Harry Potter movies, or highlight the role of influential Latinas in American society. You might help your audience to better understand autism, and introduce them to a program that marshals the talents of autistic people in computers, technology, and math to give them marketable skills.[2]

Because the topics for speeches of explanation are typically complicated, determining a clear focus is crucial to providing your audience with new information. If you try to cover a topic as broad as AIDS research in ten minutes or less, then your discussion will be inevitably superficial and less than compelling. However, if you focused on a promising new approach to treatment or a novel line of research, then you might truly provide your listeners with quality information and understanding that they will appreciate hearing. Focus on the most significant aspects of your subject: its nature, origins, presumed causes, how it works or functions, and its current state. Provide your listeners with clear definitions of important or unfamiliar terms, and representative examples to illustrate important points.[3]

Speeches of explanation sometimes incorporate characteristics of speeches of description and demonstration. In "Descent into Darkness," the powerful speech explaining Alzheimer's disease that concludes this chapter, Olivia Jackson organized her subject in the following way:

1. She opened her speech with the story of her grandfather who had contracted Alzheimer's disease.
2. She defined the disease.
3. She explained the significance of the disease both for those afflicted with it and for their families.
4. She described how the disease develops.
5. She explained how to reduce susceptibility to it.

Speeches of explanation face an additional challenge when their information runs counter to common misconceptions. Professor Katherine Rowan provides an example of how this can work in public service campaigns:

> A particularly resilient obstacle to [seat] belt use is the erroneous but prevalent belief that hitting one's head on a windshield while traveling at 30 miles per hour is an experience much like doing so when a car is stationary. . . . If people understood that the experience would be much more similar to falling from a three-story building and hitting the pavement face first, one obstacle to the wearing of seat belts would be easier to overcome.[4]

As her example indicates, analogies—such as comparing an auto accident at thirty miles per hour to falling from a building—can help break through our resistance to new ideas and behaviors. The use of such strategic comparisons and contrasts can help listeners accept new information and use it in their lives, perhaps even to *save* their lives.

Identifying Uses of Description, Demonstration, and Explanation

Identify times in your classes when professors have used description, demonstration, and explanation. What purpose did each one serve? Were they effective in conveying the information intended? How could they have been improved?

SPEAKER'S NOTES

Guidelines for Effective Informative Speaking

Keep these tips in mind as you develop your informative speech.

1. Speeches of description vividly recreate the topic for the audience.
2. Speeches of description employ colorful language.
3. Speeches of demonstration show an orderly sequence of steps.
4. Speeches of demonstration benefit from presentation aids.
5. Speeches of explanation call for clear definitions of important terms.
6. Speeches of explanation benefit from good examples.
7. Speeches of explanation can make effective use of analogies.

Helping Listeners Learn

13.3 Use different techniques to help listeners learn and remember.

Having been a student for many years, chances are you've suffered the misfortune of taking classes from boring teachers or professors. They were obviously well qualified and well prepared, but every time they started to lecture, you found yourself drifting away.

Moreover, we *hear* a lot every day, but we can only *listen* to so much. We selectively attend to messages that interest us, concern us, engage us, or even alarm us. Much of the rest of what we *hear* doesn't penetrate our listening barrier and filters.

So how can you help audience members listen to and remember your informative messages? You can start by considering some basic audience characteristics, as discussed in Chapter 5. How much, or little, do your listeners already know about your topic? Is that understanding accurate? How interested, or disinterested, are they in your topic? What preconceptions could they already have about your topic that might help or hinder your ability to reach them? How do they regard you as a speaker on this topic? Figure 13.1 charts these audience considerations and suggests possible strategies you can use.

Motivating Audiences to Listen

As discussed in Chapter 5, it is important to understand motives or deep-seated psychological impulses when adapting your message to a particular audience. To motivate members of the audience to listen, especially those who are not initially

Figure 13.1
Considering the Audience for Informative Speeches

Audience Type	Strategies
Interested but uninformed	• Provide basic information in clear, simple language. • Avoid jargon; define technical terms. • Use examples and narratives for amplification. • When communicating complicated information, use analogies, metaphors, and/or presentation aids. • Use voice, gestures, and eye contact to reinforce meaning.
Interested and knowledgeable	• Establish your credibility early in the speech. • Acknowledge diverse perspectives on topic. • Go into depth with information and expert testimony. • Offer an engaging presentation that focuses on content.
Uninterested	• Show listeners what's in it for them. • Keep your presentation short and to the point. • Use sufficient examples and narratives to arouse and sustain interest. • Use eye-catching presentation aids and colorful language. • Make a dynamic presentation.
Unsympathetic toward topic	• Show respect for listeners and their point of view. • Cite sources the audience will respect. • Present information to enlarge listeners' understanding. • Develop stories and examples to arouse favorable feelings. • Make a warm, engaging presentation.
Distrustful of speaker	• Establish your credibility early in the speech. • Rely heavily on factual examples and expert testimony. • Cite sources of information in your presentation. • Be straightforward, businesslike, and personable. • Keep good eye contact with listeners.

interested in your subject, you should tell them why your message is important to them. As you consider your audience in relation to your topic and message, ask yourself why they would want to know what you have to tell them:

- Will it improve their *health, safety, or general well-being*?
- Will it help them *understand and control* the world around them?
- Will it help them *get along better* with family and friends?
- Will it give them a feeling of *accomplishment and achievement*?
- Will it give them a sense of *personal growth and satisfaction*?
- Will it provide them with *enjoyment*?
- Will it contribute to their *financial or material well-being*?
- Will it give them a sense of *contributing to society or caring for others*?
- Will it deepen their *understanding and appreciation of tradition*?
- Will it contribute to their sense of *moral balance and fairness*?

For example, a speech offering advice for having a good job interview would appeal to your listeners' need for achievement and material well-being, whereas a speech documenting the suffering of Syrian refuges might address the need for moral balance and caring for others. Such appeals are often woven into the introductions and conclusions of presentations. For instance, Hannah Johnston opened her speech on the fast-food industry by appealing to health and safety motivations: "If you had a choice, I'm sure you wouldn't choose to eat some of the stuff that can end up in processed meat." Hannah ruined lunch for some of her classmates, but they could not help but listen closely.

Maintaining Audience Attention

Once you have motivated your audience to listen, you want to hold their attention throughout your presentation. In Chapter 9, we discussed how to attract audience attention in the introduction of your speech. Here, we focus on how to sustain that interest. You can do so by making good use of one or more of the five factors that affect attention: *relevance, intensity, contrast, repetition*, and *novelty*.

relevance
How a speech relates to an audience's specific needs, interests, or concerns.

intensity
Making aspects of a speech striking or stand out.

Relevance. A speech that relates to an audience's needs, interests, or concerns will hold its attention. You should point out the **relevance** of topics that might seem distant or obscure to your listeners. You could describe the Theremin as a musical instrument played by moving your hands between two antennas. What will make it come alive for your audience, however, is to make a connection to its use in the *Star Trek* theme song, *The Big Bang Theory*, and *Monster House*.

Nick Orobello had to work to make his speech on electronic health records relevant to his young and healthy audience at Davidson College. He grabbed their attention in his introduction by relating a common experience: having to answer the same questions over and over in the same visit to medical personnel. Then he sustained interest by showing listeners how electronic medical records would increase the efficiency and effectiveness of their own health care throughout their lives. He used vivid narratives and examples to help keep their attention.

Speakers should stress the relevance of topics that might seem distant to their listeners.

Intensity. **Intensity** in a speech can refer to its boldness, colorful language, or passionate presentation. Striking pieces of information, riveting examples, and the effective use of presentation aids can also add intensity. A presentation on bed bugs gains intensity when you call them "mattress-dwelling bloodsuckers," compare each of the hundreds of eggs laid by a female to a speck of dust, and shudder as you say it.

When one worker described the results he achieved combatting the symptoms of metabolic syndrome through his company's wellness program, he got his listeners attention by describing himself as a "tickin' time bomb." This colorful expression, which seems so simple and straightforward, actually illustrates how a number of the language techniques discussed in Chapter 11 can come together to create intensity. First, it illustrates *metaphor*. Our bodies are not literally bombs, but to think of them that way stresses the dangers of obesity and an unhealthy lifestyle. The metaphor makes us think of heart attacks and strokes as explosions that can quite literally destroy us from within. Second, the example illustrates *alliteration,* the repetition of initial sounds in adjoining words to create a striking effect. The repetition of the *t* sound drives the point home. Third, the example represents *onomatopoeia,* the use of words that sound like what they signify. "Tickin'" sounds like an ominous clock. Time was running out for this worker if he did not act.

contrast
Attracts attention and sharpens perspective by highlighting the differences between opposites.

Contrast. **Contrast** attracts and sustains attention by highlighting differences and similarities. In this text, we print important terms in bold so that they will stand out in contrast to other fonts and white paper. During your presentation, you can show contrast through abrupt changes in your voice or delivery style, or by simply speaking in terms of oppositions such as night and day or the pros and cons of a situation. Contrasting views can help dramatize ideas and abstract concepts in a way that listeners may find engaging, as when a speaker declares, "We Americans are definitely *not* communists!" Finally, again as discussed in Chapter 11, the use of antithesis to contrast opposing views in the same or adjoining sentences can be very effective for articulating positions on disputed issues. To defend their opposition to tax increases, conservative politicians often echo the words of former Speaker of the House John Boehner: "Washington does not have a revenue problem. Washington has a spending problem."[5]

repetition
Repeating sounds, words, or phrases to attract and hold attention.

novelty
The quality of being new or unusual.

Repetition. The **repetition** of sounds, words, and phrases during a speech can attract and hold attention. Skillful speakers use repetition to emphasize key words and points, to help listeners follow the flow of ideas, and to embed messages in the audience's memory. As we saw in Chapter 11, repetition is the basis of alliteration and parallel construction. Alliteration lends vividness to main ideas: "Today, I will discuss how the *M*ississippi River *m*eanders from *M*innesota to the sea." The repetition of the *m* sound catches attention and emphasizes the statement. Similarly, parallel construction, which uses the same or similar wording to open successive sentences or main points, can be very effective. Winston Churchill used parallel construction in his call to the English people to defend their country in the face of an imminent Nazi invasion: "*we shall fight* on the beaches, *we shall fight* on the landing grounds, *we shall fight* in the fields and in the streets, *we shall fight* in the hills; *we shall* never surrender."[6]

Neil deGrasse Tyson used novelty by casting Lincoln as a scientist in a speech echoing the Gettysburg Address.

Novelty. **Novelty** refers to the quality of being new or unusual. If you have a fresh way of seeing and saying something, uninterested or distrustful listeners may increase both their respect for you and their interest in your subject. Piquing their curiosity creates a gap between what they know and that they want to know, "like an itch we need to scratch."[7] Neil deGrasse Tyson, director of New York City's Hayden Planetarium, employed novelty when he characterized Abraham Lincoln as a scientist for founding the National Academy of the Sciences—in a speech precisely 272 words long, the length of the Gettysburg Address.[8] In addition, a novel twist on phrases and words can fascinate listeners and hold their attention. In a speech informing his listeners on the extent of marine pollution, Jim Cordoza noted that 19 million tons of garbage wash up on US beaches every year, concluding: "And that's just the tip of the wasteberg." His novel term *wasteberg*—clearly a twist on the term *iceberg*—helped to engaged his listeners while emphasizing the enormity of the problem.

SPEAKER'S NOTES

Techniques to Attract and Sustain Attention

Use the following strategies to attract and sustain the attention of your listeners.

1. *Motivate* listeners by showing them how they can benefit from your message.
2. *Highlight relevance* to connect your subject directly to the experience of listeners.
3. *Speak with intensity*. Develop verbal pictures that vividly depict your topic.
4. *Present contrasts* to show what your topic is not.
5. *Use strategic repetition* to amplify your message.
6. *Rely on novelty* by using fresh wording and new examples.

Helping Listeners Remember

Information is more useful when your listeners remember it. Many of the same strategies discussed above for motivating audiences to listen and attend to your messages can also be effective for promoting memory. Obviously, listeners are more likely to remember presentations when they think they might benefit from them in some fundamental way. A startling statistic or a moving real-life example will tend to linger in their minds. As illustrated by Winston Churchill's speech cited above, the repetition of key terms and phrases is perhaps the most time-tested and effective strategy for helping listeners remember the most important points and tone of a message.

Relevance is also important to memory. Our minds filter incoming information, associate it with things we already know, and evaluate it for its potential usefulness. Make the connection to what members of your audience know and care about, and they will carry your message with them. Simply put, *if you want listeners to remember your message, tell them why and how it relates to their lives.*

Finally, as we discussed in Chapter 9, a well-organized speech not only helps members of the audience follow a presentation but also helps them remember. Clear previews, summaries, and transitions are vitally important, as is the coherent organization of your main ideas and information. Suppose you were given the following list of words to memorize:

> north, man, hat, daffodil, green, tulip, coat, boy, south, red, east, shoes, gardenia, woman, purple, marigold, gloves, girl, yellow, west

Memorizing this list might be quite a challenge, but what if the words were rearranged like this?

> north, south, east, west
> man, boy, woman, girl
> daffodil, tulip, gardenia, marigold
> green, red, purple, yellow
> hat, coat, gloves, shoes

In the first example, you have what looks like a random list of words. In the second, the words have been organized by categories. Now you have five groups of four related words to remember. Material that is presented in a consistent and orderly pattern is much easier for your audience to retain—not to mention for you to present. For example, the cluster of "hat, coat, gloves, shoes" moves from the head to the feet. As you select a design for your informative speech, consider what arrangement will help your audience grasp and remember your points.

Developing a Stronger Informative Speech

Think of a time when your ears perked up at a presentation of information. What piqued your interest—the topic? The implications for you as a listener? The supporting materials? The way the presentation was structured? How can those insights help you to develop a stronger informative speech?

Finding Your Voice

Your Favorite Teacher

You can probably recall one if not several outstanding teachers (other than the instructor for this class) who have helped inspire you to learn. How did that teacher do this? What techniques did he or she use to motivate you to listen, maintain attention, and retain key ideas? How can you use these techniques to ensure that listeners hear you as well, that you have found your voice?

Designs for Informative Speeches

13.4 Understand the options for designing informative speeches.

Once you have selected your topic and conducted research, you can start to think about a potential design for your speech. In Chapter 9, we offered an overview of some of the major speech designs. Here, we offer a detailed discussion of six major speech designs that are well suited for informative speeches: *categorical, comparative, spatial, sequential, chronological*, and *causation*.

Categorical Design

categorical design
Arranges the main ideas and materials of a speech by divisions or topics.

The **categorical design**—sometimes referred to as the topical design—arranges the main ideas and materials of a speech by divisions. Sometimes divisions exist in the way the subject itself is approached by experts, such as the three most important early warning symptoms of breast cancer. Other divisions represent conventional ways of thinking about a subject, such as the four essential food groups of a given diet plan, or five strategies for maintaining the audience's attention during a speech. In some cases you may develop your own categories for discussing a subject, based on the recurring themes of emphasis you discover while conducting your research. In any case, all of us make sense of the world by arranging our knowledge and observations into patterns or groups. Categories help us classify large amounts of information so that we can better understand and communicate it to others.

When using a categorical design, each division in the presentation becomes a main point for development. You should usually limit the number of your categories to no more than five for longer presentations, and no more than three for shorter presentations. Remember, you have to develop each point with supporting material. That takes time! You don't want to overtax your listeners' willingness to give you their attention and their ability to remember. Nor do you want to go beyond the time limits set by your instructor. In her informative speech, Nicolette Fisk described architectural answers to a dilemma posed by terrorist attacks: how to keep our greatest monuments and buildings safe but still beautiful. Here is an abbreviated outline of the categorical design of her speech:

Preview. Architects have developed three innovative answers to the question of how to both guard and beautify our greatest buildings and shrines.

I. Retaining walls provide one such answer.
   A. Overlapping stone walls can provide a picturesque barrier to explosive-laden vehicles.
   B. Retaining walls have been erected to protect the Washington Monument.
   C. Architect Laurie Olin said, "The point is to turn this security thing into a beautiful walk."

II. Collapsible concrete is a second answer to the challenge.
   A. It is strong enough to support pedestrians, but collapses under the weight of heavier vehicles.
   B. It both preserves open public space and creates an urban booby trap for terrorists.
   C. It is widely used in New York City.

III. Adding street furniture offers a third answer to protect pedestrians along sidewalks.
   A. Bollards are designed to absorb huge vehicular impacts.
      1. They were first designed for military security measures.
      2. Now they function as fashionable, decorative features around buildings.
   B. Heavy benches and boulders along the street provide seating as well as protection for strollers.

Nicolette's organization thus developed three categories of defensive yet beautiful protective features, making it easy for her audience to follow her points.

Comparative Design

A **comparative design** develops the main points of a speech by exploring the similarities or differences among things, events, or ideas. Comparing the unknown to the known can be especially useful when your topic is unfamiliar, abstract, or difficult to understand. The comparative design can also be useful for describing dramatic "then and now" changes in a subject, or for comparing and contrasting the differences between subjects or ideas. Two basic variations of the comparative design develop *literal* and *figurative analogies*.

comparative design
Arranges a speech by exploring the similarities or differences among subjects.

In a **literal analogy**, the subjects compared are drawn from the same field of experience. For instance, you might track the voting records of two different politicians on an important issue such as campaign finance reform, or you might contrast the differing images of women in advertising during the 1960s with those of today. Oh-Jin Kwan offered comparisons between the American educational system and that of her native South Korea. "The French Paradox," printed in Appendix B, develops a literal analogy by comparing French and American styles of eating.

literal analogy
A comparison of subjects drawn from the same field of experience.

In a **figurative analogy**, the subjects are drawn from different fields of experience. For example, you might describe the complexities of the human circulatory system by comparing it to a city traffic system. Paul Ashdown, a professor of journalism at the University of Tennessee, used an extended figurative analogy comparing the World Wide Web to America's "Wild West."[9] In her speech on healthy eating, Thressia Taylor used a figurative analogy comparing caring for a classic car to healthy eating:

figurative analogy
A comparison of subjects drawn from essentially different fields of experience.

Preview. Providing your body with the healthy food is as important as providing a classic car with the right fuels and lubricants.

I. Getting the right proteins is like having the right octane in your gasoline.
   A. Protein builds, maintains, and repairs the tissues that keep your engine from sputtering.
   B. Three or more servings a day will act as an octane booster to keep your engine running smoothly.

II. You need carbohydrates for energy and quick acceleration.
   A. Your carbohydrates should come from whole grains, fruits, and vegetables.
   B. Eat four servings daily to keep your engine humming.

III. Finally, you need fat to keep your body well lubricated.
   A. Bad fats can gum up our systems and land us in the junkyard before our time.
   B. Good fats are necessary for the long haul.

Both literal and figurative analogy designs can be insightful and imaginative, helping listeners see subjects in surprising, revealing ways. Such designs often work by contrasting differences rather than similarities—in which case each point of difference becomes a main point. In the name of simplicity and easy comprehension, we suggest you limit yourself to just a few points of similarity or difference. You should also give careful consideration to whether your listeners will readily accept the essential similarity of your comparison. If it comes across as strained or concocted, your entire speech may collapse and your ethos may suffer.

Spatial Design

spatial design
Arranges the main points of a speech as they occur in actual space.

A **spatial design** is appropriate for speeches that develop their topics within a physical setting. The main points are arranged as they occur in physical space. Most people are familiar with maps and can visualize directions. A speech using a spatial design provides listeners with a descriptive oral map. Spatial designs can be especially useful for introducing people to new or unfamiliar locations, such as introducing incoming students to the most important locations to know on campus, or new employees to a large workplace.

To develop a spatial design that is easy to follow, select a starting point and then take your audience on an orderly journey to a destination. Once you begin a pattern of movement, stay with it to the end of the speech. If you change direction in the middle, the audience may get lost. Speakers using a spatial pattern often use such presentation aids as photographs or maps to reinforce the sense of space and direction in their speeches.

Belinda Phillip's informative speech on "Downtown Memphis Music" followed a spatial design:

Preview. When you visit Downtown Memphis, begin at the Peabody; then stroll down Beale Street to the FedEx Forum.

I. Your first stop should be at the Peabody Hotel.
   A. Take in the beautiful Renaissance Revival architecture.
   B. Watch the ducks parade through the lobby to a rousing Sousa March.
   C. Visit the Sky Room on the roof, home of big band dances.

Landmarks, such as these statues of W. C. Handy and Elvis Presley in downtown Memphis, help listeners identify the places in a spatial design.

II. Stroll over to Beale Street, "The Home of the Blues."
  A. See the classic hip-swiveling statue of Elvis Presley at the west end of Beale.
  B. Wander east to Lansky's, where Elvis shopped for his snazzy clothes.
  C. Drop in to B.B. King's and take in some quality music.
  D. Amble over to A. Schwab's on Beale for music souvenirs and a drink at the old-fashioned soda fountain.
  E. At the east end of Beale, see the statue of W. C. Handy, famed blues composer and musician.

III. Cross the street to the FedEx Forum.
  A. The Forum hosts both the Memphis Grizzlies and the University of Memphis men's basketball teams.
  B. Visit the "Rock and Soul" Smithsonian Museum to tour the history of Music City.
  C. Tour the Gibson Guitar factory, birthplace of instruments used by musicians from Chet Atkins to Frank Zappa.

Belinda's spatial design followed a linear pattern that was orderly and provided listeners with a good sense of the location of important places. Each of her main points received about the same amount of attention so that her speech seemed well balanced.

Sequential Design

A **sequential design** explains the steps of a process in the order in which they should be taken. This design is especially useful for "how to" speeches of demonstration. You begin by identifying the necessary steps in the process and the order in which they should take place; these steps then become the main points of your speech. In a short presentation, you should have no more than five steps as main points. Assigning numbers to these steps as you make your presentation will help your listeners follow the process more clearly.

sequential design Explains the steps of a process in the order in which they should be taken.

The following brief outline illustrates a sequential design for how to create a beautiful floral arrangement:

Preview. The three steps of creating an arrangement of flowers include choosing materials, arranging the stems, and finishing the display.

I. First, select your materials.
  A. Choose your flowers and foliage, either in a range of colors or in complementary hues.
  B. Get a sharp pair of clippers or scissors and an aspirin tablet.
  C. Decide on a vase or other container such as an old jar.

II. Second, cut and arrange the stems.
  A. Cut about one-half inch from the bottom of each stem to help it draw water.
  B. Place three or four stems of foliage at various angles in the container, forming a framework.
  C. Add flowers of various colors and textures to fill out the arrangement.

III. Third, complete the arrangement.
  A. Add shorter flower stems to fill in the gaps around the top of the container.
  B. Add an aspirin to the water to help the blooms stay fresh.
  C. Enjoy!

Presenting the steps in this orderly, sequential way walks your audience through the process clearly.

A chronological design is well-suited to discussing the evolution of cell phones.

Chronological Design

A **chronological design** explains events or historical developments in the order in which they occurred. Using the chronological design, you may start with the beginnings of the subject and trace it up to the present through its defining moments. Or you may start with the present and trace the subject back to its origins. In either case, chronological presentations are generally more effective when speakers keep their presentation of events simple, in the order in which they occurred, and related to the specific purpose of the speech.

Be careful not to discuss history for its own sake. Use the past to illuminate your purpose for speaking in the present. To keep your listeners' attention and meet time requirements, you must be selective. Choose landmark events for your main points, and then arrange them in the order they actually occurred.

Robert Rozinski presented a speech on the evolution of cell phones using a chronological design focusing on three major phases of development:

chronological design
Explains events or historical developments in the order in which they occurred.

Preview. The original field radios and walkie-talkies developed into more portable models, which became the smart phones we have today.

I. The predecessors of modern cell phones were field radios and walkie-talkies.
   A. These "phones" were heavy and bulky.
   B. They had a limited range of effectiveness.
   C. Messages could be easily obstructed and monitored by unknown parties.

II. In 1973 the first handheld phone was produced by Motorola.
   A. It was 9″ long, 5″ deep, 2″ wide, and weighed 2.5 lbs.
   B. It had a talk time of 30 minutes and took 10 hours to recharge.
   C. It cost up to $8,700 in today's money.

III. The prototypes of modern cell phones have evolved over the past three decades.
   A. The 1980s saw the introduction of the flip-top model.
   B. By the early 2000s cell phones could access the Internet.
   C. Apple introduced the first iPhone in 2007.

Causation Design

causation design
Addresses the origins or consequences of a situation or event, proceeding from cause to effect or from effect to cause.

Often used in speeches of explanation, a **causation design** addresses the roots and results of a situation or subject, proceeding from cause to effect or from effect to cause. The most important points of focus are the subject and either how it came about or what its results might be. The major causes and consequences become main points in the body of the speech.

Patty Lenzini used a causation design to demonstrate the positive effects of aspirin therapy. In this case, her speech proceeded from cause to effect as she touted the important health benefits of a small daily dose:

Preview. A small daily dose of aspirin can benefit your heart, prevent cancer, and protect you from strokes and brain disorders.

I. Small daily doses have been proven to benefit your heart.
   A. They reduce your risk of a heart attack by 44 percent.
   B. They lower your chance of a second heart attack by 30 percent.
   C. They decrease your risk of death during heart attack by 23 percent.

II. Small daily doses can also prevent certain cancers.
   A. They lower your risk of colon cancer by 40 percent to 50 percent.
   B. They reduce your risk of esophageal cancer by 80 percent to 90 percent.
   C. They decrease your risk of ovarian cancer by 25 percent.

III. Small daily doses can lower your risks of strokes and other brain disorders.
   A. They reduce your risk of strokes by 25 percent.
   B. They prevent dementia and Alzheimer's by increasing blood flow in the brain.

Speeches using a causation design are subject to one major drawback: the tendency to oversimplify. Any complex situation will generally have many underlying causes, and any given set of conditions may lead to many different future effects. For some people, a daily dose of aspirin may have negative health drawbacks, such as gastrointestinal bleeding or difficulty clotting. Be wary of overly simple explanations and overly confident predictions, which constitute a prominent form of rational fallacy discussed in Chapter 15.

As noted in Chapter 9, the design for your speech should fit the material you have found and your specific purpose. If you have trouble organizing your information according to a particular design, try using another one. You may find a design that better fits your topic, or you may figure out where you need more material.

The designs discussed in this chapter are often combined within a single speech. For instance, Maria Tomasso's speech on sabermetrics—the mathematical assessment of the worth of ballplayers—began by defining the subject, then traced its development chronologically, and finally explained how it is often applied in college and major league baseball. Landon West's speech on "The Battle of the Bulge" first described the extent of obesity in America and then discussed ways to combat it. If you combine designs, be sure that your transitions clearly signal the shift in focus. See Figure 13.2 for an overview of what designs to use and when to use them.

Selecting a Design for Your Informative Speech

Select two designs that you might use for your informative speech, and sketch out some ideas for each one. Then compare: What aspects of your topic does each one highlight? What aspects of your topic are less emphasized in each? Which would you choose for your informative speech—or would a third design work better? Could you combine designs?

Figure 13.2
Which Speech Design to Use When

Design	Use When
Categorical	Your topic has natural or customary divisions. Each category becomes a main point for development. It is useful when you need to organize large amounts of material.
Comparative	Your topic is new to your audience, abstract, technical, or difficult to comprehend. It helps make material more meaningful by comparing or contrasting it with something the audience already knows and understands.
Spatial	Your topic can be discussed by how it is positioned in a physical setting or natural environment. It allows you to take your audience on an orderly "oral tour" of your topic.
Sequential	Your topic can be arranged by time. It is useful for describing a process as a series of steps or explaining a subject as a series of developments.
Chronological	Your topic can be discussed as a historical development through certain defining moments.
Causation	Your topic is best understood in terms of its underlying causes or consequences. It may be used to account for the present or predict future possibilities.

Finding Your Voice

Making Sure Your Speech is Really Informative

As you complete the preparation of your informative speech, consider the following:

- What have I learned in the preparation of this speech?
- Has this experience changed my perspective on my topic?
- What have I learned about tailoring my speech to fit my audience?
- Has this experience deepened my knowledge of the subject and my sensitivity to others' needs?
- Has this experience helped me find my voice? In what ways?

Briefings: A Special Case of Informative Speaking

13.5 Appreciate briefings as a particular kind of informative speaking.

briefing
A short informative presentation offered in an organizational setting that focuses on plans, policies, or reports.

A **briefing** is a specialized form of informative speaking that is usually presented in organizational settings. It may involve description and demonstration, but the focus usually centers on explanation. Briefings often take place during meetings, as when employees gather once a month to learn about plans or policy changes.[10] At such meetings, you might be asked to give a status report on a project. After a crisis or major event, organizations often provide press briefings to explain what occurred and what steps will follow. Briefings also take place in one-on-one situations, as when you report to your supervisor at work.[11] Regardless of the setting, briefings often conclude with a question-and-answer period.

Being asked to present briefings on campus, at work, or where you volunteer provides you with the opportunity to demonstrate your leadership potential—as long as you conduct it well. Unfortunately, briefings are often *not* done well, and both business executives and experts in organizational communication offer similar lists of why they are poorly done:

- It is badly organized.
- It contains too much jargon.
- It lacks examples or comparisons.
- It is too long.
- It is not presented well.[12]

The following guidelines can help you prepare and present more effective briefings:

1. *A briefing should be what its name suggests: brief.* Cut out any material that is not related directly to your main points. Keep your introduction and conclusion short. Begin with a preview and end with a summary to help your audience follow your presentation.
2. *Organize your ideas before you open your mouth.* How can you possibly be organized when you are called on without warning in a meeting to "tell us about your project"? The answer is simple: Prepare in advance. *Never go into any meeting in which there is even the slightest chance that you might be asked to report without a skeleton outline of a presentation.* Select a simple design, and make a key-word outline of points

you would cover. Put this on a single note card or a smart phone, and take it to the meeting with you. Even if you don't use it for this meeting, the preparation likely will come in handy in other settings. The guidelines for making impromptu speeches in Chapter 12 may be helpful.

3. *Rely heavily on facts and figures, expert testimony, and short examples for supporting materials.* These forms of support relate most directly to the topics covered in briefings. Don't drift off into extended examples and long stories, which are likely to be viewed as tangents. Use comparison and contrast to make your points stand out and come alive.
4. *Adapt your language to your audience.* If you are an engineer reporting on a project to a group of managers, use the language of management, not the language of engineering. Tell them what they need to know in language they can understand. Relate the subject to what they already know.
5. *Present your message with confidence.* Be sure everyone can see and hear you. Stand up, if necessary. Look listeners in the eye, and speak firmly with an air of assurance. After all, the project is yours, and you are the expert on it.
6. *Be prepared to answer tough questions.* Anticipate and be prepared to respond to questions openly and honestly. No one likes bad news, but worse news will come if you don't deliver the bad news to those who need to know it *when* they need to know it. Review our suggestions for handling question-and-answer sessions in Chapter 12.

Using Guidelines for Effective Briefings

Go online to find a briefing by a government, corporate, or nonprofit figure. Using the guidelines for effective briefings provided in this section, assess how well the person conducted the briefing. What suggestions would you make for improvement?

Final Reflections: Bringing Fire to Your Listeners

When the gods punished Prometheus for presenting that first informative speech teaching humans the power of fire, they did so not merely for fear of humans taking command of their own destinies. They knew that knowledge and enlightenment would eventually endow us with god-like powers, and they feared that we would not exercise those powers responsibly. Finding your voice as an informative speaker means considerably more than mastering the skills of descriptive, demonstrative, and explanatory speech-making, more than motivating listeners to attend and retain your messages, and more than simply knowing what you want to say and saying it effectively. It means becoming a conscientious and accountable source of truth in a world too often drowning in partisan discord and disinformation. It means taking seriously your role and obligation as an informed voice and as a source of enlightenment before your peers. Mastering the art of informative speaking is a necessary step in finding your voice. It enables you to bring fire to your listeners.

Study Questions

CONTENT MASTERY

1 Why is informative speaking important?
2 How can you meet the challenge of informative speaking?
3 What should successful speeches of description accomplish? How do they accomplish this?
4 How do speeches that demonstrate a process proceed? What design is appropriate for them?
5 What goals, techniques, and designs are appropriate for speeches of explanation?
6 How can you assist the learning process in your informative speech?
7 What are the major design options for informative speaking?
8 How can you prepare and present effective briefings?

CRITICAL EXPLORATIONS

1. One testimonial to the power of information is how upset individuals, companies, and countries become when secret and private data are stolen or leaked through hacking or unauthorized disclosures, as when the US intelligence community declared that Russia hacked into accounts to influence the 2016 election. How much secrecy of government information can be tolerated in a society that depends on well-informed citizens? At what point does the secret surveillance of citizens violate their constitutional right to privacy? How do we resolve the conflict between individual rights and our government's need for vital information about us?
2. Develop an oral description of your hometown using a spatial design. What specific sites or attractions would you address? How would you arrange them to take your listeners on an orderly journey? What words would best help them "see" the place in their minds?
3. Have you recently used instructions that (supposedly) explained how to construct, program, operate, or repair a device? How clear and helpful were the instructions? Were there places where you got lost? Why? How could the instructions be improved?
4. Download an informative speech found on TED or YouTube. What type of informative speech is it? What design does it employ? Consider how it gains and holds attention and how it motivates learning. How could you improve its informative value? Can you suggest a different design for the speech?
5. Select an informative topic, determine a specific purpose, and develop two different outlines for the speech you might give, each illustrating one of the design options covered in this chapter. For each design, explain the motivational techniques you might use to engage your audience. Which do you prefer, and why?

INFORMATIVE SPEECH

This powerful and moving speech was presented by Olivia Jackson to her class at Phillips Exeter Academy in New Hampshire. It develops in a categorical pattern and illustrates effective use of expert testimony and narrative. Olivia's speech opens with the story of her grandfather, a brilliant man now suffering from the slow ravages of Alzheimer's. The story gives Olivia personal credibility to speak on the subject: She is personally invested in it.

DESCENT INTO DARKNESS

OLIVIA JACKSON

Reprinted with permission from Olivia Jackson, Phillips Exeter Academy in New Hampshire.

My grandfather is the smartest man I know. After skipping two grades in elementary school, my grandfather enrolled at Phillips Exeter. He was the youngest member of the class of 1948, and excelled academically, graduating *cum laude*. He went on to Harvard, and then pursued a career in finance at the Bank of Boston, where he established himself as an expert in the transportation industry. He married my grandmother, Diana Cameron, in 1959.

All his life, grandfather kept his mind active by being treasurer for a number of organizations, running balance sheets and analyzing numbers, doing crossword puzzles and Sudoku, and playing bridge, ultimately becoming a Life Master.

Olivia defines her topic and demonstrates through her grandfather's example how devastating it can be. She uses the enduring metaphor of light and darkness, combined with a metaphor based on spatial orientation (descent), to give memorable expression to the consequences of the disease.

In 1989, just six months after he had accepted an early retirement package from the bank and begun doing consulting work for his former transportation clients, my grandmother was diagnosed with an inoperable brain tumor. From 1994 until 2008, her condition got progressively worse. By 2006 she was bed-ridden, relying solely on my grandfather to care for her until she passed away. He now lives in a small house in New Hampshire, taking long walks with his dog, reading historical books, and slowly forgetting who his family is, where he is from, and who he is.

This past winter my grandfather was diagnosed with Alzheimer's disease. Alzheimer's disease, according to the *Encyclopedia of Alzheimer's Disease*, is "a progressive, degenerative disease characterized by the death of nerve cells in several areas of the brain. It is the most common of the more than 70 forms of dementia, a condition that leads to the loss of mental and physical functions." It has been incredibly hard to watch my grandfather forget how to balance his checkbook, forget information my Mom has told him several times before, and forget key family details. Something is erasing and eating away at his memory, creating a dark abyss of emptiness and forgetfulness; a world that used to be so familiar is now slipping away from him.

Today, I want to discuss four potential preventatives for Alzheimer's disease. According to Dash and Villemarette-Pitman, in their book, *Alzheimer's Disease*, the "lifestyle factors" that may possibly prevent this disease include education, physical fitness, social activity, and continual intellectual challenges. Each one of these factors plays an important role in the attempt to decrease one's chances of developing the disease or delaying the onset of Alzheimer's.

Olivia previews a discussion of preventative measures, indicating that the body of her speech will follow a categorical design. She makes good use of expert testimony, sustaining the credibility of her speech. She also demonstrates the ability to explain complex ideas with clarity and simplicity.

Education and its effect on developing Alzheimer's have been studied closely. According to Dash and Villemarette-Pitman, "people with lower levels of education have higher rates of Alzheimer's," also referred to as "AD." They support this hypothesis with several theories. One is the "synaptic reserve hypothesis," which states that a more highly educated person has more nerve cell connections in the brain because their minds have been more active. When the disease begins to deteriorate and destroy these connections, new ones can form more easily and faster due to the higher activity. It is also believed that educated people are better able to mask the dementia because, over the course of their education, they have developed strategies and skills that will help them "better compensate for any loss of ability." Education is one factor that may help prevent Alzheimer's, although it is not a guarantee, as in my grandfather's case. No matter how many years of education you have, or how little, you are still at risk of getting the disease.

Physical fitness is a second factor that is beneficial for all health concerns, lowering cholesterol, maintaining a healthy heart, and potentially preventing Alzheimer's. Dash and Villemarette-Pitman write, "exercise affects both brain structure and function." Everyone should exercise regularly, because, as the authors say, "a program of regular exercise in midlife is protective against developing AD later in life. Elderly people who exercise regularly are at a lower risk of developing AD." It is still uncertain whether physical fitness directly correlates to preventing Alzheimer's or if the exercise helps decrease the chance of getting another disease, which in turn benefits both the body and the mind. However, there appears to be some connection between the physical activity that one participates in throughout the latter half of their life and the prevention of both mental and physical diseases, AD included.

The last two preventative measures include social activity and continuing to be intellectually challenged. Social activity keeps the mind active and alert, whereas an insular person, who is not interacting with others and thus not listening and sharing ideas, is less likely to fully engage their brain all the time. Similarly, intellectual challenges keep the brain active and engaged. R. S. Wilson, from the Chicago Health and Aging Project, conducted a study of 4,000, sixty-five and older aged residents of South Chicago. He concluded, according to Dash and Villemarette-Pitman, that "those who were more intellectually active were less likely to develop AD. Those who did crossword puzzles and read books showed less cognitive decline as they aged than those who preferred less cognitively engaging activities, such as watching television." Such research suggests that maintaining an active mind for the duration of your life, as well as continuing social connections and interaction, should keep your brain alert, busy, and healthier far longer.

Olivia ponders why the various measures she has discussed did not protect her grandfather from AD. She suggests that such measures may be able only to delay, not prevent, the onset of the disease. She also wonders whether the many years of caring for her grandmother may have taken their toll, reducing his social connections with friends as well as depriving him of the stimulating conversation he had once enjoyed with his wife.

After reading about all of these things, I can't help but wonder why these things didn't help my grandfather. He is highly educated, physically fit, socially active, and still intellectually challenges himself, so how did it happen to him? Why? According to a *Time* magazine article in 2010, "the therapies that exist—drugs and lifestyle behaviors such as keeping the mind sharp with enriching social relationships and stimulating the brain with games and puzzles—can only *delay*, not stop, the onset of memory loss, confusion and cognitive decline that generally extend over a period of several years or, more often, decades." Having to care for my grandmother for over 15 years really took its toll on my grandfather. He spent much of his time caring for her, worrying about her constantly, and losing much of the social connection they had shared with friends, as well as the stimulation of conversation with her, something they had always enjoyed.

Olivia concludes that the example of her grandfather underscores the importance of finding a cure for Alzheimer's. That hope—along with the various measures that might delay, if not prevent, the disease—are what we can cling to. As she concludes, Olivia returns to the vivid composite image of darkness and descent to end her speech.

More than five million Americans are affected by Alzheimer's disease, according to *Time*. Every case is a bit different. But the disease always inevitably progresses and is eventually fatal. There are currently no cures for the disease, although researchers are frantically working to find one, and one is desperately needed because over 100,000 people die from Alzheimer's every year. The only thing a caregiver can do is watch the slow decline and make the patient as comfortable as possible. It must be terrifying to lose one's memory, although in my grandfather's case, he seems blissfully unaware of his diagnosis, which is both good and sad at the same time. My grandfather seemed to do everything right in terms of the suggested "lifestyle behaviors" that would prevent AD; we cannot know for sure whether he simply *delayed* the onset of the disease or if my grandmother's long illness also played a role. It still seems worth it to do everything possible to delay or prevent Alzheimer's by keeping one's mind active, socially and intellectually engaged, and by staying physically fit, and hope for a medical breakthrough in preventing and curing this disease. Although this will come too late to help my grandfather, hopefully others can be spared the descent into such darkness.

Persuasive Speaking

LEARNING OBJECTIVES

This chapter will help you:

14.1 Understand the ethics involved in the persuasive process.

14.2 Become aware of how the persuasive process works.

14.3 Explore the types of persuasive speaking.

14.4 Select appropriate designs for your persuasive speeches.

14.5 Appreciate how proofs can be used to develop persuasive speeches.

OUTLINE

The Ethics of Persuasion

The Process of Persuasion

Types of Persuasive Speaking

Designs for Persuasive Speeches

Proofs: The Means of Persuasion

"Because there has been implanted in us the power to persuade each other . . . we have come together and founded cities and made laws and invented arts."

—ISOCRATES

Lindsey Yoder spoke from both the heart and the head as she indicted human trafficking and exhorted her listeners to help end it. She started with a comparison between African-American slavery before the Civil War and modern sex trafficking. She then offered credible evidence of the nature and extent of the problem; invited her listeners to imagine their loved ones enduring a life of constant physical, psychological, and sexual abuse; and closed by offering specific advice for how to get involved and make a difference. Lindsey first presented her speech to her class and then to a wider audience because she won the Osborn Public Speaking contest at the University of Memphis. News of her speech then reached local activists, and soon she was speaking again at a community rally sponsored by churches and the police department. You can read a text of her speech at the end of this chapter. Through her speech, Lindsey demonstrated not only that she had found a voice but that it was destined to live on!

Over the years, we have heard thousands of strong persuasive presentations by student speakers. A number of them stand out in our minds as truly exceptional. What makes them so memorable? All of them addressed important, timely topics requiring some course of corrective thought or action. All of them were grounded in sound reasoning and evidence that was carefully adapted to the audience and situation. Finally, as exemplified by Lindsey's speech, all of them manifested a passionate commitment to their messages coupled with a desire to move their listeners to think deeply and act well.

The categories of persuasive and informative speaking often overlap. Indeed, the best persuasive speeches are typically quite informative, and the abilities you have already developed with respect to researching and using information responsibly will serve you well in your persuasive endeavors. However, persuasive speaking differs from informative in certain fundamental ways, the first of which concerns your very purpose for speaking. As discussed in the previous chapter, the primary purpose of informative speaking is to enlighten listeners by expanding their knowledge—a very important and noble function. **Persuasive speaking**, on the other hand, represents *a conscious attempt to influence the beliefs, attitudes, values, and sometimes the actions of listeners*. Whereas informative speakers might reveal and discuss options, persuasive speakers encourage us to make specific choices and commitments. Whereas informative speakers are often likened to teachers or journalists, persuasive speakers serve as advocates for causes. Whereas informative speakers use supporting materials to illustrate and explain their ideas, persuasive speakers use supporting materials as evidence to justify their proposals and recommendations.

persuasive speaking
Speaking to influence the beliefs, attitudes, values, and sometimes the behaviors of listeners.

No less important, persuasive speeches ask considerably more from listeners. It is easy enough to listen and become enlightened on interesting topics. But even thoughtful and open-minded listeners tend to resist messages that challenge their core beliefs and commitments, encourage them to embrace a new course of action, or ask them to reconsider disputed public issues such as immigration reform. When you speak persuasively, you ask your listeners to become agents of change, and

Informative Speaking	Persuasive Speaking
1. Reveals options.	1. Urges a choice among options.
2. Speaker acts as teacher.	2. Speaker acts as advocate.
3. Uses supporting material to enlighten listeners.	3. Uses supporting material as evidence to justify advice.
4. Audience expands knowledge.	4. Audience becomes agent of change.
5. Asks for little audience commitment.	5. Asks for strong audience commitment.
6. Speaker's credibility is important.	6. Speaker's credibility more important.
7. Fewer appeals to feelings.	7. More appeals to feelings.
8. High ethical obligation.	8. Higher ethical obligation.

Figure 14.1
Informative Versus Persuasive Speaking

change entails risks. The dimensions of ethos involving competence and character become progressively more important, as do appeals designed to ask your listeners to *feel* as well as *think* about your topics. Finally, because persuasive speaking can and often does influence the lives of other people, your ethical burden—as both a speaker and a listener—becomes especially high. Figure 14.1 compares informative and persuasive speaking.

In this chapter, we provide a general overview of persuasive speaking. Because ethical questions are so essential to finding your voice as a persuasive speaker, we start with those. We then discuss the persuasive process, the various types of persuasive speaking, and some commonly used designs for organizing persuasive messages. We close by considering the means or proofs that can help to make your persuasive speaking more *persuasive*.

The Ethics of Persuasion

14.1 Understand the ethics involved in the persuasive process.

Ours is a skeptical and cynical age, made more so by large-scale abuses of communication ethics. Advertisers use flashy images in place of supporting evidence to assure us that their products will make us sexier or richer. Persuasive messages disguised as journalism bombard our television sets and computer screens. So-called think tanks bribe experts into supporting their points of view, thereby contaminating a major source of responsible knowledge.[1] Public officials may present suspicious statistics, make dubious denials, or dance around questions they really don't want to answer. Such **manipulation** seeks to short-circuit our capacity for critical thinking and reasoned persuasion by avoiding the ethical burden of justification. As Al Gore writes of contemporary politics in *The Assault on Reason*:

manipulation
Strategies that short-circuit critical thinking and ethical persuasion by substituting flashy images, hidden motives, and outright dishonesty for substantive reasoning and evidence use.

> Voters are often viewed mainly as targets for easy manipulation by those seeking their "consent" to exercise power. By using focus groups and elaborate polling techniques, those who design these messages are able to derive the only information they're interested in receiving *from* citizens—feedback useful in fine-tuning their efforts at manipulation.[2]

It is hardly surprising that many people have developed a cynical attitude toward the very prospect of ethical persuasion. As communication scholars Gary C. Woodward and Robert E Denton, Jr., observe, we have a love-hate relationship with persuasion.[3] We recognize the potential value of persuasion for improving our lives and those of other people, but we cannot help but ask, "What difference can one person make? My words don't carry much weight." Yet words make ripples, and ripples can come together to make waves, as Lindsey Yoder's radiating influence on the subject of sex trafficking from class to campus to community illustrates. Or consider the example of Malala Yousafzai, the young woman who dared to speak out after being shot by the Taliban for seeking an education: "one child, one teacher, one pen, and one book can change the world."[4]

Some of our students—and some of the most respected scholars in our field—have expressed moral reservations with the very idea of persuasion. "We all have different perspectives," they say, "so why not live and let live? It's unsavory, even manipulative and unethical, to try to convince others to see the world the way I do." Others argue that the very intent to persuade amounts to little more than symbolic aggression fueled by a "conquest/conversion" mentality.[5] At its worst, manipulative persuasion can be just that—but at its best, reasoned persuasion can be so much more. It allows us to discuss and mediate our inevitable differences "rather than bringing out the fists and the weapons."[6] Better still, reasoned persuasion can help to facilitate what communication scholars Sonja Foss and Cindy Griffin call an "invitation" to engage in more constructive and more inclusive conversations.[7]

Manipulative and Ethical Examples of Persuasion

Find both manipulative and ethical examples of persuasion relevant to a topic you might choose for your persuasive speech. What makes each example either ethical or manipulative? What are the ethical implications of using or not using each example?

At the end of Chapter 1, we introduced the subject of ethical public speaking as centering on honesty and respect for the integrity of ideas and information, the responsible use of communication techniques, and the shared responsibilities of listeners. Because of the increased capacity of *persuasive* speaking to affect the lives of other people, it is particularly important that all of these standards meet the ethical burden of justification. So are discussions of ethical concerns raised in just about every chapter of this text with respect to critical thinking, audience adaptation, inclusive language use, motivational appeals, and even presentation aids. As you prepare your persuasive speech, keep these simple questions in mind:[8]

- What is my ethical responsibility to my topic?
- What is my ethical responsibility to my audience?
- Could I publicly defend the ethics of my message?
- What does this message say about my character?

The Process of Persuasion

14.2 Become aware of how the persuasive process works.

Noted social psychologist William J. McGuire argued that successful persuasion is a process involving up to twelve phases.[9] For our purposes, these phases may be condensed into five stages: awareness, understanding, agreement, enactment, and integration (see Figure 14.2). Familiarity with these stages highlights the importance of knowing where your audience stands and adapting your persuasive appeals accordingly. It also helps us to appreciate the extent to which persuasion on important

Figure 14.2 McGuire's Model of the Persuasive Process

issues is typically incremental rather than an all-or-nothing proposition. Persuasive speeches can be successful when they move listeners through the process toward your ultimate goal of accepting or acting upon your message. Indeed, just gaining a fair and considerate hearing of your point of view from an otherwise hostile audience can be a tremendous victory.

Awareness

The first phase of persuasion, **awareness**, involves calling attention to the existence of a problem. Speaking to raise awareness, also known as "consciousness raising," is especially important when listeners do not already know or believe there is a problem. If you want your listeners to support stronger measures for combatting domestic terrorism, to donate their time and money to a local animal shelter, or simply to commit to becoming more informed of your situation or issue, you should first convince them that the need is real and pressing. In such cases, startling facts, compelling examples, eyewitness accounts, and descriptive language can be effective for shaping perceptions that can help to open up listeners to accept your persuasive message or goal.

awareness
In this first stage of the persuasive process, listeners gain knowledge about a problem and pay attention to it.

For instance, you might shock your listeners into awareness for a speech on campus rape by opening with a statistic: "According to a survey conducted by the Association of American Universities, nearly 1 in 4 women report being the victim of some form of sexual assault during their college years."[10] To raise awareness of human suffering in Honduras, Alexandra McArthur offered a vivid contrast between the widely advertised paradise of "hotels, beaches, restaurants, and shopping" and the economic blight and misery she witnessed in her travels to that country. These "were not the happy, smiling faces on tourist manuals," she continued, for "far too many of them suffer from malnutrition, and have little access to medicines, running water, or electricity."

understanding
In this second phase of the persuasive process, listeners develop a broader comprehension of a problem or issue.

Understanding

The second phase of the persuasive process, **understanding**, entails developing a broader comprehension of the nature, scope, causes, and likely implications of a problem or issue, as well as the range of contrasting opinions and views of experts and opposing advocates. Beyond awareness, most listeners need to feel like they understand the situation or issue at hand before they can commit to a given proposition or course of action. In her speech opposing the U.S-funded Western Hemisphere Institute for Security Cooperation, better known as the "School of the Americas," Amanda Miller's impressive array impressive array of illustrative examples provided a broader understanding of the controversies surrounding the institute and its legacy of human rights abuses in Latin America:

Alexandra McArthur's speech helped to raise awareness of human suffering in Honduras.

> In El Salvador, the United Nations Truth Commission found that of twelve officers responsible for the massacre of nine hundred villagers at El Mozote, ten of them were graduates of the School of the Americas.
>
> I wish this were a solitary case. But according to an Inter-American Commission on Human Rights, School of the Americas graduate Raphael Samundio Molina led a massacre at the Colombian Palace of Justice, and three years later was inducted into the School of the Americas hall of fame. In the same country, an International Human Rights Tribunal found that of two hundred and forty-six officers cited for various crimes, one hundred and five of them were School of the Americas graduates.

> Finally, the School has produced at least twelve Latin American dictators in countries such as Peru, Bolivia, Argentina, and Ecuador. This is the distinguished record of the School of the Americas that we continue to fund with our taxpayer dollars.

Because her examples were so controversial, Amanda had to document them carefully, using a variety of sources to heighten their credibility. Having provided her listeners with a broader context for understanding her issue, she was now prepared to argue against continued funding for the School of the Americas.

Agreement

agreement
In this third stage in the persuasive process, listeners accept a speaker's recommendations and remember their reasons for doing so.

The third stage in the persuasive process is **agreement**, which occurs when listeners proceed from understanding to accepting your position. As they listen to you, audience members should go through a series of *affirmations*, such as: "He's right, this is a serious problem.... That's striking evidence; I didn't know about that.... I see how this can affect my life.... I've got to do something about this.... This plan makes sense. I believe it will work." These affirmations can build on each other, developing momentum toward agreement at the end of the speech.

Speakers themselves become important models for agreement. When Dolapo Olushola described the plight of orphans in her native Nigeria, she seemed a strikingly authentic spokesperson as she asked for audience support:

> Did you know the current number of orphans in the world would make a circle around the world's equator three times, if they were all holding hands? Do you know that every 15 seconds another child in Africa becomes an AIDS orphan?

enactment
In this fourth stage of the persuasive process, listeners take appropriate action as the result of agreement.

Then when listeners learned that Dolapo had helped form a service club dedicated to relieving the plight of orphans in sub-Saharan Africa, it was clear she had already walked the path she wanted them to take. As she painted verbal pictures of these abandoned children, she invited listeners to share her passion and sympathy. She convinced them that her cause deserved not just their agreement but also their commitment. She had given them a living model for their response.

Creating graphic word pictures in a speech can arouse listeners' concern and spur them to join a cause such as aiding starving orphans in Africa.

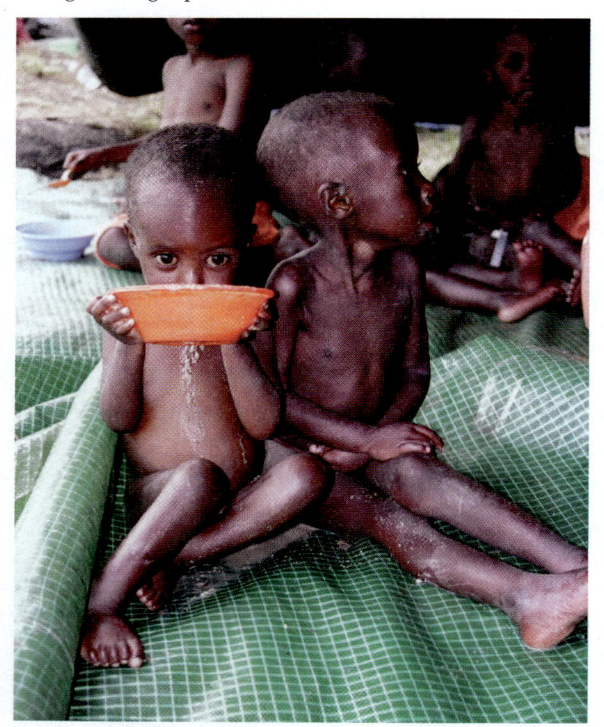

Agreement can range from small concessions to total acceptance. Lesser degrees of agreement could represent success, especially when listeners are asked to reconsider preexisting beliefs and commitments or to risk a great deal by accepting your ideas. If a reluctant listener concedes, "I guess you have a point," then that constitutes an important step in the persuasive process.

Enactment

The fourth stage in the persuasive process is **enactment** of your proposals or solutions. It is one thing to get listeners to accept what you say; it is quite another to get them to act on it. When you invite listeners to sign a petition, raise their hands, or voice assent, you give them a way to enact agreement and to confirm their commitment. The speaker who wants to mobilize the audience against a proposed tuition increase, for example, might bring a petition to sign, distribute the addresses of local legislators to contact, and urge listeners to write letters to campus leaders, alumni, and local news outlets. If you want your audience to assume the risks of getting involved, be specific in telling them not only *why* but *when, where*, and *how* they can do so. Make it easy for them to comply.

The use of emotional appeals can be very effective for moving listeners from agreement to action. Stirring stories and examples, vivid images, and colorful language can arouse sympathy. In an especially interesting use of narrative technique, Lindsey Yoder asked her listeners to imagine themselves as victims of sex slavery: isolated, helpless, and doomed to a life of abuse. Her graphic word-pictures made listeners want to join the cause of eradicating this evil.

Integration

The final stage in the persuasive process is the **integration** of new commitments into listeners' previous beliefs and values. For a persuasive speech to have lasting effect, listeners must see the connection between their core values and what you propose. By associating her opposition to human sex trafficking with the struggle to abolish slavery, Lindsey Yoder framed her persuasive speech as a reaffirmation of core American values. She urged listeners not just to accept her recommendations but to *become* the solutions she advocated. She asked for total integration of beliefs, attitudes, values, and actions.

integration
In this final stage of the persuasive process, listeners connect new attitudes and commitments with previous beliefs and values to ensure lasting change.

All of us seek consistency between our values and behaviors. For that reason, persuasive speakers might ask us to reconsider our attitudes toward abortion or the death penalty in the context of our value of respecting life, or to consider the parallels between a particular candidate's platform and our own beliefs. On some occasions, listeners might agree with your message for the moment and then revert back to their original position once they've had time to reflect on their previous beliefs and commitments. To counter this tendency, persuasive speakers often anticipate and address likely reservations or opposing views that listeners may encounter after they have tentatively agreed with their proposals. Getting your listeners to enact your message can also contribute to more lasting persuasion. Often called the "foot in the door" approach, a simple token gesture of commitment such as signing a petition or making a small financial contribution can be really effective by establishing a self-image that reverberates over time.[11]

boomerang effect
A negative reaction that occurs when speakers ask for too much persuasive change as a result of a single speech.

Understanding persuasion as a five-stage process can be helpful for developing persuasive speeches in at least two important ways. The first entails *the centrality of your listeners* in the process of communication and the importance of knowing where they stand in the process with respect to your message. Are they aware of your topic or issue? To what extent do they share your understanding of it? How disposed are they to agree with your message? How inclined are they to get involved and act on your proposed solutions? How can you associate accepting your position with reaffirming their core beliefs and values to achieve integration? Such knowledge can help you to better focus your persuasive efforts and sometimes your very purpose for speaking. The detailed discussion of audience analysis and adaptation in Chapter 5 can help you in this process.

A second related aspect involves the importance of *setting reasonable goals*. Lindsey Yoder's speech on human trafficking assumed a relatively sympathetic if sparsely informed audience, which allowed her to move her listeners through the entire process from awareness to integration. But especially when addressing controversial issues that members of the audience know and care about, listeners tend to move through the process slowly. Rarely do they move through all five stages as a result of a single speech, no matter how sensible and well-supported. Asking for too much may provoke a **boomerang effect** by which they reject you and your message altogether. We would never suggest that you compromise your convictions and motives for speaking, but we do encourage you to focus the bulk of your reasoning and evidence to the predisposition of your primary listeners. Again, just getting some listeners to hear your description of a problematic situation or to

Using the Five-Step Process of Persuasion

Think about an issue for persuasion. Using the five-step process of persuasion outlined in this section, identify a) the stage of persuasion where you think your audience probably stands, and why; b) where you yourself fall in the stages; and c) how you might focus your persuasive efforts to bridge the gap.

consider opposing views for the first time can make a tremendous contribution to moving them through the process of persuasion.

Finding Your Voice

Persuasion in Social Media

Check out social media for persuasive messages on topics of interest to you. What kind of persuasive message is each one? What stage in the process of persuasion does each seem to address most directly? Do you find the ideas expressed in these messages to be persuasive? Why or why not? Do you evaluate these comments differently from other media sources? How could these help you find your voice on a topic?

Types of Persuasive Speaking

14.3 Explore the types of persuasive speaking.

As we discussed while introducing this chapter, persuasion is a broad function of communication that often overlaps with other recognized categories of public speaking. For instance, much of the advice we offer for informative speaking in the previous chapter can be useful to you when speaking to raise awareness or to enhance understanding of problematic situations or issues. Likewise, much of the advice we offer in Chapter 16 for ceremonial speaking can be helpful when speaking to reaffirm and integrate persuasive messages with our core beliefs and value systems.

The most commonly recognized types of persuasive speaking emerge from asking three fundamental questions of a problematic situation or issue:

- What is the truth of the situation?
- How should I evaluate the situation?
- What should we do about it?

These questions in turn invite three basic and often overlapping types of persuasive speaking: speeches that focus on *facts*, speeches that emphasize *attitudes and values*, and speeches that advocate *action and policy*.

Speeches That Focus on Facts

speeches that focus on facts
Speeches that engage uncertainties and disputes surrounding questions of past, present, and future facts.

Speeches that focus on facts seek to define the truth of a given situation or issue, a function that usually corresponds to the persuasive stages of raising awareness and enhancing understanding. Important public disputes often revolve around factual information regarding (a) the nature, scope, causes, and implications of situations; (b) what the most authoritative experts have to say about it; and (c) what representative examples we should take into consideration. Is climate change happening? If so, why? How does it affect our lives and what can we expect in the future?

Speakers typically address questions of past, present, and future facts. Speeches that focus on *past* facts seek to shape the way listeners remember and interpret the meaning of previous deeds and events. Lawyers often present such speeches before courtroom juries. Did Baton Rouge police shoot and kill Alton Sterling in self-defense, or was it murder? Speeches addressing past facts are also useful for attributing the cause of a situation. When did the current trend toward gun violence begin, and how did we get to where we are?

Speeches addressing *current* facts ask us to consider or reconsider the existing state of a situation and are often crucial to deliberating public issues. What is actually happening? Is Iran attempting to develop nuclear weapons? Is our economy recovering and, if so, are working-class people sharing in the benefits? Is your university doing enough to combat sexual assault on campus?

Speeches addressing *future* facts offer predictions or forecasts based on our interpretation of the past and present. Does climate change pose a threat to our way of life? Should we expect to see more severe weather patterns as a result? Can changes in human behavior affect the course of climate change?

At times, questions of past and current facts turn not on whether something happened or is happening but on the *definition* of events. Yes, sexual activity occurred in the encounter between the celebrity and the admiring fan, but was it consensual, or did it constitute rape? Should the recent growth of the U.S. economy be defined as "promising news" or a "jobless recovery"? Is Social Security an "entitlement" or an "earned retirement benefit"? To frame the definitions of events is to influence the feelings that people have about them.

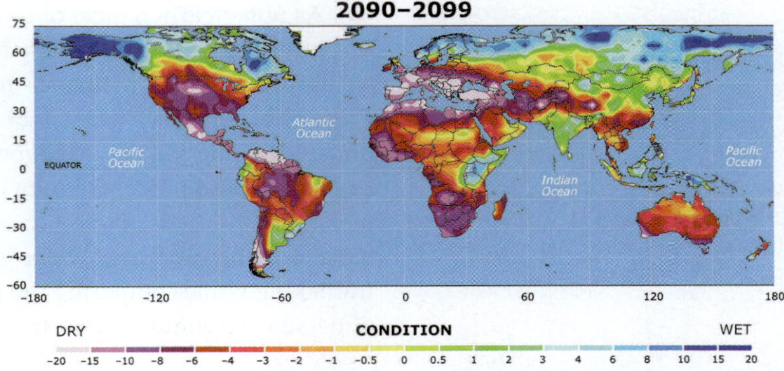

Presentation aids are useful for speeches that focus on past, present, and future facts, such as the effects of climate change.

Regardless of whether you focus on the past, present, or future, speeches that focus on facts are usually more persuasive when speakers do the following:

- **Present additional facts to support disputed claims.** Never rely on a single fact, example, or opinion to support a disputed characterization of events. As discussed in Chapter 8, supporting information is more effective when various types are presented in combination. Presentation aids can be especially useful for amplifying your most important evidence.
- **Cite authoritative experts and sources of information orally.** Citing reputable sources gives your evidence borrowed ethos. Always consider how your sources of information will be received by your listeners. With skeptical listeners, cite multiple sources that are acceptable to the audience, and stress their credentials.
- **Present a credible narrative of events to frame their presentation of the facts.** Timelines of relevant events and developments can be really useful for explaining the meaning of past, present, and future facts. Narrated examples of "real-life" people and their experiences can also be helpful. Hypothetical examples can be useful for predicting the future consequences of current situations and trends.

Speeches That Emphasize Attitudes and Values

Speeches that emphasize attitudes and values ask listeners to make evaluative judgments about a situation or issue, a function that most corresponds to the agreement stage of persuasion. These speeches often build on speeches addressing facts. For instance, once you have convinced your listeners that climate change is actually

speeches that emphasize attitudes and values
Speeches that ask listeners to make evaluative judgments on a situation or issue.

occurring and human pollution is a primary cause, you might want to further persuade them that we have an obligation to do whatever we can to slow or reverse its effects.

As discussed in Chapter 5, attitudes refer to the feelings we have toward a subject coupled with a predisposition to act, and values refer to our underlying principles or moral convictions with respect to how we should or should not behave. In the case of our example of climate change, the desired attitude would be to make your listeners feel that climate change poses a threat that warrants action, and the underlying values might be a commitment to environmental stewardship, an obligation to leave a habitable planet for future generations, or simple self-preservation. Tie your presentation to the audience's values through stories, examples, and vivid language that reawaken the audience's appreciation of how those values apply to this particular case.

As noted earlier, most of us have a natural tendency to seek consistency between our attitudes and values. For that reason, persuasive speakers might encourage us to support campaign finance reform by invoking our commitment to democratic principles. When we sense that our attitudes and behaviors are not consistent with our underlying values, we experience a sense of discomfort that psychologists call **cognitive dissonance**. Pointing out such inconsistencies can help to make persuasive messages more effective by couching them as a means to restore that consistency or balance. When Lindsey Yoder invoked the popular indifference toward human sex trafficking while comparing the practice to slavery, she tapped into a powerful source of persuasive communication.

cognitive dissonance
The discomfort we feel when we sense that our attitudes and behaviors are not consistent with our values.

Finding Your Voice

Harmonizing Attitudes and Values

Select a currently disputed issue such as gun control or immigration reform, and look up a speech by a prominent advocate on the subject. Does the speaker frame either consistency or inconsistency between attitudes and values in the presentation? If not, how might she or he have made the speech more persuasive by using the power of cognitive dissonance?

Speeches That Advocate Action and Policy

Speeches that advocate action and policy ask listeners to embrace or enact a given policy or plan of action for resolving a problem. Often building on speeches that affirm facts or actuate values, speakers advocating action and policy might ask listeners to support a disputed proposition for resolving climate change such as a tax on greenhouse gas emissions; or to get directly involved by contacting their political representatives, joining a group committed to combatting global warming, or resolving to reduce their own carbon footprints. Such speakers remind us that we should support and practice what we preach.

speeches that advocate action and policy
Speeches that encourage listeners to embrace a policy or enact a plan of action for addressing a problem or issue.

Such was the goal when Amanda Miller presented her powerful indictment of the School of the Americas. Amanda argued that the institute, conducted for many years under U.S. sponsorship at Fort Benning, Georgia, had been "implicated in gross human rights violations in Latin America." The school, she said, trained its students in "techniques for torture, false imprisonment, extortion, and intimidation" and had been "responsible for the deaths of many thousands of people and countless acts of terrorism." Amanda painted a vivid picture of the contradiction between American values and American actions as she urged her listeners to "support the cause" of shutting down the institute.

When proposing new policies for addressing such fiercely disputed topics as banning assault weapons or funding fetal tissue research, speakers may need to devote the bulk of their reasoning and evidence to engaging opposing positions as well as supporting their own. Other propositions, such as providing your listeners with advice for protecting themselves from campus crime, may be simpler and more direct. One of our students, Betsy Lyles, urged her listeners to donate hair to Locks of Love, an organization that offers hairpieces to impoverished children who are suffering from long-term medical hair loss.

Speeches that advocate action can help raise awareness and support for worthy causes. Here, Condoleezza Rice speaks at the Susan G. Komen Breast Cancer Foundation's annual National Race for the Cure.

In either case, remember that getting involved entails risks. For such speeches to be effective, you need to convince your listeners that there is a problem serious and urgent enough to warrant their involvement. You want to provide them with concrete advice or steps for taking action, and you want to convince them that your proposals are workable and will make a difference. It also helps to remind your listeners of the consequences of *not* acting and to assure them that your proposals are consistent with shared values. Finally, emphasize the importance of acting together as a community. As Lindsey moved to the conclusion of her speech on human trafficking, she exhorted her listeners:

> My words alone will not have much effect, but when we all speak together, the impact can be great.... Join the "End It Movement." Draw a red X on your hand symbolizing your stand on modern slavery. On Instagram, Twitter, and Facebook, use the hashtag *enditmovement*. The more people who become aware of this injustice, the sooner modern slavery will come to an end.

Choosing a Topic for Your Persuasive Speech

Choose a potential topic for your persuasive speech. Sketch out how you might develop a speech that focuses on facts, a speech that emphasizes attitudes and values, and a speech that advocates action and policy. What aspects are emphasized in each case? What aspects are not emphasized? How do these differences affect how you approach the topic?

Figure 14.3 The Work of Persuasive Speeches

Type	Function	Techniques
Speeches that focus on facts	Establish true state of affairs	Strengthen claims of past, present, and future facts by citing experts and other supporting evidence. Create lively pictures of the contested facts that reinforce their reality.
Speeches that emphasize attitudes and values	Apply attitudes and values to present problems	Reawaken appreciation for values through stories, examples, and vivid language. Show listeners how to apply values. Encourage them to form and re-form attitudes consistent with these values.
Speeches that advocate action and policy	Propose programs to remedy problems and put values into action	Show that the program of action will solve the problem by mentioning previous successes in similar situations. Prove that the plan is practical and workable. Picture the audience enacting the plan of action. Show the consequences of acting and not acting. Visualize success.

Designs for Persuasive Speeches

14.4 Select appropriate designs for your persuasive speeches.

In Chapter 9, we discussed the importance of choosing the right design for organizing the main ideas and supporting materials of your speeches. Many of the same designs used for informative speaking can be useful for organizing persuasive speeches—the main difference being the speaker's underlying motive to persuade. For instance, speakers seeking to raise awareness or understanding of a problem might use any combination of categorical, causation, or chronological designs. Comparative design schemes can be useful for contrasting and arguing opposing views and propositions. Sequential designs are often used for outlining the steps in a plan of action.

Three designs, however, are especially suited to persuasive speeches: the *problem–solution* design, the *motivated sequence* design, and the *refutative* design.

Problem–Solution Design

problem–solution design
A persuasive speech pattern in which listeners are first persuaded that there is a problem and are then offered solutions to resolve it.

The **problem–solution design** is useful for moving listeners to action on important issues or problems. It is a two-part design by which speakers first convince listeners that there is a problem and then offer solutions for resolving it. The solution can involve changing attitudes, beliefs, and values, or taking action.

The advice we have already discussed for addressing the facts of a situation and seeking evaluative judgments can be useful for convincing reluctant listeners that there is a problem. You should provide credible facts, statistics, examples, and expert opinions to explain the nature, scope, and causes of your problem. Use vivid language to describe the consequences of action versus inaction, and emphasize the extent to which the problem represents a threat to the interests and values of your listeners. Pictures, graphics, and other presentation aids can be particularly effective for amplifying your most compelling evidence and illustrating the impact of your problem.

Anna Aley provided a powerful description of the problem in a speech designed to encourage her classmates to stand up to the slumlords preying on her and her fellow students at Kansas State University. She opened by using vivid language to characterize her own experiences renting an apartment in an off-campus student neighborhood: the moldy carpeting, the substandard electrical wiring, and the "dead roaches in the refrigerator." She then documented the extent of the problem by providing statistics on the thousands of students in her community living under similar or worse conditions and the complaints filed by students against more than 100 landlords in the area. Finally, Anna devoted considerable attention to explaining the causes of her problem: the lax enforcement of inadequate code regulations and the fact that so many students—like herself—simply did not know what recourse of action to take. By this time, her classmates were convinced that something had to be done!

The second part of a problem–solution speech should focus on developing your proposed solutions or plan of action. As discussed above, you want to provide your listeners with clear solutions and concrete advice for enacting them, stress that your solutions are practical and will make a difference, and emphasize the value and importance of acting together. As Anna moved into the solutions phase of her presentation, she emphasized the importance of acting together to pressure the city government for stronger building codes, laws, and enforcement. She encouraged her classmates to join an Off-Campus Association, informed them of campus services that were available to student victims of substandard housing, and asked them to sign a petition to increase funding for those services. She closed with a dramatic call to action followed by a simple yet eloquent statement of affirmation: "We don't have to live in slums."

When the problem can be identified clearly and the solution is concrete and simple, the problem–solution design works well in persuasive speeches. Consider the stock

The stock issues in persuasion center around the following questions:

I. Is there a significant problem?
  A. How did the problem originate?
  B. What caused the problem?
  C. How widespread is the problem?
  D. How long has the problem persisted?
  E. What harms are associated with the problem?
  F. Will these harms continue and grow unless there is change?
II. What is the solution to this problem?
  A. Will the solution actually solve the problem?
  B. Is the solution practical?
  C. Would the cost of the solution be reasonable?
  D. Might there be other consequences to the solution?
III. Who will put the solution into effect?
  A. Are these people responsible and competent?
  B. What role can listeners play?

Figure 14.4
Stock Issues in Persuasion

Based on The structure of the stock issues design has been adapted from Charles U. Larson, Persuasion: Reception and Responsibility, 13th ed. (Belmont, CA: Wadsworth, 2012); and Charles S. Mudd and Malcolm O. Sillars, Public Speaking: Content and Communication (Prospect Heights, IL: Waveland, 1991), pp. 100–102. © Michael Osborn.

issues discussed in Figure 14.4 when preparing problem–solution speeches. Popular with debaters, the **stock issues** are simple questions that thoughtful listeners will ask before agreeing to a plan of action or a change in policy. Finally, with some problems, speakers may need to focus more attention on their causes in order to demonstrate how their solutions will work, in which case they may opt to use a variation of the problem–solution called problem–cause–solution design. Anna's speech—which is printed in full in Appendix B of this textbook—provides an excellent example of this hybrid design.

stock issues
The primary questions a reasonable person would ask before agreeing to a change in policies or procedures.

Motivated Sequence Design

The **motivated sequence design**, a variation on the problem–solution design, offers a step-by-step approach that moves listeners from attention to action.[12] In her speech at the University of Arkansas, Simone Mullinax used the five steps of the motivated sequence design to convince her listeners to become mentors.

motivated sequence design
A persuasive speech design that proceeds by arousing attention, demonstrating a need, satisfying the need, visualizing results, and calling for action.

1. *Arouse attention.* As in any speech, you begin by stimulating interest in your subject. Vivid stories or examples, surprising claims, striking facts and statistics, eloquent statements from admired leaders—all can pique the interest of your listeners. Simone aroused attention with this opening:

   > Let me share with you a simple statistic: 20 percent of our nation's children—that's one in every five kids—are now "at risk." What does that mean? It means they have no one to trust, no one to turn to. It means expectations for them are low—our expectations, and more importantly, theirs for themselves.

2. *Demonstrate a need.* Show your listeners that the situation you want to change is urgent. Arrange evidence so that it builds in intensity and taps into audience motivations to help listeners see what they have to win and lose with regard to your proposal. By the end of this demonstration, listeners should be eager to hear your ideas for change. Simone demonstrated the need in this way:

   > These are the so-called problem kids—the ones who drop out of school and drop into lives that are unproductive, unsuccessful, and often mired in crime. These are wasted lives, wasted humanity, and we all have to pay for their failures.

3. *Satisfy the need.* Present a plan to satisfy the need you have demonstrated. Set out a clear course of action, and explain how it will work. Show how this plan agrees

with audience principles and values. Offer examples that show how your plan has already worked successfully in other situations. In Simone's speech:

> So what is the answer? I'll tell you about one I know that works because I've tried it. It's called "mentoring," a person-to-person program to become that friend someone doesn't have, that person who cares. It may involve only an hour or two a week, but the mentor is a troubled child's connection to a more healthy and hopeful world.

4. *Visualize the results.* Paint verbal pictures that illustrate the positive results listeners can expect. Show them how their lives will be better when they have enacted your plan. A dramatic depiction of the future can help overcome resistance to action. You could also paint a picture of what life will be like if listeners *don't* enact your suggestions. Place these positive and negative verbal pictures side by side to strengthen their impact through contrast. Simone visualized these results:

   > Put yourself in this picture. [She tells the story of her mentoring relationship with one child.] Mentoring helps us reclaim our children, one child at a time. I'll tell you someone else who has benefited—me!

5. *Call for action.* Your call for action may be a challenge, an appeal, or a statement of personal commitment. The call for action should be short and to the point. Give your listeners something specific they can do right away. If you can get them to take the first step, the next will come more easily. Simone's call for action gave specifics:

   > The best part about mentoring is that it's so easy: Can you send an e-mail? Can you make a phone call? Can you talk to your younger sibling's friends? Can you take a child to a ball game or to the movies? Then you have the qualifications to be a mentor! Here's how you can get started [she names an organization, address, and phone number and shows material she will hand out]. I urge you, join me in this program. The good things we do in our lives radiate out from us and become magnified. The little fires we light can come together to warm the world!

Refutative Design

refutative design
A persuasive design used for arguing disputed propositions.

The **refutative design** is useful for persuasive speeches that engage disputed propositions. Whether your purpose is to address the facts of a situation, to ask for evaluative judgments from your listeners, or to promote a course of action, you may find it necessary to engage opposing views and reservations. When addressing highly contentious public issues, you may need to spend the bulk of your persuasive reasoning and evidence engaging opposing positions as well as supporting your own positions. When this is the case, a refutative design may be your best choice for organizing your speech's materials.

For the ancient Greeks and Romans, speaking to argue disputed positions before juries and deliberative assemblies became a high art form. Based on their writings and others that followed, an effective argumentative speech should contain at least five essential parts:

proposition
A clear declarative statement of your central persuasive point or thesis.

- An introduction that frames your issue in a way that predisposes your listeners to accept your message;
- A **proposition** that clearly articulates your persuasive thesis;
- arguments that engage opposing views and reservations;
- arguments that provide reasoning and support for your positions; and
- A conclusion that summarizes your arguments, emphasizes their importance, and (as appropriate) issues a call to action.[13]

We will discuss strategies for engaging disputed arguments in our next chapter on building persuasive arguments. Figure 14.5 summarizes how to select a design for a persuasive speech.

Figure 14.5 Selecting Persuasive Figure Designs

Design	Use When
Causation	• Your topic addresses disputed causes of an important problem, or you need to explain the cause as a prerequisite to offering your solutions.
Chronological	• You want to show how a persuasive issue has developed over time.
Categorical	• Your topic readily breaks into familiar patterns or categories, such as proving a plan will be safe, inexpensive, and effective; can be used to change attitudes or to urge action.
Comparative/ Contrast	• You want to demonstrate why your proposal is superior to another; especially good for speeches in which you contend with opposing views.
Sequential	• Your speech contains a plan of action that must be carried out in a specific order.
Problem–Solution	• Your topic presents a problem that needs to be solved and a solution that will solve it; good for speeches involving attitudes and urging action.
Motivated Sequence	• Your topic calls for action as the final phase of a five-step process that includes arousing attention, demonstrating the need, satisfying the need, visualizing the results, and calling for action.
Refutative	• You must answer strong opposition on a topic before you can establish your position; good for speeches engaging controversial issues.

Proofs: The Means of Persuasion

14.5 Appreciate how proofs can be used to develop persuasive speeches.

To this point, we have discussed the ethics of persuasive speaking, the nature of the persuasive process, the prominent types of persuasive speaking, and the designs for organizing them. In this section, we look at the broader resources or appeals that help to make persuasive speaking *persuasive*. The ancient Greeks referred to these resources as **proofs** that constitute the means of persuasion. They are important to all public speaking but especially to messages seeking to persuade listeners on contested topics. Each proof corresponds to important questions that thoughtful listeners will ask themselves when considering persuasive messages:

proofs
Appeals to ethos, logos, pathos, and mythos that help to enhance the persuasiveness of speaking.

- **Ethos:** Can this speaker be trusted as a source of important ideas and information?
- **Pathos:** How should I feel about the speaker's topic and message?
- **Mythos:** Is this message consistent with my community's shared values, traditions, and aspirations?
- **Logos:** Is this message supported by sound reasoning and quality evidence?

Developing Ethos

Because of its importance to all public speaking, we have already discussed **ethos** as the audience's perceptions of a speaker's competence, character, good will, and dynamism. It is difficult to overstate the importance of ethos to persuasive speaking. Before listeners will assume the risks involved with considering persuasive propositions on

ethos
A form of proof that relies on the audience's perceptions of a speaker's competence, character, good will, and dynamism.

topics they care about, they must first believe you know what you are talking about, you are honest and trustworthy, and you have their better interests at heart.

Ethos is a dynamic quality that can be nurtured and enhanced through public speaking. Speakers with relevant credentials and specialized training should cite them while introducing their presentations. Citing credible sources of information that your audience will accept and respect can also be very effective. Simply preparing good speeches and presenting them well will usually enhance perceptions of your ethos.

Speakers can also enhance perceptions of ethos by citing personal experiences to establish a sense of intimate connection to their topics. In 1851, former slave Sojourner Truth did just that when she addressed critics at a women's convention:

> That man over there says that women need to be helped into carriages, and lifted over ditches, and to have the best place everywhere. Nobody ever helps me into carriages, or over mud-puddles, or gives me any best place! And ain't I a woman? Look at me! Look at my arm! I have ploughed and planted, and gathered into barns, and no man could head me! And ain't I a woman? I could work as much and eat as much as a man - when I could get it - and bear the lash as well! And ain't I a woman? I have borne thirteen children, and seen most all sold off to slavery, and when I cried out with my mother's grief, none but Jesus heard me! And ain't I a woman?[14]

Sojourner Truth's vivid description of her experiences contradicted claims that women were too fragile to have equal rights.

A cautionary note: In some ways, ethos is similar to what some people call "your good name." While you can cultivate and enhance it through the strategies offered here, once ethos is damaged, it is difficult to restore. Once you give your listeners reason to believe you do not know what you are talking about, you are not to be trusted, or you do not speak with their better interests in mind, they are not likely to open their minds and give you a second chance to persuade them. The best way to enhance perceptions of your ethos is to practice what you preach by manifesting these virtues in all your communicative transactions.

Developing Pathos

pathos
A form of proof that relies on appeals to human emotions such as compassion or fear.

What the ancients called **pathos** includes appeals to emotions such as compassion, guilt, excitement, fear, and anger. People typically react strongly when they feel such emotions, and sometimes appeals to pathos are misused to short-circuit the reasoning process. However, emotional appeals can be both rational and ethical when presented in the context of well-reasoned persuasion. They can be helpful for involving your listeners with the human dimensions of a problem or issue, prompting them to reconsider settled beliefs and opinions, and moving them from agreement to action.[15]

Narratives and examples are often the evidence of choice for emotional appeals. Commercials for charities use narrated images of abused animals or natural disasters to arouse your involvement and financial generosity. In a student speech that won the top prize for persuasive speaking at the National Forensic League, Austin Wright aroused feelings of indignation by describing the unfair treatment received by Maher Arar, a Canadian citizen illegally detained by American authorities on unfounded suspicions of terrorist connections. His speech is reprinted in full at the end of our next chapter.

You should use pathos with caution. If an emotional appeal is too exaggerated, audiences may think you are trying to manipulate them. Overblown appeals to fear or guilt can prompt listeners to react against both you and your message. It is better to understate rather than overstate emotional appeals so that they add the human dimension without verging into theatrics. Make sure your emotional appeals are representative and backed by solid evidence, and use them to complement rather than to replace appeals to logic and reasoning.

When used as part of well-reasoned persuasion, emotional appeals can help to involve listeners with the human dimensions of a problem or issue.

Developing Mythos

In recent years, rhetorical scholars have suggested an additional type of proof by **mythos** that is grounded in the sense of identification that most of us feel with certain group traditions and the values they embody. When politicians characterize their proposals as fulfilling the will of the "founding fathers," they are invoking a powerful source of persuasive identification. As communication scholar Martha Solomon Watson has noted, "Rhetoric which incorporates mythical elements taps into rich cultural reservoirs."[16]

mythos
A form of proof grounded in the sense of connection and identification that people feel with group traditions and the values they embody.

There are many ways to invoke appeals to mythos in persuasive speeches. Simple references to group pride and loyalty can be effective, as can popular phrases such as "E pluribus unum" or "live free or die." The deeds and words of historic heroes like Ronald Reagan, Martin Luther King, Jr., Dolores Huerta, and Clara Barton can be really effective, as can references to religious narratives such as the story of the Good Samaritan. Finally, allusions to popular folk narratives and legends can enhance proof by mythos in your speeches. World War II's Rosie the Riveter, for example, offers a concise reference to women doing their part for the country. Consider, too, why so many politicians speak of their childhood upbringings in terms of the "rags to riches" narrative. It is an age-old story that has become an indelible part of the American consciousness.

Appeals to mythos do not have to be this elaborate to be effective. Simply wearing an American flag pin or a rainbow-colored shirt can serve as powerful symbols of mythic identification. As discussed in Chapter 11, the use of such powerful terms as "freedom" and "equality" can also add an element of mythos to your speeches. When John F. Kennedy characterized his vision for America as a "New Frontier," he didn't bother to offer detailed images of pioneers and cowboys struggling to conquer and settle a wild territory, but you can bet that many of his listeners thought of and identified with such images as they considered his words.

Finally, appeals to mythos can contribute to the final "integration" phase of persuasion by helping your listeners connect your messages to reaffirming core values and traditions. That said, you should be cautious of the fact that appeals to mythos are sometimes subject to gross misuse. Many scoundrels have sought to defend the indefensible by claiming they did it for God and country! As with pathos, appeals to mythos are sometimes used as a substitute for reasoning. Worse still, they can be used to propagate ethnocentrism and the exclusion of outsiders. Keep in mind that members of minority groups may have their own traditions and their own takes on popular lore. For many African Americans, Thomas Jefferson was paradoxical if not hypocritical for writing about "Life, Liberty and the pursuit of Happiness" while holding their ancestors in bondage.

While such founding fathers as Thomas Jefferson can be used as a positive source of mythos, many consider them to be hypocritical for advocating liberty while holding people in bondage.

Figure 14.6 Proofs in Reasoned Persuasion

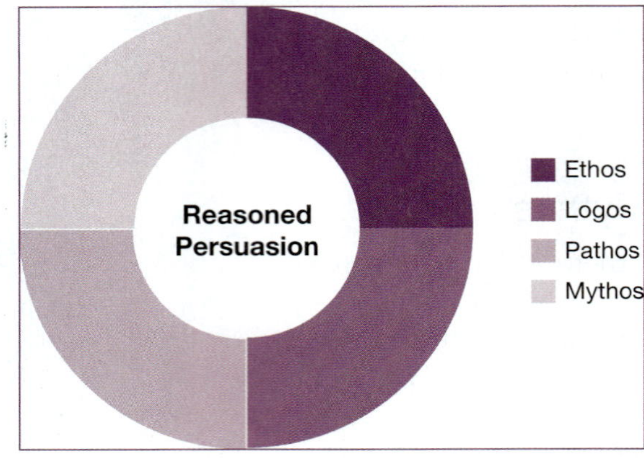

Developing Logos

logos
A form of proof that uses reasoning and evidence to provide logical support for persuasive messages.

Logos refers to the use of reasoning and evidence to support persuasive messages. Is your speech logical? Is your reasoning coherent? Does your reasoning pattern engage your topic in terms your audience will find compelling? Does your use of evidence ground your observations and assertions in the reality of the situation? Because appeals to logos are particularly important to engage skeptical audiences on such contentious public issues as domestic surveillance programs, we devote considerably more attention to the subject in our next chapter on developing persuasive arguments.

Logos is generally regarded as the most powerful and important form of proof for facilitating reasoned persuasion in part because it helps us to establish the truthfulness of our assertions and in part because it anchors the other proofs and helps to make them more reasonable. You wouldn't want to accept persuasive advice on important issues based solely on the speaker's reputation or the use of emotional and mythic appeals. We understand this reasoning but caution you not to ignore the importance of the other proofs, even as you prioritize logos. Pure reason, without regard to emotions or shared values, can sometimes lead us to make decisions that are dysfunctional, self-centered, and inhumane. What's more, appeals to logos are almost always more persuasive when supplemented by appeals to ethos, pathos, and mythos. Taken together, each type of proof lends its own strengths and contributions to persuasive speeches. The relationships among these forms of proof are indicated in Figure 14.6.

Using Proofs to Persuade Your Audience

For a topic for your persuasive speech, sketch out how you could use each of the proofs—ethos, pathos, mythos, and logos—to persuade your audience.

SPEAKER'S NOTES

When and How to Use Proof

As you consider which proofs to use in your speech, follow these guidelines:

1. *Ethos:* To reassure listeners that you are knowledgeable, trustworthy, and have their interests at heart
2. *Pathos:* To convey the human dimensions of a problem, with moving examples and stories
3. *Mythos:* To connect your message with your listeners' popular traditions, legends, and symbols
4. *Logos:* To increase understanding with well-reasoned appeals based on facts and statistics, representative examples, and expert testimony

YOUR ETHICAL VOICE

Guidelines for Ethical Persuasion

To earn a reputation as an ethical persuader, follow these guidelines:

1. Avoid name-calling: Attack problems, proposals, and ideas—not people.
2. Be open about your personal interest in the topic.
3. Don't adapt to the point of compromising your convictions.
4. Argue from responsible knowledge.
5. Don't try to pass off opinions or inferences as facts.
6. Don't use inflammatory language to hide a lack of evidence.
7. Be sure your proposal is in the best interests of your audience.
8. Remember, words can hurt.

Final Reflections: The Value of Persuasion

Recall the words of Isocrates that began this chapter. For Isocrates, the impulse to persuade was vital to the emerging nature of humanity, making possible what we now call *cultural evolution.* Persuasion, he felt, lifts us above the wild beasts in that it allows us to inspire others and resolve our disputes by words rather than by fists. Persuasion encourages cooperation and consent to bring people together, living in communities governed by laws rather than by brute force. Persuasion promotes commercial enterprises, social arrangements, and the advancement of knowledge. For Isocrates, persuasion was the key to civilization.

This chapter embraces the value of persuasion. Ethical persuasion helps us decide conflicts over facts, encourages more humane attitudes, helps correct flawed beliefs, and makes us take our values more seriously. Improving as persuaders requires that we develop a practical understanding of listeners' needs that allows us to soften opposition, convert doubters, and energize partisans. We become, as Isocrates would say, more effective human beings.

A final justification for persuasion is that we persuade because we have an ethical duty and imperative to speak. In finding our voice, we find causes to support and meaning for our lives. Not to speak, not to persuade, would deny our reasons for being. Sojourner Truth embraced that imperative more than 150 years ago when she declared, "Ain't I a woman?" Lindsey Yoder accepted that responsibility as an opportunity in her speech on sex trafficking. If you do not find and use your voice, who will?[17]

Study Questions

CONTENT MASTERY

1 What are the ethical considerations involved in persuasive speaking?

2 What are the five phases of the persuasive process?

3 What are the three major types of persuasive speaking?

4 What designs are especially appropriate for persuasive speaking?

5 What are the four proofs, and how can they help you construct persuasive messages?

CRITICAL EXPLORATIONS

1. Keep a log for one day, and record all moments when you persuade or are persuaded. Analyze these moments. Consider the following questions:
   a. What kinds of messages do the work of persuasion?
   b. How effective was the persuasion?
   c. What kinds of appeals work best for you?
   d. When are you most resistant to persuasion?
   e. How important is persuasion in your life?
2. Watch a persuasive speech on TED or YouTube. Identify the stages of the persuasive process activated during the speech. How effective was the speaker in moving the process along and making persuasion work? How could the speaker have done a better job?
3. Attend a local government meeting (e.g., student government, city or county council, or zoning board), and analyze the persuasive speeches you hear. Do the speakers argue over past, present, or future facts? Do their speeches concern attitudes, beliefs, and values? Do they propose actions? How effective are they, and why?
4. Analyze a set of advertisements for a single product category (e.g., shampoo, cars, or clothing). What proofs do they use? How effectively do they use them? What proofs do not tend to be used, and why? How would the advertisements change if you altered the proofs employed?
5. Find a speech by someone you admire, and consider its use of appeals to mythos. You might choose a historic figure like Ronald Reagan, a renowned activist such as Dolores Huerta, or any number of contemporary figures. As you read, look for references to heroic deeds, words, shared narratives, and the values they embody. How does the speaker use these appeals to strengthen his or her persuasive message?
6. Find a website for Social Venture Partners, which has multiple chapters across the country. Watch three of the videos for their SEED20 competition, through which social entrepreneurs seek funding for their nonprofit organizations in three-minute speeches. How does the discussion of ethics in this chapter apply to their appeals? What stage of the persuasive process do they target, and how? What type of persuasive speech is each one? What persuasive design do they use? How do they use the four proofs?

PERSUASIVE SPEECH

Lindsey Yoder was a junior at the University of Memphis when she gave the following speech to her public speaking class. The speech, selected for the Osborn Public Speaking contest, won first prize in that competition Soon, word of its quality reached community organizers active in the campaign against human trafficking. Lindsey was invited to speak at a rally sponsored by the local police department and area churches, right in the heart of territory notorious for such activities. What had started as a simple class assignment had become magnified beyond the moment: In terms used in her speech, the words that started as ripples had now become waves.

QUIET SCREAMS

LINDSEY YODER

Reprinted with permission from Lindsey Yoder.

Imagine yourself living during the time of slavery when African Americans were tortured, beaten, and lynched. Surely we all would be a part of the abolitionist movement that fought for their freedom. We would not leave human injustice in the dark.

Lindsey's speech begins by framing an analogy between the slavery suffered by African Americans before the Civil War and modern-day sex slavery as endured by victims of human trafficking. Her appeal is to deep values of listeners; consequently, the speech can be viewed as an appeal to attitudes and values.

Today, we are taught in our history classes that slavery ended with the Civil War. However, the quiet screams of present day slaves are all around us. According to enditmovement.com, there is more slavery in the world today than ever before. What we just imagined is not a hypothetical situation: it is our reality!

In January of this year, I attended an annual Christian conference in Atlanta called Passion. I walked into the Georgia Dome expecting to hear some of my favorite speakers and performers. I had no idea that I would soon become part of something much bigger than myself. Louie Giglio, the leader of the Passion movement, informed us—66,000 of us—about modern slavery.

There are, he said, 27 million slaves in the world today. In America alone, there are approximately 200,000, and every year 17,500 more will be sold in sex trafficking. I want you to imagine now being forced to work for someone day in and day out, only to get in return verbal, physical, and sexual abuse. No family to turn to, no friends, no one even knows you are there. Nothing belongs to you. You belong to someone else. Hundreds of thousands are trapped in this scenario.

Lindsey assumed that her audience was initially uncommitted on her topic, that listeners were indifferent because they lacked information and had not yet connected her cause to their feelings and beliefs. Here she offers vital information on the magnitude of the problem and appeals to listeners' imaginations to picture themselves as victims. In short, her major supporting materials were statistics and narratives to heighten the importance and emotional impact of her topic.

You may not care about modern slavery, but what if it were your mom? Brother? Best friend? What if it were you? If your heart does not hurt yet for these modern slaves, I hope it will by the end of my presentation.

Modern slavery is not sexy or appealing. There are no beautiful pictures to show, no humor to enjoy. Many want to avoid this issue because it doesn't make us feel good. It would be much easier to ignore it. But we can avoid this no longer. I am going to tell you how victims get caught up in modern slavery, why it is such a huge market in the U.S., and where exactly this is going on.

I would like you to meet a dear friend of mine, I will call her Kelley. When she was a child, her father began abusing her mentally and physically. By the time she was twelve, he was molesting her. He would tell her she was nothing and would never amount to anything. By the age of twenty, she was a modern slave. During that dark time, no one heard her quiet screams.

I shared Kelley's testimony so that you would understand how people just like you and me are caught up in slavery each day. People who feel unnoticed, alone, and abused. They search for acceptance, and the twenty-first-century slave traders find them. They seek them out like predators on prey. They are looking for these lost and unhappy souls that are everywhere. They find, persuade, and trick victims into believing they can provide a glamorous lifestyle. These slave traders *are* appealing and sexy. They reel the unsuspecting lost souls in by promising happiness, money, and companionship. Soon, we have yet another slave in today's world.

Having raised awareness of the problem, Lindsey extends the persuasive process by increasing the audience's understanding of how it comes about: how people become trapped into sexual slavery and what the motivations are that drive modern slave traders. Her story of her friend is especially compelling.

On *womensfundingnetwork.org*, you can find information on the Polaris Project, a nonprofit anti-trafficking organization. The Project described a man in Washington, D.C., who "owned" three slaves. Every day they would bring home to him

$500 to $2,000, approximately $24,000 every month, *all cash—tax free!* On *harrahpolicedept.com,* the FBI estimates human trafficking annually generates $9.5 billion worldwide. The demand is high because the resale value is high. You can only sell drugs once, but humans, you can sell over and over.

It is one thing to know that a serious problem exists, quite another to know that it exists in your neighborhood. That awareness is often the motivation for listeners to act. As she moves to her conclusion, Lindsey asks for the audience's involvement. But her program for action seems a bit scattered and vague. She needs to tell listeners in clearer terms what they can do: What action, for example, should they urge the university to take? How exactly could listeners join and participate in the "End It Movement"?

Furthermore, modern slavery is going on all over the world. It was easy for me to avoid getting involved until Kelley told me her story, and I suddenly realized it is all around me. She is part of an organization, Ashes to Beauty, that works here in Memphis. Yes, right here in Memphis! She is saving girls from exactly what she went through. Television website *abc24.com* recently highlighted the local hot spots for sex trafficking: Sam Cooper Boulevard, Memphis International Airport, and Wolfchase Mall Galleria. These are the top three areas where people are being picked up, transported, and sold. *Wmctv.com* says that in the last quarter of 2010 over 1,900 ads were posted on *backpage.com* listing women for sale *right here in Memphis.*

Modern slavery exists without the majority of us even being aware of it. But some of us are fighting to free these slaves. This year at Passion our youth group raised over $3 million to support seven organizations fighting the fight in different ways. You can learn more about these organizations on the Enditmovement website. In addition, the Clinton Global Initiative is now interceding for today's slaves, and President Obama has signed an executive order to strengthen our hand against trafficking.

Still, the battle to end human trafficking is hard and uphill. These organizations can't do it without our help. As the Osborn textbook says, "words make ripples, and ripples can come together to make waves." My words alone will not have much effect, but when we all speak together, the impact can be great. Think of what we, as a university, could do to help end modern slavery. We can keep these organizations going by supporting them as much as we can, but we can also take an active part. Join the "End It Movement." Draw a red X on your hand symbolizing your stand on modern slavery. On Instagram, Twitter, and Facebook, use the hashtag *enditmovement*. The more people who become aware of this injustice, the sooner modern slavery will come to an end.

Lindsey concludes her speech with an eloquent quotation that develops the enduring metaphor of light and darkness introduced in her opening. She makes effective use of parallel construction to end the speech with a powerful and graceful plea.

I wish I could end slavery today, but I cannot. Not alone. Change begins with one person, but it cannot stop there. Norman B. Rice, mayor of Seattle, once said, "Dare to reach out your hand into the darkness, to pull another hand into the light." The quiet screams of our people call to us desperately. Let us be the generation to hear them. Let us be the generation to change the world. Let us be the generation to end modern slavery.

Building Persuasive Arguments

CHAPTER

LEARNING OBJECTIVES	OUTLINE
This chapter will help you:	
15.1 Focus persuasive issues and gather evidence.	Focusing Issues and Gathering Evidence
15.2 Understand the process of constructing persuasive arguments.	Structuring Persuasive Arguments
15.3 Use various patterns of persuasive reasoning to support persuasive speeches.	Patterns of Reasoning
15.4 Address the challenges of persuading reluctant listeners.	Persuading Reluctant Listeners
15.5 Avoid common fallacies that undermine persuasive arguments.	Avoiding Defective Persuasion

"Ours is the bravery of people who think through what they will take in hand, and discuss it thoroughly."

—PERICLES

Carlos woke up early in his dorm room the morning of the big debate. He rubbed the sleep from his eyes, scratched his head, and turned on his computer when suddenly his mind snapped into focus. This was the day that the Student Council, to which he had recently been elected, was scheduled to discuss and vote on a motion to endorse the administration's call for a stronger antidiscrimination policy. He knew that many of his fellow representatives on the Council were inclined to support the idea, and he shared their concerns over recent allegations of sexism and racial bigotry on campus. Yet he was concerned the proposal would amount to a thinly veiled "speech code" that would put a chill on freedom of expression, and he was convinced it would not survive the legal challenges that were sure to follow. Carlos felt he had to speak up, but how could he argue against an idea his listeners seemed predisposed to support? How could he engage their reasons for supporting the new policy and steer their shared concerns in the direction of discussing alternative solutions for promoting a more inclusive atmosphere for all students?

Carlos' predicament represents one of the most formidable challenges to finding your voice as a public speaker. It is easy enough to discuss disputed issues with trusted friends and family who usually agree with us, but quite another to engage the concerns of skeptical listeners constructively and on their own terms. Most of us may not like to think of ourselves as "argumentative," but all of us have core values, interests, and commitments. Whether it's debating the nature and causes of gun violence in our society, funding or defunding Planned Parenthood, or proposals for promoting diversity and tolerance on your college campus, all of us feel compelled to speak out on controversial issues from time to time.

Still, few of us are as good at arguing effectively and ethically as we could or should be. Perhaps this is due to the understandable cynicism that so many of us have about the quality of public discourse in our times, or perhaps it is due to a lack of emphasis on teaching the processes of critical thinking and practical reasoning. Closer to home, perhaps it is because we care so passionately about some issues that we have a hard time appreciating that good people may have their own reasons to disagree with us. In either case, you have so much to gain by developing your ability to construct persuasive arguments. Not only will it equip you to better defend your convictions and interests in the context of public debates, but learning to engage controversial issues constructively will help you to manage personal conflicts and build better relationships, and it will enhance perceptions of your ethos and leadership potential in the workplace and other organizational settings.

In the previous chapter, we discussed the ethics, process, types, designs, and proofs of persuasive speaking in general. In this chapter, we focus on building strong persuasive arguments. We start with a brief primer on focusing persuasive issues and gathering evidence, and then address the process of constructing coherent and well-reasoned arguments and various patterns of reasoning. We then discuss some special challenges of engaging skeptical or reluctant listeners, and close by addressing some common fallacies that often undermine our efforts at effective and ethical argumentation.

Focusing Issues and Gathering Evidence

15.1 Focus persuasive issues and gather evidence.

As with any presentation, the first step in preparing a persuasive argument is to choose a general area of importance or concern to you, do some preliminary reading, and then focus on a specific question or issue. Your next step is to gather evidence to frame that issue.

Focusing Your Persuasive Issue

As we discussed in Chapter 6, the more focused and specific your topic area, the more likely you are to offer your listeners fresh ideas and information to consider. With persuasive speeches, your general convictions about controversies can be focused on the latest proposals or local applications. For instance, if you were interested in immigration, you might focus on a recent measure restricting entry into the United States or a dispute in your local area over hosting refugees. If you were interested in gun control, you might consider the latest proposals for banning assault weapons or expanding the use of background checks for gun purchases.

In Chapter 7, we discussed the process of acquiring responsible knowledge on your topics: understanding the basic facts and important issues, what the most respected authorities and advocates have to say, the latest and local developments of relevance, and how your subject might affect the lives of your listeners. Once you have developed a strong overview of your subject area, focus on your specific issue and the more prominent arguments for and against it. For instance, if you wanted to argue in favor of banning future sales of assault weapons, you would probably emphasize the high rate of gun violence in our society, the use of such weapons in highly publicized mass shootings, and the fact that they are intended for combat rather than legitimate sporting or home protection. On the other hand, opponents will likely cite their interpretation of the Constitution as guaranteeing them the right to keep and bear arms, refer to statistics showing that most gun crimes are committed with hand guns and not assault weapons, and contend that the vast majority of people who own such weapons are simply gun enthusiasts who use them for recreational purposes.

Gathering Evidence

Once you have determined the specific issue you want to address and identified the most prominent positions on its various sides, you should begin the process of gathering specific information for your presentation. It is important to be critically vigilant when researching disputed issues. If a number of people are arguing about your subject, you are bound to encounter a lot of partisan fake news and blatant disinformation, especially on social media. Read a variety of sources, explore perspectives for a balanced understanding, and critique your sources of information in terms of the 4 Rs: *relevance, representativeness, recency*, and *reliability*. Always consider the credibility and timeliness of your sources, and be sure to correlate anything you find on obscure activist sites with more reputable sources of news and information. Consciously resist the temptation to simply accept or reject ideas and information based on whether it confirms what you already believe. Finally, and perhaps most important: Read with an open mind, and don't decide where you stand on any specific proposition until you know it well enough to make that decision responsibly. Don't be like the state legislator who recently sponsored a bill to restrict abortions while admitting that he'd "never even thought about" why a woman might seek one.[1]

As noted in the previous chapter, your ability to use and interpret information effectively and ethically is crucial to all persuasive speaking. What serves as *supporting material* for informative speeches becomes *evidence* in persuasive speeches, reinforcing your claims and engaging opposing positions. Consider the forms of supporting information discussed in Chapter 8 and how you might use them as evidence for persuasive arguments.

Facts and Figures. Because facts are statements or assertions that can be verified as true or false by observation or independent experts, they offer an assumed credibility that can be invaluable in persuasion. Convincing your listeners that "the facts are in your favor" can be very influential. Statistics can be especially powerful because they offer mathematical measurements for gauging public opinion and assessing the extent or trajectory of problems. For instance, if you wanted to argue in favor of banning sales of assault weapons, you might look for credible facts and figures on their use in mass shootings over the past few years, and the growth of popular support for banning future sales.

Remember that the facts never speak for themselves. As the famous historian Carl Becker noted, "Left to themselves, the facts do not speak; left to themselves, they do not exist, not really, since for all practical purposes there is no fact until someone affirms it."[2] You want to show your listeners how the meaning of the facts and statistics support your assertions. Your facts will be more persuasive when they come from highly respected sources of information and when you cite the credentials of your sources orally while speaking. In addition, consciously distinguish the *facts* you encounter from the *opinions* or *inferences* drawn from them so that you don't conflate factual statements with judgments based on them.

Testimony. Persuasive arguments draw heavily on the use of testimony from recognized experts. Citing them lends borrowed ethos, particularly to speakers who are not already recognized authorities on a subject. Expert testimony can be especially useful for explaining the nature, causes, and likely implications of a problem or situation as well as defending the viability of disputed solutions. For a speech in support of a ban on sales of assault weapons, you might cite law enforcement experts on their accessibility to terrorists and criminal gangs, or medical experts on their destructive capacity. Remember that expertise is subject-specific; for example, most physicians aren't knowledgeable about the uses of assault weapons in combat. Stress the specific qualifications of your cited experts, and consider how they might be received by skeptical listeners. Finally, be sure to paraphrase or quote expert sources carefully, without twisting or misrepresenting their intended meaning by taking their words out of context.

reluctant witnesses
Witnesses who testify against their apparent self-interest.

While less prevalent with persuasive speaking, prestige and lay testimony can also be useful. Citing the founding fathers might add an element of proof by mythos to challenge contemporary interpretations of the constitutional right to bear arms. So could the lay testimony of victims or survivors of mass shootings, or combat veterans who know the destructive capacity of assault weapons. If you can find it, cite testimony from **reluctant witnesses**, sources more often associated with people or groups opposed to your proposition. Proponents of an assault weapons ban have repeatedly cited the words of former President Ronald Reagan, an extremely popular conservative who was known for his support of gun rights. In 1994, Reagan penned an open letter to Congress in support of a ban, arguing that "statistics prove that we can dry up the supply of these guns, making them less accessible to criminals."[3]

Gathering Evidence For Your Speech

Identify one fact or statistic, one piece of expert testimony, and one example or narrative that you could use for your upcoming persuasive speech. What value would each one bring to your presentation? What additional evidence would you like to gather for the speech?

Examples and Narratives. Examples and narratives provide concrete illustrations that help to authenticate or clarify persuasive messages. For instance, the examples or narrated experiences of actual victims of mass shootings, or perpetrators who purchased their weapons *legally* just prior to committing atrocities, might be particularly effective in support of a ban on assault weapons. While you should not use such references as a substitute for hard facts and expert opinions, they can help to involve your listeners at an emotional level and move them to action. As discussed in Chapters 8 and 16, narratives are particularly useful for invoking core values and establishing identification with listeners.

After five of his officers were killed by an angry gunman, Dallas Police Chief David Brown reached out to protestors to join with police officers to help address the problems in their community.

Because of their capacity to involve listeners and engage attention, examples and narratives are often used in the introductions of persuasive speeches to establish the desired predisposition in the audience. Wherever you use them, they should be compelling and lively, with concrete details and vividly descriptive language. Re-creating conversations with precise quotations or dialogue will be more striking than paraphrasing. As a general rule, factual examples and stories are more suitable for persuasive speaking, but hypothetical examples and figurative narratives can be effective when real illustrations are not available or appropriate. They can also invite listeners to envision the future consequences of accepting or not accepting your advice. In addition to being compelling and relevant, examples and narratives should ring true for your listeners as representative of the larger reality you are addressing rather than the exception to the rule.

As you gather evidence for persuasive speaking, keep in mind your twin objectives of establishing your main assertions and adapting them to the interests and inclinations of your listeners. What materials will make the biggest impression on them? What sources of information are they likely to find most credible? What will answer the questions they may have on this issue? Use a combination of facts, expert opinions, and factual examples from a variety of credible sources, especially when addressing skeptical listeners. Cite your sources orally, and stress their credentials. Finally, make it a point to gather more information than you will use to support your most disputed assertions, especially if your listeners will have the opportunity to ask questions after your presentation.

YOUR ETHICAL VOICE

Guidelines for the Ethical Use of Evidence

To use evidence ethically, follow these guidelines:

1. Provide evidence from credible sources.
2. Identify your sources of evidence in your speech.
3. Use evidence that can stand up under critical scrutiny.
4. Be sure evidence has not been tainted by self-interest.
5. Acknowledge disagreements among experts.
6. Do not withhold important evidence.
7. Use expert testimony to establish facts, explain issues, and promote solutions.
8. Quote or paraphrase testimony accurately.
9. Use examples that are representative of the issue.

Structuring Persuasive Arguments

15.2 Understand the process of constructing persuasive arguments.

Once you have focused your persuasive issue and gathered your evidence, you can begin the process of building your argument. A **persuasive argument** may be defined as a disputed proposition supported with reasoning and evidence. Strong persuasive arguments concentrate on building a case that will justify taking an action or adopting a point of view. They offer listeners a clear structure that invites them to examine the speaker's reasoning process.

persuasive argument
A disputed proposition supported with reasoning and evidence.

One of the most popular models for distinguishing the components and structure of persuasive arguments, from the British empiricist Stephen Toulmin, suggests that well-reasoned arguments include three core components: a *claim* or proposition, *evidence* to support the claim, and *warrants* that show how your evidence connects to your claim. These, in turn, are often elaborated by the use of *backing* to further support your warrants, and *qualifiers* that limit the certainty of your claims or recognize circumstances under which they might not apply.[4] Let's take a closer look at each of these elements and consider the role each one plays in a persuasive argument.

claim
The central point or proposition of an argument.

Claim. The **claim** is the point of your argument; it is the disputed proposition or assertion that you ask your listeners to accept. As with any thesis statement, you should be focused enough to state your main and supporting claims as concise deliberative sentences before proceeding to construct the rest of your argument. For instance, if you wanted to support a graduated license that would raise the minimum age for driving without restrictions, you might make the supporting argument that it would reduce the number of auto fatalities.

evidence
Information used in support of persuasive claims.

Evidence. As discussed in the previous section, **evidence** consists of the facts and statistics, testimony, examples, and narratives as used to support persuasive claims. To argue in support of a graduated driver's license, you might look for facts and statistics to document the disproportionate numbers of young people involved in fatal accidents, testimony from experts in law enforcement and driving instruction, and examples of horrific accidents involving young drivers or of states that have seen their driving mortality rates decline after implementing similar policies.

warrant
The stated or implied reasoning that shows how evidence connects to a persuasive claim.

Warrant. Your **warrant** provides the reasoning that shows how your evidence supports your claim, *warranting* the claim by establishing a connection between the two. Warrants provide the conceptual link between evidence and claim through such resources as shared values, commonly held beliefs, or arguments you have already established for your listeners. Our claim that a graduated driver's license would reduce the number of auto fatalities is based on at least three implied warrants: (1) we should try to reduce auto fatalities; (2) young, unrestricted drivers are a major cause of auto fatalities; and (3) restricting their driving privileges would actually reduce the number of auto fatalities.

backing
Additional evidence and reasoning to support disputed warrants.

Backing. As you develop the warrants connecting your evidence to your claim, give careful consideration to which ones your listeners may readily accept and which ones they are likely to find disputable. When listeners are apt to question a warrant or its relevance to your claim, then you should state it explicitly and provide **backing** or additional evidence and reasoning to support it. If you were arguing for a graduated license, you could probably assume that most listeners would make the connection that auto fatalities should be reduced, although you might want to provide some evidence to establish the extent or growth of the problem. However, and especially if you are addressing a younger audience with an obvious stake in your proposition, you should probably give considerable attention to backing the assumption that younger drivers are to blame for a disproportionate number of auto fatalities, or that restricting their privileges would actually decrease the number of deadly accidents.

qualifiers
Terms or statements that limit the certainty of your claims.

reservations
Qualifiers that recognize circumstances under which claims may not apply.

Qualifiers. **Qualifiers** are terms or statements that limit the certainty of your claim and are often signaled by the use of terms such as *probably* or *in all likelihood*. For instance, you might qualify an argument for a graduated license by suggesting it would *probably* reduce the number of auto fatalities, while acknowledging that other factors are at play and we can never know for certain how any proposal will shape the future. Often signaled by terms such as *unless* or *except*, **reservations** are special qualifiers that recognize circumstances under which a claim would not apply. For instance, you might argue for a graduated license "unless beginning drivers are required to take a certified course in driver's education."

While it may sound ironic, you can actually strengthen the persuasiveness of your arguments by intelligently recognizing their limitations or their specificity to a given set of circumstances. When we debate specific proposals such as signing a free trade treaty, raising or cutting sales taxes to fund educational initiatives, or improving police relations with disadvantaged communities, we are not dealing with the realm of certainty or absolute truths that apply equally in all situations. When we acknowledge as much in the course of arguing our assertions, we demonstrate a complexity of knowledge and thoughtful appreciation that will impress intelligent and discerning listeners—even those who ultimately choose not to agree with our arguments or act on our advice.

Toulmin's model of argumentation can be particularly useful for sketching out your reasoning. Much like an outline, it allows you to envision the structure of your argument as you construct it. Figure 15.1 illustrates the process by which persuasive speakers move from providing evidence, to stating warrants and (as necessary) offering backing to support them, to qualifying your assertions as appropriate, to establishing your persuasive claim. Constructing your own model will help you identify aspects that need to be strengthened before you present your arguments. You may realize that you have not shown how your evidence supports your claim or how differing circumstances might modify your claim. You can also use Toulmin's model as a critical template to help you become a more thoughtful, insightful listener.

Figure 15.1 Toulmin's Model of Argument

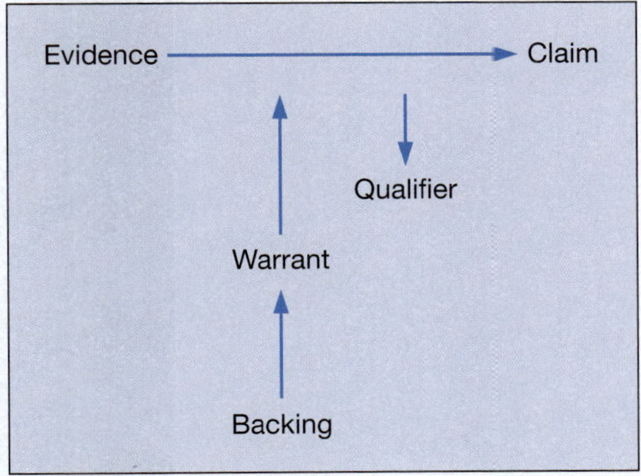

Ethical persuasion *invites* rather than *avoids* careful inspection. Think about it: you don't want to be manipulated into accepting a position. With effective, ethical arguments, such as those we can construct with Toulmin's model, we regard the audience as thinking human beings who can help us better understand the issue by their thoughtful responses. We aim for long-range commitments that will endure in the face of counterattacks. We honor civilized deliberation over verbal mudslinging, and judgment over impulses. We address our full humanity as thinking as well as feeling beings. Reason without feeling can be cold and heartless, but feeling without reason is shallow and fleeting. It is the *blend* of passion and reason that can help you find your voice.

Building an Argument Using Toulmin's Model

Select one claim for your upcoming persuasive speech, and build an argument to support it using Toulmin's model.

Finding Your Voice

Developing Your Argument

Find a news story with valuable information for your upcoming persuasive speech. Consider the following questions:

- What kind of evidence does it offer? How could you use this information as evidence to support a persuasive claim?
- What warrants should you state?
- What backing would strengthen the warrant by offering further reasoning and evidence?
- How could you better focus your argument by qualifying your claim?

Patterns of Reasoning

15.3 Use various patterns of persuasive reasoning to support persuasive speeches.

As you read through the previous section, you may have found yourself thinking, "This is really interesting and useful for analyzing arguments and gathering persuasive resources, but do effective speakers always develop such a structured and linear train of thought when addressing disputed issues?" The answer to that question, of course, is no. While all arguments should have the basic elements of claims, evidence, and warrants, those elements can be used in a variety of ways. Five of the

When persuaders find their voices, the moment can often be quite dramatic and illuminating.

most popular patterns of reasoning are *framing your issue, deductive reasoning, inductive reasoning, causal reasoning*, and *reasoning by analogy*.

Framing Your Issue

Have you ever had a heated discussion with someone, only to discover later that the two of you were not even talking about the same thing? When speakers and listeners don't share a common framework of understanding, it is difficult to communicate effectively. As we discussed in Chapter 11, the language you use shapes perceptions in powerful ways. If speakers and audiences come from different backgrounds, careful definitions create common understandings from which to work. Critics of "global warming" argue that severe winters contradict that term; in response, others suggest that the more accurate term is "climate change," in which we experience greater and greater extremes of both heat and cold. Opening his speech on "gender bending," Brandon Rader started with the following definition: "If you are a gender bender, you dress or act or think or talk like people in your community assume someone of the opposite sex would act or dress or talk." Having shared this understanding, Brandon went on to argue that most assumptions about gender benders are wrong. Brandon's definition at the beginning of his speech was essential.

As we discussed in the previous chapter, persuasive speeches often open with a narrative that is intended to frame the audience's perceptions of your issue in a manner that will predispose them to accept or appreciate your message. When artfully presented, a startling fact, quotation, example, or story can be really effective for setting the desired mood. Even simple definitions can help to frame audience perceptions. Is drug addiction a disease or a criminal act? Is an unborn fetus a human being? Is leaking classified government documents an act of treason or patriotism? In the 1968 Memphis sanitation workers' strike, which led to the assassination of Dr. Martin Luther King, Jr., the workers carried signs stating "I AM A MAN." This simple definition was the basis of a complex moral argument. The strikers asserted that they had *not* been treated like men in social, political, and economic terms.

The sanitation workers, whose strike was marred by the assassination of Martin Luther King, Jr., used the words "I AM A MAN" to effectively frame their issue.

Finding Your Voice

Controversies over Definitions

In *The Ethics of Rhetoric*, Richard Weaver observed that controversy over definitions of basic terms is a sign of social and cultural division.[5] Consider examples of disagreement over the definitions of the following terms in contemporary arguments:

1. socialism
2. marijuana
3. gun rights
4. abortion
5. government
6. feminism

Do these disagreements reflect the kind of social division Weaver suggested? Can understanding these disagreements help you find your voice?

Deductive Reasoning: Arguing from Principles

deductive reasoning
Arguing from a general principle to a specific conclusion.

With **deductive reasoning**, we reason on the basis of principles, using commonly accepted beliefs and shared values to warrant our conclusions.[6] We start with a principle, relate some specific subject to it, and draw from that relationship a conclusion about what we should do or think about the subject. Dolapo Olushola, for example, began by reminding listeners of a principle she believed they all would accept: "Children have the right to food, clothing, medical care, and loving care " Next, she offered a specific case related as evidence: "Staggering numbers of HIV/AIDS orphans in sub-Saharan Africa are left hungry, homeless, ill, and without care." Finally, she presented her claim: "We must support the Open Arms Orphanage in Malawi to give orphaned children their basic rights."

Reasoning from general principles helps establish common ground with your listeners. It can also help to leverage the power of cognitive dissonance as discussed in the previous chapter by pointing out inconsistencies between our values and our behaviors. For example, if you can demonstrate that a given proposal is inconsistent with the value your listeners place on individual freedom or environmental stewardship, then you will have provided powerful reasoning to accept your claim. *We are more likely to change a practice or attitude that is inconsistent with our principles and values than we are to change our principles and values.*

You want to invoke principles that your listeners will accept as important to them, and then help your audience accept your specific applications as relevant to those principles. A lot of people agree *in principle* with the value of social equality, environmental protection, and hard work, but they may disagree considerably on their applications to specific issues and challenging situations. In making the move from accepted principles to contested cases, focus your persuasive efforts on demonstrating the existence of relevant conditions through the use of evidence, and emphasize their connection to shared values and beliefs.

As you develop a deductive argument, ask yourself:

- Will my audience accept the principle on which I base the argument?
- How can I demonstrate the existence of relevant conditions through strong evidence?
- Am I demonstrating the connection between the principle and the evidence with clear warrants?
- Should I add backing to support the warrant between the principle and the evidence?
- Would my argument be strengthened by adding a qualifier?

Inductive Reasoning: Arguing from the Specific Case

inductive reasoning
Reasoning from specific factual instances to reach a general conclusion.

While deductive reasoning starts from a general principle and moves to a specific observation and conclusion, **inductive reasoning** starts with a close examination of the particulars—the facts and the exact circumstances—relevant to the specific case and then moves to an overall claim. We either make these observations ourselves or depend on experts who have made them for us; the important consideration is to demonstrate a commanding knowledge of your specific situation before moving to any general conclusions.

Austin Wright's speech opposing the use of faulty databases for compiling information on Americans suspected of terrorist sympathies—reprinted in full at the end of this chapter—provides an excellent example of inductive reasoning. While he does make a single reference to our "personal liberties" being at risk, the rest of his speech focuses exclusively on documenting abusive and careless practices by the companies contracted to compile the databases, examples of innocent people whose lives have been severely affected, and seemingly inexplicable court decisions allowing these abuses to proceed unchecked. The following passage demonstrates Austin's inductive prowess:

> The *Los Angeles Times* of January 27, 2006, explains that these companies also have a reputation for losing information. In 2005, for instance, Choicepoint's data system was breached by con artists, compromising more than 19 billion individual files, including social security numbers and financial histories. Although a 2007 Javelin Strategy and Research report finds that identity theft costs victims an average of $5,000, the government forced Choicepoint to pay out a mere $15 million in damages. That's an average of less than one tenth of one cent for each person whose private information was leaked by Choicepoint.

As you develop inductive reasoning for your arguments, ask yourself these questions:

- Are you taking a balanced perspective on the issues? Are you considering them from as many perspectives as possible?
- Can you present a reasonable number of observations? One or two isolated incidents cannot justify disputed claims.
- Are your observations current?
- Do your examples accurately represent the situation? The exception does not prove the rule.
- Do your specific cases justify your conclusion?
- Does your evidence come from experts, and do you establish their credentials for your audience?

While deductive and inductive reasoning are usually treated as mutually exclusive, they often work together when arguing persuasive issues. Speakers addressing like-minded listeners might lean in the direction of emphasizing shared principles, and speakers addressing skeptical listeners tend to emphasize hard facts, expert opinions, and factual examples; but the most effective arguments tend to work by emphasizing shared principles and disciplined observations simultaneously. The use of evidence is illuminated and made meaningful by its relevance to shared beliefs and principles, and abstract principles become real when we consider them in light of actual situations and specific evidence.

Causal Reasoning

In Chapter 13, we treated causation as an important design for informative speaking that addresses the causes of important events and developments, and in Chapter 14 we discussed its use in persuasive speaking that develops a problem–solution design. When addressing disturbing developments such as climate change or high rates of gun violence on American streets, we naturally look to and dispute the causes of those developments as an important precursor to assessing responsibility, predicting future developments, and debating the relative merits of proposed solutions. Is human pollution a primary cause of climate change? Or is climate change the result of a natural cycle and ultimately beyond our control? Does fracking cause earthquakes, or is the correlation between the two coincidental? The ability to make causal attributions on such issues often becomes a powerful source of persuasive reasoning.

On disputed issues, the most persuasive causal arguments are developed inductively. Speakers typically open by establishing the nature and scope of a problematic situation, or *effect*, and then proceed to address attributions of *causation*. As with all inductive reasoning, the success of your argument will likely turn on your listeners' perceptions of the quality and sufficiency of your evidence. The opinions of experts accepted by your audience are crucial to supporting attributions of causation. Facts and statistics can establish the scope and evolution of a problematic situation, and examples can illustrate its real-life consequences. Keep in mind that most problematic developments are considerably more complicated than any single cause. For example, is gun violence caused by the ready accessibility of guns in our society? Or are other factors to blame, such as poor mental health care, violence in popular culture, poverty, or a decline in family values? Or is it a combination of these? Always consider whether attributions of causation should be qualified when addressing issues that are still uncertain and fiercely contested. Finally, be particularly careful about confusing *cause* and *correlation*—a common fallacy discussed later in this chapter. The consumption of both ice cream and heart attacks increases during the summer, but that doesn't make ice cream a leading cause of heart attacks!

Analogical Reasoning

analogical reasoning
Creating a strategic perspective on a subject by relating it to something similar.

We use **analogical reasoning** when we address a threatening situation or a disputed proposal by comparing it to similar situations or proposals and drawing lessons from the similarities. Such reasoning can illuminate the new and unfamiliar in terms of what your listeners know and understand. To the extent that your audience accepts the essential similarity of what is being compared, reasoning by analogy can be a powerful source of persuasive argument.

In his speech before the American Medical Association, Dr. Richard Corlin used a vivid analogy to demonstrate how video games set the stage for a culture of gun violence. His use of analogical reasoning helped listeners understand his view of the problem:

> I want you to imagine with me a computer game called "Puppy Shoot." In this game, puppies run across the screen. Using a joystick, the game player aims a gun that shoots the puppies. The player is awarded one point for a flesh wound, three points for a body shot, and ten points for a head shot. Blood spurts out each time a puppy is hit—and brain tissue splatters all over whenever there's a head shot. The dead puppies pile up at the bottom of the screen. When the shooter gets to 1,000 points, he gets to exchange his pistol for an Uzi, and the point values go up.
>
> If a game as disgusting as that were to be developed, every animal rights group in the country, along with a lot of other organizations, would protest, and there would be all sorts of attempts made to get the game taken off the market. Yet, if you just change puppies to people in the game I described, there are dozens of them already on the market—sold under such names as "Blood Bath," "Psycho Toxic," "Redneck Rampage," and "Soldier of Fortune."[7]

Just as analogical reasoning can dramatize arguments, it can also be used to persuade listeners to accept solutions. Historic analogies offer particularly powerful sources of persuasive reasoning because they suggest that we should follow (or avoid)

Using Patterns of Reasoning to Make Your Argument

Identify a single issue from your upcoming persuasive speech, and show how you could use at least two of the patterns of reasoning identified in this section to make your argument.

the lessons of the past. Those who favor legalizing recreational drug use, for example, often base their arguments on an analogy to Prohibition.[8] They claim that Prohibition caused more problems than it solved because it glamorized drinking and led to a rise in organized crime. Moreover, they assert that legalizing drugs would help put the international drug dealers out of business, just as the repeal of Prohibition helped bring about the downfall of similar gangsters during the 1930s.

What makes analogical reasoning work? It is similar to inductive reasoning in that it seeks insight through observation, but it concentrates on *one similar situation* rather than *many*. This means that, although it seems more concrete than some forms of inductive reasoning, it can also be less reliable. Before you decide to use an analogy as part of your argument, be sure that the similarities outweigh the dissimilarities. If you have to strain to make an analogy fit, that's a sign that you should investigate another analogy or another form of reasoning.

Out of these various patterns of reasoning—framing your issue, deductive, inductive, causal, and analogical—you should be able to weave compelling arguments that make your case for the position you are defending.

SPEAKER'S NOTES

Using Persuasive Reasoning

To build strong arguments, follow these guidelines:

1. Provide clear definitions of basic terms.
2. Justify arguments with deductive reasoning based on accepted principles.
3. Use inductive reasoning to demonstrate the reality of your argument.
4. Use causal reasoning to explain the origins of problematic situations and suggest conclusions.
5. Use analogical reasoning to draw comparisons that clarify your position.

Persuading Reluctant Listeners

15.4 Address the challenges of persuading reluctant listeners.

Think about it: How often have you been persuaded by someone to actually change your mind on an important issue or do something you were not already predisposed to do? One of the biggest challenges of persuasive speaking is learning to adapt your reasoning and evidence to engage the concerns of reluctant listeners. Use the techniques of audience analysis that we introduced in Chapter 5 as you plan a persuasive argument. Begin by considering how much your listeners already know and where they stand on the issue. To what extent might they be prone to accept or not accept your arguments? Have they already made up their minds? Could they agree with you in principle but be reluctant to take action? Two of the biggest challenges of addressing reluctant listeners are *engaging opposing arguments* and *moving uncommitted audiences from agreement to action.*

Engaging Opposing Views

refutation
A strategy of engaging opposing positions and concerns by providing reasoning and evidence to argue that they are wrong or less right than your position.

When arguing controversial propositions, it is usually a good idea to engage or at least acknowledge the potential opposing arguments and prominent reservations that your listeners might raise. To the extent that listeners are sympathetic or predisposed to agree with your message, you might want to engage them directly by offering a **refutation** that provides reasoning and evidence to argue that opposing views are wrong or at least *less right* than your position. You might raise inconsistencies or fallacies in their reasoning, the representativeness or validity of their evidence, their understanding or framing of the issue itself, or (when appropriate) their underlying motives. Be sure to cite high-quality sources of information your audience will accept, to characterize opposing views accurately, and to explain the implications of your refutation before providing reasoning and evidence supporting your own position.

In her speech "The Price of Bottled Water" (the text of which appears in Appendix B), Katie Lovett offers an excellent illustration of an argumentative refutation:

> [One] main reason people want to buy bottled water is for what is *not* in it. The purity of water is the key theme for the bottled water industry. Bottlers seize upon public anxiety over municipal tap water supplies, supposedly offering us the safety that tap water cannot....
>
> Unfortunately...bottled water is not necessarily cleaner, safer, or purer than the water you get from your faucet.... In a recent four-year scientific study, the Natural Resources Defense Council tested more than 1,000 bottles of 103 brands of bottled water. In its publication, "Bottled Water or Tap Water?" the Council concluded that "there is no assurance that bottled water is any safer than tap water." In fact, a third of the brands tested were found to contain contaminants such as arsenic and carcinogenic compounds. Some of these samples contained levels of these harmful contaminants that exceeded state or industry standards. So much for "pure" and "pristine"!

When addressing less sympathetic or hostile audiences, you might consider moderating your goals and using a **co-active approach** that focuses on achieving a thoughtful and considerate hearing of your position by bridging the differences between you and your listeners.[9] With some issues, this might not be ethically acceptable to you. If you really believe that abortion is murder or that climate change threatens the survival of the human race, you may determine that you have no choice but to speak out in a confrontational manner. However, trying to move listeners too far with a single speech does risk the boomerang effect discussed in the previous chapter, and convincing an otherwise hostile audience simply to listen with an open mind can be a tremendous persuasive success. If you really want to engage such audiences constructively and on their own terms, four overlapping strategies can contribute to co-active persuasion: *establishing identification and good will early in your speech*, *reasoning from shared beliefs and values*, *emphasizing a tone of explanation over argument*, and *making a multisided presentation*.

co-active approach
An approach to persuasion that seeks to bridge differences on disputed issues by establishing identification and good will, reasoning from shared beliefs and values, emphasizing explanation over argument, and making a multisided presentation.

Establish identification and good will early in your speech. Invoking shared experiences, beliefs, and commitments can all contribute to enhancing identification and good will in persuasive speeches, as can references to shared heroes and heroines such as Martin Luther King, Jr., Ronald Reagan, or Harriet Tubman. Communication consultant Larry Tracy suggests that you try to meet with or contact key members of your audience before you speak, establishing a personal connection and seeking their advice. Then recognize them favorably during your presentation: "Nothing is so sweet to the human ear as the sound of his or her name, especially if it is mentioned positively before others."[10]

On occasions when you know your audience is predisposed to disagree, being frank and forthcoming about your differences can help to put listeners at ease and make them more receptive to hearing your message. Addressing an audience at the distinctly conservative Liberty University, the distinctly liberal Bernie Sanders opened his presentation with just such a strategy:

> I came here today because I believe from the bottom of my heart that it is vitally important for those of us who hold different views to be able to engage in a civil discourse....It is harder, but not less important, for us to try and communicate with those who do not agree with us on every issue.
>
> And it is important to see where if possible, and I do believe it is possible, we can find common ground...[on] issues out there that are of enormous

> consequence to our country and in fact to the entire world, that maybe, just maybe, we do not disagree on and maybe, just maybe, we can try to work together to resolve them.[11]

One of the most effective and time-honored strategies for establishing good will with otherwise hostile audiences is the use of humor. The late Ann Richards, former governor of Texas, told a story that illustrates how this technique can work. After she had been elected early in her career to the Travis County Commission, Richards paid a visit to a road maintenance crew at their worksite. As she entered the crew office, Richards noticed a particularly ugly dog stretched across the front door. She proceeded to make her presentation to a group of men whose popular male boss she had just defeated. After her speech, no one responded when she asked for questions. As she told the story:

> Finally, just to break the ice and get them talking, I asked them about their dog. Texas men will always talk about their dogs. Nothing. No one said a word. There was some shuffling of feet. I thought, "There must be something unseemly about the dog's name, it's the only answer." I looked around the room and they were ducking my gaze. "Let me tell you," I said, "that I am the only child of a very rough-talking father. So don't be embarrassed about your language. I've either heard it or I can top it. So what's the dog's name?"
>
> An old hand in the back row with a big wide belt and big wide belt buckle sat up and said in a gravelly bass, "Well, you're gonna find out sooner or later." He looked right at me. "Her name is Ann Richards." I laughed. And when I laughed they roared. And a little guy in the front row who was a lot younger and smarter than most, said in a wonderfully hopeful tenor, "But we call her Miss Ann!" From then on, those guys and I were good friends.[12]

Establish and reason from shared beliefs and values. It is usually a good idea to establish common ground before engaging areas of disagreement. Because values are resistant to change, you want to show listeners that your proposal agrees with principles they already accept. For example, if your audience resists an educational program for the financially disadvantaged because they think that people should take care of themselves, you might emphasize that the program is intended to promote self-sufficiency and represents "not a handout, but a hand up." Show them that your proposal will lead to other favorable outcomes, such as reductions in welfare and unemployment.

After acknowledging their differences, Bernie Sanders emphasized the values he shared with his listeners at Liberty University. He paraphrased the "Golden Rule" from Matthew 7:12 in the Bible: Do unto others as you would have them do unto you. Then he quoted Amos 5:24, "But let justice roll on like a river, righteousness like a never-failing stream." Justice became his refrain: "Justice [is] treating others the way we want to be treated, treating all people, no matter their race, their color, their stature in life, with respect and with dignity"; and given the current situation in the United States, "there is no justice." Of course, few, if any, of his listeners walked away from his presentation agreeing with everything he had to say. But by reasoning from shared beliefs and values, he managed to receive a favorable hearing as his initially skeptical audience applauded him.[13]

Emphasize a tone of explanation over argument. Instead of directly refuting opposing views and arguments your listeners hold dear, use the bulk of your persuasive evidence and reasoning to explain and support your position. This can help you avoid a defensive reaction by which they "tune out and turn off" before you have a chance to state your position. As we discussed with inductive reasoning, cite an abundance and variety of strong evidence from sources your audience will respect, looking especially for testimony from reluctant sources or revered figures usually associated with your opposition. As one communication consultant notes, "You cannot persuade people to change their mind; they must persuade themselves."[14] Help your listeners to do just that by providing them with the information they need.

We once heard a student speak against abortion to a class that was sharply divided on that issue. She began with a personal narrative, the story of how her mother had been given a drug that was later found to induce birth defects. Her mother was then faced with a decision on terminating the pregnancy. The student concluded by saying that if her mother had chosen the abortion option, she would not be there speaking to them that day. She paused, smiled, and said, "Although I know some of you may disagree with my views, I must say I am glad that you are here to listen and that I am here to speak. Think about it." If your reasons are compelling and your evidence is strong, you may soften the opposition and move at least some listeners toward your position.

Make a multisided presentation that acknowledges opposing positions. Respectfully acknowledge opposing arguments and views even as you argue for your own positions. State them accurately, as your listeners would understand them, and never question the moral sincerity of opposing advocates. You might suggest the relative superiority of your position, or you might even express agreement with underlying principles, and then explain how your positions are really not incompatible. For instance, you might agree with the audience's concerns for protecting free speech, and then argue that there are ways we can protect children from accessing Internet pornography sites without violating the First Amendment.

With co-active persuasion, your approach should be not to challenge listeners but to help them see the situation in a new light. Keep your goals modest. Ask only for a fair hearing. A co-active approach not only affirms your position but signals to listeners that you yourself are also open to persuasion and further discussion. We are not suggesting that persuading reluctant listeners is easy; it isn't. But a dispassionate first hearing can plant the seeds of future persuasion. Follow Cicero's ancient maxim to "hear the other side."[15] It can make you a stronger persuader and a better, more informed person.

Once you have emphasized commonalities with your audience and framed your proposal to address the audience's concerns, you are well on your way to creating a cooperative communication climate. Rather than trying to trick or force your listeners into agreeing with you, you are inviting them to consider your arguments and demonstrating that you have considered theirs.[16]

If you follow enough politics, you are no doubt aware that many speakers shun constructive approaches to persuasion, resorting to blatant dishonesty and character assassination when addressing disputed issues before partisan audiences. Although sometimes effective in the short run, resorting to such strategies in the long run debases the quality, standards, and constructive potential of public deliberation. When you address opposing views and concerns intelligently with reasoning and evidence, you educate and empower your listeners to do likewise, and you make them more resistant to later counter-persuasion.[17] It also enhances perceptions of your ethos as a persuasive voice worth hearing.

Finding Your Voice

Adapting to Controversy

Select a controversial subject for your persuasive speech. What resistance are you likely to face? How will you build a case for your position? What kinds of evidence will you use? What warrants will you invoke to interpret your evidence and establish your conclusions? How will you develop compelling arguments out of patterns of reasoning?

Moving from Attitude to Action

Just as partisan opponents may be reluctant to listen to opposing views, sympathetic audiences may be reluctant to act. It is one thing to agree with a speaker's message in principle, but quite another to assume the inconvenience and risk of getting involved. Listeners may not believe that the problem affects them personally, or they may not know what they should do or how they should do it.[18] To move people to action, give them reasons to act. You may have to *arouse their enthusiasm, demonstrate the need for their involvement*, and *present a clear plan of action* that makes it easy for them to comply.

SPEAKER'S NOTES

Moving People to Action

To move listeners to action, follow these guidelines:

1. Remind listeners of what is at stake.
2. Use examples and stories as models for action.
3. Visualize the consequences of acting versus not acting.
4. Demonstrate that you practice what you preach.
5. Provide a clear plan of action.
6. Ask for public commitments.
7. Make it easy for listeners to take the first step.

Spark Their Enthusiasm. To move people to action, you want to spark their enthusiasm. Demonstrate your own commitment, and ask listeners to join you. In her speech inviting her audience to become Special Olympics volunteers, Beth Tidmore anticipated that her listeners already agreed with her—*in principle*. But she had not yet won their hearts. Beth decided that the best way to arouse enthusiasm would be to help them imagine themselves enacting her proposal. So she described the experience of serving as a mentor—the pomp of the opening ceremonies, the nervous children turned serious athletes, the hard work coupled with an indescribable sense of fulfillment—before concluding:

> After the games are over, you get to see them all on the podium, because everyone gets a medal or a ribbon, everyone places. And it's great, because they're smiling and they're so proud, and there are flash-bulbs going off, and the anthem is playing. And they turn and they congratulate their fellow competitors....
>
> [On] Sunday,...when they run off the buses to show their parents their medals, and their parents walk up to you, their simplest "thank you" is a great reward. And in the end your vocal chords are shot, you have a second-degree sunburn on most of your body. Your feet hurt, your back aches, and you feel like you could sleep for a week. But you just can't stop smiling, because you know that you've just taken part in something very special.

Demonstrate the Need for Involvement. Provide evidence from credible sources to demonstrate the existence of a problem warranting their involvement. Emphasize its connection to the lives and interests of your audience, and explain its relevance to reaffirming shared values and commitments. Use factual examples, narratives, and lay testimony to invoke proof by pathos and move your listeners. As discussed in the previous chapter, most people have to *feel* as well as *think* about an issue before getting involved.

Sometimes, it only takes framing the issue in a new way to provide missing information or to answer questions that remove barriers to commitment. Show your

SPEAKER'S NOTES

How Speakers Can Bridge Divides with the Audience

Use the following strategies to establish identification with reluctant listeners:

1. Bring to life images of common heroes/heroines, enemies, and traditions.
2. Emphasize shared values, goals, and obligations.
3. Picture common problems and explain how they affect your listeners.
4. Provide a clear plan of action that they can take together, and urge them to take it.
5. Spell out an easy first step such as signing a petition or sending a text to affirm their involvement.
6. Use inclusive language, such as pronouns like "we" and "us," or family or team metaphors.

listeners how the quality of their lives depends on action, and use vivid language to help your listeners envision the future consequences of following versus not following your advice. In his final speech, Martin Luther King, Jr., offered a vision of a "Promised Land" beyond the mountain tops to help justify the sacrifices he implored his followers to endure in their fight for social justice.

Present a Clear Plan of Action. When they simply do not know how to get involved, many people tend to exaggerate the difficulty of taking action. To overcome such resistance, provide your listeners with a clear plan of action, and give them specific instructions that make it easy for them to comply. Emphasize that your plan is feasible, that it will help to resolve the problem at hand, and that it will not create more problems than it solves. As discussed in the previous chapter, consider providing your listeners with an easy first step such as signing a petition or sending a text to their political representatives. Such symbolic acts can help to reaffirm their commitment to your message and may predispose them to take further, more meaningful actions.

Figure 15.2 offers an overview of these various challenges to persuasion offered by different types of audiences and how to cope with them.

Engaging Opposing Concerns or Reluctance

Identify an issue about which you feel strongly. What strategies in this section might help you engage opposing concerns or reluctance to get involved?

Audience Type	Strategies
Reluctant to listen, possibly hostile	• Seek common ground and establish good will. • Quote sources they respect. • Emphasize explanation over argument. • Limit your goals: Ask only that listeners give you a fair hearing. • Try to weaken their resistance. • Acknowledge opposing arguments, but show tactfully why you have a different perspective.
Uncommitted, even uninterested	• Provide information needed to arouse their interest and encourage their commitment. • Connect their values with your position. • Become a model of commitment for them to follow.
Friendly but not yet committed	• Remind them of what is at stake. • Show them why action is necessary now. • Give them clear instructions, and help them take the first step. • Picture them undertaking this action successfully.

Figure 15.2
Considering the Audience for Persuasive Speaking

Finding Your Voice

Persuasive Confrontations

Are there ever times when a speaker should give up trying to persuade a hostile audience and simply confront listeners directly with the position they appear to oppose? Why would a speaker bother to do this? Could speaker and audience gain anything from such a confrontation? Look for an example of such a speech, consulting such sources as YouTube and C-SPAN. Do you agree with the strategy used in it? How would you have approached the topic differently?

Avoiding Defective Persuasion

15.5 Avoid common fallacies that undermine persuasive arguments.

fallacies
Errors in reasoning and evidence use that make persuasive messages unreliable.

As we discussed when addressing the ethics of persuasion, we live in an age of rampant disinformation and manipulation. As you research and prepare persuasive speeches, be cautious of various **fallacies**, the errors of reasoning and evidence that make persuasive messages less reliable. Such abuses can mislead your listeners, generate irresponsible decision making and action, and undermine our capacity for reasoned persuasion and more constructive discussions of important public issues. Fallacies will also undermine the persuasiveness of your efforts and can do lasting damage to perceptions of your competence and character.

Throughout this text, we have already discussed numerous abusive practices that undermine the truthfulness and reasonableness of persuasive messages. The following advice encapsulates some of our most important observations:

- Always speak from responsible knowledge with evidence that meets the standards of relevance, representativeness, recency, and reliability—and expect the same from other persuasive speakers.
- Watch out for disinformation that fabricates or distorts important facts and statistics to support persuasive claims.
- Never fabricate or exaggerate the credentials of expert sources of information.
- Don't distort the intended meaning of facts and testimony by citing them out of context.
- Make sure the examples you cite are timely and representative of the issue at hand.
- Cite a variety of high-quality evidence that is sufficient and appropriate for supporting persuasive claims.
- Watch out for presentation aids—especially pictures and graphs—that have been distorted to enhance persuasive claims.
- Watch out for misleading uses of language, including doublespeak, euphemisms, and incomprehensible jargon.
- Avoid overreliance on appeals to ethos (personal authority), pathos (emotional appeals), and mythos (appeals to tradition) at the expense of logos (reasoning and evidence).

Beyond following the above advice, take care to avoid the following commonly recognized fallacies of persuasive reasoning.

ad hominem fallacy
Attacking the character or motives of opposing advocates rather than engaging their arguments.

Ad Hominem. Sometimes called "attacking the messenger," the **ad hominem fallacy** occurs when speakers attack the character or motives of opposing advocates rather than engaging their arguments. In the heat of political campaigns, it is a lot easier to call your opponents "stupid" or "crooked" than it is to engage them on their own terms.[19] Nor are these new tactics in politics: In 1800, supporters of incumbent president John Adams called Thomas Jefferson "an uncivilized atheist, anti-American, a tool for the godless French," while Jefferson's fans dubbed Adams "a fool, a gross hypocrite, and an unprincipled oppressor."[20] Of course, sometimes underlying motives are relevant when discussing contested issues, but an overreliance on such appeals tends to divert attention from the actual subjects and undermines the prospect for constructive engagement and reasoned persuasion.

Red Herring. The **red herring fallacy** occurs when speakers raise irrelevant ideas and information to divert attention away from the real issues of an argument. Often overlapping with ad hominem attacks, politicians use red herring arguments when they respond to substantive allegations by making counter-allegations, and when they respond to bothersome revelations by attacking the source. One recent presidential candidate responded to demands she release the transcripts of various speeches delivered to gatherings of financial executives by insisting that her opponents release their tax returns.[21] She may or may not have been right to raise the issue of financial transparency, but she obviously used it to divert attention away from the issue at hand.

red herring fallacy
The use of irrelevant ideas and information to divert attention from the issue at hand.

Straw Figure. The **straw figure fallacy** occurs when speakers misstate opposing positions in a manner that makes them seem trivial, extreme, or easier to refute. Referring to all health care reforms as "socialized medicine" and proposed banking regulations as "a government takeover" are recent examples of such fallacies. When speakers extend an opponent's position to absurd lengths, attack a single example rather than the whole argument, focus only on the weakest part of a case, or shift to another problem, they engage in straw figure arguments.[22] As an ethical persuasive speaker, you should represent opposing positions fairly and fully. Remember that thoughtful listeners will likely be exposed to opposing positions stated more effectively after considering your message, and they will not be impressed if they believe that you misrepresented the issue. The straw figure fallacy is an implicit admission of weakness or desperation on the part of its user.

straw figure fallacy
Misrepresenting opposing views in a manner that makes them easier to refute.

Begging the Question. The **begging the question fallacy** occurs when speakers make claims without bothering to provide evidence to support them. We once heard a student begin a line of argument with the following statement of principle: "College athletes are not really here to learn." She was instantly in trouble. When her speech was over, the class assailed her with questions: How did she define *athletes*? How did she define *learning*? Was she aware of the negative stereotype at the center of her argument? Was she aware of the fact that student athletes perform better than average in the classroom? Needless to say, the speaker did not persuade many people that day.

begging the question fallacy
Making claims based on premises the audience may not accept without bothering to support or argue for them.

Non Sequitur. The words *non sequitur* are Latin for "it does not follow." The **non sequitur fallacy** occurs when speakers make claims that do not follow from their reasoning and evidence. Non sequiturs often emerge in arguments that are bafflingly incoherent and sometimes bizarre. A former chair of the Atomic Energy Commission once argued that nuclear power plants were safer than eating because "300 people choke to death on food every year."[23] Speaking in opposition to women serving in combat, former Speaker of the House Newt Gingrich argued that "females have biological problems staying in a ditch for 30 days because they get infections... [whereas] males are biologically driven to go out and hunt for giraffes."[24] Of course, modern combat has little to do with living in ditches, and women are no more likely to develop infections than men. We have no idea what he was talking about with respect to hunting giraffes!

non sequitur fallacy
Occurs when conclusions do not follow coherently from the speaker's reasoning and evidence.

faulty analogy fallacy
A comparison drawn between events, developments, or processes that are dissimilar in some important way.

Faulty Analogy. The **faulty analogy fallacy** occurs when speakers offer comparisons that are dissimilar in significant ways. As discussed earlier in this chapter, analogy represents a powerful form of reasoning, but you should be aware that audiences may perceive the essential similarity of events or developments in different ways. While supporters of legalizing recreational drug use offer comparisons to the prohibition of alcoholic beverages during the early twentieth century, their opponents attack the analogy by insisting that it was another time and that today's street drugs are far more dangerous than alcohol. Always consider whether your listeners will accept a given analogy before using it in persuasive speeches, and be prepared to defend the essential similarity of the components as necessary.

bandwagon fallacy
Arguing that a persuasive message must be right or wrong because of its popular acceptance.

Bandwagon. Sometimes called "argument ad populum," the **bandwagon fallacy** assumes that a proposition or course of action must be right or wrong based on its popularity. Advertisements often ask us to pay more for their products simply because more people use them. Political spin doctors tout their candidates by citing their own, often rigged polls suggesting their enhanced popularity with the people. Because we often view something as correct or valuable to the extent that we see others supporting it, such "social proof" can be enticing.[25] Don't be sucked in by such appeals. Just because something is popular doesn't make it right. Think for yourself, and respect the right of others to do the same.

either-or fallacy
Arguing that there are only two options, one of which is desirable.

Either-Or. An **either-or fallacy** creates a false dilemma. It tells listeners that they have only two choices that are mutually exclusive. Because it sets up a dramatic contrast between opposing positions, either-or thinking is attractive, but it often results in the oversimplification of important issues. It creeps into civic discussions with statements such as "It's either jobs or the environment" or "To pay off the debt, we must cut social programs." Such polarized thinking tends to preclude the possibility of constructive compromises and creative "win-win" alternatives.

slippery slope fallacy
The assumption that once something happens, an inevitable trend is established that will lead to disastrous results.

Slippery Slope. The **slippery slope fallacy** assumes that once something bad happens, it will establish an irreversible trend leading to disaster. During the Vietnam War, supporters repeatedly argued that if the tiny nation were allowed to fall to communism, the rest of Southeast Asia would inevitably follow.[26] More recently, a prominent religious leader suggested that feminism would inevitably lead women to "leave their husbands, kill their children, practice witchcraft, destroy capitalism, and become lesbians."[27] In the slippery slope fallacy, it is not logic but rather our darkest fears that drive our prediction of events.

post hoc fallacy
Occurs when speakers assume one thing caused another simply because it preceded it in close proximity.

Post Hoc. The **post hoc fallacy** presumes that when one event, development, or course of action precedes another in close proximity, it must have been its cause. It confuses simple association with causation and is often used to oversimplify important issues. For example, speakers may attribute a rise in violent crime rates to the lack of adequate gun control measures or too many gun control measures, but in either case both sides are often guilty of oversimplifying what is obviously a highly complicated and multifaceted issue. As experts will tell you, the same goes for attributing every catastrophic weather event to climate change or every period of financial growth or decline to a given president's economic policies. Of course, we have to consider the causes of troublesome events or developments as we explore appropriate solutions for dealing with them, but always remember that the world is usually more complex than it is often made to appear.

hasty generalization fallacy
An error of inductive reasoning in which general claims are based on insufficient or nonrepresentative evidence.

Hasty Generalization. A **hasty generalization fallacy** occurs when you base a conclusion on insufficient or nonrepresentative observations. For example, a student might reason, "My roommate got a D from Professor Johnson. The guy who sits next to me in history got an F from him. I'm struggling to make a C in his class; therefore, Professor Johnson is a tough grader." To avoid a hasty generalization,

The myth of the mean misuses statistical averages by ignoring the extremes.

you would need to know what the professor's grade distribution looks like over an extended period of time. Finally, as we discussed in Chapter 1, be cautious of making sweeping generalizations or stereotypes about the members of any group; people prefer to think of themselves as individuals and find such thinking offensive.

Myth of the Mean. The **myth of the mean fallacy** misuses statistical averages to mislead an audience. For example, a speaker might tell you not to worry about poverty in your hometown because the average income is well above the poverty level. However, this average could be misleading if a handful of families are extremely wealthy while the majority of citizens live at or below the poverty line. We've all been taught that "figures don't lie" when perhaps we should have been taught that "liars often figure." Averages are useful to summarize statistical information, but beware of their use to mask the reality of a situation.

myth of the mean fallacy
The deceptive use of statistical averages.

Figure 15.3 Gallery of Fallacies

Gallery of Fallacies	
1. Ad Hominem	attacks the person rather than the issue
2. Red Herring	distracts listeners with sensational, irrelevant information
3. Straw Figure	creating a likeness of an opposing position that makes it seem trivial, extreme, and easy to refute
4. Begging the Question	asserting a claim that has not been proven with evidence
5. Non Sequitor	reasoning in which the claim does not follow from the evidence
6. Faulty Analogy	comparing two aspects or events that are dissimilar in important ways
7. Bandwagon	arguing that you should do it or believe it because "every-body else" does
8. Either-Or	presenting only two options as if they are mutually exclusive
9. Slippery Slope	arguing that one bad event will inevitably lead to others
10. Post Hoc	confusing proximity in time with causation
11. Hasty Generalization	drawing conclusions based on insufficient evidence
12. Myth of the Mean	using an average to hide a problem
13. Equivocation	exploiting the ambiguity of language to mislead an audience or avoid the issue at hand

Constructing Persuasive Arguments

Intentionally construct three fallacious arguments on the topic for your upcoming persuasive speech. What kind of listeners might find your arguments persuasive? How might they reflect on your ethos as a persuasive voice? How does an awareness of such fallacies help you construct stronger, more ethical arguments?

equivocation
Exploiting the ambiguity of language to mislead an audience or avoid the issue at hand.

Equivocation. **Equivocation** occurs when speakers exploit the ambiguity of words to confuse listeners or deflect attention from the issue at hand. If you look at a dictionary, you will notice that most words have more than one definition, and sometimes clever speakers exploit the ambiguity this can create to mislead us. Former President Bill Clinton equivocated while responding to accusations of having an extramarital affair by redefining the meaning of sexual intercourse, famously concluding the answer depends on how we define the word "is"![28] More recently, a number of prominent district attorneys have been forced to defend themselves in light of revelations they suppressed evidence that might have exonerated the defendants they prosecuted at trial—in some cases sending them to death row. More often, the standard response was to ignore the question at hand by insisting they followed their understanding of "the law."[29]

Figure 15.3 lists and defines the fallacies we have been discussing.

When listening to spectacular speakers, be on the alert for fallacies.

Finding Your Voice

Fallacy Files

To learn more about the subject of fallacies, go to *The Fallacy Files*, an online site containing an extensive collection of fallacies and bad arguments. Developed by Gary N. Curtis, the well-organized, entertaining site offers definitions and examples. See especially "Stalking the Wild Fallacy," offered under the "Examples" feature on the menu. Look for either a fallacy discussed here that you aren't sure you understand or a fallacy we don't discuss here that is important to public speaking. What can you learn from this site?

Finding Your Voice

Find the Fallacies

Look for examples of fallacies in opinions expressed in blogs and online commentaries or in the "Letters to the Editor" section of your local newspaper. Consider how these fallacies affect the credibility or character of the people who commit them. Have you committed such errors? How do you think they reflect on your ethos as a persuasive speaker?

YOUR ETHICAL VOICE

Building Ethical Arguments

To demonstrate that your arguments are ethical, observe the following guidelines:

1. Develop responsible knowledge before using it as persuasive evidence.
2. Build your arguments with a genuine concern for both immediate and long-term consequences.
3. Emphasize logical reasoning built on substantive evidence.
4. Use appeals to ethos, pathos, and mythos to complement proof by logos—not to replace it.
5. Consider how your persuasive reasoning will be judged by thoughtful listeners.
6. Acknowledge when claims are based on probability rather than certainty.
7. Acknowledge conditions that might disprove your argument.
8. Understand and respect different positions.
9. Review your arguments to eradicate potential fallacies.
10. Serve as an ethical, effective listener for others, as you want them to be for you.

Final Reflections: Persuasion That Has Legs

Communication scholar Douglas Ehninger argued that the value of debating contentious issues goes beyond which side wins or loses. Instead, he posited, such contesting of views performs an *investigative function*.[30] When we build a case to support a position on policies or political candidates, we also develop a point of view that can reveal something useful about an issue. We can illuminate one facet of what are often multi-faceted controversies. The decisions that finally resolve these issues are often compromises that blend elements of the opposing positions. Many of us can "win" in the sense that we are represented in the consensus that emerges. Even when we "lose," our arguments can discipline our thinking and improve the decisions that prevail.

For these important decisions, we need persuasion that respects the power of evidence and develops patterns of reasoning into compelling arguments that constitute a reasoned case. Such effective, ethical persuasion is vital to the long-range impact of ideas. As communication scholars Josina M. Makau and Debian L. Marty contend, "deliberative communities rely on diversity and disagreement to arrive at the fullest understanding of particular issues and to make the best decision possible under the circumstances."[31] Finding your voice means more than discovering your call to a cause and learning how to make your voice heard. It also means how long your voice will be heard and the extent of its influence. Effective, ethical persuasion that uses appropriate evidence and clear reasoning offers the kind of commitment that endures. It has legs.

Study Questions

CONTENT MASTERY

1 How can you focus an issue for a persuasive speech?

2 How do the four kinds of supporting material function in persuasive speeches?

3 What are the major components of an argument as identified by Toulmin?

4 What are the five major patterns of reasoning? What are the strengths and weaknesses of each?

5 How can you approach listeners who are unsympathetic to your position?

6 How can you appeal to audiences who are sympathetic but reluctant to act?

7 What are the major kinds of fallacies, and how can you avoid them?

CRITICAL EXPLORATIONS

1. Find a persuasive speech on TED or YouTube. How well does the speaker focus the issue? What kinds of evidence are offered in support of the claims? What might have improved the speech?
2. Compile a list of public figures or sources of information you respect. Compare your high-ethos sources with those listed by your classmates, and prepare a master list for possible use in speeches. How does their subject-specific expertise influence your use of their material? How do differences in high-ethos sources point to areas and approaches you need to consider in your persuasive speech?
3. Find a recent persuasive speech in which narrative plays a prominent part. What persuasive work does the narrative perform? How well has the speaker integrated the narrative with other forms of evidence?
4. Find a segment on QVC or an episode of *Shark Tank*. Using Toulmin's model of argumentation, chart the components of the argument being made. Are components missing? How do such absences influence the effectiveness of the argument for you?
5. In the same persuasive segment from QVC or *Shark Tank* you found for #4, identify the pattern of reasoning used. How would a different pattern of reasoning affect the argument?
6. Find one message intended to win a hearing from an unsympathetic audience and another on the same topic intended to move a sympathetic audience to action. Which of the approaches outlined in this chapter do the speakers/authors use? Which are not employed? How would the addition of approaches they do not use affect the message?
7. Look for examples of fallacies in advertisements. What fallacies seem to be most frequently used? Do you think such fallacies are identified by the intended audience for the ads, or do you think most audience members fall victim to them? What does this suggest about the role of ethical considerations in effective persuasion?

PERSUASIVE SPEECH

This persuasive speech, presented during Honors Day in the Department of Communication Studies at the University of Texas at Austin, went on to win the National Championship for Persuasive Speaking presented by the National Forensic League. It is noteworthy for its reliance on well-reasoned persuasion, developing an array of proofs and evidence that emphasize facts and expert testimony, carefully documented to reassure critical listeners. Adding color and human interest to the speech are judicious uses of examples, metaphors, and appeals to fear and fairness.

KEEP BIG BROTHER OFF YOUR BACK

AUSTIN L. WRIGHT

Reprinted with permission from Austin Wright.

The speech opens with an example that raises issues of fairness over the government's use of false information and its complicity in torture. Implied in the example is a sense of violated mythos: Should the United States, which prides itself in protecting individual rights, be engaged in such egregious violations of these rights?

On September 26, 2002, Canadian citizen Maher Arar boarded a flight home from a family vacation in Tunisia. During a layover in New York City, American authorities detained Arar, interrogating him for the next twelve days. After repeatedly denying any connection to Al Qaeda, Arar was shackled and loaded onto a private, unmarked jet headed for Syria, where he was tortured for the next ten months.

As the Electronic Privacy Information Center or EPIC writes in an *amicus* brief presented before the U.S. Supreme Court on May 16, 2008, the U.S. government justified Arar's torture using patently false information. As the brief further explains, two American databases—the Department of Homeland Security's Automated Targeting System and the FBI's National Crime Information Center—track tens of millions of Americans and foreign nationals each year for things as simple as suspicious credit card charges and questionable Internet searches. Indeed, EPIC claims our government uses these databases for searches 2.8 million times every day!

Yet these databases contain widely documented errors that the government has no intention of fixing. And in 2007 the Department of Justice folded to pressure from the private intelligence companies and granted both databases blanket immunity over the accuracy of their contents, meaning no one can sue the government for the unlawful use of false information provided by private corporations.

In short: the information that our government uses to detain, interrogate, and torture suspected terrorists can be fabricated on a whim. But with more Americans being tracked as suspected terrorists than at any other point in our nation's history—writes *The USA Today* of March 10, 2009—the danger of false data to all of us is too grave to ignore.

The speech offers a clear preview of what is to come and promises to develop the main points using a categorical design.

So today we will discuss how these error-ridden databases are protected, examine the dangers they pose to our personal liberties, and discuss some ways they might be corrected.

According to *The New York Times* of January 15, 2009, the Supreme Court ruled that evidence found in faulty databases may be used to charge someone with a crime, real or imagined. These databases pose a threat to the prohibition on unreasonable search and seizure, but they are protected by the government in two ways: constraints on the exclusionary rule and the use of private companies to sidestep restrictions.

Initially, as the *Wisconsin Law Journal* of January 26, 2009, writes, the Supreme Court passed down a decision seriously limiting the scope of the exclusionary rule in the case of *Herring v. United States*. The exclusionary rule protects Americans from evidence acquired through an illegal search and seizure. But in deciding the fate of Bennie Herring—an Alabama man who was pulled over and searched using an erroneous warrant—the Court amended the exclusionary rule, writing off the government's use of false information as "reasonable" since Herring was guilty of a crime. While this new legal doctrine may sound appealing, it does expose innocent Americans as well to unreasonable search, seizure, and detention.

Additionally, the federal government hires private companies, like Choicepoint and LexisNexis, to develop these databases to circumvent legal restrictions on domestic intelligence gathering. *Washington Post* reporter Robert O'Harrow's 2005 book *No Place To Hide* clarifies that the law regulating private intelligence gathering is the Fair Credit Reporting Act. If private companies don't sell credit ratings, however, their techniques do not trigger oversight under the law, meaning that companies can use literally any means to gather information and are not legally required to verify its accuracy. As a June 1, 2007, Salon.com exposé contends, the federal government is outsourcing domestic spying to private companies that can gather any information about anyone, using any means, without any consequences for releasing false information.

When Ron Peterson, a man from California, asked Choicepoint for his private information in 2005, he was told he was a female prostitute in Florida named Ronnie, an incarcerated murderer in Texas, a stolen goods dealer in New Mexico, a witness tamperer in Oregon, and a sex offender in Nevada. All of which, thankfully, were not true. But just imagine how this so-called "information" might have been misused by a government investigator prepared already to believe the worst about Mr. Peterson!

The example that follows provides another perspective on false databases: Not only are they dangerous—but also they are sometimes patently absurd. The sardonic humor provides a touch of color and lightness in the otherwise somber wordscape of the speech.

Beyond such flagrant inaccuracies, these flawed databases threaten each of us in two ways: legal malfeasance and information leaks. Initially, given the Supreme Court's recent decision, false information contained within these databases has the same force of law as accurate information. Since the Department of Justice built a legal force field around these databases in 2007, writes the *Wisconsin Law Journal*, LexisNexis and Choicepoint are legally free to disseminate false information that can be used to fill these databases and to execute searches, seizures, and false arrests, all without a shred of truth or actual legal merit.

These databases and the private companies hired to make them are also dangerously prone to information leaks. The *North Country Gazette* of January 14, 2009, writes that a former NYPD sergeant was able to access a database through his police status and leaked top-secret documents to help a friend win a divorce battle. What's more, the *Los Angeles Times* of January 27, 2006, explains that these companies also have a reputation for losing information. In 2005, for instance, Choicepoint's data system was breached by con artists, compromising more than 19 billion individual files, including social security numbers and financial histories. Although a 2007 Javelin Strategy and Research report finds that identity theft costs victims an average of $5,000, the government forced Choicepoint to pay out a mere $15 million in damages. That's an average of less than one tenth of one cent for each person whose private information was leaked by Choicepoint.

While we may not be able to change the way the Supreme Court treats the use of false information, we can cut this problem off at its source by pressuring the private intelligence companies hired by our government and checking the information they sell. As O'Harrow explains, LexisNexis has built a virtual monopoly on American intelligence gathering. Since 9/11, LexisNexis bought most of the companies hired by the federal government to build the Automated Targeting System and NCIC, including Choicepoint. What's even worse, the CEO of Choicepoint told the *Washington Post* in 2005 that his company won't tolerate regulation under the Fair Credit Reporting Act, meaning LexisNexis subsidiaries are using any means to gather even false information without any legal consequences.

Austin anticipated the question of what listeners might do to counter the vast injustice he had described by offering his own personal action as a model. He also appealed to the pride of his Texas listeners by offering a metaphorical vision of a movement for reform starting on their campus that might then "sweep across the country."

LexisNexis charges our school about a $1.50 fee every time we use their search engine. So here's a radical idea: Let's refuse to use it! And let's ask our librarians and our college officials to cancel their contracts with LexisNexis and its subsidiary companies until they clean up their act. When I found out LexisNexis makes about $5,000 a year off my speech team, I asked my teammates to start using alternative search engines like Google News and Google Scholar. I prepared this speech using only sources taken from Google News. As an academic community that makes heavy use of their tools, we are in a unique position to

Austin concludes by raising a specter of government as a potentially abusive Big Brother, an image that might appeal to both liberals and conservatives. He offers a nice sense of closure by tying back in to his initial example of a tortured citizen and appeals for immediate action.

pressure LexisNexis for change. And we at the University of Texas—this large and prestigious university—can start a movement for reform that can sweep across this country!

If you want to take more immediate action, send a letter to Choicepoint, demanding access to your information. You can either visit their website or take one of the request forms I have printed off. All you have to do is fill in the blanks and make a copy of your driver's license and a recent bill you have paid that contains your address. If you happen to discover false information in your folder, don't hesitate to send a certified letter to Choicepoint requesting a revision of your file. Choicepoint is legally required to comply with your demands, and correcting even minor errors could help keep Big Brother off your back.

When Maher Arar was illegally detained in 2002, the dual threats posed by the Automated Tracking System and the NCIC may have seemed isolated. But today, the stakes for tens of millions of Americans are greater than ever before. We must act and act now to pressure private intelligence companies to mend the information crisis they have created. With government conducting ten searches every second using faulty data, we literally don't have a second to lose.

Ceremonial Speaking

CHAPTER

LEARNING OBJECTIVES	OUTLINE
This chapter will help you:	
16.1 Use techniques for enhancing identification and magnification in ceremonial presentations.	Techniques of Ceremonial Speaking
16.2 Prepare ceremonial presentations for a variety of special occasions.	Types of Ceremonial Speeches
16.3 Use the narrative design for developing ceremonial presentations.	Narrative Design

In her commencement address at Harvard University, author J.K. Rowling suggested that "In its arguably most transformative and revelatory capacity, [imagination] is the power that enables us to empathise with humans whose experiences we have never shared." After providing moving examples from her own life, Rowling exhorted the graduates:

> If you choose to use your status and influence to raise your voice on behalf of those who have no voice; if you choose to identify not only with the powerful, but with the powerless; if you retain the ability to imagine yourself into the lives of those who do not have your advantages, then it will not only be your proud families who celebrate your existence, but thousands and millions of people whose reality you have helped change. We do not need magic to change the world, [for] we carry all the power we need inside ourselves already: we have the power to imagine better.[1]

"[People] who celebrate . . . are fused with each other and fused with all things in nature."

—ERNST CASSIRER

Rowling celebrated the potential that each and every person in the audience had to make a difference in the world.

Far more traumatic was the agony after a student shot and killed 32 other students and faculty at Virginia Tech University in 2007. Dr. Rachel Holloway, professor of communication at that institution, contended that ceremonial speaking "has been foundational to our recovery, by revealing and calling forth our character." From the eulogies for those lost to Nikki Giovanni's powerful, poetic presentation, Dr. Holloway observed that the ceremonial speeches "reminded us of who we are and will be" by "honor[ing] our values."[2] Whether the special occasion is one of joy or of sorrow, ceremonial speaking celebrates and reinforces our common goals, beliefs, and aspirations.

---

ceremonial speaking
Speaking that celebrates the meaning of special occasions, such as speeches of tribute, award presentations, eulogies, toasts, and after-dinner speeches.

Ceremonial speaking celebrates the meaning of special occasions. Such occasions include paying tribute to special figures or group accomplishments, presenting or accepting awards, lighthearted after-dinner speeches, solemn eulogies and memorials, and simple toasts on such happy occasions as weddings or retirement dinners. Regardless of the occasion, the best ceremonial speeches celebrate the moment by reinforcing the values that bind people together in communities.[3] They strengthen our sense of connection by emphasizing those commonalities and shared aspirations. As such, ceremonial speaking addresses those four eternal questions: *Who are we? Why are we? What have we accomplished?* and *What can we become together?*

Of course, your own speaking may not be as momentous as a commencement address or mass eulogy, but you will likely be asked to make ceremonial presentations. You may be asked to present an award to an outstanding co-worker or to act as "master of ceremonies" at a banquet dinner. You may wish to say a few words at the retirement party of a former teacher or mentor, celebrate the memory of a beloved friend, or offer a congratulatory toast at a wedding reception. Ceremonial occasions offer an opportunity for you to celebrate your success in finding your voice as you discover that you can now make a contribution as a speaker to your family, to a mentor or friend, to your company, or to the life of your community. When you speak effectively on such occasions, it enhances perceptions of your ethos and leadership potential.

Regardless of the occasion, do not make the mistake of thinking that "it's just a little talk; I can do it off the cuff"—that's the reason so many ceremonial speeches are disappointing. In this chapter, we help you rise to the various challenges and opportunities of speaking on special occasions. We explore distinctive techniques of ceremonial speaking, various types of ceremonial speeches, and the unique power of narrative design for addressing special occasions.

Techniques of Ceremonial Speaking

16.1 Use techniques for enhancing identification and magnification in ceremonial presentations.

No matter what the occasion for ceremonial speaking, two basic techniques can help celebrate who we are, what we've accomplished, and what we can become: *identification* and *magnification.*

Identification

identification
When a speech creates a feeling of shared goals, values, emotions, memories, and motives between a speaker and listeners.

Identification develops when a speech creates a feeling of shared goals, values, emotions, memories, and motives between a speaker and listeners. As we noted in Chapter 1, leading theorist Kenneth Burke suggested that identification is the key component of *all* public speaking.[4] People who identify with each other are more likely to reason, rejoice, and act together. Because ritual and ceremony draw people together, identification is the heart of ceremonial speaking. Three common strategies for promoting identification in ceremonial speaking are the use of *narrative,* the recognition of *heroes and heroines,* and the renewal of *group commitment*.

Using Narrative. Narratives create strong identification between a speaker and an audience by involving the audience in the storyline and framing both the situation and the motives of those involved.[5] For example, if you were preparing a speech for a year-end sports banquet at your school, you might tell stories about a particularly discouraging loss that year and then about how your teammates worked together to triumph despite adversity. These vignettes draw listeners together as they remember the shared experience. Stories that evoke laughter can be especially effective because laughter itself is a shared phenomenon.

When Ashlie McMillan gave her speech of tribute to her class, she told the inspiring story of a cousin who was a dwarf. In her introduction, Ashlie asked listeners to close their eyes and imagine themselves shrinking to help them identify with the challenges faced by her diminutive cousin. This identification prepared the audience to accept Ashlie's eloquent conclusion: "You too may seem too short to grasp your stars, but you never know how far you might reach if you stand upon a dream." Because such effective narratives are so important for ceremonial speeches, we will explore them in more detail later in this chapter.

Recognizing Heroes and Heroines. Another strategy for promoting identification in ceremonial speaking is to invoke the words and deeds of heroes and heroines as role models. Because heroes and heroines encapsulate such admirable qualities as courage, selflessness, and notable accomplishments, they represent the best qualities of the communities that value them. A speaker might invoke such figures as Elizabeth Cady Stanton, Martin Luther King, Jr., or Mother Teresa as the personification of such virtues as dedication, steadfastness, sacrifice, and grand achievements against the odds. Remembering the lives they lived symbolizes hope, for having lived once, their values can live again in our actions and deeds.

Finding Your Voice

Why Celebrate Heroes and Heroines?

Find a ceremonial speech and read it, looking for references to heroes and heroines—past and present. Commencement addresses and presidential inaugural addresses are a rich source of heroic references and easy to find online, or you might read one of the ceremonial presentations published at the end of this chapter and in Appendix B of this textbook. As you read, consider what heroes and heroines the speaker signals out for praise and why. What deeds or words does the speaker focus on? What virtues and values are they presented to embody? How might they contribute to establishing a sense of identification or shared purpose among speaker, listener, and message? Can you think of other heroes or heroines who might have worked as well or better to embody the speaker's message?

Renewing Group Commitment. Ceremonial speaking is a time both for celebrating what has been accomplished and for renewing commitments. One way to establish identification is to engage your listeners with a vision of what the future can be like with continued commitment, by reinvigorating their identity as a group moving forward.

To renew group commitment, ceremonial speakers often contrast a challenging present to the backdrop of an idealized past. They then create a vision to guide listeners into the future. In his "Gettysburg Address," delivered to commemorate the costliest battle of the costliest war in American history, Abraham Lincoln used this technique to substantially redefine America's moral identity as a nation.

Lincoln opened with a clear reference to an idealized past: "Four score and seven years ago our fathers brought forth on this continent a new nation, conceived in Liberty and dedicated to the proposition that all men are created equal." He then moved directly to the troubled present: "Now we are engaged in a great civil war, testing whether that nation, or any nation so conceived and so dedicated, can long endure." After expounding on the sacrifices of the "brave men, living and dead, who struggled here," Lincoln closed by offering a stunning vision to guide the American future: "that this nation, under God, shall have a new birth of freedom—and that government of the people, by the people, for the people, shall not perish from the earth."[6]

SPEAKER'S NOTES

Promoting Identification

Use the following techniques to develop identification among listeners:

1. Tell stories that remind listeners of shared experiences.
2. Enjoy laughter; it bonds people together.
3. Create portraits of heroes and heroines as shared role models.
4. Revive traditions and past experiences to remind listeners of shared commitments.
5. Offer goals and visions to inspire listeners to work together.

Jesse Owens was both a great Olympic hero and a great inspirational speaker.

Magnification

In his *Rhetoric*, Aristotle noted that when speakers select certain features of a person or event and then dwell on those qualities, the effect is to magnify them in the minds of listeners.[7] Such **magnification** comes to represent the meaning of the subject for listeners. It focuses attention on what is relevant, honorable, and praiseworthy.

magnification
When speakers select and emphasize certain qualities of a subject to stress the virtues and values they represent.

Magnification relies on effective language to create dramatic word-pictures. Metaphors and similes can magnify a subject through such creative associations as "She sailed out of safe harbors and piloted us out of protected coves into deep, new seas," or "He walked on ice, but never fell."[8] Parallel structure can also help magnify a subject and embed it in our minds. For example, if you were to say of Mother Teresa, "Whenever there was hurt, she was there. Whenever there was hunger, she was there. Whenever there was desperation, she was there," you would be magnifying her dedication and selflessness.

Ceremonial speakers often use certain themes to magnify the virtues of honored figures. These themes include

- Triumph over obstacles
- Unusual accomplishment
- Superior performance
- Unselfish motives
- Benefit to society

For example, if you were preparing a speech honoring Jesse Owens's incredible track and field accomplishments in the 1936 Olympic Games, you might stress that Owens had to overcome such obstacles as racism in America to even make the Olympic team. Then you could point out that his accomplishments were unusual. No one else had ever won four gold medals in Olympic track and field competition, and Owens suffered from a headache the day he took gold in the long jump. As for superior performance, he set world records that lasted many years. His motives were unselfish because he received no material gain from his victories. He was driven solely by such personal qualities as courage and determination. Finally, you might show that because his victories repudiated Hitler's racist agenda and caused him public humiliation, Owens's accomplishments benefited our world. The overall effect would be to magnify the meaning of Jesse Owens's great performances, both for himself and for his nation.

Establishing Identification with Your Listeners

How might you establish identification with your listeners in your upcoming ceremonial speech assignment? What stories, heroes/heroines, and shared commitments could you invoke to involve them with your message?

Certain speech designs also promote magnification. Comparison and contrast designs make selected features stand out. For example, you might contrast the purity of Owens's motives with the greediness of some of today's well-paid athletes. Chronological designs that present the history of a situation magnify the themes you think are important. As Simone Mullinax, whose speech concludes this chapter, sketched certain incidents in her childhood, she gradually revealed the fascinating character of her grandmother. Causation designs magnify a person's accomplishments as the causes of important effects. For example, a speaker might suggest that Jesse Owens's victories refuted Nazi propaganda for many people. Narrative designs help to dramatize events and accomplishments.

Whatever designs ceremonial speeches use, it is important that they build to a conclusion. Speakers should save their best materials and language for the end of the speech. Ceremonial speeches should never dwindle to a close but end with a flourish.

Finding Your Voice

Magnification and Ceremonial Speaking

The way you use magnification reveals a lot about you as a person. Think of a person you might single out for praise in your upcoming ceremonial speech. You might choose an important public figure past or present, a celebrity or sports personality, a mentor or family member, or a close friend who has inspired you. What qualities or attributes would you stress or *magnify* when referencing or quoting them in a ceremonial speech? The importance or unusual nature of their accomplishments? The challenges or obstacles they had to overcome? The purity of their motives and contributions to society? What virtues and values do they inspire or embody as role models? How can recognizing and praising such figures help you to find your voice?

SPEAKER'S NOTES

Magnification

Use the following strategies to magnify a person or an accomplishment:

1. Show how people have overcome obstacles to success.
2. Point out why the accomplishments are unusual.
3. Emphasize the superior features of the performance.
4. Describe the unselfish motives behind the achievement.
5. Show how listeners and society have benefited.
6. Use speech designs—comparison, chronological, causation, and narrative—that promote magnification.
7. Use such language techniques as metaphor and parallel construction to promote magnification.

Types of Ceremonial Speeches

16.2 Prepare ceremonial presentations for a variety of special occasions.

In your personal and professional lives, you may have the opportunity to offer a variety of ceremonial presentations, including speeches of tribute (award presentations, eulogies, and toasts), acceptance speeches, introductions for other speakers,

Type	Use When
Tribute	You wish to honor a person, group, occasion, or event. Subtypes include award presentations, eulogies, and toasts.
Acceptance	You have received an award or honor and want to acknowledge it.
Introduction	You are able to introduce a featured speaker in a program.
Inspiration	You want to motivate listeners to appreciate and commit to a goal, purpose, or set of values.
After-Dinner	You want to entertain the audience while leaving a message that can guide future behavior.
Master of Ceremonies	You are in charge of coordinating a program, seeing that everything runs smoothly, and setting the mood for the occasion.

Figure 16.1
Types of Ceremonial Speeches

speeches of inspiration, after-dinner speeches, and serving as master of ceremonies (see Figure 16.1).

Speeches of Tribute

A **speech of tribute** recognizes the achievements of individuals or groups, or commemorates special events. In the process, it typically focuses on the values of individual responsibility, striving, and achievement. For example, you might be called on to honor a former teacher at a retirement ceremony, to present an award to someone for an outstanding accomplishment, to eulogize a person who has died, or to propose a toast to a friend who is getting married.

speech of tribute
A ceremonial speech that recognizes the achievements of individuals or groups or commemorates special events.

Praiseworthy accomplishments are usually celebrated in speeches of tribute for two reasons. First, *they are important in themselves*: The influence of a teacher may have contributed to the success of many of her former students; the activism of a community organizer may have led to significant improvements for the citizens of his community. Second, *they are important as symbols of the values they represent*. The planting of the American flag at Iwo Jima during some of the most intense fighting of World War II, a discrete event, resonated with the American public such that it came to symbolize the fortitude and commitment of the entire American war effort. While the event itself was no doubt significant, it became even more important as a symbol of what it represented. More often, accomplishments are celebrated for both actual and symbolic reasons. For instance, a speech praising the accomplishments of an outstanding community activist would likely focus on both the honoree's specific contributions and the value of community involvement in general.

Speeches of tribute reaffirm explicitly stated, shared moral commitments. For example, Holly Carlson chose the banning of books in public schools as the topic area for all of her speeches. In her informative speech, she demonstrated how books are banned in schools all over the country, and she cited the books and authors most often targeted. In her persuasive speech, she offered a stirring plea for intellectual freedom, urging her listeners to support the right to read and think for themselves. Then, for her ceremonial speech, she offered a tribute to one of the most frequently banned authors of the twentieth century, J. D. Salinger. Her tribute to Salinger made her listeners want to read his works themselves. It also dramatized how hurtful censorship could be. Thus, all of Holly's speeches were woven into one pattern, which gave focus to her semester's work. In the process, she found her voice forcefully.

Finally, speeches of tribute often overlap with other forms of ceremonial speaking discussed in this chapter, especially speeches of inspiration. In his speech accepting

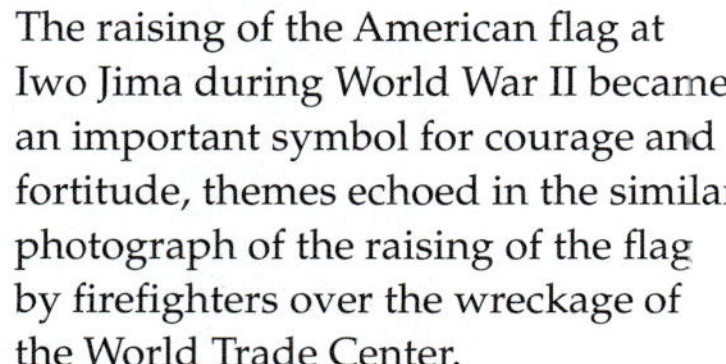

The raising of the American flag at Iwo Jima during World War II became an important symbol for courage and fortitude, themes echoed in the similar photograph of the raising of the flag by firefighters over the wreckage of the World Trade Center.

the Martin Luther King, Jr., Human Rights Award, John Bakke paid tribute to Dr. King's faith in nonviolence and to his holding fast to that faith, even in the face of criticism from friends as well as enemies. Bakke gave new life to the concept of nonviolence by expanding and exploring its meaning for our time. Note how he used parallel structure and antithesis and how he challenged his listeners to redefine their roles in the political process:

> Taylor Branch has asserted, "Nonviolence is an orphan among democratic ideas," but "Every ballot is a piece of nonviolence. . . ."
>
> It's time to make that ballot the effect of full democratic participation. It's time to reclaim our democratic processes. It's time to make the democratic processes work in America just as we are trying to make them work for others.
>
> That means more than voting. It means informed voting. It means supporting candidates and policies of our choice. It means commitment to the communication processes that give life to democracy. It means thinking of ourselves more as citizens than as just taxpayers. It means full-time citizenship. If campaigns are now permanent, citizenship cannot be cyclical. Democracy and "the vote" will always be open to criticism if people do not vote or do not know what they are voting for.

As you prepare a speech of tribute, keep the following guidelines in mind:

- **Do not exaggerate the tribute.** If you are too lavish with your praise or use too many superlatives, you may make the praise unbelievable and embarrass the recipient.
- **Focus on the person being honored, not on yourself.** Even if you know what effort the accomplishment required because you have done something similar, don't mention that at this time. The focus should be on the honoree.
- **Create vivid images of accomplishment.** Tell stories that make the honoree's accomplishments come to life, using colorful language and concrete examples.
- **Be sincere.** Speeches of tribute are a time for warmth, pride, and appreciation. Your language and your manner should reflect these qualities as you present the tribute.

award presentation
A speech that explains the nature of the award and recognizes the achievements of the award recipient.

Award Presentations. An **award presentation** calls for a speech that explains the nature of the award, honors the recipient and her accomplishments as deserving of the award, and (as necessary) presents the actual award. Suppose you were asked to present an award celebrating the volunteer work of an outstanding graduate of your university. After the customary opening greetings, you would probably expound on the meaning of the award as embodying such values as charity, community involvement, and hard work. You would then address the accomplishments and contributions of the recipient as worthy of those values and the award. As we discuss earlier under magnification, you might emphasize the importance or uniqueness of her contributions, the challenges or obstacles she had to overcome, the purity of her motives, and the public or social benefits of her work.

The actual award is usually presented at the end of the speech. Speakers often save the name of the honoree for last, which helps to build anticipation while emphasizing the shared values represented by the honor. Finally, consider whether there will be a physical presentation of the award (a plaque, a trophy, a check, etc.) and how you will present it. Determine where it will be placed during your presentation, and present it with your left hand so you can shake with your right.

Eulogies. A **eulogy** is a tribute given at a funeral or memorial service. From the ancient Greek term meaning "to praise," eulogies celebrate the life of a loved one while providing solace to those who are left behind. A sincere, heartfelt consideration of the person's distinctive qualities will embody the audience's shared feelings and appreciation. Such enduring metaphors as light and darkness, storms and the sea, or the family may provide particular power for eulogies, stressing the basic humanity that calls the mourners together.

eulogy
A speech of tribute presented upon a person's death.

When you are asked to present a eulogy, you face special challenges. In addition to dealing with natural communication apprehension, you must also control your own feelings of grief. Plan your eulogy with these thoughts in mind:

- The primary purpose of a eulogy is to offer comfort to the living. Try to provide words that will continue to warm listeners in the days, months, and years ahead.
- Share stories that highlight the humanity of the person. Use gentle humor to recall his or her endearing qualities.
- Make the eulogy a celebration of life. Focus more on how wonderful it was to have shared the life of the person than on the pain of the loss.
- Emphasize the person's life as a model for those who live on.

When pop singer Whitney Houston died in 2012, her co-star in *The Bodyguard*, Kevin Costner, addressed these challenges when he spoke at her funeral. He suggested to her children that he and their mother had a lot in common. "Really? [laughter from the audience] She's a girl, you're a boy. You're white, she's black." Costner noted that Whitney was driven by questioning whether or not she was good enough, pretty enough. "Whitney, if you could hear me now I would tell you, you weren't just good enough—you were great. You sang the whole damn song without a band. You made the picture what it was."[9]

Toasts. A **toast** is a ceremonial tribute in miniature. It is offered as an accolade to people, as a blessing for their future, or simply as a bit of lighthearted enjoyment of the present. You might want to toast a coworker who has been promoted, to congratulate a couple at their wedding reception, or to celebrate the family's gathering at a reunion. The occasion may be formal or informal, but the message should always be eloquent. It simply won't do to mutter, "Here's to Tony; he's a great guy!" or "Cheers!" As one writer has said, such a feeble toast is "a gratuitous betrayal—of the occasion, its honoree, and the desire [of the audience] to clink glasses and murmur, 'Hear, hear,' in appreciation of a compliment well fashioned."[10]

toast
A short speech of tribute, usually offered at celebrations, dinners, or meetings.

A toast, a ceremonial speech in miniature, is offered as a tribute to people, as a blessing for their future, or simply in lighthearted enjoyment of the moment.

Because toasts should be brief, every word must count. Plan your toast well in advance of the occasion. Memorize it so that you say exactly what you want to say exactly as you want to say it. Practice presenting your toast with glass in hand until it flows easily. If you have difficulty memorizing your toast, it is probably too long. Some years ago, we attended a dinner for graduating seniors. One of the speakers offered a memorable toast that made good use of metaphor:

> As you graduate, I'm offering you a gift of wisdom that some say originated with Mark Twain. Twenty years from now, you'll

> be more disappointed by the things you didn't do than by the things you did. So throw off the bowlines, sail away from the safe harbor, and catch the trade winds. Explore, dream, learn, grow, and discover. Here's to the adventurous life that awaits you!

While a touch of humor is often appropriate, a toast should never embarrass or humiliate the honoree.[11] For example, it would certainly be inappropriate at a wedding reception to say, "Here's to John and Mary. I hope they don't end up in divorce court the way I did!" Figure 16.2 offers some sample toasts.

Figure 16.2
Sample Toasts[12]

From Tom's Irish Toasts and Blessings 1998 (Tom Donaghue, Wilton ME).

- May the road rise to meet you.
  May the wind always be at your back.
  May the sun shine warm upon your face.
  And rains fall soft upon your fields.
  And until we meet again,
  May God hold you in the hollow of His hand. (Irish blessing)
- May you have warm words on a cold evening, a full moon on a dark night, and a road downhill all the way to your door. (Irish blessing)
- To get the full value of joy, you must have someone to divide it with. (Mark Twain)
- Health and love and time to enjoy it. (Latin America)
- May we be in heaven half an hour before the devil knows we're dead. (Irish)
- To absent friends! (British)
- May your home always be too small to hold all of your friends. (Buddhist)
- We are each other's harvest; we are each other's business; we are each other's magnitude and bond. (Gwendolyn Brooks)
- Make the world better. (Lucy Stone)
- May we be like mighty oaks, which, after all, are only acorns that held their ground.
- Let there be spaces in your togetherness and let the winds of the heavens dance between you. Love one another but make not a bond of love: let it rather be a moving sea between the shores of your souls. (Khalil Gibran)
- When love reigns, the impossible may be attained. (Indian proverb)
- To love someone deeply gives you strength. Being loved by someone deeply gives you courage. (Lao Tzu)
- When you realize you want to spend the rest of your life with somebody, you want the rest of your life to start as soon as possible. (Nora Ephron, in *When Harry Met Sally*)
- Live long and prosper. (Mr. Spock, *Star Trek*)

Finding Your Voice

"I propose a toast . . ."

Prepare a toast honoring someone you really admire: a friend, a mentor, a role model, or a public figure (but not the instructor of this class, please!). Keep these rules in mind: Make it short and sweet, make it striking, and, above all, toast—don't roast!

Acceptance Speeches

If you are receiving an award or honor, you may be expected to respond with an **acceptance speech**. In a speech of acceptance, you want to express your awareness of the award's significance, your appreciation of the honor, and your acknowledgment of others who made it possible. Focus on the values represented by the award, and be humble without being too self-deprecating. Saying "I don't deserve this honor" may insult the selection committee, the award, and the audience—not to mention others who may have been in the running. Both your language and your manner should reflect the dignity of the occasion.

acceptance speech
A ceremonial speech expressing gratitude for an honor and acknowledging those who made the accomplishment possible.

When Elie Wiesel was awarded the Nobel Peace Prize, he began his acceptance speech with these remarks: "It is with a profound sense of humility that I accept the honor you have chosen to bestow upon me."[13] Follow his lead, and accept an award with grace and modesty. As you accept an award, consider its deeper meaning. In his acceptance speech, Wiesel stressed the value of freedom and the importance of involvement—of overcoming hatred with loving concern.

Finally, be sure the eloquence of your language fits the dignity of the moment. Wiesel told the story of a "young Jewish boy discovering the kingdom of night" during the Holocaust. This personal, metaphorical narrative was introduced early in the speech and repeated in the conclusion when Wiesel remarked, "No one is as capable of gratitude as one who has emerged from the kingdom of night." Be inspired by the meaning of the award for you, and let your presentation contribute to the stateliness and decorum of the event.

Finding Your Voice

Your Dream Award

Think of an award you would love to receive: for your art, your volunteer work, your athletic accomplishments, your scholastic achievements, your job, or your work on behalf of a cause. Why would this award be meaningful for you? Then prepare your acceptance speech, in which you address the nature of the award, express humility, and recognize others who have helped.

Speeches of Introduction

When you are called on to introduce a featured speaker to the audience, you will present a **speech of introduction**. A good speech of introduction usually accomplishes three goals: It makes the speaker feel welcome, it strengthens the ethos of the speaker, and it prepares the audience for the speech that will follow. You make a speaker feel welcome by both what you say and how you say it. Deliver your words of welcome with warmth and sincerity.

speech of introduction
A ceremonial speech in which a featured speaker is introduced to the audience.

If the speaker is particularly well known, the introduction can be brief. For example, when Madonna introduced Muhammad Ali at a gathering of New York sports personalities, she simply said, "We are alike in many ways. We have espoused unpopular causes, we are arrogant, we like to have our picture taken, and we are the greatest."[14]

On most occasions, however, the speaker should do more to establish the speaker's ethos and create anticipation for the speech to follow. As soon as you know you will be introducing someone, find out as much as you can about that person. Perhaps Alisa Valdes will be giving a presentation on your campus, and you've been given the honor of introducing her. You may know her work well, but your audience will likely want to hear about her best-selling novels about Latina professionals, her songwriting career, and her being named one of the 25 most influential Hispanics by *Time*. You don't want to repeat her résumé, but knowing as much as possible allows you to select the most significant themes to magnify in order to build identification with your audience. And by all means, make sure you know how to pronounce her name correctly!

It's a good idea to talk with the person about what you should emphasize, and avoid making assumptions that become embarrassing presumptions. One of our favorite stories concerns the famous western artist and writer Charles M. Russell. Russell did not particularly enjoy public speaking, but on one occasion his wife, Nancy, talked him into speaking at a civic gathering in Montana. The toastmaster did not bother to talk to Charlie before the speech, deciding on his own to introduce him as a "famous pioneer." As western historian Bob Doerk described the event, this is how Charlie responded:

> "I have been called a pioneer. In my book a 'pioneer' is a man who comes to a virgin country, traps off all the fur, kills off all the wild meat, cuts down all the trees, grazes off all the grass, plows the roots up, and strings ten million miles of barbed wire. A pioneer destroys things and calls it 'civilization.' I wish to God that this country was just like it was when I first saw it and that none of you folks were here at all."
>
> About this time, he realized that he had insulted his audience. He grabbed his hat and, in the boots and desperado sash that he always wore, left the room.[15]

So much for assuming you know what the speaker values and how that person would like to be introduced!

The following guidelines will help you build the speaker's ethos and lay the groundwork for speaker–audience identification:

- Create respect by briefly discussing the speaker's main accomplishments.
- Don't be too lavish with your praise. An overblown introduction can create unreasonable expectations for the speech and embarrass the speaker.
- Mention achievements that are relevant to the speaker's message, the occasion on which the speech is being presented, and the audience that has assembled.
- Be selective! An introducer who drones on too long makes the audience tune out before the speaker ever steps to the lectern.
- End your introduction by asking the audience to welcome the speaker.

The final function of an effective introduction is to tune the audience. In Chapter 5, we discussed how preliminary tuning can put listeners in a receptive mood. You tune the audience when you arouse anticipation for the message that will follow. However, don't try to preview what the speaker will say. Let the speaker present the speech.

SPEAKER'S NOTES

Introducing a Featured Speaker

When you are called on to introduce a featured speaker, keep the following in mind as you prepare your remarks:

1. Be sure you can pronounce the speaker's name.
2. Find out what the speaker would like you to emphasize.
3. Focus on aspects of the speaker's background that are relevant to the topic, audience, and occasion.
4. Announce the title of the speech if there is one.
5. Be careful not to cross that fine line between tuning listeners and appropriating the speaker's message.
6. Make the speaker feel welcome. Be warm and gracious.
7. Be brief!

Speeches of Inspiration

speech of inspiration
A ceremonial speech designed to awaken or reawaken an audience to a goal, purpose, or set of values.

A **speech of inspiration** helps an audience appreciate, commit to, and pursue a goal or set of values or beliefs. These speeches may be religious, commercial, political, or social. When a sales manager introduces a new product to marketing representatives, pointing up its competitive advantages and its stellar market potential, the speech is both inspirational and persuasive. The marketing reps should feel inspired to push that product with great zeal and enthusiasm. Speeches at political conventions, such as keynote addresses that praise the principles of the party, are inspirational. So also is that great American institution, the commencement address. As different as these speech occasions may seem, they have important points in common.

First, *speeches of inspiration are enthusiastic*. Inspirational speakers set an example through their personal commitment and passion. Both the speaker and the speech must be lively and dynamic, with a style that demonstrates the speaker's personal dedication. Speakers offer a model for their audiences through their behavior both on and off the speaking platform.

Second, *speeches of inspiration draw on past challenges and successes to stimulate confidence and future accomplishment*. In a commencement speech at Stanford University, the late Steve Jobs, co-founder of Apple, told the story of how he had been fired when he was 30 years old and the company was worth two billion dollars. "It was devastating," he said, before expounding on how this apparent failure had opened the door to further successes:

> Then it turned out that getting fired from Apple was the best thing that could have ever happened to me. The heaviness of being successful was replaced by the lightness of being a beginner again, less sure about everything. It freed me to enter one of the most creative periods of my life.
>
> During the next five years, I started a company named NeXT, another company named Pixar, and fell in love with an amazing woman who would become my wife. Pixar went on to create the world's first computer animated feature film, *Toy Story*, and is now the most successful animation studio in the world. In a remarkable turn of events, Apple bought NeXT, I returned to Apple, and the technology we developed at NeXT is at the heart of Apple's current renaissance. And Laurene and I have a wonderful family together.[16]

Steve Jobs, speaking at a Stanford University graduation ceremony, gave an inspiring commencement address that described how past career frustrations ultimately led to his current successes.

What initially felt like defeat proved to be a great opportunity, suggesting that the graduates embrace resilience.

Third, *speeches of inspiration revitalize our appreciation for values or beliefs*. In the later years of his life, after an incredible career as a track and field athlete, Jesse Owens became known as a great inspirational speaker. According to an obituary reported in the *Congressional Record*, "The Jesse Owens best remembered by many Americans was a public speaker with the ringing, inspirational delivery of an evangelist. . . . [His speeches] praised the virtues of patriotism, clean living, and fair play."[17]

Just before his death, Jesse Owens demonstrated his inspirational prowess in a speech protesting America's withdrawal from the 1980 Summer Olympic Games. In it, he set the stage by suggesting that "What the Berlin games proved... was that Hitler's 'supermen' could be beaten. Ironically, it was one of his blond, blue-eyed, Aryan athletes who helped do the beating."

After this tantalizing opening, Owens recounted his frustration when his prowess in the broad jump proved elusive at the Berlin games. As he tried to collect himself, he was approached by "my arch enemy, Luz Long, the prize athlete Hitler had kept under wraps while he trained for one purpose only: to beat me." Yet Long did not ridicule the American; instead, he empathized and suggested putting a towel six inches before the take-off board so that Owens could "give it all I had and be certain not to foul." When Owens qualified, his competitor beamed, "Now we can make each other do our best in the finals." That they did: They broke each other's records before Owens won, a victory that Luz Long celebrated with loud cheers. Owens concluded:

> That is what the Olympics are all about. The road to the Olympics does not lead to Moscow. It leads to no city, no country. It goes far beyond Lake Placid or Moscow, ancient Greece or Nazi Germany. The road to the Olympics leads, in the end, to the best within us.[18]

Jesse Owens's powerful message incorporated identification with sport as a way to help individuals rise above ideologies, inspiring and challenging his audience to embrace international competition in the same open spirit as Luz Long, one of Hitler's "blond, blue-eyed, Aryan athletes."

After-Dinner Speeches

after-dinner speech
An often humorous ceremonial speech presented after a meal that offers a message without asking for radical changes.

Occasions that celebrate special events often call for formal dinners that provide the setting for an **after-dinner speech**. Awards banquets for work, school, and sports teams are just a few examples of such occasions. You may be asked to give an after-dinner speech because you are the leader of the group sponsoring the dinner or because you have the reputation for being an entertaining speaker. After-dinner speeches typically celebrate group accomplishments and share laughter to enrich lives and bond groups more closely together.

Almost all after-dinner speeches share certain features. In keeping with the nature of the occasion, they should not be too difficult to digest. This is not a time to introduce radical ideas that require listeners to rethink their values or to ask for dramatic changes in belief or behavior. Nor is it a time for anger or negative thoughts. Rather, it is a time for people to savor who they are, what they have done, and what they wish to do. A good after-dinner speech typically leaves a message that guides and inspires future efforts.

The Role of Humor. Humor is appropriate for most after-dinner speeches. In the introduction, humor can promote identification while putting both the speaker and the audience at ease.[19] However, speakers should play to their strengths. Humor should not be forced on a speech. It should be functional and relevant, complementing your message and purpose for speaking.

The effective use of humor can enhance identification in an after-dinner speech.

The humor in a speech is best developed out of the immediate situation. Dick Jackman, director of corporate communications at Sun Company, opened an after-dinner speech at a National Football Foundation awards dinner by warning those in the expensive seats under the big chandelier that it "had been installed by the low bidder some time ago."[20] Such references are often made more effective by a touch of self-deprecation.[21] In the spring of 2015, President Barack Obama told an annual dinner for media correspondents that "I look so old John Boehner's already invited Netanyahu to speak at my funeral. Meanwhile, Michelle hasn't aged a day. I ask her what her secret is, she says 'fresh fruits and vegetables.' It's aggravating."[22]

Effective humor requires thoughtful planning. Canned or stock jokes are rarely effective when used out of context. However intentioned, off-color references to religion, race, gender, and sexual orientation will almost always offend thoughtful listeners on formal occasions. In general, avoid any anecdotes that seem funny at the expense of others. Remember that "pc"—personal courtesy—applies throughout any presentation.

Developing an After-Dinner Speech. Like most speeches, after-dinner presentations should be carefully planned and practiced. After-dinner speeches should be more than a string of anecdotes to amuse listeners. Use stories to establish and develop a mood of celebration and a message of identification. Start with an effective introduction that commands attention, as audience members may likely be distracted by conversation and ambient noise when the speaker starts. And build to a satisfying conclusion that brings home the essence of the message.

Above all, perhaps, after-dinner speeches should be mercifully brief. Don't make them more difficult to digest than the dinner itself. Long-winded after-dinner speakers can leave the audience fiddling with coffee cups and drawing pictures on napkins. After being subjected to such a speech, Albert Einstein once murmured: "I have just got a new theory of eternity."[23]

Acting as a Master of Ceremonies

Quite often, ceremonial speeches are presented as part of a program of events that must be coordinated with skill and grace if the event is to run smoothly. It takes at least as much careful planning, preparation, and practice to function effectively as a **master of ceremonies** (or *emcee*) as it does to make a major presentation. As the master of ceremonies, you will be expected to keep the program moving, introduce participants, and possibly present awards. In the process, you will also set the tone or mood for the program.

master of ceremonies
A person who coordinates an event or program, sets its mood, introduces portions of the programming, and provides transitions.

If possible, it helps to be involved in planning the program from the beginning. Being involved will give you a better idea of what is expected of you, what the agenda will be, what the time constraints are, who the featured speakers will be, and what special logistics (such as meal service) you might have to contend with. You can also make suggestions to help the proceedings move more smoothly. The following guidelines should help you function effectively as a master of ceremonies:

- **Know what is expected of you.** Remember, as emcee, you are not the star of the show. You are the one who brings it all together and makes it work.
- **Plan a good opener for the program.** Your opening remarks as an emcee are as important as the introduction to a major presentation. You should gain the attention of those in the audience and prepare them for the program. Be sure that the mood you set with your opener is consistent with the nature of the occasion.
- **Be prepared to introduce the participants.** Find out all you can about the speakers in advance. Ask them what they would like you to emphasize, and decide how you might best prepare the audience for their speeches. Be sure you know how to pronounce the speakers' names.
- **Know the schedule and timetable so that you can keep the program on track.** You also need to be sure that the participants get this information, preferably well ahead of time. They need to know how much time has been allotted for them to speak. Review the schedule with them before the program, and work out some way to cue them in case they are running overtime. If time restrictions are strict, as in a televised or streamed program, be ready to edit and adapt your own planned comments if necessary.
- **Make certain that any prizes or awards are kept within reach.** You don't want to be fumbling around looking for a plaque or a trophy.
- **Plan your comments ahead of time.** Develop a key-word outline for each presentation on a running script of the program. Number these outlines. Print the name of the person or award in large letters at the top of each outline so that you can keep to the schedule. See our discussion earlier in this chapter on introducing featured speakers and presenting awards.

> **Making a Ceremonial Speech**
>
> Name three occasions on which you might be asked to make a ceremonial presentation, now or in the future. What kinds of ceremonial speeches would these occasions call for and how would you prepare for them?

- **Practice your presentations.** Although you are not the featured speaker, your words are important (especially to the person whom you will introduce or to the person who will receive the award you present). Practice your comments the same way you would practice any other presentation.
- **Make advance arrangements for mealtime logistics.** Speak with the director of the serving staff before the program to share the program and proposed timing and to be sure the waiters know the importance of silent service.
- **Be ready for the inevitable glitches.** Remember Murphy's Law: If anything can go wrong, it will. Be ready for problems like microphones that don't work or that squeal, trays of dishes that crash to the floor, and people who wander in and out during the course of the program. As you respond to these events, keep your cool and good humor.
- **End the program strongly.** Just as a speech should not dwindle into nothingness, neither should a program. Review the suggestions for speech conclusions in Chapter 9. When ending your presentation, thank those who made the program possible, and then leave the audience with a memorable message about the significance of the events.[24]

Narrative Design

16.3 Use the narrative design for developing ceremonial presentations.

In previous chapters, we have discussed how storytelling helps to structure and support a speech. In ceremonial speaking, narrative plays an especially important role. Because by nature we are attracted to stories, good narratives can gain and hold our attention. They describe actions, which can bring us together and emphasize the moral qualities they illuminate. Thus, narratives are central to identification and magnification, the two basic techniques of ceremonial speaking.

embedded narrative
A story inserted within a speech that illustrates the speaker's point.

vicarious experience narrative
Speech strategy in which the speaker invites listeners to imagine themselves enacting a story.

As you may recall from Chapter 8, an **embedded narrative** is a story within a speech, and a **vicarious experience narrative** invites listeners *into* a speech, asking them to imagine themselves participating in the action as it unfolds. In a commencement address before the graduating class of Tuskegee University, First Lady Michelle Obama used the embedded narrative of an early Tuskegee airman in flight to embody a vision of community, ever struggling to transcend racial barriers and serve dual commitments to patriotism and racial progress:

> One of those first pilots, a man named Charles Debow . . . said that a take-off was—in his words—"a never failing miracle" where all "the bumps would smooth off. . . . [You're] in the air . . . out of this world . . . free."
>
> And when he was up in the sky, Charles sometimes looked down to see black folks out in the cotton fields not far from here—the same fields where decades before, their ancestors [worked] as slaves. And he knew that he was taking to the skies for them—to give them and their children something more to hope for, something to aspire to.
>
> And in many ways, that never-failing miracle—the constant work to rise above the bumps in our path to greater freedom for our brothers and sisters—that has always been the story of African Americans here at Tuskegee.[25]

master narrative
A speech structured around a story that reveals some important truth.

narrative design
Structure for a speech that develops a story from beginning to end through a prologue, plot, and epilogue.

When a speaker uses a **master narrative** the entire speech becomes a story that reveals some important truth. Jesse Owens's account of his experiences at the 1936 Olympic Games provides a strong example of this. As discussed in Chapter 3, such speeches are typically developed using a **narrative design**. Whereas most designs associated with informative and persuasive speaking follow a linear pattern in which main ideas develop and follow each other in reasoned sequence, the narrative design follows a dramatic pattern of development so that the speech presents a sequence of scenes that develop a story. Such a design features three major components: *prologue, plot,* and *epilogue.*

Prologue

The **prologue** in the narrative design sets the scene for what will follow. It is the counterpart of the introduction in other speech designs. The prologue orients listeners to the context of the action so that they can make sense of it. It foreshadows the meaning and importance of the story that will follow. It also introduces the important characters who will be part of the story.

prologue
An opening that establishes the context and setting of a narrative, foreshadows the meaning, and introduces major characters.

To see these elements in action, consider the prologue to Jesse Owens's speech on the 1936 Olympics:

> What the Berlin games proved...was that Hitler's "supermen" could be beaten. Ironically, it was one of his blond, blue-eyed, Aryan athletes who helped do the beating.
>
> I held the world record in the broad jump. Even more than the sprints, it was "my" event. Yet I was one jump from not even making the finals. I fouled on my first try, and playing it safe the second time, I had not jumped far enough.

The first two sentences of this prologue foreshadow the meaning of the story. They help prepare listeners for the actions that will unfold within the plot. They also anticipate the major character who will develop within the speech, Luz Long. The final four sentences present the context and setting of the story: Because Owens held the world record, he was favored, but he now had to confront a crisis.

Plot

The **plot** acts as the body of a narrative speech. A good plot accomplishes two goals. First, *the action of the story should build suspense, leading up to a climax.* Colorful details and lively dialogue make the action come to life. Second, *the main characters should become three-dimensional as they participate in the action.* This means that they come to stand for ideas and values, just as Luz Long, Hitler's hero, ironically comes to stand for fair play, brotherhood, and the virtues of competition.

plot
The body of a speech that follows a narrative design; it unfolds in a sequence of scenes designed to build suspense.

Let's return to the Owens speech. The plot develops in three closely related scenes: (1) the time immediately before the competition, (2) the competition itself, and (3) the aftermath of the competition.

In the first scene, we see a crisis of doubt as Owens kneels to pray. We learn of the generous spirit of Luz Long, who appears on cue as though he were the answer to Owens's prayer and who offers the advice Owens needs to qualify for his event. Owens re-creates the immediacy of the moment by using dialogue as Long speaks.

The second scene, which describes the competition itself, is summarized rather quickly. In the third scene, the aftermath, the real business of the speech takes place. Its purpose is to portray Luz Long as an Olympic ideal. The fact that Long is a German, and that Hitler considers him to be the champion of Nazi ideology, adds deep irony to the portrait.

Owens's message is that sportsmanship transcends both national origin and political affiliation to join competitors together. Thus, we behold the extraordinary spectacle after the competition when Luz Long joins hands with Owens, raising their arms to the sky as he leads the crowd in chanting, "Jazze Owenz."

Epilogue

The **epilogue** of a narrative reflects on the meaning of the action and offers final comments on the character of those who participated in it. It is the counterpart of the conclusion in other speech designs. When used in ceremonial speeches, the epilogue often

epilogue
The final part of a narrative that reflects upon its meaning.

Using a Narrative Design for Your Ceremonial Speech

Consider how you might use a narrative design to organize your upcoming ceremonial speech assignment. What sequence of events would you focus on to develop the plot or body of your story? Who would your main characters be and what actions or words would you use to bring them to life? How could your prologue or introduction set the scene for your story? What moral would you seek to convey through your final reflections or epilogue?

conveys a moral. In the Owens example, we see the nobility of Luz Long reaffirmed in the final scene of the story:

> Luz Long was killed in World War II and, although I don't cry often, I wept when I received his last letter—I knew it was his last. In it he asked me to someday find his son, Karl, and to tell him "of how we fought well together, and of the good times, and that any two men can become brothers."

What Owens doesn't quite tell us, but we can infer it from what he says, is that Long and Owens had become good friends, that they corresponded often, and that Long knew his end was near. These inferences only strengthen the underlying lesson for the audience Owens addressed in 1980 in the passage cited earlier:

> That is what the Olympics are all about. The road to the Olympics does not lead to Moscow. It leads to no city, no country. It goes far beyond Lake Placid or Moscow, ancient Greece, or Nazi Germany. The road to the Olympics leads, in the end, to the best within us.

Just as the Olympic spirit could thrive in the bigoted atmosphere of Nazi Germany in 1936, so also could it blossom in the Cold War atmosphere of Moscow in 1980. Owens's speech became an argument criticizing America's 1980 boycott of the Olympic Games. A video showing this dramatic encounter may be found in the Public Broadcasting System's archive of *American Experience*.

Final Reflections: "And in Conclusion Let Us Say"

Ceremonial speaking offers us the opportunity to celebrate the history, values, and champions binding us together into communities. Being able to connect your audience with those characteristics through identification and magnification, adapting to the needs of different types of special occasions, and incorporating narrative effectively will help you speak to those values and commitments as you address the meaning of a celebrated moment. It should also help you to discover and nurture your voice as a public speaker.

We began our book by encouraging your quest to find your voice, and every chapter here has had that as its goal. We hope that your quest has been successful, one that you can see benefiting you for a long time to come.

We close with our own speech of tribute, this time to you. Public speaking may not have always been easy for you. But it is our hope that you have grown as a person as you have grown as a speaker. Our special wishes, expressed in terms of the underlying vision of our book, are that:

- you have learned to climb the barriers that people sometimes erect to separate themselves from each other and that too often prevent meaningful communication;
- you have learned to weave words and evidence into eloquent thoughts and persuasive ideas;
- you have learned to build and present speeches that enlighten others in responsible and ethical ways; and
- above all, you have found subjects and causes worthy of your voice.

And so we propose a toast: *Having found your voice, may you use your new speaking skills to improve the lives and lift the spirits of those who listen to you.*

Study Questions

CONTENT MASTERY

1 What are the values and uses of ceremonial speaking?
2 What purpose does magnification serve, and how can you make it work?
3 How can you develop a sense of identification between yourself and your listeners?
4 What are the different kinds of ceremonial speeches, and how should you prepare for them?
5 What abilities are required to be a master of ceremonies?
6 How can you use narrative design to tell an effective story?

CRITICAL EXPLORATIONS

1. Watch the commencement speech, "How to Live Before You Die," presented at Stanford University by the late Steve Jobs. (The speech can be found under "Inspirational Speeches" on TED.) Look for the processes of identification and magnification in the speech. Does Jobs use them effectively?
2. Develop a speech of tribute to yourself as you would like to be remembered. What do you hope to accomplish? What do you stand for? What values give meaning to your life?
3. Prepare a speech of tribute in which you honor a person or group significant in contributing to the cause advanced in your persuasive speech.
4. Develop an embedded narrative for use in your upcoming ceremonial speech. You might narrate the specific accomplishments or experiences of an honored figure or group hero/heroine, or you might make up your own story. How can the embedded narrative help to establish identification with your listeners?
5. For and against magnification: Some might argue that magnification is distortion, that when you select a person's achievements and accomplishments to praise in speeches of tribute, you are ignoring less desirable features and shortcomings. The effect is to revise and misrepresent reality. What is your position on this issue? Is magnification justifiable? Are there situations in which it might not be desirable? What criteria should you use?
6. Prepare a speech of introduction for a historical figure you admire, as though that person will then be speaking to the class. How can you use identification and magnification in your introductory remarks?

CEREMONIAL SPEECH

Simone Mullinax presented this speech of tribute to her grandmother in a public speaking class at the University of Arkansas. The speech develops a master narrative based on an extended metaphor and paints an endearing portrait of a complex person who—like key lime pie—combines the qualities of sweetness and tartness.

BAKED-IN TRADITIONS

SIMONE MULLINAX

Reprinted with permission from Simone Mullinax.

This brief opening does a great deal of work. Because her speech was intended for presentation at a family dinner celebrating her grandmother's birthday, Simone did not need to open with an explicit reference to the occasion or reason for gathering. Instead, she begins with a rhetorical question and a definition and establishes her personal ethos. She then previews a clever categorical design that will follow the three main ingredients of a pie.

Have you ever baked a pie? No, I don't mean one you get from the freezer section at the grocery store—I'm talking about one you bake from scratch. I learned to bake a pie at an early age. And what I learned, early on, is that there are three things you have to master: the crust, the filler, and the topping. You can't have a pie if you lack any of these.

So where do you start? You start of course in the kitchen, which is where I meet my grandmother every time we get together. I would like to tell you she's that sweet, picturesque, grandmotherly grandmother you see on television, but she's not. Rather, she's that opinionated, bold, "her-way-or-the-highway" type that scares some people off. Her salvation is that she's also insanely funny and you fall in love with her stories, her cooking, and her opinions, even when you don't agree with all of them. Just when you're ready to pack up and move on, she does or says something that makes you want to hang around.

This paragraph completes the sketch that introduces Simone's grandmother. Simone paints this portrait by offering a few glimpses of her grandmother in action, small slices of life that depict character.

She's the woman who marches to the front of the line when her "babies" don't get what they need. She's the woman who sends us care packages made up of "goodies" from Dollar General. She's the woman who offers her opinions to everyone on any occasion, whether they want them or not. She's also the woman who gathered all the family recipes together—some of them unique and over a hundred years old—and gave them to me for a Christmas present. She's my grandmother and my best friend.

As she tells us more about pies, Simone also reveals more about herself. Through the use of embedded narrative, we learn that she has been a beauty pageant contestant who has a particular fondness for key lime pies. Note how her use of dialogue instead of paraphrasing brings her story to life.

But back to baking pies. My signature pie is a key lime pie. It really isn't my signature at all because I frequently forge my grandmother's. People often think of it as a hot weather treat, but every time we are together, even if it's 23 degrees outside, we make that key lime pie. Last year before I competed in the Miss Oklahoma pageant, a reporter called and asked what I was most looking forward to eating after the competition, and I said, "A key lime pie. A whole key lime pie." It was in bold headlines the next day: "Miss Tulsa looking forward to eating a pie." For weeks afterwards, people asked me, "So did you get your key lime pie?" And I was able to answer, "Sure did." Because after the pageant, my grandmother had two pies sitting on the counter, one for now, and one for later.

This begins an elaboration of the pie as extended metaphor in order to reveal the value and values of her grandmother. Family connectedness is an underlying theme.

Grammy taught me you can't have the pie without the crust. Everything in her life is built on a firm foundation, from the love of her family to the strength of her husband and the companionship of her friends. She stands behind her word, her love, and her family. She is the crust that keeps us all together, and also—I might add—all in line. Many times I have called Grammy with problems or confessions, and then I will hear advice like, "Oh, you don't need to do that, honey." And I know that, but her reminding me makes my own foundation that much stronger. Nothing crumbles in her key lime pie, especially the crust.

These discussions of the filling and the toppings offer Simone an opportunity to develop other aspects of her grandmother's character—her urge to help others build character and her willingness to go beyond the ordinary in order to accomplish worthwhile purposes.

What would a pie be without the filling? Some are lemon or pecan or pumpkin or chocolate or apple or—of course—key lime. But that is what makes each pie unique when you take that first delicious bite. Grammy fills her own life with meaning: one of her favorite sayings is, "Comfort the afflicted and afflict the comfortable." She believes in character building and in the value of striving for improvement: "Struggle to get better, struggle to succeed," but "Don't let success prevent you from struggling to get even better." The key lime, like her advice, is sweet—but it definitely has a bite to it!

The best part of the pie is the topping. Sometimes it's another layer of crust; sometimes it's meringue or whipped cream. The topping is that something extra that finishes the pie off. For Grammy, it's doing a little bit more than is necessary, a little bit more than what's expected. Part of it is literally going that extra mile. She and I walk together at 6:30 in the morning because she says it's the only time of day when the sun doesn't beat you down. I am barely awake for some of these walks, and that extra mile she loves to walk is often uphill! Beyond that, Grammy's favorite toppings are good words, good deeds, and high expectations.

And so, as we gather together to eat this wonderful meal and celebrate her birthday, I just want to say, "Thank you, Grammy, from the bottom of my heart." Years from now, I will teach my own granddaughter to build a perfect key lime pie. As we make it, I will be thinking about the woman whose love seeps into every crust holding me together. We will mix the fillings together and we will know just what to top it off with to make it perfect. And we will bake pies like friends hold conversations, the intricacies hidden beneath the taste and the impressions lasting beyond the words.

Simone opens her final paragraph by addressing the occasion and closes with a final note of inspiration. Due to her grandmother's influence, Simone can see herself in the distant future baking pies with her own granddaughter and holding the same kinds of conversations.

Communicating in Small Groups

APPENDIX

Many of the important communication interactions in your life will occur while working in small groups. On campus, you may be assigned to collaborate with your classmates on group projects, or you may or choose to work with others in co-curricular groups. In your professional career, you may be asked to work with others in small task-oriented committees, and some day you might even find yourself elected to public office and representing the concerns of your neighbors at local school board or city council meetings. Modern technologies such as Skype and video-conferencing are making it increasingly convenient to schedule regular meetings that include people working from remote locations. Alongside the public speaking skills learned throughout this course, developing your ability to communicate in group settings will enhance your interpersonal communication skills and nurture your potential for leadership, making a valuable contribution to finding your voice.

small group
A small number of people who interact over time to achieve a goal or goals.

Of course, there are many kinds of human groups. A **small group** typically consists of *three to twelve people who interact over a period of time in order to achieve a specific goal or set of goals*. For example, small groups may be formed to work on a specific project, to perform regular tasks important to running an organization or business, or to gather ideas and information for dealing with a problem for the group. Productive small-group interactions are well structured and focused on the task at hand. They follow a well-defined format or agenda, display effective leadership and participation by group members, and occur within a climate of professionalism that fosters a rich and thorough discussion.

In this appendix, we open by considering some advantages and challenges of communication in small groups. We then discuss participating as an effective group member and leader, some techniques of group problem solving, and considerations for planning and conducting meetings (including parliamentary procedure and virtual meetings). We close by considering the various types of presentations you may be called on to make in the context of working and communicating in small groups.

Advantages and Challenges of Group Problem Solving

There are many advantages to addressing problems in small groups. When we listen to a single speaker, we hear one inherently limited version of a situation or problem. Small-group discussions provide a much broader array and interaction of ideas and perspectives. The process can stimulate creative thinking, illuminate misconceptions and biases, and even uncover areas of agreement that can help resolve differences. In short, people who engage in constructive small-group discussions tend to make better, more informed decisions to which they are more committed.

Although working in groups has many advantages, it also has some potential disadvantages. As the old saw goes, "a camel is a horse designed by committee." It takes more time for groups to generate ideas, evaluate options, and make decisions than it does for individuals, and group discussions that lack structure and focus tend to be notoriously unproductive. To be effective, groups have to balance two important forms or functions of communication: *task* and *relational* communication.[1] **Task communication** entails people working together to accomplish a goal, when they define and evaluate the problem, identify materials to address that problem, develop and consider various alternatives, and reach decisions. **Relational communication** creates the communication climate of the group, with positive relational communication enhancing the cohesion, commitment, and satisfaction of the group's members. Effective groups integrate the two types of communication, recognizing that people in groups need to accomplish tasks—and that groups accomplish tasks through people.

task communication
Group communication behaviors that focus on achieving shared goals.

relational communication
Group communication behaviors that focus on creating a positive communication climate and promoting group cohesion.

Group discussions can be particularly rewarding and challenging when groups bring together members from different social, ethnic, and cultural backgrounds. The differing perspectives, priorities, and approaches to communication can provide a rich wellspring of unique ideas and creative engagement, but they can also be a source of miscommunication and misunderstanding. The following guidelines can help to maximize the advantages of having dissimilar group members:

1. Allow time for people to get acquainted before starting to work.
2. Distribute an agenda before the meeting so people know what to expect.
3. Summarize discussions as the meeting progresses. Post key points of agreement.
4. Avoid using language that some participants may not understand.
5. Be sensitive to differences in how people relate to one another and to nonverbal communication norms.[2]

Another common drawback of group problem solving is **groupthink**, which occurs when participants uncritically accept and reinforce a single position without adequately considering reservations or alternative views.[3] Groupthink is likely to occur when the group lacks a clear set of procedures for working through problems, when members have not adequately prepared themselves for the discussion, or when participants prioritize harmonious interaction over raising and exploring contrasting views and constructive criticisms. It is especially likely to occur when a particularly dynamic or domineering leader prematurely expresses a preference for a given position and then communicates in a manner that discourages participants from expressing concerns and opposing views.

groupthink
Occurs when group members uncritically accept and reinforce a single position without adequately considering reservations or alternative positions.

Groupthink can be particularly dangerous when it leads people to believe that a given problem or proposal has been thoroughly discussed, when in fact it has not. Dealing with groupthink is difficult, but there are some steps you can take to guard against it. The first step involves group members being aware that groupthink can be a problem. The major symptoms of groupthink include pressuring dissidents within the group to conform, censoring differing ideas, defending opinions more than exploring alternate ways of thinking, and asserting the group's own moral righteousness while attacking the character of opposing groups.

Once a group is aware that groupthink is a problem, members can work to minimize its effects. The group should set standards for investigation and appraisal that discourage uncritical thinking and hasty conclusions. The following principles can help to reduce the chances of groupthink:

- Encourage critical questions from all participants.
- Encourage debate of all recommendations.
- Insist that participants evaluate the support behind recommendations.
- Urge members to delay decisions until all have expressed their views.

Participating in Small Groups

For small work groups to function effectively, the individual participants must appreciate and fulfill their responsibilities as both *members* and *leaders* in group discussions. Note that we treat membership and leadership roles together for a reason. While clearly defined leaders and procedures are sometimes necessary for facilitating group discussions, the highest quality communication tends to occur when members share leadership responsibilities to help the group accomplish shared tasks while maintaining a strong sense of group cohesion.

Working as a Group Member

Becoming an effective group participant means putting the business of the group and the question at hand ahead of your own individual agendas and concerns. That doesn't mean that you aren't yourself; it does mean that you put your needs in the context of the group. In addition, effective group members accept the following responsibilities:

- First, come to meetings prepared to contribute. This means reading background materials and completing any tasks you've accepted or been assigned before attending a meeting.
- Second, be critically engaged and open to learning from others. Contribute to discussions without dominating them, and don't get defensive or personally offended when your ideas are challenged. Be willing to accept the decisions of the group and move on constructively even when your proposals are not accepted.
- Third, listen constructively. Don't interrupt others, and do respond to what they've said. Speak up if you feel consensus is forming too quickly. You might save the meeting from groupthink.

As you participate in group discussions, avoid certain behaviors that can block or distract from constructive engagement. For instance, while there is nothing wrong with the occasional humorous comment, jokers who use every subject or comment to cue a punch line disrupt productive discussion. Participants who dominate discussions or always have to have the last word may thwart participation by other group members. And again, group members should consciously put their egos to rest and avoid getting combative in the face of constructive criticism. The self-analysis form in Figure A.1 can help you assess and improve your group communication skills.

Leading Small Groups

For many years, social scientists have been studying leadership by analyzing group communication patterns. Their findings suggest that two basic types of leadership behaviors emerge in most groups, paralleling the two kinds of communication. The first is **task leadership behavior**, which directs the activity of the group toward specified goals. The second is **social leadership behavior** (sometimes called relational leadership), which helps build and maintain positive relationships among group members. In most groups, these roles are served by the same people, and again the best communication tends to occur when members assume and share these roles as needed.

task leadership behavior
A type of leadership that directs the attention and activity of a group toward achieving specific goals.

social leadership behavior
A type of leadership that focuses on building and maintaining positive and productive relationships among group members.

Task leaders direct group communication toward achieving shared goals. They give and seek information, opinions, and suggestions, and they guide the group's discussions to keep them on track. *Social leaders* promote group cohesion, the constructive resolution of conflicts within the group, and an atmosphere in which group members feel encouraged to participate and appreciated for their contributions. In a healthy communication climate, the two kinds of leadership behavior support each other and keep the group moving toward its goal. When one person combines both styles of leadership, that person is likely to be highly effective.

Figure A.1 Analyzing Your Own Group Communication

	Need to Do Less	Doing Fine	Need to Do More
1. I make my points concisely.	☐	☐	☐
2. I speak with confidence.	☐	☐	☐
3. I provide specific examples and details.	☐	☐	☐
4. I try to integrate ideas that are expressed.	☐	☐	☐
5. I let others know when I do not understand them.	☐	☐	☐
6. I let others know when I agree with them.	☐	☐	☐
7. I let others know tactfully when I disagree with them.	☐	☐	☐
8. I express my opinions.	☐	☐	☐
9. I suggest solutions to problems.	☐	☐	☐
10. I listen to understand.	☐	☐	☐
11. I try to understand before agreeing or disagreeing.	☐	☐	☐
12. I ask questions to get more information.	☐	☐	☐
13. I ask others for their opinions.	☐	☐	☐
14. I check for group agreement.	☐	☐	☐
15. I try to minimize tension.	☐	☐	☐
16. I accept help from others.	☐	☐	☐
17. I offer help to others.	☐	☐	☐
18. I let others have their say.	☐	☐	☐
19. I stand up for myself.	☐	☐	☐
20. I urge others to speak up.	☐	☐	☐

Leadership has also been studied in terms of the way a leader handles the task and relational functions. An **autocratic leader** makes decisions without consultation, issues orders or gives direction, and controls the members of the group through the use of rewards or punishments. A **participative leader** seeks input from group members and gives them an active role in decision making. Finally, a **laissez-faire leader** lets members decide on their own what to do, how to do it, and when to do it. If you were working in an organization, you would probably say you worked *for* an autocratic leader, worked *with* a participative leader, and worked *in spite of* a laissez-faire leader.

autocratic leader
Makes decisions and gives orders without consultation; directs group behavior through the use of rewards and punishments.

participative leader
Seeks input from group members and gives them an active role in decision making.

laissez-faire leader
Leaves group members free to decide what, how, and when to act without guidance.

transactional leadership
Leadership based on power relationships that relies on reward and punishment to achieve its ends.

transformational leadership
Leadership based on mutual respect and stewardship rather than control to inspire group members.

More recent work on leadership suggests that leadership styles are either transactional or transformational. **Transactional leadership** occurs in an environment based on power relationships, and relies on reward and punishment to accomplish its ends. **Transformational leadership**, on the other hand, focuses on stewardship, mutual respect, and developing the potential of group members by appealing to their "higher levels of motivation to contribute to a cause and add to the quality of life on the planet."[4] As opposed to emphasizing *power over*, transformational leaders exhibit *power to*, by enabling group members to accomplish their goals.[5] Transformational leadership encourages communication from subordinates because they are less intimidated by their superiors and more willing to ask for advice or help.[6] Transformational leaders have the following qualities:

- They have a vision of what needs to be done.
- They are empathetic.
- They are trusted.
- They give credit to others.
- They help others develop.
- They share power.
- They are willing to experiment and learn.

Consider how effective leadership relates to the major components of ethos, as discussed in Chapter 3. An effective leader is *competent*: The leader understands the problem and knows how to steer a group through the problem-solving process. An effective leader has *integrity*: The leader is honest and places group success above personal concerns. An effective leader is perceived as a person of *good will*, concerned less about oneself and more about those the group serves. Finally, an effective leader is *dynamic*. Dynamic leaders are enthusiastic, energetic, and decisive. Most of us have each of these qualities in varying degrees and can use them when the need for leadership arises. To be an effective leader, remember two simple goals: *Help others be effective* and *get the job done.* Cultivate an open leadership style that encourages all sides to air their views.

Group Problem-Solving Techniques

Groups reach better decisions through deliberations that are systematic and thorough. To function effectively, problem-solving groups can use a variety of methods or discussion formats. One of the most influential techniques of group problem solving is called reflective thinking.

Reflective Thinking and Problem Solving

The reflective-thinking approach to group problem solving represents a modification of a technique developed by John Dewey in 1910. This systematic approach consists of five steps: (1) *defining the problem,* (2) *generating potential solutions,* (3) *evaluating options for solutions,* (4) *developing a plan of action,* and (5) *evaluating the results.*

Step 1: Defining the Problem. The first step is to define and analyze the problem. For instance, if you were assigned to a group charged with generating ideas for increasing enrollment by underrepresented groups at your university, you would first want to reach a group consensus on the meaning of "underrepresented groups." Then, you would seek reliable information on the status of enrollments of underrepresented groups at your university, the extent to which those enrollment and retention rates have risen or fallen over the past few years, and whatever measures your university has already implemented to promote and maintain enrollment by underrepresented groups.

The following guidelines can help a group define an issue or problem it needs to work on:

1. Describe the problem as specifically as possible.
2. Clarify the terms used to describe the problem.
3. Gather enough information to understand the problem.
4. Explore the causes of the problem.
5. Investigate the history and duration of the problem.
6. Determine who is affected by the problem.
7. Consider the outcomes if the problem is solved or not solved.

Step 2: Generating Potential Solutions. Once the problem has been defined, the group can begin looking for solutions. One useful technique for generating possible solutions is **brainstorming**. When brainstorming for ideas, each member contributes every idea she or he can think of, and these are recorded by a person designated by the group. Participants may combine ideas to create new ones or even repeat ideas that have already been mentioned, but at this stage of the process they should refrain from any criticism or evaluation. Freewheeling, creative, and even outrageous ideas actually benefit the brainstorming process because you never know when a productive idea will result. The point is to generate as many potential solutions as possible for later discussion.[7]

brainstorming
A technique that encourages the free play of the mind to generate a list of ideas that are then carefully evaluated.

Once the group has generated a comprehensive list of ideas, the group reviews the suggestions to clarify ideas, combine some approaches, and add new options. In the next step, the group identifies the most promising ideas and determines how to research and evaluate each one.

To save time, many small groups use **electronic brainstorming**, in which participants generate ideas online before meeting face-to-face.[8] Electronic brainstorming has the advantage of getting group members thinking about potential ideas before the actual meeting. It may be particularly helpful in eliciting more input from members who might feel inhibited in face-to-face meetings due to perceived lack of status or identification with the group. The group can also encourage participants to clarify their ideas and investigate additional supporting materials as necessary.

electronic brainstorming
A group technique in which participants generate ideas online prior to discussing them face-to-face.

Step 3: Evaluating Options for Solutions. Once your group has generated a list of potential options, the next step is to evaluate, rank, and choose the best possible solutions. With significant problems, this often means scheduling another meeting, in which case members should use the extra time to gather more information, clarify their thinking, and raise additional questions. During the evaluation session, the following criteria should be used:

- Costs of the options
- Probability of success
- Ease or difficulty of enacting options
- Time constraints
- Additional benefits of options
- Potential problems of options

As the discussion proceeds, some proposals will be quickly discarded, others will be strengthened and refined, and still others may be combined to generate new alternatives. After all of the ideas have been considered, group members will often reduce their list to the few most promising options for further discussion. Final agreement on a solution or set of solutions is often reached through consensus or general agreement, although sometimes a vote is necessary when differences of opinion persist among group members.

Participants often become personally caught up with their own solutions. During the evaluation phase, the group needs to stay focused on the ideas advanced.

Differences of opinion and conflict are a natural and necessary part of problem solving; if there aren't disagreements, the group may be engaging in groupthink or abdicating its responsibility to think critically. Discussing the strengths of an idea before talking about its weaknesses can help take some of the heat out of the process.

Step 4: Developing a Plan of Action. Once the group has selected a solution, the members should figure out how the solution can be implemented. For example, to improve company morale, a group might recommend a three-step plan:

1. Provide in-house training programs to increase opportunities for promotion.
2. Create a pay structure that rewards success in training programs.
3. Encourage more employee participation in decision making.

Once again, it is sometimes advisable to schedule a separate follow-up meeting for developing a plan of action. This gives group members more time to consider the logistics of implementing the proposed solution. Participants should consider what resources will be necessary to make their solution work, what factors might help or hinder their effectiveness, a reasonable timetable for achieving their objectives, and who will be responsible for implementing and overseeing the solution. If the group cannot develop a plan of action for the solution or if insurmountable obstacles crop up, they should return to Step 3 and reconsider other options.

Step 5: Evaluating Results. A problem-solving group also needs to decide how to evaluate results of the plan's enactment. They should establish criteria for success, a timetable of when results are expected, and contingency plans to use if the original plan fails. For example, to monitor the ongoing success of the three-part plan to improve employee morale, the group would have to determine benchmarks of progress for each stage. That way, the company can detect and correct problems as they occur, before they damage the plan as a whole. Having a scheduled sequence of benchmarks provides a way to determine results while the plan is enacted rather than waiting for the entire project to be completed.

Other Approaches to Group Problem Solving

collaborative problem solving
A group technique that gathers participants from differing backgrounds and social sectors for their input on a problem.

When a group consists of people from very different backgrounds, **collaborative problem solving** may work best.[9] For example, in many urban areas, coalitions of business executives and educators have worked together on plans to train people for jobs in the community. In such situations, the problems are important and the resources are typically limited. Because there is no established authority structure and the factions may have different expectations or goals, these diverse participants may face challenges working together. To be effective, such groups need to spend time defining the problem and exploring each other's perspectives. This should help them recognize their interdependence, while preserving the independence of each participant. The effectiveness of such groups depends on the participants not seeing themselves as members of group A (the executives) or group B (the educators), but as members of group C (the coalition). Leadership can be especially difficult in such groups.

dialogue groups
A group assembled to explore the differing interpretations and experiences that members bring to a problem.

One useful approach in such situations is **dialogue groups**. According to William Isaacs, director of the Dialogue Project at the Massachusetts Institute of Technology Center for Organizational Learning (MIT Center), "Dialogue is a discipline of collective thinking and inquiry, a process for transforming the quality of conversation, and, in particular, the thinking that lies beneath it."[10] Rather than establishing a single approach to defining or dealing with a situation or problem, dialogue groups stress understanding the different interpretations and experiences that participants bring to the interaction. Their purpose is to establish a conversation from which common ground and mutual trust can emerge.

Leadership is critical in dialogue groups. According to Edgar Schein of the MIT Center, the facilitator must take the following steps:

1. Seat the group in a circle to create a sense of equality.
2. Introduce the problem.
3. Ask people to share an experience in which dialogue led to good communication.
4. Ask members to consider what leads to good communication.
5. Ask participants to talk about their reactions.
6. Let the conversation flow naturally.
7. Intervene only to clarify problems of communication.
8. Conclude by asking all members to comment however they choose.[11]

The dialogue method is not a substitute for other problem-solving techniques. Instead, it may be used to provide an opportunity for members to understand each other well enough to be talking the same language as they work on solutions to problems.

When an organization wants to explore the feelings or motivations of customers, clients, or voters, they often hold a **focus group**.[12] Focus groups typically have six to ten members who are carefully selected to provide the type of information sought. In a focus group, the moderator asks questions and encourages all of the participants to respond. Advertisements, brochures, or video clips may be used to stimulate discussion. Interactions between members of the group often provide the most valuable information. The sessions are recorded for later analysis. Focus groups are typically face-to-face encounters, but they may also be conducted electronically.

focus group
A small group formed to reveal the feelings or motivations of customers, clients, or voters.

Effective Meetings

Many people regard meetings as dreary, boring, useless exercises in futility. Some joke that "to kill time, a meeting is the perfect weapon"; one penned an entire book entitled *Death by Meeting*.[13] Yet meetings can offer opportunities to pool group knowledge, generate fresh new insights, and build a sense of cohesion. Effective meetings are planned well, conducted effectively, use parliamentary procedure as necessary, and adapt to virtual settings.

Planning Meetings

Group meetings often become a waste of time and a source of frustration when the people who conduct them do not know when to call meetings or how to run them.[14] The first question to ask is: *Do we really need a meeting?* In this day of electronic communication, routine "housekeeping" questions and concerns can often be discussed adequately using e-mail, texting, and drop boxes—or even casual conversations among colleagues. However, traditional face-to-face meetings are still preferable for discussing issues of great importance to the group, and they help to maintain a sense of group cohesion and identification. In addition, group meetings should be called when people need to:

- discuss important developments or new information;
- decide on a common course or plan of action; or
- report on the progress of a plan, evaluate its effectiveness, and revise it if necessary.

More than just knowing when to call meetings, you need to know how to plan them. The following guidelines should help you plan effective meetings:

- *Have a specific purpose for holding a meeting.* Unnecessary meetings waste time. If your goal is simply to increase interaction, plan a social event rather than a meeting.

- *Prepare an agenda and distribute it to participants before the meeting.* Having an agenda gives members time to prepare and assemble information they might need. Solicit agenda items from participants so that each can bring questions of importance to the table. Tropman's "rule of thirds" offers a useful template for an agenda: start with announcements and acknowledgments for a sense of accomplishment; in the middle, move to the discussion of important issues; and at the end, share information and discussion without needing a resolution. This bell-shaped approach offers a way to begin and end on positive notes.[15]
- *Designate tasks that need to be completed in preparation for the meeting.* For instance, members might be asked to research and brief the group on different aspects of a problem.
- *Keep meetings short.* After about an hour, groups get tired, and the law of diminishing returns sets in. Don't try to do too much in a single meeting.
- *Keep groups small.* You get more participation and interaction in small groups. In larger groups, people may be reluctant to ask questions or contribute ideas.
- *Select participants who will interact easily with each other.* In business settings, the presence of someone's supervisor may inhibit interaction. You will get better participation if group members come from the same or nearly the same working level in the organization.
- *Plan the site of the meeting.* Arrange for privacy and freedom from interruptions. A circular arrangement contributes to participation because there is no power position. A rectangular table or a lectern and classroom arrangement may inhibit interaction.
- *Prepare in advance.* Be certain that you have the necessary supplies. These may include computers and projection equipment, in which case you need to make sure they are in working order, or such low-tech equipment as chalk, a flip chart, markers, note pads, and pencils.

Conducting an Effective Meeting

Group leaders have many responsibilities. They want to encourage deliberations that proceed in good faith toward constructive ends. When using a structured discussion format such as the reflective thinking model discussed earlier in this appendix, leaders should be prepared to guide the group through the various steps of the process, enabling productive participation from all of the members. Finally, group leaders should be well informed on the issues so that they can answer questions and keep the group moving toward its objectives.

The following checklist should be helpful in guiding your behavior as a group leader:

- Begin and end the meeting on time.
- Present background information concisely and objectively.
- Facilitate the meeting without dominating it.
- Be enthusiastic and supportive.
- Urge all members to participate.
- Get conflict out in the open so the group can deal with it constructively.
- Keep the discussion focused on the issue at hand.
- At the close of a meeting, summarize what the group has accomplished.

As a group leader, you may need to present the group's recommendations to others. In this task, you function primarily as an informative speaker. Present the recommendations offered by the group, along with the major reasons for making these recommendations. Also mention reservations that may have surfaced during deliberations. Your job in making this report is not to advocate but to educate. Later, you may

To Enhance Communication	To Impede Communication
Members seek out opinions	Members express dislike for each other
Members encourage creativity	Members personally attack each other
Members encourage participation	Members make sarcastic remarks
Members encourage opposing views	Leader intimidates members
Members provide information	Meeting becomes a gripe session
Entire group analyzes suggestions	Disagreements are ignored, not aired
Members listen to one another	Disagreement is discouraged
Members respect others' ideas	Leader sets criteria for solution
Members support others' ideas	Leader makes decision
Members thoroughly research problems	Members pursue personal goals
Group sets criteria for solution	Attention to personal disputes overtakes discussion of task
Members are knowledgeable on the issues	Members do not understand issues
Members present evidence for suggestions	Members offer no evidence for suggestions
Members focus on task	Members do not accept responsibility for success of group

Figure A.2 Communication That Enhances or Impedes Decision Making

join in any following discussion with persuasive remarks that express your personal convictions on the subject.

Finally, as you conduct meetings, keep in mind communication that either advances or impedes group effectiveness.[16] Better group decisions are made when all group members participate fully in the process, when members are respectful of each other and leaders are respectful of members, and when negative emotions are kept in check. More specific details of these principles are listed in Figure A.2.

Using Parliamentary Procedure

The larger a group is, the more it needs a formal procedure to conduct meetings. Also, if the subject under discussion is controversial or disputed, it helps to have a set of rules to follow. Having clear-cut guidelines helps to keep meetings from becoming chaotic and ensures fair treatment for all participants. In such situations, many groups conduct formal meetings by following some variation of **parliamentary procedure**.

parliamentary procedure A relatively standard set of rules for conducting formal meetings that encourages the orderly, fair and full consideration of proposals during group discussions.

Parliamentary procedure establishes an order of business for a meeting and lays out the way the group initiates discussions and reaches decisions. The point is to facilitate discussions that are inclusive and thorough as well as structured and task-oriented. Under parliamentary procedure, a formal meeting proceeds as follows:

1. The chair calls the meeting to order.
2. The secretary reads the minutes of the previous meeting, which are corrected if necessary, and approved.
3. Officers and committees present reports.
4. The group considers unfinished business.
5. New business is introduced.
6. Announcements are made.
7. The meeting is adjourned.

Business in formal meetings goes forward by **motions**, or proposals set before the group. For instance, when the chair asks: "Is there any new business?" a member might respond: "I move that we allot $500 to build a homecoming float." Before the group can discuss the motion, another group member must say, "I second the motion." The purpose of a **second** is to ensure that more than one person wants to see the motion considered. If no one volunteers a second, the chair may ask, "Is there a second?" Once a motion is made and seconded, it is open for discussion. It must be passed by

motions Formal proposals for group consideration.

second A motion must receive a "second" from another member of the group before discussion can proceed.

majority vote, defeated, or otherwise resolved before the group can move on to other business.

Let us assume that, as the group discusses the motion to build a homecoming float, some members believe the amount of money proposed is insufficient. At this point, another member may say: "I move to amend the motion to provide $750 for the float." The **motion to amend** gives the group a chance to modify a main motion. It must be seconded and, after discussion, must be resolved by majority vote before discussion goes forward. If the motion to amend passes, then the group considers the amended main motion.

motion to amend
A parliamentary move that offers opportunity to modify a motion presently under discussion.

How does a group make a decision on a motion? There usually is a time when discussion begins to lag. At this point, the chair might say, "Do I hear a call for the question?" A motion to **call the question** ends discussion, and it requires a two-thirds vote for approval. Once the group votes to end discussion, it then votes to accept or reject the motion. No further discussion can take place until the original or amended motion is voted on.

call the question
A motion that proposes to end discussion and vote on the original motion, as amended if appropriate.

Sometimes the discussion of a motion may reveal that the group is confused or sharply divided about an issue. At this point, a member may move to **table the motion** instead of calling the question. This can help dispose of a troublesome motion without further divisive or confused discussion. Once a motion is tabled, it can be reconsidered only if the member who called for the table moves to rescind that motion. At other times, the discussion of a motion may reveal that the group lacks information to make an intelligent decision. At that point, we might hear from a member: "In light of the uncertainty over costs, I move we postpone further consideration until next week's meeting." The **motion to postpone consideration** gives the chair a chance to appoint a committee to gather the information needed. The **move to adjourn** presented by a member ends the meeting.

table the motion
A parliamentary move to indefinitely suspend discussion of a motion.

motion to postpone consideration
A motion that defers discussion until some specified time.

move to adjourn
A motion that calls for the meeting to end.

These are just some of the important procedures that can help ensure that formal group communication remains fair and constructive (see Figure A.3). For more information on formal group communication procedures, consult the latest edition of *Robert's Rules of Order*.

Figure A.3 Guide to Parliamentary Procedure

Action	Requires Second	Can Be Debated	Can Be Amended	Vote Required	Function
Main Motion	Yes	Yes	Yes	Majority	Commits group to a specific action or position.
Second	No	No	No	None	Assures that more than one group member wishes to see idea considered.
Move to Amend	Yes	Yes	Yes	Majority	Allows group to modify and improve an existing motion.
Call the Question	Yes	No	No	Two-thirds	Brings discussion to an end and moves to a vote on the motion in question.
Move to Table the Motion	Yes	No	No	Majority	Stops immediate consideration of the motion until a later unspecified time.
Move to Postpone Consideration	Yes	Yes	Yes	Majority	Stops immediate discussion and allows time for the group to obtain more information on the problem.
Move to Adjourn	Yes	No	No	Majority	Formally ends meeting.

Virtual Meetings

In this age of rapidly advancing technology, you will likely be asked to participate in **virtual meetings** that are conducted and mediated using technology. Businesses and government organizations have used teleconferencing to conduct meetings among employees working from remote locations for decades. Modern software packages for video-conferencing allow for the integration of audio, visual, and written transactions among group members in real time, and there is little doubt that such technologies will continue to improve and become increasingly common in the future.

virtual meetings
Group meetings that are conducted across space and mediated using technology.

Using virtual technology for conducting group meetings offers many advantages. The most obvious, as mentioned above, is allowing group members to interact from remote locations. Virtual meetings are more convenient and less time-consuming for group participants; they minimize travel costs and other related expenses for organizations; and they leave a smaller carbon footprint, making them more environmentally friendly. The instantaneous exchange of written, audio, and visual documents can enhance the substance and efficiency of group communication, and can be especially effective for conducting group brainstorming sessions. What's more, the use of virtual communication technologies can elicit more and better input from group members who might contribute less in face-to-face discussions, and can discourage one or two group members from dominating the entire discussion.

For all the potential advantages of conducting virtual meetings, there are many challenges and potential frustrations that can undermine their effectiveness. Of course, your technical equipment must work properly, and group members need to have access to the right equipment and know how to use it. And while technology is fast closing the gap, virtual communication usually provides for less immediacy and more limited feedback than face-to-face interactions, which may cause some members to get confused, lose focus, and quit contributing to group discussions. Finally, virtual meetings are generally less effective for promoting group cohesion and resolving differences of opinion within the group.

These challenges heighten the importance of carefully planning and thoughtfully conducting virtual meetings. Because there is usually less opportunity to clarify misunderstandings, it is even more important for everyone to understand the purpose for the meeting and to have a well-defined agenda of items for discussion. Group leaders may need to be more active in eliciting input from all participants, and group members need to familiarize themselves with the technology and commit themselves to the process without the peer reinforcement of direct engagement. Experts generally recommend supplementing virtual meetings with occasional face-to-face gatherings, especially for making really important decisions or developing long-range plans.[17] See our discussion in Chapter 13 for related advice on making mediated presentations, and Chapter 10 on using PowerPoint and other forms of multimedia presentation aids.

Making Group Presentations

Group communication often overlaps with public speaking. As discussed in Chapter 13, during meetings at work you may be asked to make short informative presentations or briefings on the status of a project or some aspect of a problem. On other occasions, group members may present their findings and recommendations to larger audiences. When preparing for such presentations, the group should

- designate which group members will present which parts of the report;
- assign other duties, such as preparing or coordinating presentation aids;

- develop an outline or agenda for the presentation;
- determine who should handle questions and answers; and
- schedule and oversee a rehearsal of the group presentation.

oral report
A presentation that summarizes the deliberations or work of a small group before a larger audience.

Often, a designated spokesperson will simply present an **oral report**. This report is basically an informative speech that follows a specific design. The introduction briefly reviews the problem, introduces the members of the group (including their credentials) if they are not well known to the audience, and describes the process used by the group to study the problem. The body of the report covers the major findings or recommendations for action. The conclusion summarizes the findings and may make suggestions for further work. The report should be as brief as possible and should allow for questions and answers following the formal presentation.

symposium
A moderated group presentation format in which members present prepared speeches on different areas of a topic or issue.

In addition to a simple oral report, group presentations may follow four other formats: a *symposium*, a *panel discussion*, a *roundtable presentation*, or a *forum*. A **symposium** features a moderator and members of the problem-solving group as presenters. The primary role of the moderator is to introduce the topic and speakers at the beginning of the symposium and to summarize the findings as the presentation draws to a close. Each symposium speaker will typically cover one aspect of the topic, making a short report on the group's findings or recommendations in that area. The moderator enforces time limits and keeps the presentations on track. The symposium is usually followed by a question-and-answer session.

panel discussion
A group presentation format in which group members informally discuss a series of questions as introduced by a moderator.

A **panel discussion** is less formal than a symposium. It also has a moderator who introduces the topic and the participants, but it does not feature prepared presentations. Rather, it is a planned pattern of spontaneous exchanges. Following the brief introductions, the moderator asks questions of the group. Participants respond with brief impromptu and extemporaneous answers, often responding to other participants rather than simply to the moderator. The moderator guides the discussion, keeps the group in focus, ensures the participation of all panelists, and avoids letting a single participant dominate the discussion.

Although responses in a panel discussion are impromptu, the participants should be told in advance what general types of questions may be asked so that they can prepare with these in mind. Panelists should think back through what went on in the group and organize their ideas in advance of the discussion. They should be prepared for inquisitive and challenging follow-up questions either from the moderator or from the audience.

roundtable
An informal group presentation format in which members discuss ideas, information, and opinions before a larger audience.

A **roundtable** presentation is an interactive way of publicly exchanging information, ideas, or opinions.[18] All members of the group are considered equal and are encouraged to participate openly and fully in the proceedings. There are no formal opening statements or prepared speeches. The leader helps generate discussion, makes certain the speakers stay on track and adhere to time limits, and encourages a nonjudgmental dialogue. The Sierra Club, for example, conducted a roundtable on the climate crisis that included business and political leaders as well as environmental activists.[19]

forum
A moderated group presentation format in which designated members respond to questions from the audience.

In a **forum** presentation, questions come from the audience rather than from the moderator. The basic job of the moderator of a forum is to keep the discussion on track. The moderator may introduce the topic and participants, and during the course of the forum, recognize members of the audience who wish to ask questions. At times, the moderator may also have to actually *moderate*, acting as a referee if questions or answers become heated on contentious topics. If the group anticipates controversy, it may wish to arrange for a parliamentarian to help keep the meeting constructive. Participants should follow the guidelines suggested for handling questions and answers in Chapter 12.

Final Reflections: Your Group Voice

Over the course of our lives, all of us will develop multiple formal and informal group associations that will exert a tremendous influence on us. As you complete your education and pursue a professional or public life beyond college, you will likely be called on to participate in a variety of task-oriented small groups. Your ability to make constructive contributions to group discussions will distinguish and nurture your potential for leadership and success. In this appendix, we discussed some advantages and disadvantages of communication in small groups, ways to effectively participate as a group member and as a leader, considerations for planning and conducting meetings, and the various types of presentations by small groups. Together with the public speaking skills taught throughout this textbook, developing your group communication skills will make a valuable contribution to finding your voice.

APPENDIX B

Speeches for Analysis

Self-Introductory Speeches

1. Sandra Baltz *My Three Cultures*
2. Beth Tidmore *Lady with a Gun*
3. BJ Youngerman *To Toss or Not to Toss: The Art of Baseball Umpiring*

Informative Speeches

1. Stefan Moskowitz *The Debate on the Transpacific Partnership*
2. Joseph Van Matre *Video Games*
3. Gabrielle Wallace *The French Paradox: A Delicious Secret Revealed*

Persuasive Speeches

1. Joshua Logan *Global Burning*
2. Anna Aley *We Don't Have to Live in Slums*
3. Katie Lovett *The Price of Bottled Water*
4. Betsy Lyles *Fairly Traded Coffee*

Ceremonial Speeches

1. Ashlie McMillan *Reach for the Stars!*
2. Thomas P. O'Neill *Eulogy for Jesse Owens*
3. John Bakke *Remarks on Accepting the Martin Luther King Jr. Human Rights Award*
4. Elie Wiesel *Nobel Peace Prize Acceptance Speech*

SELF-INTRODUCTORY SPEECHES

SELF-INTRODUCTORY SPEECH 1: MY THREE CULTURES

SANDRA BALTZ

Reprinted with permission from Sandra Baltz.

Sandra Baltz first presented this self-introductory speech many years ago at the University of Memphis. She addressed the themes of cross-culturalism and family values long before these became fashionable. Sandra deftly uses comparison and contrast, and her example of foods illustrates how three cultures can combine harmoniously. As her speech developed, she built her ethos as a competent, warm person, highly qualified to give later informative and persuasive speeches on issues involving medical care. Presented at a time when tensions in the Middle East were running high, Sandra's speech served as a gentle reminder that people of good will can always find ways to enjoy their differences and to reaffirm their common membership in the human family.

Several years ago I read a newspaper article in the *Commercial Appeal* in which an American journalist described some of his experiences in the Middle East. He was there a couple of months and had been the guest of several different Arab families. He reported having been very well treated and very well received by everyone that he met there. But it was only later, when he returned home, that he became aware of the intense resentment his hosts held for Americans and our unwelcome involvement in their Middle Eastern affairs. The journalist wrote of feeling somewhat bewildered, if not deceived, by the large discrepancy between his treatment while in the Middle East and the hostile attitude that he learned about later. He labeled this behavior hypocritical. When I reached the end of the article, I was reminded of a phrase spoken often by my mother. "Sandra," she says to me, "respeta tu casa y a todos los que entran en ella, trata a tus enemigos asi como a tus amigos."

This is an Arabic proverb, spoken in Spanish, and roughly it translates into, "Respect your home and all who enter it, treating even an enemy as a friend." This is a philosophy that I have heard often in my home. With this in mind, it seemed to me that the treatment the American journalist received while in the Middle East was not hypocritical behavior on the part of his hosts. Rather, it was an act of respect for their guest, for themselves, and for their home—indeed, a behavior very typical of the Arabic culture.

Since having read that article several years ago, I have become much more aware of how my life is different because of having a mother who is of Palestinian origin but was born and raised in the Central American country of El Salvador.

One of the most obvious differences is that I was raised bilingually—speaking both Spanish and English. In fact, my first words were in Spanish. Growing up speaking two languages has been both an advantage and a disadvantage for me. One clear advantage is that I received straight A's in my Spanish class at Immaculate Conception High School. Certainly, traveling has been made much easier. During visits to Spain, Mexico, and some of the Central American countries, it has been my experience that people are much more open and much more receptive if you can speak their language. In addition, the subtleties of a culture are easier to grasp and much easier to appreciate.

I hope that knowing a second language will continue to be an asset for me in the future. I am currently pursuing a career in medicine. Perhaps by knowing Spanish I can broaden the area in which I can work and increase the number of people that I might reach.

Now one of the disadvantages of growing up bilingually is that I picked up my mother's accent as well as her language. I must have been about four years old before I realized that our feathered friends in the trees are called "birds," not "beers," and that, in fact, we had a "birdbath" in our backyard, not a "beerbath."

Family reunions also tend to be confusing around my home. Most of my relatives speak either Spanish, English, or Arabic, but rarely any combination of the three. So, as a result, deep and involved conversations are almost impossible. But with a little nodding and smiling, I have found that there really is no language barrier among family and friends.

In all, I must say that being exposed to three very different cultures—Latin, Arabic, and American—has been rewarding for me and has made a difference even in the music I enjoy and the food I eat. It is not unusual in my house to sit down to a meal made up of stuffed grape leaves and refried beans, all topped off with apple pie for dessert.

I am fortunate in having had the opportunity to view more closely what makes Arabic and Latin cultures unique. By understanding and appreciating them I have been able to better understand and appreciate my own American culture. In closing, just let me add some words you often hear spoken in my home—*adios* and *allak konn ma'eck*—goodbye, and may God go with you.

SELF-INTRODUCTORY SPEECH 2: LADY WITH A GUN

BETH TIDMORE

Reprinted with permission from Elizabeth Tidmore.

Beth Tidmore presented this self-introductory speech to her honors class in oral communication at the University of Memphis. The speech, offered as a tribute to her mother's faith in her, describes her dramatic development into a shooting champion. Beth's speech is noteworthy for its use of narrative design, especially dialogue. Her graphic descriptions, engaging her listeners' senses of sight, sound, touch, and smell, also helped her establish a vital, direct contact with her audience and transported them to the scenes she depicted. By the end of that semester, Beth had won the National Junior Olympic Championship Women's Air Rifle competition and had been named to the All-America shooters team.

I'm sure everybody has had an April Fool's joke played on them. My father's favorite one was to wake me up on April first and tell me, "School's been canceled for the day; you don't have to go," and then get all excited and say, "April Fools!" I'd get up and take a shower. Well, on April first, 2000, my mother said three words that I was sure weren't an April Fool's joke. She said, "We'll take it." The "it" she was referring to was a brand-new Anschutz 2002 Air Rifle. Now, this is $2,000 worth of equipment for a sport that I'd been in for maybe three months—not long. That was a big deal! It meant that I would be going from a junior-level to an Olympic-grade rifle.

Someone outside of the sport might think, "Eh, minor upgrade. A gun is a gun, right?" No. Imagine a fifteen-year-old who has been driving a used Toyota and who suddenly gets a new Mercedes for her sixteenth birthday. That's how I felt.

And as she was writing the check, I completely panicked. I thought, "What if I'm not good enough to justify this rifle? What if I decide to quit and we have to sell it, or we can't sell it? What if I let my parents down and I waste their money?" So later in the car I said, "Momma, what if I'm not good enough?" She said, "Don't worry about it—it's my money." Okay...

So my journey began. Most shooters start out when they're younger, and they move up through different rifles. Most of my peers had at least four years' experience on me. I had to jump right in and get a scholarship. And to get a scholarship I had to get noticed. And to get noticed I had to win, and to win, I had to shoot great scores immediately.

So my journey was filled with eight-hours-a-day practice, five days a week. On weekends I shot matches and I traveled. I had to take my homework with me to complete it before I got back to school. I had to do physical training, I had dietary restrictions. When all my friends were out at parties and at Cancun for Spring Break, I was at the shooting range. My free time—if I had any—was spent lifting weights and running.

At times I really resented my friends, because I thought they must have all the fun. But you know what, it was worth it! My friends don't know what it's like to feel the cold, smooth wood of the cheekpiece against your face. And they don't know the rich smell of Hoppe's No. 9 [oil] when you're cleaning your rifle. And they've never been to the Olympic Training Center in Colorado and seen how they embroider the little Olympic logo on *everything* from the mattresses to the plates. And they don't know the thrill of shooting in a final and having everyone applaud when you shoot a ten or even a center ten, or standing on the podium and having them put a medal around your neck, and being proud to represent your school, your country....

There's a bumper sticker that says, "A Lady with A Gun Has More Fun." After three years in this sport, I have had so much fun! I've been all over the U.S., I've been captain of a high school rifle team, I've been to matches everywhere, I've won medals, I've been to World Cups and met people from all over the world. And I've gotten to experience so many different people, places, and events through my participation in shooting sports.

So not long ago, I asked my mother, "Mom, how did you know?" She said, "Ah, I just knew." I said, "No, Mom—*really*. How did you know that you weren't going to waste your money?" She got very serious and she took me by the shoulders and she squared me up. She looked me right in the eye and she said, "When you picked up that gun, you just looked like you belonged together. I knew there was a sparkle in your eye, and I knew that you were meant to do great things with that rifle."

So, thanks, Mom.

SELF-INTRODUCTORY SPEECH 3: TO TOSS OR NOT TO TOSS: THE ART OF BASEBALL UMPIRING

BJ YOUNGERMAN

Reprinted with permission from Benjamin Youngerman.

BJ Youngerman presented this speech in his class at Davidson College. It illustrates the use of an activity as the starting point for a self-introductory speech. BJ combines effective narrative, animated gestures, and vocal contrast to carry listeners to the scene of an umpiring situation and to create the setting for his speech. He offers an impressive array of expert testimony in support of his own extensive experience to create an authentic, highly credible speech.

Me: "He's out!" [with hand motion].

Coach: "You've got to be kidding me, Blue! He was a good 10 feet beyond the base before the ball got there. That's horrible!"

Me: "Coach, shut up, you know you're being ridiculous. Get back to your dugout."

Coach: "Blue, that was the worst call I've ever seen. You're totally blind."

Me: "Coach, you're just a sore loser: Get in the dugout."

Coach: "Well just because you got cut in Little League doesn't mean you have to take it out on these kids!"

Me: "That's it! You're done!" [*swings arms to signify ejection of coach*].

Although umpiring is often considered to be a job where the sole purpose is to make judgment calls, in fact, the work includes many complexities, especially when you're dealing with angry players, coaches, and spectators. In the next few minutes, I will look into the importance of maintaining order, the importance of professionalism, and the necessity of making the right call the *first* time when working as a baseball umpire. But first let me tell you a little about my background as an umpire.

My first umpiring experience occurred with Little League when I was 13. By the time I was 16, I had been certified by the High School Federation Board and now have umpired three seasons for well over 200 games.

Some of you may be wondering: What exactly is the role of an umpire? According to Kathryn Davis, author of *The Art of Sports Officiating,* "Referees [Umpires] are the decisive directors of the game. They rule, punish, guide, and educate, all in the same split second." The U.S. Department of Labor estimates that there are roughly 16,000 umpires, referees, and other sports officials nationwide. Fred Frick, a writer for *The Baseball Almanac,* provides the "10 Commandments of Umpiring," which include the following: First, keep your personality out of your work. Second, forgive and forget and avoid sarcasm. Don't insist on the last word. Third, never charge a player, and above all, no pointing your finger or yelling. Finally, he advises to always keep your temper, as a decision made in anger is never sound.

Another important aspect of the art of umpiring is in maintaining order throughout the game. Rich Coyle and Arnie Mann, president and commissioner, respectively, for the Greater New Haven Baseball Umpires Association, offer several different techniques to use in maintaining order. Coyle recommends defusing the situation by walking away. Mann also made the infamous comment, "Don't look for boogers," or you'll encounter problems. Both Coyle and Mann agree that if someone starts attacking you personally, then eject him or her. One of the ways to avoid ever getting to the point of potentially having to eject someone is to always remain professional.

Why is it important to maintain professionalism? First and foremost, because image is crucial to success. Davis points out that you must establish your initial image at the pre-game conference. You ought to explain any new or difficult rule interpretations and ask if there are any questions. Another aspect of professionalism is the uniform, as it is a major part of your image. Davis notes, "Groomed appearance exudes competence, confidence and pride in the profession." According to Travis Hamilton, an expert on professionalism, the uniform must be tucked in and shoes must be shined. Rich Coyle jokingly comments that you can get through the first three innings even if you're the most horrible ump in the world, so long as you look good.

Attitude is also a part of image. You should be friendly but reserved. Davis says, "Coaches notice an official's rapport with the players, punctuality to the game, proper game equipment, enthusiasm, and effort." Finally, knowledge and competence are incredibly important as well, as they are components of professionalism. Aside from looking good, the other important part of professionalism is doing your job correctly. This brings up the question: How are you to make the right call and when, if ever, should you make the decision to change it?

In terms of making the right call, Rudy Raffone, rules interpreter for the Greater New Haven Chapter of the High School Umpires Federation board, suggests, "Replay the play in your head so you don't simply react, but instead actually think." Additionally, Rich Coyle recommends selling the call by showing loud verbal and physical signs.

Changing a call is a much more difficult decision. Jay Miner of *Referee* magazine asks, "When is a judgment call not a judgment call? Is it when an umpire second-guesses his own call, consults with a colleague, and changes it?"

I once encountered a similar situation to this. At age 16, I was a new umpire working a game in which the players were also 16. There was a close call at third base from which I was shielded. I made a call, but immediately went to my home plate umpire for help. After discussing the play with my co-umpire, he told me that I made the wrong call, so I did what I thought was the logical and right thing, and reversed the call. Though I probably did end up making the right decision by changing the call, my credibility was immediately gone, as the coaches, fans, and players now assumed I would overturn almost any call. Jerry Crawford, a Major League Baseball umpire says, "You don't waver… and that's how I would deal with [a close call]; there was no backing off. You've got to maintain that sense about you all the time. Your job is to maintain control out there and being weak-kneed, there's no place for that on a baseball field." It certainly seems that a Major League umpire should know best, having worked his way through the whole system.

In conclusion, umpiring requires so many different elements that one must constantly stay focused both on the game as well as on maintaining order, remaining professional, and making the right call the first time.

With this information in mind, let's do a little reenactment of the scene I portrayed a few minutes ago:

Me: "He's out!" (*with hand motion*).
Coach: "You've got to be kidding me, Blue! He was a good 10 feet beyond the base before the ball got there. That's horrible!"
Me: "Coach, it's a judgment call. I called it like I saw it. Please get back to your dugout."
Coach: "Blue, that was the worst call I've ever seen. You're totally blind."
Me: "Coach, this is your final warning: Get in the dugout."
Coach: "Well just because you got cut in Little League doesn't mean you have to take it out on these kids!"
Me: "That's it! You're done!" (wave arm)

The first scene was me, rookie umpire. The second is me, veteran umpire. In this case, the result on the field did not change. But I carried away from that second scene the knowledge that I was serving the game I love in just the right way.

INFORMATIVE SPEECHES

INFORMATIVE SPEECH 1: THE DEBATE ON THE TRANSPACIFIC PARTNERSHIP

STEFAN MOSKOWITZ

Reprinted with permission from Stefan Moskowitz.

In this informative speech, Stefan Moskowitz presented an overview of the controversial Transpacific Partnership to his Principles of Oral Communication class at Davidson College, taught by Dr. Kevin

Marinelli. His presentation provides a model of how to educate listeners about the conflicting positions on a contentious topic without trying to persuade them to accept a particular perspective.

Think about the number of items you have at home that were manufactured in China or Taiwan. I'm guessing there are quite a few. Now consider how many items you own that were manufactured here in the USA. Again I'm guessing, but I think it is safe to assume there are substantially fewer.

Today I would like to inform you about a controversial international trade agreement called the Transpacific Partnership, or TPP. While supported enthusiastically by President Obama, it has been met with stiff and determined opposition by Democrats and Republicans alike. A better understanding of the background and debate surrounding the agreement should enable you to reach a more informed and responsible conclusion on this issue.

The Transpacific Partnership was proposed to lower tariffs and to establish stronger trade relations between the US and 11 countries that border the Pacific, including [show map] Japan, Malaysia, Vietnam, Singapore, Brunei, Australia, New Zealand, Canada, Mexico, Chile, and Peru. Building upon and extending a previous agreement called the P4 that was implemented in 2006, its ultimate purpose is to promote closer ties and international trade, and to provide a buttress against the growing political and economic power of China. According to New Zealand Foreign Affairs and Trade, since joining the agreement, "New Zealand has seen its exports to Chile increase to $145 million, [and] exports to Singapore have doubled to more than $1 billion." Seeking similar benefits, the United States has been involved in negotiations to expand and join the TPP since 2008.

Now that we have a sense of the origins and purpose of the TPP, we can consider the reasons it has met with such controversy by special interest groups with conflicting agendas. Trade groups and manufacturers who support the agreement argue that eliminating tariffs will stimulate economic growth, create new jobs by increasing exports, and provide consumers with more choices and lower costs for basic household necessities. Whether we like it or not, the argument goes, globalization is inevitable and economic isolationism will only stifle our economy. As Kevin Granville of the *New York Times* explains, well-negotiated trade agreements like the TPP provide our best option to "level the playing field by imposing rigorous labor and environmental standards on trading partners, and supervision of intellectual property rights."

Those opposed to joining the TPP argue that it would be devastating to domestic industries and working-class Americans who would be forced to compete with cheaper imported products and labor. Often invoking comparisons to the North American Free Trade Agreement, known as NAFTA, opponents contend that farmers, ranchers, and small manufacturing companies would be particularly hard hit. Higher labor and environmental standards would be difficult if not impossible to enforce, and more and more manufacturers would be compelled to relocate to foreign countries where labor is cheap and regulations are lax. Sure, the cost of that next five-pack of socks might get a little cheaper, but what does that mean to an American breadwinner who just lost her job?

Not surprisingly, entry into the TPP has been difficult to marshal through Congress as both major parties have been divided on the issue. While more liberal Democrats like Elizabeth Warren and Bernie Sanders have vehemently opposed the agreement as hurtful to American jobs and small businesses, President Obama and his moderate allies insist that the TPP is fundamentally superior to previous such trade agreements, that it will strengthen our economic and political ties to an all-important region of the world, and that it will ultimately contribute to a more prosperous future and a more vibrant middle class.

While generally more supportive of the measure than Democrats, some prominent Republicans have also mounted substantial opposition to the TPP, raising a litany of concerns that include lack of measures to prevent currency manipulation, the inclusion of such countries as Vietnam with dubious human rights records, Japan's insistence on maintaining agricultural tariffs and subsides, and a simple distrust of the President and reticence to grant him "fast track" authority for conducting such deals. As political scientists Daniel Disalvo and Jeffrey Kucik write, Republican opposition to the deal is at least partially rooted in the demographic evolution of the party over the past few decades:

> As the Republican Party has increased its share of the white vote, it has taken in more working-class voters, especially in rural and small-town America. And some of those voters are skeptical of trade, reflecting a populist notion that such deals benefit corporations and wealthy individuals but shortchange working stiffs.

Members of Congress have been debating the TPP for years, but the issue has really come to the front burner of American politics during the current presidential campaign season. While many major candidates expressed support for free trade agreements in principle, they have raised overlapping concerns over lost jobs and currency manipulation. Although Democrat Hillary Clinton once referred to the TPP as the "gold standard of trade deals," her primary challenger Bernie Sanders vehemently opposed the deal, arguing that "At a time when our middle class is disappearing and the gap between the very rich and everyone else is growing wider, this anti-worker legislation must be defeated. . . . Enough is enough," he concluded, "NO to fast track, and NO to the TPP." That pressure during the primary season forced Clinton's position to evolve on the issue: "What we know about it, as of today, I am not in favor of what we have learned about it." Never at a loss for words, Republican Donald Trump disparaged the deal as misguided "Obama trade" and warned of Chinese plots to usurp our economy.

Knowing how much the legislative process and election cycles affect the implementation of the TPP will hopefully make you all realize the extent that the will of our constituency and representatives have in shaping international trade. While the fate of the TPP seems precarious at present, you can be assured that we will be debating similar trade agreements and pacts in the future as the forces of economic globalization work their inevitable will. Follow these debates and be an informed participant in them. And be a smart consumer as well: when you go to the store and buy that next five-pack of inexpensive socks, always consider where it came from as well as how much it cost. As you take stock of what you have gained, never lose sight of what we might be losing.

INFORMATIVE SPEECH 2: VIDEO GAMES

JOSEPH VAN MATRE

Reprinted with permission from Joseph Van Matre.

Joseph Van Matre presented this informative speech to his Fundamentals of Communication class at the University of Arkansas, taught by Lynn Meade. He reports that the idea for the speech "just popped into my head" after listening to a report on National Public Radio. The speech opens very effectively by using rhetorical questions and features timely and interesting research that develops in a categorical pattern.

If I say the word "gamer," what words come to mind? Antisocial? Geek? Dropout? Well, how about fitness guru, educator, or intelligence analyst?

I'm not a hardcore gamer, but I do enjoy a round of Mario Smash Bros. every now and then. So when I heard on National Public Radio one day that video games can actually help in the business world, I was intrigued and did some research. What I discovered was quite surprising.

While there have been many stereotypes associated with video games and those who play them, today I'm going to show you some of the very real benefits video games can bring to the health, education, military, and business worlds. By the end of my presentation, some of you may even be ready to break out your Game Boy!

While many people think that video games contribute to inactivity, and therefore to health problems, video games have actually helped many gamers become more active. In fact, new input systems in the twenty-first century have encouraged many players to climb off the couch. Dance Dance Revolution, for example, has become popular with many physical educators. As the *New York Times* of April 2007 reported, the West Virginia Department of Education and the Los Angeles Unified School System both use DDR as a part of their PE programs. The game "requires players to dance in ever more complicated and strenuous patterns in time with electronic dance music." Dr. Linda Carson, distinguished professor at West Virginia University, reported her first encounter with the game: "I was in a mall walking by the arcade and I saw these kids playing D.D.R., and I was just stunned. There were all these kids dancing and sweating and actually standing in line and paying money to be physically active.... It was a physical educator's dream." In follow-up studies, Dr. Carson and her colleagues have found significant health benefits for overweight children who play the game regularly.

New technologies developed by NASA can also promote mental health. While this is a little complicated, as one plays a video game, the controller gets easier to use when the player brings a healthy brainwave pattern to the game. Thus the game becomes both diagnostic and therapeutic. According to Dr. Olafur Paisson, professor of psychiatry at Eastern Virginia Medical School, "With this new [biofeedback] technology, we have found a way to package this training in an enjoyable and inherently motivating activity."

Now that you know how video games can help keep you healthy, let's consider how they can make you smarter. First, video games can be effective educational tools. A study by the British Government showed that playing games such as SimCity and Rollercoaster Tycoon can help develop creativity, critical thinking, and math skills. When played in a group, they can also develop interpersonal skills. Then if you add correct economic and human behavior algorithms, you can make these games even more effective for economics and business education.

Video games can also help people develop a knowledge of history. For example, many people are fascinated by World War II, but it's hard for them to imagine what fighting in that war must have been like. But if you place them right in the middle of simulated battle situations in which they receive the combat orders just as soldiers of that time received them under actual conditions, their imaginations are stimulated. They must act and think and fight for survival. Playing such battle games makes it so much easier to motivate them to learn about the countries and causes and underlying cultural conditions involved in the many battlefields of that war. All these types of interactive education "games" are being developed right now.

Now that you see how video games can be used in education, let's look at how they also can function in the worlds of business and national defense. Businesses are finding great uses for video games to enhance training. In 2008, for example, UPS spent over $5.5 million on new training centers that integrate "on-line learning, 3-D models, podcasts, and videos with traditional classroom learning." These training programs are effective, according to the *Emerging Technologies Center*, because they are "immersive, require the player to make frequent, important decisions, have clear goals, adapt to other players individually, and involve a social network." Obviously, these cultivate important skills in the business world.

Finally, the military is using video games to enhance training, lower costs, assist in rehabilitation, and perform dangerous tasks. Converting war games into video games allows training to focus on specific goals and can lower costs dramatically. Southern California's Institute for Creative Technologies has shown that using X-box type games can help soldiers returning from the Middle East and Afghanistan to cope with PTSD (Post-traumatic Stress Disorder). Working with video games, trainees develop skills that can help them control drone planes and tanks on the battlefield. As Dr. Alan Pope of Langley Air Force Base has reported, "Flight simulators are essentially very sophisticated video games." By developing such games, training is simplified and accelerated, and mistakes can be corrected without devastating on-site consequences.

So have you begun to change your mind about video games and gamers? We've seen that video games can make us more healthy, smarter, better trained for the business world, and more secure from international threats. The next time you see people playing World of Warcraft or Halo, try not to think of them as "geeks" or as "dropouts." Those "geeks" may have their hands on the future!

INFORMATIVE SPEECH 3: THE FRENCH PARADOX: A DELICIOUS SECRET REVEALED

GABRIELLE WALLACE

Reprinted with permission from Gabrielle Wallace.

This colorful, informative speech builds largely upon a comparative design, developing a literal analogy between French and American eating styles. It also offers a model of responsible knowledge, using facts and testimony drawn from numerous sources and experts. Gabrielle connects with the audience's dreams of a "give us the cake but spare us the consequences" lifestyle. In effect, she shows how these dreams might become reality. She presented her speech at Davidson College.

Have any of you ever fought the dreaded "freshman 15"—those unwanted pounds that seem to show up on you out of nowhere—but noticed by everyone as soon as you go home after your first year? What if I told you of a land where people eat this, drink this, and look like this [shows slides revealing delicious foods, elegant wines, and attractive people]? Would you believe me? They live like we wish we could, but don't experience the freshman 15—at least not as many of them do. If this sounds unlikely, it is nonetheless true. I call it "the French paradox." It refers to the fact that the French eat foods on a regular basis that are every bit as rich and fattening as what we eat, yet they are not nearly as prone to rapid weight gain and other negative health consequences. In order to understand the French paradox, we must consider how they combine food choices, beverage consumption, and cultural attitudes towards eating itself.

First, let's take a look at French eating habits. What they eat and how much they eat work together to make an ideal diet. The French eat as little processed food as possible. According to Roger Corder, a professor at St. Bartholomew's Hospital in London who has studied the French diet extensively, the French eat a higher quality and better variety of foods than most Americans. Like us, the French like rich fatty foods—gravies and cream sauces are common. But a much higher percentage of their diet consists of whole grains and vegetables, and they emphasize seasonally fresh and locally grown foods. This richness and variety satiates the palate and is considerably more filling than processed foods.

As a result, perhaps, the French eat smaller portions of food. According to Paul Rozin, a nutritionist at the University of Pennsylvania, French portion sizes on average are about 25% smaller than American portions—which might explain why Americans are roughly three times more likely to become obese than French people.

A factor that might account for this is the French upbringing. Mireille Guiliano, author of *French Women Don't Get Fat*, says that the French are not conditioned to overeat. Instead, they are taught to eat only until they are full, and then stop! A recent University of Pennsylvania study confirmed this tendency. The study compared the eating habits of students from Paris and Chicago. It found that French students stopped eating in response to internal cues, like when they first started feeling full or when they wanted to leave room for dessert. The American students, on the other hand, relied more on external cues. They would, for example, eat until the TV show they were watching ended, or until they ran out of a beverage. There's no question that eating habits are a vital point of difference between the French and American cultures.

The second important factor in explaining the French paradox has to do with beverage consumption. The French drink primarily two beverages: water and wine. Again according to Mireille Guiliano, they start the day with a glass of water. Water is known to have metabolic benefits: an article in *Prevention* magazine suggests that consuming 16 oz. of water increases the body's calorie burning rate as much as 30% within 40 minutes.

The second beverage of choice is red wine. According to an article published in 2008 in the *Independent*, a prominent London newspaper, the average French person drinks nearly 17 gallons of wine a year, as compared to the 7 gallons a year consumed by the average Briton. Recently scientists have discovered numerous health benefits of red wine. Studies suggest it promotes higher levels of heart-healthy HDL cholesterol, which counters the effects of bad cholesterol by preventing artery blocking plaque deposits. The World Health Organization reported that countries with the highest wine consumption—France, Italy, and Spain—had the lowest rates of heart disease. Indeed, the region of France that drinks the most wine has the highest percentage of men who live to age 90!

The third important factor in explaining the French paradox has to do with their overall attitude and approach to eating itself. Meal time in France is an elaborate event. Meals typically consist of three to four courses, including a separate course for salad, cheese, and fruit. Susan Loomis, writing in *Health* magazine, likened French meals to Thanksgiving. "[W]hat Americans do once a year," she continued, "prepare food linked to ritual and history, then gather with family and friends—the French do often, most of them at least once a week."

A meal being a social event encourages slow eating—which contributes again to less overall consumption. As Dr. Rozin argues, the French tend to eat more slowly and to include more socializing and conversation with their meals. The social etiquette of a French meal also tends to promote gradual eating. The next course is never brought out until everyone at the table has finished. Only then, usually after some delay, does eating resume.

Finally, the French thoroughly enjoy the delight of food itself. They enjoy using all five senses when eating. My stepfather, when tasting a new wine, always sticks his nose in it to take in the smell, swirls it to watch the color, and slowly takes in a small amount to absorb the flavor. The owner of a French bakery where I work back home often puts baguettes up to his ear and squeezes them to hear their crunch and test their quality. Claude Fischler, a French sociologist at the University of Pennsylvania, notes that when asked to respond to the words chocolate cake, Americans say "Guilt" whereas the French say "Celebration."

For the French, eating is about the experience of living. It is engrained in their culture and permeates their daily experience. The three factors of eating correctly, drinking wisely, and making a meal an enjoyable experience are what make the French paradox possible. It appears the French have found the secret to being able to have their cake and eat it too—along with some wine, friends, and celebration. We, as American college students, could learn from their example, especially if we want to avoid the horror of the freshman 15!

PERSUASIVE SPEECHES

PERSUASIVE SPEECH 1: GLOBAL BURNING

JOSHUA LOGAN

Reprinted with permission from Joshua Logan.

Josh Logan presented this persuasive speech on the theme of global warming in his class at the University of Memphis. "Global Burning" focuses on the problem and attempts to arouse awareness, share understanding, and secure agreement. Its strategy is to magnify the reality of global warming and its meaning for listeners. Its challenge is to remove barriers that might stand in the way of their commitment. To achieve his goals, Josh used colorful, graphic language; a presentation aid; and effective examples. This presentation, Josh's third on global warming, reflected his passion, sincerity, and commitment on this topic.

Ten years ago, five years ago, reasonable people could still argue and even disagree over some tough environmental questions: Is there really such a thing as "global warming"? Is the world really getting hotter at a rapid pace? And is it being fanned by humans? Are we really responsible for environmental conditions?

Now there's little room left for argument. The answer to all these questions is clearly YES. This definitive answer has been provided by the United Nations Intergovernmental Panel on Climate Change, reporting during the early part of 2007. This authoritative report, which correlates and tests the work of hundreds of environmental scientists from countries around the globe, concludes that the process of global warming is now in motion and is accelerating. And the fire is fed largely by humans: the IPCC supports this conclusion at a 90 to 99% level of confidence. The United States especially, with about 4% of the world's population, accounts for 25% of all global warming. We are the ones with our foot on the accelerator.

Today I want to sketch the dimensions of this problem, and what it might mean for you and your children. I will first track the causes of global warming, then trace its recent path and project its future. As recently as 2006, polls tell us that many people in the United States were in denial about global warming: yes, we believe it exists and, yes, we are concerned, but we're not that much concerned. Fifty-four percent of us think global warming is a problem for the future—but not now! Global warming is still something of an abstract, distant problem for us, and we can't see the future all that clearly.

That's the challenge I want to try to meet today. We must recognize global warming for what it is, the monster we are creating by all our action and inaction. We must become scared—really scared! We must be willing to think green and act green, from the personal everyday decisions we make on disposing trash to the big consumer decisions we make on which cars to buy, to the political decisions we make on which candidates to support. We must understand that this hot world is starting to catch fire—and we must be willing to pay the price to help put the flames out. We must be committed to the proposition that global warming must not become global burning.

Global warming begins with greenhouse gases—the tons of carbon dioxide that belch out of our smokestacks and our automobile exhausts; the vast clouds of methane gas that rise from our farms and ranches and landfills; the nitrous oxide from fertilizers, cattle feed lots, and chemical products. The world's forests are supposed to absorb much of this industrial and agricultural output, but guess what? We've also been busy cutting the rainforests and clear-cutting our own forests. We're tying nature's hands behind her back at just the wrong moment. So all these deadly gases mix and accumulate in the atmosphere, where they magnify the heat of the sun.

Now let's gain some perspective on where we now actually stand. I want to show you a chart that traces the human influence on the atmosphere over the past thousand years of history. This chart summarizes the history of greenhouse gases, according to the IPCC's *Summary for Policymakers*. Notice that the bottom border divides the time frame into two-hundred-year periods. The side frame measures the amount of the gas pouring into the atmosphere. Notice that for about eight hundred of these years, this amount is stable and even—almost a straight line. Then as the nineteenth century dawns on the Industrial Revolution, the lines begin to climb, at first gradually, then increasingly steeper until they almost reach the vertical during the past half-century. The dry technical language of the summary, speaking to carbon dioxide alone, carries the message of this chart with sharp clarity: "The atmospheric concentration of carbon dioxide (CO_2) has increased by 31 percent since 1750. The present CO_2 concentration has not been exceeded during the past 420,000 years and likely not during the past 20 million years. The current rate of increase is unprecedented during at least the past 20,000 years."

Now what does all this mean in human terms, especially if these lines continue to climb on the charts of the future? Well get your fans out, because it's going to be hot. Very hot. According to *National Geographic News* of July 2006, eleven of the last twelve years have been the hottest on record, probably reaching back for at least a thousand years. But that record won't last for long. The UN congregation of the world's scientists predicts that the earth's surface temperature could rise at least five degrees over the next hundred years—just in the last generation it has already risen two degrees on average. Can you imagine what it will be like to add five degrees to the average summer day in Memphis?

Beyond that, the world's agriculture will be profoundly changed. Fertile lands will become deserts, and vast populations will be forced to relocate. As you might imagine, and as *Time* magazine of April 2006 confirms, it is the poorest and least flexible populations—such as those one finds in Africa—who will be hardest hit initially. *Science* magazine adds that major forest fires in the West and South are more numerous and more devastating than they were a generation ago. The average land burned during a given year is more than six times what it was a generation ago.

Moreover, it will soon get more lonely here on planet earth. The latest word is that more than one-third—that's one-third—of all species in several parts of the world could be destroyed over the next fifty years. Chris Leeds, conservation biologist of the University of Leeds, says: "Our analyses suggest that well over a million species could be threatened with extinction as a result of climate change." That's over a million species.

The story becomes more tragic when we contemplate the fate of the oceans. Some scientists had previously discounted global warming because some of the most dire predictions about rising temperatures had not come true. What they forgot was the capacity of the oceans to absorb heat and smother some of the immediate impact of global warming. But a recent issue of *Science* magazine has published reports that—as they put it—"link a warming trend in the upper 3,000 meters of the world's oceans to global warming caused by human activities."

As the oceans grow warmer, especially in the Gulf of Mexico area, the threat of hurricanes grows more ominous. In its summary of conditions in 2006, *Time* reported that over the past thirty-five years, the number of category 4 and 5 hurricanes has jumped 50%. But these reports truly threaten all living creatures. In particular, they confirm the IPCC predictions that most coral reefs will disappear within thirty to fifty years. And as the oceans continue to warm and melt the great ice shelves in the polar regions, the rise in sea level—as much as three feet over the next century and perhaps even more—will wipe out vast lowland areas such as the Sundarbans in India and Bangladesh, the last, best habitat for the Bengal tiger. Large parts of Florida and Louisiana will surrender to the sea—sell your beach property soon! The barrier islands off Mobile Bay, where my parents took me camping as a boy and where I hope to take my own children, will gradually recede into memory. These are just fragments, mere glimpses, of the future global warming has in store for us, our children, and our grandchildren.

Well, I hope I have gained your attention today. We have a problem here that threatens the quality of life here on earth. Can we do anything about it? I would like to give you a happy, simple answer to this question, but it is a complex one. It's not like we can just take our foot off the greenhouse accelerator, and bring the bus to a halt. Once it is heated, the ocean does not cool quickly. Once they have accumulated, greenhouse gases can linger for a long time. But there are things we can do to change this scenario. The future is not an either-or proposition, and we can mitigate some of the worst possibilities. We can cool the fires under global warming to prevent it from becoming global burning. In my next speech I hope to show you how.

The clock is ticking, but I don't think it's too late. I hope that what I've said in the last two speeches has gained your attention. Get involved! Together we can cool the fever, and turn down the heat under our planet.

PERSUASIVE SPEECH 2: WE DON'T HAVE TO LIVE IN SLUMS

ANNA ALEY

Reprinted with permission from Anna Aley.

Anna Aley was a student at Kansas State University when she presented this persuasive speech. It is noteworthy for its vivid language; its effective use of supporting materials, especially narrative; and the way in which it focuses listeners on a program of action.

Slumlords—you'd expect them in New York or Chicago, but in Manhattan, Kansas? You'd better believe there are slumlords in Manhattan, and they pose a direct threat to you if you ever plan to rent an off-campus apartment.

I know about slumlords; I rented a basement apartment from one last semester. I guess I first suspected something was wrong when I discovered dead roaches in the refrigerator. I definitely knew something was wrong when I discovered the leaks: the one in the bathroom that kept the bathroom carpet constantly soggy and molding and the one in the kitchen that allowed water from the upstairs neighbor's bathroom to seep into the kitchen cabinets and collect in my dishes.

Then there were the serious problems. The hot water heater and furnace were connected improperly and posed a fire hazard. They were situated next to the only exit. There was no smoke detector or fire extinguisher and no emergency way out—the windows were too small for escape. I was living in an accident waiting to happen—and paying for it.

The worst thing about my ordeal was that I was not an isolated instance; many Kansas State students are living in unsafe housing and paying for it, not only with their money, but their happiness, their grades, their health, and their safety.

We can't be sure how many students are living in substandard housing, housing that does not meet the code specifications required of rental property. We can be sure, however, that a large number of Kansas State students are at risk of being caught in the same situation I was. According to the registrar, approximately 17,800 students are attending Kansas State this semester. Housing claims that 4,200 live in the dorms. This means that approximately 13,600 students live off-campus. Some live in fraternities or sororities, some live at home, but most live in off-campus apartments, as I do.

Many of these 13,600 students share traits that make them likely to settle for substandard housing. For example, many students want to live close to campus. If you've ever driven through the surrounding neighborhoods, you know that much of the available housing is in older houses, houses that were never meant to be divided into separate rental units. Students are also often limited in the amount they can pay for rent; some landlords, such as mine, will use low rent as an excuse not to fix anything and to let the apartment deteriorate. Most importantly, many students are young and, consequently, naive when it comes to selecting an apartment. They don't know the housing codes; but even if they did, they don't know how to check to make sure the apartment is in compliance. Let's face it—how many of us know how to check a hot water heater to make sure it's connected properly?

Adding to the problem of the number of students willing to settle for substandard housing is the number of landlords willing to supply it. Currently, the Consumer Relations Board here at Kansas State has on file student complaints against approximately one hundred landlords. There are surely complaints against many more that have never been formally reported.

There are two main causes of the substandard student housing problem. The first—and most significant—is the simple fact that it is possible for a landlord to lease an apartment that does not meet housing code requirements. The Manhattan Housing Code Inspector will evaluate an apartment, but only after the tenant has given the landlord a written complaint and the landlord has had fourteen days to remedy the situation. In other words, the way things are now, the only way the Housing Code Inspector can evaluate an apartment to see if it's safe to be lived in is if someone has been living in it for at least two weeks!

A second cause of the problem is the fact that campus services designed to help students avoid substandard housing are not well known. The Consumer Relations Board here at Kansas State can help students inspect apartments for safety before they sign a lease, it can provide students with vital information on their rights as tenants, and it can mediate in landlord–tenant disputes. The problem is, many people don't know these services exist. The Consumer Relations Board is not listed in the university catalog; it is not mentioned in any of the admissions literature. The only places it is mentioned are in alphabetically organized references such as the phone book, but you have to already know it exists to look it up! The Consumer Relations Board does receive money for advertising from the student senate, but it is only enough to run a little two-by-three-inch ad once every month. That is not large enough or frequent enough to be noticed by many who could use these services.

It's clear that we have a problem, but what may not seem so clear is what we can do about it. After all, what can one student do to change the practices of numerous Manhattan landlords? Nothing, if that student is alone. But just think of what we could accomplish if we got all 13,600 off-campus students involved in this issue!

Think what we could accomplish if we got even a fraction of those students involved! This is what Wade Whitmer, director of the Consumer Relations Board, is attempting to do. He is reorganizing the Off-Campus Association in an effort to pass a city ordinance requiring landlords to have their apartments inspected for safety before those apartments can be rented out. The Manhattan code inspector has already tried to get just such an ordinance passed, but the only people who showed up at the public forums were known slumlords, who obviously weren't in favor of the proposed ordinance. No one showed up to argue in favor of the ordinance, so the city commissioners figured that no one wanted it and voted it down. If we can get the Off-Campus Association organized and involved, however, the commissioners will see that someone does want the ordinance and they will be more likely to pass it the next time it is proposed. You can do a great service to your fellow students—and to yourself—by joining the Off-Campus Association.

A second thing you can do to help ensure that no more Kansas State students have to go through what I did is sign my petition asking the student senate to increase the Consumer Relations Board's advertising budget. Let's face it—a service cannot do anybody any good if no one knows about it. The Consumer Relations Board's services are simply too valuable to let go to waste.

An important thing to remember about substandard housing is that it is not only distasteful, it is dangerous. In the end, I was lucky. I got out of my apartment with little more than bad memories. My upstairs neighbor was not so lucky. The main problem with his apartment was that the electrical wiring was done improperly; there were too many outlets for too few circuits, so the fuses were always blowing. One day last November, Jack was at home when a fuse blew—as usual. And, as usual, he went to the fuse box to flip the switch back on. When he touched the switch, it delivered such a shock that it literally threw this guy the size of a football player backwards and down a flight of stairs. He lay there at the bottom, unable to move, for a full hour before his roommate came home and called an ambulance.

Jack was lucky. His back was not broken. But he did rip many of the muscles in his back. Now he has to go to physical therapy, and he is not expected to fully recover.

Kansas State students have been putting up with substandard living conditions for too long. It's time we finally got together to do something about this problem. Join the Off-Campus Association. Sign my petition. Let's send a message to these slumlords that we're not going to put up with this any more. We don't have to live in slums.

PERSUASIVE SPEECH 3: THE PRICE OF BOTTLED WATER

KATIE LOVETT

Reprinted with permission from Katie Lovett.

The persuasive speech that follows reflects a moment of self-discovery as Katie Lovett found her topic and her voice simultaneously. As Katie tells the story: "My persuasive speech topic came about after I attended a screening of the internationally acclaimed documentary 'Flow: For Love of Water,' which addresses the global water crisis. Immediately after the film ended, I knew that I wanted to design a speech persuading people against buying bottled water. The research process for that speech was incredibly interesting, and I am actually now getting more involved in the Davidson Environmental Action Coalition (EAC) as a result of our COM 101 speech assignment."

Have you heard the tired old joke about the salesperson who could sell ice cubes to Eskimos? If you think about it, that's not only a tribute to sales skills but also says a lot about our attitudes toward Native peoples—and how superior we feel towards them. These stupid people (it implies) are buying something they have no use for.

But consider this: In today's society, huge corporations like Coca-Cola, Pepsi, and Nestlé are marketing their own "ice cubes" to us with immense success. Water, a natural resource that has historically been viewed as free and open to the public, is now being bottled and sold for profit by large multinational corporations.

Why are we buying water? And what are the consequences of it? These are the questions I want to consider today. We will examine marketing strategies, consumer misconceptions, and the environmental impact of our behavior.

Let's begin by considering how the bottled water industry sells its own "ice cubes" to us. Consumers gravitate towards bottled water instead of tap water for two reasons: what's in it and what's not in it. What could possibly be inside a 20-ounce bottle of water that would compel someone to pay $3 and beyond for it? According to *The Journal of Consumer Culture,* "bottled water is a form of cultural consumption, driven by everything from status competition to a belief in magical curing." Clever advertisers feed these feelings. Since bottled water has become an affordable status symbol in today's society, companies can appeal to social distinctions of wealth and class to sell their product.

Take a look at some of the brands currently on the market: There are vitamin waters, nicotine waters, caffeine waters, electrolyte enhanced SmartWater, the "orbtastic" Aquapods that target kids, Bling H_2O which sells for $35 a bottle, "Hello Kitty" water for cats, and yes, even a "diet" water called "Skinny." And according to *The Journal of Consumer Culture,* "new water brands are entering the U.S. market at the rate of about eight per month." Now tell me, how can we possibly feel superior to Eskimos?

Another main reason people want to buy bottled water is for what is *not* in it. The purity of water is the key theme for the bottled water industry. Bottlers seize upon public anxiety over municipal tap water supplies, supposedly offering us the safety that tap water cannot. As a result, the National Resources Defense Council has found that 'pure,' 'pristine,' and 'natural' are some of the most commonly used god-terms found in marketing and on labels.

So these are some of the fantasies and feelings that support the bottled water industry. Are they justified? Unfortunately, contrary to widespread belief, bottled water is not necessarily cleaner, safer, or purer than the water you get from your faucet. The perception is that if it is off the shelf, it is somehow cleaner and tastier. But *The Bulletin of Science, Technology & Society* argues that bottles of water become "petri dishes of germs." The bottles are loaded into trucks, driven down polluted highways, and transported by many different sets of hands before sitting around gathering dust and germs in storage houses.

In a recent four-year scientific study, the Natural Resources Defense Council tested more than 1,000 bottles of 103 brands of bottled water. In its publication, "Bottled Water or Tap Water?" the Council concluded that "there is no assurance that bottled water is any safer than tap water." In fact, a third of the brands tested were found to contain contaminants such as arsenic and carcinogenic compounds. Some of these samples contained levels of these harmful contaminants that exceeded state or industry standards. So much for "pure" and "pristine"!

Another important misconception involves the regulation of tap water and bottled water. The journal *Environmental Health Perspectives,* in its article "The Price of Bottled Water," reveals the startling fact that city tap water in the United States undergoes more rigorous testing than bottled water. The Environmental Protection Agency (EPA) oversees the treatment of tap water while the Food and Drug Administration (FDA) regulates bottled water. But the FDA's standards for bottled water are actually no stricter than the EPA's health standards for public tap water: the FDA merely adopted the EPA's public drinking standards, which were first set forth in the Clean Water Act of 1978.

You may be asking, what about these reports showing that thousands of people get sick and more than one hundred of them die annually from tap water? Isn't it true that the bottled water industry has a relatively clean record in terms of outbreaks of illnesses?

According to the *Bulletin of Science, Technology & Society,* the reason for this dramatic discrepancy is that while the federal government requires all municipal water authorities to report even the mildest illnesses within 24 hours, there is no requirement for reporting sickness from bottled water. *Flow: For Love of Water,* an internationally acclaimed documentary concerning the global water crisis, also makes the shocking point that there is only one person in the FDA regulating the entire multi-billion dollar bottled water industry.

So while you are laying out the big bucks, thinking that you are protecting your health by drinking bottled instead of tap water, keep in mind that bottled water has not been proven to be any cleaner or better for you.

What about the environmental consequences of the bottled water industry? Consider that it takes an enormous amount of energy to produce a bottle of water. The process of manufacturing, transporting, and recycling plastic bottles drains fossil fuels and contributes to greenhouse gases. The bottles are often filled far away, shipped overseas, transported across the country in trucks, and then stored in refrigerators at your local convenience store. Compare that environmental impact to just turning on your kitchen faucet and we can begin to see the even larger price of bottled water.

The article "5 Reasons Not to Drink Bottled Water" warns that bottled water produces up to 1.5 million tons of plastic waste per year, since over 80% of plastic bottles are simply thrown away rather than recycled. By doing what you can to reduce that enormous pile of plastic bottles, filling a reusable bottle with tap water instead, you can make your own contribution to the quality of the environment.

I hope now, after this speech, that you will be a little less susceptible to the marketing techniques of the bottled water industry. Remember, at the very least bottled water is not safer than tap water, and instead the opposite may be true. And finally, remember the negative impact on the environment.

We pay too much—and in too many ways—for our fantasies concerning bottled water. It's time to put away these childish things. It's time to turn on our faucets instead of opening our wallets!

PERSUASIVE SPEECH 4: FAIRLY TRADED COFFEE

BETSY LYLES

Reprinted with permission from Elizabeth Lyles.

This persuasive speech by Betsy Lyles was presented in her class at Davidson College. It relies heavily on an impressive array of facts and figures to convince listeners of the ethical importance of buying fairly traded coffee. The speech might have benefited from a greater use of motivational appeals and narratives to make it come alive more powerfully for listeners.

How many of you began the morning with a cup of coffee? Many, if not most of you buy coffee every day. This daily purchase amounts to about $500 a year that you might spend on coffee. Based on a very conservative estimate that 10% of Davidson students drink coffee daily, collectively we as a student body invest more than $75,000 in the coffee industry per year.

The money we spend on coffee can go to either of two markets—the fair trade coffee market and regular trade coffee market. Today I want to urge you to support fairly traded coffee because it promotes both sustainable development and a decent lifestyle for coffee farmers in those regions that are dependent upon the export of coffee for income. I will help you gain an understanding of what fair trade is, the effect of fairly traded coffee on workers and the environment, and how you can support fairly traded coffee here on campus.

Let's start by discussing how most coffee is produced. Most coffee is produced in ways that are harmful to both the farmer and the environment. According to an article by Don Wells in *Herizons* magazine, it is grown on plantations where trees have been cut down to allow more space to plant coffee beans. After the crop is harvested the soil is depleted.

Most coffee produced this way is sold by the farmers to a big supplier. The supplier then sells it separately to importers. This means there are two more people who share the profit and the coffee farmers themselves get very little money for their work. The article in *Herizons* goes on to say that of the $7 we might pay for a pound of coffee, the coffee farmers might get 3 cents while the coffee corporations get 86 cents of every dollar consumers spend on coffee. With coffee farmers losing most of their profits to the "middle man" it creates a strain on their families, making it hard for them to maintain a sustainable lifestyle.

Now let's look at how being associated with fair trade helps the coffee farmers and the environment. Fair trade helps workers develop a lifestyle that is both sustainable and comfortable. Fair trade pays coffee farmers more per pound than they would be paid otherwise.

Andrew Downie reported in the *New York Times* last month that fair trade coffee farmers in Brazil are paid at least $1.29 a pound, compared with the regular market rate of roughly $1.05 per pound. That might not sound like much to you, but consider it from the point of view of a small farmer in Brazil, trying to raise a family. The difference mounts up into something really substantial! Downie also goes on to say that fair trade policies also create price floors to make sure that farmers will make a reasonable amount even if the coffee prices go down. The price floor is always set above the regular coffee market rate.

Coffee workers can see a noticeable difference in lifestyles as a result of fair trade. As Wells noted, coffee importers who trade fairly provide low-interest loans and credit to farmers, which helps them stay out of debt to local lenders. In a book by Alex Nicholls, *Fair Trade: Market-Driven Ethical Consumption*, a farmer from Belize remarked about how his lifestyle had changed:

> "I used to live in a thatch hut with a mud floor. Now I have two concrete houses and I have been able to educate my children.... They had to work in a shrimp farm when they were younger [to support the family], but now my children only go to school. We don't need them to work."

Another benefit of fair trade coffee is that it's grown organically, which means it has a lower environmental impact than mass produced coffee. Organic farming methods are less likely to deplete the soil and do not pollute our land and water resources.

So far we have learned what constitutes fair trade coffee farming and how it helps both the farmer and the environment. Now let's look at ways that you can personally support fair trade. There are many opportunities, right here in Davidson. To begin, it's not hard for you to buy fairly traded coffee. According to the Davidson College Dining Services website, both the Commons and the Union serve S&D coffee, which is a fair trade supplier. So we've already supported fair trade coffee if we've bought our coffee on campus. One hundred percent of Summit Coffee is fairly traded, so by purchasing this coffee you are supporting farmers.

Even if you don't like coffee, even if you never drink coffee, you can still support fair trade enterprises, because our Ben & Jerry's sells fairly traded ice cream.

A second contribution you can make is to promote awareness of fairly traded coffee. Only 3.3 percent of coffee sold in the United States last year was certified fair trade, but even that was more than eight times the level in 2001. The online campaign "Join the Big Noise" has produced a huge part of this increase, and by going online to maketradefair.com you can join the campaign to promote fair trade. Additionally, according to a study conducted last year by the New York–based National Coffee Association, 27% of Americans said they were aware of the fair trade movement, up from the 12% claiming to be aware of it just a few years earlier. I challenge every one of you to participate in making those numbers increase even more significantly.

Now you understand how fair trade is an ethical alternative, how it positively affects the workers and the environment, and what you can do to support it right here in Davidson. I will leave you with the words of Bruce Crowther of the Fairtrade Foundation:

> People see [fair trade] as charity, but it is not, it is justice. We have to get rid of the charity way of thinking. I see doing fair trade as doing two things: one, it is helping people immediately and changing their lives; then there is the bigger picture where it is a protest tool, a way of registering your vote. But now we are not boycotting something, we are supporting something positive.

Every time you drink coffee, remember the coffee farmer. Buy fairly traded coffee.

CEREMONIAL SPEECHES

CEREMONIAL SPEECH 1: REACH FOR THE STARS!

ASHLIE McMILLAN

Reprinted with permission from Ashlie McMillan.

In her speech of tribute to her cousin, Ashlie McMillan, a student at Vanderbilt University, makes use of both identification and magnification, the major techniques of ceremonial speaking. By asking her listeners to imagine themselves as dwarfs, Ashlie develops a narrative based on vicarious experiences.

Please close your eyes. Imagine now that you are shrinking. Can you feel your hands and feet getting smaller, your arms being pulled in closer to your shoulders? Can you picture your legs now dangling off the edge of your seat as your legs shrink up closer to your hips? Now you are only three feet tall. But don't open your eyes yet. This is your first day of being a diastrophic dwarf.

You wake up and get out of bed, which is quite a drop because the bed is almost as tall as you are. You go to the bathroom to wash your face and brush your teeth, but you must stand on a trash can because the faucet is out of your reach. Now you go back to your dorm room, and you're ready to put on your clothes. But again you can't reach the clothes hanging in your closet because you're too short. You have to struggle to get dressed.

Now you have errands that you must run. But how are you going to do them? If you walk, it will take you a long time because you must take many short steps. And you can't drive a car because you can't reach the pedals, much less see over the steering wheel. Finally you get to the bank. But it takes you about five minutes to get the teller's attention because she can't see you below the counter. Next you go to the grocery store. This takes forever because you can't push a cart. You're forced to use a carry basket and to find people who will reach high items for you. Frustrated yet? Okay, open your eyes.

In 1968 my cousin, Tina McMillan, was born. Today she's in her twenty-ninth year as a diastrophic dwarf. What does that mean? It means that she'll never be taller than three feet. It means that her hands will never be able to bend this way [gestures] because she will never have joints in her fingers or toes. She'll always have club feet, and she had to have a rod put in her spine because all diastrophic dwarfs are plagued with scoliosis.

So what does her dwarfism mean to my cousin? Nothing. When you first meet Tina, you might be a little shocked at how tiny she is. But after a while you forget her physical size because her personality is so large and her spirit is so bright. Today I want to tell you the story of how this small person is reaching for the stars. Her life is a miracle that should teach us never to let obstacles stand in the way of our goals and dreams.

When my aunt and uncle were told that they were going to have a baby who was a diastrophic dwarf, they prepared themselves. They were ready to tell their child that she would never be able to have a Great Dane dog because it would be three times the size that she was. That she would never be able to ride a horse. That she would never be able to drive a car. And that she might not be able to attend college because the dormitories and other facilities were not built for people three feet tall.

What my aunt and uncle were *not* prepared for was a child with a physical disability who refused to see herself as disabled. I can tell you that growing up with Tina was quite an experience. She was always the ham of the cousins, always the center of attention. I remember going over to her house and playing with her *three* Great Dane dogs in the backyard. I remember every Sunday when my grandpa would take us out to the farm and we would fight over who got to ride the horses. And Tina would even fight my grandfather so she could get up on the horse all by herself. And I remember the day, some time after her sixteenth birthday, that she slid behind the wheel of a car. She had teamed up with some engineers down in Texas to have the pedals extended as well as hand gears made on the steering wheel so that she could drive herself. But perhaps my proudest and fondest memory was watching my cousin walk across the graduation stage at Texas Christian University in 1991. She not only got her degree in English, but she went on to get a master's degree in anthropology from TCU. After she graduated, the university invited her to come back to teach in the English Department. But by this time Tina had a new challenge: She declined the teaching job so that she could enter politics as campaign manager for the mayor of Dallas.

Tina has never stopped challenging the perception that she is disabled. Next April she will be marrying a person of normal stature, and once again she will defy society's assumption that something must be wrong about such a marriage. And then in the fall she plans on attending the University of Texas law school. Want to bet against her there?

Somehow, against the odds, my cousin has led a normal life. To many people, what she has accomplished might not seem that exceptional. To me, however, she is an inspiration. Whenever I think I've got problems that are too much for me, I think of her and of what she has done, this large and vital person stuffed into such a small body. I think of how she refuses to use her disability as a scapegoat or excuse. And I remember how she does not even consider quitting if something stands in her way. She simply views the obstacle, decides the best way to get around it, and moves on. And although she will lose the ability to walk, probably by the age of forty, I believe that she will still find the way to keep moving toward her goals.

The next time a large obstacle stands in your way, remember Tina, my small cousin, who has achieved such noteworthy things. You too may seem too short to grasp your stars, but you never know how far you might reach if you stand upon a dream.

CEREMONIAL SPEECH 2: EULOGY FOR JESSE OWENS

THOMAS P. O'NEILL

Thomas P. O'Neill, speaker of the U.S. House of Representatives, Congressional Record, 1 April 1980, pp. 7459–7460.

Following the death of Jesse Owens in 1980, many tributes were presented. The following comments by Thomas P. O'Neill, then speaker of the U.S. House of Representatives, illustrate this genre. This speech was printed in the Congressional Record, 1 April 1980, pp. 7459–7460.

I rise on the occasion of his passing to join my colleagues in tribute to the greatest American sports hero of this century, Jesse Owens.... His performances at the Berlin Olympics earned Jesse Owens the title of America's first superstar.

No other athlete symbolized the spirit and motto of the Olympics better than Jesse Owens. "Swifter, higher, stronger" was the credo by which Jesse Owens performed as an athlete and lived as an American. Of his performances in Hitler's Berlin in 1936, Jesse said: "I wasn't running against Hitler, I was running against the world." Owens's view of the Olympics was just that: He was competing against the best athletes in the world without regard to nationality, race, or political view.

Jesse Owens proved by his performances that he was the best among the finest the world had to offer, and in setting the world record in the 100-yard dash, he became the "fastest human" even before that epithet was fashionable.

In life as well as on the athletic field, Jesse Owens was first an American, and second, an internationalist. He loved his country; he loved the opportunity his country gave him to reach the pinnacle of athletic prowess. In his own quiet, unassuming, and modest way—by example, by inspiration, and by performance—he helped other young people to aim for the stars, to develop their God-given potential. . . .

As the world's first superstar, Jesse Owens was not initially overwhelmed by commercial interests and offered the opportunity to become a millionaire overnight. There was no White House reception waiting for him on his return from Berlin, and as Jesse Owens once observed: "I still had to ride in the back of the bus in my hometown in Alabama."

Can one individual make a difference? Clearly in the case of Jesse Owens, the answer is a resounding affirmative, for his whole life was dedicated to the elimination of poverty, totalitarianism, and racial bigotry; and he did it in his own special and modest way, a spokesman for freedom, an American ambassador of goodwill to the athletes of the world, and an inspiration to young Americans.... Jesse Owens was a champion all the way in a life of dedication to the principles of the American and Olympic spirit.

CEREMONIAL SPEECH 3: REMARKS ON ACCEPTING THE MARTIN LUTHER KING JR. HUMAN RIGHTS AWARD

JOHN BAKKE

Reprinted with permission from John Bakke.

Professor John Bakke presented this thoughtful speech in 2006 in ceremonies held at the University of Memphis. Dr. Bakke used his acceptance speech to breathe new life into Dr. King's principle of nonviolence. Rather than a dated tactic in a long-ago civil rights struggle, nonviolence, by Bakke's interpretation, now demands full participation in the political process and acceptance of one's obligations as a citizen. Thus, what begins as an acceptance speech for an award quickly becomes a speech of tribute to Dr. King and finally a speech of inspiration to his listeners.

Thank you. It seems to me that many acceptance speeches begin with the words, "I've received many awards before, but..." Well, the truth is that I have not received many awards before, but of all the awards I have not received, this is the one I always wanted. What is more important in our lives than our rights as human beings? And who in our lifetime has done more to extend human rights than Dr. King? I'm overwhelmed by the honor. So please indulge me for a few minutes while I thank some people who are special to me before I say a few words in honor and memory of the person whom we all have reason to thank today. Dr. Martin Luther King Jr. gave me the courage to practice what he preached as best I could in and out of academia at critical points in my own life and in the life of this university and our community. And for that I am most thankful.... [Dr. Bakke acknowledges his family and friends, as well as his colleagues at the University of Memphis who shared his values and supported his work.]

We came to Memphis in 1967 and I was fortunate to be part of a progressive department at a university in a community ready for positive change. It is no accident that four members of that department, then called Speech and Drama, were previous recipients of this Martin Luther King Award.... And finally, thanks to all the seekers and holders of elected office who have given me the opportunity to work with them as well as to all the wonderful people whom I have worked with as a partisan in the political process. I got into campaign communication to help good people become more competitive in the campaign arena. I am proud of all these people for what they have done for human rights.

Dr. Martin Luther King Jr. gave to human rights his last full measure of devotion. He was devoted to nonviolence as a political strategy and as a personal philosophy because he knew the effects of violence even on those who commit violent acts as a means of necessary self defense or in a just cause. But when King was nearing his last days on earth, as Taylor Branch has recently written, in his commitment to nonviolence, King "found himself nearly alone among colleagues weary of sacrifice."

In 1968 King was increasingly under attack from all sides, by friends and foes alike. He was criticized by the Johnson Administration for opposing the war in Southeast Asia. He was under intense scrutiny by J. Edgar Hoover and the FBI. He was criticized by the white liberal establishment for his proposed Poor People's March. He was criticized by militant Black Power advocates for his nonviolent tactics and his coalitions with whites. And many of his closest friends just wanted him to back off for a while and by all means stay out of Memphis where a sanitation workers strike had been going on since February 2nd.

All such criticism came together and reached a crescendo after King's march in Memphis on behalf of the sanitation workers was disrupted by violence. The criticism came from all over, from the *New York Times* and *Washington Post* as well as the *Atlanta Constitution*, the *Dallas Morning News*, and, yes, the local *Memphis Commercial Appeal* and *Press-Scimitar* newspapers. In editorials entitled "King's Credibility Gap" and "Chicken a la King," the *Commercial Appeal*, for example, said that "King's pose as the leader of a non-violent movement has been shattered" and "The Real Martin Luther King… [is] one of the most menacing men in America today." The *Press-Scimitar* said that King's "rhetoric has lost its spell" and the *Dallas Morning News* called him "a headline hunting high priest on non-violent violence," "a press agent protester," "a marching militant" willing to "wreck everything for a spot on the evening newscast" and a "peripatetic preacher" who "could not allow the troubled waters to go unfished when there was a chance that the fisher might pick up a little publicity." You can imagine what was being said on the street at the time.

From all corners, the message was clear. "Martin Luther King! Go home! Go back where you came from. Get back in your place! At worst, you're dangerous. At best, you're history." Believe me! James Earl Ray was not the only American who wanted King out of the way. On the eve of April 4, in such a climate of violence in Memphis, Martin Luther delivered his "Mountaintop Speech" at Mason Temple. Like Socrates at his trial, like Jesus before Pilate, like Luther at Worms, King, virtually alone, had to stand up and be who he was: Dr. Martin Luther King Jr., the true apostle of nonviolent direct action.

I spent much time as a graduate student studying great speeches. I also read many treatises on the nature of eloquence. Thus I can say, personally and professionally, history knows no more eloquent speaker than Martin Luther King Jr. I never understood what Longinus meant when he wrote that "eloquence was the concomitant of a great soul" until I heard Dr. King in a context in which I knew what he was up against and what he was asking for. His last speech in Memphis was more than speech. It was "eloquence," once described by the great orator Daniel Webster as "action… noble, sublime, godlike action."

In the peroration of what became his last speech, King mentioned the threats and uncertainties that surrounded his life, but announced that he had been to the mountaintop. And from that lofty eminence he had seen "the Promised Land," a vision that would redeem all the years of pain and suffering. He might not get there with them, but assured listeners "that we as a people will get to the Promised Land."

It was perfect communication. All in his presence were filled with King's conviction and what they felt was his "truth." The striking sanitation workers would get what they deserved and so too would they as a people. That WAS more than speech. It WAS action. In Webster's words: "noble, sublime, manly, godlike action." Martin Luther King, you see, was more than just a "dreamer," more than someone who simply walked on troubled waters turning the other cheek. King was America's conscience and a powerful force for change.

In his *Ethics of Rhetoric*, published in 1953 before King became a national figure, Richard Weaver wrote that the discourse of the noble orator is about "real potentiality or possible actuality," whereas that of the "mere exaggerator" is about "unreal potentiality." In his famous "I Have a Dream" speech, King said—remember, it was 1963—that he had a dream that the sons of former slaves and former slave owners would be able to sit down together at the table of brotherhood. Unreal potentiality or possible actuality? He said little black boys and black girls would be able to join hands with little white boys and girls and walk together as sisters and brothers. Possible actuality or unreal potentiality? And he said that his four children would one day live in a nation where they would be judged not by the color of their skin but by the content of their character. A dream? Or real vision? And what about "We as a people will get to the promised land"? What about that one? Where are we on that one today? And if we are not where we want to be, whose fault is it? Certainly not Martin Luther King's nor the legitimacy of his vision.

In the last volume of his great trilogy, *America in the King Years*, Taylor Branch begins with the assertion that today "nonviolence is an orphan among democratic ideas." He says, "It has nearly vanished from public discourse even though the basic element—the vote—has no other meaning." In homage to King and for the good of ourselves, Branch strongly suggests that we commit the same time, energy, and resources to the nonviolent means of change as we now commit to the violent ones. "Every ballot is a piece of nonviolence," he says, "signifying hard-won consent to raise politics above fire power and bloody conquest."

It's time to make that ballot the effect of full democratic participation. It's time to reclaim our democratic processes. It's time to make the democratic processes work in America just as we are trying to make them work for Iraq.

That means more than voting. It means informed voting. It means supporting candidates and policies of our choice. It means commitment to the communication processes that give life to democracy. It means thinking of ourselves more as citizens than as just taxpayers. It means full-time citizenship. If campaigns are now permanent, citizenship cannot be cyclical. Democracy and "the vote" will always be open to criticism if people do not vote or do not know what they are voting for.

I don't care how much we spend on voting technology. I don't care how much we restrict campaign contributions. Special interests will always have special influence as long as we the people are not especially interested. Voting for two dead people certainly was bad [in a recent local election], but over 90% of live voters staying home was a whole lot worse.

If we work to make the democratic processes work for us at home as well as around the world, we will be on the true path—the nonviolent path—to the kind of homeland security that will keep us moving toward the Promised Land. It is nonviolence that makes civilization civil and it is through the nonviolent participation in democracy that we can live out the true meaning of OUR creed. We will be keeping alive the hope of the American dream of our founding fathers and the real potentiality in the vision of Dr. Martin Luther King Jr.

CEREMONIAL SPEECH 4: NOBEL PEACE PRIZE ACCEPTANCE SPEECH[1]

ELIE WIESEL

Elie Wiesel (1986) © The Nobel Foundation 1986.

Elie Wiesel delivered the following speech in Oslo, Norway, on December 10, 1986, as he accepted the Nobel Peace Prize. The award recognized his lifelong work for human rights, especially his role as "spiritual archivist of the Holocaust." Wiesel's poetic, intensely personal style as a writer carries over into this ceremonial speech of acceptance. He uses narrative very effectively as he flashes back to what he calls the "kingdom of night" and then flashes forward again into the present. The speech's purpose is to spell out and share the values and concerns of a life committed to the rights of oppressed peoples, in which, as he put it so memorably, "every moment is a moment of grace, every hour an offering."

It is with a profound sense of humility that I accept the honor you have chosen to bestow upon me. I know: your choice transcends me. This both frightens and pleases me.

It frightens me because I wonder: do I have the right to represent the multitudes who have perished? Do I have the right to accept this great honor on their behalf? I do not. That would be presumptuous. No one may speak for the dead, no one may interpret their mutilated dreams and visions.

It pleases me because I may say that this honor belongs to all the survivors and their children, and through us, to the Jewish people with whose destiny I have always been identified.

I remember: it happened yesterday or eternities ago. A young Jewish boy discovering the kingdom of night. I remember his bewilderment, I remember his anguish. It all happened so fast. The ghetto. The deportation. The sealed cattle car. The fiery altar upon which the history of our people and the future of mankind were meant to be sacrificed.

I remember: he asked his father: "Can this be true? This is the 20th century, not the Middle Ages. Who would allow such crimes to be committed? How could the world remain silent?"

And now the boy is turning to me: "Tell me," he asks. "What have you done with your life?"

And I tell him that I have tried. That I have tried to keep memory alive, that I have tried to fight those who would forget. Because if we forget, we are guilty, we are accomplices.

And then I explained to him how naive we were, that the world did know and remain silent. And that is why I swore never to be silent whenever and wherever human beings endure suffering and humiliation. We must always take sides. Neutrality helps the oppressor, never the victim. Silence encourages the tormentor, never the tormented.

Sometimes we must interfere. When human lives are endangered, when human dignity is in jeopardy, national borders and sensitivities become irrelevant. Wherever men or women are persecuted because of their race, religion or political views, that place must—at that moment—become the center of our universe.

Of course, since I am a Jew profoundly rooted in my people's memory and tradition, my first response is to Jewish fears, Jewish needs, Jewish crises. For I belong to a traumatized generation, one that experienced the abandonment and solitude of our people. It would be unnatural for me not to make Jewish priorities my own: Israel, Soviet Jewry, Jews in Arab lands.

But there are others as important to me. Apartheid is, in my view as abhorrent as anti-Semitism. To me, Andrei Sakharov's isolation is as much a disgrace as Iosif Begun's imprisonment. As is the denial of Solidarity and its leader Lech Walesa's right to dissent. And Nelson Mandela's interminable imprisonment.

There is so much injustice and suffering crying out for our attention: victims of hunger, or racism and political persecution, writers and poets, prisoners in so many lands governed by the left and by the right. Human rights are being violated on every continent. More people are oppressed than free.

And then, too, there are the Palestinians to whose plight I am sensitive but whose methods I deplore. Violence and terrorism are not the answer. Something must be done about their suffering, and soon. I trust Israel, for I have faith in the Jewish people. Let Israel be given a chance, let hatred and danger be removed from her horizons, and there will be peace in and around the Holy Land.

Yes, I have the faith. Faith in God and even in His creation. Without it no action would be possible. And action is the only remedy to indifference: the most insidious danger of all. Isn't this the meaning of Alfred Nobel's legacy? Wasn't his fear of war a shield against war?

There is much to be done, there is much that can be done. One person—a Raoul Wallenberg, an Albert Schweitzer, one person of integrity, can make a difference, a difference of life and death. As long as one dissident is in prison, our freedom will not be true. As long as one child is hungry, our lives will be filled with anguish and shame.

What all these victims need above all is to know that they are not alone: that we are not forgetting them, that when their voices are stifled we shall lend them ours, that while their freedom depends on ours, the quality of our freedom depends on theirs.

This is what I say to the young Jewish boy wondering what I have done with his years. It is in his name that I speak to you and that I express to you my deepest gratitude. No one is as capable of gratitude as one who has emerged from the kingdom of night.

We know that every moment is a moment of grace, every hour an offering; not to share them would mean to betray them. Our lives no longer belong to us alone; they belong to all those who need us desperately.

Thank you, Chairman Aarvik. Thank you, members of the Nobel Committee. Thank you, people of Norway, for declaring on this singular occasion that our survival has meaning for mankind.

Glossary

acceptance speech A ceremonial speech expressing gratitude for an honor and acknowledging those who made the accomplishment possible.

accidental plagiarism Various forms of unintentional academic dishonesty due to sloppy research techniques.

accuracy Criterion for evaluating the correctness of information by checking it against other information.

acronym A word composed of the initial letters of a series of words.

ad hominem fallacy Attacking the character or motives of opposing advocates rather than engaging their arguments.

advocacy website A website with the major purpose of raising awareness or persuading people to act.

after-dinner speech An often humorous ceremonial speech presented after a meal that offers a message without asking for radical changes.

agreement In this third stage in the persuasive process, listeners accept a speaker's recommendations and remember their reasons for doing so.

alliteration The repetition of initial consonant sounds in closely connected words.

amplification The art of developing ideas by restating them in a speech.

analogical reasoning Creating a strategic perspective on a subject by relating it to something similar.

analogous color scheme Colors adjacent on the color wheel; used in a presentation aid to suggest both differences and close relationships among the components.

anticipatory anxiety The fear of public speaking that occurs before the actual presentation of a speech.

antithesis A language technique that combines opposing elements in the same sentence or adjoining sentences.

appreciative listening Listening for the artistry of a message.

articulation The manner in which individual speech sounds are produced.

attitudes Strong thoughts and feelings that predispose us to respond positively or negatively toward specific subjects.

audience The listeners for whom the speaker's message is intended.

authority Criterion for evaluating the credentials of a source.

autocratic leader Makes decisions and gives orders without consultation; directs group behavior through the use of rewards and punishments.

award presentation A speech that explains the nature of the award and recognizes the achievements of the award recipient.

awareness In this first stage of the persuasive process, listeners gain knowledge about a problem and pay attention to it.

backing Additional evidence and reasoning to support disputed warrants.

balance Suggests that the introduction, body, and conclusion receive appropriate development.

bandwagon fallacy Arguing that a persuasive message must be right or wrong because of its popular acceptance.

bar graph A graph that shows comparisons and contrasts between two or more items or groups.

begging the question fallacy Making claims based on premises the audience may not accept without bothering to support or argue for them.

beliefs What we know or think we know about subjects.

body The section of a speech that contains your main ideas and the materials that support them.

body language Communication achieved using facial expressions, eye contact, movements, and gestures.

boomerang effect A negative reaction that occurs when speakers ask for too much persuasive change as a result of a single speech.

brainstorming Technique that encourages the free play of the mind to generate a list of ideas that can be carefully considered and critiqued for possible topics.

briefing A short informative presentation offered in an organizational setting that focuses on plans, policies, or reports.

bulleted list A presentation aid that highlights ideas by presenting them as a list of brief statements.

call the question A motion that proposes to end discussion and vote on the original motion, as amended if appropriate.

categorical design Arranges the main ideas of a speech so that they reflect major topics or points of emphasis.

causation design Considers the origins or consequences of a situation or event.

ceremonial speaking Speaking that celebrates the meaning of special occasions, such as speeches of tribute, award presentations, eulogies, toasts, and after-dinner speeches.

ceremonial speeches Used to celebrate or commemorate important events, people, and occasions.

channel Medium that conveys the message to listeners.

chronological design Explains the events or historical developments in the order in which they occurred.

claim The central point or proposition of an argument.

closed-ended questions Questions that stipulate a limited number of answers for respondents to select such as true-false, multiple-choice, and scaled questions.

co-active approach An approach to persuasion that seeks to bridge differences on disputed issues by establishing identification and good will, reasoning from shared beliefs and values, emphasizing explanation over argument, and making a multisided presentation.

cognitive dissonance The discomfort we feel when we sense that our attitudes and behaviors are not consistent with our values.

cognitive restructuring Replacing negative thoughts with positive, constructive ones.

collaborative problem solving A group technique that gathers participants from differing backgrounds and social sectors for their input on a problem.

communication apprehension Those unpleasant feelings and fears you may experience before or during a presentation.

communication orientation Approaching public speaking as an interactive process rather than a performance.

comparative design Explores the similarities and differences among elements.

competence The perception of a speaker as being well informed, intelligent, and well prepared.

complementary color scheme Colors opposite one another on the color wheel; used in a presentation aid to suggest tension and opposition.

comprehensive listening Listening that focuses on understanding a speaker's overall message.

computer-generated presentation The use of commercial presentation software to join audio, visual, textual, graphic, and animated components.

conclusion The ending for your speech that reinforces your main ideas and provides your audience with something to remember.

connotative meaning The emotional, subjective, personal meaning that certain words can evoke in listeners.

contrast Attracts attention and sharpens perspective by highlighting the differences between opposites.

coordination Placing statements equal in importance on the same level in an outline.

critical listening Listening that carefully evaluates a speaker's message.

cultural sensitivity The respectful appreciation of diversity within an audience.

culturetypes Terms that express the values and goals of a group's culture.

deductive reasoning Arguing from a general principle to a specific conclusion.

deliberative speeches Used to propose, discuss, debate, and decide future policies and laws.

delivery Presenting a speech to an audience, integrating the skills of nonverbal communication with the speech content.

demagogues Leaders who pander to popular prejudices and emotional appeals without regard to truth or reason.

demographics General characteristics of listeners, including age, gender, sexual orientation, education, race and ethnicity, socioeconomic background, and group affiliations.

denotative meaning The dictionary definition or objective meaning of a word.

design Standard way to arrange the main points of a speech.

dialect A speech pattern associated with an area of the country or with a cultural or ethnic background.

dialogue Having the characters in a narrative speak for themselves rather than paraphrasing what they have to say.

dialogue groups A group assembled to explore the differing interpretations and experiences that members bring to a problem.

direct quotation Repeating the exact words of others to support a point.

discovery phase Identifying broad topic areas that might generate successful speeches.

disinformation Information that has been fabricated or distorted in order to advance a hidden agenda.

distance Principle of proxemics involving the control of the space that separates speaker and audience.

documents file Contains articles downloaded from search engines or pages you scanned into your computer.

doublespeak Words that point in the direction opposite from the reality they supposedly describe.

dynamism The perception of a speaker as confident, decisive, and enthusiastic.

either-or fallacy Arguing that there are only two options, one of which is desirable.

electronic brainstorming A group technique in which participants generate ideas online prior to discussing them face-to-face.

elevation Principle of proxemics dealing with power relationships implied when speakers stand above listeners.

embedded narratives Stories inserted within speeches that illustrate the speaker's points.

empathic listening Listening to experience the speaker's perspective.

enactment In this fourth stage of the persuasive process, listeners take appropriate action as the result of agreement.

enduring metaphors Metaphors of unusual power and popularity that are based on experience that lasts over time and crosses many cultural boundaries.

enunciation The manner in which individual words are articulated and pronounced in context.

epilogue The final part of a narrative reflecting on its meaning.

equivocation Exploiting the ambiguity of language to mislead an audience or avoid the issue at hand.

ethnocentrism The tendency of any nation, race, religion, or group to believe that its way of looking at the world is right and that other perspectives are wrong.

ethos Appeals based on the perceived competence, integrity, good will, and dynamism of the speaker.

eulogy A speech of tribute presented upon a person's death.

euphemism Words that soften or evade the truth of a situation.

evidence Information used in support of persuasive claims.

examples Incidents that illustrate a speaker's points.

expanded conversational style A presentational quality that, while somewhat more formal than everyday conversation, preserves its directness and spontaneity.

expert testimony Citing the words of people or institutions qualified by training or experience to speak as authorities on a subject.

exploration phase Examining broad topic areas to pinpoint more precise topics for speeches.

extemporaneous speaking A form of presentation in which a speech is carefully prepared and practiced but not written out, memorized, or read.

facts Descriptive statements that can be verified as true by observation or by experts.

factual example An example based on something that actually happened or really exists.

fallacies Errors in reasoning and evidence use that make persuasive messages unreliable.

faulty analogy fallacy A comparison drawn between events, developments, or processes that are dissimilar in some important way.

feedback Speaker's perception of audience reactions to the message.

figurative analogy A comparison of subjects drawn from essentially different fields of experience.

figurative language Words used in surprising and unusual ways that magnify the power of their meaning.

flip chart A large, unlined tablet (usually a newsprint pad) placed on an easel so that as each page is filled up it can be flipped over the top.

flow chart A visual method of representing power and responsibility relationships or describing steps in a process.

focus group A small group formed to reveal the feelings or motivations of customers, clients, or voters.

forensic speeches Used to determine the rightness and wrongness of past actions, often in courts of law.

formal outline Represents the final, complete, polished plan of your speech.

forum A moderated group presentation format in which designated members respond to questions from the audience.

general purpose The speaker's intention to inform or persuade listeners or to commemorate some person or occasion.

general search engine An Internet search engine that allows you to enter keywords and find related websites.

god and devil terms Powerful terms that have strongly positive or negative connotations in a culture.

good will The impression that speakers have their listeners' best interests at heart.

graphics Visual representations of information, such as sketches, maps, graphs, charts, and textual materials.

groupthink Occurs when group members uncritically accept and reinforce a single position without adequately considering reservations or alternative positions.

habitual pitch The vocal level at which people speak most frequently.

hasty generalization fallacy An error of inductive reasoning in which general claims are based on insufficient or nonrepresentative evidence.

hearing A physical process in which soundwaves affect our eardrums, creating sound.

hidden agendas Actual motivations and goals that speakers keep secret, making it difficult to evaluate their intentions.

hypothetical example An example offered not as real but as representative of actual people, situations, or events.

identification A shared sense of purpose and community created between speakers and listeners.

ideographs Compact expressions of a group's basic political faith.

illusion of transparency The mistaken belief that people know what you are thinking and feeling.

immediacy A quality of successful communication achieved when the speaker and audience experience a sense of closeness.

impromptu speaking Speaking on the spur of the moment in response to an unpredictable situation with limited time for preparation.

inductive reasoning Reasoning from specific factual instances to reach a general conclusion.

inferences Assumptions or projections derived from facts and information.

information website A website designed to provide factual information on a subject.

informative speaking Functions to enlighten listeners by sharing ideas and information.

informative value A measure of how much new and important information or understanding a speech conveys to an audience.

integration In this final stage of the persuasive process, listeners connect new attitudes and commitments with previous beliefs and values to ensure lasting change.

integrity The impression of a speaker as being honest, ethical, and dependable.

intensity Making aspects of a speech striking or stand out.

interest chart Visual display of speaker or audience interests, as prompted by probe questions.

interference Distractions that can disrupt the communication process.

internal summary A transition that reminds listeners of major points already presented in a speech before proceeding to new ideas.

introduction The opening to your speech that gains attention, previews your message, and establishes a favorable connection with your listeners.

inversion Changing the normal order of words to make statements memorable.

jargon Technical language related to a specific field that may be incomprehensible to a general audience.

key-word outline Abbreviated version of a formal outline used in presenting a speech; focuses on cues and points of emphasis.

laissez-faire leader Leaves group members free to decide what, how, and when to act without guidance.

lay testimony Citing the words or views of ordinary people on a subject.

line graph A visual representation of changes across time; especially useful for indicating trends of growth or decline.

listening An active process and skill that includes attending, interpreting, evaluating, and remembering messages.

literal analogy A comparison of subjects drawn from the same field of experience.

logos Appeals based on reasoning and evidence.

magnification When speakers select and emphasize certain qualities of a subject to stress the virtues and values they represent.

main points The most important ideas developed in support of the thesis statement.

malapropisms Language errors that occur when a word is confused with another word that sounds like it.

manipulation Strategies that short-circuit critical thinking and ethical persuasion by substituting flashy images, hidden motives, and outright dishonesty for substantive reasoning and evidence use.

manuscript presentation A speech read from a prepared text or teleprompter.

master narrative A speech structured around a story that reveals some important truth.

master of ceremonies A person who coordinates an event or program, sets its mood, introduces portions of the programming, and provides transitions.

maxims Brief and particularly apt sayings.

mediated prompts Sources such as newspapers, magazines, and electronic media that can suggest ideas for speech topics.

memorized text presentation Speeches committed to memory and delivered word for word.

message The main ideas and information a speaker wants to convey.

metaphor An implied comparison that connects subjects not usually related to create a surprising perspective.

metasearch engine A search tool that compiles results from multiple search engines.

mind mapping Changes customary linear patterns of thinking into visual representations of relationships to encourage creative exploration.

mirror question A question that repeats part of a previous response to encourage further discussion.

model A replica used to represent an object.

monochromatic color scheme Use of variations of a single color in a presentation aid to convey the idea of variety within unity.

motion to amend A parliamentary move that offers opportunity to modify a motion presently under discussion.

motion to postpone consideration A motion that defers discussion until some specified time.

motions Formal proposals for group consideration.

motivated sequence Expanded version of the problem-solution design that emphasizes the steps of attention, need, satisfaction, visualization, and action.

motives Widely shared psychological needs, desires, and impulses.

move to adjourn A motion that calls for the meeting to end.

myth of the mean fallacy The deceptive use of statistical averages.

mythos A form of proof grounded in the sense of connection and identification that people feel with group traditions and the values they embody.

narrative design A speech structure that develops from beginning to end through a prologue, a plot, and an epilogue.

narratives Stories that illustrate the ideas or theme of a speech.

neologism An invented word that combines previous words in a striking new expression.

non sequitur fallacy Occurs when conclusions do not follow coherently from the speaker's reasoning and evidence.

novelty The quality of being new or unusual.

objectivity Criterion for evaluating whether or not a source provides an unbiased or balanced perspective.

objects Specific items that illuminate an article or parts of a process.

onomatopoeia Words that sound like the subjects they signify.

open-ended questions Questions that allow respondents to answer in as much detail as they choose.

opinions Personal evaluations or judgments based on facts and inferences.

optimum pitch The level at which people can produce their strongest voice with minimal effort and that allows variation up and down the musical scale.

oral citations Providing your listeners with essential information about the sources you use in your speech.

oral report A presentation that summarizes the deliberations or work of a small group before a larger audience.

order A consistent pattern used to develop a speech.

panel discussion A group presentation format in which group members informally discuss a series of questions as introduced by a moderator.

parallel construction Using the same or similar word patterns to articulate and contrast your main ideas.

paraphrase Rephrasing or summarizing the words of others to support a point.

parliamentary procedure A relatively standard set of rules for conducting formal meetings that encourages the orderly, fair, and full consideration of proposals during group discussions.

participative leader Seeks input from group members and gives them an active role in decision making.

pathos Appeals based on emotions.

peer review Process by which articles in scholarly journals are checked by experts in the field for quality and accuracy before being approved for publication.

perfectionism Believing that your presentations must be perfect to be effective.

personification A figure of speech in which nonhuman or abstract subjects are given human qualities.

persuasive argument A disputed proposition supported with reasoning and evidence.

persuasive speaking Speaking to influence the beliefs, attitudes, values, and sometimes the behaviors of listeners.

pie graph A circle graph that shows the size of a subject's parts in relation to each other and to the whole.

pitch The position of the human voice on a scale ranging from low and deep to high and sharp.

plagiarism Presenting the ideas and words of others as though they were your own.

plot The body of a narrative that unfolds in a sequence of scenes designed to build suspense.

post hoc fallacy Occurs when speakers assume one thing caused another simply because it preceded it in close proximity.

preliminary tuning effect The effect of previous speeches or other situational factors in predisposing an audience to respond positively or negatively to a speech.

PREP formula A technique for making an impromptu speech: State a *p*oint, give a *r*eason and *e*xample, and restate the *p*oint.

presentation aids Visual, auditory, and tactile supplements intended to enhance the clarity and effectiveness of a presentation.

presentation anxiety The discomfort you feel while actually giving a speech.

prestige testimony Citing the words of an admired public figure or text.

preview The part of the introduction that identifies the main points to be developed in the body of the speech and presents an overview of the speech to follow.

probe A question that asks a person to elaborate on an answer.

problem-solution design Focuses attention on a problem and offers a solution for it.

prologue The opening of a narrative that establishes the context and setting, introduces the main characters, and foreshadows the meaning.

pronunciation The use of correct sounds and of proper stress on syllables when saying words.

proofs Appeals to ethos, logos, pathos, and mythos that help to enhance the persuasiveness of speaking.

proposition A clear declarative statement of your central persuasive point or thesis.

proxemics The study of how human beings use space during communication.

psychographics The beliefs, attitudes, values, and motives that influence the behavior of listeners.

public speaking ethics Standards for judging the rightness or wrongness of public speaking behaviors.

qualifiers Terms or statements that limit the certainty of your claims.

quoting out of context An unethical use of a quotation that changes or distorts its original meaning.

rate The speed at which words are uttered.

red herring fallacy The use of irrelevant ideas and information to divert attention from the issue at hand.

refinement phase Framing the general and specific purposes of a speech's topic and a thesis statement.

refutation A strategy of engaging opposing positions and concerns by providing reasoning and evidence to argue that they are wrong or less right than your position.

refutative design A persuasive design in which the speaker engages opposing views.

reinforcer A comment or action that encourages further communication from someone being interviewed.

relational communication Group communication behaviors that focus on creating a positive communication climate and promoting group cohesion.

relevance How a speech relates to an audience's specific needs, interests, or concerns.

reluctant testimony Invoking the words of sources who appear to speak against their own interests.

reluctant witnesses Witnesses who testify against their apparent self-interest.

repetition Repeating sounds, words, or phrases to attract and hold attention.

research log File in which you jot down ideas, list key terms, and prioritize readings.

reservations Qualifiers that recognize circumstances under which claims may not apply.

responsible knowledge An advanced state of awareness concerning a topic, understanding its major features, issues, latest developments, and local applications.

rhetorical questions Questions that have a self-evident answer or that provoke curiosity, which the speech then proceeds to satisfy.

rhetorical situation The perception that an effective speech provides an appropriate response to the public speaking situation.

rhythm Rate and stress patterns of vocal presentation within a speech.

roundtable An informal group presentation format in which members discuss ideas, information, and opinions before a larger audience.

second A motion must receive a "second" from another member of the group before discussion can proceed.

selective relaxation Practicing muscle control techniques to help you reduce physical and psychological tension by relaxing on cue.

self-awareness inventory A series of questions that allow speakers to explore specific ideas for developing their speech of self-introduction.

self-sabotage Focusing on anxieties to the extent that your communicative behaviors confirm and reinforce them.

sequential design Explains the steps of a process in the order in which they should be taken.

setting Physical and psychological context in which a speech is presented.

sexist language Using disparaging labels and references to gender, making irrelevant references to gender, or using masculine nouns or pronouns when the intended reference is to both sexes.

simile A language tool that clarifies something abstract by comparing it with something concrete; usually introduced by *as* or *like*.

simplicity Suggests that a speech has a limited number of main points and that they are short and direct.

slang The informal style and vocabulary used by a particular group.

slippery slope fallacy The assumption that once something happens, an inevitable trend is established that will lead to disastrous results.

small group A small number of people who interact over time to achieve a goal or goals.

social leadership behavior A type of leadership that focuses on building and maintaining positive and productive relationships among group members.

source citations Brief references to your sources within a formal outline.

source file Contains complete information for citing your consulted sources on your bibliography.

spatial design Arranges the main points of a speech as they occur in actual space, creating an oral map.

speaker Initiates the communication process by framing an oral message for the consideration of others.

speaking situation The occasion for speaking as well as the physical and psychological settings.

specific purpose The speaker's particular goal or the response that the speaker wants to evoke.

speech of demonstration An informative speech that shows the audience how to do something.

speech of description An informative speech that uses vivid language to illustrate an activity, object, person, or place.

speech of explanation An informative speech that offers information about the nature, workings, and implications of abstract and complex subjects.

speech of inspiration A ceremonial speech designed to awaken or reawaken an audience to a goal, purpose, or set of values.

speech of introduction A ceremonial speech in which a featured speaker is introduced to the audience.

speech of tribute A ceremonial speech that recognizes the achievements of individuals or groups or commemorates special events.

speeches that advocate action and policy Speeches that encourage listeners to embrace a policy or enact a plan of action for addressing a problem or issue.

speeches that emphasize attitudes and values Speeches that ask listeners to make evaluative judgments on a situation or issue.

speeches that focus on facts Speeches that engage uncertainties and disputes surrounding questions of past, present, and future facts.

statistics Facts that can be measured mathematically.

stock issues The primary questions a reasonable person would ask before agreeing to a change in policies or procedures.

straw figure fallacy Misrepresenting opposing views in a manner that makes them easier to refute.

subject directory An organized list of links to websites on specific topics.

subject files Contains the precise information you discover and gather while conducting your research.

subordination Arranging materials in an outline in an order of descending importance from the general to the specific—from main points to subpoints to sub-subpoints, and so on.

subpoints The major divisions of a speech's main points.

sub-subpoints The major divisions of a speech's subpoints.

supporting materials The facts and statistics, testimony, examples, and narratives that are the building blocks of substantive speechmaking.

symbolic racism Indirect racism that uses code words or subtle contrasts to suggest that one race is superior to another.

symposium A moderated group presentation format in which members present prepared speeches on different areas of a topic or issue.

table the motion A parliamentary move to indefinitely suspend discussion of a motion.

task communication Group communication behaviors that focus on achieving shared goals.

task leadership behavior A type of leadership that directs the attention and activity of a group toward achieving specific goals.

testimony Citing the words and ideas of others to support a point.

textual graphics Visuals that contain words, phrases, or numbers.

thesis statement The central idea of a speech stated as a simple declarative sentence.

toast A short speech of tribute, usually offered at celebrations, dinners, or meetings.

topic analysis Using questions often employed by journalists (*who, what, when, where, why,* and *how*) to explore topic possibilities for speeches.

topic area inventory chart A means of determining possible speech topics by listing topics you and your listeners find interesting and then matching them.

topic areas Promising but broad subjects that need to be honed into topics for briefer presentations.

transactional leadership Leadership based on power relationships that relies on reward and punishment to achieve its ends.

transformational leadership Leadership based on mutual respect and stewardship rather than control to inspire group members.

transitions Connecting elements that cue listeners that you are finished making one point and are moving on to the next.

trigger words Words that arouse powerful feelings and may interfere with our ability to listen effectively.

understanding In this second phase of the persuasive process, listeners develop a broader comprehension of a problem or issue.

values The moral principles that suggest how we should behave or what we should believe.

vicarious experience narrative Speech strategy in which the speaker invites listeners to imagine themselves enacting a story.

virtual meetings Group meetings that are conducted across space and mediated using technology.

visualization Systematically picturing yourself as a speaker and practicing your speech with that image in mind.

vocal distractions Filler words, such as "er," "um," and "you know," used in place of a pause.

warrant The stated or implied reasoning that shows how evidence connects to a persuasive claim.

working outline A tentative plan that allows you to see the structure of your message as you develop it.

works cited A list of the sources mentioned in your presentation.

works consulted A list of all the works you read in preparation for your presentation.

Notes

Chapter 1

1. Weaver, Richard M. *Ideas Have Consequences* (Chicago: University of Chicago Press, 1948) and *The Ethics of Rhetoric* (Chicago: Henry Regnery, 1953).
2. Hart, Roderick P. "Why Communication? Why Education? Toward a Politics of Teaching." *Communication Education* 42 (1993): 101.
3. Adapted from Karen Kangas Dwyer, "Communication Apprehension and Learning Style Preference: Correlations and Imp lications for Teaching." *Communication Education*, 47 (April 1998), 137.
4. "Employers Say Verbal Communication Most Important Candidate Skill." National Association of Colleges and Employers, 1 March, 2016, http://naceweb.org/about-us/press/2016/verbal-communication-most-important-candidate-skill.aspx?terms=communication%20 skills#sthash.1Cti397i.dpuf (accessed March 29, 2016); and Press Release, National Association of Colleges and Employers, 15 March 2007, www.naceweb.org/press/display .asp?year=2007&prid=254 (accessed 7 May 2007).
5. "Employers Complain About Communication Skills." *Pittsburgh Post-Gazette*, 6 February 2005, www.post-gazette .com/pg/pp/05037/453170.stm (accessed 7 May 2007).
6. McMillan, Jill J. and Katy J. Harriger. "College Students and Deliberation: A Benchmark Study." *Communication Education* 51 (2002): 237–253.
7. From Kathleen Peterson, ed., *Statements Supporting Speech Communication* (Annandale, VA: Speech Communication Association, 1986).
8. See, for example, Taylor Cox, Jr., and Ruby L. Beale, *Developing Competency to Manage Diversity* (San Francisco: Berrett-Kohler Publishers, 1997); and Taylor Cox, Jr., *Creating the Multicultural Organization: A Strategy to Capturing the Power of Diversity* (San Francisco: Jossey-Bass, 2001).
9. Allen, Brenda J. *Difference Matters*, 2nd ed. (Long Grove, IL: Waveland Press, 2011).
10. *Our Voices: Essays in Culture, Ethnicity, and Communication,* ed. Alberto Gonzalez, Marsha Houston, and Victoria Chen, 3e, Oxford University Press, 2000.
11. Flaherty, Colleen. "'A More Perfect Union.'" *Inside Higher Ed*, April 7, 2015, https://www.insidehighered.com/news/2015/04/07/anna-deavere-smith-delivers-nehs-jefferson-lecture (accessed April 7, 2015).
12. *On Justice, Power, and Human:* Selections from *The History of the Peloponnesian War, Thucydides,* Paul Woodruff, Hackett Publishing, 1993.
13. Osborn, Michael, and Suzanne Osborn. *Alliance for a Better Public Voice: The Communication Discipline and the National Issues Forums* (Dayton, OH: National Issues Forums Institute, 1991).
14. Aristotle. *On Rhetoric*, trans. George A. Kennedy (New York: Oxford University Press, 1988).
15. Cicero. *De Oratore*, trans D.W. Sutton and H. Rackham (Cambridge, MA: Harvard University Press, 1988).
16. Prof. Pat Baker, Department of Communication Studies, Davidson College.
17. See, for example, Lauren Broussell, "Why Social Media Could Swing the 2016 Presidential Election," *CIO*, 27 August, 2015, http://www.cio.com/article/2976083/social-networking/why-social-media-could-swing-the-2016-presidential-election.html (accessed 3 April 2016); Hadas Gold, "Sanders Bests Clinton on Social Media," *Politico,* March 4, 2016, http://www.politico.com/blogs/on-media/2016/03/social-media-2016-elections-220286 (accessed 3 April 2016); and Antoaneta Roussi, "The Twitter Candidate: Donald Trump's Mastery of Social Media is His Real Ground Game," *Salon*, 18 Feb, 2016, http://www.salon.com/2016/02/18/the_twitter_candidate_donald_trumps_mastery_of_social_media_is_his_real_ground_game/ (accessed 3 April, 2016).
18. "Twitter Usage Statistics," Internet Live Stats, http://www.internetlivestats.com/twitter-statistics/ (accessed 29 March, 2016)
19. Bitzer, Lloyd F. "The Rhetorical Situation," in *Rhetoric: A Tradition in Transition*, ed. Walter Fisher (Michigan State UP, 1974), pp. 247-60.
20. See especially Burke's discussion of identification and consubstantiality: "The Range of Rhetoric," in *A Rhetoric of Motives* (Berkeley: University of California Press, 1969), pp. 3–43.
21. King, Jr., Martin Luther. "I Have a Dream," www .americanrhetoric.com/speeches/mlkihaveadream.htm.
22. "Credo of Ethical Communication," National Communication Association. Reprinted by permission of the National Communication Association. www.natcom.org.
23. "Rewriting the Science, Scientist Says Politicians Edit Global Warming Research," *60 Minutes*, 19 March 2006, www.cbsnews.com/news/rewriting-the-Science/ (accessed 31 March 2016).
24. Schlesinger, Robert. "The Myth of JFK as Supply Side Tax Cutter." *U.S. News and World Report*, 26 Jan. 2011, www .usnews.com/opinion/articles/2011/01/26/the-myth-of-jfk-as-supply-side-tax-cutter (accessed 31 March 2016).
25. Kessler, Glenn. "President Obama: Quoting Reagan Out of Context." *The Washington Post*, 12 April 2012, https://www .washongtonpost.com/blogs/fact-checker/post/president -obama-quoting-reagan-out-of-context/2012/04/11/glQAaOsZBT.html (accessed 31 March 2016).
26. Hinman, Lawrence M. "How to Fight College Cheating." *Washington Post,* 3 September 2004, http://ethics.sandiego.edu/LMH/op-ed/CollegeCheating/index.asp (accessed 29 June 2006).
27. Miller-Henningsen, Mary Lynn, Kathleen S. Valde, and Jason Akst Denbow. "Academic Misconduct: A Goals-Plans-Action Approach to Peer Confrontation and Whistle-Blowing." *Communication Education, 62*, 148–168.

28. This theme develops in Richard L. Johannesen, Kathleen S. Valde, and Karen E. Whedbee, *Ethics in Human Communication*, 6th ed. (Long Grove, IL: Waveland, 2007).
29. *The Years of Lyndon Johnson: The Path to Power,* Robert A. Caro, Random House Inc., 1983.

Chapter 2

1. McCroskey, James C. "Communication Apprehension: What We Have Learned Over the Past Four Decades," *Human Communication* 12 (2008): 157–71; Roper Starch, "How Americans Communicate" May 2008, teachingfsem08.umwblogs.org/files/2008/05/roper-poll-on-communication(1).pdf (accessed 11 January 2016).
2. Peterson, Ginny. "Speaking With Ease: Local Clubs Help With Fear of Presentations." *Star News* 28 February 2007, 1–2. Print.
3. "Celebrities' Stage Fright Secrets," 19 Nov. 2003, NCBuys Worldwide Newsdesk Reporting, www.ncbuy.com/news/2003-11-19/1008286.html (accessed 5 May 2007); and "Famous People" Shyness and Social Anxiety Treatment (updated posting) www.social anxietyassist.com.au/famous_people.shtml (accessed 5 May 2007).
4. Colbert, Stephen. *CBS Sunday Morning*, September 6, 2015.
5. Cited in Scott Berkun and Liz Danzico. "Training the Butterflies: Interview with Scott Berkun," 23 February 2010, http://allstapart.com/article/interview-with-scott-berkum (accessed 8 February 2013). Emphasis added.
6. Behnke, Ralph R. and Chris R. Sawyer. "Milestones of Anticipatory Public Speaking Anxiety." *Communication Education*, 48 (April 1999), pp. 165–72.
7. Kangas Dwyer, Karen. *Conquer Your Speech Anxiety*, 2d ed. (Belmont, CA: Thomson Wadsworth, 2005), p. 18.
8. Knowles, Beyoncé. Quoted in the *Charlotte [NC] Observer*, September 4, 2013, p. 1C.
9. Finn, Amber N., Chris R. Sawyer, and Paul Schrodt. "Examining the Effect of Exposure Therapy on Public Speaking State Anxiety." *Communication Education* 10 (2009): 92–109; Karla M. Hunter, Joshua Westwick, and Laurie Haleta, "Assessing Success: The Impacts of a Fundamentals of Speech Course on Decreasing Public Speaking Anxiety," *Communication Education*, 63(2) (2014), pp. 124–135.
10. Bratskeir, Kate. "This App Could Help You Get Over Your Public Speaking Anxiety." *Huffington Post*, March 1, 2016, http://www.huffingtonpost.com/entry/fear-of-public-speaking-app-virtualspeechus_56d0b01be4b0871f60eb59df (accessed 19 June 2016).
11. Braiker, Harriet. *Charlotte Observer*, August 14, 2012, p. C1.
12. Semple, Dean. American Choral Directors Association convention, Los Angeles, February 2005.
13. Wooden, John. *Charlotte Observer*, April 10, 2014, p. C1.
14. Ferderbar, Pam. "Public Speaking: The Horror." *Huffington Post*, October 22, 2015, http://www.huffingtonpost.com/pam-ferderbar/public-speaking-the-horror_b_8363992.html (accessed 19 June 2016).
15. Gilovich, Thomas, Kenneth Savitsky, and Victoria Husted Medvec. "The Illusion of Transparency: Biased Assessments of Others' Ability to Read One's Emotional States." *Journal of Personality and Social Psychology*, 75:2 (1998), pp. 332–346.
16. Beaver, H. Dennis. "Got Stage Fright" Resource Library, Graduate School of Banking, University of Wisconsin–Madison, www.gsb.org/articles/Stage_Fright.htm (accessed 15 February 2007).
17. Our thanks to Dr. Karen Bernd, Department of Biology, Davidson College, for this suggestion.
18. Kolligian, Jr., John. "Perceived Fraudulence as a Dimension of Perceived Incompetence," in Robert J. Sternberg and John Kolligian, Jr., eds., *Competence Considered* (New Haven, CT: Yale University Press, 1990), pp. 317–39; and Barry J. Zimmerman, Albert Bandura, and Manual Martinez-Pons, "Self-Motivation for Academic Attainment: The Role of Self-Efficacy Beliefs and Personal Goal Setting," *American Educational Research Journal*, 29:3 (Fall 1992), pp. 663–76.
19. Daly, John A., Anita L. Vangelisti, and David J. Weber. "Speech Anxiety Affects How People Prepare Speeches: A Protocol Analysis of the Preparation Processes of Speakers." *Communication Monographs* 62 (1995), pp. 383–397; and Hunter, Westwick, and Haleta, "Assessing Success."
20. Winans, James Albert. *Public Speaking: Principles and Practice* (Ithaca, NY: Sewell Publishing, 1915).
21. Borchard, Therese J. "Conquering Performance Anxiety: A Primer for All Phobias," 10 May 2011, http://psychcentral.com/blog/archives/2011/05/10/conquering-performance-anxiety-a-primer-for-all-phobias/ (accessed 5 February 2013).
22. Mochari, Ilan. "The Fascinating Pregame Routine of NBA MVP Stephen Curry." *Inc.*, June 5, 2015, http://www.inc.com/ilan-mochari/nba-finals-flow.html (accessed 17 June 2016); and Elizabeth Quinn, "Why Do So Many Athletes Have Superstitions and Rituals?" 28 October 2008, http://sportsmedicine.about.com/od/sportspsychology/a/superstitions.htm (accessed 4 November 2009).
23. Anderman, Joan. "Yo-Yo Ma and the Mind Game of Music." *New York Times*, October 10, 2013,http://www.nytimes.com/2013/10/10/booming/yo-yo-ma-and-the-mind-game-of-music.html?_r=0 (accessed 21 June 2016).
24. Grohol, John M. "Visualize Your Goal in Order to Attain It," 16 August 2011, http://psychcentral.com/news/2011/08/16/visualize-your-goal-in-order-to-attain-it/28624.html (accessed 6 February 2013).
25. Ayers, Joe. "Speech Preparation Processes and Speech Apprehension," *Communication Education*, 45 (1996), pp. 228–235.
26. Choi, Charles W., James M. Honeycutt, and Graham D. Bodie. "Effects of Imagined Interactions and Rehearsal on Speaking Performance." *Communication Education*, 64:1 (January 2015), pp. 25–44.
27. Researchers have found that students who rehearsed in front of real live listeners received higher evaluations than those who did not. See Tony E. Smith and Ann Bainbridge Frymier, "Get 'Real': Does Practicing Speeches Before an Audience Improve Performance?" *Communication Quarterly*, 54:1 (February 2006), pp. 111–125.
28. Abrahams, Matt. *Matt Abrahams: Tips and Techniques for More Confident and Compelling Presentations*, Stanford Graduate School of Business.
29. Whitworth, Randolph W., and Claudia Cochran. "Evaluation of Integrated Versus Unitary Treatments for Reducing Public Speaking Anxiety." *Communication Education*, 45 (1996): 306–314; Tim Hopf and Joe Ayres, "Coping with Public Speaking Anxiety: An Examination of Various Combinations of Systematic Desensitization, Skills Training, and Visualization," *Journal of Applied Communication Research*, 20:2 (May 1992), pp. 183–198.
30. Li, Ding. "What's the Science Behind a Smile?" *Voices: British Council* (April 2, 2014), https://www.britishcouncil.org/voices-magazine/famelab-whats-science-behind-smile (accessed 21 June 2016).
31. Hsu, Chia-Fang (Sandy). "The Relationship of Trait Anxiety, Audience Nonverbal Feedback, and Attributions to

Public Speaking State Anxiety." *Communication Research Reports*, 26 (2009), pp. 237–246.

32. Peterson, Wilfred Arlan. *Adventures in the Art of Living: A Fourth Book of New Essays*. (New York: Simon and Schuster, 1968).

Chapter 3

1. "John F. Kennedy, Inaugural Address, January 20, 1961." *Great Issues in American History, 1864–1981*. Richard and Beatrice K. Hofstadter, editors, New York: Random House, 1982, p. 549.
2. McCroskey, James C., and Mason J. Teven. "Goodwill: A Reexamination of the Construct and Its Measurement." *Communication Monographs*, vol. 66, 1999, pp. 90–103.
3. Burke, Kenneth. *A Rhetoric of Motives*, Berkeley: University of California Press, 1969, pp. 20–23.
4. Obama, Barack. "Reclaiming the Promise to the People." *Vital Speeches of the Day*, vol. 70, 1 Aug. 2004, p. 625.

Chapter 4

1. Janusik, Laura. "Time Spent on Listening and Communicating." http://d1025403.site.myhosting.com/files.listen.org/Facts.htm (accessed 16 February 2016).
2. Chambers, Harry E. *Effective Communication Skills for Scientific and Technical Professionals*. Cambridge: Perseus Publishing, 2001.
3. Hayakawa, S.I. https://www.goodreads.com/author/quotes/310553.S_I_Hayakawa (accessed 17 March 2016).
4. Purdey, Michael. "The Listener Wins." Undated, http://career-advice.monster.comm/in-the-office/workplace-issues/the-listener-wins/article.aspx (accessed 15 February 2013).
5. Thoreau, Henry David. "Life Without Principle." 1863, http://xroads.virginia.edu/~hyper/walden/Essays/life.html (accessed 7 March 2016).
6. See, for example, Blubaugh, Jon A. "Effects of Positive and Negative Audience Feedback on Selected Variables of Speech Behavior." *Speech Monographs*, vol. 36, June 1969, pp. 131–47; and Julia T. Wood, *Communication Mosaics*, 7e, Boston: Wadsworth Cengage, 2014, p. 115.
7. Mueller, Pam A., and Daniel M. Oppenheimer. "The Pen Is Mightier Than the Keyboard: Advantages of Longhand Over Laptop Note Taking." *Psychological Science*, June 6, 2014, http://pss.sagepub.com/content/25/6/1159.full?keytype=ref&siteid=sppss&ijkey=CjRAwmrlURGNw (accessed 18 November 2016).
8. Eisenberg, Eric M., Alexandra G. Murphy, Kathleen Sutcliffe, Robert Wears, Stephen Schenkel, Shawna Perry, and Mary Vanderhoef. "Communication in Emergency Medicine: Implications for Patient Safety." *Communication Monographs*, vol. 72, no. 4, December 2005, pp. 390–413.
9. Bristol-Smith, Dana. "Listening: The Overlooked Communication Skill." *Speak for Success*, undated, www.speakforsuccess.net/a-listng.htm (accessed 15 February 2013).
10. Kossoff Smith, Amy. "Are You a Bad Listener?" *Chicago Tribune*, March 16, 2012, www.chicagotribune.com/features/tribut/sc-fam-0313-listen-month-20120312,0,50772773.story (accessed 15 February 2013).
11. Flora Wei, Fang-Yi, Y. Ken Wang, and Michael Klausner. "Rethinking College Students' Self-Regulation and Sustained Attention: Does Text Messaging During Class Influence Cognitive Learning?" *Communication Education*, vol. 61, no. 3, July 2012, pp. 185–204.
12. Professor Halley discussed this triggering stimuli assignment on the website of the International Listening Association in 1998. The article is no longer available online.
13. Shachtman, Tom. *The Inarticulate Society: Eloquence and Culture in America*. New York: The Free Press, 1995, p. 36.
14. Bodie, Graham D., and Susanne M. Jones. "The Nature of Supportive Listening II: The Role of Verbal Person Centeredness and Nonverbal Immediacy." *Western Journal of Communication*, vol. 76, no. 3, May–June 2012, pp. 250–269; and Graham D. Bodie, "The Active-Empathic Listening Scale (AELS): Conceptualization and Evidence of Validity Within the Interpersonal Domain," *Communication Quarterly*, vol. 59, no. 3, July–August 2011, pp. 277–295.
15. "The Discipline of Listening." *Harvard Business Review Blog Network*, 21 June 2012, http://blogs/hbr.org/cs/2012/06/the_discipline_of_listening.html (accessed 15 February 2013).
16. Norton, Mary Beth, David M. Katzman, Paul D. Escott, Howard P. Chudacoff, Thomas G. Paterson, and William M. Tuttle, Jr. *A People and Nation: A History of the United States*. Boston: Houghton Mifflin Company, 1990, pp. 842–844, 859–861.
17. Garver, Eugene. *For the Sake of Argument: Practical Reasoning, Character, and the Ethics of Belief*. Chicago: University of Chicago Press, 2004.
18. Dobson, Andrew. *Listening for Democracy: Recognition, Representation, Reconciliation*. Oxford, England: Oxford University Press, 2014, p. 122.
19. Epictetus, http://www.brainyquote.com/quotes/quotes/e/epictetus106298.html#qsChQ7LAq6FS4SrX.99 (accessed 18 February 2016).
20. Wilferd A. Peterson, http://www.wow4u.com/peterson2/index.html (accessed 18 November 2016).
21. Dr. Raymond Sprague, Professor of Music, Davidson College, in many choral rehearsals.

Chapter 5

1. Woodward, Gary C., and Robert E. Denton, Jr. *Persuasion & Influence in American Life*, 3rd ed., Prospect Heights, IL: Waveland Press, 1996, p. 189.
2. Kennedy, George, trans. *The Rhetoric of Aristotle*, New York: Oxford University Press 1992, bk. 2, chs. 11–14, pp. 163–169.
3. Simons, Herbert W., and Jean G. Jones. *Persuasion in Society*, 2nd ed., New York: Routledge, 2011, p. 276; Rokeach, Milton *The Open and Closed Mind*, New York: Basic Books, 1960; and Tyler, T. R. and Schuller, R. A. "Aging and Attitude Change," *Journal of Personality and Social Psychology*, vol. 61, 1991, pp. 689–697.
4. Germond, Jack W. "Clinton Was Able to Expand Appeal to Suburbs, Whites, Independents." *Baltimore Sun*, 5 November 1992, http://articles.baltimoresun.com/1992-11-05/news/1992310208_1_clinton-young-voters-white-voters (accessed 6 June 2013); and Scott Keeter, Juliana Horowitz, and Alec Tyson, "Young Voters in the 2008 Election," Pew Research Center, 13 November 2008, www.pewresearch.org/2008/11/13/young-voters-in-the-2008-election/ (accessed 6 June 2013).
5. Larson, Charles U. *Persuasion: Reception and Responsibility*, 10th ed., Boston: Wadsworth, 2004, p. 275.
6. "How Millennials Today Compare with Their Grandparents 50 Years Ago," Pew Research Center, 19 March 2015, http://www.pewresearch.org/fact-tank/2015/03/19/how-millennials-compare-with-their-grandparents/ (accessed 29 February 2016).

7. See, for example, http://www.heri.ucla.edu/infographics.php (accessed 29 February 2016).
8. See such sources as Marketing Charts, http://www.marketingcharts.com/traditional/how-do-millennials-and-other-generations-see-themselves-58789/ (accessed 29 February 2016); William Schrorer, "Generations X, Y, Z, and the Others." http://www.socialmarketing.org/newsletter/features/generation1.htm (accessed 29 February 2016); and ValueOptions,http://www.valueoptions.com/spotlight_YIW/traditional.htm, http://www.valueoptions.com/spotlight_YIW/baby_boomers.htm, http://www.valueoptions.com/spotlight_YIW/gen_x.htm, and http://www.valueoptions.com/spotlight_YIW/gen_y.htm (accessed 29 February 2016).
9. "Current Glance at Women in the Law," Commission on Women in the Profession, American Bar Association, July 2014, http://www.americanbar.org/groups/women/resources/statistics.html (accessed 1 March 2016); and Catherine Rampell, "U.S. Women on the Rise as Family Breadwinner," *New York Times*, May 29, 2013, http://www.nytimes.com/2013/05/30/business/economy/women-as-family-breadwinner-on-the-rise-study-says.html?_r=0 (accessed 1 March 2016).
10. See Julia T. Wood, *Gendered Lives: Communication, Gender, and Culture*, 8th ed., Belmont, CA: Wadsworth Cengage Learning, 2009; Diana K. Ivy and Phil Backlund, *Exploring GenderSpeak: Personal Effectiveness in Gender Communication*, 4th ed., Boston, MA: Pearson/Allyn and Bacon, 2008; and Sonja Foss and Cindy Griffin, "Beyond Persuasion: A Proposal for an Invitational Rhetoric," *Communication Monographs*, vol. 62, 1995, pp. 2–18.
11. "The Gender Gap: Three Decades Old, As Wide as Ever," Pew Research Center, 29 March 2012, www.people-press.org/2012/03/29/the-gender-gap-three-decades-old-as-wide-as-ever/ (accessed 29 February 2016); "The Gender Gap: Attitudes on Public Policy Issues," Center for American Women and Politics, 2012, www.cawp.rutgers.edu/fast_facts/voters/gender_gap.php (accessed 6 June 2013); and Kelly Ditmar, "The Gender Gap: Gender Differences in Vote Choice and Political Orientations," Rutgers Center for American Women and Politics, 15 July 2014, http://www.cawp.rutgers.edu/research/women-voters-and-gender-gap (accessed 1 March 2016).
12. Lowen, Linda. "Who's More Likely to Vote—Women or Men? Gender Differences and Voter Turnout." About.com, 30 November 2011, http://womensissues.about.com/od/thepoliticalarena/a/GenderVoting.html (accessed 6 June 2013).
13. Goldman, Russell. "Here's a List of 58 Gender Options for Facebook Users." ABC News, 13 February 2014, http://abcnews.go.com/blogs/headlines/2014/02/heres-a-list-of-58-gender-options-for-facebook-users/ (accessed 1 March 2016); and see, for example, *The Danish Girl, Orange Is the New Black, Modern Family, Glee, Transparent, Ellen DeGeneres,* and *The Bold and the Beautiful*.
14. Kalbfleisch, Norm, and Terri Schmidt. "Cultural Competency on Lesbian, Gay, Bisexual or Transgender (LGBT)," University of Virginia Medical School, virginia.edu (accessed 1 March 2016), p. 2.
15. Yep, Gust A., Karen E. Lovaas, and John P. Elia. "Introduction: Queering Communication: Starting the Conversation." In G.A. Yep, K.E. Lovaas, and J.P. Elia, eds., *Queer Theory and Communication: From Disciplining Queers to Queering the Discipline(s)*, Binghamton, NY: Harrington Park Press, 2004, p. 4.
16. Kurtzleber, Danielle. "Gay Couples More Educated, Higher Income Than Heterosexual Couples." *U.S. News and World Report*, March 1, 2013, www.usnews.com/news/article/2013/03/01/gay-couples-more-educated-higher-income-than-hetereosexual-couples (accessed 16 March 2016).
17. Stenner, K. *The Authoritarian Dynamic*, New York: Cambridge University Press, 2005; and J. F. Dovido, P. Glick, and L. A. Rudman, eds., *On the Nature of Prejudice: Fifty Years After Allport*, Malden, MA: Blackwell, 2005.
18. Antonsich, Marco. "Identity and Place." *Oxford Bibliographies*, 29 October 2013, DOI: 10.1093/obo/9780199874002-0030, http://www.oxfordbibliographies.com/view/document/obo-9780199874002/obo-9780199874002-0030.xml (accessed 19 March 2016).
19. "Quick Facts," United States Census Bureau, http://www.census.gov/quickfacts/table/PST045215/00 (accessed 1 March 2016); also see "Immigrants to U.S. by Country of Origin," Infoplease, http://www.infoplease.com/ipa/A0201398.html (accessed 1 March 2016).
20. Onwuachi-Willig, Angela. "Race and Racial Identity Are Social Constructs." *New York Times*, 17 June 2016, http://www.nytimes.com/roomfordebate/2015/06/16/how-fluid-is-racial-identity/race-and-racial-identity-are-social-constructs (accessed 1 March 2016); Coates, Ta-Nehisi *Between the World and Me*, New York: Spiegel and Grau, 2015, p. 115.
21. "2014 Highlights," United States Census Bureau, http://www.census.gov/hhes/www/poverty/about/overview/index.html (accessed 16 March 2016).
22. Saez, Emmanuel and Gabriel Zucman. "The Explosion of U.S. Wealth Inequality Has Been Fueled by Stagnant Wages, Increasing Debt, and a Collapse of Asset Values for the Middle Class." London School of Economics U.S. Centre, blogs/ise.ac.uk/useppblog/2014/10/29/the-explosion-of-us-wealth-has-been-fueled-by-stagnent-wages-increaing-debt-and-a-collapse-of-asset-values-for-the-middle-classes/ (accessed 16 March 2016).
23. Houston, Marsha, and Julia T. Wood. "Different Dialogues, Expanded Horizons: Communicating Across Race and Class." *Gendered Relationships*, ed. Julia T. Wood, Mountain View, CA: Mayfield P, 1996, pp. 47–49.
24. Palus, Shannon. "Nine Out of Ten Americans Consider Themselves Middle Class." *Smithsonian*, 13 April 2015, http://www.smithsonianmag.com/smart-news/nine-out-10-americans-consider-themselves-middle-class-180954970/?no-ist (accessed 18 March 2016).
25. Jones, Jeffrey M. "In U.S., New Record 43% Are Political Independents." *Gallup Poll*, 7 January 2015, http://www.gallup.com/poll/180440/new-record-political-independents.aspx (accessed 1 March 2016).
26. Newport, Frank. "Mormons Most Conservative Religious Group in the U.S." *Gallup*, 11 January 2010, www.gallup.com/poll/125021/mormons-conservative-major-religious-groups.aspx (accessed 16 March 2016).
27. Foster, Peter. "Is America Losing Faith? Aetheism on the Rise But Still in the Shadows." *The Telegraph*, 17 March 2016, www.telegraph.co.uk/news/worldnews/northamerica/usa/10626076/is-america-losing-faith-aetheism-on-the-rise-but-still-in-the-shadows.htm (accessed 17 March 2016).
28. Murray, Henry A. *Explorations in Personality*, New York: Oxford University Press, 1938. Interest in Murray's research

continues, and the Radcliffe Institute for Advanced Study maintains a website for the Murray Research Center at www.radcliffe.edu/.

29. Maslow, Abraham H. *Motivation and Personality*, 2nd ed., New York: Harper & Row, 1970.
30. Zaki, Jami. "The Altruism Instinct: An Antidote to the Tragedy of the Commons." *Psychology Today*, 23 November 2009, www.psychologytoday.com/blog/your-brain-us/200911/the-altruism-instinct (accessed 17 June 2013).
31. Colby, Sandra L., and Jennifer M. Ortman. "Projections of the Size and Composition of the U.S. Population: 2014 to 2060," March 2015, https://webcache.googleusercontent.com/search?q#x003D;cache:N9N3mfOmIzYJ:https://www.census.gov/content/dam/Census/library/publications/2015/demo/p25-1143.pdf+&cd=9&hl=en&ct=clnk&gl=us (accessed 2 March 2016).
32. Obama, Barack. "2004 Democratic National Convention Keynote Address, delivered 27 July 2004, Fleet Center, Boston," www.americanrhetoric.com/speeches/convention2004/barackobama2004dnc.htm (accessed 6 June 2013).
33. Yousafzai, Malala. 12 July 2013, https://secure.aworldatschool.org/page/content/the-text-of-malala-yousafzais-speech-at-the-united-nations/ (accessed 10 February 2016).
34. Associated Press, "Gore Promotes Benefits of Good Storytelling," Memphis *Commercial Appeal,* 8 October 1995, B2.
35. Joyner, James. "Romney Bungles Castro Quote in Miami." *Outside the Beltway*, 19 March 2007, www.outsidethebeltway.com/romney_bungles_castro_quoteP_in_miami/ (accessed 17 June 2013).
36. Adams, Tyrone, and Sharon Scollard. *Internet Effectively: A Beginner's Guide to the World Wide Web,* Boston: Pearson, 2006.
37. "Winston Churchill's Command of the English Language Was Arguably One of the Greatest Weapons in His Arsenal."*Military History Monthly*, 20 November 2010, http://www.military-history.org/articles/winston-churchill-quotes.htm (accessed 2 March 2016).
38. Cross, Jody. *Leaders Speak: How to Transform Your Career and Life Through Public Speaking* (n.p.: Author, 2012), pp. 36–39.
39. Bryant, Donald C. "Rhetoric: Its Function and Its Scope." *Quarterly Journal of Speech*, vol. 39, December 1953, p. 413.

Chapter 6

1. If you're curious about what resulted, see Kathleen J. Turner, '"The Only Thing I've Learned...': The Central Tenet of a Liberal Arts Education." Address to the Spring Convocation, College of Arts and Sciences, Queens University of Charlotte, February 2004, *Vital Speeches of the Day*, vol. 70, 1 June 2004, pp. 500–502.
2. Humphrey, Judith. "Executive Eloquence: A Sevenfold Path to Inspirational Leadership." *Vital Speeches of the Day*, vol. 64, 15 May 1998, p. 469.
3. The concept of mind mapping takes somewhat different directions in books that develop the technique. See, for example, Joyce Wycoff, Steve Cook, and Michael J. Gelb, *Mindmapping: Your Personal Guide to Exploring Creativity and Problem-Solving* (New York: Berkley, 1991); and Tony Buzan and Barry Buzan, *The Mind Map Book: How to Use Radiant Thinking to Maximize Your Brain's Untapped Potential,* New York: Plume Books, 1996. For a judicious summary of recent developments, see "Mind Map," *Wikipedia, undated* https://en.wikipedia.org/wiki/Mind_map (accessed 27 November 2016).
4. Corporate mind mappers often refer to this space as "landscape." They think of the central concept as a tree and its associated ideas as "branches." See, for example, the mind map provided in "Mind Maps: A Powerful Approach to Note-Taking," undated www.mindtools.com/pages/article/newISS_01.htm (accessed 21 February 2013).
5. Porter, Jeremy. "Five Ws and One H: The Secret to Complete News Stories." *Journalistics*, August 5, 2010, http://blog.journalistics.com/2010/five-ws-one-h/ (accessed 15 March 2016).
6. Booth, Wayne C., Gregory G. Colomb, and Joseph M. Williams. *The Craft of Research,* Chicago: University of Chicago Press, 1995, p. 42.
7. Ibid., p. 38.

Chapter 7

1. See, for example, Daniel Zwerding and Margot Williams. "Conditions Allow for More Sustainable Seafood." *NPR*, 12 February 2013, www.npr.org/2013/02/12/171376617/condition-allow-for-more-sustainable-labeled-seafood?ft=1&f=1025 (accessed 9 April 2016); and "Greenwashing Index." EnviroMedia Social Marketing and the University of Oregon. http://greenwashingindex.com/about-greenwashing/ (accessed 20 May 2016).
2. Thanks to Robin Winks, ed., *The Historian as Detective* (New York: Harper Colphon, 1969).
3. "Wikipedia Statistics." http://stats.wikimedia.org/EN/TablesArticlesTotal.htm (accessed 31 March 2014); "Special Report: Internet Encyclopedias Go Head to Head." *Nature*, vol. 438, December 2005, pp. 900–901, www.nature.com/nature/journal/v438/n7070/full/438900a.html (accessed 14 April 2016); Charles Arthur, "Wikipedia: An Old-Fashioned Corner of Truth on the Internet." *The Telegraph*, 15 January 2016, http://www.telegraph.co.uk/technology/wikipedia/12101712/Wikipedia-an-old-fashioned-corner-of-truth-on-the-internet.html (accessed 31 March 2016).
4. Hadas Gold, "Bloomberg Falls for Fake Nancy Reagan Report," *Politico*, 15 April, 2015, www.politico.com/blogs/media/2015/04/bloomberg-falls-for-fake-nancy-reagan-report-205356 (accessed 15 April, 2016).
5. Wayne C. Booth, Gregory G. Columb, and Joseph M. Williams, *The Craft of Research*, 3rd ed. Chicago: University of Chicago Press, 2008, p. 71.

Chapter 8

1. "Childhood Obesity Facts." Centers for Disease Control, 14 March 2016. http://www.cdc.gov/healthyschools/obesity/facts.htm; and Cynthia L. Ogden, Margaret D. Carroll, Cheryl D. Fryar, and Katherine M. Flegal. "Prevalence of Obesity Among Adults and Youth: United States, 2011–2014." National Center for Health Statistics Data Brief, No. 219, November 2015. https://www.cdc.gov/nchs/data/databriefs/db219.pdf (accessed 4 January 2017).
2. "The Unemployment Situation, February 2, 2016." U.S. Department of Labor.
3. Bain, Robert. "Statistics—Lost in Translation?" *Populus*. 9 November 2011. https://www.research-live.com/article/features/statistics-lost-in-translation/id/4006362 (accessed 9 March 2016).
4. D'Arcy, Jan. "Using Statistics in Your Speech." http://www.cfug-md.org/speakertips/783.html (accessed 17 March 2016).

5. Simons, Herbert W., and Jean G. Jones. *Persuasion in Society*, 2nd ed. New York: Routledge, 2011, pp. 290–291.
6. Kemp, Simon. "Digital, Social, and Mobile Worldwide in 2015." *WeAreSocial*. http://wearesocial.com/uk/special-reports/digital-social-mobile-worldwide-2015 (accessed 17 March 2016).
7. Bankrate Money Pulse survey, Sept. 15–18, 2016, http://www.bankrate.com/finance/consumer-index/money-pulse-1016.aspx#ixzz4OJjrRDh1 (accessed 27 October 2016).
8. McKean, Erin, ed. *Totally Weird and Wonderful Words*. New York: Oxford, 2006, p. 217.
9. Perrin, Andrew, and Maeve Duggan. "Americans' Internet Access: 2000–2015." *Pew Research Center*. 26 June 2015. http://www.pewinternet.org/2015/06/26/americans-internet-access-2000-2015/ 17 March 2016; and "Internet Users in the World by Region." *Internet World Stats*, November 2015. http://www.internetworldstats.com/stats.htm (accessed 17 March 2016).
10. Heraclitus. http://www.goodreads.com/quotes/336994-the-only-thing-that-is-constant-is-change– (accessed 17 March 2016).
11. Mintz, Anne P., ed. *Web of Deception: Misinformation on the Internet*. Medford, NJ: CyberAge, 2002, p. 8.
12. Andrews, Wilson, and Thomas Kaplan. "Where the Candidates Stand on 2016's Biggest Issues." *New York Times*. 15 December 2015. http://www.nytimes.com/interactive/2016/us/elections/candidates-on-the-issues.html?_r=0 (accessed 17 March 2016).
13. Hattersley Gray, Robin. "Sexual Assault Statistics." *Campus Safety Magazine*. 5 March 2012. www.campussafetymagazine.com/article/Sexual-Assault-Statistics-and-Myths# (accessed 26 March 2016).
14. "Best Cars." *U.S. News & World Report*. http://usnews.rankingsandreviews.com/cars-trucks/Mazda_MX-5-Miata/ (accessed 17 March 2016).
15. Benoit, William L., and Kimberly A. Kennedy. "On Reluctant Testimony." *Communication Quarterly*, vol. 47, 1999: pp. 376–387.
16. Moyers, Bill. "Best of Jobs: To Have and Serve the Public's Trust." Keynote address at the PBS Annual Meeting. 23 June 1996. Reprinted in *Current*, 8 July 1996.
17. McGee, Michael Calvin. "In Search of 'The People': A Rhetorical Alternative." *Quarterly Journal of Speech*, vol. 61, 1975, pp. 235–249.
18. "Barack Obama's Speech on Race." *The New York Times*. www.nytimes.com/2008/03/18/us//politics/18text-obama.html (accessed 19 March 2008).
19. "On the Campaign Trail." *Reader's Digest*. March 1992, p. 116.
20. Mill, John Stuart. *On Liberty*. http://www.bartleby.com/130/1.html (accessed 1 March 2016).
21. Bono. "Remarks to the 2006 National Prayer Breakfast: February 2, 2006." http://usliberals.about.com/od/faithinpubliclife/a/BonoSermon.htm (accessed 15 March 2007).
22. Christie, Governor Chris. "State of the State Address." www.nj.com/politics/index.ssf/2013/01/full_text_of_chris_christies_2.html (accessed 15 May 2013).
23. Jimenez, Joseph. "When Your Reputation Doesn't Match Your Ideals . . . Something Has to Change." *Vital Speeches of the Day*, vol. 78, July 2012, p. 230.
24. Ibid., p. 229.
25. Fisher, Walter R. *Human Communication as Narration: Toward a Philosophy of Reason, Value, and Action*. Columbia: University of South Carolina Press, 1987.
26. Kerpen, Dave. "13 Quotes to Inspire Your Inner Storyteller." http://www.inc.com/dave-kerpen/you-need-to-become-a-better-storyteller-heres-some-inspiration.html (accessed 21 March 2016).
27. Ibid.
28. Fisher, pp. 62–69.
29. Kerpen, Dave. "13 Quotes."

Chapter 9

1. Kearney, Patricia, Timothy G. Plax, Ellis R. Hayes, and Marilyn J. Ivey. "College Teacher Misbehaviors: What Students Don't Like about What Teachers Say and Do." *Communication Quarterly*, vol. 39, 1991, pp. 309–324.
2. Thompson, Ernest C. "An Experimental Investigation of the Relative Effectiveness of Organizational Structure in Oral Communication." *Southern Speech Journal*, vol. 26, 1960, pp. 59–69.
3. Sharp, Jr., Harry, and Thomas McClung. "Effects of Organization on the Speaker's Ethos." *Speech Monographs*, vol. 33, 1966, pp. 182–183.
4. Yun, Kimo Ah, Cassie Costantini, and Sarah Billingsley. "The Effect of Taking a Public Speaking Course on One's Writing Abilities." *Communication Research Reports*, vol. 29, October–December 2012, pp. 285–291.
5. Alan Monroe introduced the concept of the motivated sequence in *Principles and Types of Speech*. New York, NY: Scott, Foresman, 1935.
6. Cited in Arthur M. Schlesinger, Jr. *A Thousand Days: John F. Kennedy in the White House*. Boston: Houghton Mifflin, 1965, p. 733.
7. "The Speech Pope Francis Gave to Congress." September 24, 2015. http://time.com/4048176/pope-francis-us-visit-congress-transcript/ (accessed 25 March 2016)
8. American Presidency Project. http://www.presidency.ucsb.edu/ws/?pid=25860 (accessed 30 March 2016).
9. Bergson, Henri. *Laughter: An Essay on the Meaning of the Comic*, trans. Cloudsley Brereton and Fred Rothwell. London: Macmillan, 1911, p. 56.

Chapter 10

1. "Dyslexia." *Black's Medical Dictionary*, 42nd ed. Allen and Unwin, 2010. http://ezproxy.lib.davidson.edu:3668/entry/blackmed/dyslexia (accessed 18 May 2010).
2. See the classic study conducted by Wharton Business School's Applied Research Center and the Management Information Services Department of the University of Arizona, cited by Robert L. Lindstrom, "The Presentation Power of Multimedia," *Sales and Marketing Management*, vol. 51, September 1994, p. 7. These findings are reinforced by Gina Poirier, "The Advantages of Multimedia Presentation Aids," (n.d.), www.ehow.com/info_12012601_advantages-multimedia-presentation-aids.html and" "Presentation Aids," Changing Minds and Persuasion (n.d.), http://changingminds.org/techniques/speaking/preparing_presentation/presentational_aids.html (accessed 20 May 2013).
3. Hamilton, Cheryl, and Cordell Parker. *Communicating for Results*, 9th ed. Belmont, CA: Wadsworth, 2011. p. 341.
4. Mzoughi, Nabil, and Samar Abdelhak. "The Impact of Visual and Verbal Rhetoric in Advertising on Mental Imagery and Recall." *International Journal of Business and Social Science*, vol. 2, no. 9, 2011, p. 257.
5. Bumiller, Elisabeth. "We Have Met the Enemy and He Is PowerPoint." *New York Times*. 26 April 2010, www.nytimes

.com/2010/04/27/world/27powerpoint.html (accessed 18 May 2010).

6. Bolte-Taylor, Jill. "Stroke of Insight." February 2008. www.ted.com/speakers/jill_bolte_taylor.html (accessed 18 May 2010).
7. Bump, Philip. "Jim Inhofe's Snowball Has Disproven Climate Change Once and for All." *The Washington Post*. 26 February 2015. https://www.washingtonpost.com/news/the-fix/wp/2015/02/26/jim-inhofes-snowball-has-disproven-climate-change-once-and-for-all/ (accessed 29 May 2016).
8. Ratecliff Barr, Kathryn. "Teaching Parenting Skills to Adolescents." *Our Everyday Life*. 2016. *oureverydaylife.com/teaching-parenting-skills-adolescents-2988.html* (accessed 31 May 2016).
9. Cited in Laurence J. Peter. *Peter's Quotations: Ideas for Our Time.* New York: Bantam, 1979, p. 478.
10. Reynolds, Garr. *Presentation Zen Design: Simple Design Principles to Enhance Your Presentations.* Berkeley, CA: New Riders, 2010, p. 139.
11. An excellent resource on understanding, preparing, and using charts and graphs is Gerald Everett Jones, *How to Lie with Charts* (Lincoln, NE: iUniverse, 2000).
12. Our thanks for this example go to Professor Mary Katherine McHenry, Northwest Mississippi Community College, Senatobia, Mississippi.
13. Ganzel, Rebecca. "Power Pointless." *Presentations.* February 2000, pp. 53–58.
14. Tessner, Franklin N. "PowerPoint 2008 vs. Keynote '08." 16 April 2008. www.macworld.com/article/1132979/office_presentation.html?page=2 (accessed 21 May 2013.); Robin Williams, *The Non-Designer's Presentation Book: Principles for Effective Presentation Design.* Berkeley, CA: Peachpit Press, 2010, pp. 12–13.
15. Norvig, Peter. "The Gettysburg PowerPoint Presentation" and "The Making of the Gettysburg PowerPoint Presentation." 2000. http://norvig.com/Gettysburg/ and http://norvig.com/Gettysburg/making.html (accessed 18 May 2010).
16. Atkinson, Cliff. *Beyond Bullet Points,* 3rd ed. Redmond, WA: Microsoft, 2011, pp. 1–16.
17. Reynolds, Garr. *Presentation Zen: Simple Ideas on Presentation Design and Delivery.* Berkeley, CA: New Riders, 2008, p. 68. See also Reynolds' website at www.garrreynolds.com/; and William Earnest, *Save Our Slides: PowerPoint Design That Works,* Dubuque, IA: Kendall/Hunt, 2007.
18. Williams, *The Non-Designer's Presentation Book,* p. 131.
19. Boyd, Ty. "Are You Addicted to PowerPoint?" 28 January 2012 e-newsletter.
20. Duarte, Nancy. *Slide*ology: The Art and Science of Creating Great Presentations.* Sebastopol, CA: O'Reilly Media, 2008, p. 152.
21. Ibid., p. 140.
22. Manjoo, Farhad. "No More Bullet Points, No More Clip Art." 5 May 2010. http://www.slate.com/id/2253050/ (accessed 21 May 2013).
23. Duarte. *Slide*ology,* p. 2.
24. Titsworth, Scott. Ohio University. CRTNET posting #11325. 10 May 2010. Reprinted by permission of Scott Titsworth, Director of the School of Communication Studies at Ohio University.
25. Apostel, Shawn P. "Visual Presentation Aids in the Communication Center: Tips and Techniques for Providing Useful Design Feedback." National Association of Communication Centers Conference. Eastern Kentucky University, Richmond, KY. 20 April 2012.
26. Apostel, Shawn P. "Avoiding Prezilepsy: Organizational Strategies to Reduce Motion Sickness Caused by Prezi." National Association of Communication Centers Conference. Eastern Kentucky University, Richmond, KY. 21 April 2012.
27. Apostel, Shawn P. "Prezi Design Strategies." https://prezi.com/bm9alx1pbtmc/prezi-design-strategies/ (accessed 7 June 2016).
28. Apostel. "Avoiding Prezilepsy."
29. Williams, George. "Use Haiku Deck for Simple, Elegant Presentations." *Chronicle of Higher Education.* 19 June 2013. http://chronicle.com/blogs/profhacker/use-haiku-deck-for-simple-elegant-presentations/50383 (accessed 21 May 2013).
30. Newton, Eric. "Commencement Address." 3 May 2013. http://queens.edu/News-and-Information/Flash-Philanthropy.html (accessed 5 May 2013).
31. See, for example, Reynolds, *Presentation Zen Design,* p. 20; Williams, *The Non-Designer's Presentation Book,* p. 19.
32. Diamond, Stephanie, *Prezi for Dummies,* Hoboken, NJ: Wiley, 2010, p. 40; and John Tollett, "Foreward" in Williams, *The Non-Designer's Presentation Book,* p. viii.
33. Paradi, Dave."Latest Annoying PowerPoint Survey Results: Results of the 2011 Annoying PowerPoint Survey" (May 2011), "Results from the 2009 PowerPoint Survey" (17 May 2010), "Survey Shows How to Stop Annoying Audience with Bad PowerPoint" (14 March 2004), www.thinkoutsidetheslide.com/articles/ (accessed 22 May 2013), and "Results of the 2015 Annoying PowerPoint Survey" (October 15, 2015) http://www.thinkoutsidetheslide.com/free-resources/latest-annoying-powerpoint-survey-results/ (accessed 7 June 2016).
34. White, Alex. *The Elements of Graphic Design: Space, Unity, Page Architecture, and Type.* New York: Allworth Press, 2002, p. ix.
35. Paradi. "Latest Annoying PowerPoint Survey Results."
36. Ibid.
37. Ibid.
38. Williams. *The Non-Designer's Presentation Book,* p. 46.
39. Dirksen, Julie. *Design for How People Learn.* Berkeley, CA: New Riders, 2012, p. 41.
40. Reynolds. *Presentation Zen Design,* p. 19.
41. Paradi. "Latest Annoying PowerPoint Survey Results."
42. Alliance for Board Diversity. "Missing Pieces: Women and Minorities on Fortune 500 Boards—2010 Alliance for Board Diversity Census. (2011. www.catalyst.org/knowledge/people-colors-share-fortune-500-board-seats (accessed 24 May 2013).
43. Brunner, Cornelia. "Teaching Visual Literacy." *Electronic Learning,* vol. 16, November–December 1994, p. 16.
44. Novak, Matt. "76 Viral Images from 2015 That Were Totally Fake." Gizmondo. 15 December 2015. gizmodo.com/76-viral-images-from-2015-that-were-totally-fake-1747317711 (accessed 9 January 2017).
45. Ehrenfreund, Max. "Obama's Skin Tone Darker in GOP Ads, Study Shows." *The Times-Picayune.* 29 December 2015. www.nola.com/politics/index.sff/2015/12/president-obamas-skin-tone-dar.html/ (accessed 30 May 2016).

Chapter 11

1. Raspberry, William. "Any Candidate Will Drink to That." *Austin American Statesman,* 11 May 1984, p. A–10.

2. Pinker, Steven. *The Stuff of Thought: Language as a Window into Human* Nature. New York: Viking, 2007, p. 24.
3. Davis, Viola. "'Hunger Is' at Power of Women Awards Luncheon," https://www.youtube.com/watch?v=AMtKz54UcxQ (accessed 12 January 2016).
4. "Conversations From the Moon," www.v-j-enterprises.com/astro2.html, 5 April 1996 (accessed 17 June 2008).
5. Smith, Stephen A. *Myth, Media, and the Southern* Mind. Fayetteville: U of Arkansas P, 1985, pp. 5–45.
6. "Paula Deen Racist Comments, Use of N-Word Allegedly Caught on Video," 6 June 2013, www.huffingtonpost.com/2013/06/19/paula-deen-racist comment (accessed 25 June 2013).
7. Adapted from *The American Heritage Dictionary*, 2nd ed. Boston: Houghton Mifflin, 1985, p. 92.
8. "President Obama's Address at Boston Memorial Service," 18 April 2013, www.huffingtonpost.com/2013/04/18/obama-boston-address-full (accessed 24 June 2013).
9. Reagan, Ronald. "Second Inaugural Address." *Vital Speeches of the Day*, vol. 51, 1 February 1985, pp. 226–228.
10. Listeners whose lives seem dull and unrewarding are especially susceptible to such dramas. See the discussion in Eric Hoffer. *The True Believer: Thoughts on the Nature of Mass Movements*, New York: Harper, 1951.
11. Ronald C. White argues that creating speeches for the ear rather than the eye was key to Abraham Lincoln's success. See *The Eloquent President*, New York: Random House, 2005.
12. See, for example, Peter A. Andersen and Tammy R. Blackburn, "An Experimental Study of Language Intensity and Response Rate in E-Mail Surveys," *Communication Reports*, vol. 17, no. 2, Summer 2004, pp. 73–82.
13. Tarver, Jerry. "Words in Time: Some Reflections on the Language of Speech." *Vital Speeches of the Day*, vol. 54, 15 April 1988, p. 410.
14. Lutz, William. *Doublespeak: From "Revenue Enhancement" to "Terminal Living": How Government, Business, Advertisers, and Others Use Language to Deceive You*. New York: Harper & Row, Publishers, Inc., 1981.
15. Moyers, Bill. "Commencement Address." University of Texas, cited in *Time*, 19 June 1985, p. 68.
16. "Find Your Bold: Gabby Murnan Helps Welcome a New Generation of Honors Hawks to Campus." *Honoread*, Fall 2015, p. 1.
17. http://www.plainlanguage.gov/resources/quotes/historical.cfm (accessed 26 January 2016).
18. http://www.usewisdom.com/fun/insults.html (accessed 26 January 2016).
19. Cockerham, Haven E. "Conquer the Isms That Stand in Our Way." *Vital Speeches of the Day*, 1 February 1998, 240.
20. "Wrestling Showman, Innovator Fargo Dies." *Commercial Appeal*, Memphis, 25 June 2013, p. B1.
21. Lee, Jennifer. University of New Hampshire Commencement Speech, 17 May 2014. https://www.youtube.com/watch?v=TLwsrVVgeQs (accessed 24 May 2016).
22. "Death Takes Carl Sandburg." *Reading Eagle*, Reading, PA, 23 July 1967, A1.
23. Shields, Mark. "Bush Can't Talk (Alas!), Gore Can (Alack!)." *The Freelance Star*, Fredericksburg, VA, 31 March 2000, A14.
24. Sheridan, Richard. *The Rivals: A Comedy* (1775), *The Project Gutenberg*, 6 March 2008, www.gutenberg.org/ebooks/24761 (accessed 26 January 2016).
25. Will, George. "Kerry Will Say Whatever It Takes to Become President." *Beaver County Times*, PA, 6 June 2004, A7.
26. Ivins, Molly. "Language That Can Derail the Ship of State." *Observer-Reporter*, Washington, PA, 7 Sept. 1989, B5.
27. See http://public.wsu.edu/~brians/errors/ (accessed January 28, 2016).
28. Maggio, Rosalie. *Talking About People: A Guide to Fair and Accurate Language*. Phoenix, AZ: Oryx Press, 1997, p. 26.
29. "Paula Deen Loses Major Endorsement Deal," *The New York Times*, 25 June 2013, www.nytimes.com/2013/06/25/us/paula-deen-loses-major-endorsement (accessed 25 June 2013).
30. Ignatius, David. "Sequestration is Feeding a Slow-Motion Decay." *Washington Post*, 21 June 2013, www.washingtonpost.com/opinions/david-ignatius-sequestration--s-feeding-a-slow-motion-decay/2013/06/21/87547be74c-d9ef-11e2-a016-92547bf094cc-story.html?utm-term=.2b4208d823f5 (accessed 8 December 2016).
31. Haslam, Nick, Steve Loughnan, and Pamela Sun. "Beastly: What Makes Animal Metaphors Offensive?" *Journal of Language and Social Psychology*, vol. 30, pp. 311–25.
32. Bytwerk, Randall L. "Rhetorical Aspects of the Nazi Meeting: 1926–1933." *Quarterly Journal of Speech*, vol. 61, no.3, 1975, pp. 307–318.
33. For additional discussion of such metaphors, see Michael Osborn, "Archetypal Metaphor in Rhetoric: The Light-Dark Family," *Quarterly Journal of Speech*, vol. 53, 1967, pp. 115–126, and "The Evolution of the Archetypal Sea in Rhetoric and Poetic," *Quarterly Journal of Speech*, vol. 63, 1977, pp. 347–363.
34. Bush, George W. "Inaugural Address." *Vital Speeches of the Day*, 1 February 2001, p. 226.
35. See another side of this image in J. Vernon Jensen. "British Voices on the Eve of the American Revolution: Trapped by the Family Metaphor," *Quarterly Journal of Speech*, vol. 63, 1977, pp. 43–50.
36. Barack Obama's Speech on Race, www.npr.org/templates/story/story.php?storyld=8847867 (accessed 20 March 2008).
37. Kennedy, John F. "Democratic National Convention Acceptance Address: 'The New Frontier,'" delivered 15 July 1960, Memorial Coliseum, Los Angeles, americanrhetoric.com (accessed 27 January 2016).
38. "The World," PRI Radio, 16 September 2015.
39. McGee, Michael Calvin. "The Ideograph: A Link Between Rhetoric and Ideology." *Quarterly Journal of Speech*, vol. 66, 1980, pp. 1–16.
40. See Celeste Michelle Condit and John Louis Lucaites, *Crafting Equality: America's Anglo-African Word*, Chicago: U of Chicago P, 1993.
41. See, for example, "Do you have a favorable or an unfavorable opinion of *socialism*?" YouGov survey, Cloudfront.net, Jan. 25-27, 2016, tabs_OP_Socialism_20160127(1).pdf (accessed February 5, 2016). Of those under the age of 30, 43% had a favorable opinion of socialism, perhaps associating it with prosperous Scandinavian countries rather than with the Cold War.
42. Kennedy, John F. "Inaugural Address, January 20, 1961." *Great Issues in American History: From Reconstruction to the Present Day*, New York: Random House, Inc., 1982, p. 549
43. Moyers, Bill. "Pass the Bread." Baccalaureate address presented at Hamilton College, 20 May 2006.
44. Tarver, Jerry. "Words in Time: Some Reflections on the Language of Speech." *Vital Speeches of the Day*, 15 April 1988, p. 411.

45. Vagt, Bobby. Commencement Address. Davidson College, 15 May 2005.
46. "British Officials Divided on EU," *Commercial Appeal,* Memphis, 12 December 2011, p. A5.

Chapter 12

1. James A. Winans used the term "enlarged conversation style" in *Speechmaking.* New York: Appleton-Century-Crofts, 1938.
2. Dwyer, Karen Kangas. *Conquer Your Speech Anxiety,* 2nd ed. Belmont, CA: Thomson Wadsworth, 2005, pp. 79–80.
3. McCroskey, James C. *An Introduction to Rhetorical Communication,* 9th ed. Boston: Allyn & Bacon, 2006.
4. Peck Richmond, Virginia, James C. McCroskey, and Mark L. Hickson. *Nonverbal Behavior in Interpersonal Relations,* 7th ed. Boston: Allyn & Bacon, 2011.
5. Ringle, Ken. "George Bush and the Words of War." *Washington Post.* 9 March 2003. http://pqasb.pqarchiver.com/washingtonpost/access/303554101.html?dids=303554101:303 (accessed 18 May 2007).
6. Annie Lennox's 2013 commencement address is available through her website, www.annielennox.com.
7. Angelou, Maya. (n.d.) www.brainyquote.com/quotes/quotes/m/mayaangelo140532.html (accessed 20 May 2013).
8. Lennox, 2013 commencement address.
9. Momaday, N. Scott. *The Way to Rainy Mountain.* Albuquerque: University of New Mexico Press, 1969, p. 5.
10. Thanks to Dr. Christopher Gilliam, Director of Choral Music, Davidson College.
11. Adapted from Stuart W. Hyde, *Television and Radio Announcing,* 10th ed. Boston: Houghton Mifflin, 2003.
12. Hargitay, Mariska. "No More!" National Press Club. 13 March 2013. www.youtube.com/watch?v=uOE4x6hfSxE (accessed 18 April 2013).
13. Douglis, Carole. "The Beat Goes On: Social Rhythms Underlie All Our Speech and Actions." *Psychology Today,* November 1987, pp. 36–41.
14. Colbert, Stephen. "A Funny Farewell to Wake Forest University Class of 2015." https://www.youtube.com/watch?v=VbzrmIqstd8f (accessed 24 May 2016).
15. Richardson, Ralph. http://bigfishpresentations.com/2012/05/03/25-awesome-public-speaking-quotes/ (accessed 25 May 2016).
16. Hecht, Michael L., Peter A. Andersen, and Sidney A. Ribeau. "The Cultural Dimensions of Nonverbal Communication," in *Handbook of International and Intercultural Communication,* ed. Molefi Kete Asante and William B. Gudykunst. Newbury Park, CA: Sage, 1989, pp. 163–185; and Samovar, Larry A., Richard E. Porter, and Edwin R. McDaniel. *Communication Between Cultures,* 6th ed. Belmont, CA: Wadsworth, 2007.
17. Golden, James L., Goodwin F. Bergquist, and William E. Coleman. *The Rhetoric of Western Thought,* 4th ed. Dubuque, Iowa: Kendall/Hunt Publishing Company, 1989, p. 10.
18. Hillman, Ralph. *Delivering Dynamic Presentations: Using Your Voice and Body for Impact.* Boston: Allyn & Bacon, 1999.
19. *NBC Handbook of Pronunciation,* 4th ed. New York: Harper, 1991.
20. Taylor, Kate. "Why Does Bush Go 'Nucular'?" *Slate,* 18 September 2002. www.slate.com/articles/news_and_politics/explainer/2002/09/why_does_bush_go_nucular.html. (accessed 19 May 2016).
21. Burgoon, Judee K., Laura K. Guerrero, and Kory Floyd. *Nonverbal Communication.* Boston: Allyn & Bacon, 2010, pp. 141–42.
22. Griffith-Roberts, Carolanne. "Let's Talk Southern." *Southern Living,* February 1995, p. 82.
23. Boyd, Ty. *The Million Dollar Toolbox.* n.p.: Alexa Press, 2001, p. 93.
24. Quillen, Carol. "Inaugural Remarks," Davidson College, 19 October 2011, www3.davidson.edu/cms/x44303.xml (accessed 21 October 2011).
25. Samovar, Porter, and McDaniel. *Communication Between Cultures,* p. 177.
26. Bernstein, Constance. "Winning Trials Nonverbally: Six Ways to Establish Control in the Courtroom," *Trial* 30, January 1994, pp. 61–65. Constance Bernstein-Synchronics Group Trial Consultants.
27. Knapp, Mark L., Judith A. Hall, and Terrence G. Horgan. *Nonverbal Communication in Human Interaction,* 8th ed. Belmont, CA: Wadsworth, 2014, p. 8.
28. See, for example, Burgoon, Guerrero, and Floyd. *Nonverbal Communication,* pp. 43–44; and Orbe, Mark P. and Tina M. Harris, *Interracial Communication: Theory into Practice,* 2nd ed. Belmont, CA: Wadsworth, 2007, pp. 112–14.
29. Research psychologist Carolyn Copper has found that newscasters influence voters when they smile while speaking of candidates, further evidence of the power of facial expression. "A Certain Smile." *Psychology Today,* January–February 1992, p. 20.
30. Carney, Dana, Amy Cuddy, and Andy Yap. "Power Posing: Brief Nonverbal Displays Affect Neuroendocrine Levels and Risk Tolerance." *Psychological Science,* October 2010, vol. 10, pp. 1363–1368. http://www.ncbi.nlm.nih.gov/pubmed/20855902 (accessed 10 June 2016); and Rosenberg, Robin S., "Why You May Want to Stand like a Superhero." *Psychology Today,* 13 July 2011. https://www.psychologytoday.com/blog/the-superheroes/201107/why-you-may-want-stand-superhero (accessed 10 June 2016).
31. Dinklage, Peter. "Peter Dinklage '91 Addresses Bennington College's Class of 2012." June 5, 2012. https://www.youtube.com/watch?v=CuEfEv0OlsY (Accessed 24 May 2016).
32. Gasarabwe-Laroche, Edouard. "Meaningful Gestures: Nonverbal Communication in Rwandan Culture." *UNESCO Courier,* September 1993, pp. 31–33.
33. Klein, Richard B. "Winning Cases with Body Language: Moving Toward Courtroom Success." *Trial,* vol. 31, July 1995, p. 84.
34. The literature supporting this conclusion is reviewed by Virginia Kidd, "Do Clothes Make the Officer? How Uniforms Impact Communication: A Review of Literature," presented at the Visual Communication Conference at Pray, MT, 8 July 2000.
35. Goffman, Erving. *The Presentation of Self in Everyday Life.* London: Penguin Press, 1969, p. 21.
36. Kawasaki, Guy. "How to Get a Standing Ovation." 7 September 2010. http://holykaw.alltop.com/how-to-get-a-standing-ovation-O (accessed 21 May 2013).
37. Goffman, pp. 1–14.

38. See, for example, Gallo, Carmine. "Body Language: A Key to Success in the Workplace." 14 February 2007. http://finance.yahoo.com/news/pf_article_102425.html (accessed 20 May 2013); and Jones, Charisse. "Face Off: Hotel Staff Taught to Read Guests' Body Language." *USA Today,* 24 October 2011 http://travel.usatoday.com/hotels/story/2011-10-24/Face-off-Hotel-staff-taught-to-read-guests-body-language/50896514/1 (accessed 24 November 2011).
39. Burgraff, Wayne, http://bigfishpresentations.com/2012/05/03/25-awesome-public-speaking-quotes/ (accessed 24 May 2016).
40. Gallo, Carmine, "The Presentation Secrets of Steve Jobs: How to Be Insanely Great in Front of Any Audience," 29 November 2009 www.slideshare.net/cvgallo/the-presentation-secrets-of-steve-jobs-2609477 (accessed 21 May 2013).
41. Behnke, Ralph R., and Chris R. Sawyer, "Public Speaking Procrastination as a Correlate of Public Speaking Communication Apprehension and Self-Perceived Public Speaking Competence," *Communication Research Reports* 16 (1999): 40–47.
42. Bernstein, 61+.
43. Smith, Tony E., and Ann Bainbridge Frymier. "Get 'Real': Does Practicing Speeches Before an Audience Improve Performance?" *Communication Quarterly,* vol. 54, 2006, p. 113.
44. Wallis, Claudia, and Sonja Steptoe. "The Case for Doing One Thing at a Time," *Time,* 16 January 2006, p. 76.
45. Cross, Jody. *Leaders Speak: How to Transform Your Career and Life Through Public Speaking.* n.p.: Author. 2012, p. 167.
46. These guidelines for handling questions and answers are a compendium of ideas from the following sources: Body, Stephen D. "Nine Steps to a Successful Question-and-Answer Session." *Management Solutions,* May 1988, pp. 16–17; Brady, Teresa. "Fielding Abrasive Questions During Presentations." *Supervisory Management,* February 1993, p. 6; Ragsdale, J. Donald, and Alan L. Mikels. "Effects of Question Periods on a Speaker's Credibility with a Television Audience." *Southern States Communication Journal,* vol. 40, 1975, pp. 302–312; Sarnoff, Dorothy. *Never Be Nervous Again.* New York: Ballantine, 1987; Schloff, Laurie, and Marcia Yudkin. *Smart Speaking: Sixty-Second Strategies.* New York: Holt, 1991; and Zaremba, Alan. "Q and A: The Other Part of Your Presentation." *Management World,* January–February 1989, pp. 8–10.
47. Hutson, Matthew. "How to Dodge a Question." *Psychology Today,* October 2009, p. 24.
48. "South Carolina Democratic Debate transcript," MSNBC, p. 7, 27 April 2007. www.msnbc.msn.com/id/18352397 (accessed 20 May 2007).
49. Ross, Tom, to COM 101: Principles of Oral Communication, Davidson College, 2 December 2008.
50. The authors are indebted to Professor Roxanne Gee of the television and film area in the Department of Communication at the University of Memphis; much of this section rests on her observations and suggestions. In addition, McDermott, Virginia, and Rachel A. Wegter's *Public Speaking: Preparation and Presentation in a Digital Age* (Dubuque, IA: Kendall Hunt, 2012) provided helpful information.
51. Noonan, Peggy. http://www.poemhunter.com/quotations/famous.asp?people=peggy%20noonan (accessed 25 May 2016).

Chapter 13

1. Carr, Caleb. http://goodreads.com/quotes/tag/information-age (accessed 9 March 2016).
2. NonPariel Institute. http://www.npitx.org/ (accessed 11 March 2016.)
3. Rowan, Katherine E. "Goals, Obstacles, and Strategies in Risk Communication: A Problem-Solving Approach to Improving Communication About Risks." *Journal of Applied Communication Research,* vol. 19, 1991, p. 314.
4. Ibid.
5. Weigel, David. "It's Not a Revenue Problem. It's a Spending Problem: Tracing the History of a GOP Talking Point." *Slate,* vol. 18, April 2011. www.slate.com/articles/news-and-politics/politics/2011/04/its-not-a-revenue-problem-its-a-spending-problem.html (accessed 10 May 2016.)
6. Churchill, Winston. "We Shall Fight on the Beaches." House of Commons, June 4, 1940. http://www.winstonchurchill.org/resources/speeches/128-we-shall-fight-on-the-beaches (accessed 9 March 2016).
7. Simons, Herbert W., and Jean G. Jones. *Persuasion in Society,* 2nd ed. New York: Routledge, 2011, p. 289.
8. "Neil deGrasse Tyson Pays Homage to Abe Lincoln, the Science Guy." http://mentalfloss.com/article/71387/neil-degrasse-tyson-pays-homage-abe-lincoln-science-guy (accessed 1 March 2016.)
9. Ashdown, Paul. "From Wild West to Wild Web," *Vital Speeches of the Day,* vol. 66, 1 September 2000, pp. 699–701.
10. Gamble, Paul R., and Clare E. Kelliher. "Imparting Information and Influencing Behavior: An Examination of Staff Briefing Sessions." *Journal of Business Communication,* vol. 36, July 1999, p. 261.
11. Sparks, Ancil B., and Dennis D. Staszak. "Fine Tuning Your News Briefing: Law Enforcement Agency Media Relations." *FBI Law Enforcement Bulletin.* http://www.highbeam.com/doc/1G1-69441917.html December 2000 (accessed 10 July 2013).
12. Gardner, Howard. *Changing Minds: The Art and Science of Changing Our Own and Other People's Minds.* Cambridge, MA: Harvard Business School Publishing, 2006; and Timothy J. Koegel.
13. Koegel, Timothy J. *The Exceptional Presenter.* Austin, TX: Greenleaf Book Group Press, 2007.

Chapter 14

1. Hargreaves, Steve. "Exxon Linked to Climate Change Pay Out." *Fortune* (CNN.Money), 2 February 2007, http://money.cnn.com/2007/02/02/news/companies/exxon_science/index.htm?cnn=yes (accessed 23 May 2007).
2. Gore, Al. *The Assault on Reason.* New York: Penguin Press, 2007, pp. 245–246.
3. Woodward, Gary C., and Robert E. Denton, Jr. *Persuasion & Influence in American Life,* 3rd ed. Prospect Heights, IL, 1996, p. 16.
4. Malala Yousafzai's speech at the Youth Takeover of the United Nations, 12 July 2013, http://secure.aworldatschool.org/page/content/the-text-of-malala-yousafzais-speech-at-the-united-nations/ (accessed 10 February 2016).

5. Johannesen, Richard L. *Ethics in Human Communication*, 5th ed. Long Grove, IL: Waveland Press, 2002, pp. 217–218.
6. Nelson, Elizabeth Jean. Syllabus for Persuasion and Argumentation in Public Speaking. University of Minnesota–Duluth, Spring 2006.
7. Foss, Sonja K., and Cindy L. Griffin. "Beyond Persuasion: A Proposal for an Invitational Rhetoric." *Communication Monographs,* vol. 62, 1995, pp. 2–18.
8. Adapted from Richard L. Johannesen, Kathleen S. Valde, and Karen E. Whedbee. *Ethics in Communication*, 6th ed. Prospect Heights, IL: Waveland, 2007.
9. McGuire, William J. "Attitudes and Attitude Change," in *The Handbook of Social Psychology*, ed. Gardner Lindzey and Elliot Aronson, New York: Random House, 1985, vol. 1, pp. 258–261.
10. Hattersley Gray, Robin. "Sexual Assault Statistics." *Campus Safety Magazine.* 5 March 2012. campussafetymagazine.com/article/Sexual-Assaults-Statistics-and-Myths (accessed 10 June 2016).
11. Cialdini, Robert B. *Influence: Science and Practice*, 5th ed. Boston: Pearson, 2009, pp. 64–66.
12. The motivated sequence design was introduced in Alan Monroe's *Principles and Types of Speech*, New York: Scott, Foresman, 1935, and has been refined in later editions.
13. Golden, James, Goodwin F. Berquest, and William E. Coleman, *The Rhetoric of Western Thought*, 4th ed. Dubuque, IA: Kendall/Hunt Publishing Co., 1989, pp. 61–63; also see Thomas Wilson, "From *The Arte of Rhetorique*," *The Rhetoric Tradition: Readings from Classical Times to the Present*, edited by Patricia Bizzell and Bruce Herzberg, New York: St. Martin's Press Inc., 1990, pp. 593–594.
14. Truth, Sojourner. "Ain't I a Woman?" Speech at the Women's Convention, Akron, Ohio, 1851. http://www.sojournertruth.com/p/aint-i-woman.html (accessed 3 January 2017).
15. Damasio, Antonio R. *Descartes' Error: Emotion, Reason, and the Human Brain*. New York: Putnam, 1994.
16. Solomon, Martha. "The 'Positive Woman's' Journey: A Mythic Analysis of the Rhetoric of STOP ERA." *Quarterly Journal of Speech,* vol. 65, 1979, pp. 262–274.

Chapter 15

1. Gray, Emma. "Co-Sponsor Of Heartbeat Bill 'Never Even Thought About' Why Women Get Abortions." Huffington Post, December 9, 2016. http://www.huffingtonpost.com/entry/jim-buchy-co-sponsor-of-ohio-heartbeat-bill-never-even-thought-about-why-women-get-abortions_us_584af889e4b0e05aded3c31f (accessed 14 December 2016).
2. Becker, Carl. "What Is Evidence?" *The Historian as Detective: Essays on Evidence*, ed. Robin W. Winks. New York: Harper Colophon, 1970, p. 19.
3. Davis, Janel. "Did Reagan Support an Assault-Weapons Ban?" *Politifact Georgia.* 5 February 2013. www.politifact.com/georgia/statements/2013/Feb/05/barck-obama/did-reagan-support-assautl-weapons-ban/ (accessed 12 July 2016).
4. Toulmin, Stephen. *The Uses of Argument.* Cambridge: University Press, 1969.
5. Weaver, Richard. *The Ethics of Rhetoric* 1953. Davis, CA: Hermagoras Press, 1985.
6. Some argue that the terms *deduction* and *induction* should no longer be used in speech textbooks because modern logic has changed its use of these words. Such logicians are concerned with accounting for certainty in conclusions, such as one seeks in mathematical reasoning. Since the time of Aristotle, rhetorical theorists have recognized that speakers deal with a world of contingency in which degrees of uncertainty and probability are the sole concerns. Systems of nomenclature such as *induction* and *deduction* should be measured by their usefulness in specific fields of inquiry and are not subject to decree by any other privileged field.
7. Corlin, Richard F. "The Secrets of Gun Violence in America." *Vital Speeches of the Day,* vol. 67, 1 August 2001, p. 611. Reprinted by permission of Richard Corlin.
8. Ross, Lisa M. "Buckley Says Drug Attack Won't Work." *Commercial Appeal.* Memphis, 14 September 1989, p. B2.
9. Adapted from Herbert W. Simons and Jean G. Jones, *Persuasion in Society*, 2nd ed. Thousand Oaks, CA: Sage, 2011.
10. Tracy, Larry. "Taming Hostile Audiences: Persuading Those Who Would Rather Jeer than Cheer." *Vital Speeches of the Day*, vol. 71, 1 March 2005, p. 311.
11. Sanders, Bernie. Liberty University. 14 September 2015. https://www.washingtonpost.com/news/the-fix/wp/2015/09/14/bernie-sanders-liberty-university-speech-annotated/ (accessed 5 February 2016).
12. Ann Richards, *Straight from the Heart*, Simon and Schuster, 2013.
13. Sanders.
14. Tracy.
15. Kelly, John M. "Audi Alteram Partum: Note." *National Law Forum*, Paper 84, 1964, pp. 103, 106–107.
16. Ibid.
17. Compton, Joshua A., and Michael W. Pfau. "Inoculation Theory of Resistance to Influence at Maturity," in *Communication Yearbook 29*, ed. P. J. Kalbfleisch, Mahwah, NJ: Erlbaum, 2005, pp. 97–145.
18. Rowan, Katherine E. "Goals, Obstacles, and Strategies in Risk Communication: A Problem-Solving Approach to Improving Communication About Risks." *Journal of Applied Communication Research,* vol. 19, 1991, p. 322.
19. Itkowitz, Colby. "'Little Marco,' Lyin' Ted,' 'Crooked Hillary': How Donald Trump Makes Name Calling Stick." *The Washington Post,* 20 April 2016. www.washingtonpost.com/news/inspired-life/wp/2016/04/20/little-marco-lying-ted-crooked-hillary-donald-trump-winning-strategy-nouns/ (accessed 23 June 2016).
20. Raley, Yvonne. "Character Attacks: How to Properly Apply the Ad Hominem." *Scientific American*, 1 June, 2008. http://www.scientificamerican.com/article/character-attack/ (accessed 21 July 2016).
21. Caldwell, Leigh Ann. "Bernie Sanders and Hillary Clinton Spar Over Transparency, Judgment." *NBC News.* 14 April 2016. www.nbcnews.com/politics/2016-election/sanders-release-tax-returns-clinton-won-t-commit-releasing-paid-n556286 (accessed 23 June 2016).
22. Gula, Robert J. *Nonsense: Red Herrings, Straw Men, and Sacred Cows: How We Abuse Logic in Our Everyday Language.* Mount Jackson, VA: Axios Press, 2007.
23. Ray, Dixy Lee. "Quotes by Dixy Lee Ray." *Gaiam Life: Your Guide to Better Living*." 2016. blog.gaiam.com/quotes/authors/dixy-lee-ray (accessed 23 June 2016).
24. Seelye, Katherine Q. "Gingrich's 'Piggies' Poked." *The New York Times,* 19 Jan. 2016. www.nytimes.com/1995/

01/19/us/gingrich-s-piggies-poked.html (accessed 23 June 2016).

25. Cialdini, Robert B. *Influence: Science and Practice*, 5th ed. Boston: Pearson, 2009, p. 99.
26. Brinkley, Alan. *American History: A Survey*, 11th ed. New York: McGraw-Hill, 2003, pp. 846–847.
27. Cranberg, Gilbert. "Even Sensible Iowa Bows to the Religious Right." *Los Angeles Times*, 17 August 1992, p. B5.
28. Noah, Timothy. "Bill Clinton and the Meaning of 'Is.' " *Slate*, 13 September 1998. www.slate.com/articles/news_and_politics/chatterbox/1998/19/bill_clinton_and_the_meaning_of_is.html (accessed 23 June 2016).
29. Thompson, April. "District Attorney Amy Wyrick Testifies on How She Handled Murder Case." *News Channel 3*. 25 November 2014. wreg.com/2014/11/25/district-attorney-amy-wyrick-testifies-on-how-she-handled-murder-case/ (accessed 23 June 2016).
30. Ehninger, Douglas, and Wayne Brockriede. *Decision By Debate*. New York: Dodd Mead & Company, 1963.
31. Makau, Josina M., and Debian L. Marty. *Cooperative Argumentation: A Model for Deliberative Community*. Long Grove, IL: Waveland Press, 2001, p. 40.

Chapter 16

1. Rowling, J. K. "The Fringe Benefits of Failure, and the Importance of Imagination." *Harvard Gazette*, 5 June 2008.
2. Holloway, Rachel. "Clarity through Tragedy: Honoring Our Work." Southern States Communication Association Awards Luncheon, 5 April 2008.
3. Condit, Celeste Michelle. "The Functions of Epideictic: The Boston Massacre Orations as Exemplar." *Communication Quarterly*, vol. 33, 1985, pp. 284–299; Gray Matthews, "Epideictic Rhetoric and Baseball: Nurturing Community Through Controversy," *Southern Communication Journal*, vol. 60, 1995, pp. 275–291; Chaim Perelman and Lucie Olbrechts-Tyteca, *The New Rhetoric: A Treatise on Argumentation*, South Bend, IN: University of Notre Dame Press, 1971, pp. 47–54; and Richard M. Weaver, *The Ethics of Rhetoric*, Chicago: Henry Regnery, 1953, pp. 164–185.
4. See Burke's discussion in "The Range of Rhetoric," in *A Rhetoric of Motives*, Berkeley: University of California Press, 1969, pp. 3–43.
5. Fisher, Walter R. *Human Communication as Narration: Toward a Philosophy of Reason, Value, and Action*, Columbia: University of South Carolina Press, 1989; Kirsten Theye, "Shoot, I'm Sorry: An Examination of Narrative Functions and Effectiveness within Dick Cheney's Hunting Accident Apologia," *Southern Communication Journal*, vol. 73, no. 2, April–June, 2008, pp. 160–77.
6. *Selected Speeches and Writings by Abraham Lincoln*, New York: Vintage Books, 1992, p. 405; and Abraham Lincoln, "Gettysburg Address," americanrhetoric.com/speeches/gettysburgaddress.htm (accessed 16 December 2016).
7. See the discussion in The Rhetoric of Aristotle, trans. Lane Cooper, New York: Appleton-Century-Crofts, 1932, I.7, I.9, 1.14, pp. 34–44, 46–55, 78–79.
8. Osborn, Michael. "Tribute to Janice Hocker Rushing," Southern States Communication Association convention, Tampa, April 2004; and Ta-Nehisi Coates, "My President Was Black," *The Atlantic*, 11 December 2016.
9. Costner, Kevin. "Eulogy for Whitney Houston Presented February 19, 2012," posted 19 February 2012, http://transcripts.cnn.com/TRANSCRIPTS/1202/18/se.07.html (accessed 1 July 2013).
10. Edwards, Owen. "What Every Man Should Know: How to Make a Toast." *Esquire*, January 1984, p. 37.
11. The advice that follows is adpated from Jacob M. Braude, *Complete Speaker's and Toastmaster's Library: Definitions and Toasts*, Englewood Cliffs, NJ: Prentice Hall, 1965, pp. 88–123; and Wendy Lin, "Let's Lift a Glass, Say a Few Words, and Toast 1996," [Memphis] *Commercial Appeal*, 28 December 1995, p. C3.
12. Selected from www.theknot.com/content/traditional-cultural-wedding-toasts; thechive.com/2015/08/27/toasts-from-around-the-world-12-photos/; heavy.com/social/2014/03/best-funny-drinking-toasts-memes/7; quotations.about.com/od/WeddingQuotesandWishes/a/Fill-The-Cup-Of-Matrimonial-Harmony-With-Wedding-Wishes.htm; www.etiquettescholar.com/dining_etiquette/toasting_etiquette/toasts_for_all_occassions/dedication_toasts.html; http://www.brainyquote.com/quotes/quotes/k/khalilgibr136982.htmll; www.theweddingdirectory.co.za/planning-tools/wedding-planning-advice/_okes-one-liners-speech-toast-2 (accessed 1 March 2016).
13. Wiesel, Elie. "Nobel Peace Prize Acceptance Speech." *New York Times*, 11 December 1986, p. A8.
14. *Commercial Appeal* (Memphis), 23 October 1995, p. D2.
15. Dobie Frank. "The Conservatism of Charles M. Russell," in *Charlie Russell Roundup: Essays on America's Favorite Cowboy Artist*, ed. Brian Dippie, Helena, MT: Montana Historical Society Press, 1999, p. 256.
16. Jobs, Steve. "Commencement Address at Stanford University." *Stanford Report*, 14 June 2005.
17. *Congressional Record*, 1 April 1980, p. 7249. Although Owens wrote this speech, he died before he could deliver it.
18. Ibid., p. 7248.
19. Ailes, Roger. *You Are the Message*, New York: Doubleday, 1988, pp. 71–74.
20. Jackman, Dick. "Awards Dinner of the National Football Foundation and the Hall of Fame." *Harper's Magazine*, March 1985.
21. Gruner, Charles R. "Advice to the Beginning Speaker on Using Humor—What the Research Tells Us." *Communication Education*, vol. 34, 1985, pp. 142–147; and Christie McGuffee Smith and Larry Powell, "The Use of Disparaging Humor by Group Leaders," *Southern Speech Communication Journal*, vol. 53, 1988, pp. 279–292.
22. www.washingtonpost.com/news/reliable-source/wp/2015/04/25/the-funniest-lines-in-president-obamas-white-house-correspondents-dinner-speech/(accessed 21 January 2016).
23. *Washington Post*, 12 December 1978.
24. Adapted from Joan Detz, *Can You Say a Few Words?* New York: St. Martins, 1991, pp. 77–78.
25. Obama, Michelle. "Remarks by the First Lady at Tuskegee University: Commencement Address, May 9, 2015," www.whitehouse.gov (accessed 5 February 2016).

Appendix A

1. See, for example, Lawrence R. Frey and J. Kevin Barge, eds., *Managing Group Life: Communicating in Decision-Making Groups*, Boston: Houghton Mifflin, 1997, p. 45.
2. Adapted from Marc Hequet, "The Fine Art of Multicultural Meetings," *Training*, July 1993, pp. 29–33.

3. For additional insights on groupthink, see the following sources: Irving L. Janis, *Victims of Groupthink: A Psychological Study of Foreign-Policy Decisions and Fiascoes,* Boston: Houghton Mifflin, 1972; John A. Courtright, "A Laboratory Investigation of Groupthink," *Communication Monographs,* vol. 45, no. 3 (1978), pp. 229–246; Moya A. Ball, *Vietnam-on-the-Potomac,* Santa Barbara, CA: Praeger, 1992; Judith Chapman, "Anxiety and Defective Decision Making: An Elaboration of the Groupthink Model," *Management Decision,* vol. 44 (2006) pp. 1391–1404; Jack Eaton, "Management Communication: The Threat of Groupthink," *Corporate Communications,* vol. 6 (2001), pp. 183–192; and Steve A. Yetiv, "Groupthink and the Gulf Crisis," *British Journal of Political Science,* vol. 33 (2003), pp. 419–442.
4. Schuster, John P. "Transforming Your Leadership Style." *Association Management,* January 1994, pp. 39–43.
5. Boulding, Kenneth. *Three Faces of Power,* Thousand Oaks, CA: Sage, 1990; Charles Conrad and Marshall Scott Poole, *Strategic Organizational Communication in a Global Economy,* 7th ed., New York: Harcourt, 2004.
6. Madzar, Svjetlana. "Subordinates' Information Inquiry: Exploring the Effect of Perceived Leadership Style and Individual Difference." *Journal of Occupational and Organizational Psychology,* June 2001, pp. 221–232.
7. For more information on face-to-face brainstorming, see J. M. Hender et al., "Improving Group Creativity: Brainstorming versus Non-brainstorming Techniques in a GSS Environment," *Proceedings of the 24th Annual Hawaii International Conference of Systems Sciences, 2001;* Thomas J. Kramer, Gerald P. Fleming, and Scott M. Mannis, "Improving Face-to-Face Brainstorming Through Modeling and Facilitation," *Small Group Research,* vol. 32 (2001); and Paul A. Paulus et al., "Social and Cognitive Influences in Group Brainstorming: Predicting Production Gains and Losses," *European Review of Social Psychology,* vol. 12 (January 2002).
8. For additional information on electronic brainstorming, see Nicolas Michinov and Corine Primois, "Improving Productivity and Creativity in Online Groups Through Social Comparison Process: New Evidence for Asynchronous Electronic Brainstorming," *Computers in Human Behavior,* vol. 21 (2005), pp. 11–28.
9. Lasker, Roz D., and Elisa S. Weiss. "Broadening Participation in Community Problem-Solving: A Multidisciplinary Model to Supportive Collaborative Practice and Research." *Journal of Urban Health,* March 2003, pp. 14–47; Nikol Rummel and Hans Spada, "Learning to Collaborate: An Instructional Approach to Promoting Collaborative Problem Solving in Computer-Mediated Settings," *Journal of the Learning Sciences,* vol. 14, 2005, pp. 201–241.
10. Issacs, William M. "Taking Flight: Dialogue, Collective Thinking, and Organizational Learning." *Organizational Dynamics,* Autumn 1993, pp. 24–39.
11. Schein, Edgar H. "On Dialogue, Culture, and Organizational Learning." *Organizational Dynamics,* Autumn 1993, pp. 40–41. For additional information on dialogue groups, see Joseph H. Albeck, Sami Adwan, and Dan Bar-on, "Dialogue Groups: TRT's Guidelines for Working Through Intractable Conflicts by Personal Story Telling," *Peace and Conflict: Journal of Peace Psychology,* vol. 8, 2002, pp. 301–322.
12. Stewart, David W., Prem N. Shamdassani, and Dennis W. Rook. *Focus Groups: Theory and Practice,* 2nd ed., Thousand Oaks, CA: Sage, 2006; Thomas L. Greenbaum, *Moderating Focus Groups: A Practical Guide for Group Facilitation,* Thousand Oaks, CA: Sage, 2000; and Claudia Puchta and Jonathan Potter, *Focus Group Practice,* Thousand Oaks, CA: Sage, 2004.
13. Seibold, Dave, and Dean H. Krikorian. "Making Meetings More Successful," in *Managing Group Life: Communicating in Decision-Making Groups,* eds. Lawrence R. Frey and J. Kevin Barge, Boston: Houghton Mifflin, 1997, pp. 274–275; and Patrick Lencioni, *Death by Meeting,* San Francisco: Jossey-Bass, 2004.
14. Much of the material in this section is adapted from Gregorio Billikopf, "Conducting Effective Meetings," August 2005, www.cnr.berkeley.edu/ucce50/ag-labor/7labor/11.pdf (accessed 30 June 2007); Don Clark, "Meetings," 20 May 2007, www.nwlink.com/~donclark/leader/leadmet.html (accessed 30 June 2007); and Carter McNamara, "Basic Guide to Conducting Effective Meetings," copyright 1997–2007, www.managementhelp.org/misc/mtgmgmnt.htm (accessed 30 June 2007).
15. Renz, Mary Ann, and John B. Greg. *Effective Small Group Communication in Theory and Practice.* Boston: Allyn and Bacon, 2000, pp. 257–258.
16. Mayer, Michael E. "Behaviors Leading to More Effective Decisions in Small Groups Embedded in Organizations," *Communication Reports.* Summer 1988, pp. 123–132.
17. Niesche, Christopher. "Virtual Meetings on the Rise." *The Sydney Morning Herald,* 1 November 2012, www.smh.com.au/business/momentum/virtual-meetings-on-the-rise-20121023-2832v.html (accessed 9 August 2013); J. Dan Rothwell, *In the Company of Others: An Introduction to Communication,* 3rd ed., New York: Oxford University Press, 2010, pp. 328–329.
18. "Roundtables," 4 Dec. 2003, www.sdanys.org/Archive_Round/NYPWAGuidelines.htm (accessed 30 June 2007).
19. Berlin Snell, Marilyn. "Climate Exchange." *Sierra,* May/June 2007, pp. 44–53, 73–74.

Appendix B

1. Page 410, Nobel Peace Prize Acceptance Speech, December 10, 1986.

Credits

Chapter 1 p.001: Tetra Images/Getty Image; p.03: Source: Employers complain about communication skills, Post-Gazette. http://www.post-gazette.com/business/businessnews/2005/02/06/Employers-complain-about-communication-skills/stories/200502060145.; p.004: Stephen Lovekin/Getty Images Entertainment/Getty Images; p.005: Hero Images Inc./Alamy Stock Photo. p.05: Source: Our Voices: Essays in Culture, Ethnicity, and Communication, ed. Alberto Gonzalez, Marsha Houston, and Victoria Chen,3e,Oxford University Press,2000.; p.06: Source: On Justice, Power, and Human Nature: Selections from The History of the Peloponnesian War, Thucydides, Paul Woodruff, Hackett Publishing, 1993.; p.18: Source: The Years of Lyndon Johnson: The path to power, Robert A. Caro, Random House Inc., 1983.; p.007: Panos Karas/Shutterstock; p.011: Rawpixel.com/Fotolia.

Chapter 2 p.021: Davidson College; p.022: Everett Collection Inc/Alamy Stock Photo; p.22: Reprinted with permission from Betsy Lyles.; p.24: James C McCroskey, Measures of Communication Bound Anxiety, Speech Monographs, 37 (1970), p. 276. The Speech Communication Association.; p.25: Pam Ferderbar, "Public Speaking: The Horror," Huffington Post, October 22, 2015.; p.030: bst2012/Fotolia; p.31: Source: Matt Abrahams," Matt Abrahams: Tips and Techniques for More Confident and Compelling Presentations, Stanford Graduate School of Business.; p.32: Reprinted with permission from Betsy Lyles.; p.034: Davidson College.

Chapter 3 p.036: WavebreakmediaMicro/Fotolia.; p.039tl: Lida Salatian/Fotolia.; p.039bl: Mark Wilson/Getty Images.; p.040: Photo Researchers, Inc/Alamy Stock Photo.; p.043: GoGo Images Corporation/Alamy Stock Photo.; p.046: Racorn/Shutterstock.; p.049: Alekuwka83/Fotolia.; p. 52: Reprinted with permission from Sabrina Karic, University of Nevada–Las Vegas.; Stock Montage, Inc./Alamy Stock Photo.; Library of Congress Prints and Photographs Division Washington, D.C. 20540 (LC-USZ62-5513).

Chapter 4 p.054: Fuse/Corbis/Getty Images.; p.059: Tomalu/Fotolia.; p.064: Alin Dragulin/FogStock/Alamy Stock Photo.; p.066: Rido/Fotolia.; WavebreakmediaMicro/Fotolia; Monkey Business/Fotolia.; Andrey Popov/Fotolia.

Chapter 5 p.34: Reprinted with permission from Gabrielle Wallace.; p. 35: Source: Congressional Record: Proceedings and Debates of the ... Congress, Volume 113, Part 1. U.S. Government Printing Office.; p.069: The Washington Post/Getty Images; p.077: Spike Mafford/UpperCut Images/Alamy; p.082: Peter Casolino/Alamy Stock Photo; p. 82: Reprinted with permission from Beth Tidmore.; p. 82: Reprinted with permission from student speaker Stephanie Herrera.; p.088: Adrian Sherratt/Alamy.; p.090: Robert Daly/Caiaimage/OJO+/Getty Images.; p.073: antoniodiaz/Shutterstock.

Chapter 6 p.098: corepics/Fotolia.; p.100cl: PCN Photography/Alamy.; p.100cr: Galyna Andrushko/Fotolia.; p.096: Photodisc/Getty Images.; p.105: Roger Bacon/Reuters/Alamy Stock Photo.; p.108: Reprinted with permission from Benjamin Youngerman.; p.111: Reprinted with permission from Jessica Bradshaw.; p.112: Source: Dr. Seuss: American Icon, 2005, Continuum International Publishing.; p. 97: Reprinted with permission from Lindsey Yoder.; p.98: Reprinted with permission from Graham Honeycutt, a student at Davidson College.

Chapter 7 p.113: Creativa/Shutterstock.; p.115: Bruce Chapman/The Winston-Salem Journal/AP Images.; p 118: Barton Seaver.; p.121: goodluz/Fotolia.; p.122: Source: Abraham Lincoln.; p.123: Reprinted by permission of the Sierra Club.; p.123: Source: Sierra Club, www.sierraclub.org. Used with permission.; p.124: Reprinted by permission of the Mayo Clinic.; p.124: Source: By permission of Mayo Foundation for Medical Education and Research. All rights reserved.; p.127: Randy Duchaine/Alamy; p.129: Goodluz/Shutterstock; Konoplytska/iStock/Getty Image; Konoplytska/iStock/Getty Image.

Chapter 8 p.135: Mariusz Blach/Fotolia; p.137: Source: "Childhood Obesity Facts," Centers for Disease Control, http://www.cdc.gov/healthyschools/obesity/facts.htm.; p.138: Based on data from Bankrate Money Pulse survey, Sept. 15-18, 2016,http://www.bankrate.com/finance/consumer-index/money-pulse-1016.aspx#ixzz4OJjrRDh1 (accessed October 27, 2016).; p.141: Pikselstock/Shutterstock; p.142: Ric Francis-File/AP Images; p.142: Ric Francis-File/AP Images; p.142: Source: "Barack Obama's Speech on Race," the New York Times, http://www.nytimes.com/2008/03/18/us//politics/18text-obama.html.; p.142: Source: "Best of Jobs: To Have and Serve the Public's Trust," keynote address at the PBS Annual Meeting, 1996. American University School of Communication.; p.145: Monica Schipper/Getty Images Entertainment/Getty Images; p.145: Monica Schipper/Getty Images Entertainment/Getty Images.; p.145: Source: "Remarks to the 2006 National Prayer Breakfast: February 2, 2006.; p.146: Source: Governor Chris Christie, "State of the State Address," www.nj.com/politics/index.ssf/2013/01/full_text_of_chris_christies_2.html.; p.147: Reprinted with permission from Joseph Jimenez.; p.148: David Quinn/AP Images; p.149: Reprinted with permission from Sandra Baltz.

Chapter 9 p.155: Darren Baker/Fotolia; p.167: Adrian Weston/Alamy Stock Photo; p.174: RosaIreneBetancourt 8/Alamy Stock Photo.; p.158: Dave/Les Jacobs/Getty images.; p.169: RealyEasyStar/Fotografia Felici/Alamy Stock Photo;169: "Source: The Speech Pope Francis Gave to Congress," Sept. 24, 2015, http://www.informationclearinghouse.info/article42951.htm.; p.170: Jason DeCrow/AP Images; p.170: Reprinted with permission from Joseph Van Matre.;

p. 171: Reprinted with permission from Guy Britton.; p.171: Reprinted with permission from Ashlie McMillan.; p.174: Reprinted with permission from Beth Tidmore.; p.173: Jessica Hill/AP Images.; p.174: Reprinted with permission from Anna Aley.; p.175: Reprinted with permission from University of Arkansas student, Simone Mullinax.; p. 177: Reprinted with permission from Elizabeth Lyles.

Chapter 10 p.186: Andresr/Shutterstock; p.191: Jim West/ Alamy Stock Photo; p.192: David L. Moore/Alamy; 193: Source: U.S. Geological Survey, Department of the Interior/ USGS.; 194: Source: Percent of People 25 Years and Over Who Have Completed High School or College, by Race, Hispanic Origin and Sex: Selected Years 1940 to 2015, U.S. Census Bureau. U.S. Department of Commerce.; 200: Reprinted with permission from Peter Norvig, "The Gettysburg Powerpoint Presentation," http://norvig.com/Gettysburg/.; 202: Prezi Designed by Dr Shawn Apostel.; p.195: Jonathan Mitchell/ Alamy; 202: Reprinted with permission from Scott Titsworth, Director of of the School of Communication studies at Ohio University.; 207: Courtesy of La Puerta Books and Media.; 210: Based on Alliance for Board Diversity, "Missing Pieces: Women and Minorities on Fortune 500 Boards—2010 Alliance for Board Diversity Census, (2011).

Chapter 11 p.213: ZUMA Press, Inc./Alamy Stock Photo; p. 214: Source: "Any Candidate Will Drink to That," Austin American Statesman, 11 May 1984, p. A–10.; 216: Reprinted with permission from Sally Duncan.; p.217: AdMedia/Splash News/Newscom; p. 217: AdMedia/Splash News/Newscom; 217: Source: "President Obama's Address at Boston Memorial Service," 18 April 2013, https://www.whitehouse.gov/the-press-office/2013/04/18/remarks-president-interfaith-service-boston-ma.; p.217: Source: "Second Inaugural Address," Vital Speeches of the Day 51 (1 February 1985): 226–228.; p. 218: Reprinted with permission from Anna Aley; 219: Reprinted with permission from Stephanie Lamb.; p.221: Source: "Commencement Address," University of Texas, Time, 19 June 1985, p. 68.; p. 222: Reprinted with permission from Alexander McArthur.; p.223: Wavebreak-MediaMicro/Fotolia; p.223: Reprinted with permission from Olivia Jackson, Phillips Exeter Academy in New Hampshire.; p. 224t: Eric Isselee/Shutterstock; p.224c: Andres Rodriguez/ Fotolia; p.225: Image Source/Getty Images; p.228: Sea Wave/ Shutterstock; p.228: Reprinted with permission from Wade Steck, University of Memphis Frosh Camp Program; p.230: Reprinted with permission from Katie Lovett.; p. 236: Ashley Smith; Used with permission from the National Communication Association, www.natcom.orgp. Pearson Education; Pearson Education.

Chapter 12 p.238: GreenPimp/E+/Getty Images; p.244: Allstar Picture Library/Alamy Stock Photo; p.255: Jordan Strauss/ Invision for MTV/AP Images; p. 246: Source: N. Scott Momaday, The Way to Rainy Mountain (Albuquerque: University of New Mexico Press, 1969); p.248: Christy Bowe/Polaris/Newscom; p.249: Davidson College; p.250: Reprinted with permission from Davidson student BJ Youngerman; p.252: Steven Senne/ AP Images; p. 253: Source: "Winning Trials Nonverbally: Six Ways to Establish Control in the Courtroom," Trial, 30 (January 1994), pp. 61–65. Constance Bernstein-Synchronics Group Trial Consultants.; p.256: Digital Vision/Photodisc/Getty Images; p.262: ZUMA Press, Inc/Alamy Stock Photo.

Chapter 13 p.266: Monkey Business Images/Shutterstock; p.267: Justin Sullivan/Getty Images News/Getty Images; p.271: Source: Katherine E. Rowan, "Goals, Obstacles, and Strategies in Risk Communication: A Problem-Solving Approach to Improving Communication About Risks," Journal of Applied Communication Research 19 (1991): 314.; p.273: epa european pressphoto agency b.v./Alamy Stock Photo.; p. 276: Reprinted with permission from Nicolette Fisk.; p. 277: Reprinted with permission from Thressia Taylor; p.278bl: Michael Osborn; p.278br: Michael Osborn; p. 278: Reprinted with permission from Belinda Phillip.; p.278bl: Michael Osborn; p.278br: Michael Osborn; p.280: Victor Watts/Alamy Stock Photo; p.280: Reprinted with permission from Robert Rozinski.; p.280: Reprinted with permission from Patty Lenzini.; p.285: Reprinted with permission from Olivia Jackson: Descent Into Darkness, Phillips Exeter Academy in New Hampshire.; p.274: Kristin Callahan/Everett Collection/Alamy Live News/Alamy Stock Photo.

Chapter 14 p.287: Hill Street Studios/Blend Images/Getty Images.; p.290: Source: Al Gore, The Assault on Reason (New York: Penguin Press, 2007).; p.291: Davidson College.; p.292: Mark H. Milstein/ZUMAPRESS/Newscom .; p.292: Reprinted with permission from Amanda Miller.; p.292: Reprinted with permission from Dolapo Chizoba Olushola.; p.295: Ho New/Reuters Pictures.; p.296: Reprinted with permission from Amanda Miller.; p.297: Kevin Wolf/AP Images.; p.297: Reprinted with permission from Lindsey Yodar.; p.299: Based on The structure of the stock issues design has been adapted from Charles U. Larson, Persuasion: Reception and Responsibility, 13th ed. (Belmont, CA: Wadsworth, 2012); and Charles S. Mudd and Malcolm O. Sillars, Public Speaking: Content and Communication (Prospect Heights, IL: Waveland, 1991), pp. 100–102. © Michael Osborn.; p.302: Source: Sojourner Truth, Albumen silver print, circa 1870 from the National Portrait Gallery, Smithsonian Institution.; p.303br: National Geographic Creative/Silverfish Press/National Geographic Creative/ Bridgeman Images.; p.303tr: dpa picture alliance/Alamy Stock Photo.; p.307: Reprinted with permission from Lindsey Yoder.

Chapter 15 p.309: Stockbyte/Getty Images.; p.313: Erik s. Lesser/epa/Newscom.; p.316tr: Paul Hudson/Getty Image.; p.316bl: Barney Sellers/The Commercial Appeal/ZUMA-PRESS.com/Newscom.; p.319: Reprinted with permission from Dr. Richard Corlin.; p.321: Reprinted with permission from Katie Lovett.; p.322: Source: Ann Richards, Straight from the Heart, Simon and Schuster, 2013.; p.324: Reprinted with permission from Beth Tidmore.; p.334: Reprinted with permission from Austin Wright.; p.329tl: Andrea Izzotti/Fotolia; p.329bl: demerzel21/Fotolia; p.331: Lightworks Media/Alamy Stock Photo.

Chapter 16 p.334tc: Joe Rosenthal/Library of Congress Prints and Photographs Divison [LC-USZC4-4835].; 334tl: Ronald Asadorian/Splash/Newscom.; p.337: JGI/Jamie Grill/ Blend Images/Getty Images.; p.338: Source: "The Fringe Benefits of Failure,and the Importance of Imagination," Harvard Gazette, 5 June 2008.; p.340: Source: Selected Speeches and Writings by Abraham Lincoln.; p.341tc: Library of Congress Prints and Photographs Division [LC-USZ62-27663].; p.341tl: Dean Conger/The Denver Post/Getty Images.; p.344: Taylor Branch; At Canaan's Edge: America in the King Years

1965–68; Simon & Schuster; 2006.; p.345: Photodisc/Getty Images.; p.346: From Tom's Irish Toasts and Blessings 1998 (Tom Donaghue, Wilton ME.; p.349: Jack Arent/Palo Alto Daily News/AP Images.; p.349: Steve Jobs, Commencement Address at Stanford University, Stanford Report, June 14, 2005.; p.350: Stuart Ramson/AP Images; Bettmann/Contributor/Getty Images; Keystone Pictures USA/Alamy Stock Photo.; p.352: Michelle Obama, "Remarks by the First Lady at Tuskegee University: Commencement Address, May 9, 2015," www.whitehouse.gov.; p.353: Congressional Record, 1 Apr. 1980, p.7248.; p.356: Reprinted with permission from Simone Mullinax.; Tim Graham/Alamy Stock Photo.

Chapter Appendix A p.361: © Michael Osborn.; p.367: © Michael Osborn.; p.368: © Michael Osborn.

Chapter Appendix B p.372: Reprinted with permission from Sandra Baltz.; p.373: Reprinted with permission from Elizabeth Tidmore.; p.375: Reprinted with permission of BJ Youngerman.; p.376: Reprinted with permission from Stefan Moskowitz.; p.378: Reprinted with permission of Joseph Van Matre.; p. 380: Reprinted with permission of Gabrielle Wallace.; p.381: Reprinted with permission from Joshua Logan.; p.383: Reprinted with permission from Anna Aley.; p.385: Reprinted with permission of Katie Lovett.; p.387: Reprinted with permission of Elizabeth Lyles.; p.389: Reprinted with permission from Ashlie Mcmillan; p.390: Thomas P. O'Neill, speaker of the U.S. House of Representatives, Congressional Record, 1 April 1980, pp. 7459–7460.; p.391: Reprinted with permission of John Bakke.; p.393: Elie Wiesel (1986) © The Nobel Foundation 1986.

Index

O

P

T